THE A+ CERTIFICATION AND PC REPAIR HANDBOOK

LIMITED WARRANTY AND DISCLAIMER OF LIABILITY

THE CD-ROM THAT ACCOMPANIES THE BOOK MAY BE USED ON A SINGLE PC ONLY. THE LICENSE DOES NOT PERMIT THE USE ON A NETWORK (OF ANY KIND). YOU FURTHER AGREE THAT THIS LICENSE GRANTS PERMISSION TO USE THE PRODUCTS CONTAINED HEREIN, BUT DOES NOT GIVE YOU RIGHT OF OWNERSHIP TO ANY OF THE CONTENT OR PRODUCT CONTAINED ON THIS CD-ROM. USE OF THIRD-PARTY SOFTWARE CONTAINED ON THIS CD-ROM IS LIMITED TO AND SUBJECT TO LICENSING TERMS FOR THE RESPECTIVE PRODUCTS.

CHARLES RIVER MEDIA, INC. ("CRM") AND/OR ANYONE WHO HAS BEEN INVOLVED IN THE WRITING, CREATION, OR PRODUCTION OF THE ACCOMPANYING CODE ("THE SOFTWARE") OR THE THIRD-PARTY PRODUCTS CONTAINED ON THE CD-ROM OR TEXTUAL MATERIAL IN THE BOOK, CANNOT AND DO NOT WARRANT THE PERFORMANCE OR RESULTS THAT MAY BE OBTAINED BY USING THE SOFTWARE OR CONTENTS OF THE BOOK. THE AUTHOR AND PUBLISHER HAVE USED THEIR BEST EFFORTS TO ENSURE THE ACCURACY AND FUNCTIONALITY OF THE TEXTUAL MATERIAL AND PROGRAMS CONTAINED HEREIN. WE, HOWEVER, MAKE NO WARRANTY OF ANY KIND, EXPRESS OR IMPLIED, REGARDING THE PERFORMANCE OF THESE PROGRAMS OR CONTENTS. THE SOFTWARE IS SOLD "AS IS" WITHOUT WARRANTY (EXCEPT FOR DEFECTIVE MATERIALS USED IN MANUFACTURING THE DISK OR DUE TO FAULTY WORKMANSHIP).

THE AUTHOR, THE PUBLISHER, DEVELOPERS OF THIRD-PARTY SOFTWARE, AND ANYONE INVOLVED IN THE PRODUCTION AND MANUFACTURING OF THIS WORK SHALL NOT BE LIABLE FOR DAMAGES OF ANY KIND ARISING OUT OF THE USE OF (OR THE INABILITY TO USE) THE PROGRAMS, SOURCE CODE, OR TEXTUAL MATERIAL CONTAINED IN THIS PUBLICATION. THIS INCLUDES, BUT IS NOT LIMITED TO, LOSS OF REVENUE OR PROFIT, OR OTHER INCIDENTAL OR CONSEQUENTIAL DAMAGES ARISING OUT OF THE USE OF THE PRODUCT.

THE SOLE REMEDY IN THE EVENT OF A CLAIM OF ANY KIND IS EXPRESSLY LIMITED TO REPLACEMENT OF THE BOOK AND/OR CD-ROM, AND ONLY AT THE DISCRETION OF CRM.

THE USE OF "IMPLIED WARRANTY" AND CERTAIN "EXCLUSIONS" VARIES FROM STATE TO STATE, AND MAY NOT APPLY TO THE PURCHASER OF THIS PRODUCT.

The A+ Certification and PC Repair Handbook

Christopher A. Crayton
Joel Z. Rosenthal
Kevin J. Irwin

FIREWALL MEDIA
(An Imprint of Laxmi Publications Pvt. Ltd.)
BANGALORE • CHENNAI • COCHIN • GUWAHATI • HYDERABAD
JALANDHAR • KOLKATA • LUCKNOW • MUMBAI • RANCHI
NEW DELHI • BOSTON, USA

Published by :
FIREWALL MEDIA
(An Imprint of Laxmi Publications Pvt. Ltd.)
113, Golden House, Daryaganj,
New Delhi-110002

Phone : 011-43 53 25 00
Fax : 011-43 53 25 28

www.laxmipublications.com
info@laxmipublications.com

Economy Edition Price : **Rs. 495.00** *Only.* *Edition* : 2007

Offices :

India

- **Bangalore** (*Phone* : 080-26 61 15 61)
- **Chennai** (*Phone* : 044-24 34 47 26)
- **Cochin** (*Phone* : 0484-239 70 04)
- **Guwahati** (*Phones* : 0361-254 36 69, 251 38 81)
- **Hyderabad** (*Phone* : 040-24 75 02 47)
- **Jalandhar City** (*Phone* : 0181-222 12 72)
- **Kolkata** (*Phones* : 033-22 27 37 73, 22 27 52 47)
- **Lucknow** (*Phone* : 0522-220 95 78)
- **Mumbai** (*Phones* : 022-24 91 54 15, 24 92 78 69)
- **Ranchi** (*Phone* : 0651-230 77 64)

USA

- **Boston**
  11, Leavitt Street, Hingham,
  MA 02043, USA
  Phone : 781-740-4487

FA+-2890-495-A+ CERT. & PC REP. HANDBOOK **C—12989/06/08**
ISBN : 81-318-0076-8 ***Printed at*** : Sanjeev Offset Printers, Delhi.

This book is dedicated to all of my former students
who are now managing networks and fixing computers all over the world.
It is also dedicated to all certification exam hopefuls who seek to change
their lives by achieving certification success!

To Amanda and Rachael Hutchinson, Nancy and Ken Crayton, Sean Reilly,
Rickey Johnson, Scott Barr, Jim Krick, Jerry Adams, and Rob Metty (Hawkeye)—
thank you for your love, guidance, and continuing support.

To the families of Joel Rosenthal and Kevin Irwin-Risë,
Laura, Karen, Olivia, and Lincoln.

Acknowledgments

First and foremost, I would like to thank David Pallai, founder and president of Charles River Media, for directing and editing yet another fantastic project. It has been an awesome learning experience to work with both David and his magnificent team at CRM. Their strict attention to detail and dedication to producing only the highest quality of work is truly apparent in this book and all other projects I have had the privilege of being involved with.

Very special thanks to authors Joel Rosenthal and Kevin Irwin for writing Part I, *PC Repair and Maintenance*. Simply put, never in my life have I seen better training material for those who wish to learn about or pursue a career in computer maintenance and repair. The easy-to-understand diagrams and intuitive video tutorials are superb. This is by far the best "hands-on" learning material available on the market today. From the heart, thanks again, gentlemen.

Joel and Kevin would like to thank Dave Pallai, not the least for suggesting that Joel write Part I of this book. They would also like to thank Bryan Davidson and Beth Roberts for helping get this book out in the form you see it in. Additionally, they thank Max Hersch, Roman Martynenko, Kelman Khersonsky, and Brian O'Connor for technical advice.

Joel would like to thank Steve Irwin for advising us along the way; Michael Rosenthal for steering Joel in the direction of computers; Rina Youngner and Andy Weiss, Joel's high school English teachers, who helped turned Joel into a good writer; his daughter Laura Rosenthal for helping to make sure the cross-references were valid, and for her love and support; his wife, Risë; and parents Estelle and Daniel Rosenthal for being a great cheering section.

Kevin would like to thank his wife Karen, daughter Olivia, son Lincoln, brother Steven Irwin, and parents Myrna and Larry Irwin for all their love, support, and dedication. Additionally, he would like to thank Steve Zelicoff for keeping Kevin in shape enough to be able to work on the book.

Contents

Preface

Welcome and congratulations! You hold in your hands the most powerful, user-friendly combination PC repair/A+ certification tool available. It is crafted to teach you the basics of PC repair and maintenance as well as prepare you to take and pass the current Computing Technology Industry Association's (CompTIA's) A+ certification computerized exams.

This practical, no-nonsense book focuses on and teaches you specific topics that will prepare you well to fix computers and prepare for a career as a computer technician. It also targets topics that are most likely going to be addressed on the current A+ exams. The authors' main objective is to prepare the reader by isolating and focusing on these specific topics without adding all of the "fluff" found in other books. It is not designed to fill your head with unnecessary information before you fix specific computer-related issues or enter a computerized testing site (this type of preparation is usually accompanied by confusion, lost time, and certification exam failure).

HOW TO USE THIS BOOK

This book is divided into two main parts.

Part I, *PC Repair and Maintenance,* is an easy-to-read "hands-on" approach to learning, repairing, and maintaining PCs. It is loaded with detailed figures and diagrams that make even the most complicated of tasks easy to understand. In Part I, you will learn important industry terminology. You will learn how to install and troubleshoot hardware. You will learn how to solve many of the most common operating system-related problems that occur when you are running Windows 95, 98, Me, 2000, or XP. You will also learn how to acquire computer replacement and expansion components inexpensively.

After every few chapters in Part I, you will notice cumulative A+ Certification Review Questions. These questions are in place to build upon your acquired knowledge of the subject matter discussed and ultimately prepare you for deeper discussion of those topics in Part II. The review questions are followed by answers and a cross-reference as to where the topics are located in Part II. It is very likely that you will have to do a little work to find the supporting theory behind the correct answers!

Part II, *The A+ Certification Exams*, is a powerful resource specifically designed to prepare you to ace the current CompTIA A+ certification exams. This section is further separated into two parts: Part II A, which covers A+ Core Hardware Service Technician Study (Exam 220-301), and Part II B, which covers A+ Operating Systems Technologies Study (Exam 220-302). All of the CompTIA A+ certification objectives are covered in detail in Part II of this book. You will be able to reinforce your acquired knowledge of these objectives by answering certification review questions at the end of every chapter.

It is important to note that you will see important subject matter in this book covered more than once. Remember that you learn the basics in Part I and build upon that knowledge in Part II. In other words, you will learn to walk before you run.

WHAT'S ON THE CD-ROM?

The CD-ROM included with this book features a plethora of video tutorials that will, among other things, show you how to properly open cases and towers, install memory, remove and replace expansion cards, install motherboards and CPUs, and properly maintain your computer.

ON THE CD

The CD-ROM also includes A+ practice exams that will prepare you well for the CompTIA A+ Hardware Service Technician and Operating Systems Technologies examinations. There are four practice exams. The first two exams contain practice questions for the A+ Core Hardware Service Technician test (Part II A, Chapters 15 through 22). The second two exams contain practice questions for the Operating Systems Technologies test (Part II B, Chapters 23 through 28). Each exam has 80 questions and has a review feature to identify incorrect answers. It is recommended that you take these tests until you score 100% every time. This will ensure your best chance to score well on the real CompTIA A+ examinations. For more information regarding the CD-ROM, please see the Appendix: About the CD-ROM.

Introduction

Personal computers are, at once, horrendously complicated yet simpler than one might expect. How can this be? Computer professionals spend years working on computers, but never learning all there is to know. There's just too much information for one human being to absorb in a lifetime, especially because the technology changes continually and there are so many different types of each component. However, it is not necessary to know anything close to "everything" to be able to repair or even build computers. Because the parts are all modular, most technicians rarely, if ever, use a soldering iron. When a component such as a modem has a hardware problem, you wouldn't spend hours trying to repair it. You simply replace it—a procedure that normally takes a few minutes. Other problems can be corrected through software. So, while it cannot be said that repairing computers is "simple," it is nowhere near as complicated as the complexity of the computer would suggest.

Part I of this book, *PC Repair and Maintenance,* is designed to enable the reader to repair personal computers running Microsoft® Windows®, primarily Windows 9x (which includes 95, 98, and Millennium Edition, or "Me"), 2000 (mainly 2000 Professional), and XP. This book gives you hints and tricks that few other books provide. Many actions that Microsoft documentation would seem to suggest are impossible are often quite possible with software that is available for download, sometimes even at no charge, from the Internet. These kinds of tips might help you succeed in repairing a computer, or at least saving data, when other technicians might fail.

We don't believe it is necessary to have a deep understanding of every facet of how a computer works in order to diagnose and repair computer problems, so we explain only as much as necessary for each scenario. Furthermore, it is impossible for any book to cover all computer issues. Our goal with this book is to give you the basic information needed to make common repairs and to help you to be able to find information necessary to make other repairs. We decided not to spend much time with monitors, printers, imaging devices, or networking; repairing these devices takes highly specialized skills. Moreover, the software that comes with these devices often modifies the Windows interface from the standard, so configuration screens can differ from one computer to another. Additionally, there are many different types of these devices, each requiring different skill sets. In fact, there are entire books on some of these and on networking, so we don't feel that mere chapters can do them justice. We will limit our coverage to some common issues regarding these devices.

One theme evident throughout the book can be summed up in the phrase "Quality in, performance out." We explain how to select quality replacement and expansion components—even some relatively unknown manufacturers make satisfactory components. Moreover, it is often not necessary to pay top dollar to get quality components. Additionally, we want to make it clear that there's no shame in asking for advice from manufacturers and other experts. Getting appropriate advice can prevent serious problems and save huge amounts of time and money.

This book and accompanying CD-ROM contain many photographs, diagrams, and videos showing the right and wrong ways to perform various tasks, even to the level of physically connecting connectors.

SPECIAL NOTES

Here are some things to keep in mind as you use this book:

1. Due to version and configuration differences, some computers might not have items described in tutorials. In this case, please use Windows Help if you can't find what you're looking for.
2. This book often uses greater-than signs (>) to indicate the next step in a software command. For example, Start > Settings > Control Panel > System.
3. Windows versions are usually referred to by the following designations:

   9x: Windows 95, 98, and Me. These versions are sometimes referred to individually.

   2000: Windows 2000 Professional. Much of the information also covers Windows 2000 Server and Advanced Server.

   XP: Windows XP Home and Professional Editions. These are also referred to individually in places.
4. We use URLs in this book to direct you to helpful Web sites. In Part I of the book, we leave out the "http://www." from each URL that starts that way. URLs without "www" are shown in full. Please note that just as telephone directories are out of date by the time they are printed, some of these URLs won't be in service by the time you read this book. However, there is little or no exclusivity on this type of information, and we encourage you to look up any information you need.
5. Most changes in 2000 and XP require that the user be logged on as an administrator. We don't point that out in subsequent chapters.

Part I

PC Repair and Maintenance

1 Overview

In This Chapter

- The PC
- Computer Repair Tools
- General Advice
- It's No Shame to Seek Assistance

This chapter describes the basic structure of a personal computer, along with a list of tools needed by a PC technician, and some general advice on computer repair.

THE PC

Figure 1.1 shows a typical personal computer.

Proper Terminology

Some terms are commonly misused. The most basic of these is the computer itself, which is the box containing all the main components. All peripherals are connected

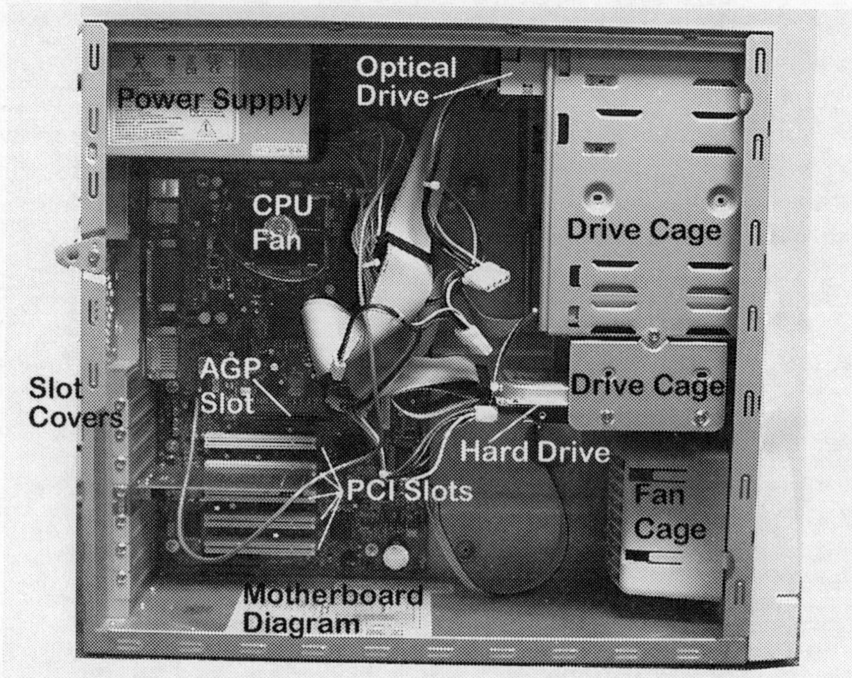

FIGURE 1.1 A typical PC system.

to the computer. The computer is not the modem, hard drive, or CPU. These three terms represent individual components that are part of the computer. They, along with other terms, are defined here.

Case: The cabinet that holds the main components of a computer.

Power supply: A box-shaped device that converts wall-outlet AC power to low-voltage DC used to power the devices in the computer.

Motherboard (system board, main board, desktop board): The large printed-circuit board to which all other parts are connected.

Expansion slots: Slot connectors on the motherboard for attaching various components. Motherboards typically have several expansion slots.

Central Processing Unit (CPU, or processor): The chip that performs all of the calculations necessary for the computer to do its job.

Random Access Memory (RAM, or memory): Chip assemblies that store data for very quick recall. The main memory in a computer requires constant power to be able to hold data. Every task performed by a computer requires the program and data to be loaded into memory.

Hard drive (hard disk drive, HDD): A device that stores data on permanently enclosed magnetic disks. The vast majority of computers have at least one hard drive. Data stored on a hard drive remains after the power is disconnected. The *operating system* (OS) (such as Windows), along with programs and data, are almost always stored on a hard drive.

Basic Input Output System (BIOS): A program that works as soon as the computer is powered on to test hardware, locate the OS startup files on the hard drive in order to start the OS, and support the transfer of data among hardware devices. The BIOS is usually stored on a *Complementary Metal Oxide Semiconductor* (CMOS) flash memory chip. *Flash memory* is expensive memory that holds its data indefinitely after the power has been disconnected, but the data can be changed. See Chapter 2, "System Configuration and Computer Hygiene," and Chapter 3, "Motherboards and Their Components," for more information.

Optical drives: Including CD-ROM, CD-RW, DVD-ROM, and various writable DVD drives, optical drives are devices that read, or read *and* write data from or onto discs using laser beams.

Floppy disk drives (FDD, floppy drives, diskette drives): Devices that store data on removable magnetic disks. Virtually all floppy drives sold since the mid-1990s have been of the 3.5" variety. These floppy disks are enclosed in a thin, hard plastic shell. Because of this, they are sometimes confused with hard drives. However, because of their limited capacity, their susceptibility to data loss, and other reasons, floppy disks have become much less useful in recent years. However, as you will see in subsequent chapters, floppy disks can be indispensable for certain repairs.

Ports: Connectors, usually on the back of the computer, to which peripheral devices can be connected.

Modem: A device that allows the computer to access a telephone line for the purpose of faxing, Internet access, data transfer between computers, or other telephone-related uses. Internal modems plug into expansion slots, while an external modem connects to a port on the computer.

Monitor (display): A device resembling a television that displays the computer's video images.

Sound card (multimedia device): A device whose primary function is to allow a computer to play and record sound. A sound card can either be a separate card that plugs into an expansion slot, or a component built into the motherboard.

Video card (video adapter, graphics adapter, display adapter): A device whose primary function is to generate a video signal ("picture") to be shown on the monitor. A video card can either be a separate card that plugs into a slot on the motherboard, or a device built into the motherboard.

Network card (network adapter, network interface card, NIC): A device that connects the computer to the network. A *network* is a group of computers connected together so that they can communicate with each other. Network cards either come as a separate card, or are built into the motherboard.

COMPUTER REPAIR TOOLS

Table 1.1 lists various PC repair tools and the importance of each.

TABLE 1.1 PC Repair Tools

Tool	Comments
Standard screwdrivers (not magnetic)	High-quality Phillips® screwdrivers are indispensable. At the very least, you'll need small and larger Phillips screwdrivers with various shaft lengths. A few different sized flat-head screwdrivers are very helpful to have. *Do not use magnetic screwdrivers inside computers.*
Cordless rechargeable screwdriver	Saves time and effort; especially useful when fixing multiple computers.
Paper clips	An unbent paper clip makes a perfect tool for releasing the drawer of an optical disc drive (see Chapter 7, "CD and DVD Drives").
Multitesteı/voltmeter	Essential. A multitester has many uses, the most common of which is testing power supplies. It can test voltage, continuity, resistance, and more. Unlike a multitester, a voltmeter's only function is to measure voltage.
ATX power supply tester	A simple tool that indicates whether the power supply is indeed outputting power, and provides convenient terminals that allow you to easily test the voltage using a voltmeter or multitester.

TABLE 1.1 PC Repair Tools *(continued)*

Tool	Comments
Cable testers	Testers are available for most types of cables used with a computer. While there are other ways to test cables, such as swapping them with known good cables, cable testers save time and trouble.
Port-testing software	Used to determine whether various ports are working correctly.
Breakout boxes	Another device used for testing cables and ports. Allows complete flexibility in changing the electrical configuration of cables and ports for testing purposes.
Loopback adapters	Available for serial and parallel ports, loopback adapters simulate signals that are input into a computer. Works with port-testing software, described earlier.
Anti-static (ESD) wristbands or anklebands	Tool to protect computer circuits against the damage even carpet shocks can cause.
Anti-static (ESD) spray	Very effective in reducing static electricity on fabric and carpet.
Anti-static (ESD) mats	Provides a static-free surface. Can be used with anti-static wristbands. Includes anti-static floor mats.
POST card	A card that can be plugged into an expansion slot and contains a small display to a show a problem code, POST cards are timesavers that provide accurate and specific diagnoses.
Diagnostic software such as Micro-Scope and PC Certify	A worthwhile investment. These products can significantly reduce the time needed to diagnose all sorts of computer problems.
Disk drive installation software	Software utilities that are provided by the drive manufacturers and from other sources, many of which are available at no charge. These sometimes come with the drives, but can also be downloaded.

TABLE 1.1 PC Repair Tools *(continued)*

Tool	Comments
BIOS flashing utilities (by companies such as MR BIOS®)	Use these to flash BIOSs and to perform other rescue operations on BIOSs and CMOS chips with problems. See Chapter 3.
USB network adapter	Allows for easy network access on a computer that has USB ports but no internal network adapter. Used for data transfer and Internet access on networks set up for it.
Internet access	Allows access to Web-based virus-scanning software and other utilities, and easy downloads of device drivers. See Chapter 2. It is also essential for obtaining technical support. See Chapter 11, "Troubleshooting."
Data transfer cables	Cables of various types such as serial (null-modem), parallel, and USB that allow for different methods of data transfer. Very often, the best solution for a computer with serious OS trouble is to format the hard drives (which erases all content), and reinstall the OS and all software. Data transfer is often the most efficient method of saving data that will be erased by formatting the drive. Various software utilities, some of which are supplied with Windows, allow for data transfer through these cables.
Cleaning and maintenance tools: vacuums and dust-cleaning sprays	Computers get dusty inside, and dust build-up interferes with proper cooling. Use sprays such as Blow Off™ while vacuuming to clean out the dust. See Chapter 2 for details. In addition, the accompanying CD-ROM has a visual presentation of the proper cleaning methods.
CD/DVD scratch repair kits	These can often save damaged software and data discs.
Uninterruptible Power Supply (UPS)	These provide continuous power to a computer when there is a power failure. Indispensable when making changes to a computer's BIOS, because a power failure during these operations will render a computer useless unless a replacement BIOS chip is obtained, which isn't always possible.

TABLE 1.1 PC Repair Tools *(continued)*

Tool	Comments
Data-recovery software	Software that can often recover data from damaged hard drives.
Data-recovery companies (such as Ontrack®)	When a hard drive crashes and the data on the drive is extremely valuable, these companies can often recover data from these drives for a substantial fee.
Problem-solving software	Various software programs such as Norton Utilities™ and McAfee® Clinic that solve many different computer problems and optimize performance.
Infrared temperature sensor	Available from companies such as Raytek® *(raytek.com)*, this uses a laser to point at an object such as a CPU to detect its temperature. Can be very helpful in detecting bad connections or heat-related problems.
Emergency boot disks	These are floppy disks that allow the user to boot a PC when it can't boot on its own or to boot an Me machine to DOS when a repair can't be made in Windows. See Chapter 11 for more information.

GENERAL ADVICE

There are some basic recommendations that will make repairs run as smoothly as possible and ensure good post-repair performance.

Quality In, Performance Out

Obviously, the quality of replacement parts is one factor in determining performance after the repair. When it comes to selecting replacement parts, there can be dozens or even hundreds of choices, and naturally, there are wide variations in quality and price. For example, while most computer-literate people can differentiate hard drives solely by their data-storage capacity, overall computer performance is affected by differences in hard drives such as rotation speed and whether the manufacturer uses quality components and quality production methods.

How to Spot Quality Components

How do you determine which parts are high quality? It's not necessarily a matter of selecting the most expensive components. There are many clues to help guide you in this matter. The most obvious are that the components come with some type of manual or guide, and the company supplies you with a way of contacting them for support or warranty needs. The manual might be in the form of a file on the installation CD, and the contact might be an address, a telephone number, or more likely these days just a Web site or e-mail address. You want to be able to reach customer service and tech support. Some vendors have excellent customer service and tech support, but other vendors are virtually impossible to reach. Often, you can't reach the company unless you can provide the product's serial number.

Additionally, look at the packaging and the actual components themselves. If they look cheap and shoddy, you should be wary. Moreover, if the price is so low that it seems too good to be true, then most times it is. However, that doesn't mean that real bargains aren't available. Let common sense be your guide.

Be Careful with Components

While hardware components are not extremely delicate, they aren't indestructible either, or else you wouldn't need to replace them. They are susceptible to physical and electrical damage due to mishandling and power surges. Follow these guidelines to minimize the risk of damage:

Make sure the power supply is set to the correct voltage: In North America, electric utilities provide 110–120 volts AC to wall outlets. In much of the rest of the world, the standard is 220–240 volts. Check the power supply at the back of the computer. Most have switches labeled 120/240. Make sure the voltage setting matches the actual voltage, or you could face catastrophic results.

Use surge suppressors and UPSs whenever possible: Power surges and undervoltages can damage or even destroy components. See Chapter 2 for more information.

Don't force components: Connectors should be pushed in directly, not at an angle, and most go in only one way. Match up the pins with the holes. If you try to force a connector in the wrong way, you can bend or push in pins, damaging the connector and most likely causing the device to malfunction. In the case of a device with a permanently connected cable, which is common with monitors, damaging the connector requires that a qualified monitor technician repair the monitor.

There are different procedures for inserting expansion cards, memory chips, and CPUs, although the same "no-force" warning applies. See Chapter 3 for more information.

Prevent static damage: Discharge as much static as possible by touching a ground—any large metal object. Avoid carpet. Use anti-static floor mats, surface mats, and wrist ground straps. Make sure all circuits are wired correctly, including grounding.

Wire organizing tip: Do not use rubber bands or metal twist-ties inside a computer. Use plastic wire ties and snip off the ends to avoid scratching your hands and arms.

Document all changes: Keep a record of every change you make; you might have to undo certain changes. Mark all jumper and wire positions, before changing them, with a fine-tipped permanent marker. Make notes and diagrams of wire and jumper positions, and keep a record of all software configuration changes.

IT'S NO SHAME TO SEEK ASSISTANCE

Obtain the correct information before starting or continuing with a repair. This saves not only time but even damage that can sometimes be caused by doing something wrong. In addition to the information found in this and other books, a vast amount of information is available on the Internet from manufacturer's Web sites and from sites dedicated to assisting computer technicians. See Chapter 11 for information on finding assistance. The Industry Contacts document on the accompanying CD-ROM has contact information for many hardware and software providers, along with helpful Web sites.

ON THE CD

2 System Configuration and Computer Hygiene

In This Chapter

- BIOS Overview
- Windows Control Panel
- Device Drivers (Drivers) Overview
- Windows Performance
- System Tools
- Windows Update
- MS-DOS (DOS) and the 2000/XP Command Prompt
- Overview of Viruses and Other Hazardous Programs
- Surge Suppressors and UPSs
- Hardware Hygiene

BIOS OVERVIEW

When a computer is first started, it needs some direction as to what to do. It needs to know where to find the OS's startup files, how hardware is to be accessed by the OS, and what hardware is installed on the system, among other things. It is the job of the BIOS to perform these tasks. BIOSs are made by a number of different companies, often customized by the motherboard manufacturers or system builders for a particular motherboard or computer. Some common BIOS brand names are Phoenix™, AMIBIOS®, Award™, IBM®, and MR BIOS®. They are in the form of CMOS chips that store the information.

Power On Self Test (POST)

The first event that happens when a computer is powered on is the POST, performed by the BIOS. The POST consists of a quick series of diagnostic tests, mostly to make certain that essential hardware is present and operating. The most essential hardware is the BIOS itself, processor, memory, video system, and a source of OS startup files (almost always a hard drive). The POST first checks the BIOS, and then the other items. If any of these are not operating correctly, the computer might not start or run correctly. As long as the BIOS program is not set to "Quiet Boot," the POST will give a single beep to let you know that all the tests were successful. If the POST detects problems, it will give a beep code and/or a text message to let you know what is wrong. You can find a list of common beep codes on the accompanying CD-ROM.

ON THE CD

Setup Program

The program run by the BIOS is usually called the *setup* program. Different motherboard manufacturers vary as to how to access the setup program. The most common method is to press a given key just after the first information appears on the screen after the computer is powered on. Often, the screen will give a prompt such as "Press Delete to access Setup." <Delete> is the most common key. Others include <F2> on Dells and Hewlett-Packards, <F10> on Compaqs, and <F1> on some Gateways. Setup screens vary widely, so we will cover the most common and important BIOS settings.

NOTE

Before you go into a setup program, make sure that you are ready to write down any changes you make. Some setting changes can render a computer unbootable, and if you don't know which changes you made, you'll have a difficult time finding the change that caused the problem.

To help prevent changes from causing serious problems, BIOS manufacturers offer a way out. After you have changed BIOS settings, setup programs offer you a choice to accept or discard changes as you exit the program. Use this function if you are unsure of any changes you have made, or if you haven't recorded those changes on paper. You can always go back and make the changes again. Figures 2.1 and 2.2 show examples of setup screens.

Important BIOS Settings and Information

Because there is so much variability among setup programs on different BIOSs, we will cover common and important items only:

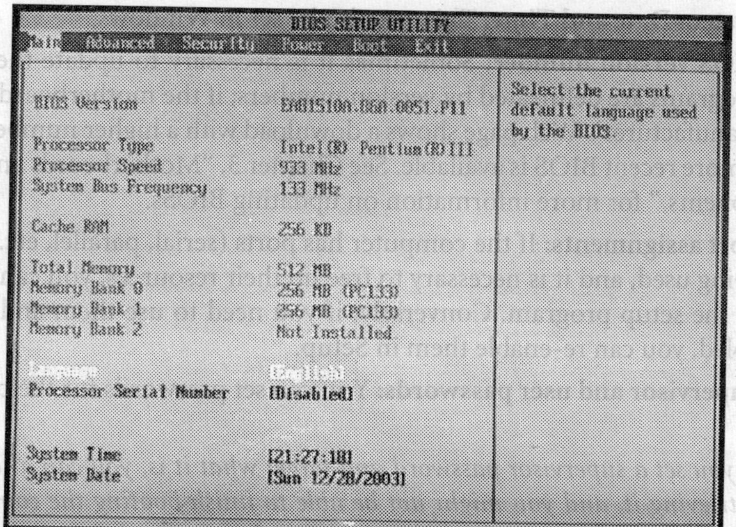

FIGURE 2.1 A sample of a setup screen.

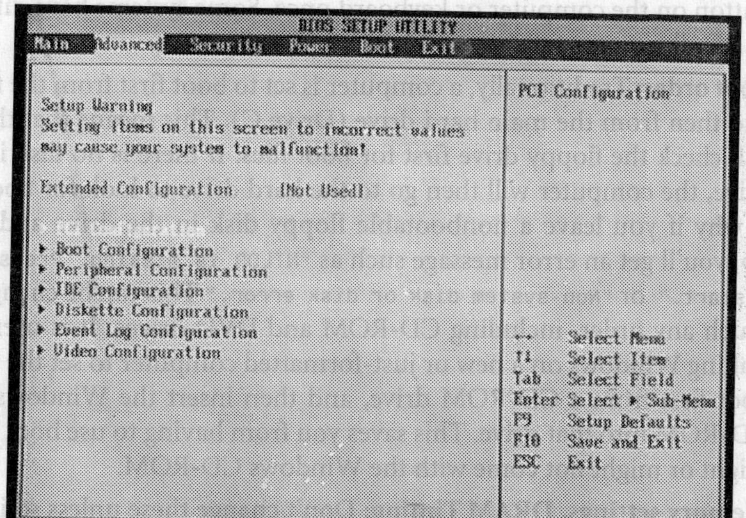

FIGURE 2.2 Another setup screen.

System Date and Time: This can also be set in Windows.

BIOS version number: Sometimes it is necessary to update the BIOS. BIOS programs are delineated by version numbers; if the motherboard or computer manufacturer's Web page shows a download with a higher number, that means a more recent BIOS is available. See Chapter 3, "Motherboards and their Components," for more information on updating BIOSs.

Port assignments: If the computer has ports (serial, parallel, etc.) that are not being used, and it is necessary to free up their resources, you can disable them in the setup program. Conversely, if you need to use them and they are disabled, you can re-enable them in Setup.

Supervisor and user passwords: You can set passwords for the computer.

NOTE

If you set a supervisor password and forget what it is, you can also forget about retrieving it, and you might not be able to finish booting the computer. Sometimes, there are steps you can take to reset the password. See Chapter 3 for more information.

Power settings (Advanced Configuration and Power Interface, ACPI): Contains power use settings including those for hibernation, standby, and in battery-powered computers, power conservation settings. Often, BIOSs contain settings that allow proper shutdown of Windows just by pressing the power button on the computer or keyboard once. Some systems have different levels of standby types.

Boot order: Traditionally, a computer is set to boot first from the floppy drive, and then from the main hard drive (Drive C). This means that the computer will check the floppy drive first for boot files. If there is no disk in the floppy drive, the computer will then go to the hard drive to look for boot files. That is why if you leave a nonbootable floppy disk in the drive and try to boot up, you'll get an error message such as "`NTLDR is missing. Press any key to restart.`" or "`Non-system disk or disk error.`" This can be changed to pretty much any order, including CD-ROM and DVD drives. It is useful when installing Windows on a new or just-formatted computer to set the computer to boot first from a CD-ROM drive, and then insert the Windows installation CD-ROM into that drive. This saves you from having to use boot floppies that might or might not come with the Windows CD-ROM.

Memory settings, DRAM Timing: Don't change these unless so instructed by a support technician.

AGP Aperture Size: Don't change this unless you are familiar with troubleshooting techniques and feel comfortable in this area. The main thing to remember here is that the AGP Aperture Size should almost always be set to at least 16MB and never to more than the actual physical RAM installed in the system. This setting will allow a possible increase in graphics (video) performance by permitting the graphics system to share system memory if needed. A higher setting often (but not always) means better graphics performance, so test the results of any change you make here by viewing the graphics performance.

CPU Frequency, Voltage Control, and other settings such as frequency (speed): On many BIOSs, this can be set automatically or manually. If you're setting them manually, you have to know the exact settings for your CPU so you don't damage your motherboard or CPU. Settings other than those specified by the CPU manufacturer should be made only by very experienced technicians.

PC Health: These include CPU and system temperatures at which warnings are made and shutdowns occur.

Integrated peripherals: These are items such as sound "cards" and network adapters that are part of the motherboard. The most common use of these settings is to disable these devices when additional peripherals of the same type are installed. For example, if the user installs an expansion sound card on a system that has onboard sound (because the onboard sound device has failed or because the user wants to upgrade to a better sound device), the onboard sound needs to be disabled to prevent problems that can occur with two active sound cards.

Interrupts (IRQs): These settings can also be changed in the Windows Device Manager (we provide more information later in this chapter).

Extended System Configuration Data (ESCD): If this setting is available, it should be enabled every time a new component is installed in the computer. Each time ESCD is enabled, the configuration resets at next boot. If a computer won't boot after installation of a new component, enabling ESCD and rebooting the system can sometimes solve the problem.

IDE Detection: This is normally set to Auto for automatic detection of IDE disk drives. Disabling auto-detection on unused drive channels can speed the boot process. See Chapter 6, "Magnetic Disk Drives," for more information on IDE drives.

Self-Monitoring Analysis and Reporting Technology (S.M.A.R.T.) drives: This technology, incorporated into most modern IDE hard drives, can alert the user of possible impending hard drive failure and most likely allow for data backup before this happens. Because of this, S.M.A.R.T. drive support should always be enabled in the setup program. Interestingly, computers are often delivered from the factory with S.M.A.R.T. drive support disabled.

Plug and Play (PnP) settings: We describe Plug and Play capability later in this chapter. PnP should be enabled in the vast majority of cases. Sometimes in Windows 95, you will have to disable Plug and Play support. There are certain other unusual situations that require you to disable Plug and Play, as you might find when researching certain problems or reading installation manuals.

Load defaults: Setup programs have default settings. Loading default settings is a good way to get your computer back to its original configuration. Do this only if all else fails. Before loading the default settings, *go through each screen and write down every setting.* Some devices might not work with the default settings.

WINDOWS CONTROL PANEL

Control Panel is one of the most important areas in Windows for configuring your computer. Although many of the applets in Control Panel can be accessed from elsewhere, Control Panel is the central location for these tools. There are several ways to access Control Panel, and these vary depending on Windows version and configuration. Tutorial 2.1 explains three ways to access Control Panel. If none of these applies to the computer you're working on, please consult Windows Help.

TUTORIAL 2.1: ACCESSING CONTROL PANEL

A. **Windows 9x, 2000, and XP with classic Start menu:** Go to Start > Settings > Control Panel.
B. **Windows XP with standard Start menu:** Go to Start > Control Panel.
C. **All versions if so configured:** Open My Computer and click or double-click Control Panel.

Applets

In Control Panel, *applets* are small programs that are used to configure individual components of the OS and hardware. Control Panel contains many applets. The applets and their names vary from version to version. Certain third-party programs install additional applets in Control Panel. This section covers pertinent applets not covered elsewhere in the book.

Wizards

A *wizard* is a program that leads the user through various steps of configuring software or hardware by prompting for answers to questions. Wizards facilitate simpler configuration of hardware and software by making sure that all of the necessary components are properly configured and that none are missed. Many of the applets in Control Panel contain wizards. The disadvantage to wizards is that they sometimes can limit options available in traditional configuration screens. However, most components can be configured from traditional screens after the wizard has been completed.

The remainder of this section deals with the more important applets.

NOTE *For XP users, if you reach Control Panel and find that it shows none of the applets described in the following paragraphs, click the Switch to Classic View link that should appear at the top of the menu on the left side of the screen. The default "Category View" is designed more for end users than for technicians.*

Accessibility Options

Accessibility Options are aids for people with various disabilities. They are also available in most versions in Start > Programs > Accessories, along with an Accessibility Wizard. This applet is fairly self-explanatory. Check here if you are experiencing unusual keyboard behavior such as ignored brief or repeated keystrokes, sounds such as beeps when certain keys are pressed, exceptionally large or high-contrast video, and so forth. Make sure the user doesn't need these settings before disabling them. If you do need to disable them to work on the machine and the user needs them, make sure to write down all settings and restore them before returning the machine to the user.

Add/Remove Hardware

This goes by different names in the various versions of Windows. Its purpose is to scan the computer for new hardware components and to install the drivers for them. In the event that Windows doesn't automatically detect new hardware, compatible hardware can often be installed by following the wizard. This applet is becoming less important as Windows installs almost all Plug and Play hardware automatically. We cover this and related wizards, plus Plug and Play technology, in greater detail in the upcoming section on device drivers.

Administrative Tools: Computer Management

The Administrative Tools folder is available in 2000 and XP only, although there are versions of a few of the tools in 9x. This is a series of tools, most of which are not intended for the average end user. These tools are accessible by themselves, and many are accessible through one of them: Computer Management. Computer Management is also accessible by right-clicking the My Computer icon and clicking Manage from the menu that appears, and from the programs list in the Start menu if so configured. Computer Management is divided into the following three categories:

System Tools

System Tools comprises a collection of tools allowing you to monitor performance and events, view information about hardware and software, and manage shared folders and user and group accounts.

NOTE

There is another set of tools in all versions called System Tools. These are accessible from the programs in the Start menu and are discussed later in this chapter.

The pertinent tools in this folder vary between 2000 and XP and are:

Event Viewer: You might be directed by a support technician or article to use Event Viewer. For detailed information on Event Viewer, go to *http://support.microsoft.com,* click the link for searching Knowledge Base articles by number, and enter 308427.

Device Manager: We discuss Device Manager in detail later in this chapter.

Storage

Disk Management: Disk Management is the one very useful program here that isn't readily available elsewhere. It allows you to view a graphical depiction of the condition of all disk drives installed in the computer. Indicators show the type of partition (system, logical, primary, etc.), its condition (healthy, failed, formatting, healthy [at risk], etc.), file system (FAT, FAT32, NTFS), and other information. As long as the system is bootable, Disk Management allows you to repair some types of disk problems (of course, if the system isn't bootable, you won't be able to start Disk Management).

Management of hard drives at this level is rather complicated. To understand more, see reference books on Windows 2000. We discuss some disk restoration techniques in Chapter 6.

Services and Applications

Services: Shown in Figure 2.3, this is the important subcomponent here. It allows management of services on the computer. A *service* is a small program or part of a program whose purpose is to support larger programs or OS components. Many services need to run for Windows and certain installed programs to operate. Some should start automatically with Windows, and some should be started manually only when called on by a program or OS process. If you get

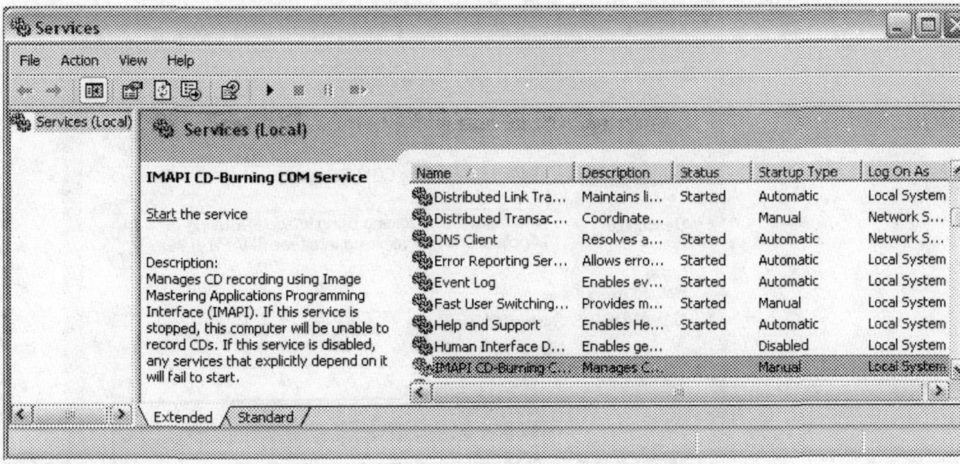

FIGURE 2.3 Services applet.

a message that says that something isn't working because a needed service isn't started, go to Services. Locate the service (hopefully the error message identified the particular service) and double-click on its line in the list. Here, as shown in Figure 2.4, you'll see controls that allow you to start the service manually, set it to automatic so it starts when Windows starts, set it to manual so it waits for a command to start, or disable it so it never starts. If you attempt to start the service and it won't start, it's time to troubleshoot. See Chapter 11, "Troubleshooting," for general troubleshooting information.

TIP

You can also use the XP version of MSConfig to set services to start or stop with Windows. We discuss MSConfig later in this chapter.

Add/Remove Programs

Known as "Add or Remove Programs" in XP, this applet is used most often for uninstalling programs. One mistake many Windows newbies make is to delete program files rather than uninstalling them. This can cause problems with the Windows registry (we discuss the registry in Chapter 11). This applet has several uses:

Installation of programs: This applet is no longer frequently used for installing programs. Usually, to install programs, you can simply insert the program installation disc and follow the prompts, or double-click on a program installation file icon and follow the prompts. If you do decide to use this to install a

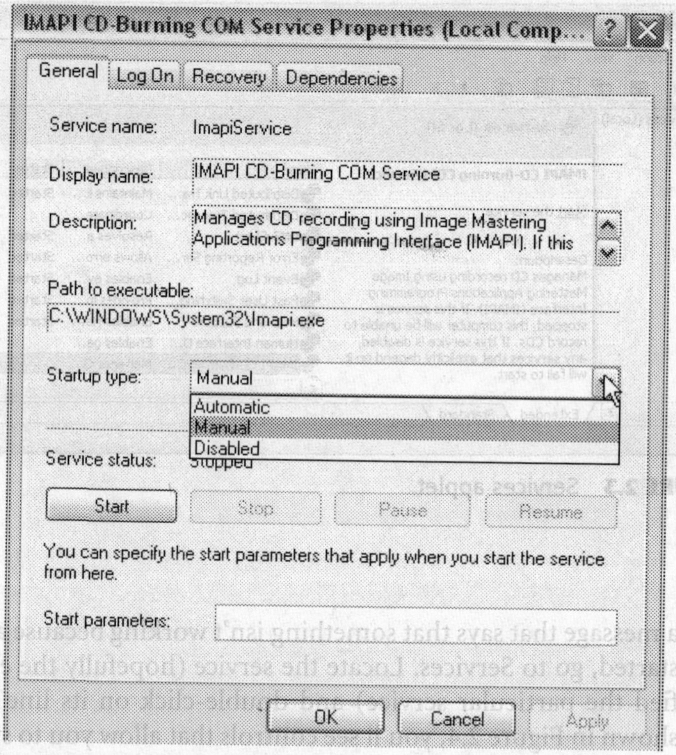

FIGURE 2.4 Configuring a service.

program, click the Install button on 9x or the Add New Programs button on 2000 or XP, and follow the simple prompts.

Uninstallation of programs: The Uninstall Wizard is a very useful tool. It is a good idea to uninstall programs that are no longer likely to be used, in order to free up space on the hard drive. One common problem computers have is that their hard drives become nearly full. A computer might run badly or not at all unless the hard drive has enough free space to hold the *swap file* for *virtual memory* (we define these terms later in this chapter). Other reasons to uninstall programs are if they are causing problems on the computer or if installation of a new version of the program requires that the old version be uninstalled first. Click the name of the program in the list and follow the prompts. You might be asked while running this wizard to decide if certain files should be retained or deleted. Usually, your choices will be "Yes" (delete the file), "Yes to all" (delete all such files), "No" (retain the file), or "No to all" (retain all such files). Unless you are certain, it is safest to select "No to all." At the end, you'll usually get the message that not all of the items were deleted and that you should remove the remaining items manually. You can safely forgo doing so, although you might want to delete shortcuts. *Shortcuts* are small files that allow you to access other files. Most of the icons on the desktop are shortcuts, as are the programs listed in Start > Programs. If there are still shortcuts on the desktop for a program you have uninstalled, right-click the shortcut icon and click Delete.

If you absolutely must uninstall a program that doesn't show up in the list, you can locate the program's folder and delete it. First, make sure that the program's name isn't different from what you expect—for example, different components of McAfee products might be called McAfee or Network Associates. If it is truly not in the list, the program's folder is most likely in the root directory (main folder) of the main hard drive, but it could be on the desktop, the Program Files folder, or elsewhere. If you have error messages during boot or other problems after deleting the program folders, you can try to fix the problem using a registry cleaning program (see Chapter 11). If that doesn't solve your problems, reinstalling the program (assuming you have the installation media) might help until you can get assistance in properly uninstalling it. It is generally a good practice, however, not to delete programs unless you know how to deal with the aftermath.

Addition and removal of Windows components: Most people don't need every component that comes with Windows to be installed on their computer. Sometimes, you might need to remove an unused component to free up disk space. Other times, a user will need a Windows component that wasn't installed originally. This is where you make these additions and subtractions. On 9x, click the Windows Setup tab, as shown in Figure 2.5. In 2000 and XP, click the Add/Remove Windows Components button. This calls up a list of installable components, as shown in Figure 2.6. Note the check boxes next to each item. Empty white check boxes mean that none of the components in that category are installed or set to be installed. White check boxes with a check mark mean that all of that category's components are installed or set to be, and gray check boxes with a check mark mean that some of the components are installed or set to be installed. When you have selected a category, clicking the Details button provides a list of items in that category, and a description appears under the list. Make your decisions, click Next, and then follow the remaining prompts. In many cases, you'll be asked for the Windows installation disc. In 9x, rather than using the Windows CD-ROM, you often can navigate to the folder C:\Windows\Options\Cabs, where C: is the hard drive partition where Windows is installed. Cabs refer to Cabinet files. Cabinet files are highly compressed files, in this case containing all of the Windows installation files.

Creating an emergency boot disk (9x only): You might recall from Chapter 1, "Overview," that the emergency boot disk is an essential tool when the

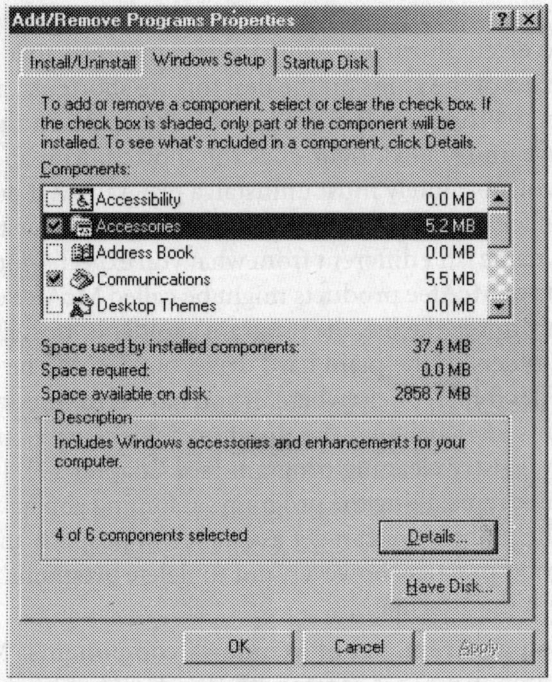

FIGURE 2.5 9x Windows Setup tab.

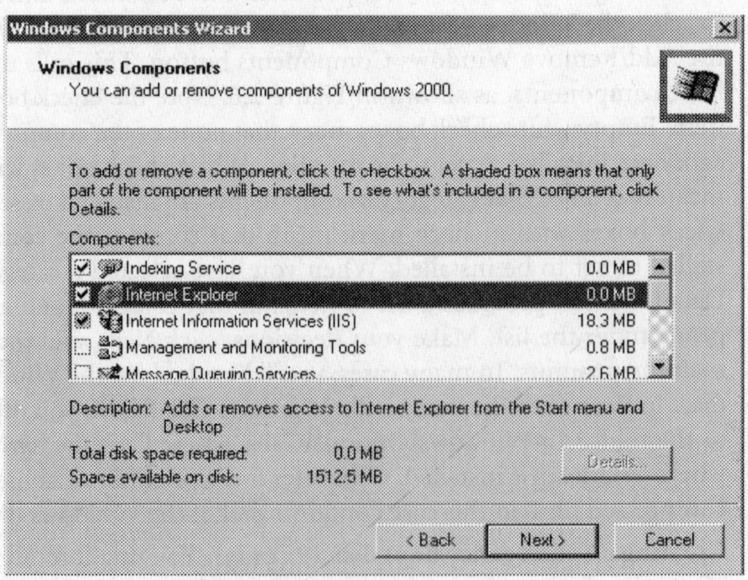

FIGURE 2.6 XP Windows Components Wizard.

computer won't boot. This is where you create it; the wizard is straightforward. As we discuss in Chapter 11, 2000 and XP don't have this applet, although it is possible to make an emergency boot disk for these versions. Make sure you have boot disks for each version of Windows 9x you will be working with. See Chapter 11 for more information on boot disks.

Windows Update: Although present on all versions, it is accessible from here on XP only. We discuss Windows Update later in the chapter.

Automatic Updates: (Can be in Control Panel in Me and 2000 Only) This is covered later in this chapter.

Folder Options

This applet has two useful tabs. The View tab has a list of items with check boxes. To see all folders and files that could be needed for repair, it is very helpful to clear the following check boxes: "Hide file extensions for known file types," and "Hide protected operating system files [Recommended]." You might also want to select the "Show hidden files and folders" option button. It's probably a good idea to change the latter two settings back to their defaults before returning the machine to the user, however.

The other useful tab is the File Types tab. Have you ever noticed that when you double-click on a data file, Windows starts the correct program to open the file? This is where those file-program associations are stored. One of the best uses for this tab is undoing the unwanted file associations that certain applications, especially media players, make. Select the file extension you want to configure and click Advanced. Click the function in the Action list (usually "open" and/or "play," in the case of a media file). Click Edit, and browse for the program you want to perform this function. You might want to change the icon as well. Then, click OK. With a lot of luck, your file-program associations will remain the way you set them. Unfortunately, programs have a tendency to change these settings without your knowledge.

TIP

To select the program to play audio CDs automatically when you insert a CD in the drive, edit both the file type called Audio CD (with no file extension), and the file type described as "CD Audio Track," bearing the CDA extension. If you want to use the basic Windows CD player rather than Windows Media Player, you can usually find the program cdplayer.exe in the folder C:\Windows (or Windows NT in 2000)\System32, or C:\Windows.

Game Controllers

This applet is fairly self-explanatory—it's used to configure game joysticks and other controllers. However, one point about game controllers must be stressed: follow the game controller manufacturer's instructions to the letter, especially if the instructions say to install the software before plugging in the device. Although installation is usually simple, an incorrectly installed game controller can be a nightmare to reinstall correctly. You might find yourself at the manufacturer's Web site or making a toll call for support if directions are not followed carefully.

Power Options

Power options are settings related to A/C and battery power, standby and hibernation, and UPS (battery backup) configuration. *Standby* is the function that shuts off power to almost everything but the memory. When full power is restored, by moving the mouse or using the keyboard in most cases, or pushing the power button on some notebook computers, the computer is left in the same state it was in before it was placed in standby. All of the same programs will be open to the same places. *Hibernation* (also known as *suspend*) is similar to standby, but the entire memory is written to the hard drive and the power is shut off completely. Like standby, when power is restored (usually by pushing the power button), the computer returns to the same state it was in before hibernation. The options that appear in this applet depend on whether the hardware and BIOS support them—if they don't, the functions sometimes simply don't appear. For example, if there is no UPS installed on the computer (and connected via USB or serial port), the UPS tab either doesn't appear or else it shows no UPS installed and the UPS options are dimmed. Notebook computers tend to have the most functions in this applet because of the data loss that can occur if the battery were to die while files are open. Peruse the available tabs to see all the configurable properties here.

NOTE

Some computers don't restart properly from hibernation. If you discover one of these computers, disable hibernation.

System

System is perhaps the most important applet in Control Panel. Accessible from here and also by right-clicking My Computer and clicking Properties, System has a number of useful components. Figure 2.7 shows the 9x version, Figure 2.8 shows the 2000 version, and Figure 2.9 shows the XP version. The different tabs are as follows:

General tab: The General tabs are nearly identical on all the versions, and contain some helpful information. The exact OS version plus installed *service packs* are identified. Service packs are significant updates to Windows OSs that are offered by Microsoft. We discuss them later in the chapter. Other information on this page is the name the OS is registered to with the registration code num-

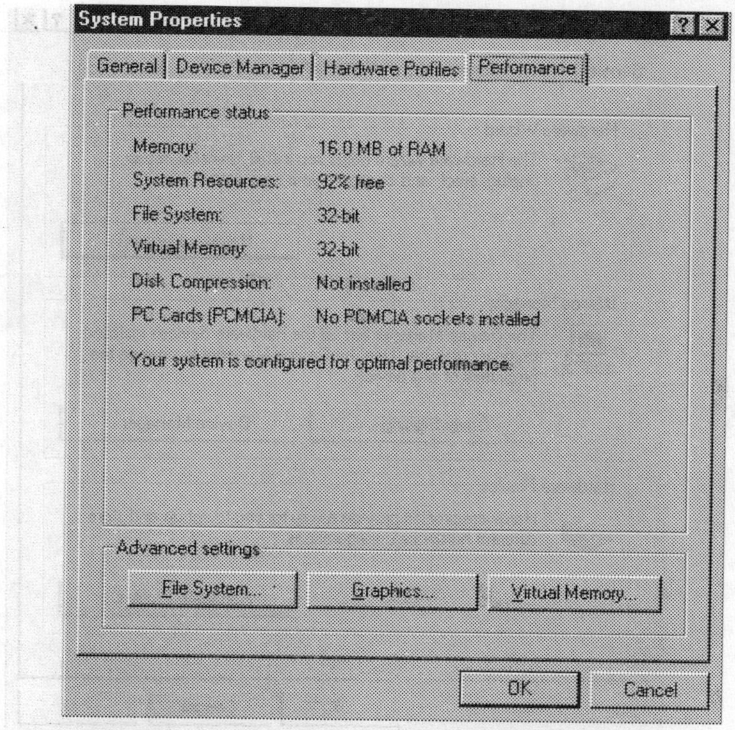

FIGURE 2.7 System Properties in Windows 9x.

ber, the general category of CPU and amount of RAM installed on the machine, and sometimes, contact information for the computer's manufacturer.

Computer Name (XP)/Network Identification (2000): These tabs contain network settings that are beyond the scope of Part I of this book, but if you will ever deal with networks, you should familiarize yourself with them.

Hardware (2000 and XP): This tab contains the Add Hardware Wizard (XP) or the Add/Remove Hardware Wizard (2000). They are the same wizards described earlier in this section under Add/Remove Hardware and are covered in detail in the next section. Another important function here is Device Manager, which is also covered in the next section. The Driver Signing button allows you to determine how the system reacts to drivers that aren't digitally signed by Microsoft when you attempt to install them. See the note in Tutorial 2.4b for more information.

Remote (XP only): This tab contains authorization settings for Remote Assistance and Remote Desktop. These should be enabled on any XP computer if you want to be able to view someone's computer screen from a remote location

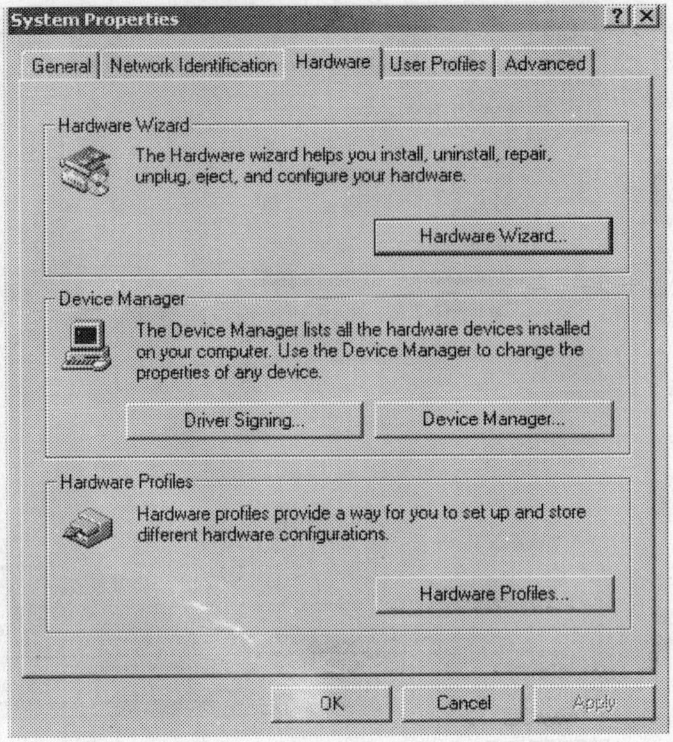

FIGURE 2.8 System Properties in Windows 2000.

through a network or even over the Internet. Click the Advanced button and select the appropriate check boxes. We discuss Remote Assistance and Remote Desktop in Chapter 11.

Advanced (2000 and XP): The most important function is Startup and Recovery. Click the Startup and Recovery button in 2000, or the third Settings button in XP. The System Failure settings on the bottom part of this dialog box apply to the "blue screen of death." The *blue screen of death,* officially known as a stop error, can happen on XP and 2000 machines when something serious occurs. Windows suddenly shuts down and the contents of memory are dumped into a file called memory.dmp located by default in C:\Windows [or Winnt]\System32. It is recommended to clear the "Automatically reboot" check box on 2000; it is important to be able to read the entire blue screen, and automatic rebooting doesn't leave the screen on long enough for anyone to write the entire error code. The error code consists of a cryptic statement such as KMODE_NOT_LESS_OR_EQUAL followed by several long *hex* numbers (we define hex numbers later in this chapter). If you get this dreaded screen, write down the

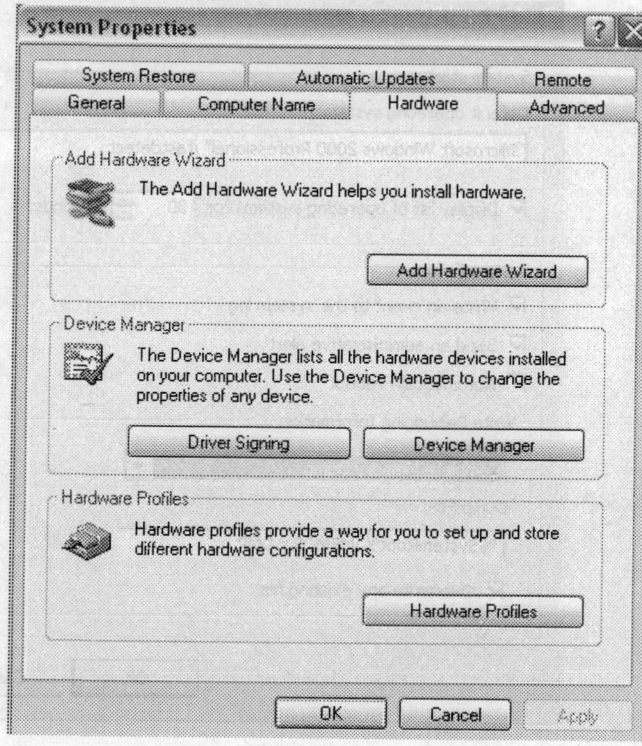

FIGURE 2.9 System Properties in Windows XP.

entire error code and search for it either on Google™ or on Microsoft's Knowledge Base. More information on searching for error messages is available in Chapter 11. If you don't get useful information and want to get support from Microsoft, they'll ask you for the memory.dmp file so they can diagnose the problem by reviewing everything that was in memory at the time the stop error occurred. Note that this file can be very large. Figure 2.10 shows the 2000 Startup and Recovery page.

Performance (9x only): We discuss the Performance tab in the Windows Performance section later in the chapter.

System Restore (XP only): System Restore is covered later in this chapter and in Chapter 11. This tab allows you to enable or disable System Restore and set the disk space allocated to it. Instructions on configuring System restore in Windows Me can also be found in Chapter 11.

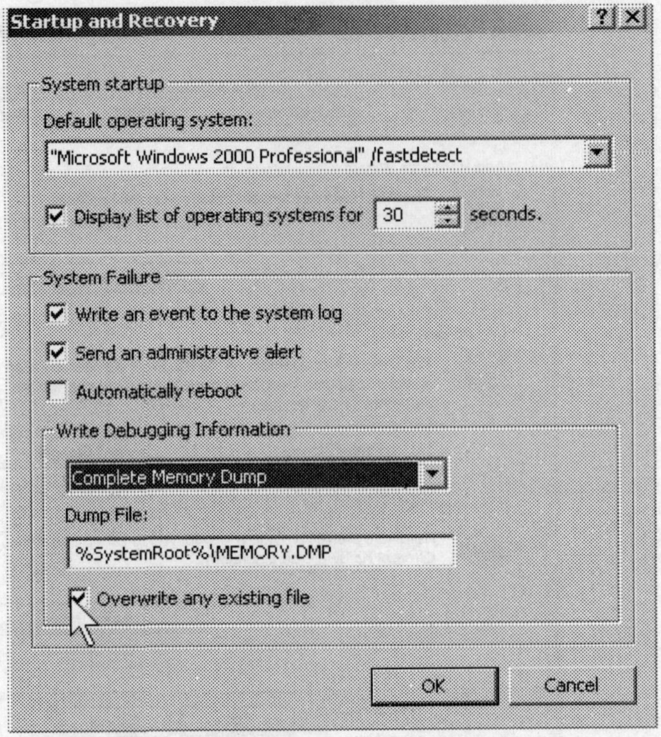

FIGURE 2.10 Windows 2000 Startup and Recovery settings.

Automated Updates (XP only): This tab allows you to configure if and how Windows Critical Updates are made. The choices are self-explanatory. Windows Update is covered later in this chapter. In Me and 2000, Automated Updates can often be found in the main portion of Control Panel.

DEVICE DRIVERS (DRIVERS) OVERVIEW

Device drivers are software files that contain instructions that allow the OS to interact with hardware. For example, it takes one or more mouse drivers for the OS to understand what to do when you move the mouse. The printer driver tells the printer what to do when you click Print. Almost all devices need some type of driver in order to operate, so virtually every new device comes with a driver disk or disks. Windows also contains a large selection of drivers for all types of hardware.

Some devices are so important that generic drivers are available immediately after powering on the computer. These are the video and keyboard drivers. Generic drivers for these devices are built into the BIOS. That is because, barring the presence of devices used by those with certain disabilities, a computer is useless without a monitor running at least at some point during its operation, and cannot be controlled without a keyboard. A *generic driver* is a driver that will work with many or all of its class of devices, but will usually not allow for full functionality of a particular device. To illustrate this, you might notice that, while booting, your monitor might display larger text and few colors. Then, toward the end of boot-up, you'll see much better color and smaller, sharper text. That is because the generic drivers that allow for video as soon as the machine is powered on aren't designed to take full advantage of the capabilities of the video card and monitor. Once the device-specific drivers are loaded into memory, later on in the boot process, you should see more colors and greater resolution. You can find more information about video in Chapter 8, "Video, Sound, Modems, and Network Adapters."

Drivers are also usually specific to the OS version, or version group. In many cases, a driver will work in all versions of Windows 9x, while another driver will work with Windows 2000 and XP. In some instances, there is one driver for all of these versions, and in others, there is a separate driver for each version. This all depends on the individual device.

You will notice that many devices come with "software." Usually, this includes both drivers to make the device operational and programs to make them functional. For example, a CD-RW drive with just its device driver installed will work only as a CD-ROM drive. To be able to "burn" (record) CDs, you need a program that will give you controls that allow you to use the device for all of its intended purposes. Often, the software that ships with a hardware device includes one or more third-party programs that are certified by the device manufacturer to be compatible with that device. The drivers to operate the device, and sometimes drivers for competing devices, are included in the program. However, some devices, most notably printers, come with software that is designed by the printer manufacturer solely for that device. And in some cases, Windows will have built-in software components that can be used to perform the tasks of the hardware device. For example, the most recent versions of Windows Media Player™ can be used to burn multimedia CDs on a CD-RW.

Installing Drivers

All of the versions of Windows discussed in this book are PnP OSs. Often disparagingly called "Plug and Pray" when introduced in Windows 95, Plug and Play refers to the capability of a device to be recognized and installed automatically by the OS without the user having to manually configure the resources used by the device. A computer's BIOS, OS, and the device all have to be Plug and Play compatible for Plug and Play to work; nearly every PC BIOS, OS, and virtually every device sold since Windows 95 became common is so compatible. If everything is working as it should, Windows will automatically detect any newly installed Plug and Play device and attempt to install the drivers for it.

NOTE *Manufacturer's installation instructions always supercede the instructions in this chapter in case there are any differences.*

Installing a driver is part of installing a device. In fact, when Windows messages refer to "installing or uninstalling a device," they mean primarily installation and uninstallation of the drivers for that device. Here are the most common ways that device drivers are installed on Windows PCs:

Automatically by Windows: Windows detects the device on bootup and installs the drivers for it.

Almost automatically by Windows: Windows detects the device and prompts for the location of the driver. The user supplies the disk or location of the driver files on the hard drive, and answers the prompts.

Manufacturer-supplied installation CD: The installation CD starts automatically upon insertion. The user follows the prompts to install the software. Often, there is more than one program to install in this situation.

Installation program on the hard drive: The user runs the program, usually by double-clicking, and installation proceeds in the same manner as the previous method.

When installing or reinstalling a driver, make sure you know where the drivers are. If they are on a floppy or CD, make sure you know which drive the disk is in along with the path to the driver files. If the drivers are on the hard drive, which is common if you downloaded them from the Internet, make sure you know the path to the files.

TIP *If you download a file from the Internet, make sure to navigate to a folder that you can easily find when prompted for a location. Otherwise, Windows might direct the file to a hidden temporary Internet folder that is almost impossible to find, even if you know where to look and your system is configured to show hidden and system files.*

Reinstalling a Driver

One very common problem that occurs with PCs is for a device to stop working correctly or at all. In most cases, there is nothing wrong with the hardware; instead, the driver has become corrupted. Corrupted drivers can sometimes even affect the functioning of the entire computer.

There are various degrees of reinstalling drivers. Try these in order if you haven't solved the problem:

1. Reinstall the existing driver.
2. Uninstall and reinstall the driver.
3. Uninstall the driver from your system and reboot. When Windows restarts, it should detect the new hardware and start to install the drivers again.

If you have the documentation and driver disks from a device, follow the provided directions. For example, corrupted drivers are common with Hewlett-Packard printers. Tutorial 2.2 describes a typical case of reinstalling a printer driver.

TUTORIAL 2.2 REINSTALLING PRINTER SOFTWARE

Make sure you have the driver disk or have downloaded the file before proceeding with these steps:

1. In Windows XP with the standard Start menu, go to Start > Printers and Faxes. If Printers and Faxes isn't there you can find it in Control Panel. In all other versions, go to Start > Settings > Printers.
2. Right-click the icon for the printer you want to uninstall and select Delete from the pop-up menu that appears.
3. Follow the prompt to confirm deletion.
4. Insert the driver disk or execute (run) the installation file on the hard drive.
5. Follow the prompts to install the printer software.

In other situations, follow the procedures outlined in Tutorial 2.4a, *Reinstalling a Known Driver in Device Manager*, or Tutorial 2.4b, *Letting Windows Select the Best Driver to Install.* The procedures vary slightly with different versions of Windows.

NOTE

The one place where almost all drivers can be accessed is Device Manager. There are many ways to get to Device Manager, not all of which can be used on every computer, depending on Windows version or configuration. A few methods are described in Tutorial 2.3. If none of these methods applies to the computer you're working on, please search Windows' Help for Device Manager.

TUTORIAL 2.3 Accessing Device Manager

A. **Windows 9x:** Right-click the My Computer icon on the desktop and select Properties from the pop-up menu that appears. Click the Device Manager tab.

B. **Windows 2000 and XP:** Right-click the My Computer icon on the desktop and select Properties from the pop-up menu that appears. Click the Hardware tab, and then the Device Manager button. In XP, you can right-click My Computer in the Start menu to view the pop-up menu. Alternately, in either version, you can right-click My Computer, click Manage from the popup menu, and select Device Manager in the left pane of the Window that appears.

C. **All versions:** You can access Device Manager through the System applet in Control Panel. See Tutorial 2.1 for instructions for opening Control Panel.

NOTE

Some computer owners rename My Computer to their own names.

TUTORIAL 2.4A Reinstalling a Known Driver in Device Manager

1. Follow the appropriate procedure described in Tutorial 2.2 to access Device Manager.
2. In Device Manager, click the "+" sign next to the category of hardware whose driver you want to reinstall. One or more devices appear under the category name.
3. Double-click the name of the device. The device's Properties page appears.
4. Click the Driver tab. The driver page appears. You will have various options here, depending on the Windows version.
5. Click the Update Driver button. You'll be prompted to search for a suitable driver or to select a driver from a list, except in XP, which will prompt you to install a driver automatically or to select from a list. If you have a driver disk, insert it now.
6. Follow the instructions for your system:
   A. **Windows 9x and 2000:** Select the "Display a list..." or "No. Select driver from list" option button and click Next.
   B. **Windows XP:** Select the "Don't Search..." option button and click Next.

   A list of drivers might appear in the window.

7. The existing driver usually appears first in this list. If you want to reinstall it, click Next and follow the remaining prompts. If you have inserted a disk, or know where you can find the driver on the hard drive, click Have Disk.
8. If you know the path to the driver, enter it in the text box. To browse for the driver, click Browse, and then locate the driver. In case the driver is on your desktop, know that the default path to the desktop in Windows 9x is C:\Windows\Desktop. In Windows 2000 and XP, the default path is C:\Documents and Settings\[logged-on username]\Desktop. Once you find the file, its name should appear in the text box. Note that only a file with the extension ".inf" will be considered a driver.
9. Click OK and follow the remaining prompts.

If you get warning messages, consider them carefully. Some Windows warning messages are critical (but see the note immediately following Tutorial 2.4b).

TUTORIAL 2.4B LETTING WINDOWS SELECT THE BEST DRIVER TO INSTALL

1. Follow Steps 1 through 5 of Tutorial 2.4a.
2. In the Update Device Driver wizard that appears, select the option button appropriate for your version:
   A. **Windows 95/98:** Select the "Yes (Recommended)" option button that answers the question, "Do you want Windows to search for the driver?"
   B. **Windows Me:** Select the "Automatically search for a better driver (Recommended)" option button.
   C. **Windows 2000:** After clicking Next, select the "Search for a suitable driver for my device (Recommended)" option button.
   D. **Windows XP:** Click the "Install the software automatically (Recommended)" option button.

   Then, click Next.
3. Windows 9x and XP start the search at this point. If Windows doesn't find a driver, it prompts you to search in other locations. Windows 2000 allows you to specify a location here. If you don't, it will search the hard drive only.
4. If you haven't inserted a disk and Windows has found a driver it says will work, follow the prompts to install that driver. If you have inserted a disk, or Windows hasn't located a suitable driver, and you know where the driver is, browse or otherwise specify the location of the file. Then, follow the prompts to install or not install the driver.

NOTE

If Windows warns you that a driver might not be suitable for your hardware, don't attempt to install it. However, Windows might give you a message that says that the driver is not digitally signed. While a driver with a digital signature will almost certainly work, other drivers intended for the specific Windows version will probably work also. You can ignore this particular warning in the vast majority of cases. Better yet, in 2000 and XP, you can configure these warning messages in 2000 and XP in System Properties, Hardware tab (see Figures 2.8 and 2.9). Click the Driver Signing button and choose either to be warned or not to be warned. The third choice is to block unsigned drivers altogether. Don't choose this unless you have a compelling reason to.

If using one of these methods doesn't solve the problem, the next step is to uninstall the device and then reinstall. The procedure is similar to that in Tutorial 2.4a. In Windows 9x, select the device in Device Manager and click the Remove button. Follow any prompts you see, and then click the Refresh button. In 2000 and XP, right-click the device and click Uninstall from the pop-up menu. Then, close Device Manager. The Hardware tab of the System applet should be visible. Click the Hardware Wizard button and go through the wizard. Follow all the prompts. Then, run Add/Remove Hardware in Control Panel and install the driver following the directions in Tutorial 2.4a.

The last thing to try before suspecting bad hardware is to uninstall the device following the methods just mentioned. Then, restart the computer. Windows should recognize the device as newly installed and start the process to install the driver. If you have an installation program disk, cancel the Windows installation and run the installation program after the computer has finished rebooting.

If you have tried all of these things and the device still doesn't work, there is a good chance that the device is broken. Uninstall the device again, only this time, shut down the computer and physically remove the device. If you have a similar device handy that you know is good, you might want to try to install it. If the newly installed device works, that is more evidence that the previously installed device is defective. Then, obtain a permanent replacement device and install as directed. For more information on installing devices, see the chapter in this book appropriate to the device you want to install.

Rolling Back a Driver (XP Only)

In case there is a new problem with the computer after the installation of a new driver, Windows XP gives you the option of "rolling back the driver." Double-click the device name in Device Manager and click the Rollback Driver button on the property sheet. The previous driver will be reinstalled.

NOTE

Occasionally, Windows will automatically select the wrong driver for the OS. For example, one customer reported that he attempted to install an MPX chipset-based network adapter on a Windows 95 machine, but despite following the directions, the network adapter didn't work. It turned out that Windows pulled drivers for the wrong OS off the network card's installation CD. We fixed the problem by removing the wrong driver, manually selecting the driver in the CD's /drivers/win95 directory, and restarting the computer.

Obtaining Device Drivers

Computer technicians often spend a great deal of time searching for drivers. Many times, the driver disks are lost, and other times, upgrading the OS requires new drivers. Additionally, new drivers can often improve the functionality of existing devices (but sometimes, new drivers can cause problems too).

There are some standard locations to find drivers. The first place to look is the Web site of the device manufacturer. See the Industry Contacts document on the accompanying CD-ROM for a list of manufacturer contact information. Some Web sites make it easier to find driver downloads than others do. Note that a high-speed Internet connection is extremely valuable when downloading large files. If you don't have access to such a connection, and you need a large file, you might be better off attempting to order a disk from the manufacturer, if available. The cost usually isn't prohibitive, but you'll have to wait for delivery.

ON THE CD

Another good source for drivers is Windows itself. For example, an old printer might come with drivers only for 9x and previous versions. If you need that printer to work with 2000 or XP, run the Add Printer Wizard in the Printers folder (see Tutorial 2.2 for instructions on accessing the Printers folder). If Windows doesn't install the device automatically, you will eventually be able to reach a page allowing you to select the device manufacturer and model name/number. Sometimes, you'll need to insert the Windows disc in the drive for Windows to use this driver, unless you browse for the appropriate files. In Windows 9x, these are often in C:\Windows\Options\Cabs or C:\Windows\Options\Install. A driver for a close model number might or might not work with your hardware. For example, an HP DeskJet 660 driver will work with an HP DeskJet 672C printer.

This procedure isn't limited to printers. Run the Add Hardware Wizard (or equivalent) from Control Panel to install other types of devices in the same way.

Microsoft also keeps a huge selection of drivers. If you search *Microsoft.com* for "drivers," you'll get a wealth of pages where you can find drivers, including third-party companies that sell drivers.

When you download drivers, there are different types of files you can download. Some downloads are compressed files in .zip form. XP, Me, and 98 with the Microsoft Plus! option have the built-in capability of opening .zip files. Otherwise, you need to have a program such as WinZip® (winzip.com) or Stuffit® (aladdinsys.com) to expand them. More common is the executable file. These files have the .exe extension and must be run, usually by double-clicking the icon. These come in two types: the setup program and the self-extracting zip file. If the file is a setup program, once executed, usually by double-clicking the icon, it will immediately start the process of installing the device driver and perhaps the operating program. If it is a self-extracting zip file using WinZip, you'll see a text box displaying the destination path of the extracted files. Figure 2.11 shows this process. Change the path to a folder that you can easily locate, such as the desktop. Note that you do not need to have WinZip to extract the files from this type of file—a dedicated WinZip program is part of the file.

Occasionally, you'll run a self-extracting file and see a command prompt or MS-DOS prompt window. To be able to locate the extracted files after extraction, create a new folder and put the self-extracting file in this folder before running it. The extracted folders and files will be placed in the new folder as well.

Often when you download files from a self-extracting file, you'll see folders bearing the names of various OSs and versions. You can delete any folders for OSs that you won't be using, such as Windows 3.1, OS/2, Solaris, and so forth. One title you might see is Win32. This refers to 32-bit Windows OSs, which include all of the versions covered in this book. You install these drivers using the Windows Add/ Remove Programs applet in Control Panel, or by navigating to the drivers when Windows has detected the new hardware on boot.

Chipset Manufacturers

If you searched everywhere else for a driver but had no luck, there is another place to try: the chipset manufacturer. A chipset is the set of integrated circuits used on a

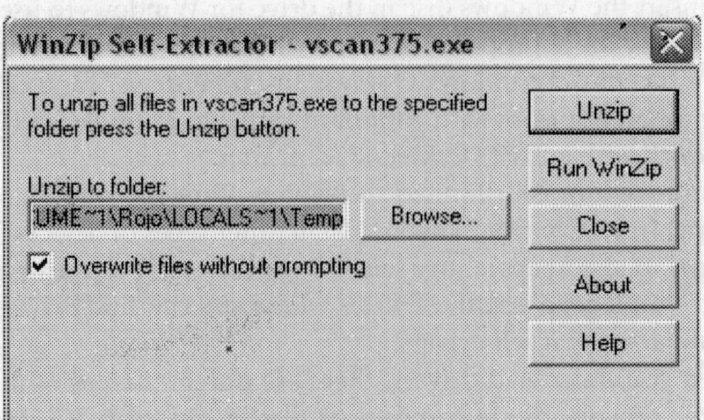

FIGURE 2.11 A WinZip self-extracting file.

particular device, and is often made by a manufacturer other than the device manufacturer. Look at the device and try to read the name and numbers on the larger chips. If the item is identified in Device Manager, it sometimes is identified by chipset rather than by device manufacturer. If that fails, search on the Internet (we recommend *google.com*) for information about the device; you can often find the chipset manufacturer and model number from the device manufacturer's Web site. You can also run a diagnostic program such as Micro-Scope™ (*micro2000.com*) or PC Certify® (*pccertify.com*) to identify the hardware. This is especially helpful on a laptop, which you will be unlikely to open.

Locating the chipset manufacturer and model number is no guarantee that the manufacturer's Web site will have a driver, and if it does, that the driver will work with your device—but it's certainly worth a try.

FCC ID

Another way to help find the manufacturer of a device, and thus, ultimately the proper device drivers, is by the FCC ID printed on the circuit board or on a label on the device. Make a note of the ID number and search at *fcc.gov/oet/fccid*.

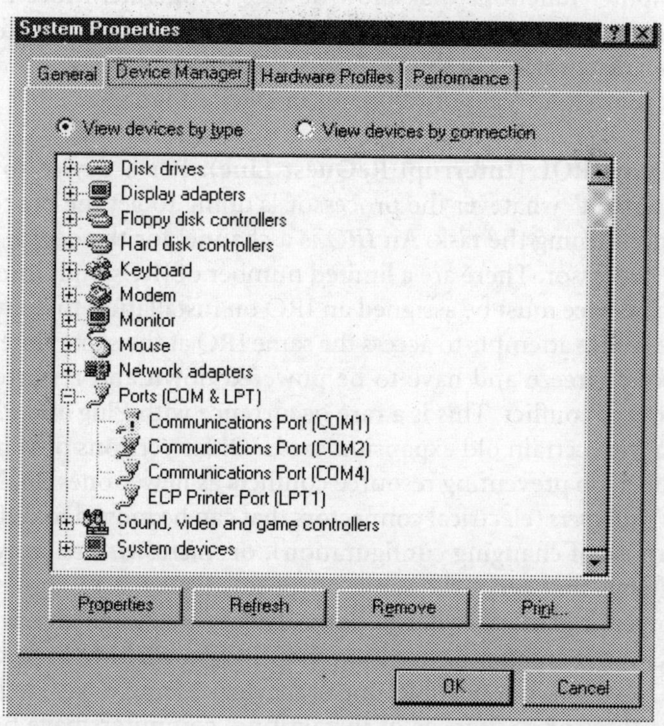

FIGURE 2.12 Device Manager indicating problematic hardware.

Device Status

When you look in Device Manager, you might sometimes see a yellow question mark or exclamation point, or a red "x" next to a device listing (see Figure 2.12). The red "x" or yellow exclamation point indicates a resource conflict (discussed later in this section), a problem with the device and/or its driver, or that the device has been disabled in Device Manager. The yellow question mark indicates that Windows has detected a newly installed device but cannot determine the nature of that device. Use the procedures described earlier in this section to diagnose and remedy the problem.

TIP

If you see the "This device is working properly" comment on a device's property page, don't count on it. The device might or might not be working properly. However, a comment stating that there is a problem with the device will always be correct.

Device Manager Resources

Every device uses some of the computer's resources. *Resources,* in Device Manager, are computer functions that allow devices to operate. More than one device attempting to access the same resource at the same time is called a *resource conflict,* which we discuss later in this section.

There are four types of resources in Device Manager:

IRQ or IRQL (Interrupt ReQuest Line): For a device to operate, it has to "interrupt" whatever the processor is doing to get the processor to do its part in performing the task. An *IRQ* is a channel for the device to use to interrupt the processor. There are a limited number of IRQs built into the motherboard. Each device must be assigned an IRQ on installation to do its job. If more than one device attempts to access the same IRQ at the same time, the computer will *lock up* (freeze and have to be powered down and restarted) because of this resource conflict. This is a rare occurrence with Plug and Play, but it can happen with certain old expansion cards. Older versions of Windows didn't do as good a job preventing resource conflicts as newer ones do. Many older devices have *jumpers* (electrical connectors that can be moved to different places for the purpose of changing configuration), or *microswitches* (very small mechanical switches that serve the same purpose). Figure 2.13 shows a card with both jumpers and microswitches. Some devices are designed to work only on certain IRQs, so if another device is on that IRQ, it will have to be changed to another IRQ. If that is not possible, one of the devices might have to be replaced. For the past three or so years as of this writing, computers have been able to reliably share IRQs to some extent. However, IRQ sharing can occasionally be problematic. Figure 2.14 shows an IRQ list in the Resource View in Device Manager.

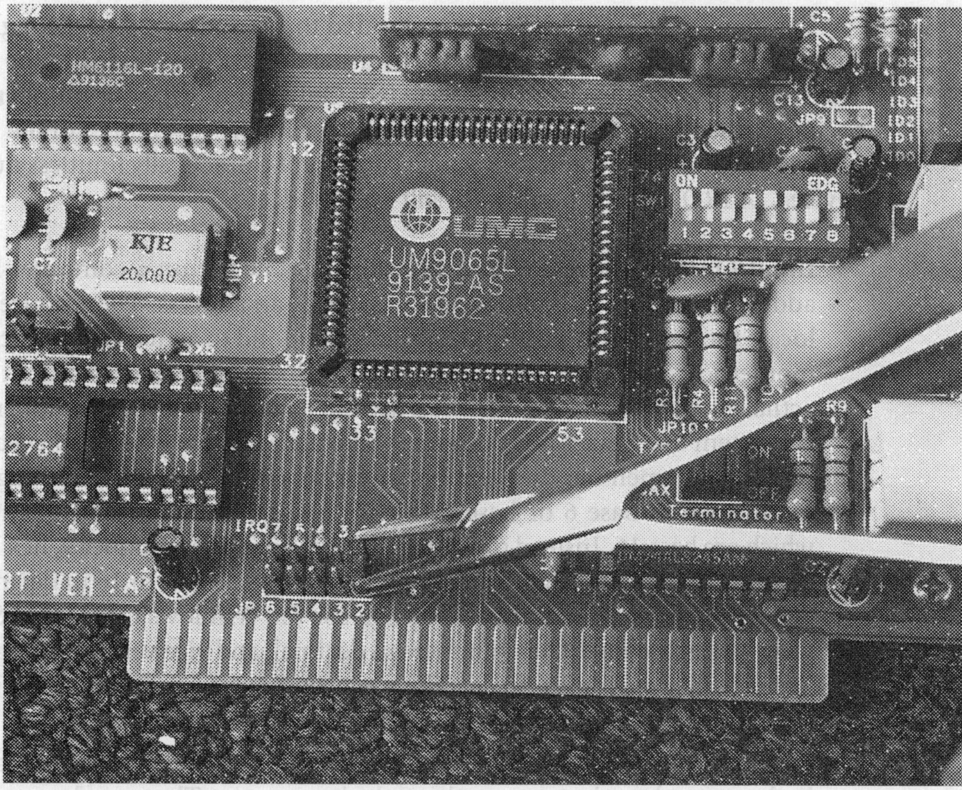

FIGURE 2.13 Jumpers and microswitches.

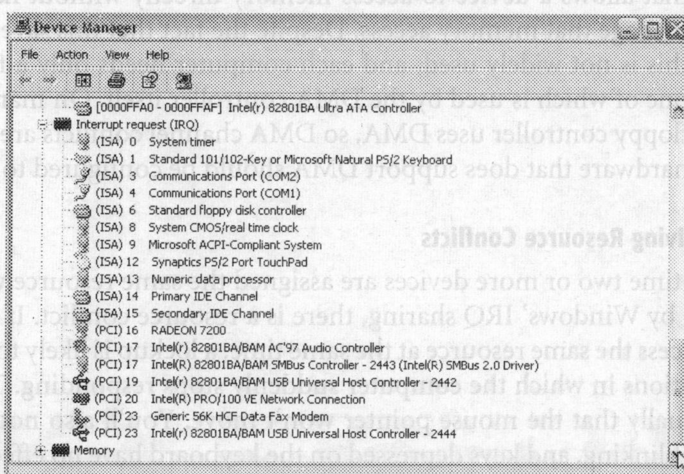

FIGURE 2.14 Device Manager IRQ View in newer computer.

For many years, usable IRQs were limited to 14, numbered 00 through 15, but with 02 and 09 not available. After all the usual devices were added to the required system devices, very few free IRQs were left. Only recently has the number of IRQs been increased to 24 (see Figure 2.14). Considering the capabilities of the USB and IEEE 1394 (FireWire) interfaces, which can accept a practically limitless number of devices, 24 IRQs should be all a PC will ever need.

Input/Output Address (I/O Address): Every device on a computer needs an address just as every building in a city needs an address. These addresses help locate the devices on a computer, and correspond to actual solder traces on the motherboard. They are often confused with memory addresses, but they are actually not related. They are measured in hexadecimal (hex) numbers, which is a system that makes huge numbers take up less space when displayed or written. If you remember different base numbers in grade school and high school math, such as base 6 or base 2 (binary), you will understand hex numbers, which are base 16. Instead of adding another digit after number 9, hex numbers continue with A through F. For example, F hex is equal to 16 in decimal (base 10); 11 in hex is 17 in decimal. You can use the Windows Calculator, Scientific view, to easily convert hex numbers to decimal, and vice versa, although there's not usually a reason to do so. The main thing you need to know is that, like IRQs, I/O addresses must be unique on a given computer.

Memory Addresses: Memory addresses are a way to specify the exact location in the system's main memory that a device accesses. They are also measured in hex numbers and cannot be duplicated on the same system.

Direct Memory Access (DMA) Channels: Direct Memory Access is a system that allows a device to access memory directly without having the processor manage that memory access. Despite the fact that this saves processing power, this is not widely used, and each computer needs only a few DMA channels, one of which is used by the DMA controller itself. On many systems, only the floppy controller uses DMA, so DMA channel conflicts are rare. However, any hardware that does support DMA should be configured to use it.

Resolving Resource Conflicts

Any time two or more devices are assigned the same resource without being managed by Windows' IRQ sharing, there is a resource conflict. If the devices attempt to access the same resource at the same time, a lockup is likely to occur. Lockups are situations in which the computer suddenly stops responding. The first sign of this is usually that the mouse pointer won't move. You'll also notice that the cursors stop blinking, and keys depressed on the keyboard have no effect. These symptoms can sometimes happen temporarily, however, so there is an easy test to determine if the computer is really locked up (as long as your keyboard has a working Num Lock or Caps Lock light): press the <Num Lock> or <Caps Lock> key on the keyboard. If the light doesn't go on or off, you can bet that your computer is locked up. If the Num Lock light responds, wait a minute or two to see if the computer starts responding again, and then try the Num Lock test again. If the computer is truly locked up, the only alternative is to shut off the power to the computer and reboot. You can shut off the power on all newer computers (those with a soft power switch) by pressing and holding the power switch for several seconds until the power goes off. A soft power switch is one that activates an electronic circuit to start or stop the computer, as opposed to a mechanical switch that simply shuts power on and off by opening or closing the circuit. On computers with mechanical switches, simply pressing the button once will do the trick. Many computers have a mechanical power supply switch on the back that can be used. If all else fails, turn off the surge suppressor/power strip switch, or pull out the plug.

Reconnect the power, if disconnected, and restart the computer. To avoid another lockup, go into Safe Mode. *Safe Mode* is a mode of Windows in which only essential hardware is activated. This will allow you to resolve many problems with a greatly reduced risk of the computer locking up in the middle of your efforts. Follow the instructions in Tutorial 2.5a or b as applicable to boot into Safe Mode.

TUTORIAL 2.5A Booting into Safe Mode in Windows 9x

1. As soon as the computer powers back on, press and hold the <F8> key. This should call up the Windows Startup menu. If this doesn't work, try pressing <F8> repeatedly, or consult the documentation for the computer on the Internet, if available.
2. Enter the number for Safe Mode and press <Enter>. The computer should then boot into Safe Mode. In Windows 9x, ScanDisk will probably run to detect and repair errors on your hard drive that result from powering down the computer without shutting down Windows. Go ahead and wait for ScanDisk to run. If you don't have time, you can cancel ScanDisk and run it later—the sky won't fall.

If you miss the opportunity and Windows starts to boot into normal mode, press <Ctrl> + <Alt> + <Delete> to restart the computer and try again. To do this, press and hold <Ctrl> and <Alt> simultaneously; then, while they're still depressed, press <Delete>.

TUTORIAL 2.5B Booting into Safe Mode in Windows 2000 and XP

1. After restarting power, watch for a black screen with the message "Starting Windows." Underneath will be a message that says, "For troubleshooting and advanced startup options for Windows ____, press F8." You'll have to press <F8> in the few seconds that the message appears. Once the progress bar starts, it is too late and you'll have to press <Ctrl> + <Alt> + <Delete> as described in Tutorial 2.5a to restart and try again. Some configurations cause systems not to show any of these messages. In this case, repeatedly press <F8> as soon as it starts to boot. Figure 2.15 shows the Windows Startup menu.

Assuming you can successfully boot into Safe Mode, you can then open Device Manager and attempt to resolve the resource conflict. If you can't even boot into Safe Mode, see Chapter 11 for troubleshooting information. You can manually assign resources through Device Manager, but it's generally better to let Windows make resource assignments if possible. If you have legacy expansion cards that work only on one IRQ, or cards that have jumpers or DIP switches to select between only two IRQs, you'll have to do a bit of planning to resolve the conflict. Make the selection to view devices by resource in Device Manager. In 9x, select My Computer in the Device Manager Window and click the Properties button below. Then, make sure the Interrupt Request (IRQ) option button is selected. In 2000 and XP, click "Resources by type" in the View menu. This displays a list of IRQs and the devices

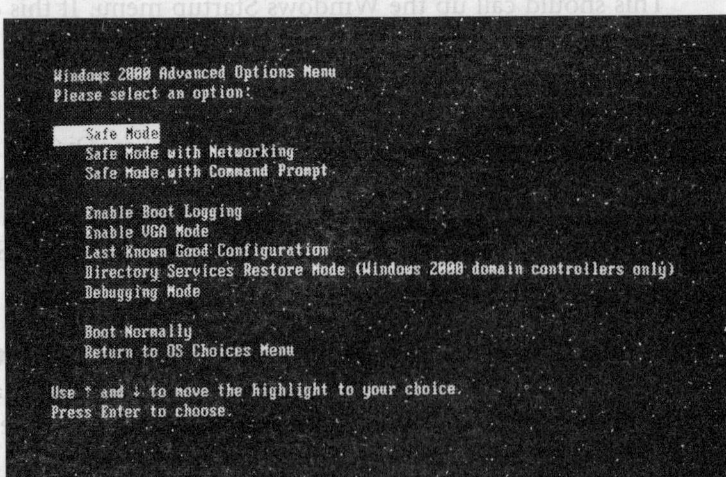

FIGURE 2.15 Windows 2000 Startup menu.

assigned to them. Then, make a note (literally—write it down on paper) of all devices in which a yellow exclamation point indicates a problem. By double-clicking each of these devices and then the Resources tab on the dialog box that appears, you'll see which resources the device is using, and a list of conflicts on the bottom of the dialog box. If you don't see the resources used, click the Manual configuration button and the conflict list should appear. Write down all this information. Then, review the list of IRQs for unused numbers, noting that there are certain IRQs that are reserved and cannot be reassigned, and that some devices must have certain IRQs and I/O addresses and can accept no others. Then, write down a list of problem devices and plan for them to use free IRQs and I/O addresses. Configure manually in the Resources tab of the device's Properties dialog box by clearing the "Use automatic settings" check box, highlighting the Resource type in the Resource settings windows, and clicking the Change Setting button, as shown in Figure 2.16. Note that many devices will not let you change settings, and often the Automatic settings check box is dimmed (grayed out). Table 2.1 lists typical resource reservations on a typical 16 IRQ computer.

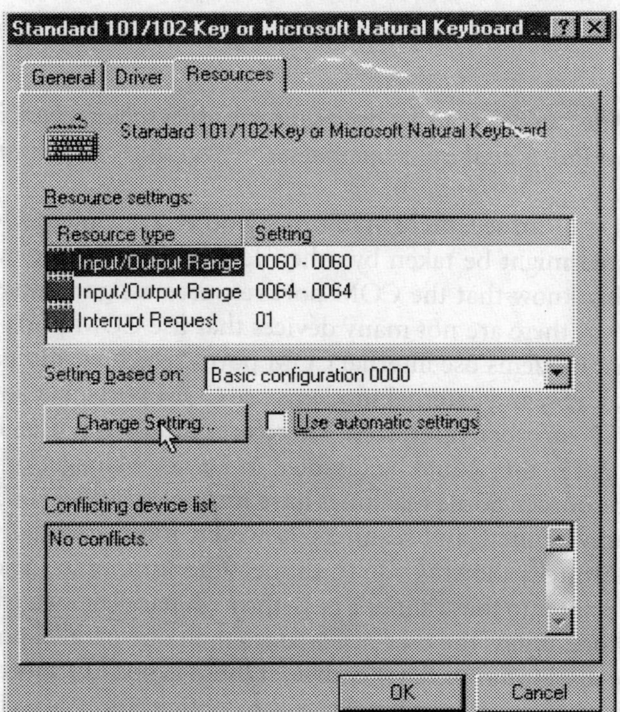

FIGURE 2.16 Changing resources manually.

TABLE 2.1 Common Reserved Resources

IRQ	Device	I/O Address Range
00	System timer	0040 – 0043
01	Keyboard controller	0060 and 0064
02	Unavailable	——
03	COM 2	02F8 – 02FF
03	COM 4	02E8 – 02EF
04	COM 1	03F8 – 03FF
04	COM 3	03E8 – 03EF
07	LPT1	varies
08	Real-Time Clock	0070 – 0071
13	Numeric Data Processor	00F0 – 00FF
14	Primary IDE Controller	01F0 – 01F7, 03F6
15	Secondary IDE Controller	0170 – 0177, 0376

TIP

If you can't seem to get the resource conflict solved, check in the BIOS to make sure that PnP is enabled. Sometimes, PnP can shut off spontaneously.

As you can see, there aren't many other available IRQs, and some of the ones not listed might be taken by other devices. If you have taken an A+ course, you probably know that the COM port resource assignments are almost set in stone. However, there are not many devices that use COM ports 1 through 4 these days. Internal modems use internal COM ports, which we discuss in Chapter 8. Certain PDAs, UPSs, and external modems use COM ports, but some of these devices also use USB or other interfaces. Therefore, unless the user has and needs multiple COM ports, they could be disabled in Device Manager or in the BIOS, freeing up their resources. Some machines have multiple parallel (LPT) ports. These are good for many printers and scanners; however, most or all parallel port scanners have pass-throughs allowing you to connect the scanner to the computer's parallel port and a printer to the scanner's pass-through parallel port, while using only one IRQ. Therefore, unless the user needs more than one parallel port, additional LPT ports can be disabled as well. Of course, if there is no IRQ shortage or problem with resource conflicts, it is best to leave the configuration as is. In other words, if it ain't broke, don't fix it.

If you still have resource conflicts, you can remove (uninstall) all Plug and Play devices with conflicts and reboot the computer. Depending on the Windows version, you might be asked to reboot after each device is recognized and reinstalled. Reboot as soon as you are prompted. You might have to try many different configurations until you eliminate all the conflicts.

WINDOWS PERFORMANCE

Performance drains can make even the newest and best computers run more slowly than they should. There are many ways to gauge a computer's performance, and many ways to improve it.

System Properties, Performance Tab (9x Only)

The quickest way to gauge performance of 9x computers is by viewing the Performance tab, shown in Figure 2.17. Notice in Figure 2.17 where it displays "System

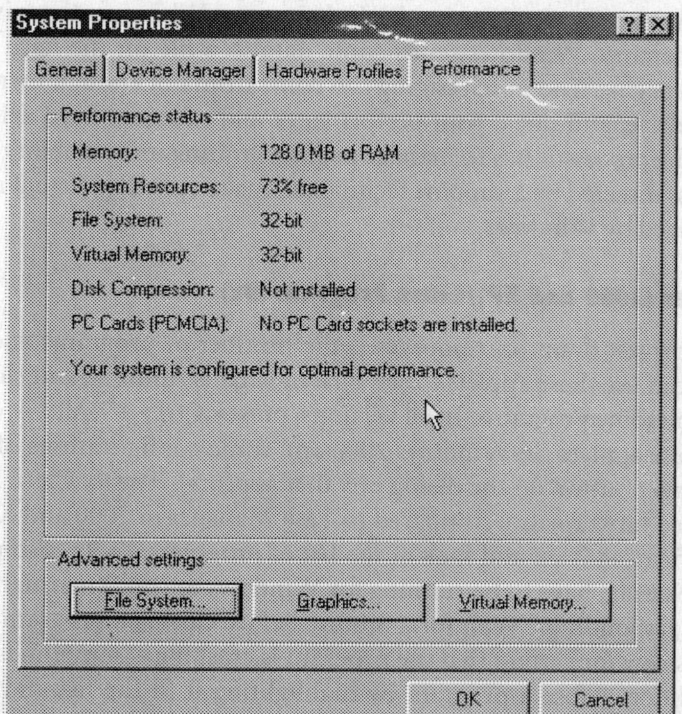

FIGURE 2.17 9x System Properties, Performance tab.

Resources: 73% free." This is an average of processor time and memory used. Programs that start with the computer, such as antivirus software, have a significant effect on this number. However, a 9x computer that has just booted should have a number ranging from the low 80s to the mid 90s. Lower numbers indicate that something is using too much resources. As you make the performance-enhancing changes described in this section, keep checking this tab for changes. Hopefully, the number will increase.

Note the additional two buttons in this tab. These open a host of other settings that should almost always be set to their defaults. In File System properties, set the typical role of the computer in the text box. Set Read-ahead optimization to Full, and System Restore disk space use (Me only) to Max unless there is a shortage of hard disk space. In the Floppy Disk tab (Me and 98 only), leave the check box cleared. In the CD-ROM tab, set the Supplemental Cache size to large and, unless the computer actually has a CD-ROM drive that is slower than 4x, set the access pattern to be optimized for quad speed or better. On Removable Disk (Me and 98 only) and in Troubleshooting, leave all check boxes cleared. Close this and the File System tab and click the Graphics button. The Hardware acceleration should be set to Full. Close this and click the Virtual Memory button. *Virtual memory* is the use of disk space to supplement physical memory. Whenever there is not enough physical memory, Windows sends some data to a file on the hard drive in a process called *paging*. Too much paging can come from not enough memory and/or a slow hard drive, and cause poor performance and excessive hard drive wear. Additionally, the processor has to manage paging, limiting its availability to other processes. Unless directed by a support technician, make sure that virtual memory is set to be managed by Windows.

Task Manager (2000 and XP)/Close Program (9x)

The biggest drain on resources is the number of programs and services running. You can use these applets to see a list of what is running, and close unimportant or troublesome programs. In all versions, press <Ctrl> + <Alt> + <Delete> to get one of these applets (in Windows 2000 and some configurations of XP, click the Task Manager button on the dialog box that appears). The 9x Close Program applet has limited functionality compared to Task Manager in 2000 and XP, but it is still very helpful. Call it up and look at the list of programs. In 9x, two programs, Explorer and Systray, have to be running for Windows to run. You might see the indication "not responding." Wait for a minute before closing a program so indicated unless you know for certain that the program is crashing—sometimes this is a temporary condition. Close a program by highlighting it in the list and clicking End Task. You'll usually get a box that says, "This program is not responding," prompting you to end the program or return to Windows and wait. This box appears whether or not the program is responding. Click End Program. If you want to close several programs, you don't have to wait for each to close. Keep highlighting them and clicking End Task, and respond to the prompts as they occur. If you can't immediately identify a program by its name in the list, you can try to discover it by searching the computer for a file by that name. Go to Start > Find (or Search) and enter the name of the file exactly as shown in the Close Program box. Then, perform the search. Once the file is found, choose the option to open the containing folder. This should tell you the program the particular file is from, and from that, you can determine if you want to close it.

Application Tab

The 2000 and XP Task Manager provides much more information. The Application page lists all running applications and the status of each. If you need to view information that is covered up, move your mouse pointer to the line between the words *Task* and *Status,* and then click and drag to move the dividing line (this can be done in many Windows dialog boxes).

Processes Tab

The Processes tab shows much more detail than the Applications tab does. Generally, only the System Idle Process should be using a large amount of CPU time for an extended period of time. If you see another process using an extraordinary amount of CPU time or memory for more than several seconds, there might be a problem with that process. Figure 2.18 shows a Windows Task Manager Processes screen with a problematic process. You can highlight the process and click End Process. You will be warned that stopping a process can cause the computer to become unstable. Generally, it is safe to end any process that is running with an actual user listed, although you'll want to save any of that process's open files first, if applicable. If the User column indicates SYSTEM, LOCAL SERVICE, or NETWORK SERVICE, closing the process might cause the system to be shut down. You can right-click a process and change its priority. If you increase its priority, the process you select will get CPU time before others of lower priority. Changing priority to Realtime might cause the computer to stop responding. Select this only if directed to do so by a support technician.

Performance Tab

As shown in Figure 2.19, the Performance tab contains graphical displays related to memory and processor usage. If you watch these graphs while you work on other programs, you'll see processor use and possibly memory use react to certain actions. If processor use is excessive (over 50%) for continued periods of time and there is no obvious explanation for it, you'll have to try to find the culprit. It could

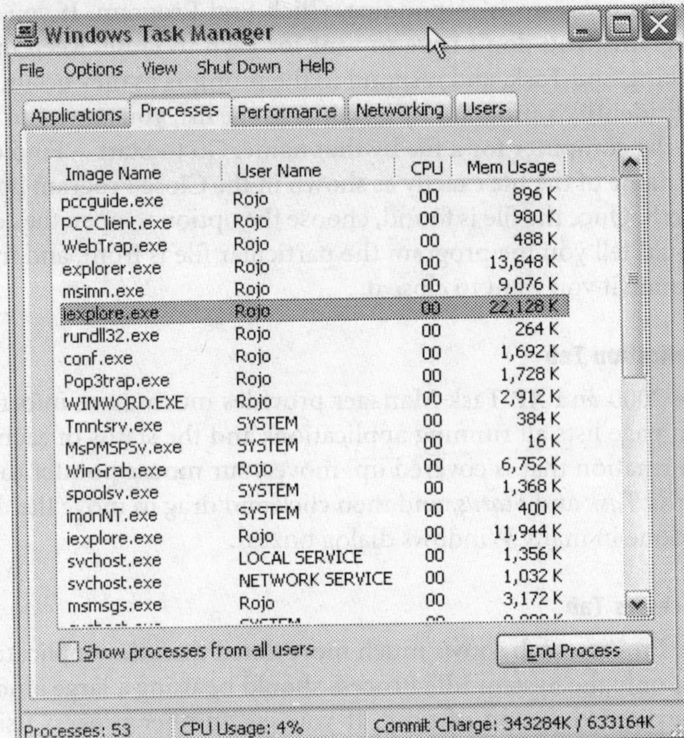

FIGURE 2.18 Processes tab of Windows XP Task Manager.

be a process or program that's causing the problem, or it could be that the processor is not up to the job. If memory use is also excessive, the problem could be a slow hard drive or inadequate memory. However, if the user is running Windows XP Professional on a 300 MHz Celeron machine with 64MB of RAM and a 5400 RPM hard drive with a small cache, and trying to use the computer for video editing or as a network server, you don't have to do any serious troubleshooting to know why it runs slowly. A newer machine might be upgradeable, but in a case like this one, advise the user to find a less demanding use for this computer and to get a new one. Chances are good that it wouldn't pay to upgrade a computer like this one to be able to handle rigorous duty.

System Tray

Now, look at the system tray on your computer. By default, it is located in the bottom right-hand corner of the screen, and it usually displays the clock. Then, look at Figure 2.20. If your system tray has that many or more icons, especially just after

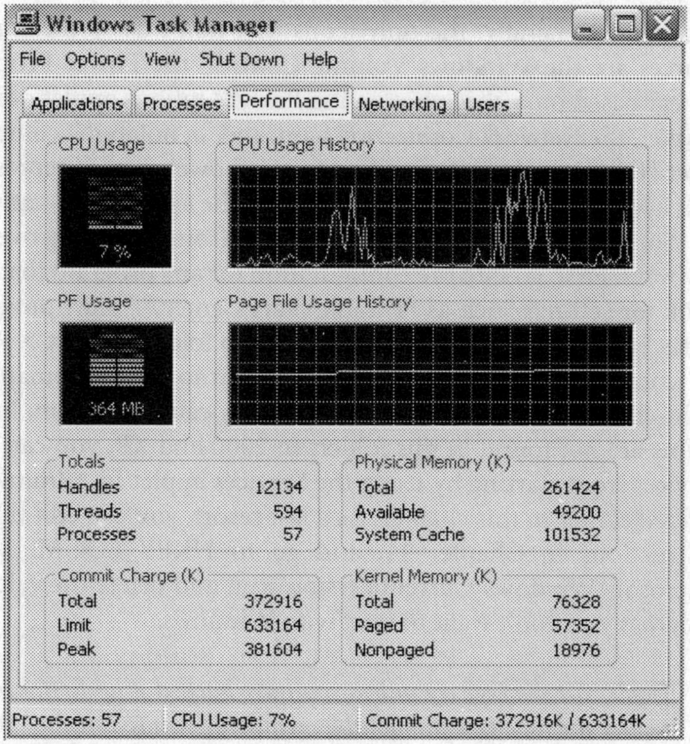

FIGURE 2.19 Performance tab of Windows XP Task Manager.

FIGURE 2.20 Overloaded system tray.

booting, chances are your computer does not have much resources remaining—the computer this came from has 35%. Most of these icons represent a process that has reserved some memory. The problem is that many programs are designed to constantly remind you that they are there, and thus they place an icon in the system tray. Many of these icons, however, don't serve much of a purpose while they aren't being used. For example, if you have dial-up Internet service and go online for an hour a day, but use the computer for other activities while not online, there is no reason to have an instant messenger (IM) program running in the background. It makes more sense to start the IM program when you go online and turn it off when you go offline. Some video adapter software puts an icon in the tray, but it is rarely necessary. Generally, the only icons that don't use a meaningful amount of resources are the Windows Volume Control, the Power Properties icon that can appear based on a check box in the Power Options applet described earlier in this chapter, the Network Connection icon, and, in notebook computers, the Unplug or Eject Hardware icon. There is one icon, however, that represents a program that uses a lot of resources that should stay in the system tray-antivirus software.

So, how do you prevent a system tray from becoming overloaded? There are a few ways. First, go into the configuration for any program that places an icon there. Look for settings such as "Disable Start Center," "Start program when Windows starts," and so forth. Second is the Startup folder in Start > Programs. If you find an icon for a program that you don't want to start automatically with Windows, right-click the icon and delete it. This can cause no harm, but most startup programs are not found in this folder. In 2000 and XP, you can prevent unnecessary services from starting by using the Services applet in Administrative Tools, as described earlier in this chapter. As a last resort, you can edit the registry. Follow the instructions in Chapter 11, and go to HKEY_LOCAL_MACHINE\Software\Microsoft\Windows\CurrentVersion\Run and delete the values for any service or program you don't want to start with Windows.

NOTE

Don't edit the registry unless you have backed it up first, because one mistake can render the machine unbootable, requiring you to reinstall Windows. You can find information on backing up the registry in Chapter 11. A better way to remove icons is by using MSConfig.

MSConfig (98, Me, and XP, Can Be Added to 2000)

This applet provides a convenient graphical interface to allow you to easily stop a program from loading with Windows. Go to Start > Run and enter msconfig. Then, click OK. When the program appears, click the Startup tab. You'll see a list of programs, each with a check box next to it as seen in Figure 2.21. As you might have guessed, each selected check box indicates that the program will start with Windows. Clear any that you don't want to start, but do so one check box at a time.

NOTE

Don't clear any check boxes on any of the tabs unless you know that the program or file you are disabling from startup is not necessary for startup. This is not common, but on certain machines with Windows 9x, most notably Sony VAIO® computers, files such as config.sys and autoexec.bat must be set to start with Windows or the machine won't boot and Windows might have to be reinstalled. On certain Compaq Presarios®, a file called sxgdsenu.exe appears in the startup. Do not disable this from starting, or the computer won't shut down. Other essential programs can be found here as well.

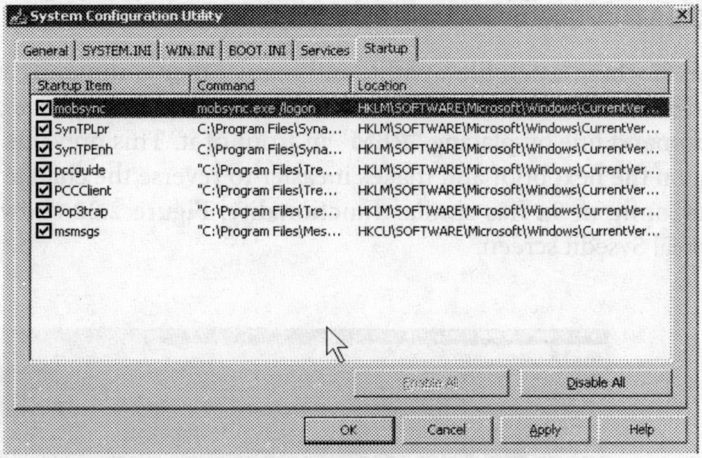

FIGURE 2.21 MSConfig.

Some notes and tips on MSConfig:

- Certain versions of MSConfig have a Cleanup command. Do not use it—it can cause problems.
- If you have XP and 2000 machines, you can copy the msconfig.exe file from the XP machine to the 2000 machine. Use the Windows Search function to search the Windows folder in XP for msconfig.exe. When you find it, copy it to the System32 folder in 2000 (usually C:\Windows\System32 or C:\Winnt\System32). It should work normally in 2000.
- The Windows XP version of MSConfig also allows you to set services to start or not start with Windows. We discussed services earlier in this chapter.
- After making changes in MSConfig, you will be prompted to restart your computer. However, there is no need to reboot until you are finished with everything you want to do. After you do reboot, check to see if the changes you made solved the problems you were attempting to resolve.

Sysedit

Sysedit is a helpful tool accessible by typing *sysedit* from the Run dialog. When run, a text editor opens the system startup files autoexec.bat, config.sys, win.ini, system.ini, and sometimes protocol.ini so they can be easily modified. If a support Web site or technician tells you to edit any of these files, using Sysedit is the best method.

AUTOEXEC.BAT

This is where batch files, paths, and many other commands are placed to start up and load before Windows. For troubleshooting here, you would remark out the command line by placing "REM" in front of it. This prevents that line from loading on the next boot and makes it easier to reverse the change if needed. Note that MSConfig in 9x has similar functionality. Figure 2.22 shows autoexec.bat on a typical Sysedit screen.

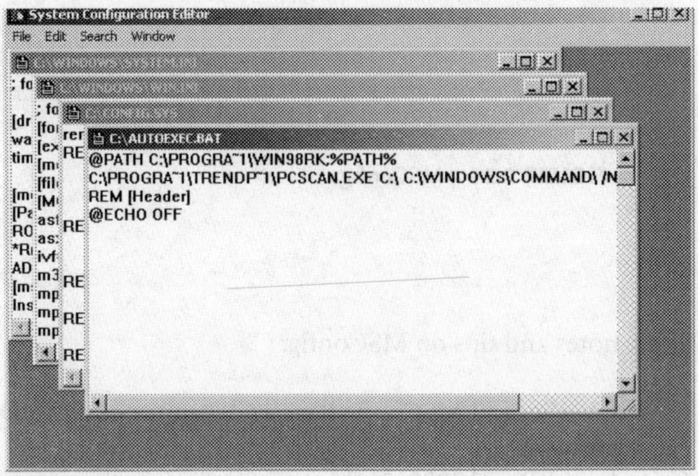

FIGURE 2.22 Sysedit open to AUTOEXEC.BAT.

Config.sys

This is where device drivers such as DOS mouse drivers and CD-ROM drivers as well as the buffers and files command are placed. The "REM" method is used in config.sys as well.

Other INI Files

System.ini: This file tells Windows about your system, such as which desktop interface (called a *shell*) will be loaded at boot. Each section has a specific name in brackets with the information below. Unlike the REM statement in autoexec.bat and config.sys, a line is commented out by placing a semicolon ";" as the first character in the line. This is safer than deleting the line, because if you comment out a line and find that it is causing problems you can easily reverse the change by running Sysedit again and removing the semicolon.

Win.ini: This is the file that tells Windows about the default settings, window positions, colors, ports, printers, and installed software. Microsoft recommends that the Win.ini file be 32KB or smaller, and it should never be larger than 64KB. Each section has a specific name in brackets with the information below. Unlike the REM statement in autoexec.bat and config.sys, a line is commented out by placing a semicolon ";" just in front of the line. Again, this is safer because if you comment out a line and find that it is causing problems, you can more easily reverse the change by just running Sysedit again and removing the semicolon.

Boot.ini: This is used only in 2000 and XP, and tells Windows which hard drive partition contains the boot files. Unless you know how and have a reason to, never edit this file, or your computer won't boot. You can find more information in Chapter 11.

SYSTEM TOOLS

In addition to the system tools available in the Administrative Tools folder, Windows has a series of system tools accessible through Start > Programs > Accessories. Many of these are helpful for the proper operation of a computer.

Backup

This comes with all versions except XP Home. For more information on backing up and restoring data using Backup, see Chapter 11. However, on 2000 and XP Pro, there are more pertinent uses for this program, such as the emergency repair process and the Recovery Console, which we also cover in Chapter 11.

Disk Hygiene

Included in System Tools and in other locations are tools for maintenance and repair of hard drives, including those we discuss next.

Disk Cleanup

Disk Cleanup is a simple applet that facilitates deletion of unnecessary files. Call it up, select the hard drive(s), and let it find files to delete. Temporary Internet files are always good to delete. Make sure that the user doesn't need to save any of the files already in the Recycle Bin before deleting them for good. Run this before running a defragmentation program (covered next).

NOTE

On many 2000 and XP machines, Disk Cleanup will often "hang." This means that it will keep working but never finish. To solve this problem, follow the instructions in Chapter 11, "Troubleshooting," for editing the registry and do the following: Navigate to HKEY_LOCAL_MACHINE\SOFTWARE\Microsoft\Windows\CurrentVersion\Explorer\VolumeCaches\Compress old files and delete the Compress old files subkey. Close the Registry editor and run Disk Cleanup. It should now work quickly.

Disk Defragmenter (Defrag)

As files and folders are added, created, and deleted from a hard drive, they tend to get *fragmented;* that is, they end up in pieces spread out all over the drive. This causes slow performance, because the hard drive heads have to move all over the drive just to read one file. Run this applet to put all fragments back together in order on the disk and increase performance. There is one interface for 9x and another for 2000/XP, but both are user friendly. A badly fragmented drive could take hours to defragment. It is best to run Defrag in Safe Mode, or at least shut off all screen savers and other programs, including those in the system tray. Advise users to run this monthly, or after deleting large amounts of data or uninstalling large programs. Running this more frequently causes unnecessary wear and tear on the drive.

There are also third-party utilities that perform defragmentation. Diskeeper® from Executive Software (*execsoft.com*) claims to defrag drives three to five times faster than "built-ins." It also has the capability of scheduling defrag jobs and performing continuous defragging to prevent a drive from ever becoming fragmented. Executive has a Lite version, which does not have the scheduling or continuous defragging capability, and a full-featured trial version with a limited operating life.

NOTE

Our tests show that the Windows 2000/NT defrag utility works similarly to Diskeeper, but the 9x defrag utility will arrange files much differently than Diskeeper does, at least when 9x's "Rearrange my files so that my programs start faster" check box is selected.

ScanDisk/Chkdsk/Error-checking

These are applets that can solve certain hard disk problems. Windows 9x comes with *ScanDisk*. Anyone who has ever had a lockup or a power failure on a Windows 9x machine causing the computer to be powered off without shutting down Windows first will be familiar with ScanDisk, because it starts automatically during boot after such an incident. For general maintenance of Windows, however, you can run ScanDisk from System Tools. There are three check boxes in the interface: Standard, Thorough, and Automatically fix errors. Standard looks for problems with files, and Thorough adds a scan of the disk surfaces for errors. It is usually advisable to leave the "Automatically fix errors" check box selected unless you need to see each individual error and confirm whether or not to fix it. Running in Thorough mode can take hours.

If a 9x computer won't boot and gives a hard drive-related error message, this often means that a file needed for Windows is on a damaged sector on the drive. Boot to DOS (covered later in this chapter) and run ScanDisk by typing scandisk from a command prompt. After it runs its standard file scan, it will prompt you to run a surface (Thorough) scan. Do so, and follow the subsequent prompts to fix the problem.

In 2000 and XP, you have two choices: Chkdsk and Error-checking. To run Chkdsk, open a command prompt or the Run dialog and type *Chkdsk /f /r* (/f sets Chkdsk to automatically fix errors it encounters, and /r sets it to attempt to recover data from bad sectors). To run Error-checking, right-click the drive you want to check, click Properties from the menu that appears, click the Tools tab, and then the Check now button in the Error-checking section. Neither will be able to accomplish much right away if there are open files such as when Windows is running on the disk being checked. In this case, you will be prompted to schedule the program to run the next time you start Windows. Do so, and then reboot. You have 10 seconds to cancel Chkdsk by pressing any key, but if you don't, you'll have to wait for Chkdsk to complete its tasks. When run after rebootings, there is no difference between Chkdsk and Error-checking. In fact, the only difference between the two is that when run in Windows, Error-checking uses a *Graphical User Interface* (GUI), and Chkdsk uses a command prompt.

NOTE *There is a version of Chkdsk available on Windows 9x, but it's not particularly useful. Use ScanDisk instead.*

We discuss other system tools in subsequent chapters.

WINDOWS UPDATE

Microsoft is constantly coming out with updates to virtually all but its oldest software, which it makes available on the *windowsupdate.com* Web page. The purposes of updates are to patch "security holes," improve functionality, fix bugs, update drivers, and so forth. In 95, there is no link to Windows Update; you'll have to go to *microsoft.com/windows95/downloads* for Windows updates, but in the other versions, you'll almost always find a link to Windows Update in the Start menu. In XP, it will be above the All Programs list and also in Add or Remove Programs in Control Panel. Another link to Windows Update is in the Tools menu in Internet Explorer. Microsoft divides its updates into three categories: Critical Updates, Windows (version) Updates, and Driver Updates. At some point, you will also be prompted to install software to install these automatically, which is convenient for the end user. Critical Updates should usually all be installed. For example, computers that had the appropriate critical update were immune from the Blaster worm that caused so much trouble in the summer of 2003. Windows (version) Updates should be chosen—for example, there is no need to install Internet Explorer support for the Danish language if the user doesn't read it. Driver updates aren't necessarily a good idea; if a hardware component is functioning correctly, it is best not to install a Windows driver update for it. There are situations in which the new driver will stop the component from functioning.

TIP

It is highly recommended to have a high-speed Internet connection to install updates, because some updates can take hours when using a dial-up connection.

MS-DOS (DOS) AND THE 2000/XP COMMAND PROMPT

The Microsoft Disk Operating System (MS-DOS) is Microsoft's original OS. It is a variation of the OS used on the original IBM PC back in 1981. It is a 16-bit OS. It is not necessary to understand exactly what the terms 16 and 32 bits mean in relation to OSs. It is enough to know that 32-bit systems are much more capable and less troublesome than their 16-bit predecessors. The original consumer versions of Windows (1.0–3.11) were 16-bit OSs. They were actually nothing more than graphical interface shells that used DOS as the OS. Windows 9x versions are 32-bit OSs that still make use of DOS, while 2000 and XP are true 32-bit OSs. You'll notice that the command prompts in 9x are called "MS-DOS Prompt," while the other two versions' command prompts are called "Command Prompt." This means that while the 9x command prompts actually use DOS, the 2000/XP command prompts are 32-bit programs that emulate DOS. 2000 and XP can run many 16-bit programs that don't attempt to access hardware directly; they have built-in emulators for DOS and Windows 3.x programs.

NOTE

In 2000 and XP, when you access the command prompt from Programs (or All Programs) > Accessories, or if you type cmd in the Run dialog, you get the 32-bit DOS emulation program. However, if you type command in the Run dialog, in most cases you get actual DOS.

There are four different ways to run a 9x computer in DOS:

A. **Reboot to DOS:** Go to Start > Shut Down and select the "Restart the computer in MS-DOS mode" option button (95 and 98 only).
B. **Use the MS-DOS prompt:** Go to Start > Programs > MS-DOS Prompt (95 and 98), or Start > Programs > Accessories > MS-DOS Prompt (Me).
C. **Boot to a DOS disk:** Use the emergency boot disk or a rescue disk from software such as an antivirus program to boot the computer.
D. **Boot to Command Prompt or to Safe Mode, Command Prompt Only:** Safe Mode is described earlier in this chapter. Power on the computer, press F8 repeatedly as soon as it starts to boot, and select either of these options from the boot menu (95 and 98 only).

So, what is the purpose of using text-based commands on Windows machines? There are several uses from a repair standpoint. First, many utilities have no graphical interface so they must be controlled with commands. Second, there are times when it is necessary to boot into DOS to fix problems that can't be fixed in Windows 9x. For example, an earlier section discussed running ScanDisk in DOS when Windows wouldn't boot because of a hard disk problem. Certain procedures, such as restoring damaged registries, must be done in DOS. Remember, early PCs ran on DOS alone, so DOS has many commands to manipulate files, folders (which it calls *directories*), and disks. A program called FDISK is necessary to format and partition as well as view the status of hard disks. We discuss FDISK in Chapter 6. Some DOS files, including config.sys and autoexec.bat among others, are still used to varying extents in all versions.

TIP

You can use an emergency boot disk to start a 2000/XP machine, but the default hard drive file system on those OSs, NTFS, is not compatible with DOS disks. Therefore, you won't normally be able to do anything useful unless at least one of the disk partitions is formatted as FAT or FAT32. However, there is a freeware utility available called Active@ *NTFS Reader for DOS from ntfs.com that will allow you to read but not write files on an NTFS partition while in DOS. You can copy this utility to any 9x boot disk and use it to boot the computer. Then, you can start the utility and use it to read files. If there is a FAT partition available on the machine, or if there is room on the boot disk, you can copy a file to it. You can also run this utility from Windows 9x in the event you have a 9x machine with an NTFS partition.*

Paths

The system of paths used by all versions of Windows originated in DOS. A typical path looks like the following:

```
C:\Documents and Settings\User\Documents\long file name A.tiff
```

where C:\ represents the C partition on the hard drive, Documents and Settings is the top-level folder, User and Documents are subfolders, and long file name A.tiff is a file. Note, however, that this path is *not* a valid DOS path. In DOS, all file and directory names must fit the 8.3 standard. 8.3 means that directory names have a maximum of eight characters, and filenames have a maximum of eight characters followed by a maximum three-character extension. The sample path, converted to 8.3, might look like this:

```
C:\DOCUME~1\USER\DOCUME~1\LONGFI~1.TIF
```

For more information on 8.3 conversion, go to *http://support.microsoft.com*, click the link for searching the Knowledge Base by article number, and enter the article number KB142982 into the search box.

Using DOS and Command Prompt Commands

Most DOS and Command prompt commands are simple to use. Unfortunately, most articles and the help files in DOS and command prompts describe these commands using excessive punctuation to delineate the portions that require substitution by actual information. Consequently, if you are not proficient in these commands and you are following one of these articles, you will likely type in punctuation that wasn't intended to be there, resulting in nothing but error messages. Moreover, the instructions might not work, even when typed correctly. Here is an example of a badly described command, the ATTRIB command, which is used to view and set the read-only, archive, system, and hidden attributes of a file or folder/directory:

```
ATTRIB [+R|-R] [+A|-A] [+S|-S] [+H|-H]
[[d:][drive:][path]filename][/S[/D]]
```

This is a typical description of a DOS command—too bad it doesn't work as described. The actual command works only by first navigating to the file or directory you want to configure by typing *CD SYSTEM* after the opening C:\WINDOWS prompt where CD is the Change Directory command, and SYSTEM is the folder you want to navigate to. To use it to remove the Read Only, Hidden, and System attributes of the file ccapi.dll in C:\WINDOWS\SYSTEM, you would type the following after the C:\WINDOWS\SYSTEM prompt:

```
attrib -r -h -s ccapi.dll
```

For more information on using DOS and command prompts, see Chapter 13 "Command-Line Tutorial." You can also search the Internet for DOS tutorials or command-line tutorials. There is a good page at *glue.umd.edu/~nsw/ench250/dostutor.htm#2a*. Another good one is *pcnet-online.com/content/general.htm*. Select the appropriate articles from the list.

OVERVIEW OF VIRUSES AND OTHER HAZARDOUS PROGRAMS

Unfortunately, there are many conscience-free people out there with nothing better to do than write and circulate programs designed to harm computer data, software, and even hardware. Many of today's computer problems come from viruses and could have been prevented by proper use of good antivirus software. The virus situation is so bad that any unprotected computer that has been connected to the Internet for awhile is likely to have some kind of virus. Simply avoiding opening e-mails from unknown senders and not opening attachments is nowhere near enough. Besides that, people who do delete such messages and attachments probably end up deleting important messages and attachments. Yet many people either don't install antivirus software or never update the program they have. People need to realize that, to be effective, antivirus software needs a file written to deal with nearly every different virus. Virus developers are at work 24/7. That is why antivirus program developers offer "pattern updates" from their Web sites as often as several times a week. Most of these programs offer some type of automatic updates—they check to make sure programs are up to date every day the user logs on to the Web, and prompt the user to accept the update if available. Just follow the instructions supplied with the program.

The program will also prompt the user to scan for viruses regularly. In fact, any prompts from antivirus programs should be heeded as soon as possible. This doesn't mean that you should let a program start a routine scan or some other time-consuming process while you're in the middle of an important task, but you should let it scan as soon as you're finished.

If the program finds a virus, it will probably attempt to clean, quarantine, or delete the file(s) and prompt you to scan the entire system for additional infection. This should be done as soon as possible to avoid further contamination. These programs also offer virus encyclopedias both in their user interface and on their Web pages. If the program tells you it cannot effectively deal with the virus, search your program's encyclopedia for instructions and follow them if possible. If your program's encyclopedia doesn't have helpful information, you can search the encyclopedia of one of its competitors.

If you have a spare computer with a good virus scanning program, a great way to scan for viruses is by removing the hard drive to be scanned and connecting it to the spare as an additional hard drive (see Chapter 6 for information on installing hard drives). For ease in connection, the spare should have a hard drive cable connected by itself to the secondary IDE controller, and a power connector, both coming out of a space on the front of the computer. Find something stable to prop up the hard drive and run the virus scan. There are several advantages to doing it this way. First, you know that no files will be in use on the scanned hard drive, error messages are much less likely, and rebooting is unnecessary to clean infected files. Use 2000 or XP so that Windows will recognize any file system. A computer like this is also good for backing up data. Figure 2.23 shows an example of such a computer.

Sometimes, virus scan programs report infected files in the hidden _Restore folder in Me or XP, but cannot clean or delete the files. While the file can be safely deleted in DOS in Me, it might not be possible to delete the individual file in XP. It

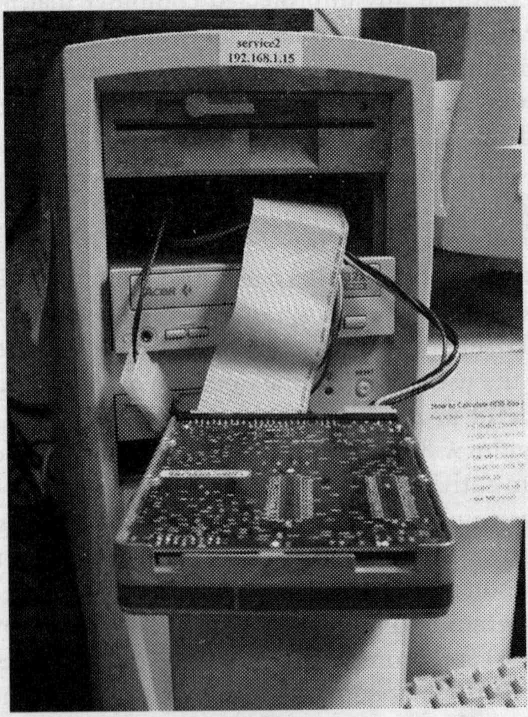

FIGURE 2.23 A computer dedicated to virus scanning and data backup.

is easier to disable System Restore, reboot the computer, and re- enable System Restore to delete the entire _Restore folder. See Chapter 11 for instructions on disabling and enabling System Restore.

Popular Antivirus Programs

Here are four effective antivirus programs:

McAfee® Virus Scan® by Network Associates: This is available in both a CD-ROM version and an online version. Web page: *mcafee.com*

Norton Antivirus™ by Symantec: This is one of many antivirus and other helpful products available from Symantec. Web pages: *symantec.com* and *norton.com*

PC-Cillin™ by Trend Micro™: Trend Micro has a wide range of antivirus and other security-related products in its line. Web page: *antivirus.com*

AVG Anti-Virus™ by Grisoft: This one leaves no excuses not to have antivirus protection—one version is available free of charge! Web page: *grisoft.com*

Spyware, Malware, and Other Malicious Programs

Spyware consists of programs that do things such as steal your private information. Malware are programs that can cause harm to a computer, yet they aren't considered viruses. There are other types of problematic programs as well. These programs often end up on the computer from the user visiting, and especially downloading from, two types of Web sites: porn sites (adult sites), and the ones most likely to be installed when teenagers get to the computer, such as:

- Bonzi Buddy
- Comet Cursor
- Date Manager
- Gator
- Gnutella
- Kazaa Desktop
- Precision Time
- Weather Bug
- Xupiter
- Any dialer.exe program the user didn't install on purpose

Although some of these provide valuable services, it is still better not to have them. Some of these don't show up in installed program lists in Add/Remove

Programs. If that is the case, you'll have to go into Program Files and delete their folders, and then use a registry cleaner to delete their entries (see Chapter 11 for information on the registry).

Another way to deal with them is to install and run a program called Ad-Aware™ from Lavasoft (*lavasoft.nu* or *lavasoft.de*). There is a free version and an inexpensive version; both are worth the weight of a hard drive in gold (there are also other programs for this purpose). Download the latest version and install it (make sure to read and comply with the terms of the license). Then, run the program. You'll most probably discover many junk programs even if you have no idea how they got there. Make the choice to remove everything unless you find something you know you need. Instruct the user to update the signature file and run Ad-Aware regularly—once a month or more will be advisable, depending on the frequency of surfing and the types of Web sites visited.

SURGE SUPPRESSORS AND UPSs

Every computer should be connected to a good surge suppressor, and preferably a UPS. A *surge suppressor* is a device that absorbs abnormally high voltages that can damage a computer. You plug the surge suppressor into a wall outlet and plug the computer and other peripherals such as monitor and printer into it. A *UPS* is a device that provides a battery backup to keep your computer running for a few minutes in case of a power failure. Except for very expensive models, UPSs provide power just long enough to allow the user to save work and shut down the computer—most can do this automatically. The advantage to this is the prevention of lost data, and the capability of allowing users to work uninterrupted in the event of very brief power failures. Most or all UPSs provide surge suppression, so you don't need a separate surge suppressor. Most or all UPSs also provide brownout protection—that is, they take over from the wall outlet and supply power when the wall voltage dips below a minimum acceptable level.

Selecting a Quality Surge Suppressor or UPS

There are hundreds of outlet strips available for less than $10, even as low as $2 or $3. Except in very rare instances, these provide little or no protection. When selecting a surge suppressor and/or UPS, there are many things to consider.

For both UPSs and surge suppressors:

- The needed number of regular outlets and, for transformers, widely spaced outlets.

- The necessary specifications. For an instructive article, go to *howstuffworks.com/surge-protector.htm.*

For UPSs only:

- The amount of time you need the system to continue to run after the power fails.
- Add up the total wattage of the computer, monitor, and other essential peripherals, and make sure the UPS is designed to work with at least that amount of wattage.
- In most UPSs, some outlets have battery backup and some have surge suppression only. Make sure that you have enough backed-up outlets to serve your purposes.

Lightning Protection

It is nearly impossible to protect against a direct lightning strike. By having a good computer grade surge protector installed between all equipment and the outlets, including the telephone and network connections, you will minimize your risk of loss. If you are going to be leaving the computer equipment unused for an extended period, it is safest to unplug everything from the outlets, thus eliminating the risk altogether.

HARDWARE HYGIENE

Computers can get dirty inside. While even computers in particularly clean environments get dusty inside, computers in dirty environments, such as industrial settings or homes of people who smoke, get extraordinarily dirty. This dirt and dust can interfere with cooling and even electrical connections inside a computer.

Vacuuming and Spray Cleaning

This dirt and dust should be cleaned out periodically using compressed air sprays of the non-flammable and non-CFC type, and by vacuuming. Mini Shop Vac® vacuums are particularly good for this task. It is best to spray and vacuum simultaneously. Spray in cooling fans and in any spot where you see dust buildup. One place dust seems to accumulate is behind the front panel. If you are cleaning a computer whose front panel can be removed, doing so allows easier access to the dust. There are a few precautions to consider:

- Turn off the computer and disconnect power first before vacuuming to prevent damage from flying debris or rapid cooling.
- Make sure the vacuum doesn't pull cables off their connectors.
- Do not rub the nozzle or brush directly on components.
- Do not invert the spray can. Doing so can emit harmful freezing gas.

ON THE CD

For a video demonstration of how to vacuum the dust from computers, see the video entitled Vacuuming and Cleaning Computers on the accompanying CD-ROM. The file is called vacuuming.mpg.

3 Motherboards and Their Components

In This Chapter

- Motherboard (Main Board, System Board, Desktop Board) Overview
- Removal and Replacement of Motherboards
- Diagnosing Motherboard Problems
- BIOS Overview
- Central Processing Units (CPUs, Processors)
- Some Cool-Looking Fans Don't Cool Any Better
- Expansion Slots
- Ports (Input/Output, or I/O) Overview

MOTHERBOARD (MAIN BOARD, SYSTEM BOARD, DESKTOP BOARD) OVERVIEW

The motherboard is the part of the computer to which every other component is connected. It contains the processor socket(s), memory slots, expansion card slots, ports for mouse, keyboard, printer, et cetera, and electronic parts, known as the *chipset*, to make everything run. Most motherboards contain some built-in components such as video, sound, network adapter, and others, and they therefore have ports for whatever built-in components they have. For example, if a motherboard has built-in sound, it will have built-in audio connectors as well.

NOTE

Laptop/notebook motherboards are not covered in this chapter unless otherwise noted.

Form Factors

Since the first PC was introduced, several types of motherboards have been used; the types referred to as *form factors*. What differentiates form factors of motherboards is their size, arrangement of components on the boards, and other details. Cases and power supplies are also classified into the same form factors; they all have to match to some extent for the components to fit properly into the case. The following form factors of motherboards are among those that have been used for PCs: AT, ATX, LPX, Micro ATX, Mini-ITX, NLX, and Flex ATX, in addition to proprietary boards by Dell, Compaq, Gateway, Hewlett-Packard, IBM, and others. Mini-ITX is a standard that allows for very small computers. Newer proprietary boards are based on the aforementioned standards, so some substitution is possible. Many sites on the Web explain the differences among form factors, such as *motherboards.org* and *formfactors.org*. Search *Google.com* for "motherboard form factors."

Motherboard Components

It is important for technicians to be able to identify the parts of any motherboard. Figure 3.1 shows an ATX motherboard.

While there are wide differences among the various brands and form factors, all motherboards have certain components in common:

CPU slot/socket: We discuss CPUs in detail later in this chapter.

Memory slots: Physical configurations of memory chips have changed over the years, but the industry seems to have settled on *dual inline memory modules*

FIGURE 3.1 ATX motherboard.

FIGURE 3.2 DIMM slots.

(DIMMs). These chips have 72 or more pins per side, although the two sides are so close to each other that it is not readily apparent that there are two sets of pins. Memory slots can accept one type of memory chip. Board design further limits the compatible memory chips. See Chapter 5, "Memory (RAM)," for more information on memory. Figure 3.2 shows DIMM slots.

BIOS chip: We discuss BIOS chips in greater detail later in this chapter.

Chipset: Every motherboard has a number of *integrated circuits* (chips or ICs) permanently installed on different parts of the board. Each chip has a separate function. It is most common for these chips to all be from a single manufacturer. You might see ASUS® brand motherboards, for example, with chipsets from Intel® or VIA. Some companies such as Intel make their own motherboards in addition to chipsets for competitors' products. Manufacturers such as these virtually always use their own chipsets in their motherboards.

AGP slot: All motherboards made in the last several years that don't have built-in video, and some that do, have an *accelerated graphics port* (*AGP*) slot. This is the slot for a video adapter. Figure 3.3 shows an AGP slot. See Chapter 8, "Video, Sound, Modems, and Network Adapters," for more information on video adapters.

FIGURE 3.3 AGP video slot.

DVO connector: Some motherboards have header connectors for digital video adapters. The connectors are called *DVO* and the adapters are called *DVI*. Figure 3.4 shows a DVO connector.

Expansion slots (ISA and PCI): Expansion devices in card form, such as modems and network adapters, go into these slots. Newer motherboards have only *Peripheral Component Interconnect* (*PCI*) slots, while some middle-aged boards have a combination of PCI and the older *Industry Standard Architecture* (*ISA*) slots. Some boards have expansion slots that give a choice between the two, as shown in Figure 3.5. In this case, ISA cards have to be inserted upside down (with the soldered-on components facing the bottom of the computer) as compared to PCI cards. As you can see in Figure 3.6, ISA slots are often dark colored, and PCI slots are usually white or off-white. The cards are also easy to differentiate; compared with ISA pins, PCI pins are much smaller and closer together, as shown in Figure 3.6. This is important, as the slots can accept only cards of the same type.

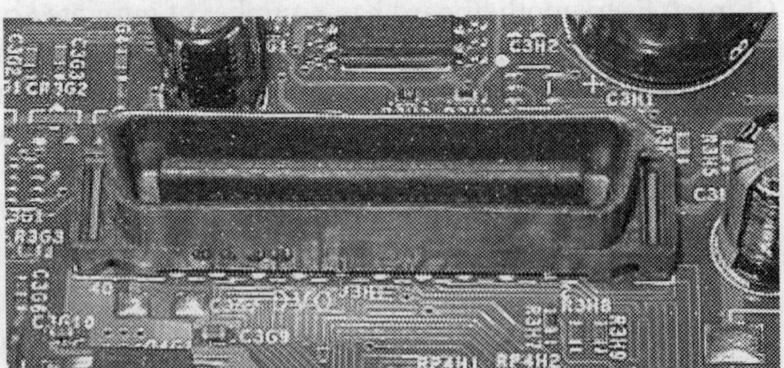

FIGURE 3.4 DVO video header connector.

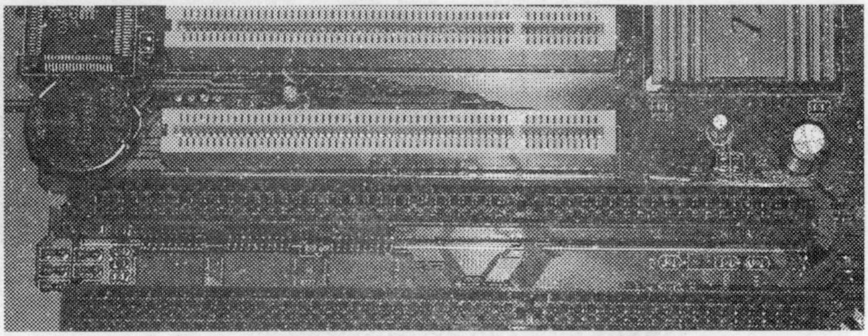

FIGURE 3.5 A combination ISA/PCI slot.

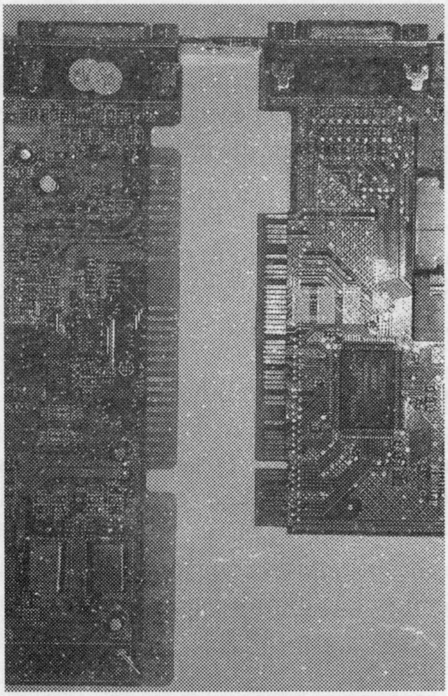

FIGURE 3.6 ISA cards' pins are much bigger and farther apart than PCI cards' pins.

PCI slot and card standards are constantly being reviewed and updated. Several new versions of PCI slots are out or coming out soon. Low Profile PCI devices, for example, are designed to fit in newer small computers. The first iterations of these cards will fit in the original PCI slots, but future versions might not. Another new version is the Mini-PCI standard for devices such as network adapters and modems

FIGURE 3.7 ATX power connector.

in laptops and other small computer-type devices. Also changing is the cards' operating voltage. Newer devices are running at 3.3 volts rather than the older standard 5 volts. Moreover, 64-bit computers are available, although very expensive as of this writing, and there are necessarily 64-bit PCI cards to fit them. All of these new standards will be important to keep up with, as compatibility between cards and slots will become more of an issue. For more information on the PCI standards, see *pcisig.com/news_room/faqs.*

ON THE CD

See the video "Removal and Replacement of Expansion Cards" on the accompanying CD-ROM for more information. The filename is Removal_and_Replacement_of_Expansion_Cards.mpg.

Power connectors: Every motherboard has power connectors that look something like the one shown in Figure 3.7. Those of you who have taken A+ courses might know this as P-8 and P-9, although the actual designations vary from board to board. Some newer boards have a 12-volt connector like the one in Figure 3.8. The one in Figure 3.8 must be connected to the proper connector on the power supply for the motherboard to receive power. If the board has a 12-volt connector, it must be connected to the power supply to avoid damage to the board.

Note that an AT (form factor) motherboard power connector is different from an ATX connector. The AT connector has two parts, each with black wires on one end. They must be installed with the black wires next to each other at the center of the motherboard's connector, as shown in Figure 3.9.

Battery: We discuss the motherboard battery later in this chapter.

Disk drive connectors: Virtually every motherboard has two IDE connectors for up to four IDE devices, usually one or two hard drives and one or two op-

FIGURE 3.8 If the motherboard has this 12-volt connector, it must be connected. The connector from the power supply is in the inset.

tical (CD or DVD) drives. With the proper cables, each connector can support two drives. Many new boards are coming with connectors for SATA drives as well. In addition, there is a connector for the floppy drive. See Chapter 6, "Magnetic Disk Drives," and Chapter 7, "CD and DVD Drives," for more information on disk drives. Figure 3.10 shows IDE connectors.

Header connectors: These are multi-pin connectors that are similar to but smaller than the disk drive connectors for ports such as serial, parallel, USB, audio, case speaker, and so forth. If you can't locate the connection instructions on a sticker on the board or in the case, refer to the motherboard documentation in hard-copy form or on the manufacturer's Web site.

Ports: Motherboards have some or all of the following ports: serial, parallel, game, PS/2 mouse, PS/2 or AT keyboard, and USB. We discuss these later in this chapter.

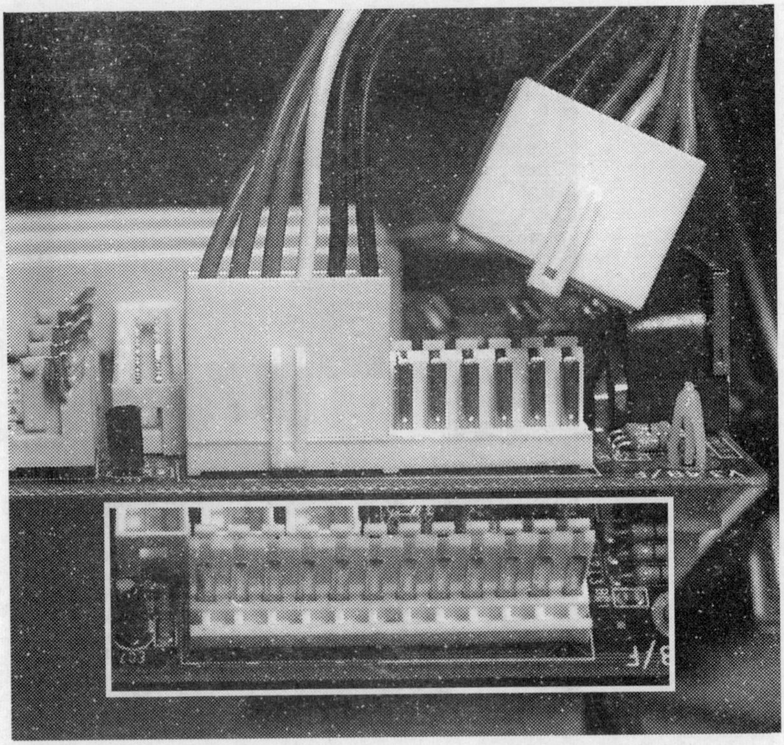

FIGURE 3.9 AT power connector.

FIGURE 3.10 IDE and floppy disk drive connectors.

Identifying a Motherboard

While many motherboards are easily identifiable, a few aren't. Here are some identification methods:

- Look for the brand name, model number, and revision number printed on the circuit board.
- Look for a sticker underneath the lowest expansion slot. It might not be visible without disassembling the computer and removing the board, or at least by using a small mirror on a handle (preferably nonconductive).
- On bootup, look on the first screen—if the information does appear, you won't have long to see it unless you press the Scroll Lock key.
- The information might appear somewhere in the BIOS.
- If the computer is a brand-name computer, you can often find the board used by going to the computer manufacturer's Web site.

Selecting a Quality Motherboard

While the chipset manufacturer can make a difference in the quality of a motherboard, the manufacturer of the board itself makes the most difference. To select the best, most appropriate board, first decide on the features the user needs such as type and number of expansion slots, plus the needed built-in components. Also note that motherboards take only one type of memory. Generally, the faster the memory, the more expensive it is. Therefore, decide on the best memory you can afford and select the motherboard accordingly. See Chapter 5, "Memory (RAM)," for more information on memory.

Next, evaluate the manufacturer based on its available technical support and its Web site. Live technical support should be available without long waits. Web sites should have technical specifications and information, plus driver and BIOS downloads, and these should be easy to find and download, if needed. Then, consider warranty and cost.

Another useful method is to go to the processor manufacturer's Web sites for recommendations of motherboards (*intel.com*, *amd.com*). Note that Intel doesn't limit recommendations to Intel motherboards and that AMD doesn't make motherboards. There are also customer reviews and professional evaluations of motherboards on Web sites such as *tomshardware.com* and *motherboards.com*.

Built-In (Onboard) Components

Just about all motherboards these days have some built-in components that were available only on expansion cards on earlier PCs. The most common of these are video, sound, network adapters, and modems. It is easy to tell when a board has

FIGURE 3.11 A computer with built-in sound and video.

these systems built in—just look for the appropriate connectors. If the computer is fully assembled, look at the back to determine the functions that are built in. The computer shown in Figure 3.11, for example, has built-in video and sound. This is apparent because these connectors are closer to the top of the computer. Other connectors are lower down, in the stack of expansion cards. By the way, the shiny metal plate surrounding the ports for the built-in components is called the I/O shield. Although this comes with a new motherboard, we'll cover this in Chapter 4, "Cases and Power Supplies."

Certain instances call for replacement of a built-in component, usually when that component fails or when the user desires a better component or one with more features. It is practically impossible to replace the individual parts on the motherboard, so the answer is to add an expansion card with the desired function. For example, if the built-in video system becomes troublesome, you can add a PCI or AGP video card. On some boards, you can add a video card and still use the built-in video in order to use two monitors. In the case of a sound card especially, if you add one you should go into the BIOS setup program (see Chapter 2, "System Configuration and Computer Hygiene") and disable the built-in sound device to prevent any conflicts.

Modem Riser

Some motherboards have modems that are not quite built in. You will see a slot that appears to be a very short PCI slot with a small modem attached. The slot is called a *modem riser*. The modem will not work on any non-identical motherboards. Replace a bad modem of this type by removing the card and installing a new modem in an unused expansion slot.

REMOVAL AND REPLACEMENT OF MOTHERBOARDS

When would you need to replace a motherboard? There are a few situations when doing so makes sense; for example, when the board fails while under warranty, or the user wants to upgrade a good quality computer but the motherboard won't support a faster processor or more memory.

TIP

Unless the new motherboard is identical to the old one, most or all drivers will be different. For this reason, you'll want to back up data on the hard drive containing Windows, if necessary, and format (erase) the hard drive before going any further. When you have installed a new board, be prepared to install Windows and all programs from scratch and to restore data from the backup. Although it is possible to replace the motherboard without following this procedure, you can expect reduced performance and other configuration problems if you do.

When replacing a motherboard, there are some general precautions to take and procedures to follow.

Removing the Existing Motherboard

ON THE CD

This is a fairly simple matter. First, with the power off, disconnect *every* cable from the outside of the computer. After opening the case (see Chapter 4 and the accompanying CD-ROM for more information on opening cases), make sure to use a grounding strap and perhaps other anti-static devices as described in Chapter 1, "Overview." Then, disconnect all cables you can access from inside the computer, including the disk drive cables and small audio cables. You will most probably have to remove the drive cage (see Chapters 4 and 6). Remove any remaining cables and all cards in expansion (PCI, ISA, AGP, etc.) slots and place them on an anti-static surface. It is probably best to leave the processor and memory in their places for now. Next, remove the screws holding the motherboard to the case, and carefully remove the board. If it is still usable and/or the CPU and memory are still in place, place it on the anti-static surface.

ON THE CD See the "Motherboard Installation" video on the accompanying CD-ROM for an example of installing a motherboard.

Installing the New Motherboard

First, make sure that the new motherboard is the same form factor as the case. Then, make absolutely certain that the power supply is set for the correct voltage to avoid zapping the new board. Look at the back of the case for a small switch that says 115V and 230V, or something similar, as shown in Figure 3.12. This should be set to the voltage available in the country in which it is used; in North America, this voltage is 115.

Next, make sure that no conductive surface comes in contact with any metal parts of the case. While some cases have elevated mounting holes that hold the board away from the case wall (see Figure 3.13), other cases call for standoffs. *Standoffs* are small spacers that go between the board's and the case's mounting holes (see Figure 3.14).

After screwing in the screws, you need to install the power connectors and then follow the manufacturer's instructions for setup, which we discuss next. After you've done this, reinstall all of the compatible peripheral devices (if any) that were connected to the old motherboard. For more information on installing peripherals, see the rest of this chapter, Chapter 2, and the chapter appropriate for the type of device in question.

FIGURE 3.12 Power supply voltage switch.

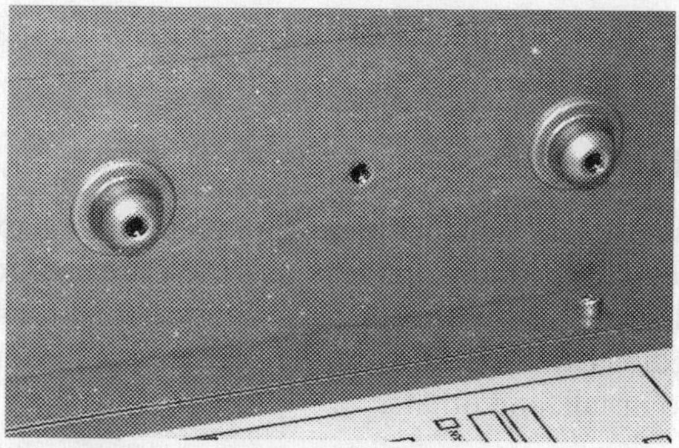

FIGURE 3.13 Elevated mounting holes.

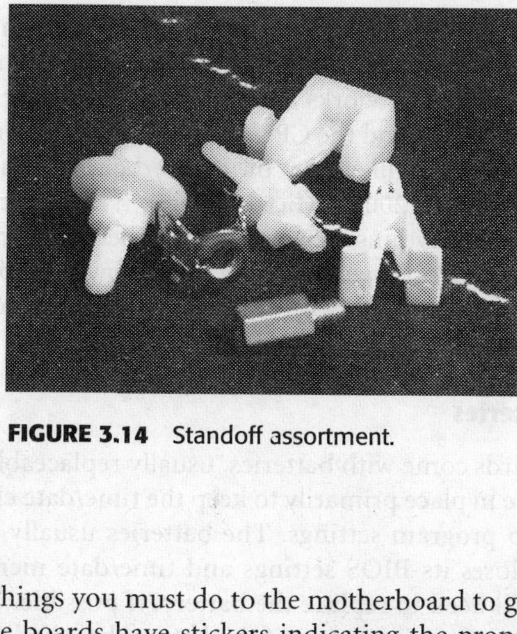

FIGURE 3.14 Standoff assortment.

Motherboard Setup

There are certain things you must do to the motherboard to get everything working together. Some boards have stickers indicating the proper positions of DIP switches and jumpers, but in most cases, the documentation (manual) is essential. If you don't have the manual, you can usually find information on the manufacturer's Web site.

TIP

In some cases, the board was manufactured by one company but sold by another under a different trade name. In this case, you might be able to find the actual brand and model number by peeling off a brand/model-number sticker on the board to reveal the actual manufacturer's sticker. Make sure the board is not under warranty when you do this; peeling off the sticker might void an active warranty.

ON THE CD See the Industry Contacts document on the accompanying CD-ROM for manufacturer contact information.

DIP Switches and Jumpers

All boards have DIP switches and/or jumpers (see Chapter 2 for general information on these). Depending on the board, these are used to select such settings as the speed and family of the processor, and there might also be jumpers to reset the CMOS, redirect the sound from the rear to front connectors, select the type of memory to install, and others.

DIAGNOSING MOTHERBOARD PROBLEMS

The most obvious sign of a damaged motherboard is a burnt or otherwise visibly damaged part. Naturally, motherboards can die without any visual signs. If you are sure the power supply works and is turned on, set for the correct voltage, and is connected correctly, and the CPU is good, but you attempt to boot and absolutely nothing happens, it is likely that the motherboard is dead. In this situation, a POST card such as Micro 2000's Micro-Scope™ (see Chapter 11, "Troubleshooting") might not show anything. The only answer here is to try to replace the board with one that is compatible with the case, CPU, power supply, memory, and peripherals. If this is not feasible, a new computer can often be built with at least some of the existing parts.

Motherboard Batteries

Motherboards come with batteries, usually replaceable lithium coin cells. These batteries are in place primarily to keep the time/date clock running and maintain BIOS setup program settings. The batteries usually last at least six years. If a computer loses its BIOS settings and time/date memory every time it is shut down, you'll need to replace the battery, if possible. The POST (see Chapter 2) might show an error message if the battery has died. Moreover, if someone has set a supervisor password in the setup program, and now has forgotten it, and the computer cannot boot, the only way to reset or cancel the password is to remove and replace the battery. You might be able to use a battery tester to test the voltage of the battery without removing it. Make sure the polarity of the probes matches the polarity of the battery, and check to see if the battery is still good. Double-check the motherboard documentation to make sure the battery is the right type.

Battery Replacement

If the BIOS settings are still valid and you need to replace the battery, know that the motherboard *might* have a capacitor that will hold a charge just long enough for you to replace the battery without losing your settings. However, whether or not it has such a capacitor, it is recommended to write down all non-default BIOS settings before changing the battery. Changing a replaceable battery is a simple but delicate operation. Carefully remove the old battery and insert the new one, as shown in Figure 3.15. Just make sure that the new one is of the correct type and that it outputs the correct voltage.

NOTE

There is a long narrow tab on some battery holders that at first glance looks as though it should be pulled up to remove the lithium coin cell. It is really just a spring tab, and if pulled up will permanently lose its ability to hold the battery down and make contact, thus almost always ruining the board. In this case, slide the battery to the open side and remove it, as shown in Figure 3.15.

Some motherboards have batteries soldered in place. Many of these boards have terminals for connection of a replacement battery; in these cases, the dead battery is left in place, as shown in Figure 3.16.

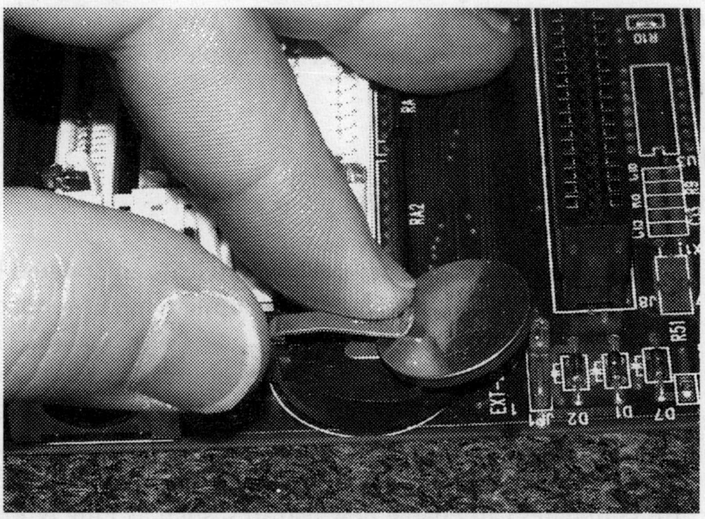

FIGURE 3.15 Replacing a lithium coin cell battery.

FIGURE 3.16 Permanently installed battery and replacement battery terminals (four pins).

BIOS OVERVIEW

We discussed the BIOS setup program in Chapter 2. Here we cover the physical BIOS chip and the updating of the BIOS.

Updating (Flashing) the BIOS

While the BIOS seems permanent, it can almost always be updated. That is why the BIOS is called *firmware*, rather than software or hardware. The process of replacing firmware is called *flashing*. It is often a simple, albeit delicate, matter to flash the BIOS.

Why Update the BIOS?

There are three main reasons to update a BIOS:

- The motherboard manufacturer might release an updated BIOS to correct bugs in the original. For example, a BIOS update might reduce the operating temperature of the computer.
- BIOS updates sometimes allow the computer to use hardware or software that wasn't available when the original BIOS was released. Examples are a new version of Windows, a hard drive with greater storage capacity than the previous BIOS allowed for, or a processor that didn't exist at the time the BIOS was written.
- BIOS updates can enable new features, such as Plug & Play technology or *hibernation* (storing the contents of the memory on the hard drive and shutting off the power so that when the user restarts the computer, the session is left as if the computer had not been shut down).

A Reason *Not* to Update the BIOS

If everything is working well, then in most cases you should leave the BIOS alone and not update it. Updating the BIOS for no reason other than the fact that there is a new version available could actually *cause* problems.

Determining Your Current BIOS

There are various ways to view your current BIOS version number. If you have access to your computer or motherboard manual in hard copy, disk, or on the Web, you might be able to find the recommended method. Otherwise, try these until you have found it:

- Go to Start: > Programs: > Accessories: > System Tools: > System Information, and with System Summary highlighted, find BIOS Version/Date in the right-hand pane.
- Run an information-gathering utility (see Chapter 11 for more information) and look at the BIOS information under Main Circuit Board.
- Boot or reboot the computer. When you see the BIOS information on the screen, early in the boot process, press the Scroll Lock key as soon as you can to pause the boot process. Then, write down the number and date.
- While the computer is booting up, press the appropriate key for your system and enter the BIOS setup program (see Chapter 2). Usually, the current BIOS version number will appear on the very first screen you will see.
- Go to *unicore.com* and run the BIOS Agent. *Unicore.com* is covered next.

Obtaining an Updated BIOS

The first place to look for a BIOS update is on the computer or motherboard manufacturer's Web site. Check the update's date and the version number. If the date is later and the version number is higher than on the existing BIOS, you might want to update. If the manufacturer doesn't have an updated BIOS, *and you have a compelling reason to update it*, the next step is to go to the BIOS manufacturer's Web site. With most BIOSs, doing so will eventually take you to *unicore.com*. This site provides a free utility to find the existing BIOS version on your computer and direct you to the latest upgrade, which is not free. The upgrade might be downloadable, or might be available only by purchasing a new BIOS chip.

Wherever you obtain your update, follow the instructions on the Web page. If there is a downloadable update, it will probably be accompanied by a BIOS *flash* utility (program) such as awdflash.exe or the Intel Express BIOS update utility (which runs in Windows). Download the BIOS update and the flash utility and follow the instructions. The traditional flash utility runs only in DOS, so you'll need a DOS boot disk with the flash utility and the BIOS BIN file copied onto it. Interestingly, a Windows Me boot disk won't work. Use either a Windows 95 or 98 boot disk to start the computer, regardless of the OS. If you don't have access to a 95/98 boot disk, any DOS disk will work. Particularly useful is DrDflash™, available free from *bootdisk.com*. The advantage to DrDflash is that there are no drivers on the disk to get in the way. Follow the directions, paying close attention to these warnings:

Use a UPS or else: *UPS* stands for *Uninterruptible Power Supply*; it is also known as a battery backup. If power is interrupted during the updating of the BIOS, your computer will likely be rendered unbootable, and the only solution will be to get a replacement BIOS chip, if replacement is even possible with your motherboard. Make sure that the UPS is working properly, and that the battery is fully charged.

NOTE

If you are updating a laptop's BIOS, a UPS is unnecessary as long as the laptop's battery is working properly and the laptop is plugged in to AC power.

Back up the current BIOS first: Many BIOS update utilities allow for backing up the original BIOS. Do this if possible; you should be able to go back to the original BIOS if there is a problem with the new one.

Follow the directions exactly: Updating the BIOS is probably the most delicate operation you can perform on a computer. Make sure that you read *all* of the instructions before starting. If you are typing commands, make sure that the syntax of every command is exactly as written in the instructions.

What to Do About a Failed BIOS Update

Unfortunately, sometimes BIOS updates are not successful. If you saved the original BIOS, you can usually run the flash utility to restore it. If this doesn't work, you will probably have to replace the chip. Some Gigabyte™ brand motherboards have a backup BIOS that automatically takes over in the event of a primary BIOS failure, but this feature is not common. In other boards, if the chip is permanently attached to the motherboard, you'll either have to send the motherboard back to its manufacturer for chip replacement, or buy a new board.

If you have a replaceable BIOS chip, then you can hopefully find a replacement. First, try the motherboard or computer manufacturer for a replacement. If they cannot supply one, try *unicore.com*. You'll also need a chip puller to remove the chip, as shown in Figure 3.17.

FIGURE 3.17 Removing a BIOS chip.

CENTRAL PROCESSING UNITS (CPUs, PROCESSORS)

Often called the brains of the computer, the CPU is the device that performs the calculations that make computing possible. Although there are several CPU manufacturers, Intel and Advanced Micro Devices (AMD) make the vast majority of processors used in Windows-based PCs, so we will limit our discussion mostly to Intel Celeron and Pentium II, III, and 4 processors, and AMD K6-2, K6-3, Athlon, and Duron processors. For more information, go to *intel.com* or *amd.com*. One other processor family worth mentioning is the very inexpensive VIA C3 family from VIA Technologies (*via.com.tw*), which has started to show up in some similarly inexpensive systems. Time will tell if the quality will match that of Intel or AMD.

Selecting an Appropriate Processor

When selecting a processor, the first consideration is compatibility with the motherboard.

Motherboard-CPU Compatibility

A given motherboard can accept certain CPUs. The most obvious limitation is whether the motherboard has a CPU socket or slot, and which type of either it has (we discuss sockets and slots later in this chapter). Of the two most popular CPU brands, Intel and AMD, some boards can accept one and some can accept both. CPU compatibility is further limited by design elements of the board that require certain models and speed (gigahertz, or GHz) ratings. The motherboard manual will specify the processors that are compatible with it. However, you should check the board manufacturer's Web site for updated information. Sometimes a motherboard will accept a processor version that didn't exist when the manual was printed.

CPU Terminology

For you to be able to select the most appropriate CPU, it will be helpful to understand some terminology:

Front Side Bus (FSB): Measured in megahertz (MHz), the FSB is the channel that connects the processor with main memory. The faster this is, the better the performance will be. This number will range, as of this writing, between 33 and 800 MHz.

Cache (pronounced "cash"): All new CPUs have cache memory. *Cache*, as it pertains to CPUs, is expensive high-speed memory used for storing frequently used instructions. This saves the time needed for the CPU to get all of its instructions from slower main memory. All other things being equal, the more cache a CPU has, the better its performance will be. The less expensive CPU lines, Intel, Celeron, and AMD Duron, have less cache than their otherwise equivalent Pentium and Athlon cousins. L2 Cache, the most variable number, ranges from 128 to 512 KB on relatively recent processor models.

Sockets and slots: As discussed in the motherboard section, processors either fit in a socket or slot, depending on their construction. There are quite a few different socket and slot types.

For more information on slots and sockets, see *itp-journals.com/ sasample/ T1053.pdf*. There is also a very helpful presentation available at *ccc. commnet. edu/DL/~moriber/pc_3e_03b.ppt.*

Pins: Within the categories of sockets and slots, there are different types of each. The types vary by size, and number and configuration of pins.

Fans and heat sinks: All processors made in the recent past require heat sinks and fans. *Heat sinks* are little radiators used to radiate the heat away from the processor. Heat sinks are crucial; remove the heat sink from some processors while they're running and they will melt, or even catch fire almost immediately.

Some Intel processors have built-in temperature protection; they will shut down if the temperature gets too high, but they could still sustain damage. The heat sink and fan work together to keep the processor's temperature within a safe range. It is necessary to use a thermal pad, thermal grease, or silver thermal compound between a processor and the heat sink, which not only helps to transfer heat from the processor but also evens out the surface to reduce the possibility of cracking the processor. *Use the compound sparingly*. The silver thermal compound has the highest heat transfer capacity of all of these. Figure 3.18 shows the thermal pad on the bottom of the heat sink.

NOTE *A very helpful article on these heat-transfer materials appears at antec-inc.com/info_DIYArticle2.html. We highly recommend that you read it.*

CPU families: CPU manufacturers create *families* of processors for both technical and marketing purposes. Examples of family names are Intel's Pentium 4 and Celeron, and AMD's Athlon and Duron. Generally, each member of a family has the same internal design with the only differences being speed and perhaps some

FIGURE 3.18 The thermal pad goes on the bottom of the heat sink.

less-publicized specifications. Celerons don't fit that definition exactly, however; all of Intel's lower priced processors since Pentium IIs were current have been called Celerons. Therefore, Celerons have the same general internal design as other Celerons of the same particular generation and form (socket, slot, etc.). Celerons and Durons are less expensive than Pentiums and Athlons of the same speed and form. The differences are in such specifications as cache memory and front side bus speed. They are suitable for basic computing.

Selecting a Replacement CPU

When building or buying a new computer, it might make more sense to select the CPU first, and then select a motherboard to accommodate it. However, in the context of repair, you'll usually have to find a CPU that matches an existing motherboard. Therefore, the first consideration is to review the motherboard documentation to see which processors are compatible with it, as discussed earlier in the chapter. You'll then want to select the best of the compatible processors you can afford. "Best" is usually defined as fastest with the most cache. However, you should also consider the usage of the computer. A computer used primarily for e-mail, to read news on the Web, and to write letters does not need as good a processor as one used for heavy-duty number crunching or video production, for example.

CPU Removal and Replacement

CPUs are often very easy to remove and replace. Currently used sockets are called *zero insertion force (ZIF)* sockets. The processor can be gently placed in the socket, and then a lever is lowered and locked to hold the CPU in place. Slot processors should be gently inserted in their slots. Make sure to use proper grounding protection and be careful not to touch the pins.

ON THE CD

See the "Installing CPUs" video on the accompanying CD-ROM to see examples of installing a slot-type and a socket-type CPU.

There are three ways to set motherboards for the processor in use: automatically, manually with jumpers or micro DIP switches, or in the BIOS setup program. Some motherboards offer more than one of these methods. With the boards with jumpers to set processor parameters, the manuals have charts to show the jumper settings for the processors it takes.

Diagnosing CPU Problems

CPUs are generally trouble-free. The most likely problem is heat damage that can happen when the fan wears out. The most common symptom of heat damage is a computer that starts out working normally, but after awhile performs erratically.

Eventually, the computer will lock up. When hearing a report like this, with the power disconnected, open the case and check to make sure that the fan and heat sink are in place—put them in place if they aren't. Attempt to spin the processor fan by hand. The fan should spin freely and continue spinning when you let go, and not make any noise. If you encounter resistance and/or hear noise, replace the fan.

If the fan blades spin freely, the next step is to power on the computer and see if the fan actually spins. Some BIOS setup programs have CPU temperature gauges, and some motherboard manufacturers provide Windows programs to monitor the CPU temperature, among other things. If the fan does spin, you can check these gauges, if present, to determine if the processor's temperature is in the safe zone, which will be indicated on the gauge. Another way to measure the processor temperature is to use a laser temperature gauge. While the computer is running, aim the laser at the space between the processor and heat sink. Compare your result to the processor documentation's temperature specifications. If the temperature is too high, the processor isn't being cooled properly.

If there is any problem with the fan spinning, shut down the computer immediately and replace the fan. Then, start up the computer and let it run for at least two hours. Next, open some programs and try to use them. If the computer works normally, you can be reasonably sure that the processor didn't sustain any major damage. If you still have problems, it is possible that the processor has been damaged, or that the computer has other problems. If you have a used replacement available, and you are sure that the CPU is now being properly cooled, temporarily replace the CPU. If the problems go away, there's a very good chance that the old CPU has sustained damage and will need to be replaced. Products such as Micro-Scope and its POST card can give you accurate diagnoses.

If the power supply fan spins, but the computer won't otherwise power on, the problem could be a dead or disconnected CPU or motherboard. If everything is connected, the only way to diagnose the problem, after ruling out a bad power supply (see Chapter 4), is to swap a known good CPU or motherboard, one at a time, with the original items. If the replacement device causes the system to work, then you have found the problem.

CPU Fan Replacement Tips

When replacing a fan on a socket processor, you might need to press hard on the retaining clip. Make sure you don't slip and damage the motherboard. Figure 3.19 shows the steps for installing a processor, fan, and heat sink.

Fans can have 2-, 3-, or 4-pin power connectors. Figure 3.20 shows the 3-pin connector. The two basic types are the 3-pin that connects to a connector on the motherboard, and the 4-pin type that connects to any of the 4-pin connectors from the power supply. Adapters are available to connect one to the other.

FIGURE 3.19 Installing a processor, fan, and heat sink.

FIGURE 3.20 3-pin processor fan connectors.

Socket to Slot Adapters

There are adapters available that allow you to use a Socket 370 processor in a motherboard that otherwise would accept only a slot processor. These can work well when they are first installed, but we have found that they are often the cause of lockups as time goes on. If you are troubleshooting lockups on a machine with one of these adapters, it is a good idea to reseat the adapter in the slot, making sure the slot processor retention mechanism is properly secured and holding the assembly securely in place. If the problem persists, the solution is to get a compatible slot-type processor and install it in place of the socket processor with the adapter.

SOME COOL-LOOKING FANS DON'T COOL ANY BETTER

A few computer owners seem concerned about the appearance of the inside of their computer case. This is fine if the components both work well and look good, but many cool-looking fans don't cool any better than lower cost models. Rather than worrying about the appearance of a fan, check to see if it is approved by the processor manufacturer.

EXPANSION SLOTS

As stated earlier, expansion slots consist of AGP video slots and DVI video header connectors, and PCI and ISA slots. PCI and ISA slots are used primarily for modems, network adapters, sound cards, additional ports (such as USB or parallel), and video cards. You will likely encounter other types of cards as well.

Removal and Installation of Expansion Cards

Removal and replacement of expansion cards is usually simple. You might want to use an anti-static wristband for this. With the computer powered off and disconnected, open the case and remove the screw (if present) holding the card in place, as shown in Figure 3.21.

Next, pull out the card, using only as much force as necessary. Do not bend the card. After removing the card, if you plan on reinstalling it or installing another card, you are ready. However, if you plan to leave the slot empty, you'll want to install a slot cover, as shown in Figure 3.22.

To install another card, just follow the procedure in reverse.

NOTE *This procedure works for the vast majority of tower and desktop computers. However, if you encounter a computer for which this doesn't, you might need to seek assistance from the computer manufacturer's Web site. Certain Sony VAIO and Gateway towers require removal of a single panel on the outside back of the computer to unlock all of the cards.*

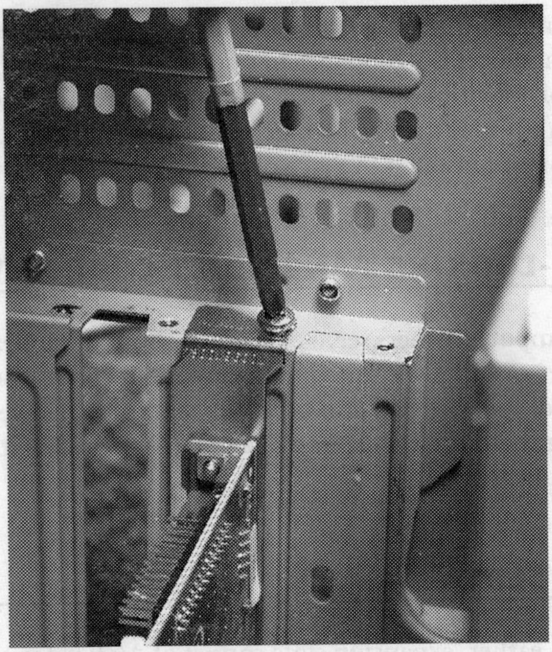

FIGURE 3.21 Removing the screw that holds an expansion card in place.

PORTS (INPUT/OUTPUT, OR I/O) OVERVIEW

Ports, for the purpose of this chapter, are physical connectors and their corresponding software that conduct signals into and out of computers. Figure 3.23 shows the most common ports, and some are described in the upcoming list. These are often built into the motherboard, but are also on expansion cards.

Serial: 9-pin serial ports carry electrical pulses one at a time and therefore tend to be slow. They are used for older pointing devices (mice), connections to UPSs, Personal Data Devices (PDAs), digital cameras, and external modems. Serial ports are associated with software COM ports (see the *Device Manager* discussion in Chapter 2). Serial devices can be plugged in and unplugged without risking damage to the device or the computer.

Parallel: Used mostly for printers and scanners, 25-pin parallel ports carry eight electrical signals at one time. Associated with LPT ports in Device Manager and printer software, parallel devices can be plugged in and unplugged without risking damage to the device or the computer.

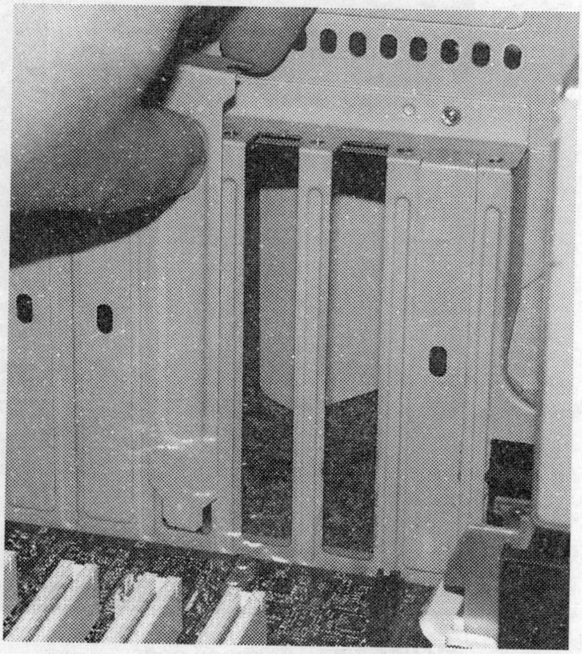

FIGURE 3.22 Installing a slot cover.

Universal Serial Bus (USB): USB ports are very versatile. Unlike serial and parallel devices, which require a separate IRQ per device, USB ports can be expanded through the use of USB hubs (adapters that convert one USB port to several), yet all devices connected to a single USB port on the computer safely share one IRQ. USB 2.0 is a newer standard for much faster USB devices. Most USB 2.0 devices run if connected to older USB 1.1 ports, although they will be limited to the speed of the slower port. Slower USB devices work normally in USB 2.0 ports. Additionally, USB provides power to devices that don't use a lot of it. Another advantage to USB is that it is hot-pluggable or hot-swappable, meaning that devices can be plugged in and removed while powered on, without risking damage to the device or the computer. Although later versions of Windows 95 might support USB, most USB devices don't support Windows 95.

Video Graphics Adapter (VGA) ports: VGA is the standard for all analog monitors used since the early 1990s. VGA connectors have 15 pins and can be plugged and unplugged without risk of damage.

DVI ports: These are for digital monitors and also can be plugged and unplugged without risk of damage.

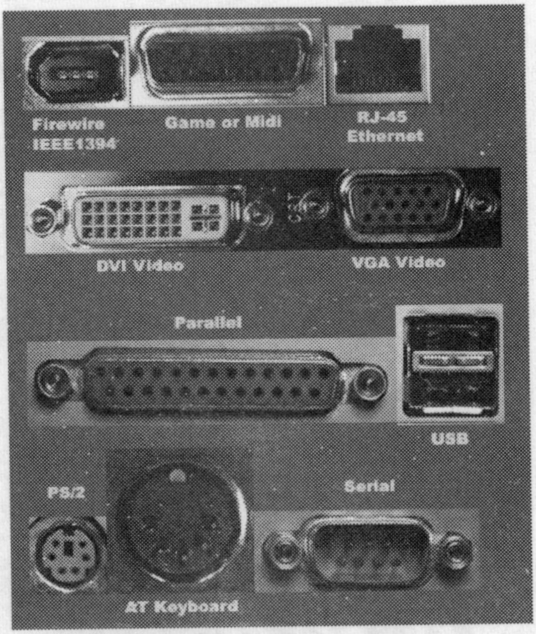

FIGURE 3.23 Common ports.

FireWire (IEEE 1394): Similar to USB, but much faster than USB 1.1. Used for all the types of peripherals as USB, plus digital audio and video cameras and other devices that require high-speed data transfer.

PS/2: Mouse and keyboard connectors. Plug and unplug only with computer power off.

DIN AT keyboard connectors: Used in older PCs.

PCMCIA (PC Card, CardBus): Present almost exclusively in laptops, these are used mainly for modems, network adapters, and for tiny hard drives. These cards can usually be inserted in their slots without any special steps, but they should be stopped in Windows Control Panel, PCMCIA or PC Card applet before removing to prevent Windows problems such as lockups, or possible damage to the card.

Game Controller/MIDI port: These are 15-pin ports used for older game controllers and MIDI musical instrument devices.

SCSI (pronounced "scuzzy"): There are no fewer than seven different types of SCSI connectors, so chances are good that if you see a connector not covered here, it's a SCSI.

RJ-45 (Ethernet): This is a connector for a network cable.

4 Cases and Power Supplies

In This Chapter

- Cases
- Power Supplies

CASES

A computer's case is more than a box. The case includes the *drive cage*, the internal compartment that holds disk drives, and almost always the power supply, among other features, all of which we discuss in this chapter. As discussed in Chapter 3, "Motherboards and Their Components," cases come in various types called form factors, which differ in layout of components. The case's form factor needs to match that of the motherboard and the power supply. Just as with motherboards, some cases are proprietary and require proprietary power supplies and motherboards.

FIGURE 4.1 A typical ATX case.

Case Components

Cases come with various components, as shown in Figure 4.1.

Most of these components are self-explanatory. Drive bays are slots, usually in the front, for installation of disk drives. There are bays for removable media drives such as optical, floppy disk, and Zip drives. These have openings in the front and usually come with plastic covers in case they are not used. The 5¼-inch bays are primarily for optical drives. There is at least one hard drive bay and almost always a 3½-inch floppy drive bay. Cases usually come with a small speaker, which is there to provide very basic sounds to the user. About all this speaker plays are warning beeps and the sound of a modem connecting. This speaker is very important, because multimedia speakers don't work before Windows has booted, if Windows is in Safe Mode (see Chapter 2, "System Configuration and Computer Hygiene"), or if there is a problem with the sound card (or if there isn't a sound card). If the computer won't boot due to a hardware problem, there is usually a beep code that plays through this speaker. See Chapter 11, "Troubleshooting," and the Beep Codes list on the CD-ROM for more information.

ON THE CD

NOTE *Some motherboards have extremely small speakers soldered onto the board. These are little black plastic cylinders with a hole at the top. These boards don't use case speakers.*

While many older PCs had key locks, few newer ones do. Locking a computer prevents it from being booted. The most important indicator lights are the ones that show that power is on and that the main hard drive is active. Constant flashing of the hard drive indicator shows that the drive is running too much (churning). If the indicator either doesn't light at all or glows continuously, that usually means the computer is locked up.

On recent cases, the only button is the power button. Older cases might have a Reset button, which simply turns power off and on, and a "Turbo" button. Leave the Turbo button in the On position unless a tech support technician tells you to turn it off.

I/O Shields

I/O shields are the metal plates that surround the ports that are built into the motherboard. These snap in place, as shown in Figure 4.2. They are used to shield these ports from radio frequency interference (RFI) and to provide openings in the case in the correct size and configuration for the motherboard's built-in ports.

Case Quality

A good quality case can have a big impact on the performance and durability of the computer. Cases sold have to meet requirements for shielding against both RFI that

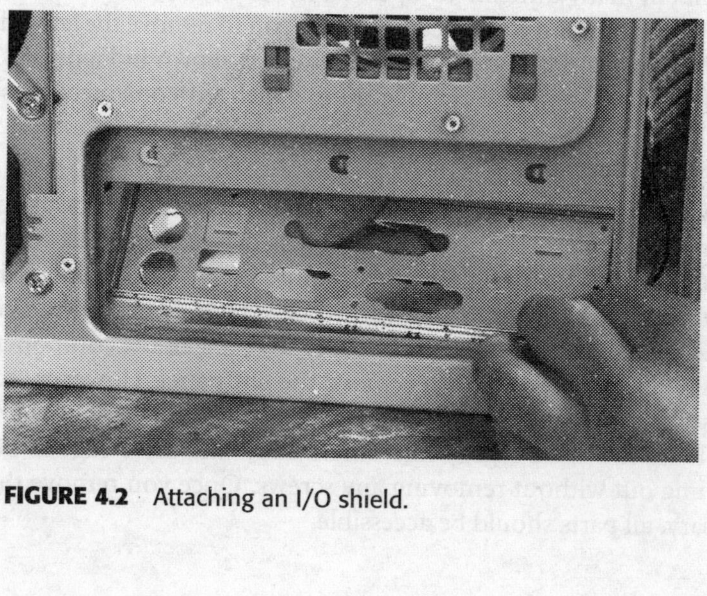

FIGURE 4.2 Attaching an I/O shield.

comes from external devices, and from interference generated by the computer that affects external devices. Good cases are designed to provide for proper airflow to keep the components from overheating. Well made cases do not have a thin tinny feel or sound when you tap on them. They have rolled edges to prevent injury. Panels should fit together well without requiring excessive effort. When the computer is running, a good case does not make excessive vibration noises. Other attributes of good cases include ease in opening and ease in accessing internal components (we discuss opening cases later in this chapter).

ON THE CD

See the video "Opening Different Types of Cases and Accessing Internal Parts" on the accompanying CD-ROM. The file is called opening_the_Case.mpg.

Case Form Factors and Styles

Cases come in many form factors, the most common being AT, ATX, and Micro ATX. For more information on case form factors, see *formfactor.org*. Available styles include mid-tower, small footprint, desktop (horizontal), and those cases integrated with a monitor.

Opening Different Types of Cases

Cases also vary in the difficulty of opening and accessing internal components. While most cases open easily after removing screws from the back, you will undoubtedly come across cases whose method of opening is not the least bit apparent. Some require removal of the plastic faceplate to access screws behind it, and others are so unusual that you could look at the case for an hour and not figure out how to open it. A few manuals tell you how to open the case, but the problem with that is that in many difficult-to-open cases, the manufacturer is unidentifiable.

One common style of case requires you to remove the left-side panel only (as you are looking at the front of the computer (as shown in Figure 4.3), while many other styles combine the left, right, and top panels into one piece, as shown in Figure 4.4.

Accessing Components

Once you have opened the case, you might be stumped about how to access blocked parts, particularly the processor and disk drives. Some cases are extraordinarily difficult in this respect. These often require you to remove the drive cage. Sometimes you have to disassemble the case, while others, even ones the same size on the outside, need only to be opened in order to reach all the components. In a majority of cases, all you have to do is remove the left panel. However, you might find some cases that require you to remove both the left and right panels to access the screws holding the drive cage, while others allow the drive cage to be easily removed or swung out without removing any screws. Once you remove the drive cage, if necessary, all parts should be accessible.

FIGURE 4.3 Removing a side panel.

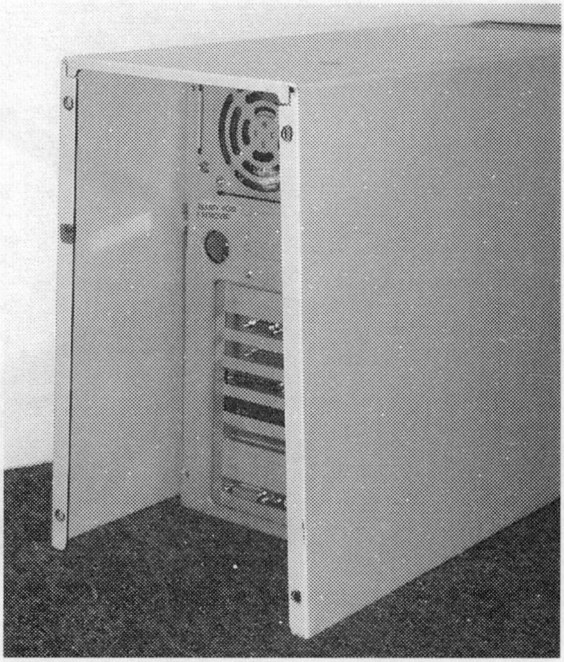

FIGURE 4.4 One-piece case cover.

ON THE CD See the video "Opening Different Types of Cases and Accessing Internal Parts" on the accompanying CD-ROM. The file is called opening_the_Case.mpg.

Choosing a Case

If you decide to replace a case, simply match the form factor to the motherboard and make sure it has the needed number of internal and external drive bays, physical size, power supply capacity (in watts), and front-panel ports. In addition, check the processor and motherboard documentation. There very well might be further limitations on the type of case that can be used.

POWER SUPPLIES

The *power supply* connects to an AC outlet and provides power to the components of the computer through a gaggle of DC connectors. AC is connected through a standard CEE three-pronged power cord (see Figure 4.5), which is used with almost all PCs, including Macs, some laptop power supplies, and many other devices, computer-related and otherwise. New cases come with power supplies, but power supplies often wear out and need to be replaced.

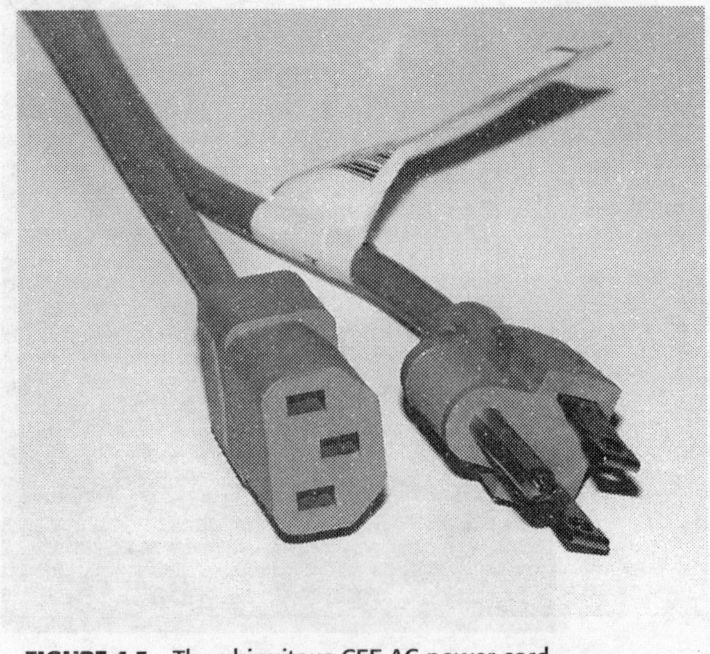

FIGURE 4.5 The ubiquitous CEE AC power cord.

DC Power Output Connectors

The DC power connectors vary somewhat between AT, ATX, and proprietary form factors. While the disk drive connectors are all the same, the motherboard connectors are different and incompatible between major form factors, although subversions of ATX have the same connectors. Figure 4.6 shows different ATX DC power connectors.

In addition to the power connector variants, different cases require power supplies of different shapes and sizes, or they won't fit in the case.

Determining Power Supply Power Requirements

Common power supplies come in a range of about 80 watts to 600 watts. How do you determine how much you need? First, determine the number of drives, the processor, number of expansion cards, and so forth. Know that it never hurts to have more capacity than you need. Check the motherboard and processor documentation. Some power supplies are overrated. For example, if you find a 300-watt power supply at a very low price, and you notice that it is physically light in weight, it is likely to fail under load.

Proprietary Power Supplies

Many brand-name computers require special power supplies in order to fit in the case or properly power the computer. These power supplies might or might not be more expensive than generic supplies. For example, certain Dell power supplies

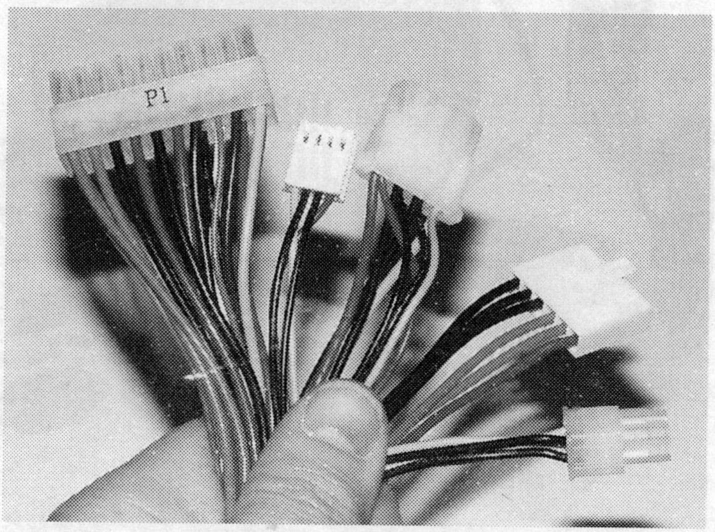

FIGURE 4.6 ATX DC power connectors.

have an extra connector that fits into a connector on a proprietary Dell motherboard. Unfortunately, this connector matches a connector found on standard ATX power supplies, but the wiring differs. Therefore, don't try to plug in a generic power supply in a Dell motherboard unless you want to fry the board. The good news is that Dell sells replacement power supplies on its Web site for a very reasonable price. However, a particular Hewlett-Packard computer takes a power supply available only from Hewlett-Packard at a rather high price. Sometimes you can get proprietary power supplies from generic manufacturers. Just make sure to do all your homework before connecting a power supply to a motherboard on a brand name computer. Figure 4.7 shows an assortment of power supplies.

Diagnosing Power Supply Problems

The most obvious symptoms of a failed power supply occur when you turn your computer on and hear a loud noise, smell something burning, and/or see smoke, and the computer won't power on. Disconnect the power immediately; you likely

FIGURE 4.7 Power supply assortment.

have a blown power supply. If there is smoke, you'll want to ventilate the room—it is toxic. Usually, however, the symptoms of a blown power supply aren't nearly so dramatic; you turn on the computer and nothing happens.

Always Check the Voltage Switch!

We've said it before and we'll say it again: Make sure the power supply is set for the correct voltage.

Unusual Noises

If you hear a grinding noise, or there is excessive vibration, the power supply fan might be going bad. Visually check the rotation of the fan. Don't try to replace the fan, replace the power supply. A loud hum that changes pitch while you're doing different things usually indicates a bad power supply.

Testing the Power Supply

Testing a power supply is straightforward. Antec (*Antec-inc.com*) offers a simple, inexpensive ATX power supply tester, although it is helpful to have a voltmeter or multitester to use with it. Simply connect the tester to the power connector and view the LED. If it lights, the power supply is working. For a better reading, while the tester is in place, touch a voltmeter's or multimeter's probes to the tester's leads to read the voltage. Voltage should be 12v, 5v, or 3.3v, depending on the connector. Tested voltage should be very close to the rated number.

Removal and Replacement

This is usually straightforward. Make sure the power cord is disconnected. With most tower or desktop cases, you'll have to open the case and remove the screws from the back around the power supply. Because some manufacturers have special connectors attached to the motherboard and other devices inside the system, you should draw a diagram of the colors of the wires and positions of the connectors as you are disconnecting them so you can match the power supply and connect it, or a new one, properly. Then, remove all of the power connectors. The power supply should come right out. In some computers, the power supply is mounted to a bracket. You'll have to remove the power supply from the bracket. Replacing the power supply, or installing a new one, is done the same way, in reverse.

NOTE

For a useful discussion on PC power supplies, go to http://computer.howstuffworks.com/power-supply.htm.

Chapters 1–4 A+ Certification Review Questions

The following A+ Certification Review Questions are related to the general topics introduced in Part I, Chapters 1 through 4, of this book. The answers and supporting references are provided after the review questions. You will notice that all of the answer references specify chapters that are located in Part II of this book: The A+ Certification Exams. It is likely you will need to refer to these chapters in Part II to correctly answer the questions. The real A+ exams are not easy to pass unless you prepare yourself well. Likewise, these questions are not easy to answer unless you prepare yourself well by researching the material. When you finish this book, successfully complete the A+ practice exams located on the CD-ROM, and finally take the real exams, you will be glad you followed this proven format.

ON THE CD

1. **Which of the following will work with Slot 1 architecture? (Choose Two)**
   - □ A. AMD AT
   - □ B. AMD K6
   - □ C. Pentium II
   - □ D. Pentium III
2. **What advantages does the ATX form factor have over AT? (Choose Two)**
   - □ A. Dual power supplies
   - □ B. PS/2 integration
   - □ C. Micro channel
   - □ D. "Soft Switch" power support
3. **You are plugging the connectors from an AT power supply into the motherboard. What wire colors must match up?**
   - ○ A. Red and red
   - ○ B. Orange and orange
   - ○ C. Black and red
   - ○ D. Black and black

4. Where are the system settings stored when the computer is off?

- o A. CMOS
- o B. RAM
- o C. A permanent swap file
- o D. Disaster recovery site

5. You are planning to upgrade the CPU on your motherboard. What else must you consider?

- o A. SCSI chain priorities
- o B. Upgrading the CMOS chip
- o C. Upgrading the operating system
- o D. Adding an RS232c

6. Intel's Single Edge Connector technology design incorporates a processor and?

- o A. CMOS
- o B. Level 2 cache
- o C. Centronics D-shell
- o D. Level 3 caches

7. A major difference between the original Pentium (I) and the Pentium II is?

- o A. IEEE 1394
- o B. LBA support
- o C. Pipeline cache size
- o D. File allocation table

8. The Pentium III is designed for what type of technology?

- o A. Slot A
- o B. Slot B
- o C. Slot 1
- o D. Slot III

9. IRQ 4 is reserved for?

- o A. COM2 and COM4
- o B. COM3 and COM4
- o C. COM1 and COM4
- o D. COM1 and COM3

10. What is used to fill the area between a CPU and a heat sink in order to transfer heat from the CPU to the heat sink?

- o A. Liquid nitrogen
- o B. CNR
- o C. L3 cache
- o D. Thermal compound
- o E. All of the above

11. You connect to the Internet with a 56Kbps modem. At times, your access speed is faster than others. What can you do to maximize your potential access speed? (Choose Two)

- □ A. Get the most recent driver-update for your modem
- □ B. Use a crossover cable
- □ C. Change your RJ11 connector to RJ45
- □ D. Resolve your IRQ5 conflict
- □ E. Have your telephone company clear the phone line
- □ F. Grant full-access permissions to your 56Kbps modem

12. By default, which IRQ is reserved for the Real Time Clock?

- o A. IRQ0
- o B. IRQ1
- o C. IRQ7
- o D. IRQ8

13. How many USB devices will one system resource (IRQ) support?

- o A. 1
- o B. 15
- o C. 2
- o D. 127
- o E. None of the above

14. Which is considered the newest battery type that produces hydrogen converted from methanol or alcohol?

- o A. NiCad (Nickel-cadmium)
- o B. NiMH (Nickel Metal Hydride)
- o C. Fuel cell
- o D. Lithium ion
- o E. None of the above

15. What type of technology do all of the processors in the AMD Athalon XP line use?

- o A. Pentium IV technology
- o B. Slot technology
- o C. Socket A technology
- o D. AMD Duron technology
- o E. None of the above

16. Which of the following is a motherboard installable module that regulates the electrical voltage that is fed to the system's microprocessor?

- o A. VRM
- o B. CNR
- o C. AMR
- o D. LCA (Liquid Cooling Apparatus)
- o E. None of the above

17. Which of the following represent possible printer connections?

- o A. Centronix
- o B. DB25
- o C. USB
- o D. All of the above

18. What IRQs by default are available for additional devices in a computer system? (Choose Three)

- □ A. IRQ9
- □ B. IRQ11
- □ C. IRQ15
- □ D. IRQ10
- □ E. IRQ4

19. Which of the following is used to translate drive information such as sectors, cylinders, and heads into BIOS understandable format?

- o A. Power-on Self-Test
- o B. ROM BIOS
- o C. CMOS Checksum
- o D. LBA
- o E. None of the above

20. What is the default IRQ for COM2?

- o A. 3
- o B. 4
- o C. 2
- o D. 5

21. Which is a specification for motherboard architecture that allows analog I/O functions to be separate from the motherboard by placing them on a riser?

- o A. Plug and Play
- o B. MCA
- o C. AMR
- o D. ISA
- o E. None of the above

22. How does AGP differ from PCI?

- o A. AGP uses a point-to-point dedicated channel to directly access RAM.
- o B. AGP offers a faster NIC card support.
- o C. PCI specifications include 2x, 4x, and 8x.
- o D. PCI offers faster video acceleration speeds.

23. In Windows 9x, what files can you edit by using the text editor SYSEDIT? (Choose Two)

- □ A. MSDOS.SYS
- □ B. WIN.INI
- □ C. IO.SYS
- □ D. AUTOEXEC.BAT

24. SCANDISK is a utility that scans and fixes problems with which? (Choose Two)

- □ A. Hard drives
- □ B. Tape drives
- □ C. CD-ROM drives
- □ D. Floppy drives

25. You want to make changes to the AUTOEXEC.BAT and WIN.INI files. What Windows text editors can be used? (Choose Two)

- □ A. SYSEDIT
- □ B. REGEDIT
- □ C. EDITPAD
- □ D. NOTEPAD

26. How can you start the Disk Defragmenter utility in Windows 9x? (Choose Three)

- □ A. Start, Programs, Accessories, System Tools, Disk Defragmenter
- □ B. Control Panel, System, Performance, Virtual Memory
- □ C. My Computer, right-click on drive, Properties, Tools, Defragment Now...
- □ D. Start, Run, type in "defrag", click OK, click OK again
- □ E. Start, Programs, Accessories, System, Device Manager

27. What is the overall system starting order?

- o A. POST, BIOS, Boot Sector, GUI
- o B. Boot Sector, POST, BIOS, GUI
- o C. POST, GUI, MBR, BIOS
- o D. Push the button, hope the magic happens

28. In Device Manager, your NIC card has a yellow circle with a black exclamation point on it. Why?

- o A. It is not working properly and is in a problem state.
- o B. It has been disabled.
- o C. It is not recognized by the system at all.
- o D. Windows doesn't support cards from NIC anymore.

29. Which of the following versions of Windows was the first to feature System Restore?

- o A. Windows 95
- o B. Windows 98SE
- o C. Windows Me
- o D. Windows XP

30. Your USB printer has been detected but Windows XP will not install the printer driver. What should you do?

- o A. Check the Device Manager for your printer, and perform an "Uninstall" on it.
- o B. Check Peripheral Management for your printer, and perform a "Reinstall" on it.
- o C. Disconnect and reconnect the printer.
- o D. Roll back the driver.

31. Driver signing and testing in Windows XP is also known as?

- o A. Windows Logo Testing
- o B. Windows Hardware Quality Labs (WHQL)
- o C. Windows Logo Compatible
- o D. Windows Driver Testing

32. What will you often see when a Windows operating system suddenly halts or terminates?

- o A. A Red, white, and blue screen
- o B. A Unix or Linux replacement
- o C. The infamous BSOD
- o D. The message "Boot could not find NTLDR. Please insert another disk."

33. Where in Windows Me, Windows 2000, and Windows XP would you go to easily add or configure a digital camera or scanner?

- o A. Command prompt
- o B. DOS prompt
- o C. Control Panel > Scanners and Cameras
- o D. Control Panel > Cameras and Scanners
- o E. None of the above

34. How much memory can a PCI 32-bus access?

- o A. Up to 1GB
- o B. Up to 4GB
- o C. 512K
- o D. Up to 17 billion GB
- o E. All of the above

35. Which operating systems have Device Manager? (Choose Four)

- □ A. Windows 9x
- □ B. Windows Me
- □ C. Windows 2000
- □ D. Windows NT
- □ E. Windows XP

36. Which of the following Windows XP utilities would you first use in troubleshooting hardware related issues?

- o A. Automated System Recovery
- o B. Cmd.exe
- o C. Sysprep.exe
- o D. Computer Management

37. Recently, manufacturers such as Intel have developed technology that brings an additional 1MB (512K) on to the CPU chip. This addition has dramatically increased the speed at which a processor can access stored information. What is the new addition being described as?

- o A. MICRODIMM
- o B. L3 cache
- o C. SODIMM
- o D. L5 cache
- o E. Direct Memory Address (DMA)

38. An EEPROM chip on a network interface card is capable of storing certain settings. Name three of these settings. (Choose Three)

- □ A. MAC address
- □ B. IRQ
- □ C. I/O
- □ D. IP address

39. In Windows 9x how can you terminate a stuck or "hung" program without powering down or restarting the system?

- o A. Keep pressing Ctrl+Alt+Delete until the problem goes away.
- o B. Press Ctrl+Alt+Delete: Select Task Manager: Select the stuck or "hung" program and click the End Task button.
- o C. Use the KTHP (Kill The Hung Program) built-in Windows utility to end the task.
- o D. Unplug the unit's power cable from the AC wall outlet.
- o E. Run a thorough ScanDisk.
- o F. None of the above.

40. When you press the F5 key, just before the Windows 9x splash screen, and enter Safe Mode, which of the following are not loaded? (Choose Four)

- □ A. NIC driver
- □ B. Modem driver
- □ C. AUTOEXEC.BAT
- □ D. CONFIG.SYS
- □ E. HIMEM.SYS
- □ F. Keyboard driver

A+ CERTIFICATION REVIEW ANSWERS AND REFERENCES

Answer Key	References Taken from Part II: The A+ Certification Exams
1. C and D	Chapter 15, "Slots and Sockets"
2. B and D	Chapter 15, "Motherboards and Form Factors"
3. D	Chapter 15, "Electricity and the Power Supply"
4. A	Chapter 15, "Complementary Metal Oxide Semiconductor (CMOS)"
5. B	Chapter 15, "Complementary Metal Oxide Semiconductor (CMOS)"
6. B	Chapter 16, "SEC and SEP"
7. C	Chapter 16, "Processors and Modes"
8. C	Chapter 16, "Processors and Modes"
9. D	Chapter 18, "Interrupt Requests (IRQs)"
10. D	Chapter 16, "Thermal Compounds"
11. A and E	Chapter 18, "Modems"
12. D	Chapter 18, "Interrupt Requests (IRQs)"
13. D	Chapter 21, "USB Connections"
14. C	Chapter 18, "Batteries and Power"
15. C	Chapter 16, "Processors and Modes"
16. A	Chapter 16, "VRM (Voltage Regulator Module)"
17. D	Chapter 19, "Laser Printers"
18. B, C, and D	Chapter 18, "Interrupt Requests (IRQs)"
19. D	Chapter 15, "Power-on Self-Test (POST) and Error Codes"
20. A	Chapter 18, "Interrupt Requests (IRQs)"
21. C	Chapter 15, "Expansion Bus Architecture"
22. A	Chapter 15, "Expansion Bus Architecture"
23. B and D	Chapter 23, "Windows Initialization Files"
24. A and D	Chapter 23, "DOS Windows Utilities"
25. A and D	Chapter 23, "Windows Initialization Files"
26. A, C, and D	Chapter 23, "DOS Windows Utilities"
27. A	Chapter 23, "DOS System and Configuration Files"
28. A	Chapter 24, "Utilities and Settings"
29. C	Chapter 27, "Windows Me Tools and Utilities"
30. A	Chapter 28, "Printers"
31. A	Chapter 28, "Windows XP Tools and Utilities"
32. C	Chapter 24, "Diagnosing and Troubleshooting Test Tips"

A+ CERTIFICATION REVIEW ANSWERS AND REFERENCES *(continued)*

Answer Key	References Taken from Part II: The A+ Certification Exams
33. C	Chapter 18, "Digital Cameras"
34. B	Chapter 15, "Expansion Bus Architecture"
35. A, B, C, and E	Chapter 26, "Windows 2000 Tools and Utilities"
36. D	Chapter 28, "Windows XP Tools and Utilities"
37. B	Chapter 16, "Cache, Levels 1, 2, and 3 "
38. A, B, and C	Chapter 22, "Network Interface Cards"
39. B	Chapter 24, "Utilities and Settings"
40. A, B, C, and D	Chapter 24, "The Windows 9x Start-up Process"

5 Memory (RAM)

In This Chapter

- Memory Overview
- Memory Installation
- Troubleshooting Memory Problems
- BIOS Memory Settings

MEMORY OVERVIEW

Computer *memory* is electronic circuitry that holds binary data. It does this by setting the positions of microscopic electronic switches to on or off. The on position represents the binary 1, and the off position represents the binary 0. Each 0 and 1 is called a *bit*. The switches are divided into groups of eight bits, called *bytes*. A byte is an 8-bit number that can equal any decimal number between 0 (all 0s) and 255 (all 1s), and is the basis of all computer data. For more information on binary numbers, go to *http://computer.howstuffworks.com/bytes.htm*.

Main memory in computers comes in modules, often called *sticks*, which can contain billions of switches. Memory sticks are measured in megabytes (MB) and gigabytes (GB). One MB equals, oddly enough, 1,048,576 bytes. One GB equals 1,073,741,824 bytes.

The acronym *RAM* stands for random access memory. This means that any part of memory can be accessed directly, as opposed to data stored on tape, which requires fast winding to the appropriate segment.

When selecting memory for a computer, there are several items to consider:

Type: Motherboards can accept certain types of memory, such as SDRAM, DDR SDRAM, Rambus, EDO RAM, and burst-EDO RAM. Check the motherboard documentation or the motherboard manufacturer's Web site. We discuss these types later in this chapter.

Speed: Motherboards can accept memory modules in certain ranges of speed; for example, 100 or 133 MHz. The faster the memory, the faster the performance of the computer. As in memory type, all memory installed in a single computer should be the same speed. If you install two different speeds of memory on the same motherboard, all chips will run at the slower speed.

Quantity (as measured in megabytes): Unlike medication, with memory, more is better, although you can reach a point of diminishing return. The motherboard documentation will specify the maximum amount of memory it can accept. We discuss how to determine the optimum amount of memory later in this chapter.

Quality: Memory rarely fails unless it is exposed to static electricity. The most common problem with memory is when brand new modules are bad—so a good warranty is essential. Kingston, Crucial, and PNY are examples of good brands.

Error detection: Memory comes in ECC or parity, or non-ECC or non-parity. *ECC* and *parity* are systems for detecting and correcting memory errors. Parity memory can compensate for single-bit errors. This parameter is specified by the motherboard manufacturer, but is changeable in some BIOSs. If the BIOS is set for ECC/parity memory, only ECC/parity memory will work. Again, even if the motherboard will accept either, it likely will accept only one of these at a time. If you have a DIMM (see the next item in this list) and you want to determine if it is ECC/parity or non-ECC/non-parity, simply count the number of black chips soldered to the module. If the number of chips is evenly divisible by three or five, then the module contains ECC or parity memory. If the number of chips is *not* evenly divisible by three or five, you have non-ECC/non-parity memory.

Physical module size and pin layout: Almost all currently used memory comes in Dual Inline Memory Module (DIMM) form (see Figure 5.1). However, size and number of pins vary. This parameter must match that of the motherboard. Rambus® memory comes in RIMM™ form, which is Rambus' version of DIMMs. Prior to DIMMs, Single Inline Memory Modules (SIMMs) were prevalent. Notebook computers take very small DIMMs, called SODIMMs.

FIGURE 5.1 A 184-pin DIMM.

CAS Latency: Measured in numbers such as CL2 and CL3; make sure these match the requirements of the motherboard.

Serial Presence Detect (SPD): This is memory with an additional chip that contains information used by some motherboards to set certain memory parameters. This can be used on any motherboard, but if the motherboard requires this type of memory and non-SPD memory is used, the computer will display an error message when attempting to boot. We discuss the error message later in this chapter.

Single- or double-sided module: Some motherboards take either kind, but with a restriction. The Intel D815EEA motherboard, for example, has four memory slots. You can use up to four single-sided modules, but the motherboard will recognize only two double-sided modules. If you install two double-sided modules on slots 0 and 1, any modules in slots 2 or 3 will be ignored. Interestingly, you might not be able to determine this parameter by looking at the module. For more information, go to *kingston.com* and use the Memory Search function to search for memory for the Intel D815EEA motherboard.

Memory Types

There are many types of memory used today. They differ mainly in available speeds and cost. Motherboards are limited to one type of memory. Common memory types include SDRAM, DDR SDRAM, Rambus, EDO RAM, and burst-EDO RAM.

How to Determine the Optimum Amount of Memory

More memory, up to the maximum specified by the motherboard manufacturer, can never hurt a system. More memory allows the computer to keep more programs and processes running simultaneously. Additional memory is usually the easiest way to boost performance of a computer. With the price of memory being so low as of this writing, there is little reason to skimp, except in older computers getting limited use. For example, a Windows 95 computer used mainly to check e-mail, or a Windows 95 computer used only to run a business program designed for the OS version installed on that machine, probably doesn't need more than 32MB of RAM. Once a computer is used for more activity, especially running several programs at the same time, it will definitely need more. The most obvious factor is the performance of the computer. If it runs just fine, there is little or no reason to upgrade it. If performance or booting is sluggish, especially after new programs have been installed, this is a good time to add more memory.

Microsoft sets minimum and recommended amounts of memory for all its Windows versions, and developers set minimum levels for their programs. Recognize that Microsoft's minimums are absolute minimums; computers with this amount of RAM can pretty much run the OS and little else. Even recommended levels are on the low side. Minimum RAM levels for programs are often based on only the OS, that program, and other background processes, such as virus protection running. With current computers running Windows 2000 or XP, as of this writing, 128MB is the minimum amount of memory needed to provide adequate performance—256MB or more is recommended. If the computer is being used for memory-intensive programs such as video editing or multimedia, or if it is a busy server, 512MB to 1024MB (1GB) would be advisable. Again, any time a computer runs slowly, adding memory is a very safe bet. See software boxes or developers' Web sites for minimum hardware requirements.

Windows Virtual Memory Settings

Computers often temporarily need more memory than they have. For this reason, Windows manages virtual memory. *Virtual memory* is the use of a *swap file* on the hard drive for extra memory when needed. The action of moving data between physical RAM and the swap file is called *paging*. If there is not enough physical memory for the normal use of the computer, paging will increase, adding stress to the hard drive containing the swap file, and reducing the overall performance of the computer. Also note that the processor has to manage all the paging, so it doesn't have as much time to perform its other duties when there is too much paging. Therefore, if you run into a situation in which the hard drive is *thrashing* or *churning*, which is visible when the hard drive indicator light flashes continuously for extended periods of time, it is possible that the computer needs more memory. It is also possible, however, that the problem is a cheap hard drive. A hard drive without an adequate built-in buffer (2MB or more of cache memory), or one that skimps on other performance-related elements could be inadequate for the job of paging. Therefore, it is best to make sure that the computer has a good hard drive and enough memory. If, however, you need to test the system to see which one is the culprit, use Windows System Monitor (9x), Performance (2000), or Performance Monitor (XP). For more information about these utilities, go to *support.microsoft.com*, select Advanced Search and Exact Phrase, and search for "Chapter 27—Overview of Performance Monitoring." Make sure to type the phrase exactly as shown.

Finding the Right Memory for a Computer

The usual methods apply to determining the memory specifications that will work in a given computer: check the computer or motherboard manual, the manufacturer's Web site, or call the manufacturer. Where memory is concerned, however, there is an extraordinarily simple method in addition to these. Go to a memory manufacturer's Web site such as Crucial's (*crucial.com*), Kingston's (*kingston.com*), or PNY's (*pny.com*), access the memory upgrade, memory search, or "configurator" program on the home page, and enter the requested information (computer or motherboard brand, model number, etc.). The program will list all of the different memory modules that will work in the computer or specified motherboard. You can purchase memory from some of these sites, or you can go to a bricks-and-mortar retail store to buy them.

Determining the Amount of Memory Installed

There are several ways to see how much physical memory is installed in a computer:

- On Windows 9x, right-click My Computer and click the Performance tab. The amount of physical memory should be displayed.
- In any Windows menu, select Help: > About.
- On bootup, before Windows starts, many BIOSs will test the memory and display it.
- Open the BIOS setup program and go to the page with memory settings.
- In Windows 2000 and XP, start the Task Manager (<Ctrl>+<Alt>+<Delete>). The Performance tab shows the amount of physical memory (see Figure 5.2).

The Computer Reports the Wrong Amount of Memory

There are several reasons that a computer might report an amount of memory that doesn't match the actual amount installed.

- On some computers, the on-board video uses a portion of the main memory, so the computer indicates the amount minus the memory reserved for video. In some of these cases, the amount reserved for video can be changed in the BIOS Setup program.

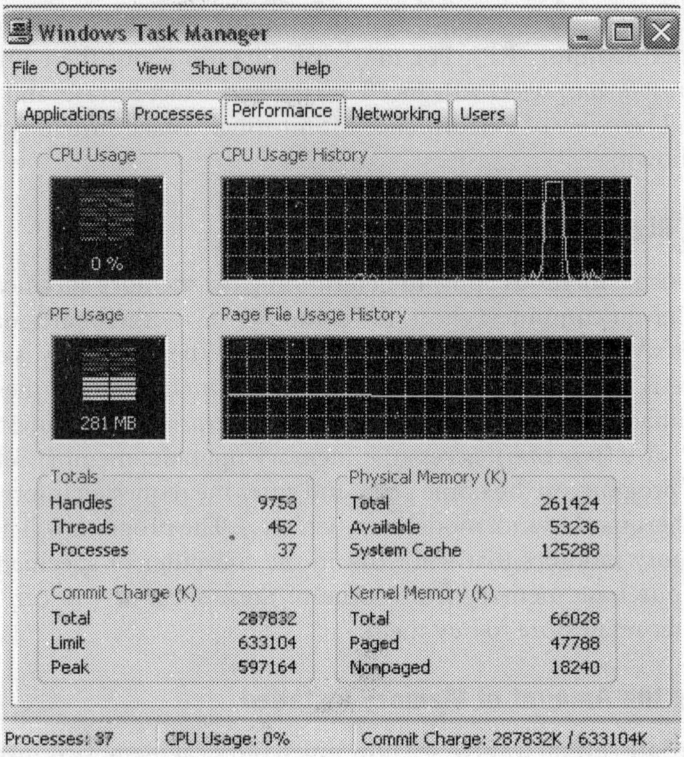

FIGURE 5.2 This computer has 261,424 KB of physical memory.

- In the event that the number seems just a bit off, remember that one kilobyte is 1024 bytes, and that one megabyte is 1024 kilobytes. Therefore, if your computer shows 262,144 KB of memory, that is actually 256MB of RAM.
- If the amount of memory is off by the size of a whole memory module or large portion of one, there is a problem. Check to make sure the modules are installed correctly, the memory is of a type compatible with the motherboard, and that it matches the other memory installed. Some memory on certain motherboards has to be installed in pairs. On some boards, the memory modules have to be installed starting with the lowest numbered slot; in other words, the lowest numbered slot must have a module in it. While you're checking for this, check to see if your slots are numbered starting at 0 or 1. In still other cases, the memory must be installed in capacity order. For example, if you have three modules of 128MB, 64MB and 32MB, the 128 would have to be in slot 0, the 64 in slot 1, and the 32 in slot 2. Even if a motherboard doesn't have these restrictions, it can't hurt to follow them anyway as a matter of course. Figure 5.3 shows numbered DIMM slots. Moreover, if you install more memory than

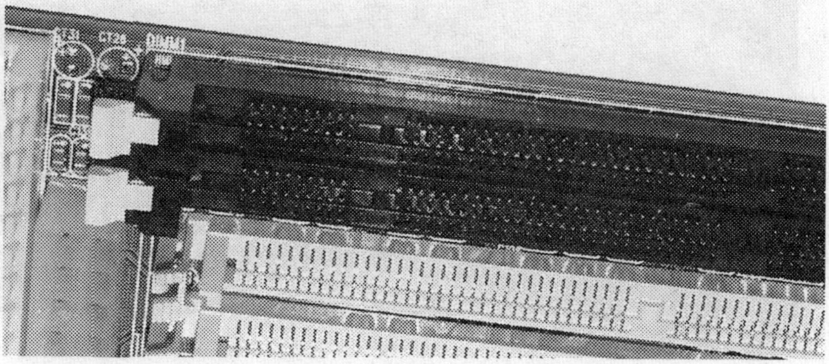

FIGURE 5.3 Numbered DIMM slots.

the motherboard allows, your computer will likely show only the maximum amount of memory allowed by the motherboard.

- If all else fails, you might have a bad memory module. If your computer boots, a diagnostic program such as Micro-Scope or PC Certify will test the memory. Also, some brand-name computers come with their own diagnostic programs such as Hewlett-Packard's HP Diagtools. If the computer won't boot, a POST card can diagnose the memory problem. We discuss these testing methods later in the chapter. Naturally, if you determine that a new memory module is bad, you'll want to contact the manufacturer for warranty replacement. The companies mentioned in this chapter are very good about honoring their warranties as long as the customer has handled the module properly.

MEMORY INSTALLATION

Memory isn't hard to install. First, make sure to take the usual static-avoidance measures, including wearing an anti-static wrist strap. Touch a piece of bare metal on the case before proceeding. With DIMMs, insert the module straight in the slot, taking care to match up the indentation in the module with the notch in the slot (see Figure 5.4). Then, make sure the plastic clips are closed as shown in Figure 5.5.

In old computers that take SIMMs, insert at an angle, and then straighten out. Do this very carefully, as old-style memory modules are exceptionally delicate.

Notebook Computer Memory Installation

Check the documentation for the notebook to find the memory slot—they are usually on the bottom. With the power off, remove the screw(s) to access the slot. Insert the modules at an angle and then straighten out, as shown in Figure 5.6.

FIGURE 5.4 Match the indentation with the notch.

FIGURE 5.5 An installed module.

General Rules for Memory Installation

- Use the correct memory for the motherboard.
- Follow all instructions from the computer/motherboard and memory manufacturers.

FIGURE 5.6 Inserting a SODIMM in a notebook computer.

- Make sure all the memory modules match as described earlier in the chapter.
- Start at the lowest number memory slot, either 0 or 1.
- Insert the memory in capacity order starting with the highest-capacity module in the lowest number slot.
- After you have installed the memory, boot the computer and check the memory. If you don't have a diagnostic program, run some memory-intensive programs such as office programs, photo or video, or games with a lot of graphics.

For more help with memory installation, go to *kingston.com* and select Install Guides from the Support menu.

TIP *Some motherboards with the Intel 865 and 875 chipsets take DDR SDRAM in a dual-channel configuration. There are two channels of memory, A and B, and two slots for each channel, 0 and 1. For best performance, make sure to follow the motherboard manufacturer's instructions. This means that chips in channel A, slot 0, and channel B, slot 0, should match exactly. The same goes for the DIMMs in the two slots 1. The best advice is to follow the instructions in the motherboard manual.*

ON THE CD See the video "Installing Memory" on the accompanying CD-ROM.

TROUBLESHOOTING MEMORY PROBLEMS

So, how do you know when memory is a problem? First, if a problem occurs just after you installed new memory, you know that memory is a possible culprit. Other signs of a memory problem include frequent *lockups* (when the mouse pointer won't move and the Num Lock light on the keyboard is stuck on or off), or there is suddenly no video. Of course, neither of these symptoms is a certain indication of memory problems. There can be many reasons why these things could happen, such as viruses or corrupted Windows files. For more information, see Chapter 11, "Troubleshooting."

> TIP
>
> *This applies only to old SIMMs: don't install SIMMs with tin contacts in slots with gold contacts, or gold contacts into tin slots. These two metals react and lose conductivity, resulting in memory failure.*

If you get memory error messages, especially early in the boot process, you might have a memory problem.

> TIP
>
> *Many memory error messages are misleading and don't indicate a problem with the memory. Before you attempt to troubleshoot any memory error messages, make sure to read the next section.*

Memory Error Messages

Error messages are not always useful. Many are vague or cryptic, and some don't even represent a problem, while others are right on the money. It is also not always apparent whether the error message comes from Windows or from a program. This section will help you interpret memory error messages.

One type of error message that you'll be forced to heed is the type that appears early in the boot process and often prevents the computer from booting. Examples of these are the memory mismatch or memory parity error. They usually mean that the wrong type of memory is installed in the computer, incompatible modules are combined in the same machine, or that a module is faulty or not correctly installed.

If you see the following error message when attempting to boot the computer, the motherboard requires SPD memory for normal operation:

```
SERIAL PRESENCE DETECT (SPD) device data missing or inconclusive. Prop-
erly programmed SPD device data is required for reliable operation. Do you
wish to attempt to boot at XXXMHz bus speed? Y/N [Y] Type [N] to shut down.
```

Either non-SPD memory is installed, or the data in the SPD chip has been corrupted. You can continue to operate the computer, but you risk data loss. It is best to replace the module(s).

Sometimes, on Windows NT, 2000, and XP, you'll get a stop error, better known as "the blue screen of death." See Chapter 2, "System Configuration and Computer

Hygiene," and Chapter 10, "Troubleshooting Internet Connections," for more information about these errors. There are other types of errors as well. Some of these can be memory related. In the case of stop errors, copy the exact text of the message (encompassing the long hexadecimal numbers at the top of the screen). Regardless of the type, copy the entire error message exactly and search Microsoft's Knowledge Base (*http://support.microsoft.com*) or on *google.com* for the problem. Make sure to either use quotation marks around the error message, or use the Advanced Search function to search for the exact phrase—and don't make any typos.

One common error message category is the out-of-memory error. A message might warn you to save a document because the system is almost out of memory. Often, these messages occur on systems with lots of memory and few programs running. These messages usually indicate a program error, not a problem with memory. If this happens, close the program. The error messages should disappear. Reopen the program and see if the problem returns. If the error messages recur, go to the developer's Web site or contact tech support (if possible) to see if there are any fixes for the problem.

Memory Testing Hardware

Available from companies such as CST (*simmtester.com*), these devices are the quickest, most efficient way to accurately test memory. They can usually tell you quickly exactly what is wrong and also locate the offending module. However, because they are priced in the thousands of dollars, they are cost-effective only if you are testing large amounts of memory every day. For this reason, small repair shops are unlikely to have them. If you need to have memory tested with one of these devices, you might be able to find a business, such as your memory supplier, that has one and will test the memory for you for a fee. Just make sure you transport the memory in an anti-static container and have the container marked to identify whose memory is in it.

Memory Testing Software

Memory-testing software doesn't have all the capabilities of the hardware testing devices, but the price is right.

Also from CST (*simmtester.com*) is a program called DocMemory. As of this writing, this can be downloaded and used free, although the Web site warns that this offer is for a limited time only. Make sure to download the user guide in *PDF* form, and then read it before attempting to use the software. If you don't read it and configure it correctly, the memory test could go on for hours, even days. This is a highly professional program, but note that the Web site might indicate that it does not work with all versions of Windows, although our tests indicate that it does work.

Memtest86 (*memtest86.com*) is also freeware, and is a little rougher around the edges than MemoryDoc, although it too will give you valid results. Read the readme file that comes with the zipped download before using.

Both of these are used in the same way: download and expand the .zip file, and run the install program to install the memory test program onto a floppy. Then, making sure that the BIOS boot order is set to boot first from a floppy, restart the computer and run the program.

A diagnostic kit such as Micro-Scope (*micro2000.com*) and PC Certify (*pccertify.com)* is a great investment because it can not only test memory, but virtually everything on a PC that needs testing. Additionally, the available POST Card can be used to test the system even if the system won't get beyond the earliest stage of booting. We discuss Micro-Scope and PC Certify in detail in Chapter 11.

Resolving Memory Problems

When you try any of the following, do so with the power off. If you change anything, test the system each time to see if the problem is resolved. Keep a list of each change you make so you don't have to repeat them.

First, make sure that each module is installed correctly. Then, remove the modules one at a time, making sure to continue to follow the rules of memory installation listed earlier in this chapter. If you are using DIMMs, try cleaning the memory contacts (pins) with a pencil eraser. Then, use compressed air, such as Blow Off to blow the dust out of the slot. Reinsert the module and try again. If none of these procedures helps, or if a memory test indicates a bad module, replace the module with a new one, and then test the system to make sure the problem doesn't recur.

BIOS MEMORY SETTINGS

Some BIOS setup programs have settings for memory. Normally, most of these settings are to be left alone. In fact, manuals for Award BIOSs warn the technician never to alter the memory settings on the Chipset Features Setup page unless data is being lost. Data loss from memory is extraordinarily rare, so we also recommend leaving these settings alone unless directed to change them by support technicians *from the computer/motherboard manufacturer or the BIOS manufacturer.*

One memory setting you can change, as discussed earlier, is whether the memory should be ECC/parity or not. ECC/parity memory is not usually necessary except on file servers. An example of when you might change this setting is if you have some good non-parity memory from an otherwise irreparable computer and a computer that needs new memory of that type and speed, but that computer normally took ECC or parity memory. In the event that its BIOS has such a setting, change it to non-parity/non-ECC before removing all of the old parity/ECC memory and replacing it with the non-parity/non-ECC memory from the irreparable computer. Under normal circumstances, however, it is advisable to leave BIOS memory settings at their defaults.

For more information about BIOS settings, see your BIOS manufacturer's Web site, your motherboard/computer manufacturer's Web site, or access tech support at unicore.com.

6 Magnetic Disk Drives

In This Chapter

OVERVIEW OF HARD DRIVES (HARD DISK DRIVES, HDDs)

Hard disk drives are so named because they contain hard magnetic disks inside the housing. They are designed to store large quantities of information, and they don't need to be continuously powered in order to hold that data. The vast majority of PCs used today have at least one hard drive, and in almost all of these, the hard drive is used to store the OS, programs, and data. When a computer boots, depending on BIOS settings, the computer searches for boot files on different disk drives, most commonly the floppy drive first, then the hard drive, and then a CD drive. For regular use on any modern PC, the hard drive is the only

FIGURE 6.1 A standard PC EIDE hard drive.

one that is big enough to hold the required files. In fact, PCs that don't use hard drives are beyond the scope of Part I of this book. Figure 6.1 shows a typical PC hard drive. Note that laptop hard drives are physically much smaller.

Basic Hard Drive Characteristics

Externally, hard drives have a power connector, a data connector, and jumpers. We discuss jumpers later in this chapter. The power connector is connected to one of the drive connectors from the power supply, and the data connector is connected to the appropriate drive connector on the motherboard. Internally, hard drives have spinning magnetic platters and heads. *Heads* are small devices that store and pick up magnetic information from the platters; they have similarities to heads on cassette tape machines. Storage areas on the platters are divided into portions called *cylinders, sectors,* and *clusters.* Information about these parameters appears in the hard drive documentation and often on the paper label on the housing. When you go to the BIOS setup page that shows hard drive information, an example of which is shown in Figure 6.2, you might see some or all of this information and possibly more. Under the "type" category, there are usually three or more settings: User,

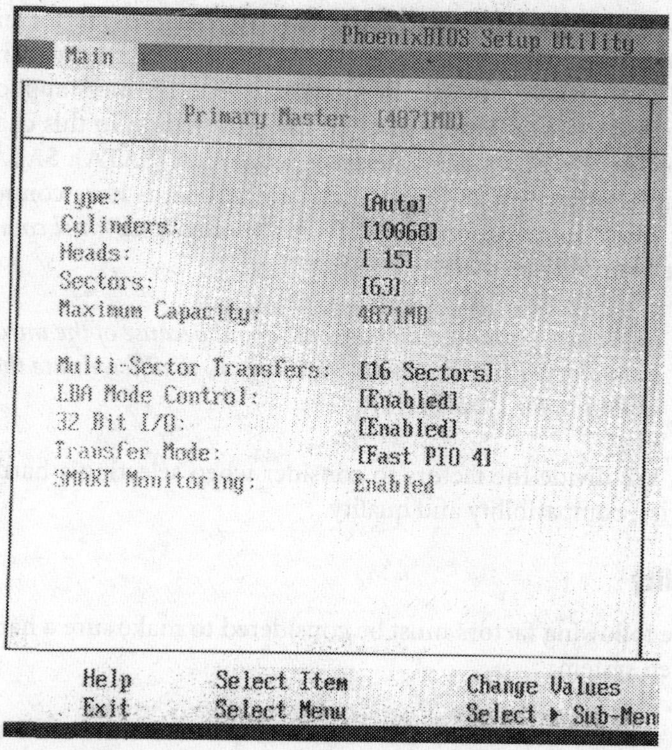

FIGURE 6.2 Hard drive information in a BIOS setup program.

None, and Auto (other settings might not apply to stationary hard drives). The None setting disables the drive. User allows the user to input the settings manually. If you choose User, the settings must match those of the drive exactly. Auto has the computer detect the drive information; on the vast majority of newer computers, Auto is the best setting.

NOTE

This book is concerned only about what you need to know about hard drives in order to fix PCs. However, it will be very helpful to see the clear and simple explanation of how hard drives work at howstuffworks.com/hard-disk.htm, or search howstuffworks.com for "hard drive."

SELECTING A HARD DRIVE

There are two main interfaces used today: Enhanced Integrated Drive Electronics (EIDE), and Small Computer System Interface (SCSI, pronounced "scuzzy"). SCSI drives perform better and have features that provide for higher reliability than EIDE drives. Not surprisingly, they are much more expensive than EIDE drives, and thus are used mostly in mission-critical business applications, and rarely in standard PCs—although some of the information in this chapter applies to SCSI, also. There is also a new interface: Serial ATA (SATA). SATA drives are set to replace EIDE drives, and many new motherboards have connectors for both types. For more information on SATA technology, see *intel.com/technology/serialata/index.htm?iid=sr+ata&*.

NOTE

In the new parlance that has come about because of the introduction of Serial ATA technology, EIDE drives are now known, to differentiate them from SATA drives, as PATA, for Parallel ATA.

We divide the factors to consider when selecting a hard drive into two categories: compatibility and quality.

Compatibility

The following factors must be considered to make sure a hard drive will work in a given system:

Form factor: Hard drive form factors aren't the same as other form factors. They have to do only with fitting the drive in the case, and thus are applicable only with internal hard drives. Desktop and tower computers are standardized for the 3.5-inch form factor, although it is possible to use smaller drives in one of these computers. (We discuss installing a small hard drive in a full-sized system later in this chapter). Laptops take 2.5-inch drives or smaller; check with the laptop documentation or Web site, or remove the drive and look at the label.

Ultra Direct Memory Access (UDMA) speed rating: This refers to the speed of data transfer between system memory and the hard drive buffer measured in megabytes per second and, at the time of this writing, has possible values of 33, 66, 100, and 133. Check the motherboard's maximum transfer speed and select the fastest hard drive the user can afford. Motherboards can accept any drives rated at their maximum speed or slower.

EIDE or SATA: Some new motherboards have connectors for both, but older boards accept EIDE only. As of this writing, most SATA drives have both the standard 4 pin power connector and the newer SATA power connector, but others come with only the SATA power connector. When the drive has only the new type power connector and the power supply does not, an inexpensive adapter is required. But many new power supplies are starting to show up on the market with at least one or two SATA power connectors built into the wiring harness.

Quality

Any time you are purchasing a hard drive that is to be the main or only hard drive in a computer, you should take the following quality indicators into account. A cheap hard drive will provide poor performance in most cases, but might be well suited for file archiving when the files aren't accessed often.

Here are factors to consider when attempting to purchase the highest quality hard drive for the money:

Warranty: Previously, many hard drives came with a three-year manufacturer's warranty. More recently, one-year warranties have become most common. Try to get three years if possible.

Buffer (cache memory): This is high-speed memory that is used to store a small amount of data while it is waiting to be read from or written to the drive. As this significantly improves performance of the computer, the bigger the buffer, the better. 2MB is good; 8MB is much better, especially when the user works with graphics-intensive programs such as video editing or games, or other high-stress programs. Drives with less than 2MB of cache will likely provide poor performance.

Platter speed: The most common speeds are 5400 and 7200 revolutions per minute (RPM). The faster the platter spins, the faster data can be accessed and transferred.

EIDE or SATA: EIDE drives are the ones that PCs have been using for many years now. SATA technology is a much more recent innovation. SATA drives perform faster and more accurately than EIDE, and are *hot-swappable.* This means that they can be connected to and disconnected from computers when the computer is running. Another advantage is that SATA data cables are small, making for easier installation and better airflow than the standard ribbon cables used on EIDE devices. The smaller cables also allow for smaller computers.

HARD DRIVES AND OPERATING SYSTEMS

For it to store and retrieve data on a hard drive, and keep track of multiple partitions and multiple drives, significant portions of OSs have to be dedicated to managing hard drives. A *partition* is a portion of a hard drive recognized by the OS as a separate and complete entity; it is not the divider between these portions as the name suggests.

File Systems

The OS has to have a method of storing and organizing files on a drive. There are different *file systems* used by Windows and DOS to serve that purpose:

File Allocation Table (FAT): Better known today as FAT16 for its 16-bit file storage, this is the original DOS and Windows file system. Its storage efficiency is the lowest of all file systems in use and it is highly susceptible to fragmentation (portions of files spread out all over the drive resulting in slow performance and additional wear). Additionally, FAT16 limits file names to eight characters, plus a three-character extension. The maximum partition size for FAT16 is 4GB. FAT16 is the only file system accessible in all versions of Windows and DOS, and is the only file system usable by the original version of Windows 95 and older. It is also the file system for floppy disks.

FAT32: FAT32 stores files more efficiently than FAT16 and has support for long filenames. FAT32 drives can be read by every version of Windows since the second version of Windows 95 (except for NT 4.0), and is the default file system for 98 and Me. The maximum partition size for FAT32 is very large, although there is a 32GB limit in Windows XP.

NTFS: The original version of NTFS was introduced with Windows NT. A newer version was introduced in Windows 2000, and it is the default file system for 2000 and XP. NTFS is somewhat resistant to fragmentation and allows for many of Windows 2000 and XP's security features not available in FAT16 or 32. The maximum size for an NTFS partition is two terabytes (TB), which is 240 bytes, or 2048GB. Windows 9x and DOS cannot use NTFS.

To select a file system for a hard drive, you have to *format* the drive. When installing Windows 9x, you can use the DOS program FDISK, covered later in this chapter. When installing 2000 or XP, the OS setup program provides this service. You'll be shown a graphical display of all the hard drives installed on the system, and you'll be given your choice for installation of the OS. You'll also have the choice of file systems, and NTFS will be recommended.

Partitions and Drive Letters

Here are definitions of the terms used in this area:

Active partition: This is the partition that needs to contain the OS's boot files because the BIOS looks to this partition for them. You can, however, designate any partition as the active partition; if it is the wrong one, the computer won't be able to boot from the hard drive.

Basic disk: A physical disk that is accessible by any version of Windows.

Dynamic disk: A disk used in 2000 or XP that can use special features, such as logical disk volumes, that span more than one physical disk.

Extended partition: A partition that can exist only on a drive containing the *master boot record*. An extended partition does not get a drive letter. To use an extended partition, you must create one or more logical drives on it; logical drives are assigned drive letters. There can be only one extended partition on a physical disk and you cannot install an OS on an extended partition. The only reason to create an extended partition is if you want to have more than four partitions on a physical hard drive.

Logical drive: A partition created on an extended partition. A logical drive can be assigned a drive letter.

Master Boot Record (MBR): The area on a hard disk that contains boot files; this is the first sector on the disk.

Physical disk: A hard drive.

Primary partition: A partition that functions as a physically separate disk. You can create up to four primary partitions on a physical disk that contains the MBR, or three if you create an extended partition, also. Primary partitions normally are assigned a drive letter by the OS.

Volume: Any area on a hard drive that has a drive letter assigned to it.

The most important thing to know here is that you must designate a partition as active in order to boot from it. However, the other items are likely to come up at some time or another.

Drive Letters

In a PC, physical disks are designated a number starting from 0. Primary partitions, logical drives, optical drives, and network drives are assigned drive letters between C and Z (a *network drive* is a folder or drive on another computer on a network that can be accessed as if it were a local partition on the hard drive). A and B are reserved for floppy drives. The order of automatic letter assignment is as follows:

1. The first primary partition on drive 0 gets C.
2. Subsequent primary partitions on any drive get D, and so on.
3. Logical drives get the next available letters.
4. Optical drives get the next available letters.
5. Network drives get any available letters.

NOTE

This lettering system can cause the following complications: suppose drive 0 has one primary and one extended partition with one logical drive. Drive 1 has one primary partition. Because primary partitions come first, the primary partition on drive 0 is C, the primary partition on drive 1 is D, and the logical drive on drive 0 is E. Furthermore, if you add a second hard drive to a system with a logical drive on drive 0, the new primary partition takes the drive letter formerly held by the logical drive.

OS Hard Drive Control and Configuration

There are several Windows and DOS programs and commands to use to control and configure hard drives. When you are dealing with the only hard drive on a system, you are limited to what you can do in Windows. The reason for this is that Windows files are in use. In many cases, major changes won't be made until the computer is rebooted. The following sections are overviews of the programs.

FDISK

FDISK is a program that runs in DOS, and is useful mainly in 9x. Very old versions of FDISK aren't compatible with FAT32; if you run into this problem, it shouldn't be difficult to obtain a newer version from a Windows 98 or Me boot disk. No version of FDISK is compatible with NTFS. FDISK allows you to view partition information, create or delete a partition or logical drive, and set a partition to active status. FDISK is available on all 9x boot floppies, and in 95 and 98 by booting to DOS from the hard drive. When you get the command prompt, type FDISK. The first thing you'll see, unless you have a tiny hard drive, is a message asking if you want to enable support for large disks (larger than 504MB). Always answer yes (Y) to this prompt. The main menu then appears. You should usually start by viewing partition information by selecting number four from the menu. If you are installing a new hard drive, partition the drive as desired. Unless you have a compelling reason to have multiple partitions, such as setting up a *dual-* or *multiple-boot system*, create a single partition.

NOTE

Partitioning with FDISK effectively deletes all data on the drive. If you are working with a used drive, make sure that the data is either backed up or unneeded before doing anything with FDISK other than viewing partition information or setting the partition as active.

FORMAT

Once you have completed partitioning with FDISK, your drive is not yet usable. The drive must be formatted with a file system. You do this with the FORMAT command. From the DOS command prompt, type FORMAT. For a list of switches, type FORMAT /?. Here is the syntax to use when formatting the C drive as FAT32:

```
FORMAT C: /FS:FAT32
```

After you press <Enter>, drive C, as shown in FDISK's partition information, will be formatted as a FAT32 partition. This will take some time, but when it is done, the partition will be usable. If you have set it active, you can install Windows on it. If you haven't set it to active, you can always run FDISK again and do so.

NOTE

Any time you format a partition you necessarily delete all data on it. There are, however, programs such as Norton Unformat that can sometimes retrieve data from a formatted drive.

CONVERT (2000 and XP Only)

CONVERT is a command available in 2000 and XP that is used to convert a partition from FAT or FAT32 to NTFS. This is done in Windows at a command prompt. This cannot be undone in Windows without formatting the drive and deleting the data, although third-party software such as PartitionMagic® can be used to convert the file system back to FAT or FAT32 while preserving the data. The syntax to convert drive C to NTFS is as follows:

```
CONVERT C: /FS:NTFS
```

Press <Enter> and if the drive contains files that are in use, the conversion will occur at the next reboot; otherwise, it will start immediately.

My Computer

My Computer is available in all versions of Windows. If you select a partition and right-click it, you can perform a few tasks, which vary a bit from version to version. If you select Format from the menu that appears, you can format a partition. Naturally, you won't want to do this on a drive that you want to continue using, as this will delete all data on it. If you select Properties from the menu, the General tab shows you a pie chart showing used and free space on the drive. If you see a check box to enable DMA support, select it. *DMA* is a system that increases performance by reducing the amount of work done by the processor. If the drive doesn't support DMA, the box will be cleared at the next reboot. The Tools tab gives you access to error checking (ScanDisk), backup, and defrag programs.

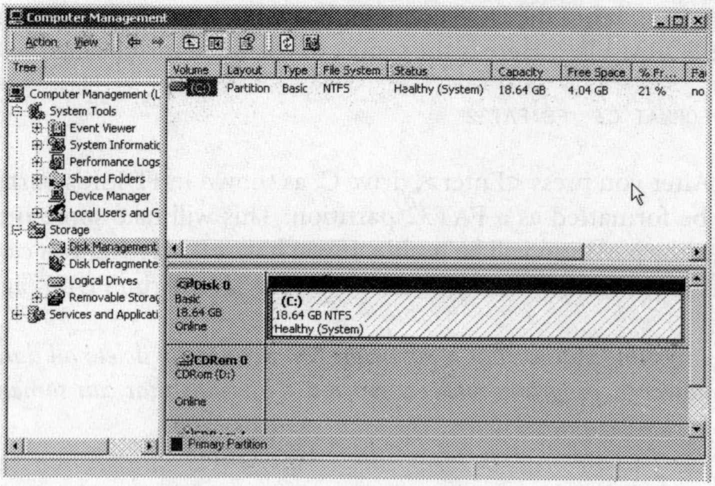

FIGURE 6.3 Disk Management on a simple Windows 2000 system.

Disk Management (2000 and XP Only)

All available disk-related tasks can be done in Disk Management. You can get there through Administrative Tools in Control Panel, and opening Disk Management from Computer Management, or by right-clicking My Computer, selecting Manage from the menu that appears, and opening Disk Management from Computer Management. This will show you a graphical depiction of all disks and partitions on your system. Note that by right-clicking a drive, you have access to certain commands, as shown in Figure 6.3.

If you make any changes in your disk configuration, make sure to edit the boot.ini file to match your changes. This can be a complicated procedure, but if you don't, the computer probably won't boot afterwards. The only way to boot the computer after this happens is to use a Windows XP/2000/NT boot disk, with the boot.ini file on it edited to match the new disk configuration. Fortunately, Windows will remain intact. For information on making a boot disk for 2000 and XP, and on editing the boot.ini file, see Chapter 11, "Troubleshooting."

Disk Tools: ScanDisk, CHKDSK, and Defrag/Disk Defragmenter

We discussed these tools in Chapter 2, "System Configuration and Computer Hygiene."

HARD DRIVES AND MOTHERBOARDS

All standard PC motherboards today come with two EIDE channels, primary and secondary, as evidenced by connectors on the board. Each channel can handle two EIDE devices, one as the *master* and one as the *slave*. In this context, the terms *master* and *slave* really don't mean much, as everything a master drive can do, a slave drive can do also, although traditionally, the hard drive with the OS/boot files is installed as the primary master. This is not a rule, however. If the BIOS is set to detect any device as a boot device, then any one of the four can have the OS. The only restriction is that each channel cannot have more than one master and one slave drive. EIDE devices that can be connected to the EIDE connectors include hard drives, optical drives (CD and DVD), and Zip drives. Additional EIDE drives can be added to motherboards by using an EIDE expansion card (one manufacturer is Promise Technology, Inc. at *promise.com*). To use SCSI devices, a SCSI controller expansion card must be installed.

As we said before, many newer boards come with SATA connectors as well. With this interface, there is no such thing as master and slave, and only one device can be attached to each SATA connector.

HARD DRIVE REMOVAL AND INSTALLATION

It is *usually* not difficult to remove a hard drive from a desktop or tower computer for testing, virus scanning, data transfer, or disposal. The biggest problems you might run into are accessing the screws or having enough room to slide the drive out of the back of the cage. There are a number of steps to follow to install a new or replacement drive, but it usually isn't difficult either.

Hard Drive Removal

The first step in removing a hard drive is, with all the cables and power disconnected, to open the case and access the drive, as instructed in Chapter 4, "Cases and Power Supplies." You will probably have to remove four screws, two on each side of the drive, as shown in Figure 6.4. Then, remove the power connector and the data connector as shown in Figure 6.5.

Handle the hard drive with care. It shouldn't be subjected to physical shocks.

ON THE CD See the video "Opening Different Types of Cases and Accessing Internal Parts" on the accompanying CD-ROM. The file is entitled Opening_the_Case.mpg.

FIGURE 6.4 Removing the screws that secure the drive to the cage.

FIGURE 6.5 Removing the power and data connectors from an EIDE hard drive.

Hard Drive Installation

There are several steps you need to take depending on whether the drive is new or you are reinstalling an existing drive.

Setting Jumpers

The first thing you'll want to do before installing a hard drive is to decide whether you want it to be a primary or secondary, master or slave, based on the other EIDE devices that are or will be installed in the machine. Then, make sure the jumpers are set correctly for master, slave, or cable select. Figure 6.6 shows a jumper panel that is set for the drive to be a master.

Cable Select is a setting that allows the slave or master condition to be determined by which connector on the ribbon cable the EIDE device is connected to. The cable and motherboard or IDE controller must support cable select in order to use it. Most cables that do support cable select have three different colored connectors: black at one end for master, gray in the middle for slave, and blue at the other end for the motherboard (see Figure 6.7). Other cables with three connectors might support cable select. If you have two EIDE devices on one channel (primary or secondary), both or neither must be set to cable select. That is, you can't mix cable select and master or slave jumper settings on the same channel. Jumper settings are usually displayed on the drive label. If not, go to the drive manufacturer's Web site. For example, go to *seagate.com* and enter "cable select" in the search box. Then, open the article entitled "What is Cable Select and How Do I Configure my Seagate Drive to Use It?" This article gives an explanation of cable select, along with a jumper diagram for Seagate hard drives.

You can select whether a drive is primary or secondary by connecting the data cable to the appropriate connector on the motherboard or controller.

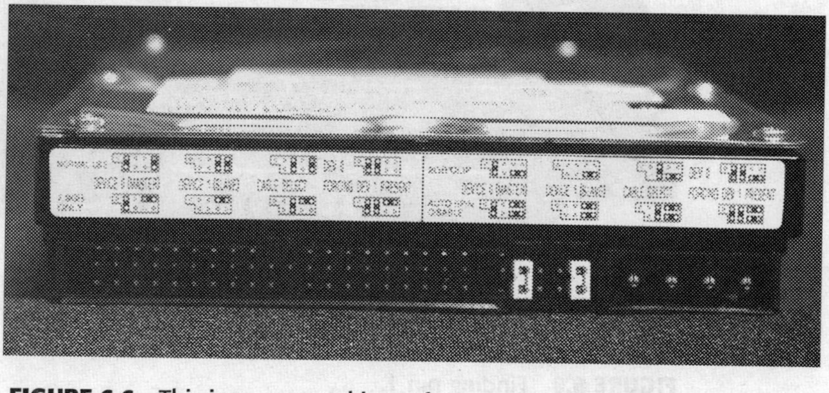

FIGURE 6.6 This jumper panel is set for master.

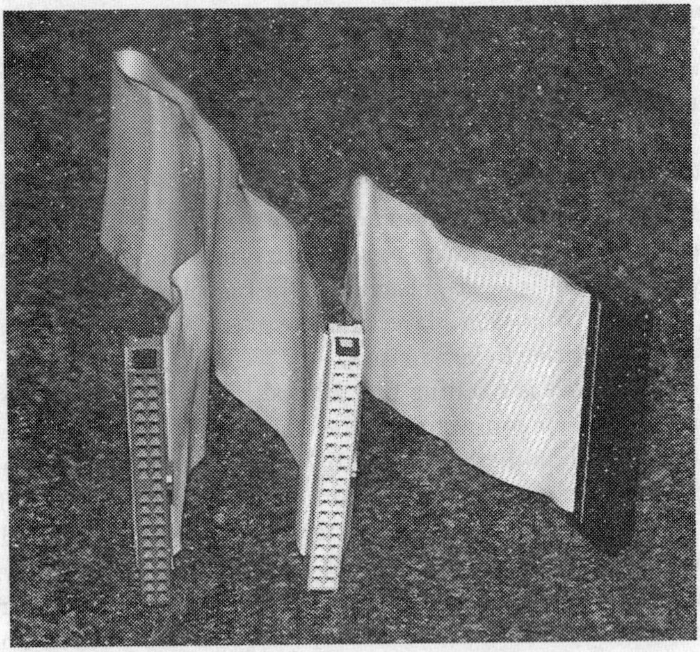

FIGURE 6.7 This ribbon cable supports cable select.

FIGURE 6.8 Finding pin 1.

Ribbon Cables

When installing the data connector with a ribbon cable, you'll notice that one edge is colored differently from the others. That indicates pin 1. If you don't match up pin 1 on the connector with pin 1 on the drive, the hard drive will not work and might cause damage in some systems. In all full-sized hard drives, pin 1 is next to the power connector, as shown in Figure 6.8; notice that the stripe on the cable is next to the power connector.

Of course, it is just as important to connect the ribbon cable correctly to the motherboard, in the event you have removed it. The motherboard will also have a pin indication, as shown in Figure 6.9.

Also, notice the notch in the connector. This is for the ridge in the cable connector, called the *key*. The key should fit in the notch. Some well-designed connectors are actually polarized—they will go in only the correct way. Thankfully, all SATA connectors are polarized.

There are two types of EIDE ribbon cables. Make sure that the ribbon cable is rated for the UDMA capacity of the hard drive and motherboard. Although all the connectors at the ends of the cables have 40 pins, cables for UDMA 66 through 133 have 80 conductors (wires). UDMA 33 cables have 40 conductors. The speed is printed on the cable. If the cable says 66, it is good for the higher speeds. If you use a 33 cable with a 66 hard drive or higher on a motherboard that supports the higher speed, the UDMA speed of the hard drive will still be held to 33.

FIGURE 6.9 An EIDE ribbon cable connected to the connector on the motherboard. Notice the "40" on the opposite side of the cable's stripe, indicating pin 40.

NOTE

You might see the term UltraATA in place of UDMA. For the purposes of this discussion, there is no difference.

Round Cables

Round cables are likely to all be designed to handle UDMA133. The rules for connecting them are basically the same as ribbon cables, but pin 1 is marked on the connector rather than on the wire. Round cables are much more expensive than ribbon cables, but are easier to work with and allow for better airflow. Search the Internet for round EIDE cables.

TIP

Make sure to tie off cables neatly. Use plastic wire ties, never rubber bands or twist-ties.

Hard Drive Bays

PC cases have a few different locations for hard drive bays. The most common is in a cage that holds drives horizontally at the front of the case. The second most common is the bay that holds drives vertically at the front of the case. The vertical bay is often used in smaller cases, or in larger cases for additional hard drives. If you are placing the drive horizontally, the label side should face up and the controller side should face down, unless it was previously installed and running in the opposite position. Then, connect the power connector.

Sometimes it might be necessary to install a hard drive in a 5.25-inch bay, the type usually used for optical drives (CD and DVD). There are adapters that allow you to do this. See Chapter 7, "CD and DVD Drives," for more information on optical drives and 5.25-inch bays. There may come a time when you want to install a 2.5-inch laptop drive into a regular computer. This requires an adapter for the data connector for a temporary situation, and a full kit for a permanent installation. To find an adapter, search the Internet for "2.5 hard drive to 3.5 adapter." If you can't determine which pin on the notebook hard drive is pin 1, consult the manufacturer's Web site. Unlike others, 2.5-inch laptop style hard drives do not have a separate power connector; the power connector is part of the data connector. There are two rows of pins with a space between it and the 4-pin jumper block. The first pin after the jumper block is pin 1, and the last pin at the opposite end on the bottom row is the positive power. If you connect this wrong, you might be connecting a power lead to a data pin, which, once the computer is powered on, will damage the drive and possibly the motherboard. Figure 6.10 shows the connector on a 2.5-inch hard drive.

TIP

We recommend to always remount a hard drive in the same position (right-side up, upside down, vertical) it was in originally, or it might fail sooner than it would otherwise. This is based solely on our personal experience.

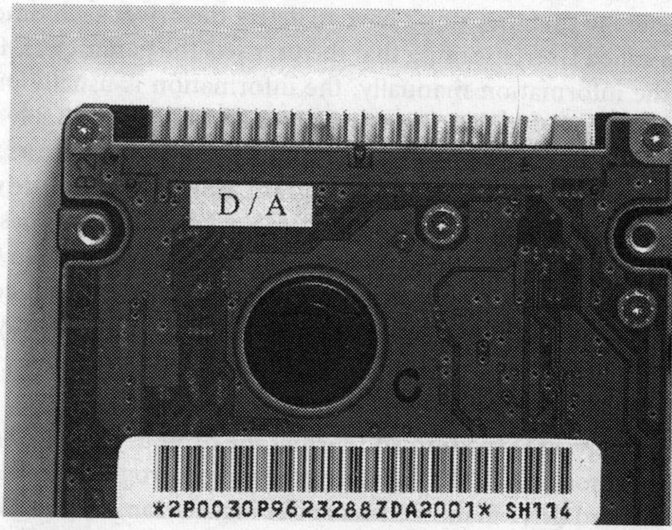

FIGURE 6.10 2.5-inch hard drive connector.

Notebook/Laptop Hard Drive Installation

Unfortunately, there is no standard location where notebook manufacturers put their hard drives. On some machines, you might find that simply removing a single screw on the bottom of the machine and removing the plastic plate gives you full access to the hard drive. Other machines require you to remove the keyboard (see Chapter 9, "Input Devices," for more information). Still others have the hard drive in a slot on a side panel. Unless you have the first type, you will probably have to go to the manufacturer's Web site for service information. Once you find the hard drive, however, replacing it should be easy; the connector is usually polarized (goes in the correct way only). For more information, search the Web for notebook hard drive installation.

Hard Drive Setup

Once the drive is in place, there is a series of steps to perform to set up the drive and prepare it for use. The first is to make sure the BIOS recognizes the drive.

Hard Drive BIOS Settings

As long as it has such a setting, it is best to set the BIOS to Auto, so that it detects the hard drive settings itself. Manually entering these settings might slightly reduce the time it takes for a computer to boot, but it won't be significant enough to make it worthwhile. Some motherboards auto-detect the drive the first time and set the parameters so that they don't have to detect the drives each time. The other option is often called User, meaning that the user sets the parameters. If you feel you need to set the information manually, the information is usually printed on the drive label, or is available from the drive manufacturer's Web site and includes such items as cylinders, heads, write precomp, landing zone, sectors, and size mode.

Also, look in the BIOS setup program for a S.M.A.R.T. drive setting. This feature reports potential problems with the hard drive. Sometimes it will report that a hard drive is ready to fail. This will hopefully give you time to back up the data to another drive before you lose it all. Certainly, no harm can come from enabling S.M.A.R.T., so as long as the setting is available, it should always be enabled.

Disk Partitioning and Formatting

The next step is to partition and format the drive as described earlier in this chapter. In addition to FDISK, there are other setup programs you can use. In fact, just about all hard drive manufacturers offer installation, diagnostic, and other utilities free for download from their Web sites. Ontrack Data Recovery Services (*ontrack.com*) has enhanced versions of some of these utilities for sale. These utilities have many advantages over FDISK and FORMAT, including the capability of formatting partitions as NTFS.

ON THE CD

The Industry Contacts document on the CD-ROM lists hard drive manufacturers. Visit their Web sites and look for downloads for installation, diagnostic, BIOS size limitation, and other utilities.

When you set up Windows 2000 or XP from scratch or perform a *clean install* (installing an OS on a formatted drive, as opposed to running an upgrade), you can boot from an installation floppy or CD and follow the prompts. At a certain point you'll be shown a graph of available partitions and you'll be asked how you want to proceed. You might be able to use existing partitions or delete them and let Setup create new ones for you. You simply answer the prompts concerning the installation partition and file system you want. Then, Setup formats the partition as set. There is no need to pre-format a drive before installing 2000 or XP.

NOTE

You might come across a function in a BIOS setup program or elsewhere called "low-level formatting." Never do this; it would likely ruin the drive and invalidate the warranty. The point of low-level formatting is to do a complete format and erase everything to eliminate a virus or prepare the drive for a new user. This includes data that the manufacturer wrote onto an otherwise inaccessible portion of the drive. If you need to perform this operation, use the drive manufacturer's utility. In Seagate's case, for example, the procedure is called "Zero Fill" because it replaces all data with zeroes, and is done with Seagate's Disk Wizard software.

NOTE

When installing a SATA drive, make certain to follow the drive's and motherboard's instructions exactly. Intel motherboards that support SATA, for example, require that SATA drives be set up as RAID drives, even if there is only one drive in the system. RAID is covered later in this chapter.

Third-party disk management programs such as Symantec Corporation's PartitionMagic (*powerquest.com* or *symantec.com*—PowerQuest was acquired by Symantec Corporation in December, 2003) have many features that aren't available in Windows or from any of the utilities that come with new hard drives. You can use PartitionMagic to create, delete, undelete, re-size, hide, merge, or move partitions, as well as change the file system or drive letters, all without losing data. These and many other features make it an especially useful tool for a technician to have, especially if you have finished installing an OS only to discover that you made an error in partitioning or formatting. You can use PartitionMagic to correct the error without having to start all over.

Once you have installed, formatted, and partitioned the drive, you should be ready to install the OS.

Installing 2000 or XP on a SCSI Drive

Early in the 2000/XP installation process, you are prompted to press <F6> if you need to install any third-party SCSI drivers or RAID drivers. This prompt appears for only a few seconds. You will have to provide the drivers for the SCSI controller at this point if you want the installation to be successful. See the upcoming RAID section for more information.

TROUBLESHOOTING HARD DRIVES

Hard drives are a common culprit in PC problems. These problems can range from easily correctable to disastrous. As mentioned earlier in this chapter, making sure S.M.A.R.T. drives are enabled in the BIOS could be helpful to catch some of these problems sooner than they otherwise would be caught. This section covers some common hard drive problems and solutions.

Operating System Is Missing

One of the most obvious signs of a hard drive problem is an error message early in the boot process saying that the system can't find an OS. However, before jumping to conclusions, make sure there is no floppy in the floppy drive. It is most common for a BIOS to be set to boot first from a floppy, so if there is a non-bootable floppy in the drive, you'll probably get a message such as "Non-system disk or disk error," or "ntldr is missing." Remove the floppy and restart before taking any other measures.

TIP *If a computer is in early stages of booting or is running in DOS, pressing <Ctrl> + <Alt> + <Delete> will restart the system.*

If there is no floppy in the drive and you continue to get a missing OS message, it is time to check the hard drive for problems. You can try the following:

A. Listen for hard drive activity and look at the indicator light on the case. The light should flicker and you should hear some sounds. Buzzing or clicking, however, is a possible sign of drive failure.
B. Check the BIOS to make sure that it recognizes the hard drive. Set the BIOS to auto-detect the hard drive and to enable S.M.A.R.T. drives.
C. Check the power and data cables. Make sure they are plugged in correctly and securely. If the data cable looks damaged, try a replacement cable. Try disconnecting the power cable and using another one from the power supply.
D. Check the hard drive jumpers. Make sure there aren't two slaves, two masters, or a mixture of slave or master and cable select.
E. Run a diagnostic program such as Micro-Scope or PC Certify, or a utility offered by the hard drive manufacturer or Ontrack (*ontrack.com*). Also helpful are the PartitionMagic Rescue floppies. You can boot the machine with these and run the program even if PartitionMagic isn't installed on the system. You can access drive information and check for errors, as well as perform other operations. Just make sure to use a version of PartitionMagic as recent as the OS installed on the system. For example, running a version of PartitionMagic older than 7.0 on Windows XP or 2000 with Service Pack 2 or later will likely produce false error messages.

TIP *If you use a hard drive software utility, make sure to read the directions carefully, and, if so instructed, back up the data before running tests. In addition, make sure to follow the terms of the software license for any program you run.*

F. Use a hardware-based EIDE hard drive tester such as the Western Digital Quick Tester (*http://support.wdc.com/order/drivestester.asp*).
G. Run FDISK and select number four from the menu to view partition information. Note that if the partition is formatted as NTFS, FDISK will label the partition only as a non-DOS partition. Sometimes the use of drive overlay software such as EZ-BIOS will actually interfere with the system's recognition of the drive.

H. Remove the hard drive and check it on another computer. Look for the Windows folder to make sure it is intact, and scan the drive for viruses.

I. Try a different EIDE device in the same channel to make sure the problem isn't in the motherboard or EIDE controller.

J. If there is another EIDE device on the same channel, disconnect it and boot the computer. One malfunctioning drive can cause the other device to stop working.

The System Doesn't Recognize the Full Capacity of the Hard Drive

There are a few different reasons why a computer might not make full use of a hard drive.

Many BIOSs are limited as to the maximum size of a supported partition. In the past, the only way to get around these limitations was to partition the drive so that each partition fit into the size limitation. However, today, unless the computer is very old, there are more satisfactory ways to get around this problem. The following list will be a helpful guide.

Enable large drive support in the BIOS, if available. This includes a setting called LBA support.

Check for a BIOS update. The source of the update should show a list of changes from the previous BIOS version. If there have been any BIOS versions released after the one installed on the computer but before the newest update, you might have to view them to see if any of them have a fix to this problem.

Install drive overlay software. This is available for download from the hard drive manufacturers, although it's not always called "drive overlay" software. If the computer locks up on boot and the hard drive is larger than 33GB, check to see if the BIOS is Award 4.5x. If so, drive overlay software should solve the problem.

Remove drive overlay software. Oddly enough, this software can sometimes cause the problem it was designed to solve, especially if it is installed on a newer computer. You will probably have to boot the computer with the drive overlay floppy and elect to uninstall the software once you get to the main program page.

Other Hard Drive Problems

Disk too full: Whenever a system runs poorly or if you get Windows Protection errors, check to make sure that at least 10 percent of the drive is unused. The paging file and other temporary files need this space. If less than 10 percent of the disk capacity remains, you will have to delete or transfer some data to another location. You might have to install the hard drive on another computer to do this. Another choice is to copy all or some of the data onto a larger drive and install the new drive in the computer. We discuss data backup later in this chapter.

The system suddenly can't read data on the drive: This is a sign of possible hard drive failure. If Windows is still running, run ScanDisk (9x), or Error-Checking/CHKDSK (2000, XP) (see Chapter 2 for more information). Make sure to select the "Thorough" and "Automatically fix errors" check boxes on ScanDisk, or the "Automatically fix file system errors" and "Scan for and attempt recovery of bad sectors" check boxes on Error-Checking/CHKDSK before running. You can also try the methods described in the previous list under "Operating system is missing."

If you have removed a hard drive from a Gateway computer with 98 or Me, and installed it in another machine and find that the second machine can't read any data from the drive, Gateway's Go Back utility might have been installed on the drive. Reinstall the drive in the Gateway machine, boot to Windows if possible, and uninstall Go Back. To do this, go to Control Panel, Add/Remove Programs.

If Windows stops running, you can boot a system with a Windows 98 or Me startup disk and scan a FAT or FAT32 partition by typing SCANDISK at the command prompt and pressing <Enter>. With NTFS partitions, you'll have to use a third-party program such as Norton Utilities or Partition Magic. Diagnostic programs such as Micro-Scope and PC Certify can also be very helpful.

Hard Drive Trouble Indicators

Some hard drive problems are indicated by blue screens or a message in 2000 or XP's Disk Management. This will usually require you to write down the entire error message and search Microsoft's Knowledge Base. In Disk Management, there is a status indicator on each partition's graph. Underneath the drive letter, size, and file system you'll see a word; hopefully the word is "Healthy," although you could see words such as "Failed" or "Unreadable." For more information, access the Help files in Computer Management and search for "healthy." Then, select "Disk status descriptions" or "Volume status descriptions" and click the Display button.

If you get these indicators or other serious error messages, but the drive appears to work, there is no time to waste to back up important data, covered next.

For more help with hard drive problems, go to *computerhope.com/help/hdd.htm*.

SAVING DATA

Anyone who has important data is advised to back it up regularly. Few of us, however, do so. However, if you have an indication that a drive is about to fail, you might be able to save the data before it does. There are various ways to do this. First, you could copy the data directly. You can install the replacement hard drive into a separate computer on its own channel and transfer the data over a network, or barring that, you could install the replacement hard drive into the same computer on the other channel. Disconnect an optical drive if you have to. The XCOPY command is particularly good for this.

XCOPY

While you could manually transfer data in Windows, the XCOPY command gives you the advantage of certain options that streamline the process. Using the following switches when copying from the C drive to the E drive causes the system to copy hidden and system files, and continue copying even if some files are bad, among other benefits:

```
XCOPY C: E: /E /V /C /I /F /H
```

For more information, see the description of XCOPY in Chapter 13, "Command-Line Tutorial." You can also open the command prompt and type XCOPY /?. This will provide the command's syntax and list the switches.

Another way to copy blocks of data is by using software such as Drive Copy™ or Drive Image® (*powerquest.com* or *symantec.com*). These programs have to be installed, but they work much faster than XCOPY.

Backup Programs

There are also backup programs that take all the data to be backed up and create a single highly compressed file. These programs provide a way to back up and restore data, including OSs and programs, exactly the way they were. Early Windows Backup programs could store the backup only on the local drive, floppies, or on a network drive, although the backup file can always be moved to another drive (assuming the media is big enough for the entire file) once the backup is complete. The most common backup program is Backup Utility for Windows, better known as Windows Backup, available in Start: > Programs (All Programs in XP Professional): > Accessories: > System Tools. The interface for Windows Backup is simple (see Figure 6.11). Just follow the wizard. See Chapter 11 for more information on Windows Backup.

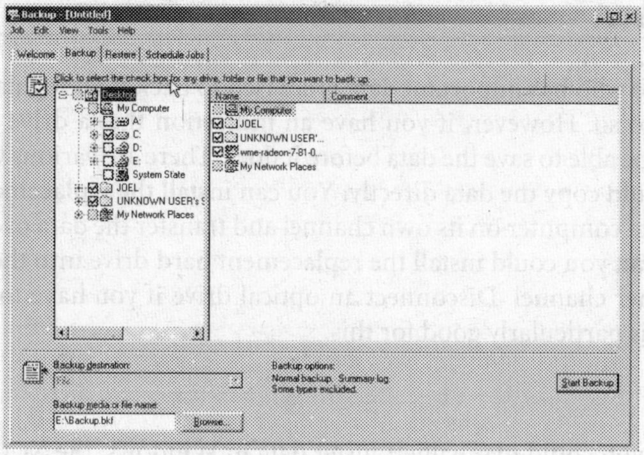

FIGURE 6.11 Windows Backup.

There are many third-party backup programs on the market, most of which offer more features than Windows Backup does.

Hard Drive Crash

If you have a hard drive that has absolutely ceased to work no matter what steps you have taken to restore it, it has probably *crashed*. To recover the data, your only option might be to send the drive to a recovery company such as Ontrack (*ontrack.com*). This is an expensive operation, so it is done mainly when the data is critically important.

File and Settings Transfer Wizard

Introduced with Windows XP, the File and Settings Transfer Wizard allows you to set up a new computer running Windows XP as close as possible to the old one running Windows versions 95 through 2000, including NT 4.0. Available in Start > Programs (All Programs in XP) > Accessories > System Tools, this wizard is easy to follow. Early versions have been troublesome, however. To correct any problems, make sure to install Service Pack 1 or later on Windows XP before proceeding.

RAID

RAID stands for "Redundant Array of Independent (formerly "Inexpensive") Disks." RAID is a collection of hard drives in a computer that is used for performance enhancement and/or fault tolerance. Windows server versions (Windows

NT and 2000 Server, and Windows Server 2003) have built-in support for some levels of RAID, but hardware-based RAID systems provide better performance. The most basic level of RAID uses two hard drives to increase performance, while higher levels store data on two or more drives so that if one fails, the data won't be lost. SCSI or SATA drives are usually used in RAID systems. In hardware-based RAID systems, it is common for the drives to be removable; they are kept in a caddy that is accessible through an opening in the case. When one fails, it can easily be replaced. More advanced systems employ *hot-swappable* drives. These are drives that can be removed and replaced without shutting down the system. Naturally, all this technology is much more expensive than standard PCs, so it is used mainly in business and government situations in which downtime and/or data loss would be catastrophic to the operation of the organization. For more information on RAID, see *raidweb.com*, and search the Web for more articles; there are many.

TIP

Early in the Windows 2000/XP installation process, you are prompted to press the F6 key in case you want to install drivers for a special drive controller. You must do this if you want to install the OS on a SCSI drive. If you are setting up hardware RAID with SCSI or SATA drives, or could be using RAID later, make sure you supply the RAID drivers at this point or you will probably have to reinstall the entire system when you do want to use RAID. The option to press <F6> is available for only a few seconds. Also, if there is such a setting, make sure RAID is enabled in the BIOS.

REMOVABLE STORAGE DEVICES

There are several different types of removable storage devices. We discussed removable full-sized hard drives in the section on RAID. There are additional uses for these. One is for drives containing data only (no OS or programs) that can be easily switched from machine to machine, although networks usually do that job. Another use is as an easy way to switch OSs on a single computer, a job usually done by setting up the different OSs on different partitions.

USB and FireWire (IEEE 1394) Drives

USB and FireWire are external drives that connect easily into the appropriate port. They are especially good for backup and transferring large amounts of data from one machine to another without using a network connection, and they are hot-swappable (consult the manual to be sure). These take drive letters, just as internal hard drives. They cost a bit more than internal drives because of the housing and external power supply. When installing one of these drives, make sure you follow the directions exactly, especially order of installation. You can expect problems if you don't. If you are asked to get one of these drives working after someone installed it incorrectly, you'll have to uninstall the drive and start over again.

PC-Card (PCMCIA) Hard Drives

PC-Card hard drives are credit card sized drives that fit into the appropriate Type II or III PC-Card slots on notebook computers and the occasional full-sized computer. Recent models by Kingston (*kingston.com*) and other companies hold several gigabytes of data. However, because of their extraordinarily small size, they don't have much buffer, so they are good mainly for data archiving on notebooks. These drives are usually easy to set up and they do get a drive letter from the system. They are also hot-swappable, but if Windows is running, make sure to stop the device by clicking the Eject or Unplug Device icon in Windows' system tray, or in the Add/Remove Hardware wizard (or equivalent depending on Windows version) in Control Panel. Failure to stop a PC-Card device before ejecting it can damage the device.

Microdrives

Microdrives are even smaller drives used in certain computers and digital cameras. A tiny Hitachi 4GB drive using a single 1-inch platter is available (search *hgst.com* for "Microdrive"). There are adapters available to plug microdrives into PC-Card slots.

TIP

When formatting an external hard drive, take into account the different computers in which it might be used. You wouldn't want to format a drive as NTFS if it will be shared with a notebook running Windows 9x.

Flash Memory Cards

Flash memory is memory that doesn't need continuous power to maintain its data. Therefore, it can be used in place of a disk drive. Flash memory has the advantage over disk drives of having no moving parts, so it is much more resistant to damage than the spinning platters and fast-moving heads of a hard drive. If flash memory eventually gets to the point where it exceeds the speed of hard drives for a comparable cost, it will possibly replace hard drives and possibly all disk drives. Flash memory is also adaptable to PC-Card slots.

Diagnosing Removable Storage Device Problems

These devices can fail just as regular hard drives can. Follow all drive troubleshooting instructions that apply to these devices. Moreover, with the USB and FireWire drives, drivers could be a problem—either the driver could be corrupted or the installer didn't follow the instructions. Uninstall the device and reinstall the drivers, making sure to follow the directions to the letter. See Chapter 2 for more information on device drivers.

FLOPPY DISK DRIVES (DISKETTE) OVERVIEW

Floppy drives were the original storage drive type in PCs. The IBM PC, circa 1981, had two 5.25-inch floppy drives, each with a capacity of 360KB. There were no other storage devices. 1.2MB versions of these came out years later, and the 3.5-inch version that we use today came out after that. There was an attempt to circulate 2.88MB floppies, but they really didn't catch on.

These days, floppy drives are on their way out, although the vast majority of new computers still come with them, with the exception being notebooks. While many of the most common uses for floppies have been taken over by CD-RWs, removable hard drives, Zip drives, and network connections, at the moment, floppies are still essential for tasks such as starting computers that won't boot otherwise, or running programs such as disk utilities that can't run in Windows. This is because the drivers to run floppy disks are included on all BIOS chips, meaning that floppy disks can run as soon as the BIOS gets to them. More recently, however, this has become true for optical drives as well.

Selecting a Floppy Drive

New floppy drives available today are nearly all good quality. If the case has an opening that shows the entire floppy faceplate, as shown in Figure 6.12, the only consideration is that the color of the faceplate matches the computer case, if that is important to the user. Many cases, however, have openings for proprietary floppy drives, an example of which is shown in Figure 6.13. In this case, if you have a selection of used drives, you can try to match up a faceless drive, such as the one shown in Figure 6.13, or try to order a new drive from the case or computer manufacturer.

Floppy Drive Installation

Motherboards have one floppy connector, and many newer motherboards support only one floppy drive. A computer can have no more than two floppy drives. About the only need these days for two floppy drives is if the user has 5.25-inch disks to access. In this case, the 3.5-inch drive should be A and the 5.25-inch should be B. A small power connector (see Figure 6.14) is used for 3.5-inch floppy drives. A standard floppy drive ribbon cable has three connectors: one for A, one for B, and one for the motherboard connector (see Figure 6.15). You'll see that a floppy cable has

FIGURE 6.12 Standard opening, standard drive.

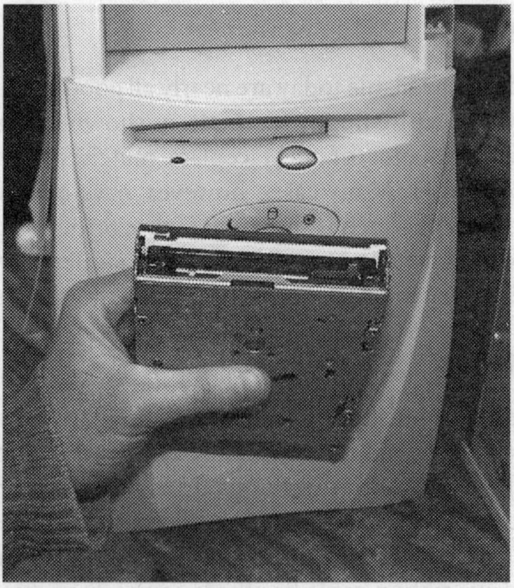

FIGURE 6.13 Proprietary opening, proprietary drive.

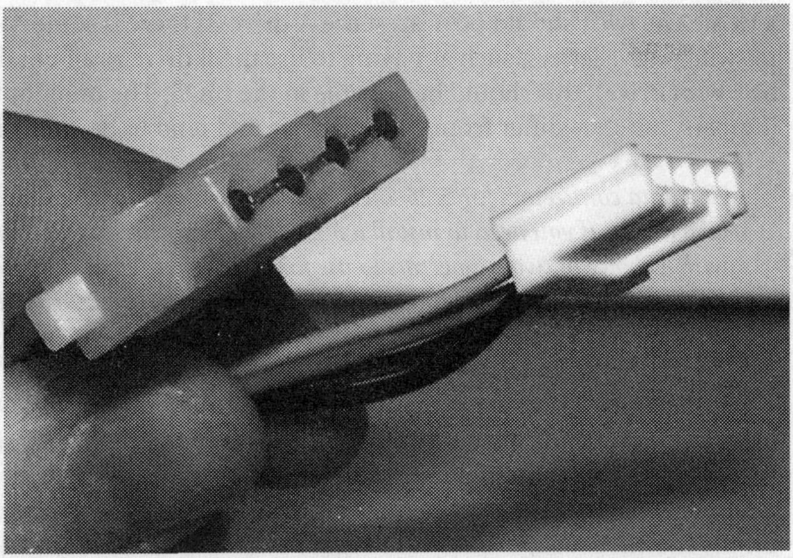

FIGURE 6.14 The large connector is for hard drives, optical drives, and 5.25-inch floppy drives. The small connector is only for 3.5-inch floppy drives.

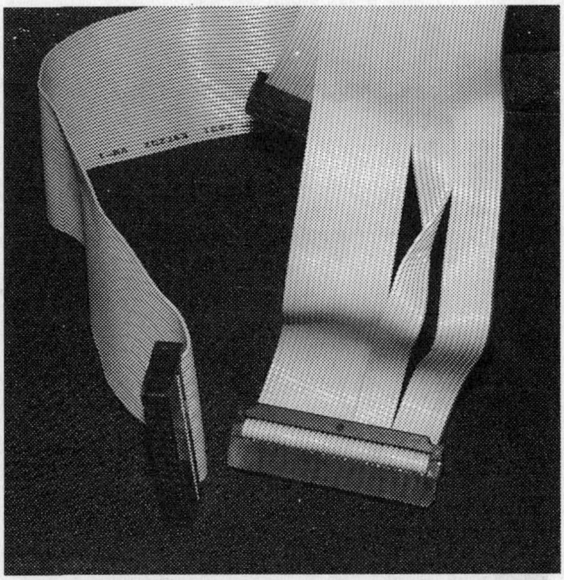

FIGURE 6.15 One floppy cable with a twist.

a twist. The twist should be nearest the A drive. If there is some compelling reason to switch drive letters, such as having to use the B drive as a boot drive (only A can be a boot drive), this should be possible in the BIOS. The other option is to change jumpers, but they differ from drive to drive and tend to be confusing.

NOTE

The data connectors for 5.25-inch floppy drives are not the same as those for 3.5-inch drives. If you need to install a 5.25-inch floppy drive, you'll need a floppy cable with a choice of two connectors to use for the B drive. That type of cable allows connection of either a 3.5-inch or a 5.25-inch device as the B drive. Remember, the A drive is always the one nearest the twist in the cable.

Just about every case has a space dedicated to a floppy drive. Look for a 3.5-inch bay that corresponds to an opening in the front of the case (shown in Figure 6.16). Just as in hard drives, you'll have to match up pins 1. Pin 1 on the cable has a stripe, and there will be some type of marking on the drive as shown in Figure 6.17, and on the motherboard, as shown in Figure 6.18. The drive markings can be cryptic, but know that if pins 0 and 34 are marked, pin 1 will be next to pin 0, and on the opposite end from pin 34. Other drives have only a red mark. Once you ascertain which side pin 1 is on, it is a good idea to mark it on the drive with a fine-tipped permanent marker. However, damage won't occur if you make a mistake with the data cable; if the floppy drive light stays on continuously, it means that one end of the data cable is in backward.

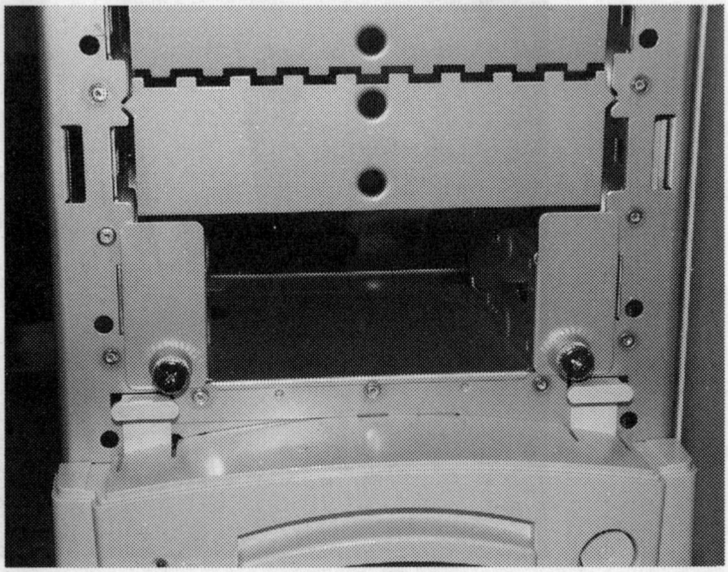

FIGURE 6.16 A bay usable for a floppy drive.

FIGURE 6.17 Pin 1 markings can be vague.

Finally, make sure that the BIOS is set correctly for the floppy drive(s) in the system.

Diagnosing Floppy Problems

There aren't many different types of problems with floppy drives. The one mentioned previously is that of the light staying on continuously, indicating that one of the data connectors is in backward. If the drive doesn't seem to work at all, either the data or power cable might not be in all the way. The only other problem is trouble reading from or writing to the disk. First, try a new disk—floppy disks are prone to damage. If that doesn't work, try using a cleaning kit. Search the Web for "floppy drive cleaning kit." These should be very inexpensive.

TIP

Don't use an important floppy to test a drive; a bad drive can damage a floppy disk and/or its data.

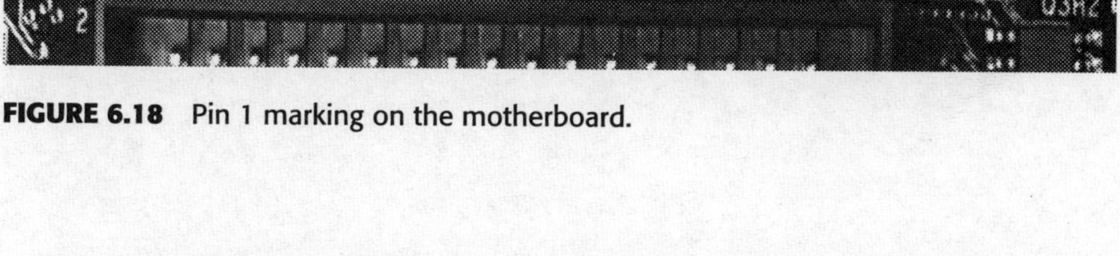

FIGURE 6.18 Pin 1 marking on the motherboard.

Formatting Floppies

Floppy disks come from the factory already formatted for PCs or Macs. The easiest way to erase all the data on a floppy is to format it again. In Windows, right-click the drive in My Computer and click the Format command. If the disk has been working and you are in a hurry, select the Quick Format check box. Quick Format skips the step of checking the disk for bad sectors. If the data has been corrupted, or you have the time, leave this box clear. You can also do this at a command prompt, which is important if you are in DOS. The command is as follows:

```
FORMAT A: /Q
```

The Q switch instructs the system to do a quick format.

NOTE

All floppies will be formatted as FAT16.

Making a Windows 9x Startup Disk

To make a Windows 9x startup disk, insert a floppy in the drive of a Windows 9x computer. Then, go to Add/Remove Programs in Control Panel, and click the Startup Disk tab.

For more information on floppy drives, go to *pcmech.com/floppy.htm.*

ZIP® AND JAZ® REMOVABLE DISK DRIVES

Zip and *Jaz* drives use proprietary removable disks in sizes running from 100MB to 2GB. These drives get a drive letter and are fast and easy to use. Windows Me and later versions don't need to have software installed in order to use them. Mac-formatted disks and PC-formatted disks are available. A Mac can usually use a PC disk, but a PC needs third-party software to be able to use a Mac disk. The disks are rather reliable, but of course are subject to bad sectors and magnetic or physical damage. The disadvantage to these drives is that the removable disks are much more expensive than CD-RWs and recordable DVDs, which can be had for under $1 apiece, and can be formatted to act as a regular magnetic disk.

7 CD and DVD Drives

In This Chapter

- CD/DVD Drive Overview
- Selecting Optical Drives
- Removal and Installation
- Backups onto Optical Discs
- Maintenance of Optical Disc Drives and Discs
- Diagnosing Optical Disc Problems
- Booting from a CD-ROM

CD/DVD DRIVE OVERVIEW

Compact Disc (CD) and Digital Versatile Disc (DVD, formerly Digital Video Disc) drives are called *optical* drives because microscopic pits embedded into the discs are read by measuring reflected laser light. Read-Only Memory (CD-ROM) drives became popular around 1994 and represented a major improvement over floppies for program installation. They can also be used to read from CD data discs. Eventually came CD-R drives, which allowed discs to be *burned* (recorded) once only. There weren't too many of these made as they were quickly replaced by CD-RWs, which can be used with both single-use and rewritable discs. DVD-ROM drives were next. These are used to play DVD videos and read from data DVDs. More and more programs are becoming available on DVDs as well.

NOTE: *The term ATAPI refers to IDE optical drives.*

Unfortunately, there are several different incompatible types of DVD writable drives available, and the industry has not settled on a standard. The different types include the following:

DVD-R: Can write to a blank disc once. The discs are compatible with most recent DVD video players.

DVD-RW: Can be written and rewritten to. The discs are compatible with most recent DVD video players.

DVD+RW: Can be written and rewritten to. They can read and write to DVD-Rs. The discs are compatible with some DVD video players.

DVD-RAM: Can be written and rewritten to. The discs are *not* compatible with most DVD video players as of this writing.

Blu-ray Disc: A format not yet available as of this writing that allows for up to 27GB of data to be stored on a single DVD disc.

Go to *dvdrw.com* for more information on the DVD+ standards, *dvdforum.org* for information on the DVD- standards, and *blu-raydisc.info* for information on Blu-ray standards.

Some multi-standard drives are available. There are also discs with multiple layers and discs that can be flipped over to record on the other side, increasing the data capacity. Stay tuned; the industry will probably eventually come to an agreement on a single standard.

SELECTING OPTICAL DRIVES

There are only a few considerations in selecting an optical drive.

Interface

So far, internal drives come only in two interfaces: IDE and SCSI. IDE is the same interface as EIDE as it applies to hard drives, and thus the optical drives are connected to the same cables as the hard drives. See Chapter 6, "Magnetic Disk Drives," for more information on the IDE interfaces. SCSI drives are simply additional devices in the SCSI chain. SCSI controllers and consequently, SCSI drives, are found almost exclusively in heavy-duty business computers. Serial ATA optical drives will be available eventually.

External drives once came with parallel interfaces (they connect to a parallel port on the computer) and SCSI, but now are available in USB and FireWire. You should select the fastest interface the user can afford. Also note that USB 2.0 is much faster than USB 1.1, so if you are using a USB 2.0 drive with a computer that has only a USB 1.1 interface, the drive will operate at the slower speed.

Speed

Speed of optical drives is based on the data transfer rate of the original CD-ROM drives, 150 kilobits per second (Kbps). For example, the data transfer rate of a 52x CD-ROM drive is 52 × 150, or 7.8 megabits per second (Mbps). Even the fastest optical drives, however, are slower than hard drives.

CD-RW Speed

A CD-RW, also known as a *CD burner*, has three speeds listed in its specifications. The first number represents the speed of writing to a CD-R, the second is the speed of writing to a CD-RW, and the third is the speed it reads a disc. In the case of a combo drive that offers a DVD-ROM along with a CD burner, a fourth number is the speed the drive reads a DVD, but see the next item for an explanation of DVD speeds.

DVD Speed

There are combo drives available that offer DVD and CD-burning capabilities. In these cases, there are so many numbers in the specifications that each is spelled out (or should be) wherever it is displayed. The single DVD-burning speed, however, is much faster than the CD's 150 Kbps, and can vary from standard to standard. The actual speed in Mbps should be spelled out in the documentation.

NOTE *The maximum speed of the blank media (writable discs) in any format must match or exceed that of the burner in order for the burner to operate at its maximum rated speed.*

REMOVAL AND INSTALLATION

IDE optical drives are connected the same way as EIDE hard drives, so see Chapter 6 for more information. Set the jumpers for primary/secondary, master/slave, or cable select, just as you do with EIDE hard drives. The BIOS should be set for autodetect for each optical drive. Also, pin 1 is almost always next to the power connector, which is the same type of power connector used for hard drives. Screws are used on each side of the cage to secure the drive. The only differences are that optical drives have to be installed in a 5.25-inch bay with an opening in the front of the case, and that an audio cable usually has to be connected. Figure 7.1 shows a typical example of an installed optical drive.

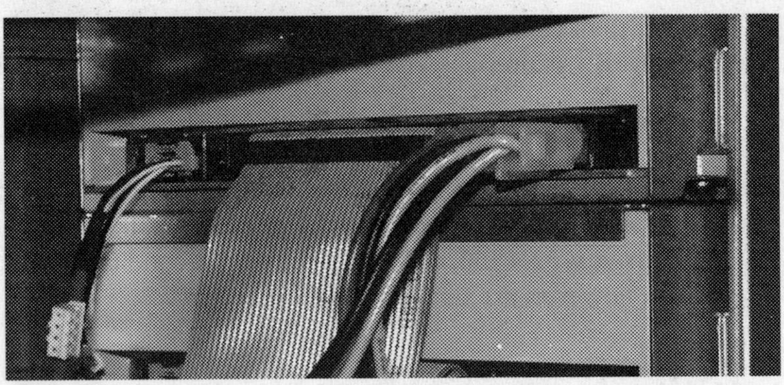

FIGURE 7.1 A typical CD-ROM drive installation.

To remove a drive, shut off the power, remove all cables from the computer, and open the case. If there could be any question about reconnecting the drive, make a diagram of which connectors are connected where. Make a note of the drive's jumper position. This is especially important if you will be removing other drives as well. Next, remove the data, power, and audio cables. Then, remove the screws fastening the drive to the cage and pull out the unit. To replace a drive, follow the instructions in Chapter 6 for installing a hard drive, except for the differences described here.

Mixing Drives with Different UDMA Ratings

As is true with hard drives, you normally wouldn't want to have drives of different UDMA ratings—for example, an Ultra ATA UDMA 100 drive on the same IDE channel as an Ultra ATA UDMA 66—unless the motherboard or IDE controller came with a program such as Intel's Application Accelerator. See Chapter 6 for more information.

Audio Cables

For most optical drives to play analog audio from audio CDs or video discs with audio, there is an audio connector on these drives. These get connected to the audio header connectors on the motherboard or sound card. Some motherboards have two or more of these, as shown in Figure 7.2.

If you have one drive and two connectors, use the header connector for CD-ROM in. If you have two drives and two connectors, connect the drive that will be most likely used for audio playback to the CD-ROM in and the other to the AUX in. If you have two drives and only one connector, the user will be limited to one of the drives for analog audio playback (digital audio playback can be heard without

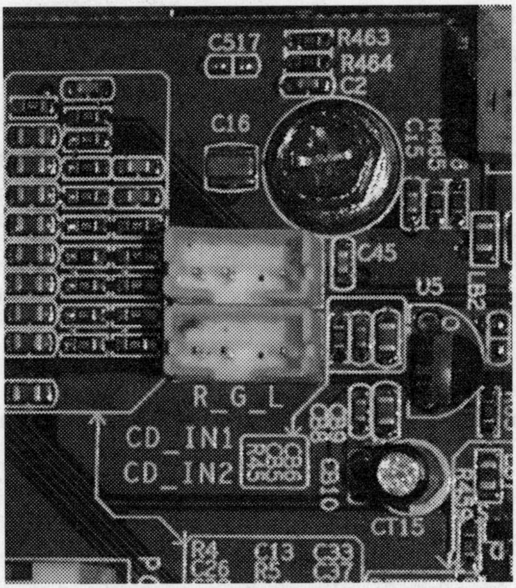

FIGURE 7.2 Audio header connectors on a motherboard.

an audio cable being connected at all; it is transmitted via the data cable). If one of the drives is a DVD drive, you'll want to connect the audio connector to it. In this case, instruct the user to play audio CDs in the DVD drive. Figure 7.3 shows an audio connector on an optical drive.

Proprietary Faceplates

Often, a computer manufacturer will design their cases for aesthetics and will include an odd-shaped front opening for optical drives. It is often hard to acquire a

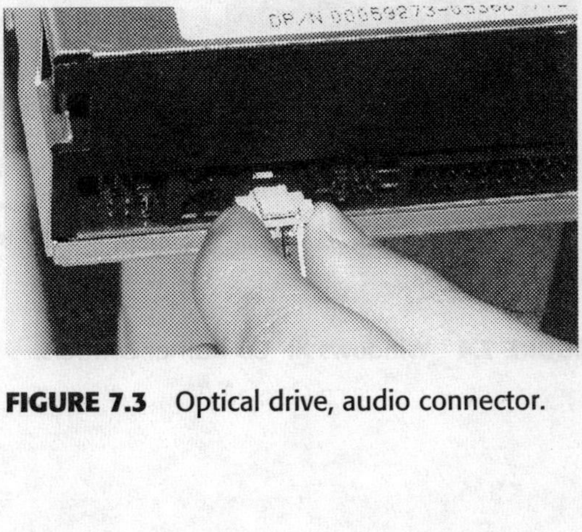

FIGURE 7.3 Optical drive, audio connector.

replacement for these drives by the time they fail. If you have a large supply of used drives or can match the original manufacturer's drive closely enough, you might be able to get a good match by removing the faceplate carefully from the original and fitting it on the replacement. Usually, you will need to modify the case slightly or place the drive in a different drive bay if available. There have been times that we have opted to get a brand new high-quality case with a power supply, and transfer the motherboard and all internal parts to the new case as well as install a new standard optical drive. This might actually be a better and more aesthetic long-term solution as long as all the components will fit properly in the new case.

Driver, Firmware, and Software

Windows, in almost all cases, will automatically install all necessary drivers for optical drives. Once the drive is installed, the programs supplied by the manufacturer that allow for use of the drive's features can be installed. These are usually "lite" versions of programs. The user can purchase full versions of these programs for added functionality. In addition, newer versions of Windows Media Player and other media players such as RealPlayer™ (*real.com*) have the *multimedia* functions built in. Windows Media Player is standard with Windows, and updates are frequently available either through Windows Update (see Chapter 2, "System Configuration and Computer Hygiene"), *microsoft.com/downloads*, or *microsoft.com/windows/windowsmedia*. In addition, data-burning capabilities are built into My Computer in Windows XP, as shown in Figure 7.4.

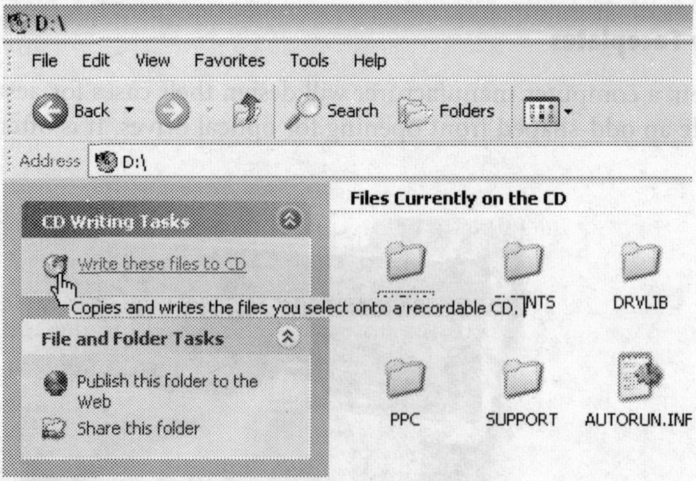

FIGURE 7.4 Windows XP CD burner controls.

In most cases, a drive's firmware should be left alone. If you are researching a problem and find that a firmware update is necessary, go to the manufacturer's Web site and follow the directions exactly.

NOTE *Remember, you run the same risks when updating component firmware as when you update a motherboard BIOS. If you make a mistake, you might render the drive useless!*

Installing and Configuring External Optical Drives

USB and FireWire drives can be very simple to install. Follow the manufacturer's instructions carefully and *read them first* before you connect anything. In most cases, USB drives will require that the software be installed before the drive is ever connected to the computer. Some USB drives might be able to be plugged into a PC with Windows Me, 2000, or XP directly without any driver installation at all because the drivers are built right into the firmware of the drive.

With FireWire, the drive is usually plugged into the computer after it is running and the OS will recognize the drive and install Windows native drivers. If the drivers were not installed originally with Windows, you will probably be asked to insert your Windows installation CD. After your drive is properly detected, you can install any applications needed to use the drive, such as software for CD burning, movie editing, music production, and so forth.

BACKUPS ONTO OPTICAL DISCS

Windows Backup, which comes with Windows except for XP Home Edition (Start > Programs/All Programs > Accessories > System Tools > Backup), can use optical drives. Many third-party backup programs have this capability as well. Elect to back up to a file and then store the file, if it will fit, on a CD-RW or writable DVD. With Windows Backup you will probably have to use a formatted rewritable disc. Most or all CD-burning software has a function for formatting the disc. To format a disc could take between 25 and 45 minutes. When it is completed, files and folders can be dragged and dropped, or cut/copied and pasted into and out of the rewritable disc. This makes these discs very convenient to use for backups. Keep in mind that formatting a rewritable optical disc will preclude its use in a DVD or CD video/music player. Some other backup programs have the capability of using nonformatted discs.

Windows Backup can be installed on XP Home Edition. See Chapter 11, "Troubleshooting," for more information.

MAINTENANCE OF OPTICAL DISC DRIVES AND DISCS

The same cleaning kits you use to clean lenses in audio/video optical disc players can be used to clean lenses in computer drives. It is also helpful to spray the inside of the disc drawer with Blow Off or a similar air spray. Do not use any chemicals or solvents anywhere near a drive unless it is designed for it. Cleaning doesn't need to be done often unless the computer is exposed to dust, tobacco smoke, or other pollutants.

DIAGNOSING OPTICAL DISC PROBLEMS

The list of problems that can occur with optical drives isn't huge.

Disc Read Problems

The most common problems are related to reading from discs.

Repairing Disc Scratches

If you find that a drive cannot read a disc, the first thing to do is to examine the disc for damage. If the disc has a crack, there is little hope of saving it. If there is no serious visible damage, try the disc in another drive you know to be working. If the disc still can't be read, the problem is most likely to be in the disc. Scratches can often be repaired using a scratch repair kit. Follow the directions on the kit. This might be a good time to copy the files to a hard drive folder and then burn a new disc, as long as this doesn't violate copyright laws. Most computer supply stores stock or can order you a hand-operated or motorized CD cleaner. Be aware that you might have to get a different type of tool for data CDs and DVDs.

Drive-Related Disc Read Problems

If the disc is good in other drives, the problem *should* be in the drive. Try another known good disc in the drive. If the drive still will not consistently read the disc, you should start by using a compressed air spray and a vacuum hose to blow out the dust. If all else fails and you feel comfortable with it, you can sometimes carefully disassemble the drive and find hair and dust in the works of the drive and remove it. If you then carefully reassemble the drive, it might work again. This step should be used only as a last resort.

Read Failures of CD-R or RW Discs in ROM Drive

You might run into a situation in which you try to read a CD-R or CD-RW in a CD-ROM drive, but the disc isn't recognized. There are a few reasons why this could occur. One is that the disc was not finalized after being burned. The disc should be taken back to the machine it was burned on, and then finalized. Another possibility is that the CD-ROM drive is so old that it was not designed to read these discs. While there is an outside chance that the drive manufacturer might have a firmware update that will allow the drive to recognize these, your best bet is usually to replace the drive with a new one, especially considering how inexpensive they have become.

If all else fails, the operating system may be corrupted. This is especially true if you find that discs can be read in Safe Mode or when the computer is booted to a 9x boot disk, and if the floppy drive is similarly affected. Another symptom of this is when the drive can read audio discs but not other discs. Follow the instructions in Chapter 11, "Troubleshooting," to fix or reinstall the operating system.

Problems Writing to a Disc

It is common, when writing to a disc, to get *buffer underrun* errors. These errors indicate that the data is being read at a different rate than it is being written. The result of these errors is that the destination discs become beverage coasters. Newer drives are designed to avoid these errors, but if you have this problem, there are a few ways to reduce the chance of this occurring. One way is to copy all the files to a single folder on the hard drive first. The other is to lower the writing speed in the burner program. Another is to free up resources by closing all unneeded programs that are running. For ways to free up resources, see Chapter 2. These steps can be taken individually, or together to gain the best results. For troubleshooting a particular problem, it is recommended to try them one at a time to see what gives the best results. If you consistently have problems writing to CD-R and CD-RW discs, it might be more cost effective, due to lower prices, to purchase a newer, faster CD-RW drive with more buffer memory. Today's drives often come with 4 or 8MB of buffer, and other technology designed to minimize failures.

Occasionally, a particular drive might have a problem with a certain brand of disc. Once you find a disc brand that works, try to stick with it and you will be likely to have fewer failures.

Other Drive Problems

Does a drive simply fail to work or even open? Try going into Device Manager, removing the drive, and then rebooting the system. The drive might very well work normally again. In Windows 9x, the IDE controller might not have the appropriate drivers. If the optical drive is connected to the secondary IDE controller in some versions of 9x, Windows might not be able to recognize the drive if the IDE drivers for the chipset are corrupt or not installed. You can usually test this by attaching the optical drive as a slave to the hard drive on the primary IDE controller and restarting Windows. If the drive is now recognized and working properly, this is most likely the problem. The solution is to reinstall the IDE bus mastering controller software drivers, or if you have only two IDE devices in the system, you can leave the optical drive connected as a slave on the primary.

Certain CD-burning programs can cause problems opening the drive. For example, Roxio Easy CD Creator™ 5.0 on XP might cause the drive not to open after a CD is burned. Roxio offers a software *patch*, at *roxio.com*, that solves this problem, but you can open the drive before downloading the patch by opening the Direct CD application and clicking Eject.

In case a disc gets stuck in the drive, if you need to remove a disc while the computer's power is off, or if there is a disc in a drive that's not installed in a computer, you need a highly specialized tool to open the drawer. The tool is a straightened paper clip. If you look closely at the front of the drive, you'll find a tiny hole. Insert the clip in this hole and push until the drawer opens, as shown in Figure 7.5.

In case an Me, 2000, or XP user wants to listen to audio CDs through the front panel headphone jack, and it doesn't work, it's probably because the CD-ROM drive is configured for digital playback. Either instruct the user to use the speaker or headphone jack on the soundcard or speakers, or disable digital playback by accessing the drive's properties in Device Manager and clearing the "Enable digital CD audio for this CD-ROM device" check box.

Another problem that can occur is excessive noise when the disc is spinning. Although some noise is normal, if you hear a loud buzzing or grinding noise, there are two main possibilities: either the disc has a loose label that is flapping against the top of the drive, or the drive is broken or worn out.

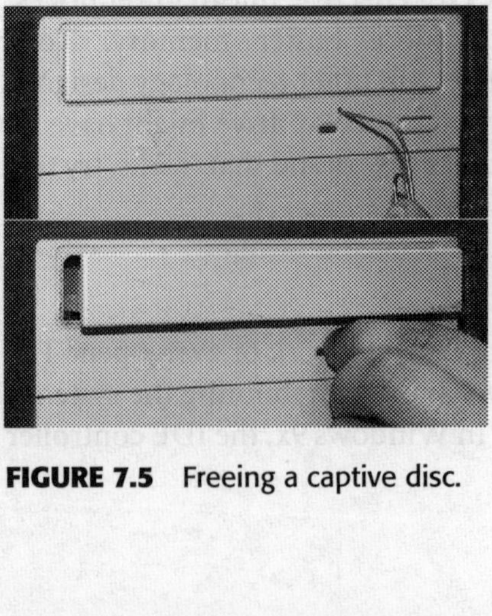

FIGURE 7.5 Freeing a captive disc.

BOOTING FROM A CD-ROM

In older DOS-based systems, including Windows 9x, you often couldn't boot from a CD. This is because DOS CD drivers couldn't be loaded before DOS boots. The *El Torito* specification allows that problem to be overcome. Most CD drives for many years meet that specification. Furthermore, in newer machines, the BIOS is designed to load drivers needed to allow the CD drive to work. This makes it possible to install Windows 98SE/Me/2000/XP without using installation boot floppies. Simply set the BIOS to boot first from a CD drive, insert the installation CD, and boot the machine. This also makes floppy drives obsolete; you can make boot CDs for Windows 9x or for 2000 and XP. In 9x, you will need to either copy the boot files from a boot floppy or from the hard drive, because the Windows Setup boot disc creation function won't work directly with a disc other than a floppy.

CD-ROM Doesn't Work in DOS

If you have a boot floppy for Windows 9x and you need to access files on a CD, simply select "Start computer with CD support" when you are so prompted. If you still do not have access to the CD-ROM, your drive might be too old to support the generic drivers on the Windows 9x boot floppy. If this option does not appear with your boot floppy, which would occur if the boot floppy were from an old version of 95, then you might have to manually install the device drivers that come from the manufacturer of the CD-ROM drive. Visit their Web page for DOS CD-ROM drivers and follow their instructions. Other options include borrowing a boot disk from a newer version of Windows, or downloading a boot disk from a Web site such as *bootdisk.com*. For more information on boot disks, see Chapter 11.

8 Video, Sound, Modems, and Network Adapters

In This Chapter

- Video Overview
- Sound Overview
- Modem Overview
- Network Adapters (Network Cards, Network Boards, Network Interface Cards, NICs, Ethernet Adapters)

VIDEO OVERVIEW

Video is the single most important feature of a PC. Even in the two situations that don't require video, servers and blind people's computers, video is still essential. In the case of servers that aren't regularly accessed by users, you still need video on occasion for configuration, repair, and other operations. Blind people use screen readers and keyboards to use their computers, but screen readers don't work until the OS boots. Consequently, repairs and other operations often require a sighted technician to see the monitor. It is because of video's high level of importance that the BIOS allows the video adapter to provide base VGA video as soon as the computer is powered on. *Base video* is enough for clear text: 640 x 480 *pixels* (the smallest picture elements) and 16 colors. *Video Graphics Adapter* (*VGA*) is a video standard used by PCs for many years. *Super VGA* (SVGA) is a major improvement, but it is based on VGA and the monitor connectors are the same. (See the end of Chapter 3, "Motherboards and Their Components," for more information on ports.) Figure 8.1 shows a monitor plug and a corresponding VGA connector.

Video Adapter (Graphics Adapter, Video Card) Overview

Many computers come with video built into the motherboard. However, many motherboards don't have built-in video, and some that do also have AGP slots for additional or replacement video adapters. There are also PCI video adapters available, although PCI isn't considered the best interface for video. There are several reasons to use separate video adapters:

- Users may want better video performance than their motherboard's built-in video provides.
- If built-in video fails or is troublesome, it can be disabled in the BIOS and an expansion card used.

Sometimes, inserting an expansion video card automatically disables built-in video in the BIOS.

- Users might need to use two or more monitors simultaneously, and multiple adapters or a specially designed video adapter is necessary for two or more

FIGURE 8.1 VGA connectors.

monitors. Recent Windows versions support multiple monitors for different purposes, including having all monitors show the same screen, having one screen spread across more than one monitor, or even having a different screen on each monitor. For more information on multiple monitors in Windows XP, search Windows XP's Help and Support for "multiple monitors."

NOTE

Dualview in XP is similar to multiple monitors, but works with laptop/notebook computers. With Dualview, the laptop's built-in screen is the primary monitor, and a monitor that the user attaches to the external VGA port is the secondary monitor. For more information on Dualview, search for it in XP's Help and Support.

As covered in Chapter 3, there are also DVO header connectors for DVI digital video adapters in some motherboards, and built-in DVI ports in others. As of the time of this writing, most PC motherboards have either built-in VGA ports or AGP slots for VGA video cards. Digital video capability might or might not be present.

Selecting a Video Adapter

High-quality video is necessary for any graphics-intensive activities such as Web surfing, high-graphics games, video and photographic editing, and others. High-quality video has two main components: general quality of the video adapter and monitor including the chipset, and amount and type of video memory. To understand the importance of sufficient video memory, it is necessary to understand how the amount of video memory affects the screen resolution and *color depth* (the total number of different colors a video adapter can output to the monitor). The easiest way to show this is through Tutorial 8.1.

TUTORIAL 8.1 Setting Display Properties in Windows (All Versions)

1. Access Display Properties in one of two ways:
   A. Double-click Display in Control Panel (see Chapter 2, "System Configuration and Computer Hygiene," for information on Control Panel).
   B. Right-click any spot on the desktop with no icons and select either Properties or Active Desktop: > Customize my desktop from the menu that appears.
2. On the Display Properties page, click the Settings tab. A page such as the one shown in Figure 8.2 appears.

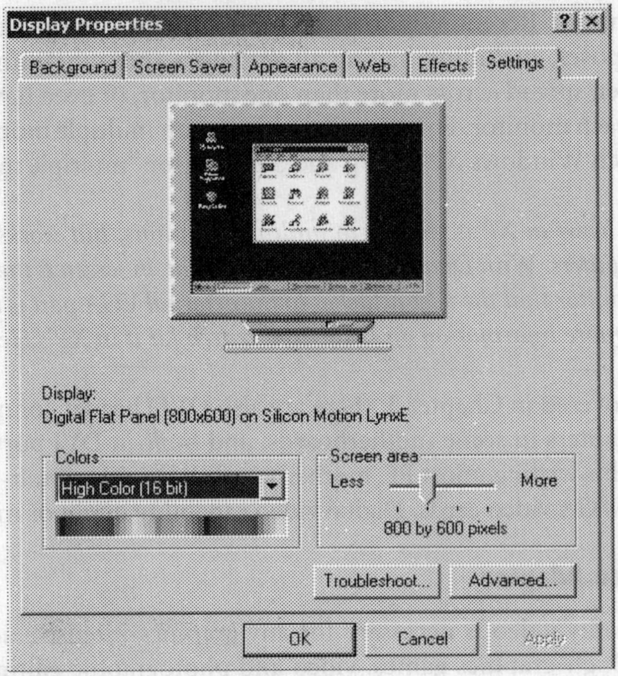

FIGURE 8.2 Display Properties.

3. Click the down arrow next to the Colors box. You should see a choice of color depth. Table 8.1 lists the possible choices.

TABLE 8.1 Display Colors

Color Depth	Number of Colors	Useful For
16 Colors	16	Text and very simple graphics
256 Colors	256	Text and simple graphics
Medium (16 bit)	65,535	Text and most general graphics use, plus video editing and most photography editing
True Color (24 bit) or High Color (24 bit)	16,777,216	Text and any but the most demanding graphics use
Highest (32 bit) or True Color (32 bit)	4,294,967,295	Text and the most demanding graphics use

It is most doubtful that you will see all of these choices. Old video adapters don't support the higher color levels, and newer ones might not show the lower or even support some of the intermediate levels.

4. Move the slider in the area labeled "Screen area," "Screen resolution," or equivalent. You'll see that as the numbers change, the image in the sample screen on the page changes in size correspondingly.
5. Click OK or Apply. Regardless of whether you have changed color depth or resolution, in most or all cases, you'll be shown the new screen and will be prompted to accept or reject the change. In some cases, the results will be unsatisfactory and you'll have to change back. Other things that could happen include lowering of one parameter as you raise the other, or having few or no choices at all. These conditions could be caused by several factors, as listed in Table 8.2.

Video Memory

So, you can see that the capacity to display high-quality video depends on video memory. Fortunately, you can get the highest color depth and excellent resolution

TABLE 8.2 Display Setting Anomalies

Anomaly	Possible Causes
No choices in either resolution or color depth, or both.	Certain LCD screens can display video at only one preset resolution.
	Design limitation of the video adapter or monitor.
	The computer is in Safe Mode.
	There is a problem with the adapter or its driver.
One parameter decreases as the other one is increased.	Lack of sufficient video memory to support high resolutions and large color palettes simultaneously.
The image is odd-shaped.	The aspect ratio of the selected screen resolution does not match that of the screen (4x3 for most computer monitors except for the new wide-screen models). The problem could also be a maladjustment of controls on the monitor itself.
The page displays unusable or poor quality video.	The settings exceed the capability of the video adapter or monitor.

with amounts of memory that are modest by today's standards. People successfully use computers with 2 to 8MB of video memory, although they might see slower loading of graphics on the screen and slower Web surfing. Video adapters with enormous amounts of memory—in the 1GB range—are available. For consumer use, 256MB is the most available at this time, although this number will probably be higher by the time you read this. These high-powered adapters can provide good resolution for large-screen high definition television (HDTV). They are great for three-dimensional and other special effects, and those who are into the latest computer games will want the most video memory they can get. However, a mere 8MB allows for 1024 x 768 resolution and 32-bit color simultaneously with memory to spare, settings that are good for the vast majority of computer users with typical monitors.

Just as in main computer memory, video memory comes in different types. Single Data Rate (SDR) and Double Data Rate (DDR) are the most common types. DDR is faster, so its performance will be better. Video cards with more and faster memory have the potential to provide better performance than others, but there is a point of diminishing returns. It is probably not worthwhile to have a great video card installed in a computer with a slow processor and limited amount of main memory.

NOTE *In some computers with video built into the motherboard, video memory is part of the main memory. There might be a BIOS setting to determine how much of the main memory to dedicate to video. Unless there is a large amount of main memory, the decision becomes a trade-off between video performance and overall computer performance.*

Other Elements of Quality Video Adapters

When your motherboard comes with built-in video, you basically choose graphics by the quality, features, and reputation of the manufacturer in much the same way you would choose a video adapter card to install on the motherboard. With a separate video card, however, you have more choices, and that can be confusing.

One big manufacturer of video chipsets, ATI, makes their own video cards and sells chipsets to other video card manufacturers. Even though the chipsets might be identical, video cards from different manufacturers might be different. The same is true for video chipset makers such as nVidia® who do not manufacture their own video cards. Be careful to choose a company that has great support and supplies driver updates readily.

Video Adapter Interfaces

Video adapters are available in AGP, PCI, and other older interfaces.

Accelerated Graphics Port (AGP)

AGP represents an advancement over previous video interfaces. It allows for more efficient transfer of data between the chipset and the graphics controller. There have been three different connectors used for AGP. These are designed so that only the correct card can be inserted into a given slot. Each connector represents a different standard that includes a different signal voltage and other parameters.

PCI Video Cards

PCI video cards are rarely used for primary video adapters anymore; they are almost always used when built-in video fails or to feed video to second monitors. In the late 1990s, however, there were systems in which the video did come in PCI.

DVI Video

DVI video is becoming more popular, especially as digital flat-panel monitors become more commonplace. DVI video is available mainly in AGP video cards and as built-in video. DVI video can be better and faster than analog video. A computer's VGA port outputs analog video that the video adapter has converted from digital using a *Random Access Memory Digital-to-Analog Converter* (*RAMDAC*) chip. All flat-panel monitors are digital, but those with VGA connectors have to convert the analog signal back to digital. Video that has been converted from digital to analog and back to digital again loses some quality. Therefore, it is best to use a digital flat panel monitor with a DVI output. Early digital flat panel monitors used oddball video connectors: the MDR-20 and the Plug & Display connector. The DVI connectors shown in Chapter 3 aren't compatible with these, but a few adapters are available. Search the Internet to find them.

For more information on DVI, see Chapter 3, or go to *matrox.com/mga/products/tech_info/dvi_backgrounder.cfm*.

Older Video Interfaces

The only other interfaces you could run into on PCs built since the mid-1990s are ISA, which fit into ISA slots, and VESA Local (VL) Bus. VL Bus adapters fit only into VL Bus motherboard slots. These rather long slots are found only on PCs from the mid-1990s.

Speed

Video speed comes from the type of AGP port, the chipset, the RAMDAC chip, and the type and amount of video memory. With applications that are used to manipulate images, greater speed and memory amount allows for much faster loading and manipulation of images. Moreover, the faster the RAMDAC chip, the faster the refresh rate. We discuss *refresh rates* later in this chapter.

Removal and Installation of Video Adapters

Video adapters are removed and installed similarly to other expansion cards. AGP slots might have retention clips to hold them in place (retention clips are covered later in this chapter).

To upgrade a video driver, go to Add/Remove Programs in Control Panel and uninstall the drivers, if present. If prompted to restart the computer, say No, and shut down instead. Remove the existing video card and install the new one, following the manufacturer's directions exactly. For onboard video, follow the same instructions, obviously omitting the step of removing the video card. Install the new card, start the computer, and go into the BIOS and look for a setting to disable onboard video. If there is such a setting, disable it. Then, finish booting the computer to test the new video.

Video chipset maker nVidia (*nvidia.com)* provides a single set of drivers, called Detonator™, which will work with any card with an nVidia chipset, regardless of the card's manufacturer. ATI (*atitech.com*) has a similar driver set called Catalyst™, although it doesn't cover all ATI chip cards.

Diagnosing Video Problems

The best thing about video problems is that you know immediately if your computer has them. An additional plus is that it is usually easy to troubleshoot video problems; compared to many other categories of computer problems, there aren't that many things that can go wrong. Table 8.3 lists many common video problems and possible solutions.

Viruses can sometimes affect video. One virus causes a pinwheel image to almost completely cover the screen. Use the usual antivirus procedures as covered in Chapter 2.

Bent Pins

If, in a VGA connector, one pin is not making contact with the corresponding terminal in the socket, the video will be degraded. It is common to be missing one color in the event this happens. Use a small probe such as a thick sewing needle, needle-nosed pliers, tweezers, or hemostats to try to gently straighten the pin. Know, however, that such a pin has been weakened and runs the risk of breaking off. In the event that the cable is permanently attached to the monitor, it is recommended to attach a VGA extension cable and never remove it. This protects the pin from breaking off, which would require an expensive monitor repair or replacement, and also protects the video port from getting a pin fragment stuck in it, which would also require replacement.

TABLE 8.3 Common Video Problems and Solutions

Problem	Troubleshooting and Possible Solution
No video	Make sure the monitor is powered on, connected to the computer, and that the brightness control is not turned all the way down. If the power indicator is blinking or glows orange, that means there is no video signal coming from the computer. Try another monitor or connect the dark monitor to a different computer. If there is no video at boot, listen for the POST beep code and/or use a POST card (see Chapter 11, "Troubleshooting," for more information on POST beep codes and POST cards). Try removing the hard drive and scanning for viruses. Try installing a known good video adapter.
Video at low resolution with splotchy colors	Try to adjust the settings from 640 x 480 resolution and 16 colors. The video driver might be corrupted. Update or reinstall the driver. Try installing a known good video adapter.
Artifacts (parts or shapes of windows continue to appear on screen after the window is closed); other unwanted spots appear on screen	Reinstall or upgrade the video driver. Scan for viruses.
Line appears on screen	Swap the monitor with a known good monitor. Reinstall or update the video driver.
One or more colors missing	Check the VGA connector pins. If the monitor cable is replaceable, swap it with a known good cable. If not, swap the monitor with a known good monitor.

Troubleshooting Specialty Video Devices

For *video capture devices* (video cards that include *composite video* inputs for connection to VCRs and older video cameras, or cards with FireWire ports that connect to digital video cameras), and video cards with TV outputs, a common problem is that Windows installs the wrong driver. Uninstall the existing driver and follow the manufacturer's instructions to install the correct driver.

Monitor Settings

Today's CRT monitors (those with television-like picture tubes) can handle the highest settings computer users are likely to want to use. If you run into a situation, however, in which an old monitor is displaying unusable video, it is possible that the Windows video settings exceed the capabilities of the monitor. You will have to diagnose the source of the problem. If you are able to read the text that appears on screen as the system is starting but the video becomes distorted and unreadable once Windows starts up, then the settings are most likely too high for the monitor. If the image is distorted from the moment you start up the computer, then it is possibly a video adapter issue. If it is the former, you will have to start Windows in Safe Mode, which will give you basic settings that almost all monitors will work with. While in Safe Mode, set the Display Properties to a lower setting and restart Windows. At this point, you might very well decide to get a new monitor that can display higher settings rather than live with a low resolution monitor. You can try to find the monitor's specifications on the Web and set the Display Properties accordingly. If you can't find this information, which is possible, you'll have to try lower settings until you find a combination that works.

The monitor itself will have settings for shape and size of the picture, brightness and contrast, and others. In addition, virtually all monitors manufactured for the last several years have an energy saving system. When the video signal from the computer stops, the monitor goes into a low-power state, and the power indicator light begins to blink or turns from green to orange. Some monitors, however, show a test pattern or no-video message in certain circumstances such as when the power comes back on after a failure and the computer is still off.

Refresh Rate

A monitor (or television, for that matter) produces a picture by having an electron beam scan a grid of microscopic light-emitting elements. The *refresh rate* is the rate at which the beam scans all the elements—the entire screen—once. The rate is expressed in Hertz (Hz), which means cycles per second, so that a rate of 60 Hz means that the electron beam scans the screen 60 times every second. Rates that are too low have noticeable flicker. If the rate is set too high for a given monitor, the video can be unusable and the monitor can be damaged. The higher the refresh rate, the less apparent the flicker will be. Rates of 70 Hz or higher should provide flicker-free video for most people. The refresh rate should be set only as high as necessary to minimize flicker—higher rates, even if all the components support it, can cause other problems such as reduced contrast. To adjust the refresh rate, follow Tutorial 8.2.

TUTORIAL 8.2 SETTING THE REFRESH RATE

Note that some systems don't have a refresh rate setting.

1. Follow Steps 1 and 2 of Tutorial 8.1 to access the Settings page of Display Properties.
2. Click the Advanced button.
3. Click the Monitor tab (if there is one).
4. Click the down arrow next to the frequency and select a new frequency.

AGP Retention Clip

Loose adapters in AGP slots are often the culprits for video problems. Retention clips that retrofit to most AGP slots were introduced to hold them in place. Figure 8.3 shows an AGP retention clip in place. If a PC with this type of AGP slot loses its video for no apparent reason, try a retention clip. The video adapter you use must have a notched tab to work with the retention clip.

Dot Pitch

Dot pitch is a measurement of how close the picture elements are to one another. The closer they are, the higher the resolution can be, so the lower the number, the better. Cheap monitors have larger dot pitches and are harder on users' eyes. Select .028 mm or lower.

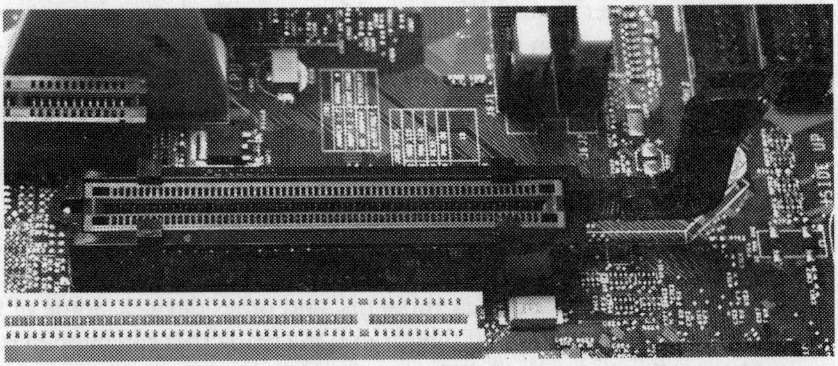

FIGURE 8.3 AGP retention clip.

Testing Displays

There are a few ways to test monitors. DisplayMate® (*displaymate.com*) offers testing utilities and hardware for any type of video display. They have products for end users, technical users, and advanced users. If you plan to test monitors, their products are definitely appropriate.

General computer testing utilities, such as products from PC Certify and Micro-2000, and even some products that are released by computer makers also include video tests. See Chapter 11 for more on general diagnostic products.

Monitor Installation

In the vast majority of cases, monitors need only to be plugged into the video adapter outputs, be they SVGA or DVI. Some monitors are recognized and installed automatically by Windows. In some situations, Windows will need a driver in order for the monitor to display more than *base video*. This is most likely to happen with an older version of Windows, or a monitor that uses new technology.

SOUND OVERVIEW

Sound cards range from simple built-in models to elaborate two-piece devices with physical control panels that mount into a 5¼-inch drive bay. The basic purpose of sound cards is to allow the user to hear sounds played by the OS and programs, along with music from audio CDs and other audio files, plus sound from DVD and other types of videos. They are also used for sound recording. In addition, these allow for voice communication using software such as Yahoo Messenger™, AOL Instant Messenger™, and Windows Messenger™, along with Internet telephone calls, voice-recognition software, and other uses.

Sound Card Removal and Installation

Sound cards are physically installed and removed in the same way as any other card using the same interface (PCI or ISA), except that there are likely to be analog audio cables connected to it inside the computer. On a motherboard with onboard sound, there will also be audio connectors. These connectors are for connecting analog audio to optical drives, modems, and other devices. Some of these connectors are polarized, but even if they aren't, the worst that can happen is that the right and left audio channels could be reversed. Figure 8.4 shows the audio connectors on a sound card.

FIGURE 8.4 A sound card's audio connectors.

External Sound Connections

Sound cards can vary as to the number and type of external inputs and outputs. The most basic, usually found on motherboards with built-in sound, have three:

Microphone input: This is for a computer microphone, although battery-powered condenser mics usually work in these jacks.

Line input: This is for an external line source such as a cassette deck or CD player's line outputs.

Speaker/headphone output: This is a headphone-level output that can sometimes drive small, non-amplified speakers. They are usually connected to amplified speakers.

A sound card with a built-in amplifier would have full-power speaker outputs, able to drive most non-amplified speakers. More advanced cards have a whole assortment of inputs and outputs. On many cards, the icons that identify each jack are very difficult to see and interpret, especially when you are struggling just to see any part of the back of the computer. Consult the manufacturer's documentation. Figure 8.5 shows sound card jack panels.

Now look carefully at Figure 8.5. The concentric arcs represent sound waves. An arrow pointing toward the center indicates a line input, while an arrow pointing away from the center represents a line output. The microphone and speaker icons are more illustrative than are the others.

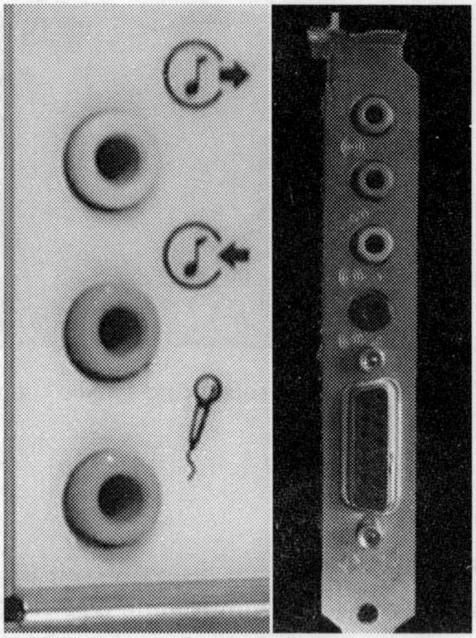

FIGURE 8.5 A sound card jack panel.

Diagnosing and Repairing Sound Problems

There are a number of steps you can take to correct sound problems. First, make sure the speakers are powered, turned on, and turned up. Make sure all external connections are correct, and that the cables aren't damaged. Run System File Checker (see Chapter 11). Reinstall the sound drivers. Sometimes, you'll have to remove the device in Device Manager, shut down the computer, remove the card, restart the computer and uninstall any programs that came with the sound card, and then shut down the computer again. Then, follow the manufacturer's directions for installing the card, or just re-install it physically, reboot, and see if Windows will install it correctly. If you have any trouble with resource conflicts, which would be evidenced by instant lockups, go into the BIOS and make sure Plug and Play is enabled.

Selecting a Sound Card

A basic sound card is good for most people. High-end models are good for gamers and musicians. Some people like to have surround sound with their computers, so surround sound models are common.

MODEM OVERVIEW

Oddly, modems are often confused with the computer itself. A *modem*, as discussed in this chapter, is a device that connects a computer to a standard analog telephone line, the kind to which your telephone is connected. Modems are used for dial-up Internet service, telephone use such as faxing, wide area network (WAN) connections, and the antiquated, but still-used terminal connections, which are beyond the scope of this book. You might have noticed that modem speed has been stuck at a maximum of 56 Kbps for several years. That is because the amount of data that can be transmitted across an analog telephone line might have reached a physical limit. Consequently, although there have been improvements in accuracy of data transfer and the capability of connecting and holding onto a telephone line, modems haven't gotten any faster than 56K. Because of this limit, Internet service has moved away from dial-up and toward different broadband technologies. As a result, modems are now not usually built into newer motherboards (except in laptops, which are often used where the only network access is through telephone lines). There are a few motherboards out there with modem risers. These are slots that take proprietary modem cards. If one of these modems fails, it is cheapest and easiest to remove it and install a standard modem in a PCI or ISA slot, if possible.

Internal vs. External Modems

Internal modems are PCI or ISA expansion cards. They tend to be simple to install; just follow the manufacturer's directions if available. They receive their power from the slot. External modems are less common today, but are still around because internal modems are often optional these days. External modems traditionally plug into a serial port on the computer, although there are USB modems available today as well. The advantages to external modems are that you don't have to be a technician to install one and they can easily be moved from computer to computer. The disadvantages to external serial-port modems are that they require external power and are more expensive. Most or all USB modems are powered by the USB ports and aren't as expensive as serial-port modems. Figure 8.6 shows a PCI modem, a USB modem, and an external serial-port modem.

PC-Card modems are designed for laptops without built-in modems, or those whose built-in modems are broken. They tend to be expensive. Many of these come with *dongles*, which are small cable assemblies that connect the card to the telephone jack assembly. Dongles are usually delicate and replacements have to be ordered from the manufacturer. Better designs are available that have the phone jacks built into the card. Figure 8.7 shows two PC-Card modems.

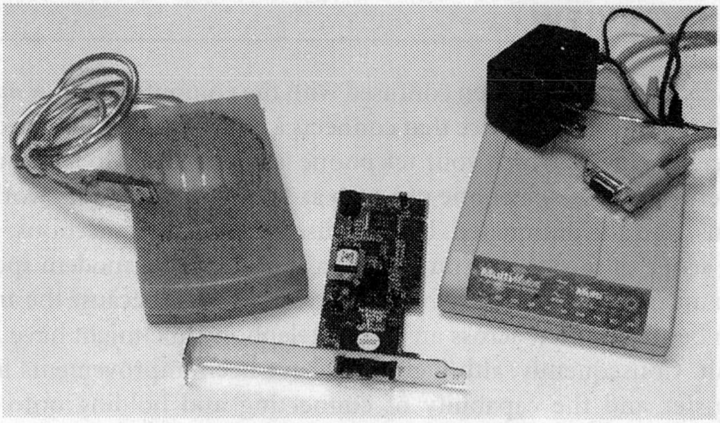

FIGURE 8.6 Three different types of modems.

FIGURE 8.7 PC-Card modems.

TIP

For an alternative to PC-Card modems, try an external USB modem.

Use of Serial Ports

Older PCs often came with up to four serial ports, while newer machines usually come with one. These ports are referred to as COM 1 through COM 4. Traditionally, COM ports 1 and 4 use IRQ 3, and COM ports 2 and 3 use IRQ 4. If you have ever installed an internal modem, you have probably noticed COM ports with numbers up to 12. These COM ports that are numbered higher than the highest numbered physical COM port are called *logical* COM ports.

Selecting a Modem

Even though modem speed hasn't changed since 1998, modems have gotten better. You might recall that picking up a telephone while an early 56K modem was connected to the Internet on the same line caused the modem to instantly disconnect the connection. Fortunately, that problem was abated in subsequent modems.

WinModems vs. Controller-Based Modems

If you look at modems, you might notice that some have very few components soldered onto the circuit board. If these have PCI or ISA connectors, then they are probably WinModems (if they don't have PCI or ISA connectors, they are probably riser modems). If they have a lot of components, they are probably controller-based modems. As you might have guessed, controller-based modems are more expensive than WinModems. WinModems let Windows do much of the work that controllers do in the more expensive modems. Consequently, that means that the processor has extra work to do. For that reason, WinModems don't work well in any systems with slow processors, and should never be used in a computer with a legacy Cyrix processor. Therefore, if an old computer needs a new modem, don't install a WinModem.

Faxing and Voice

Virtually all modems sold in the last several years have faxing capability. Using supplied "lite" software, retail software, or fax programs built into newer versions of Windows, users can send and receive faxes. Fax software installs itself as a printer; to send a fax, open a document or image file and use the Print command. There are three ways to access the Print command in almost all programs:

- Click File: > Print.
- Click the printer icon.
- Press <Ctrl> + <P>.

You will see a dialog box similar to the one shown in Figure 8.8. Select the fax software as a printer and click Print. The fax program should open. Many users with scanners print documents, scan them, and then fax them. This is necessary only if you have to write something, such as a signature, on the document. There are sketch programs available that allow you to store a signature image that you can paste on a document. For example, if you have a Synaptics touchpad (pointing device), a program is available free from *synaptics.com*.

Modem Removal and Installation

External modems are simple to install; just plug in and install the software, with the order depending on the instructions to the particular model. Internal modems are installed physically just as any other expansion card. Many will be installed automatically by Windows.

Software that uses modems, such as faxing programs or dial-up Internet software like AOL, have provisions to search for the modem. Therefore, it is a good idea to look in Device Manager to see how many COM ports are installed in the machine. Look for the Ports (COM & LPT) listing and click the plus sign. Hopefully, you won't see any more than the number of physical COM ports installed on the system. Then, when you install the modem or modem-using software, look for the COM port the system uses. If the port number is the same as one of the physical COM ports, it is usually wise to change it. To do this, open up Modem Properties in Device Manager or in Control Panel > Phone and Modem (or equivalent). Click the Advanced tab to get a page similar to the one shown in Figure 8.8.

If you change it, make sure to change it in modem-using software, too. Then, check all programs that use the modem: dial-up Internet, telephone networking, telephone dialing and answering systems, and fax programs. Either change the COM port manually in these or have the programs redetect the modem.

Diagnosing Modem Problems

Modems can be troublesome. If you have a telephone communications problem, there are a number of things you can do to check to see if the modem is working.

NOTE

It bears repeating that the message often seen in the properties of any hardware device, "This device is working properly," is often wrong. However, if you see "This device is not present, not working properly, or does not have all the drivers installed. See your hardware documentation (Code 10.)," you can bet that it is right.

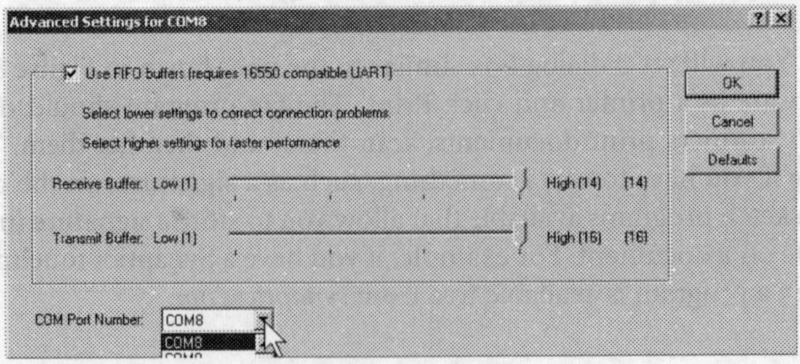

FIGURE 8.8 Advanced modem properties.

Here is a list of places in Windows where you can check to see whether a modem is working:

A. **Modem Properties in Device Manager, General page:** If you see a message that indicates a problem, the modem might need to be reinstalled or replaced. Follow the directions in Chapter 2 or from the modem manufacturer to reinstall the driver.

B. **Query Modem:** Go to Modem Properties from either Control Panel or Device Manager and click the Diagnostics tab if one is present. Then, click the Query Modem button and wait for the report. If the last couple entries in the report indicate OK, the query hasn't detected a problem. You will often see the line "COMMAND NOT SUPPORTED" at one point in the report. You can ignore this.

C. **HyperTerminal:** Go to Start > Programs (or All Programs) > Accessories > Communications > HyperTerminal, if it is installed. You will be prompted to set up a connection. Give it a simple name; you won't be saving it. Figure 8.9 shows this page.

Then, enter a single-digit telephone number. Make sure your modem is listed in the Connect using box. Click OK and you will be prompted to dial the number you

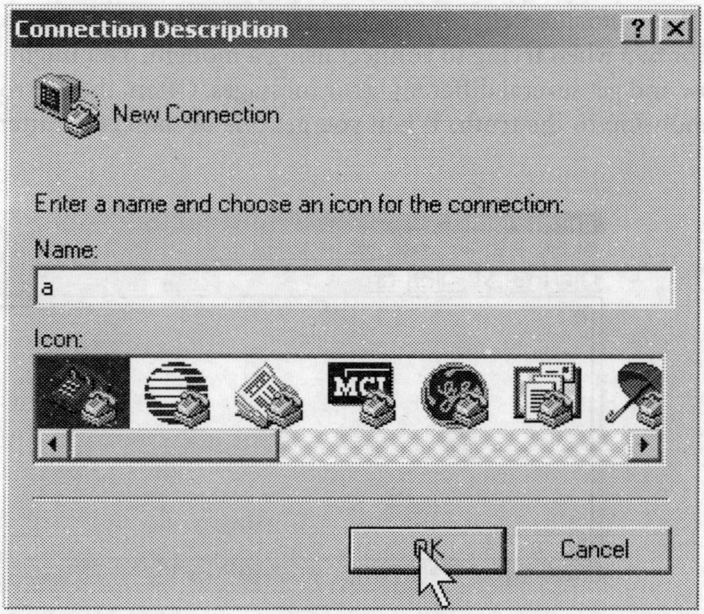

FIGURE 8.9 Naming a HyperTerminal connection.

entered. Click Cancel. You will see a blank HyperTerminal window. Type "AT" and then press <Enter>. A working modem should respond with "OK," as shown in Figure 8.10. Then, you can close HyperTerminal and elect not to save the connection.

NOTE

Some malfunctioning modems can nonetheless pass every one of these diagnostic tests.

It is also a good idea to test a suspect modem with every function in which it can be used on the computer. This is to rule out the possibility that a program, rather than the modem, is malfunctioning. For example, if a modem works with faxing and Phone Dialer (Start > Programs (or All Programs) > Accessories > Communications > Phone Dialer), but not on the Internet, it is likely that the problem is in the Internet software or service rather than with the hardware.

NOTE

You might find that Phone Dialer doesn't work properly in Windows 2000 on certain machines no matter what you do. However, Windows 9x's Phone Dialer (dialer.exe) might work in the newer Windows versions. If the modem will dial a number in Phone Dialer but do nothing else, the problem might very well be the hardware; we had a batch of new PCI modems that did this. The modems weren't recognized by the Plug and Play system and had to be installed manually because they were defective.

It is unfortunately common to get certain numbered error messages such as 619 or 693 when trying to connect using a modem. You might try several times in a row and get several different error messages. Often, these error messages bear no relationship to the truth. When you get one of these, first attempt to rule out the

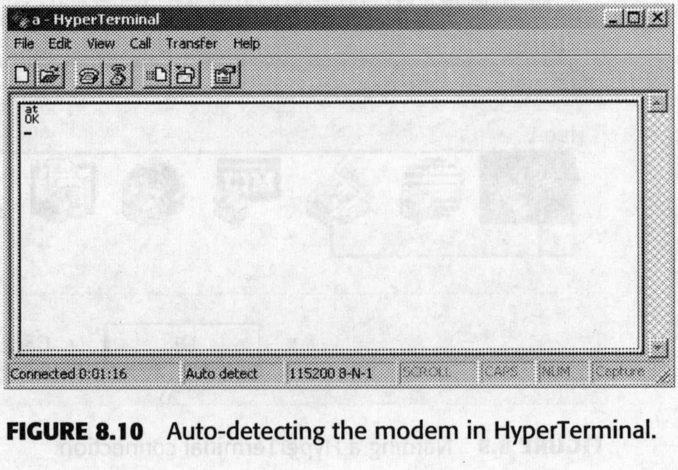

FIGURE 8.10 Auto-detecting the modem in HyperTerminal.

problem that the message indicates, assuming you can understand the message. The problem could be as simple as a bad telephone cord, the Caps Lock being on and altering the password, or that the telephone line is in use. Other possibilities include problems with the remote computer or service, or incorrect password or username. If the computer locks up every time you try to connect, you probably have a resource conflict. See Chapter 2 for information on resolving it.

NOTE *Make sure that the user doesn't plug a modem into a PBX telephone line. Even though PBX systems can use RJ-11/14 telephone connectors, the voltage and signal are different. This can damage the modem, but it might merely cause the computer to lock up.*

Once you have ruled these out, the next step is to reboot the computer, especially if you have a laptop. With some laptops, a design flaw causes certain functions not to work after the computer comes out of standby or hibernation. Rebooting might solve other problems as well. If none of these steps works, delete the connection and recreate it. If you still have the problem, it is time to try new hardware. Swap the modem for a known good unit and retry the connection. This is the perfect time to try an external modem if you have one. If you still can't connect, and the modem is removable, try it in another system.

If a built-in modem on a laptop fails and you have reinstalled the driver to no avail, unless the laptop is under warranty or the modem is a mini-PCI type, which is replaceable, your only recourses are to install a PC-Card modem or use an external serial or USB modem. You might want to disable the built-in modem in the BIOS, if such a setting exists. Note, however, that sometimes seemingly permanent modem failures can occasionally resolve themselves over time.

Modem Cables

Different external serial modems use an assortment of different types of cables. Make sure the cable is actually a modem cable; other cables might fit, but that doesn't mean they'll work. Also try testing the cable in a cable tester. With USB cables, it is often easy to swap with a known good cable.

For information on troubleshooting network connections, see Chapter 10, "Troubleshooting Internet Connections."

Modems and Windows Installation

When Windows is installed on a computer with the modem already present, especially the recent Windows versions, Windows tends to correctly install most hardware devices. One of the most common exceptions to this is the modem. Often, Device Manager will show a yellow question mark with a notation such as "PCI

Communications Controller." Other times, a generic modem chipset driver will install and Device Manager will indicate that the modem is working properly even though it really isn't. You know it should be working because it is a new modem. This same problem may occur when you search for a driver by chipset (see Chapter 2) and the driver you found does not seem to work with the modem properly. If you follow the manufacturer's instructions for properly installing the driver from the installation floppy or CD, or download the latest driver from the manufacturer's Web site for the exact model, and install it per instructions given by the manufacturer, the modem usually works. This is because in some cases the components on the modem other than the chipset require custom drivers supplied only by the manufacturer.

Cable and DSL Modems

Cable and DSL modems are external devices used to connect computers to a broadband (high-speed) Internet connection. DSL models connect to the telephone line *without a DSL filter*. A *DSL filter* is a device that blocks the DSL signal from interfering with regular telephone conversations; these are usually provided by the DSL provider. DSL modems are connected to the computer either through a USB cable or an Ethernet network cable. Cable modems are similar to DSL modems, but they connect to a television cable instead of a telephone line.

Modem/Sound Card Combinations

No longer manufactured, modem/sound card combinations are very difficult to get drivers for. The best way to deal with failed modem/sound card combos is to replace it with individual components. If you have only one free slot, you can probably replace the modem with an external modem.

NETWORK ADAPTERS (NETWORK CARDS, NETWORK BOARDS, NETWORK INTERFACE CARDS, NICs, ETHERNET ADAPTERS)

Considering how complicated networking can be, network adapters are rather simple. They are among the easiest devices to install; simply follow the manufacturer's directions. Cards made by 3Com and Intel are often installed automatically by Windows. Others, including external USB models, require driver disks, but are still easy to get up and running.

Selecting a Network Adapter

Older network adapters came in myriad types, but today's cards are mostly Ethernet cards. *Ethernet* is a network standard that almost exclusively uses *Cat 5/Cat 5e* UTP (unshielded twisted pair) cables with RJ-45 connectors. *RJ-45* connectors are very similar to standard RJ14 modular telephone plugs, but are twice as wide and have eight wires. Many of today's motherboards come with built-in Ethernet adapters. Ethernet transmission speeds have increased from 10 to 100 to 1000 Mbps. Older cards worked at a fixed speed, preventing their connection with any network device running at a different speed. Newer cards, however, can automatically switch to a lower-than-maximum speed to match the device they are directly connected to, be it a router, switch, hub, or other Ethernet adapter. The vast majority of Ethernet network adapters on the market will work fine for most users with home or small business networks, or high-speed Internet service that requires network adapters.

Wireless Network Adapters

Wireless models come in various types to work in desktops or laptops. They require wireless routers to work. They work similarly to cordless telephones; they have to stay within a certain distance of the base (wireless router or access point) to maintain a connection.

Diagnosing Network Adapter Problems

Many things can go wrong with networks, but not many problems can occur with the adapters; usually, they either work or they don't. Check in Device Manager to see if there is a problem. If reinstalling the driver doesn't fix the problem, it is probably time to replace the card.

If Device Manager indicates a working adapter, it is a good idea to check the cable. Use a tester, or swap it with a known good cable.

NOTE

Make sure to use the right cable for the job. RJ45 telephone cable, if it is not Cat5 or Cat5e, will not be reliable for network transmission. There is also such a thing as a crossover cable, which is used only for a direct connection between two computers with Ethernet adapters, or between two central devices such as hubs, switches, or routers. A crossover cable won't work for a connection between a central device and a computer, and a straight-through cable won't work with a two-computer network or between two central devices, unless the two devices have a setting allowing use of a straight-through cable. Crossover cables should be marked on the cables' insulation. If there is any doubt, you can check it with a cable tester.

Chapters 5–8 A+ Certification Review Questions

The following A+ Certification Review Questions are related to the general topics introduced in Part I, Chapters 5 through 8, of this book. The answers and supporting references are provided after the review questions. It is important to remember that all of the answer references specify chapters that are located in Part II of this book: The A+ Certification Exams.

1. **What is the memory bus width of a 30-pin SIMM?**
   - o A. 8-bits
   - o B. 4-bits
   - o C. 1-bit
   - o D. 1,024
2. **What is the memory bus width of a 72-pin SIMM?**
   - o A. 8-bits
   - o B. 4-bits
   - o C. 32-bits
   - o D. 64-bits
3. **There are three programs running in "protected mode." One program fails. What happens to the other two programs?**
   - o A. Both programs fail
   - o B. One fails, one does not
   - o C. Neither program fails
   - o D. Only the program in slot 1 fails

4. **There are two SODIMM memory module configurations mentioned in Table 17.3 of Chapter 17. What are the number of pins and memory bus widths associated with the SODIMMS? (Choose Two)**
   - □ A. 72 pins and 32 bits
   - □ B. 144 pins and 64 bits
   - □ C. 184 pins and 16 bits
   - □ D. 168 pins and 64 bits

5. **These memory modules are often used in sub-notebook computers. They have 144 pins and provide a 64-bit data path. What are they?**
   - o A. DIMMs
   - o B. RIMMs
   - o C. MicroDIMMs
   - o D. L3 cache SIMMs

6. **If the Memory Manager in Windows 9x cannot provide memory to an application, what will occur?**
   - o A. A book fault
   - o B. A hard drive crash
   - o C. A page fault
   - o D. A black screen of death

7. **In what order should you prepare a hard drive before a Windows 9x installation?**
   - o A. FDISK, FORMAT, Reboot the system
   - o B. Reboot the system, FDISK, FORMAT
   - o C. FORMAT, FDISK, Reboot the system
   - o D. Simply run the DOS program PREPARE.BAT before installation

8. **Which Backup type is the fastest and requires the least amount of tape storage space?**
   - o A. FULL Backup
   - o B. Incremental Backup
   - o C. Differential Backup
   - o D. Full/Copy Backup

9. **What is characteristic of an Incremental Backup?**
   - o A. Will only back files up to a ZIP drive
   - o B. Backs up all files no matter what
   - o C. Backs up all files with the archive bit set to off
   - o D. Backs up all files with the archive bit set to on

10. Your computer is Plug and Play. You install a second hard drive. What will determine its drive letter?

- o A. You
- o B. The ribbon cable position
- o C. The jumpers and dip switches
- o D. The Plug-and-Play Operating System

11. You need to terminate a SCSI bus that has an external CD-ROM and an internal hard drive. What devices would you terminate?

- o A. The SCSI controller and the motherboard.
- o B. The hard drive and the CD-ROM.
- o C. The motherboard, the SCSI controller, and CD-ROM.
- o D. You do not have to terminate both ends of a SCSI chain.

12. You want to install two new IDE drives on the same ATA controller and configure them as master/slave. You install drive 1 as master and drive 2 as slave. Your BIOS does not detect drive 2 on bootup. What would you do next to troubleshoot drive 2?

- o A. Install an IDE add-on card.
- o B. Set up drive 2 to be the master. Remove drive 1 and reboot.
- o C. Configure both drives to be master.
- o D. Set the BIOS hard drive detection method to cable select.

13. What would you have to enable on a SCSI controller card in order to use a tape device?

- o A. Direct Memory Access
- o B. Termination
- o C. C000-C7FFF
- o D. The INT 13h support

14. You are trying to access your "A" drive. You keep getting an error message "Drive not ready, abort, retry or Fail." What is causing this problem? (Choose Two)

- □ A. You need to change the jumpers on your floppy drive back to slave.
- □ B. You have bad media inserted in your floppy drive.
- □ C. The spindle motor needs adjustment.
- □ D. Your physical floppy drive needs cleaning. Use compressed air.

15. Which of the following devices are compatible with SCSI technology? (Choose Three)

□ A. A tape drive unit
□ B. A modulation device
□ C. A network interface card
□ D. A hard drive
□ E. A CD-ROM

16. What is the highest ID assignment on a SCSI 1 device with a block of three jumpers?

o A. 0
o B. 7
o C. 1,024
o D. 15

17. Which of the following commands will remove MBR infector viruses and replace a systems boot loader with a generic boot loader?

o A. Erase MBR
o B. FDISK /?
o C. Format C:\MBR
o D. ScanDisk /MBR
o E. FDISK /MBR
o F. None of the above

18. Which RAID level is known as disk mirroring?

o A. RAID Level 0
o B. RAID Level 1
o C. RAID Level 3
o D. RAID Level 5
o E. None of the above

19. There is no sound coming from your speakers as you play your favorite CD. What is most likely the problem?

o A. Your floppy drive cable is connected backwards.
o B. You need to refresh your sound card RAM.
o C. Your CD-ROM audio cable is disconnected.
o D. Your sound card drivers have become corrupt.

20. What should your first troubleshooting step be if you have installed a new CD-ROM, CD-RW, or DVD device into a computer and it doesn't work?

- o A. Insert a pin or paper clip into the tiny hole on the front of the unit.
- o B. Verify that the jumper settings on the device are correct.
- o C. Purchase a new device.
- o D. Verify that the CD, CD-RW, or DVD's audio cable is connected to an installed sound card.
- o E. None of the above.

21. Which key must you press during text-mode setup of Windows XP in order to load RAID or SCSI drivers from a floppy?

- o A. F3
- o B. F4
- o C. F5
- o D. F6

22. Which of the following are valid types of video memory? (Choose Three)

- □ A. RWAM
- □ B. VRAM
- □ C. XRAM
- □ D. WRAM
- □ E. XGRAM
- □ F. SGRAM

23. You need to manually reset your modem. Which AT modem command would you use?

- o A. ATA
- o B. ATH
- o C. ATZ
- o D. ATREST=ALL

24. Modems use which type of connector?

- o A. BNC
- o B. RJ-45
- o C. RJ-11
- o D. Kevlar

25. Using a video resolution of 800x600 is equivalent to using which video mode?

- o A. Raster
- o B. Vector
- o C. VGA
- o D. SVGA
- o E. MCA
- o F. None of the above

26. How many pins does a VGA connector have?

- o A. 7
- o B. 9
- o C. 10
- o D. 15
- o E. None of the above

27. Which of the following choices is not a touch screen technology?

- o A. Surface Wave.
- o B. Resistive.
- o C. Capacitive.
- o D. Foam element.
- o E. All of the above represent touch screen technologies.

28. If a device such as a network interface card has an ST or SC connector, it will most likely be used with which type of cable?

- o A. Thicknet
- o B. 100BaseTX
- o C. Fiber optic
- o D. Shielded twisted pair

29. What does 10/100 mean?

- o A. 10 users for peer-to-peer, 100 for server based
- o B. 10 or 100Mbps transmission
- o C. A processor that utilizes 10 threads and 100 processes
- o D. A Sonet technology term for high-speed access

30. What is considered the hub in a wireless network?

- o A. Router
- o B. Server computer
- o C. Access point
- o D. Wireless NIC card
- o E. WAP
- o F. None of the above

31. What type of connector is most commonly used with twisted-pair cabling?

- o A. RJ-11
- o B. RJ-45
- o C. BNC
- o D. STP

32. A customer is trying to access a Novell network using a NIC card with the IPX/SPX protocol bound to it. The customer cannot access the network. What is most likely the problem?

- o A. Incorrect frame type setting.
- o B. Incorrect IP configuration.
- o C. The IPX/SPX protocol should be the first in the binding order.
- o D. IPX/SPX and TCP/IP cannot run together.

33. What is DMA channel 2 assigned to?

- o A. Second DMA controller (cascades to DMA channels 0–3)
- o B. Floppy drive (possible tape drive)
- o C. Available
- o D. Port 1024
- o E. None of the above

34. What is the command used to make a bootable floppy system disk?

- o A. FORMAT A: /S
- o B. FORMAT /S A:
- o C. SYS A: /FORMAT
- o D. MAKEFLOPPYBOOTABLE.BAT

35. Which version of Windows does not include NT Backup by default?

- o A. Windows XP Professional
- o B. Windows XP Home
- o C. Windows NT 4.0
- o D. Windows 98

36. Which type of memory uses 184 pins and has a memory bus width of 16 bits (or 2 bytes wide)?

- o A. SIMM
- o B. DIMM
- o C. RIMM
- o D. SODIMM
- o E. NOSDRMM
- o F. None of the above

37. What would a bent or broken DB-15 male connector pin cause?

- o A. FRU displacement
- o B. Monitor problems
- o C. 800x600 pixels
- o D. Fragmentation

38. Which of the following relates to the measurement of time that it takes for the electron gun to redraw the display?

- o A. Interlace
- o B. Refresh rate
- o C. Dot pitch
- o D. Pixel triad

39. You have changed your display settings while using Windows 98 and have rebooted your system. Windows will not come up. What mode would you use to troubleshoot this problem?

- o A. 386 enhanced mode
- o B. Safe mode
- o C. Graphics mode
- o D. SVGA mode

40. Which RAID level is not considered fault tolerant?

- o A. RAID 32
- o B. RAID 0
- o C. RAID 1
- o D. RAID 5
- o E. None of the above

A+ CERTIFICATION REVIEW ANSWERS AND REFERENCES

Answer Key	References Taken from Part II: The A+ Certification Exams
1. A	Chapter 17, "Memory Packaging"
2. C	Chapter 17, "Memory Packaging"
3. C	Chapter 16, "Processors and Modes"
4. A and B	Chapter 17, "Memory Packaging"
5. C	Chapter 17, "Memory Packaging"
6. C	Chapter 23, "Memory Management Utilities"
7. A	Chapter 24, "Installation and Upgrading"
8. B	Chapter 24, "Utilities and Settings"
9. D	Chapter 24, "Utilities and Settings"
10. D	Chapter 20, "The Hard Drive"
11. B	Chapter 20, "Drive Controllers and Interfaces"
12. B	Chapter 20, "Drive Controllers and Interfaces"
13. D	Chapter 20, "Drive Controllers and Interfaces"
14. B and D	Chapter 20, "The Floppy Drive"
15. A, D and E	Chapter 20, "Drive Controllers and Interfaces"
16. B	Chapter 20, "Drive Controllers and Interfaces"
17. E	Chapter 20, "The Hard Drive"
18. B	Chapter 20, "RAID (Redundant Array of Independent Disks) "
19. C	Chapter 18, "Sound Cards"
20. B	Chapter 20 , "Optical Storage Devices"
21. D	Chapter 28, "Windows XP Installation Process"
22. B, D, and F	Chapter 17, "Memory Types and Characteristics"
23. C	Chapter 18, "Modems"
24. C	Chapter 21, "Networking Connectors and Cables"
25. D	Chapter 19, "Liquid Crystal Display"
26. D	Chapter 19, "Liquid Crystal Display"
27. D	Chapter 18, "Touch Screen"
28. C	Chapter 21, "Networking Connectors and Cables"
29. B	Chapter 22, "Network Interface Cards"
30. C	Chapter 21, "Wireless Connectivity"
31. B	Chapter 21, "Networking Connectors and Cables"
32. A	Chapter 22, "Protocols"

A+ CERTIFICATION REVIEW ANSWERS AND REFERENCES *(continued)*

Answer Key	References Taken from Part II: The A+ Certification Exams
33. B	Chapter 18, "Direct Memory Access Channels (DMAs)"
34. A	Chapter 23, "DOS Windows Utilities"
35. B	Chapter 28, "Windows XP Tools and Utilities"
36. C	Chapter 17, "Memory Packaging"
37. B	Chapter 19, "Video Display Devices"
38. B	Chapter 19, "Cathode Ray Tube (CRT)"
39. B	Chapter 19, "Monitor Shapes and Sizes "
40. B	Chapter 20, "RAID (Redundant Array of Independent Disks) "

9 Input Devices

In This Chapter

- Pointing Devices
- Keyboard Overview

Input devices are devices that allow the user to input data into a computer. The most obvious input devices are pointing devices (mice and their equivalents) and keyboards. Other input devices include such things as microphones used in the case of voice recognition systems. This chapter is limited to discussion of keyboards and common pointing devices.

POINTING DEVICES

The most common pointing device is the mouse. Others include the trackball, touchpad, and track stick ("pencil eraser") controls found on some laptops. All but the last one come in different forms.

Pointing Device Types

Pointing devices can be divided into interface type, features, and detection system.

Mouse Interfaces

Mice can be connected to PCs in at least one of four ways: serial (DB-9 female connector), PS/2 (the small, round, 5-pin connector), USB, and infrared or radio frequency wireless. Many mice come with adapters so that an individual mouse can be used in both PS/2 and serial ports, or both PS/2 and USB ports. More information about these follows:

Serial: This is the original interface used in personal computers. Serial devices are hot-pluggable. Although new computers no longer come with serial mice, the vast majority of computers have serial ports, so a serial mouse is the perfect choice when the built-in PS/2 port fails. Serial mice used to come with drivers on floppy disks, although Windows 95 and later have the drivers.

PS/2: This is the standard mouse interface for the vast majority of computers with ATX and similar motherboards. These computers have dedicated PS/2 mouse ports that can be used only for PS/2 pointing devices and those adapted to PS/2. These devices *are not hot-pluggable*; plug in and remove only with the computer's power off. There is no guarantee that ignoring this warning will fry the motherboard, but it is not worth the risk. Windows installs PS/2 mice transparently to the user unless the device has unusual features, in which case, a software disk might be needed for the features to work.

NOTE

Many laptops have one PS/2 port. A keyboard or a pointing device can be plugged into this port. Y-connectors are available that allow both a pointing device and a keyboard to be plugged in simultaneously. However, not all Y-connectors work with all brands of laptops; there are at least two types of Y-connectors for this purpose. Make sure to match up one that will work with the brand you're using.

USB: This is the standard mouse port for many new computers. However, because most computers still have PS/2 mouse ports, unless the mouse you want is available only in USB, it is a good idea to use a PS/2 mouse. This is because there are many devices that use USB ports, but only one that can use a PS/2 mouse port, so you might as well save the USB port for some other device. Most of the feature-laden mice use USB. USB devices are recognized and installed by Windows, and many come with software disks. Windows, however, has drivers for almost all commercially available mice. USB mice are also good choices for replacements when PS/2 ports fail.

Wireless: Wireless mice use one of the other interfaces in this list. They come in two varieties, infrared and *radio frequency* (*RF*). The RF types are usually preferred because the receiver and mouse do not have to be directly in line of site of each other. The mouse runs on battery power, so plan to have spare batteries on hand or at least hold on to a basic wired mouse in case of an emergency.

Detection Types

Mice come in two detection types: mechanical (ball) and optical. Ball mice have rubber-coated metal balls that roll over a surface. This is the cheapest and most common type. It is also the most troublesome because the mechanical parts get clogged with dust, lint, and hair, and they also break. They usually need mouse pads, or at least table or desktops of a certain texture to work well.

Optical mice use a reflected red LED light to detect movement. Early optical mice sometimes required certain types of surfaces, but since then, optical mice have become easy to use and much more reliable than ball mice.

Mouse Features

The most common feature is a scroll wheel. This allows the up-and-down scrolling of a window by turning the wheel with your thumb, rather than clicking on the scroll arrows or moving the scroll bars on the screen. The next most common feature is an ergonomic shape.

Non-mouse Pointing Devices

Trackpads, touchpads, and track sticks are the most common. The track sticks are found in the center of laptop keyboards, and are available built into keyboards. Touchpads are commonly found on laptops, although they are also available built into separate keyboards, or as freestanding devices. Trackballs can also be found in any of those locations. These devices, shown with others in Figure 9.1, are often very helpful for people who experience wrist pain from excessive use of mice.

Touchpads have no moving parts, so they tend to be very reliable. The most common manufacturers of touchpads are Synaptics (*synaptics.com*) and Alps (*alps.com*). Free software available from the manufacturers or the computer maker provide touchpad users with many features such as scrolling, tapping for left-clicks, and click-and-drag operations with one finger (not requiring the use of the mechanical mouse button).

Pointing Device Configuration

Although there is considerable configuration possible in the Control Panel Mouse applet, most settings are typically left at their defaults. Microsoft has done a good

FIGURE 9.1 Pointing device assortment.

job of setting these defaults. It is helpful to be familiar with these settings so that you aren't bewildered when you encounter unusual pointing device behavior. This applet looks like the one in Figure 9.2 unless extra pointing device software is installed.

The most useful settings in this applet include double-click speed, which is useful for older people and others who have trouble double-clicking. There is also a setting for right- and left-handers that reverses the functions of the left and right mouse buttons. There is a whole host of settings of pointer appearance and speed. Windows Me and XP come with a check box that causes a circle to appear

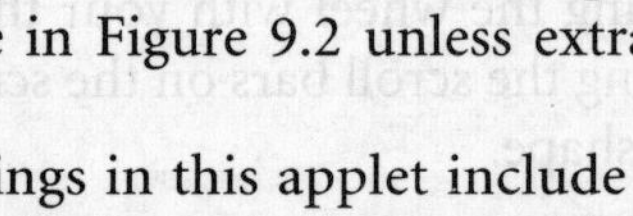

FIGURE 9.2 A typical Mouse applet from Windows Me.

around the pointer when the Ctrl key is pressed, although it doesn't always work in Windows Me. There is also a Click Lock setting that allows clicking and dragging without holding down the button. Another setting is in more than one place in some versions of Windows: single- or double-click to open an item is both in the Mouse applet and in the Tools > Folder Options command in any Windows Window.

Removal and Installation of Pointing Devices

As covered earlier in this chapter, removal and installation of these devices isn't complicated unless you are trying to replace a pointing device that is built into a laptop, a repair that is beyond the scope of this book. The main point to remember is never to plug in or unplug a PS/2 device with the computer powered on. Other points to remember are:

- Don't reverse pointing device and keyboard PS/2 connections. This will cause neither device to work, and you'll have to shut off the power, usually without a proper shutdown to switch the connectors. You might see badly labeled connections, such as the one shown in Figure 9.3. In this case, the keyboard port is on the bottom and the mouse port is on the top.

FIGURE 9.3 Badly labeled PS/2 ports.

- USB devices are hot-pluggable and are recognized as new hardware.
- Serial mice can be safely plugged in or removed while the computer is running.

Diagnosing Pointing Device Problems

Pointing devices are not the culprit in most computer problems, but because they are almost indispensable, the problems they do have are important to repair quickly.

Error Messages

There is only one common error message related to pointing devices, a message indicating that Windows didn't detect a mouse. The message is accompanied by a note that a serial mouse can be attached right away, but that to install a PS/2 mouse, you'll have to shut down the machine. If there actually is no mouse connected, the solution is obvious. If a PS/2 mouse is connected, the first thing to check is that the mouse and keyboard connectors aren't reversed. Again, switch them only once the computer has been shut down. If the pointing device is installed correctly, however, there is a problem. The pointing device could be dead, so swapping a known good device should confirm that. For this reason, it is a good idea to keep various types of mice around any computer shop. If a known good mouse doesn't work either, then the problem could be in the port. First, check the BIOS setup program to make sure that the port in question hasn't been disabled. Then, unless the port is PS/2, check in Device Manager for the same thing. If the port is disabled or not installed in Device Manager, attempt to enable it or reinstall it. If you still can't get it to work, the port might be disconnected or broken. In an older computer, the serial port might not be part of the motherboard. The cable from the port to the header connector on the motherboard might be detached, damaged, or connected to the wrong header connector. Of course, these possibilities are unlikely unless someone opened the case and made changes. If the port cannot be fixed, the simplest solution is to use a pointing device with a different interface. In an AT computer that accepts only serial pointing devices, you can try a different serial port, if there is one available. If not, you might be able to replace the port or add a new one. Search the Web for these replacement parts if you don't have old ones available. But remember, AT computers are probably not worth the time involved to fix.

Jerky Pointer

There are two possibilities for jerky pointers. One is a dirty or damaged mechanical ball mouse or trackball, and the other is that a computer's CPU and memory are being used heavily. The latter should be ruled out first. Often, use of memory- or processor-intensive hardware such as printers, scanners, or optical disc burners cause the pointer to be jerky. There are several ways to determine if this is the case. First, a damaged or dirty mouse will not spontaneously start working normally; if it does, the problem is probably not in the device. Another way to tell is if the computer reacts slowly or erratically to everything you try. For example, if you press the Windows key (shown in Figure 9.5, appearing in the section on keyboards) or click Start, but the Start menu takes a noticeable amount of time to appear, the problem is probably not related to the mouse. In 2000 and XP, you can check Windows performance in Task Manager; look for a high percentage of CPU time being used. In 9x, look at the Performance tab of the System applet for the percentage or resources remaining. If the number is low, something might be draining resources. Sometimes, Windows will run poorly for no apparent reason.

If everything appears to be working normally, except for a jerky pointer, and the pointing device is a ball mouse or trackball, try cleaning the device. It is probably a good idea to save your open files and close all programs to avoid clicking anything that can cause problems. You could also clean the device while the computer is shut down.

To clean a ball mouse, twist and remove the bottom plate in the direction of the arrow as shown in Figure 9.4. Remove the ball. You will probably find grit and stringy substances around the rollers. Pull out this debris. Air spray such as Blow

FIGURE 9.4 Opening the bottom of a ball mouse.

Off can be helpful. Replace the ball and plate and try the mouse again. If this doesn't help, try a new or known good mouse. If the new mouse solves the problem after a cleaned old mouse is still jerky, discard the old mouse. If the new mouse doesn't solve the problem, you'll have to go back to the drawing board. It will be helpful to try both mice in a different computer. Make sure to note which mouse is which; if necessary, mark the bottom of the old mouse with a permanent marker.

Similar problems will occur in mechanical trackball-style pointing devices. The balls can be removed by pulling them out, or by pushing from a hole in the bottom. Use an air spray and blow out the dust.

Of course, to avoid the problem of contaminated mice, recommend an optical mouse or touchpad to the user.

Lockups

Lockups are when the computer stops responding to any input. The mouse pointer freezes, keyboard commands are ignored, and the screen doesn't change. The telltale sign of a lockup is when the Num Lock light on the keyboard (if there is one) doesn't change when the <Num Lock> key is pressed. However, because the most obvious sign of a lockup is the frozen pointer, many users are convinced that the problem is in the mouse. Many mice are sold to consumers who want to repair a lockup. In fact, a bad mouse can lose the capability to move the pointer, but the screen will still change and keyboard commands will still be accepted. However, lockups are much more common culprits of frozen pointers. We discuss lockups in more detail in Chapter 11, "Troubleshooting."

The Center Mouse Button

You have most probably noticed that some mice have three buttons. Software that comes with the mouse can be used to configure the center button for a number of different functions such as the Enter key. Most people didn't program these, so this type of mouse never really caught on.

KEYBOARD OVERVIEW

Keyboards are also crucial devices in the vast majority of computers. Keyboards can be had for around five dollars, and for several hundred dollars. Keyboards come in versions for different languages. There are *Dvorak* keyboards, which have the alphabet laid out in a pattern conducive to faster typing than the QWERTY type, which was designed for old typewriters to keep the typebars from jamming. Some keyboards come with features such as ergonomic shapes or built-in touchpads. Some have extra buttons used for turning the computer on and off, connecting to the Internet, controlling audio CDs, or opening any program designated by the user.

Not everyone is familiar with all the keys on a keyboard, so an explanation of some of the lesser-known keys follows:

Windows key: Opens the Windows Start menu. See Figure 9.5.

<Print Screen|Sys Rq>: There are various abbreviations of this key label. This key doesn't actually cause the screen to print, at least in Windows. If it is enabled, pressing this key copies the screen to the clipboard so that if you open any document or image program and use the Paste command <Ctrl> + <V> or Edit > Paste), the screen image appears in the document or image program. Holding the <Alt> key when you press Print Screen stores just the active window in the clipboard.

<Pause>: If Quiet Boot or its equivalent isn't enabled in the BIOS, lots of valuable information about hardware can appear on the screen early in the boot process. Some of this information moves down the screen at about the same

FIGURE 9.5 The Windows key.

pace as the credits after a television show. Use the Pause key to stop this movement so you can actually read it.

<Num Lock>: This key toggles the numeric keypad on and off. It also, as stated earlier in this chapter, can be used to test for a lockup as long as there is a working Num Lock light. If pressing the key has no effect, you can be almost certain that the machine is locked up. If the Num Lock light responds to the key, the computer isn't locked up, although it could be in a virtual lockup condition in which the pointer moves, but nothing really responds in a reasonable amount of time. The <Caps Lock> key can be used for the same purpose.

<Home>, <End>: These keys move the cursor to the beginning and the end of a line in a document, respectively. Holding down the <Ctrl> key when pressing these causes the cursor to move to the beginning and end of the entire document, respectively.

Keyboard Interfaces

There are four main interfaces for keyboards:

PS/2: All varieties of ATX motherboards, except "legacy-free" models, come with PS/2 keyboard connectors. The same rules that apply to PS/2 mice apply to PS/2 keyboards. Plug in and unplug these only when the power is off, and don't attempt to plug any other device into a PS/2 keyboard port. Windows installs these keyboards transparently. Models with extra features need software disks from the manufacturer for the extra features to work. Adapters exist to plug a PS/2 keyboard into an AT port, or vice versa.

5-Pin DIN (AT): All varieties of AT motherboards come with these keyboard connectors. These are the only type of keyboard that can be used in a computer with one of these motherboards. Although there should be no problem hot plugging an AT keyboard, it is better to be safe and turn off the computer first.

USB: These are hot-pluggable devices. Some have their own auxiliary USB connectors, which are handy for USB mice.

Wireless: These come in the USB and PS/2 varieties and can be either infrared or RF controlled.

Keyboard Maintenance

There is one overriding rule that must be followed when cleaning a keyboard: *don't let it get wet*! Keys and the body of the keyboard can be cleaned with a slightly damp cloth, but don't let water get underneath the keys. The most common damage that occurs to keyboards is when someone spills liquid into them. Air sprays such as Blow Off are great for removing dust. Sprays are available to clean the surfaces of keyboards; make sure they are designed specifically for computer keyboards.

Troubleshooting Keyboard Configurations

What little configuration that can be done for the main functions of a keyboard can be done in the Keyboard applet in Control Panel. Figures 9.6 and 9.7 show a typical Keyboard applet from Windows 2000. As with pointing devices, it is helpful to be familiar with these settings.

Repairing Keyboard Problems

Keyboards are generally trouble-free unless subjected to liquids or physical shock. If a broken keyboard is an inexpensive model, it is probably best to replace it. The

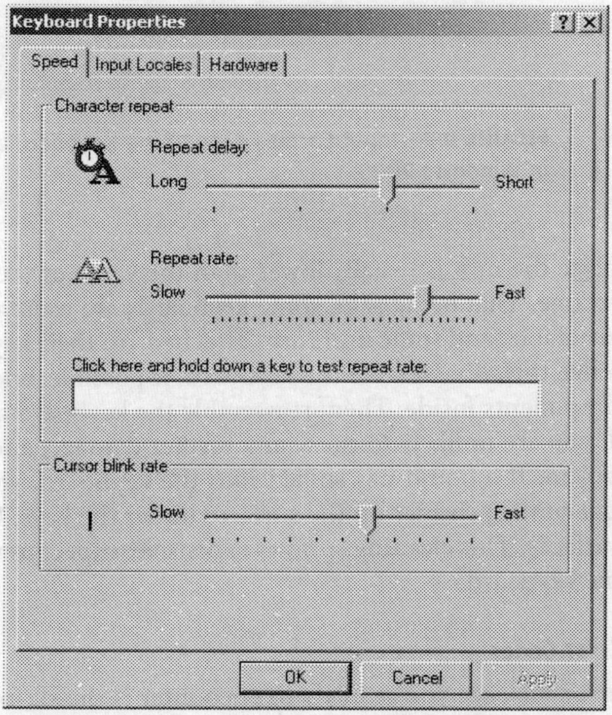

FIGURE 9.6 Speed page of the Keyboard applet in Windows 2000.

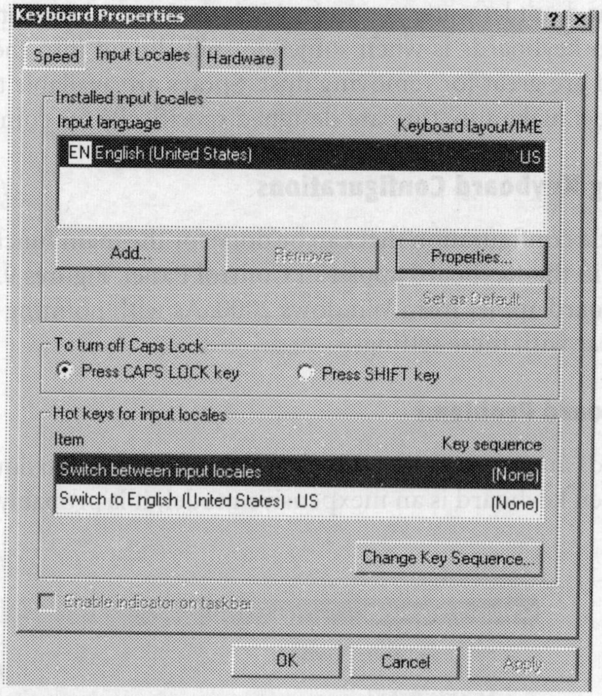

FIGURE 9.7 Input Locales page of the Keyboard applet in Windows 2000.

cost to replace the unit is usually lower than the value of the time it takes to attempt to fix one. That being said, some keyboards are more expensive, some are no longer available, and some users are "attached" to their keyboards. If you have a situation like this, disassemble the keyboard, if possible, and carefully clean the internal components inside. Then, reassemble the keyboard and try it out. If you are careful, you are unlikely to cause any further damage, and hopefully you can fix the problem. If a liquid has spilled into the keyboard, you should spray the non-residual contact cleaner on the surfaces under the keys. Use cotton swabs to clean the surfaces. This cleaning spray is expensive; expect to use up to $10 worth cleaning one keyboard.

Keyboard Error Codes

The only error message you're likely to encounter is the six-beep (usually) POST code indicating a keyboard or keyboard controller problem. If this happens, and replacing the keyboard doesn't help and there are no other obvious problems such as the heat sink having fallen off the processor, unless the motherboard is under warranty, your only solution will be to use a USB keyboard if the computer has a USB port. If not, it is probably time to retire the motherboard.

Laptop Keyboards

Laptop keyboards are essential to the portability of a laptop. Imagine trying to tote a laptop or use one on a plane if you have to use a separate keyboard. The most common reason to have to replace a laptop keyboard is if liquid spills on it, but the rest of the machine still works. Laptops vary widely in how to remove the keyboard, and laptop manufacturers vary widely in providing such information. For example, IBM makes detailed service instructions for its ThinkPad® laptops available on its Web site (*ibm.com*), while many other companies do not make this information available on the Web. There are two common ways to remove a laptop keyboard. One is, with the power off and battery removed, to look for a removable panel around the keyboard. There might be a screw or two holding it in place (see Figure 9.8).

Remove the screw(s) and then the panel. You might then see a screw holding in the keyboard. Remove the screw and lift the keyboard slightly. Look underneath to see where the ribbon cable is, as shown in Figure 9.9. Make certain not to stress the ribbon cable as you lift the keyboard out of the way. Another common method is to look at the bottom of the laptop and remove any screws marked with "K" (see Figure 9.10). Then, gently lift the keyboard out following the previous instructions to prevent damage to the ribbon cable.

FIGURE 9.8 The removable panel type of laptop keyboard removal.

FIGURE 9.9 Treat the ribbon cable with care.

FIGURE 9.10 The "K" screw.

NOTE

If liquid has spilled on a laptop, do not attempt to power it on until you or a technician experienced in portable computers has determined that there is no liquid present anywhere in the system. See Chapter 11 for more information on attempting to rescue a laptop that has been exposed to liquid.

10 Troubleshooting Internet Connections

In This Chapter

INTERNET CONNECTION PROBLEM OVERVIEW

Failure to connect to the Internet is a very common reason why people request service for their computers. We'll cover two main types of Internet connections here: dial-up and high speed. Each type has its own problems, with some overlap. The problems can be put into main categories:

- You cannot connect to the *Internet Service Provider* (*ISP*).
- You can connect to the ISP, but you can't open Web pages and/or use e-mail.
- You can connect to the ISP and open Web pages and use e-mail, but your connection is very slow, and/or you get disconnected frequently.

There are many causes of each of these problems, too many to cover them all here. We will attempt to cover common problems. However, as is the case with other problems, there are times that everything is set correctly, and the hardware is OK, but Internet connections still don't work. When this happens, it might be because of OS corruption serious enough to require a clean install, or it might be one of those Windows things that happens for no real reason, and sometimes resolves itself with no real reason either.

NOTE

We don't cover wireless Internet specifically in Part I of this book, although some of the information in this chapter does apply to it.

When setting up or troubleshooting a connection, there are some simple rules to follow, as we discuss in the following sections.

Basic Connection Problems

- **Call the ISP first:** There could be an outage in your area. There is no point in troubleshooting before you rule out an outage.
- **ISP settings:** Every ISP has its own requirements and specifications for connection configuration. Make sure you follow them.
- **Username and password:** Many connection problems could be avoided if users always used the correct username and password. This means that typos must be avoided and that the Caps Lock shouldn't be toggled on. In addition, some ISPs require you to enter your entire e-mail address (such as name@domain.com) as a username, and some require only the username (the part before the "@").

DIAL-UP CONNECTIONS

Although high-speed Internet service is becoming much more common and affordable, dial-up is still the most common as of this writing. In many rural areas, dial-up is the only option. Additionally, if you have high-speed Internet service at home, but you take your laptop to a distant location such as a motel or a relative's house, your only Internet access might be through dial-up.

Problems Dialing Up to an ISP

The first thing you need to do to troubleshoot a dial-up connection is to make sure that the hardware is connected correctly. If you are using a built-in modem in a desktop computer, make sure the telephone line is connected to the jack on the modem labeled *line*, or with a picture of a telephone jack, as shown in Figure 10.1.

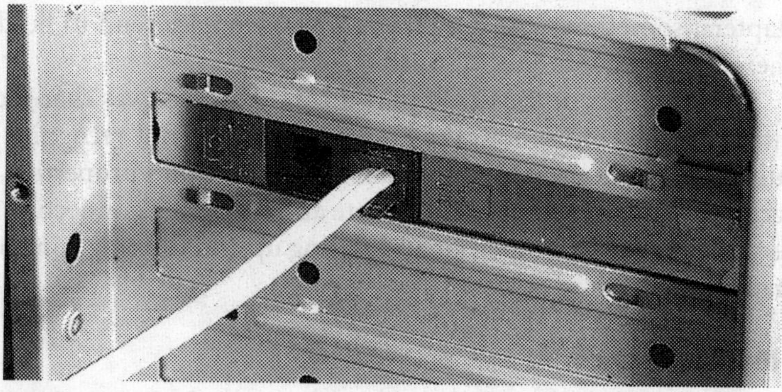

FIGURE 10.1 Connect the phone line to the phone jack.

In addition, make sure that the other end of the cable is connected to the wall jack. If the installation has a surge suppressor with telephone line protection, the telephone line needs to be connected to the line jack on the surge suppressor, with another telephone cord connecting the surge suppressor's output jack to the modem's line jack. If there is a telephone, hook it up to the telephone jack on the modem; it's the one labeled *Tel, Phone*, or with a picture of a telephone. Sometimes, there is a problem with the surge suppressor. To test it, plug a telephone into the output jack on the surge suppressor and listen for a dial tone. If you get no dial tone, and the line jack is connected to the telephone line, there might be a problem with the surge suppressor. Bypass the problem by connecting the telephone line directly to the computer.

Try connecting a telephone to the telephone line and dial the access number and listen to be sure you hear a modem on the other end. If you do not connect to a modem on the other end, you might have to modify the telephone number you are calling to reach the access number. If the call connects but you do not hear a modem, you will have to find an alternative access number to dial.

NOTE

Never connect a computer modem to a PBX business telephone line. The voltage is different that that of a regular telephone line, and it could damage the modem, or at the very least, lock up the computer.

If you still get no connection, plug a telephone directly into the wall jack to make sure the telephone line works.

Other items to check include the telephone cords themselves: make sure they're good. If you are using a PC-Card modem with a dongle in a laptop, make sure it's working. A *dongle* is a cable that plugs into the end of the PC-Card and has a telephone connector on the other end (other PC-Card devices, such as network adapters, sometimes use dongles as well). Dongles tend to be delicate, especially where they plug into the PC-Card.

If the modem or the COM port the modem uses was changed at any time after setting up the connection, the connection might not recognize the new modem. Attempt to select the new modem in the connection's properties, have the ISP software detect the new modem, or delete and set up the connection from scratch. We discuss connection properties and setting up and deleting connections later in this chapter.

Does the Modem Work?

Obviously, if the modem doesn't work properly, you're not going to be able to connect. Follow the instructions in Chapter 8, "Video, Sound, Modems, and Network Adapters," for troubleshooting modems.

The Hardware Is OK, but I Still Can't Get Online

There are a myriad of different problems you can have connecting to the Internet related to configuration. The first thing to consider is whether you use a program provided by the ISP, such as AOL, or if you are using Windows dial-up networking. The programs vary greatly, so if you do have a problem, you'll have to consult the program vendor. Windows configuration can, however, play a big part in connecting, even if you're using third-party software.

ON THE CD

The Industry Contacts file on the accompanying CD-ROM has a section on ISPs.

NOTE

If you're using a free ad-based Internet service, you'll probably have a difficult time getting anything beyond automated technical support.

The main configuration problems are related to the following:

- Selecting the modem.
- Dialing the correct numbers, including the area code if necessary, the code to disable call waiting, codes required to get an outside line, even calling card numbers.
- Username and password.
- Any other settings required by the ISP.

Windows Dial-Up Networking (9x), Network Connections (2000/XP)

Access Internet connection wizards in these places:

9x: Dial-up Networking is accessible in Control Panel, and often in My Computer. Create new connections and access existing ones in Dial-up Networking.

2000: Create new connections using the Internet Connection Wizard. Although this can be started in several places, it is always available through Start > Programs > Accessories > Communications > Internet Connection Wizard. View existing connections in Network & Dial-up Connections, also accessible through the Communications folder.

XP: Create new Internet connections by using the New Connections Wizard, accessible through Start > All Programs (or Programs) > Accessories > Communications > New Connection Wizard. Access existing connections in Network Connections, also accessible in the Communications folder. XP also has a Network Setup Wizard, which allows some Internet configuration such as sharing an Internet connection with other computers and enabling or disabling the built-in *Internet Connection Firewall* (*ICF*). We discuss the ICF later in this chapter.

The 9x wizard is rather simple. The 2000 and XP wizards are also simple, although they offer more choices. Early in each wizard, you'll be prompted to select a modem. If there is no modem installed, or the modem is dead, Windows will attempt to detect and install the modem. Install or troubleshoot the modem before starting the wizard. If there is more than one modem, make sure to choose the correct one.

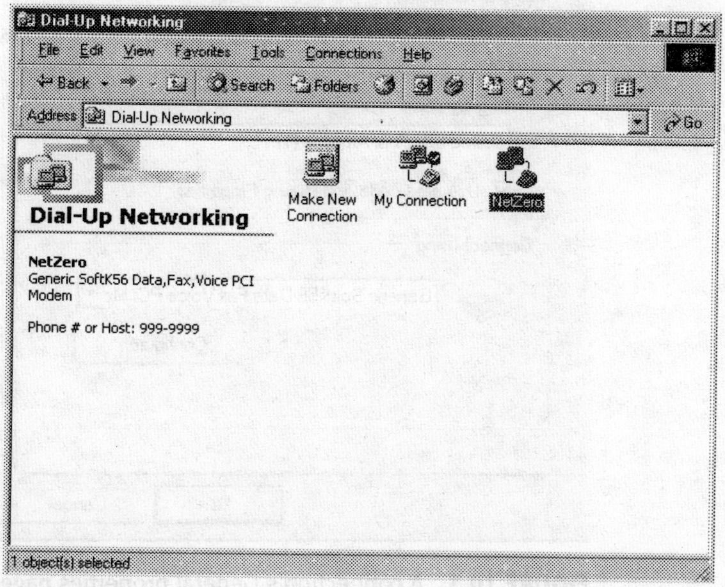

FIGURE 10.2 Dial-up Networking in Windows Me.

The main issues with dial-up connections are dialing the correct numbers, using the right username and password, and setting up any requirements from the ISP and local telephone company. To see a connection, open Dial-up Networking or Network Connections. You should see all the dial-up connections on the computer along with an icon to add a new connection, as shown in Figure 10.2.

Right-click a connection and click Properties from the menu that appears. You'll see a page like the one in Figure 10.3. (The dialog boxes that appear vary among the Windows version, but they are similar.)

Some of the other tabs in this dialog box have settings that might prevent connection if set improperly. Look at Figure 10.4. This page is very useful if you use the computer in different areas where other numbers need to be dialed. Click the Area Code Rules button, shown in Figure 10.5.

Area Code Rules can be a very important page now that more and more areas require 10-digit dialing for local calls. The settings are self-explanatory. Another important page is the Dialing page, shown in Figure 10.6. The three option buttons

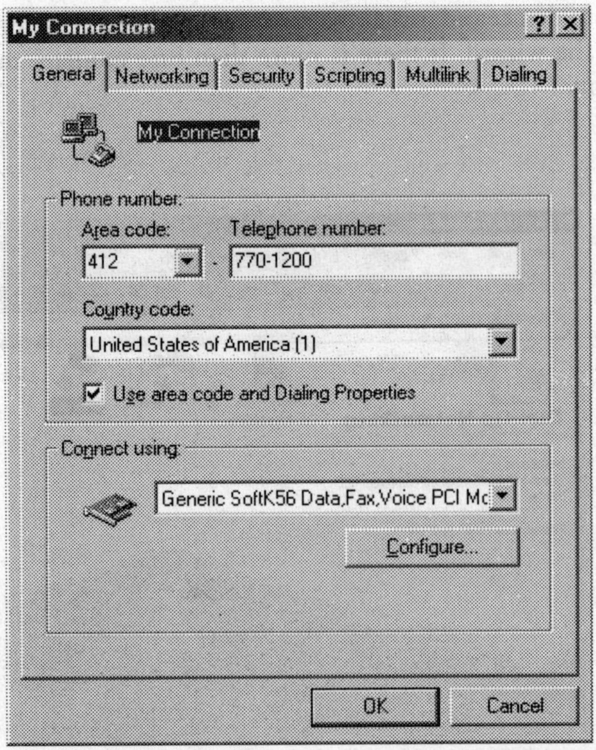

FIGURE 10.3 A connection's General properties page in Windows Me.

at the top of this page don't affect the capability of connecting, but setting them correctly can make the difference between an unhappy and a happy computer user:

Never dial a connection: Selecting this button means that Windows will never dial a connection unless the user chooses to connect.

Dial whenever a network connection is not present: This is the setting to choose if you want to always be connected whenever Windows is running. This is great for high-speed Internet, and occasionally useful with dial-up, but it can also be extremely annoying to the user, especially when using a laptop that is not connected to a telephone line, high-speed line, or wireless network source.

Always dial my default connection: This setting will cause the computer to dial the default connection whenever the user opens a Web browser (such as Internet Explorer) or clicks an Internet link in a document, whenever the computer is not already connected to the Internet. Many people like this setting, although some don't.

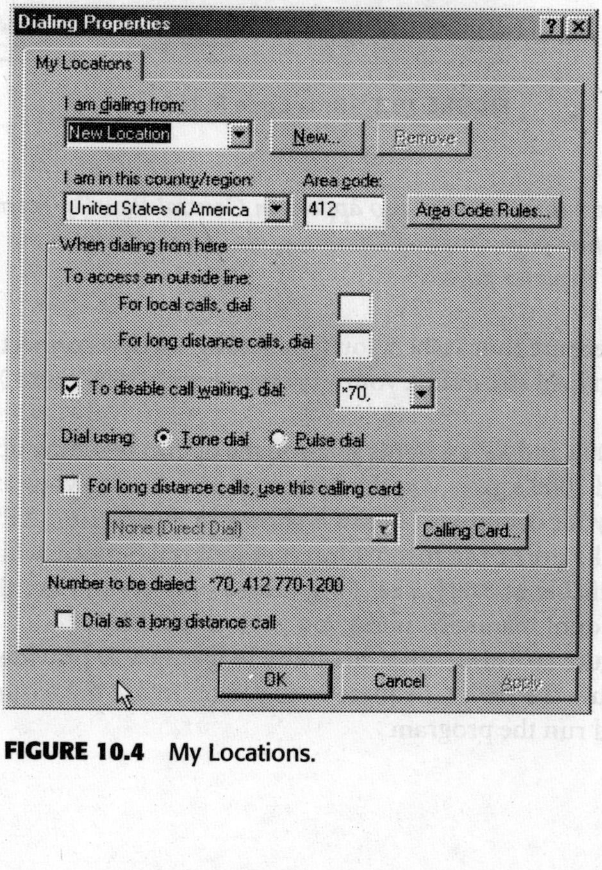

FIGURE 10.4 My Locations.

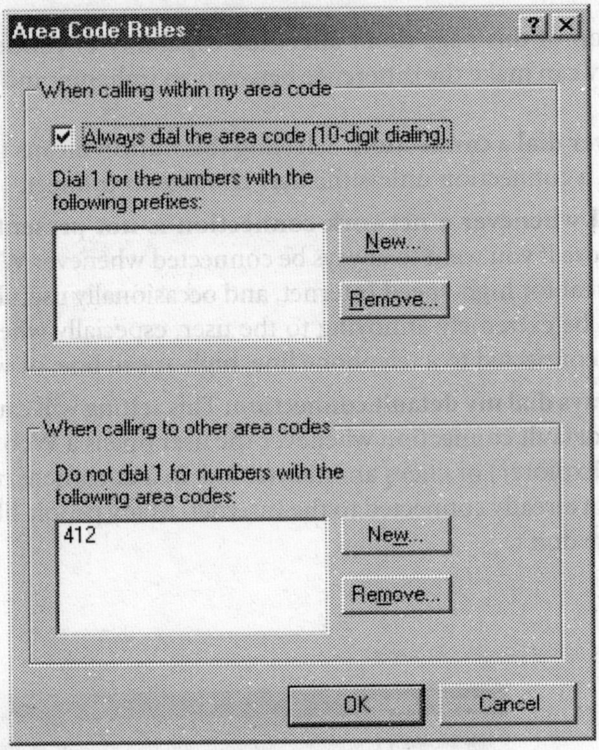

FIGURE 10.5 Area Code Rules.

NOTE

These three settings also appear in Control Panel > Internet Options on the Connection page. Internet Options is also accessible from the Tools menu in any Internet Explorer page.

There are times when you'll be setting up new connections. Here are a few tips that can help streamline your experience with 2000's and XP's wizards:

- 2000's and XP's wizards give you the option of setting up a new Internet account, and 2000's gives you the option of transferring your existing Internet account to your computer (2000's is shown in Figure 10.7, XP's in Figure 10.8). These make use of Microsoft's Internet Referral Service, which doesn't list every ISP available in every area. Forgo these options and use the choice to set up your account manually unless you want to use MSN®.
- Figure 10.8 also shows an option to use the CD provided by the ISP. If you want to use the ISP's CD, there is no reason to use the wizard. Simply insert the CD and run the program.

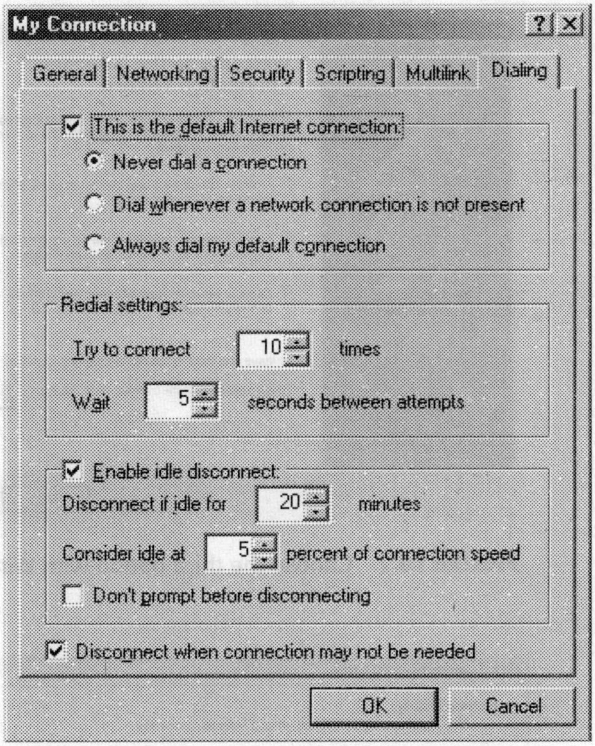

FIGURE 10.6 The Windows Me Dialing page.

- When running XP's wizard you'll be prompted to enable the ICF. It is a good idea to enable this for any *direct* connection to the Internet, as long as no other firewall is running on the system. If you dial up to an ISP or have one computer that connects to a DSL or cable modem, this is considered a direct connection. We discuss firewalls later in this chapter.

Dialing Rules

Dialing rule settings are accessible from the Phone and Modem applet (or equivalent) in Control Panel, and from buttons in the wizards and the connection pages. These rules purport to give the user control of exactly how the computer dials numbers, including the appropriate area code, calling card numbers, and other codes. These settings are supposed to be in effect for any connection on the computer with the "Use area code and dialing rules" (or equivalent) check box selected, as shown in Figure 10.9.

In 2000, it sometimes doesn't seem to matter how you have Dialing Rules configured and if you have the connection configured to use them; the rules will often be ignored.

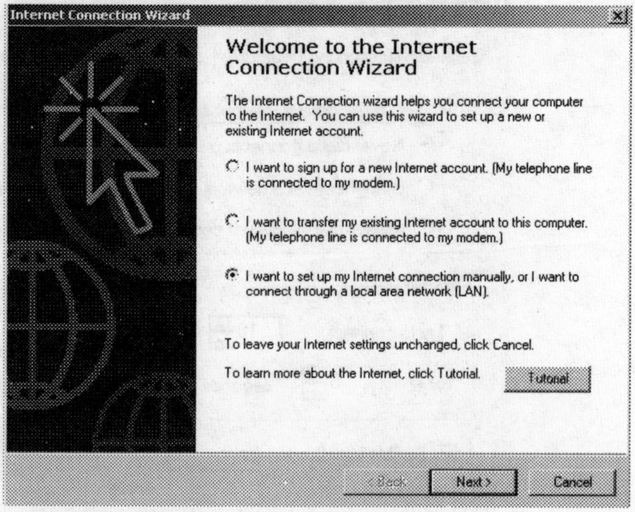

FIGURE 10.7 Choose the third option with Windows 2000.

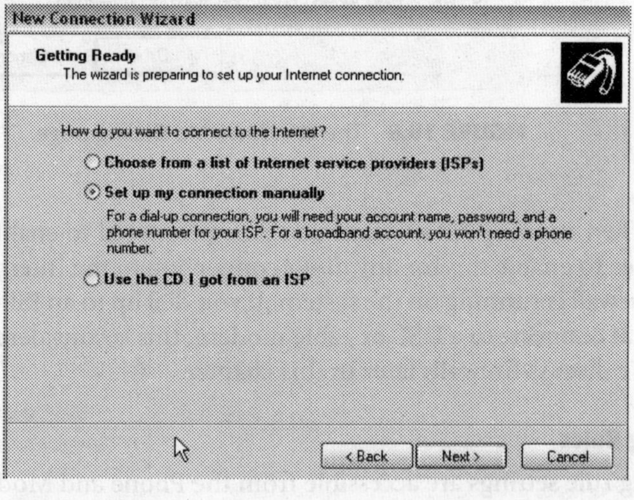

FIGURE 10.8 Choose the second option with Windows XP.

TIP *If you run into the problem of Dialing Rules being ignored in 2000, and you're sure that everything has been correctly configured, try rebooting—it sometimes helps.*

Dialing Rules also allows you to set up separate rules for different locations as shown in Figure 10.10; select the one you want for your location.

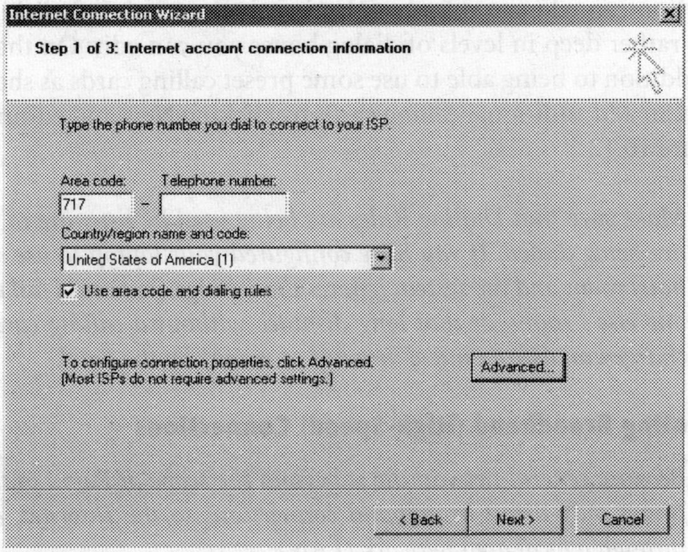

FIGURE 10.9 2000's wizard page with the "Use area code and dialing rules" check box selected.

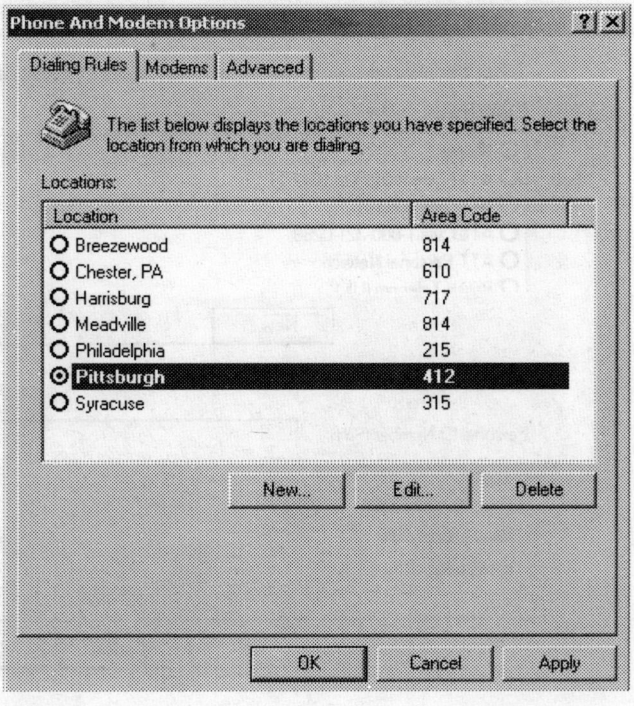

FIGURE 10.10 Configure a separate set of rules for each location.

You can edit the rules by selecting the location and clicking Edit. This applet gets rather deep in levels of dialog boxes you can edit. On the Calling Card page, in addition to being able to use some preset calling cards as shown in Figure 10.11, you can add additional calling cards by clicking New and editing the page shown in Figure 10.12.

TIP

Make sure that Dialing Rules are being used by listening to hear if enough digits are being dialed. If you have configured your laptop to use a calling card from a hotel room and the system ignores the settings, you could fail to connect, call someone else's room, or dial long distance without a calling card and most likely be charged an astronomical amount of money by the hotel.

Troubleshooting Broadband (High-Speed) Connections

NOTE

Because general networking is beyond the scope of Part I of this book, this section covers only direct broadband connections to the Internet, and not connections through a local area network (LAN).

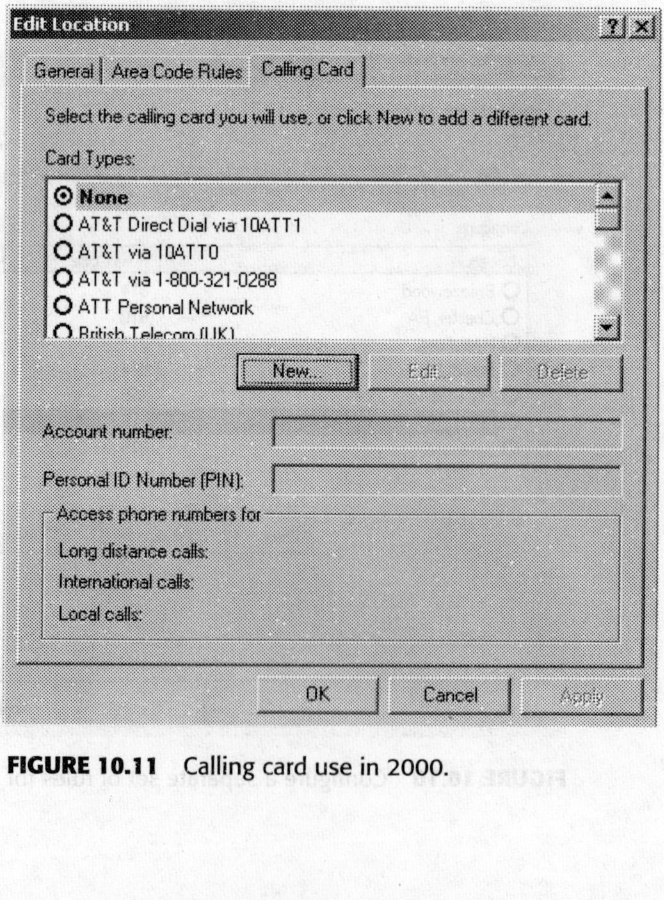

FIGURE 10.11 Calling card use in 2000.

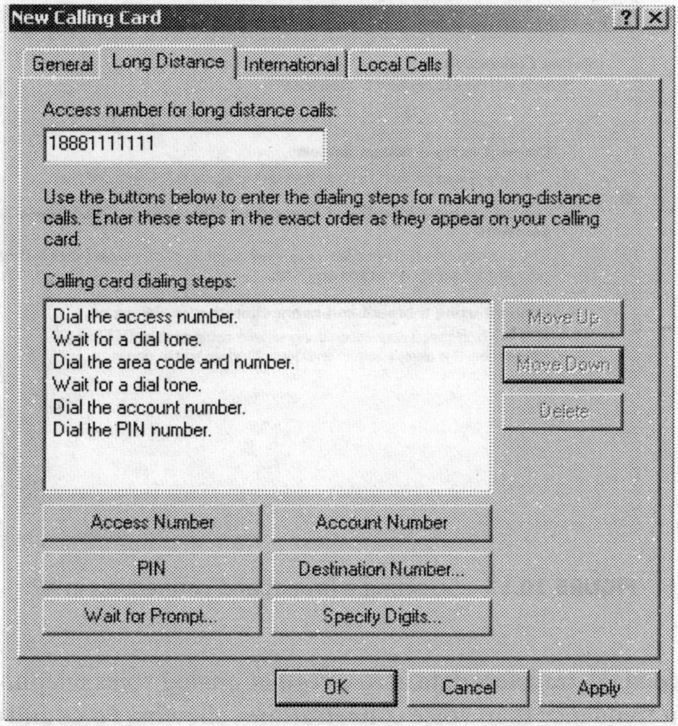

FIGURE 10.12 Adding a new calling card in 2000.

Generally, broadband Internet connections are made with ISP software. This software can vary widely; therefore, most troubleshooting should be done with the assistance of the ISP's technical support department. However, Windows XP allows broadband connections without the use of ISP software, as shown in Figure 10.13.

Using XP's broadband feature is desirable any time the ISP's software becomes troublesome. Regardless of whether you're using the ISP's software or XP's feature, you'll get a connection dialog that could be similar to a dial-up connection dialog. Sometimes a "phone number" is displayed, usually 111-1111. As mentioned earlier, the most common configuration problems in this type of connection are incorrect use of username and password, and the Caps Lock function being toggled on in the event of case sensitivity of either.

Broadband Hardware Issues

The two most popular types of consumer and small business broadband connections are *Digital Subscriber Line* (*DSL*) and *Cable Internet*.

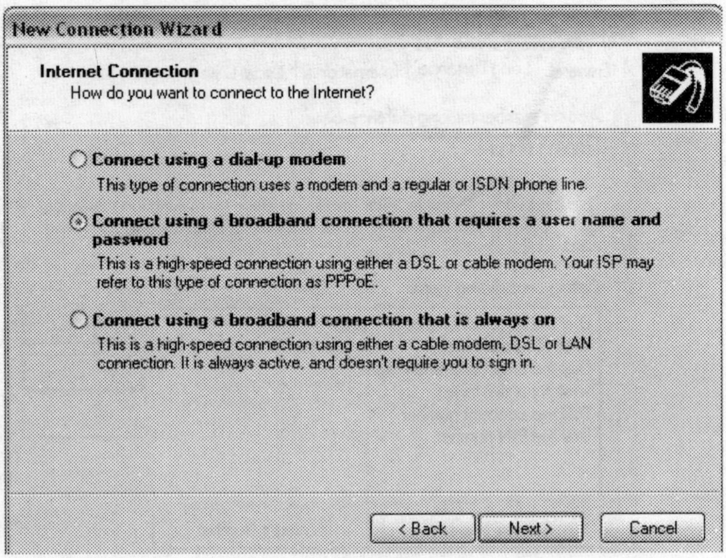

FIGURE 10.13 Selecting a broadband connection in XP.

DSL: DSL transfers data across regular analog voice telephone lines at a different frequency than voice conversations, allowing voice and data to flow simultaneously. To keep the Internet signals from interfering with voice, fax, and even dial-up signals, *DSL filters* must be attached to every telephone jack on that telephone line (or one heavy-duty filter used for all the other jacks). Don't forget to install filters on *every device connected to the telephone line except the DSL modem.* This includes fax machines, computer modems, alarm systems that dial the telephone, and utility (water, gas, electricity, etc.) meters. The individual DSL filters should be connected between the telephone jack and the device. Figure 10.14 shows an assortment of DSL filters.

To connect DSL to your computer, use a standard telephone cable to connect the wall telephone jack to a DSL modem (or DSL router). *Do not* use a DSL filter on this connection. The modem connects to the computer either with an Ethernet cable to an Ethernet adapter (see Chapter 8) or to a USB port (unless the DSL modem is an internal expansion card). Any of these cables or devices represents a potential point of failure. If you rule out everything else, it is likely that the modem (or router) is the problem. Make sure the modem is powered and connected, and that all cables are intact. You can also check the telephone line by unplugging the telephone cable from the DSL modem and plugging it into a telephone. You should hear a dial tone with no interference. (The interference comes from the modem, not the telephone line.)

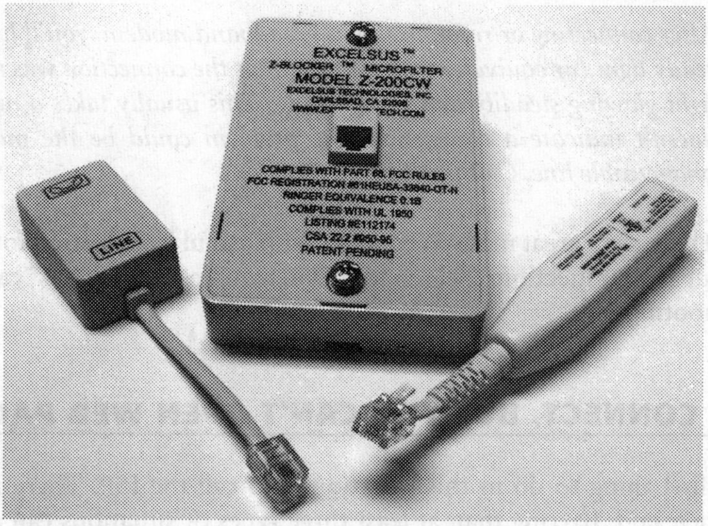

FIGURE 10.14 An assortment of DSL filters.

TIP

If DSL is being used where there are multiline telephone jacks, make sure the DSL modem is connected to the correct telephone line.

Cable Internet: This makes use of cable television cables, which already have a great deal of *bandwidth.* A television cable gets connected to a cable modem that connects to the computer either through an Ethernet cable to an Ethernet adapter (see Chapter 8), or through a USB port. Because televisions and VCRs have tuners, there is no problem with interference. Cable modems simply tune to a frequency not used by television channels.

Here are some items to check when troubleshooting suspected cable Internet hardware problems:

- Check for a damaged television cable.
- Did anyone install or remove a cable splitter? Cable modems can be finicky. If the signal is too strong or weak, the Internet connection might fail. Splitters reduce the signal strength by a factor equal to the number of extra outlets in use.
- Make sure the Ethernet or USB cable is good. The Ethernet cable in most cases must not be a crossover cable (see Chapter 8).
- Check the cable modem for power (or if the modem is an internal expansion card, check its status in Device Manager.

TIP

After connecting or reconnecting a broadband modem, you'll have to wait for the ready light (or equivalent) to indicate that the connection was made, often by the light glowing steadily and not flashing. This usually takes a minute or two. If it doesn't indicate a connection, the problem could be the modem or the telephone/cable line. Call the ISP.

There are a great many Web pages with useful information for troubleshooting broadband connections. Search for "DSL troubleshooting" or "cable modem troubleshooting."

YOU CAN CONNECT, BUT YOU CAN'T OPEN WEB PAGES

The first thing to do in this situation is to call the ISP. There might be a glitch on their end. Barring that, at least three types of situations can cause this type of problem:

- Configuration
- Malware
- Virus infection

Solve the latter two by using procedures described in Chapter 2, "System Configuration and Computer Hygiene," and Chapter 11, "Troubleshooting." We discuss configuration here.

Internet Options

NOTE

The information here applies to Internet Explorer 6.0, but most will apply to other versions.

Internet Options is a group of settings accessible from Control Panel or from the Tools menu of any Internet Explorer page. Its settings can affect the performance of the Internet. Figure 10.15 shows the General page of Internet Options.

The General Page

This page has the following pertinent settings:

Home page: Use this to select the Web page that appears when Internet Explorer is opened. If a rogue program changes it, you can change it back here.

Temporary Internet files: These files can take up a surprising amount of disk space, and large amounts of files can even slow Internet performance. *Cookies*

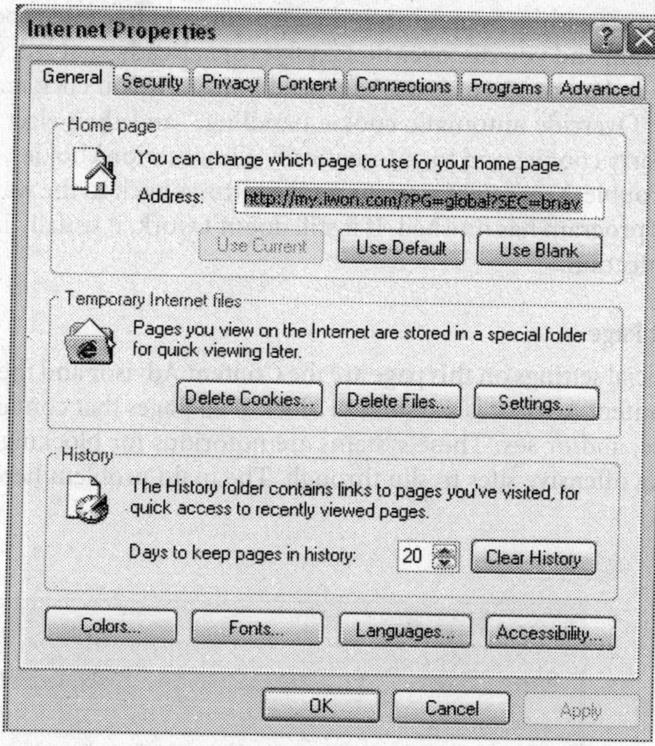

FIGURE 10.15 The Internet Options General page from XP.

are small files that remember data the user entered for the next time the user visits the same Web site where the cookie came from. For example, when a user regularly visits a Web page that makes use of a logon, such as Yahoo.com, cookies are the files that allow Yahoo! to recognize the user every time he visits (if the page is so configured). Some cookies are used for nefarious purposes, but we'll discuss that later in this chapter.

History: History allows a user to click on the arrow next to the address bar and select a previously viewed Web page. Clearing the history will clear this list.

Security and Privacy Pages

These pages are used to set various options related to security. Keep the sliders too low, and malware and viruses can become easier to contract. Keep the bars too high, and you won't connect to too many pages or be able to download files. If you are prompted to "enable cookies," these pages are where it's done. It's possible that you'll have to use a custom level by clicking the button and selecting or clearing the check boxes within. Sometimes, you are prompted to enable cookies by a Web page or program and you discover that cookies are already enabled. On the Privacy page (shown in Figure 10.16) is an Advanced button. If you click it and select the check box to "Override automatic cookie handling," and then elect to accept first- and third-party cookies and to automatically allow session cookies, you should have no more trouble. You might want to set the settings back to the way they were after the page or program has finished. If it still doesn't work, it usually indicates malware or virus infection.

Content Page

The crucial settings on this page are the Content Advisor and the Certificates section. The Content Advisor is a system to block Web pages that contain profanity, nudity, violence, and/or sex. These systems are notorious for blocking legitimate sites and allowing offensive sites to slip through. The main problem here is if the user wants

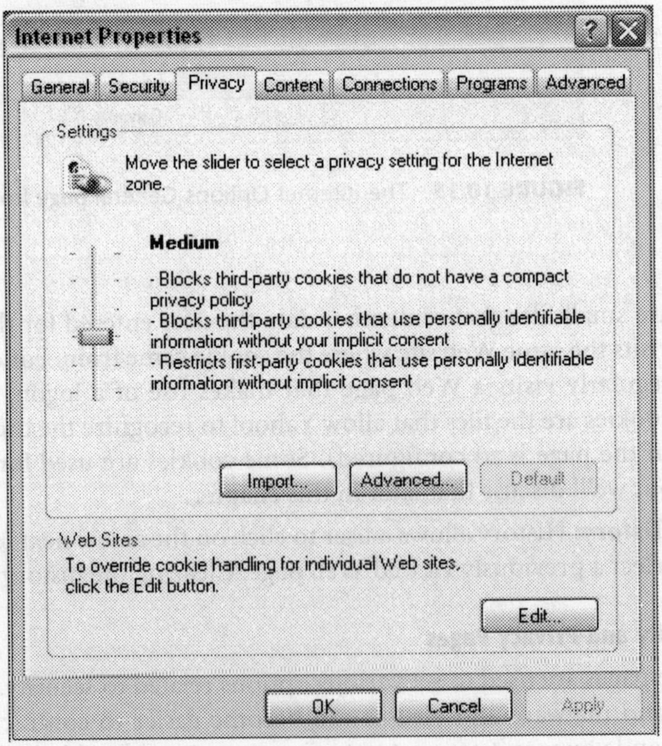

FIGURE 10.16 The Pri ac pa e

to disable or configure the advisor but can't remember the password. Search the Internet for "lost Content Advisor password," or see Microsoft Knowledge Base article 155609 (See Chapter 11 for information on viewing Knowledge Base articles).

Certificates are documents that certify that an entity communicating via the Web is who it purports to be. Too high of a setting on the Security page and you'll have Web pages blocked or you'll receive prompts to block them based on problems with certificates. Sometimes, even Microsoft pages can be blocked by too high a setting. Figure 10.17 shows the Content page.

We have all seen the prompt when attempting to download files to accept or reject the download. Each of these dialog boxes contains a check box to "Always trust content from..." Selecting these check boxes is desirable when the content provider is a known trustworthy entity such as Microsoft or your antivirus program provider—doing so will eliminate these prompts. The content providers (called *publishers*) are stored on the page that appears when you click the Publishers button.

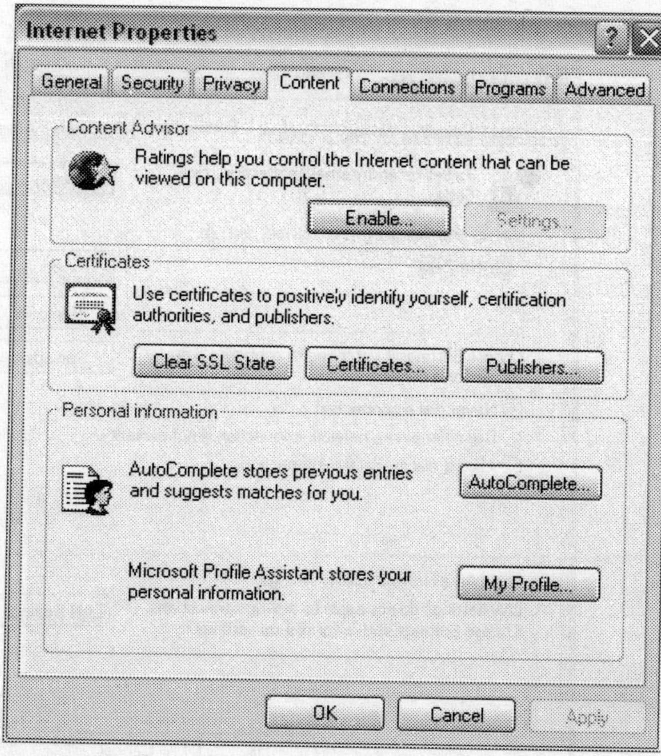

FIGURE 10.17 The Content page.

Connections Page

The pertinent settings on this page are the Setup button, which opens up the Internet Connection Wizard; the option buttons in the middle, which are the same as the ones discussed earlier in this chapter except that they apply to any Internet connection; and the LAN settings, which are used only if the computer is connected to the Internet via a LAN. By clicking the LAN settings button and selecting the "Automatically detect settings" check box within, the computer should be able to connect to the Internet simply by having a network cable carrying an Internet signal connected to the network adapter. Figure 10.18 shows the Connections page.

Programs and Advanced Pages

The Programs page is used to set the default programs for certain activities. The most important one is the e-mail program. If you click an e-mail address link anywhere in Windows, a document, or a Web page, the program displayed here should appear automatically. However, this is one of those settings that, in 2000 and XP,

FIGURE 10.18 The Connections page.

has to be made in one other place as well. If you click the Start menu and look at the top portion, you will usually see a command called *Set Program Access and Defaults.* This option seems to have priority over the one in Internet Options.

The Advanced page has highly technical settings that should be left at their defaults unless you are instructed by Microsoft support personnel or documents to change them.

DATA TRANSFER SPEED ISSUES

Speed of data transfer is affected by viruses and malware, just as the inability to get Web pages at all. There are, however, some other steps you can take to try to resolve these issues.

Telephone Line Problems

Windows Dial-up Networking and most Internet software have an indicator of connection speed. Usually, you can view the speed by moving the pointer over the appropriate icon in the System Tray, as shown in Figure 10.19.

If you have slow speeds, such as under 38 Kbps with a 56K modem, and/or the Internet connection is frequently dropped for no apparent reason, the problem might be in the telephone line. Hotel room telephone lines often have extraordinarily slow speeds; it is unusual to connect at *faster* than 19 Kbps from a hotel room, regardless of whether the property is a cheap motel or a four-star property (although some hotels are installing new telephone systems allowing faster connections). There is nothing that the user can do about it unless the hotel has a high-speed network connection, as a small, but increasing number, do. The user should test the connection speed from different residential telephone lines. Chances are that most will be faster than hotel lines are. If, however, the connection speed is very slow or the connection gets dropped frequently in a residence, there might be

FIGURE 10.19 Viewing the Internet connection speed.

a problem with either a noisy telephone line or with the ISP. To attempt to rule out the ISP, the user should sign up for a free ISP such as NetZero™ (*netzero.net*) or Juno™ (*juno.com*) just to test the connection speed and reliability (assuming that the free service isn't using the same telephone number to connect as the primary ISP is). If they are significantly faster or more reliable, the problem is most likely with the ISP. If they are no faster or better, the problem is probably in the telephone line. This could be a problem with internal house wiring or with external telephone company wiring, or both. Have the user check with the telephone company, noting the possibility that there could be a substantial charge in some cases for the telephone company to repair house telephone wiring.

Call Waiting and Voice Mail

When setting up a dial-up Internet connection, the user must know if the line has Call Waiting from the telephone company. *Call Waiting* is the feature that signals someone during a telephone call that another call is coming in and allows switching between one call and another. Normally, those users with Call Waiting wouldn't want to be disconnected from the Internet every time another call comes in, so most or all connection programs have a provision to dial the deactivation code before the telephone number. In most or all cases, this code is *70 (1170 with a pulse-only line). However, having the software programmed to dial this on a laptop will likely cause the connection attempt to fail when dialing from a telephone line without Call Waiting, such as a hotel room. Therefore, the user should not use *70 when setting up a connection to use on a line without Call Waiting.

Telephone company voice mail is very helpful for those who have dial-up Internet service. With voice mail, the telephone will never be busy. If the user has both Call Waiting and voice mail, the Call Waiting should be disabled in an Internet connection. A problem that can occur with voice mail is if the telephone company uses a pulsing dial tone to indicate a new message. In some cases, the modem will not detect a dial tone. To solve this problem, either listen to all your messages before trying to connect, or add three commas to the beginning of the telephone number to dial. Commas are seen as pause indicators by the system.

There are also Internet answering machines and software. We haven't tested any of the hardware devices, but their advertisements say that they allow incoming calls to come in when the telephone line is connected to the Internet. The most notable software-based system is the CallWave® Internet Answering Machine® (*callwave.com*). This software requires Call Forwarding from the local telephone company. You simply forward the calls from the telephone line to a toll-free number provided by CallWave, and callers will hear an announcement prompting them to leave a message. Their message will then be played on your computer while you are online. AOL has a feature to accomplish this as well for an extra charge.

FIREWALLS

A firewall is a program or hardware device that keeps hostile attackers from accessing a computer's data. Firewalls can help prevent virus transmission, and overall, they are good to have. Unfortunately, configuration of some firewalls can be painstaking. Without proper configuration, certain firewalls can block all Internet access.

Certain products come with firewalls. For example, Linksys routers act as firewalls, but the router firmware also makes available a trial version of a software-based firewall. Trend Micro's PC-Cillin antivirus program comes with a firewall that, at least in recent versions, won't deactivate even when the program settings indicate that it is disabled. (To disable it in 2000 or XP, go into Services and disable the Trend Micro personal firewall service there.) In the most recent version, however, it is possible to configure PC-Cillin's firewall to protect your computer and still allow satisfactory Web surfing. As mentioned earlier, Windows XP comes with the ICF.

Here are some basic recommendations about use of firewalls:

- Use of more than one firewall on a system will probably stop most or all Internet traffic. Stick with one.
- If you are using Internet Connection Sharing in 2000/XP, enable the ICF or use another firewall product.
- If you use a *proxy server* to connect to the Internet, don't use a firewall, except on the proxy server. (It is not necessary to know what a proxy server is for our purposes.)

See XP's Help and Support for more information about the ICF.

TROUBLESHOOTING E-MAIL

Although there are several e-mail programs (called *clients*) that people use, in addition to Web-based e-mail such as Hotmail® and Yahoo®, Outlook® Express is the most common (besides AOL). The reason is that Windows and Internet Explorer come with Outlook Express. There are a few common problems with Outlook Express, as we discuss here.

Outlook Express and General E-Mail Information

NOTE

We will be covering Outlook Express version 6 here, the latest as of this writing. Much of this information applies to other e-mail programs as well.

The problem most people have with Outlook Express has to do with a change in their account. If there are any errors, you might not be able to send or receive e-mail. You must set up new accounts using the wizard. The wizard is very simple to use, as long as you have all the correct information from the ISP. To access the wizard, open Outlook Express. There might be icons for it all over the Desktop, but you should be able to find it in the Start menu program list. The first time you start it, the wizard will open. Just follow the prompts. If Outlook Express has already been configured, you can access the wizard by going to Tools > Accounts > Mail and clicking the Add button (see Figure 10.20). This adds another e-mail account to Outlook Express. If the ISP has any unusual configuration requirements, you might have to configure the account manually anyway. To do this, select the name of the account in the Mail page and click Properties. You'll get a page like the one shown in Figure 10.21.

The key to successful configuration of most of these pages is not to make any typos. If there are connection problems, compare what is entered in these text boxes to the information provided by the ISP, letter by letter if you have to.

> **NOTE** *Some ISPs require the full e-mail address to be entered in the username box, and some require just the username portion (the part before the @). Sometimes, such as when the ISP is separate from the e-mail domain, you might be required to use a % in place of the @.*

The Servers page (Figure 10.22) contains some of the most important information. The server names must be right. Don't use @ in place of periods in the server name; normally, only the e-mail address itself will use the @. In addition,

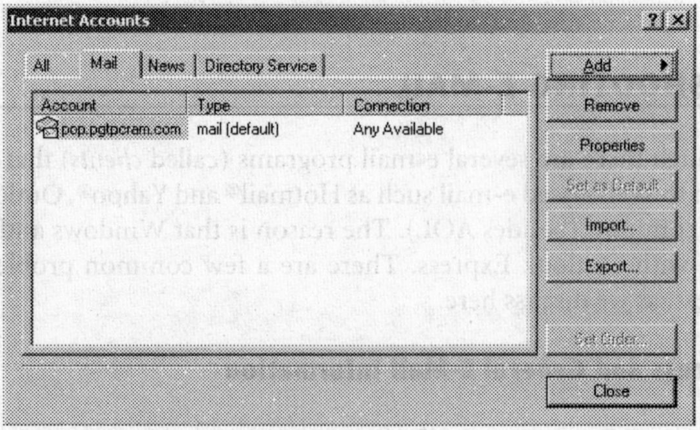

FIGURE 10.20 Add an e-mail account.

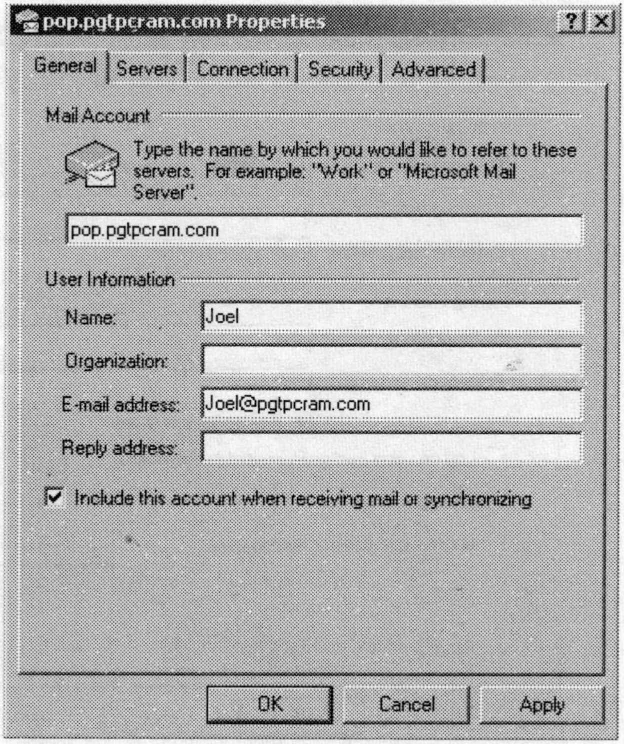

FIGURE 10.21 General properties.

don't select the "My server requires authentication" check box unless the ISP requires it or you are checking e-mail for an ISP different than the one you are connected to.

The Connection page (Figure 10.23) gives the option of selecting the Internet connection to be used for the particular account. If you have multiple ISPs and multiple e-mail accounts, this is where you match them up.

The Security page has various options that you would configure based only on instructions from the ISP. The same goes for the Advanced page (Figure 10.24), except for the setting at the bottom. Most ISPs allow you to get e-mail on your local computer and on the Web. Many business e-mail accounts are monitored by more than one person. Selecting the "Leave messages on server" check box allows other users to download the same messages on their computers, and keeps the messages available on the ISP's Web page. Users who have this box selected will have to regularly delete the messages from the server to keep from using up their quotas and/or disk space unless they also select the additional option to remove messages from the server when deleted from the Deleted Items folder. In most cases this will remove any mail from both the mail server and the Deleted Items folder.

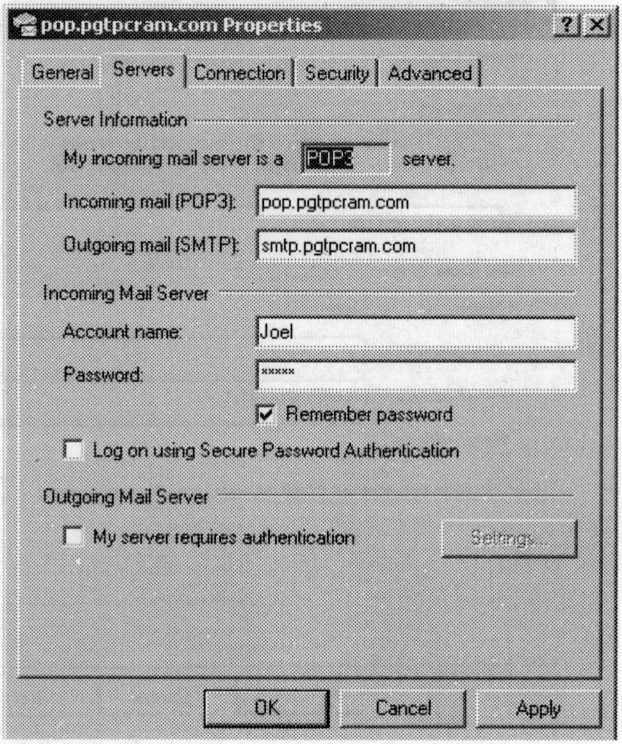

FIGURE 10.22 The Servers page.

Common Outlook Express Problems

Incoming attachments won't download: Especially after updating Outlook Express in Windows Update, you might find that attachments won't download. This is because the update selects the "Do not allow attachments to be saved or opened that could potentially be a virus" check box. Go to Tools > Options and click the Security tab to find this check box. See Microsoft Knowledge Base article 329570 for more information (Chapter 11 has instructions for searching the Knowledge Base).

Attachment pages are blank: Sometimes, attachments download but aren't visible. This usually indicates a problem in the attachment as sent. If you can't get it to appear, download it to a folder, right-click it, click Open With, and select Notepad from the list. Among all of the useless characters you should find the message, as long as there are no images.

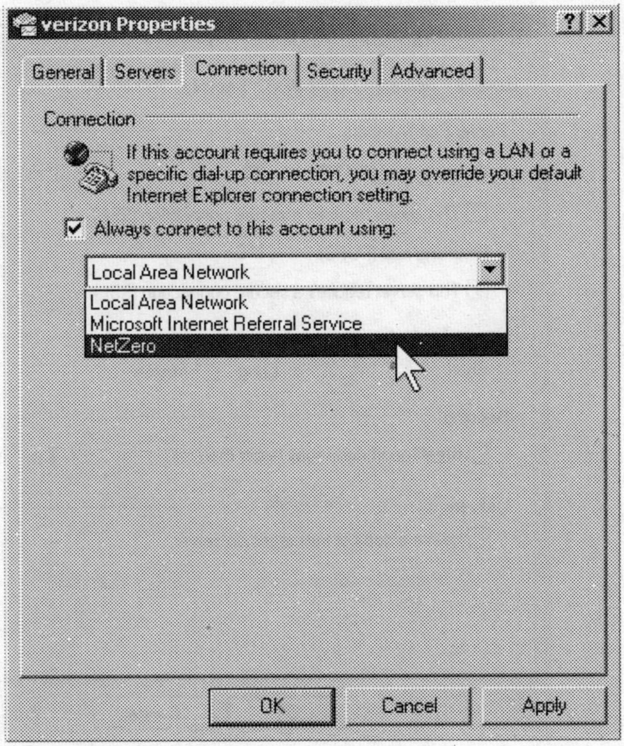

FIGURE 10.23 The Connection page.

Attachments come up with many pages full of numbers or nonsense characters: The computer doesn't have a program capable of opening the attachment. Contact the sender and ask what program the attachment was created in.

Dial-up settings are wrong: Different users have different needs as far as how they read their e-mail. Many dial-up users prefer to open Outlook Express and have the system automatically dial their ISP, download their messages, and then disconnect. This way, they can read their mail and write replies without tying up their telephone lines. After they finish their replies, they click to send and the system again dials up to the Internet just long enough for the messages to be sent. The problem occurs when these settings are reset. Users can become rather unhappy when that happens, because it's not always easy to find the location to change these settings. Go to Tools > Options and click the Connection tab. If you want the connection to disconnect after downloading or uploading, select the "Hang up after sending and receiving" check box. The Change button on this page directs you to Internet Options as discussed earlier

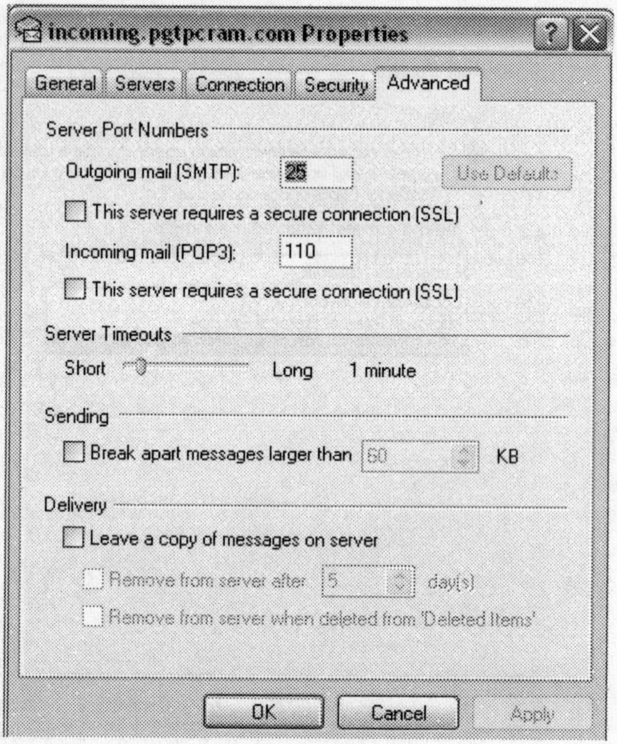

FIGURE 10.24 The Advanced page.

in this chapter. Make changes to suit the user, but remember that these changes will affect Internet Explorer as well.

Backing Up Outlook Express

Full system backups will include Outlook Express data files. Outlook Express folders aren't real Windows folders. Messages and Outlook Express folders are actually stored in a single or a few files. The same goes with address book information. If you are doing a manual backup of Outlook Express data, in 2000 and XP, copy the Documents and Settings\[username]\Application Data\Microsoft\Outlook Express folders. It's a little harder to find in 9x; you can look in Windows\Application\Data\Identities\ and Windows\Profiles\[username]\Application Data\Identities. The easier way is to click Find or Search from the Start menu and enter *.dbx in the text box. This will search for all files with the .dbx extension, which is where Outlook Express' data is stored. Copy the contents of all folders with these files.

When restoring, make sure to put these files back in the same or equivalent folders, or open Outlook Express on the restored machine and import the folders. To do this, in Outlook Express, click File > Import, and follow the prompts for each item you want to import: settings, messages, address book, and/or mail account settings.

TROUBLESHOOTING AOL CONNECTIONS

AOL is the most popular ISP in the United States and in many other countries.

> **NOTE** *Because AOL took over CompuServe™, virtually everything we say about AOL applies to CompuServe as well.*

If you have connection problems in AOL and you have tried some of the hints provided in this chapter to no avail, you can try uninstalling and reinstalling the program. Use the Add/Remove programs applet in Control Panel and let it completely remove all copies it finds. In AOL versions 6 through 9, and possibly in earlier versions as well, you can go to Start > Programs > America Online (or equivalent) > AOL System Information and then clear the browser cache and check the error messages. You can even uninstall the AOL adapter from the Utilities tab as shown in Figure 10.25, and then reboot the computer and reinstall the AOL software.

If you are able to sign on to AOL but get an error message when you try to load a Web page, there might be a problem with *TCP/IP*. AOL uses a software device called an *AOL adapter* that actually shows up in Device Manager as a network adapter. There are two AOL adapters in all versions since AOL 5. Removing these and restarting the computer might solve the problem. The best place to do this is AOL System Information, shown in Figure 10.25.

If you have been using AOL 6 or later, after uninstalling AOL, your address book and most of your settings will be saved. If you are using an earlier version, copy the contents of your address book before uninstalling. You will then need to redo all your settings after installation.

Since Windows 95B and C allow a maximum of four TCP/IP connections by default and AOL will try to use two of them, you might run into a problem if your computer has too many other TCP/IP connections. Check to see if there are any unused TCP/IP connections in the network settings and remove them. To do this, double-click Network in Control Panel. The applet will open to the Configuration page. Look for any TCP/IP listings in the network components box, highlight it, and click Remove. Click OK. You'll have to reboot the computer for the new settings to take effect.

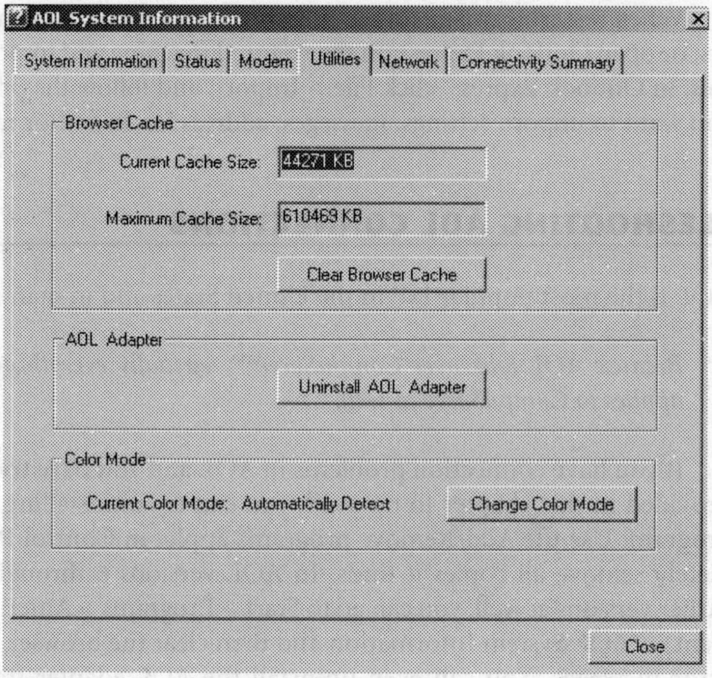

FIGURE 10.25 AOL System Information.

If AOL is unable to find your modem, you might need to reinstall or replace the modem. If you have tested the modem and determined it to be okay, then you might need to go into Setup, remove the modem, and let AOL find your modem again. Depending on what version of AOL you are using, the dialog boxes vary slightly, but the option to get into Setup is at the bottom of the Sign On screen window in all versions.

If AOL has been installed for awhile and suddenly you keep getting disconnected, and you have ruled out faulty cables and modem, you might need to select the access numbers button on the Sign On screen and get updated telephone numbers to dial.

If you get a message that the modem would not initialize, you can turn the power to the modem off and on again if it is an external. If it is an internal modem, restart the computer.

If you click the Help button from the Sign On screen, you can get lots of help there. Go to Setting up your computer to connect to AOL > Resolving Connection Problems > Disconnections to the AOL service > I get disconnected from the AOL service. Doing so attempts to repair your AOL connection automatically.

MISCELLANEOUS ITEMS

As discussed in Chapter 2, certain hardware devices, including modems and network adapters, have problems working with certain programs and Windows versions. If you search for support articles (see Chapter 11), be sure to specify the modem brand and model number, or the chipset's identifying information.

Some ISPs require a *terminal window* to be called up to log on to the Internet. Hyperterminal, discussed in the modem troubleshooting section of Chapter 8, is a terminal program. When setting up a connection to this type of ISP, you'll notice a check box on one of the wizard pages that will call up a terminal window. Select it. The ISP should be able to provide instructions.

11 Troubleshooting

In This Chapter

- Troubleshooting Overview
- Obtaining Assistance
- Boot Floppies
- Basic Repairs That Might Help (And Couldn't Hurt)
- Diagnosing System Crashes and Lockups
- Remote Troubleshooting
- Troubleshooting Printing Problems
- Access Denied (2000 and XP only)
- The Windows Registry
- Windows Repair Utilities and Procedures
- Rescuing a Wet Laptop
- A Final Comment
- Practical Troubleshooting Tables

TROUBLESHOOTING OVERVIEW

So, you have a computer with a problem. Where do you start? Sometimes, that answer is obvious. If you have a machine that won't power on, the first thing to check is if the power is connected. Then, check the power supply. Is the voltage switch set correctly? Is the power supply on-off switch in the on position? If the answer to these is yes, the next thing to do is try a known good power supply. If that works, you have found the problem. Occasionally, that won't work either, but then you have reason to suspect a bad motherboard; there aren't too many other possibilities.

More often, however, the source of the problem won't be so obvious, or it will seem obvious, but nothing you try works. While experience helps more than anything else, there are certain principles and concepts that ease the job of diagnosing a computer.

All Might Not Be What It Seems

All might not be what it seems. The best example of this is when the computer locks up, as discussed in Chapter 9, "Input Devices." Many people see that the pointer freezes and assume that their mouse just broke. They buy a new mouse, and unless the computer locks up immediately, they think the problem is solved. Here's what happened to me on two laptops. The machines wouldn't go into standby or hibernation, and attached printers stopped printing. In every case, the error messages blamed the problem on the driver of an item that was working normally: in one case, it was the keyboard driver; in another, a COM port driver; in the third, a network adapter driver. The problem, however, had nothing to do with these drivers. In fact, keyboard and COM port drivers rarely, if ever, exhibit any problems. The problem in each case turned out to be the recent installation of a USB device: a scanner, a Web cam, and a hard drive. Even with the device disconnected, the mere presence of one of these drivers in the system caused these problems. Uninstalling the drivers, and in the case of the Web cam, removing every vestige of the software, solved the problem. The oddest thing is that all three of the USB devices worked perfectly.

So, to repeat the question, how do you know where to start? For those who work in technical support for certain notorious hardware and software companies, the answer is anywhere but with their product. However, if you're trying to find the real reason, the first thing you'll have to accept is that a given problem could be caused by almost any component in a system. Therefore, the troubleshooting procedure should start with the most likely culprit and then proceed to the next most likely once the most likely has been ruled out. If nothing is obvious, there are other ways to find the problem, which we discuss throughout this chapter.

TIP

There comes a point at which it is not worthwhile to diagnose a problem, such as when you'll be spending more time and/or money than the computer is worth, or when it would be easier to simply back up the data, if desired, format the hard drive, reinstall the OS and programs, and restore the data.

Basic Troubleshooting Rules

There are basic rules to follow when troubleshooting:

Make only one change at a time: If you make more than one change at a time, you won't know which change solved the problem. If a change you made didn't help, undo the change before trying the next one.

Record all changes: It can be very difficult to remember all the changes you've made, especially if you've tried several. There's no sense in repeating changes; and if you haven't solved the problem and need to turn the machine over to another technician, the machine should be the same as when you got it.

Keep a record of all error messages: We discuss error messages later in this chapter.

Seek assistance: Others might have experience with the problem you are having. Ask colleagues. Look on the manufacturer's or developer's Web site for their knowledge base or *frequently asked questions* (*FAQs*), or call the company. In many cases, there is a simple fix or software patch to solve your problem. You can also search the Internet for the problem; in many cases, there are forums where people post problems and others give recommended solutions. You can find tips on obtaining tech support later in this chapter.

ON THE CD See the Industry Contacts document on the accompanying CD-ROM for a list of helpful Web sites.

Questions to Ask

There is a series of questions to ask when you begin to troubleshoot a problem:

Is there an error message or beep code? We discuss error messages and beep codes later in this chapter.

Had the computer been physically moved just before the problem started? When a computer is moved, cables often become disconnected, including the power cord. If the computer has been moved from one place to another and the case sustains enough shock, internal components can become partially or fully dislodged.

Were any changes made to the computer just before the problem surfaced? These changes include configuration changes, or installation or uninstallation of hardware or software.

Diagnostic Tools

Thankfully, trial and error isn't the only way to diagnose a problem. Many hardware- and software-based tools exist to let you know what is wrong. Many of these were discussed in previous chapters. A few others are described here:

CheckIt (*smithmicro.com/checkit*): There is a series of programs designed to help you diagnose and fix PC problems. The most relevant title is *CheckIt Professional*, which has a battery of tests for just about every aspect of the computer. Additionally, it has professional features such as the capability of running from a bootable floppy. This is similar to Micro 2000's Micro-Scope. CheckIt offers a POST card as well.

AMI Diag (*ami.com*): This is very similar to CheckIt Professional.

Diagnostic Utilities from Hardware Manufacturers: Many computers come with their own diagnostic utilities. For example, HPDiag comes with Hewlett-Packard computers and some other HP products.

Norton SystemWorks (*norton.com* or *symantec.com*): This is a set of programs including Norton Anti-Virus and Norton Utilities. Norton Utilities has a set of tools that can be used to solve hard drive and other problems. It is a useful program, but one of its main features, the capability of running in the background to prevent problems, can be troublesome. There was a case in which a user found that he had only 3GB of space left just one day after having 24GB left, but Windows showed no evidence of additional files. It turned out that a program he ran was creating and deleting 1GB temporary files, and a feature of Norton Utilities, Delete Protect, was rescuing these temporary files from deletion. The user finally found the files in the Norton Recycle Bin. In fact, if you encounter a computer with an inexplicably small amount of remaining hard drive space, and the computer is running Norton Utilities, check the Norton Recycle Bin. Of course, the anti-virus program is particularly important (see Chapter 2, "System Configuration and Computer Hygiene," for more information on viruses). Norton and others even have a program that can "unformat," possibly saving data from a drive that has been formatted.

Registry cleaners: There are many other registry-cleaning utilities available, most of which work with all versions of Windows. A notable one is RegCleaner™, available free from *jv16.org*.

McAfee QuickClean™: This is a program that performs several very useful functions. It removes unnecessary files, cleans unused registry entries, and removes unwanted programs.

Information-gathering Utilities

There are also utilities designed simply to obtain information from your computer. This information includes installed hardware and software and even some software registration codes. Again, some of these were discussed in previous chapters:

System Information: Available from Start > Programs (or All Programs) > Accessories > System Tools, this applet provides a comprehensive report of many aspects of the computer. Figure 11.1 shows a System Information report.

Belarc Advisor: Belarc is a great program that can be used to get a wealth of very useful information from a computer. Download free from *belarc.com*, but note that Belarc's license allows personal use of Belarc Advisor only; it is not licensed for any commercial purpose. Therefore, use it only on your own personal computers.

Norton SystemWorks: This has an information-gathering program.

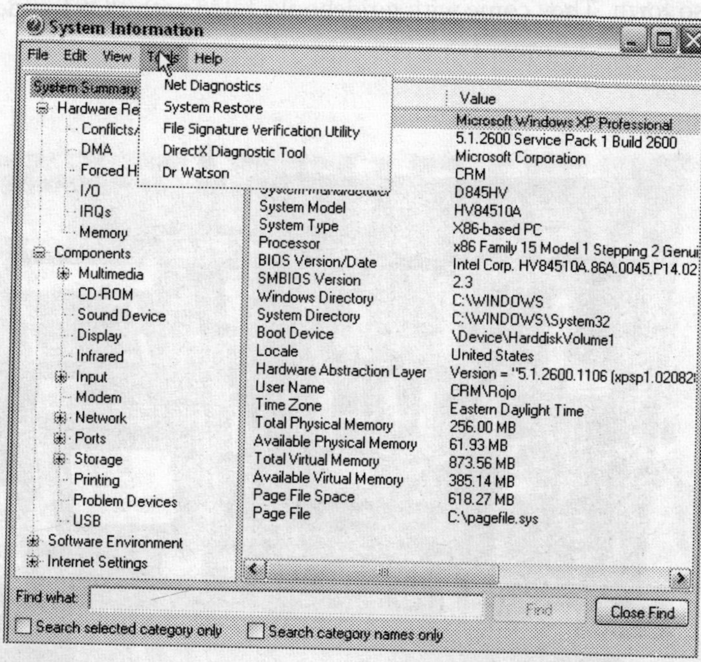

FIGURE 11.1 A sample System Information report on Windows XP. Note the open Tools menu.

Two Excellent Diagnostic Programs

PC Certify (*pccertify.com*) and the Micro-Scope diagnostic program by Micro 2000 (*micro2000.com*) are useful in many ways. They operate by using their own proprietary OSs that bypass DOS and Windows problems. Their OSs read the system hardware and report a complete list of information that can help to diagnose the PC. They can also run hundreds of tests on components such as memory, video, hard drives, floppy drives, and CD drives. They will also help to determine if you have hardware conflicts, and will allow you to see which IRQs are being used and which are available so you can get things straightened out. They also can be used to perform a low-level format and a secure wipe (complete erasure) of a hard drive. They are useful in running burn-in tests and creating a report of the results. A *burn-in test* is a series of individual tests run over a course of several hours for the purpose of certifying a newly built computer.

POST cards are available from each company (Micro 2000's is shown in Figure 11.2). They are used when a system will no longer boot up or run the diagnostic software. They will help in determining the cause of a dead system and can tell you whether the problem lies in memory, processor, a PCI or ISA slot, video system, and so forth. They come with guidebooks filled with POST codes for most BIOSs.

FIGURE 11.2 The Micro 2000 POST card.

The guidebooks list the meaning of each code and provide recommended solutions. They are big time savers and can eliminate many hours that would be spent swapping components.

Many other companies make products designed to perform the same functions. They range in price and vary from slight to great in their abilities to diagnose different problems.

The biggest advantage to this type of software and a POST card is that you can rule out or correct hardware issues before you try to deal with software issues. For example, if you are installing a new component and are having trouble with it, you can first see if the component is defective. You can then see if it needs to have jumpers changed, if applicable. Afterward, you can go ahead and troubleshoot the software and driver issues. You can see that this process will save you lots of time compared with installing and uninstalling drivers and software over and over again when the problem was hardware related all along.

TIP

It is a good idea if you do this type of work on a regular basis to have tools such as these available so you can get the problems diagnosed quickly and cost-effectively. If you are just an occasional hobbyist, then you might find that swapping components and trial and error are just fine for you.

OBTAINING ASSISTANCE

As covered elsewhere in this book, obtaining assistance is crucial to effective and timely repair. There are two categories of assistance sources: manufacturers and information sharing groups.

Manufacturers

This includes hardware manufacturers, software developers, ISPs, and any organization that provides a product or service that you are troubleshooting. Help can be available in any form, including telephone support, live chat, e-mail, Usenet newsgroups, Web page form submission that leads to various types of responses, and others. Manufacturers prefer that their customers use self-service help such as FAQ pages and knowledge base searches, and often, this provides the information you need. A *knowledge base* is a collection of articles providing all information made available by a manufacturer. Many businesses force you to try self-service support before they supply contact information. This is usually reasonable, because some people will ask questions the answers to which are easily found in the product's documentation. With some other companies, however, important information is nowhere to be found; self-service support pages contain nothing but a rehash of the product's inadequate help files; and even if you can locate contact information, getting personalized support is about as easy as having your teeth pulled. Some other companies are easy to contact but often provide useless or incorrect information, and still others give you the runaround either because of incompetence or because they apparently hope you'll just go away. Fortunately, there are enough businesses that make good quality products and provide good or excellent support, that there is usually no need to buy from the bad ones.

TIP *When visiting a Web page, you'll almost always find assistance under the "Support" heading.*

Some support is free of charge, especially under warranty, but some requires payment. Charges can be prohibitive. For example, one company charges $25 to troubleshoot an out-of-warranty inkjet printer, and there is no guarantee that the printer will work when you're done. With the cost of these printers so low today, you're usually better off buying a new printer, even if that means you've just wasted $60 on new ink cartridges. We discuss printer troubleshooting later in this chapter.

Knowledge Base Searches

The best way to search a knowledge base, and for that matter, the Internet, is to use few keywords to start with. Do not use "and," "or," "the," and so forth. If you get too many responses, you can narrow the search with exact phrases. (Here you can use the aforementioned small words.) If you get too few responses, or none at all, broaden the search with fewer keywords. Also realize that many sites' search engines don't work well. Sometimes you won't get anything no matter how you search.

To reach Microsoft's Knowledge Base, go to *http://support.microsoft.com.* Advanced searches can be very helpful. Click Advanced Search in the upper left-hand corner. You'll have options such as specifying the Microsoft product, searching for any of the words, all of the words, or the exact phrase, among others. Despite the fact that Microsoft's Knowledge Base has literally hundreds of thousands of articles, there will still be situations in which you can't find what you're looking for.

TIP *Microsoft numbers its Knowledge Base articles with six-digit numbers. To search for a specific article, go to* http://support.microsoft.com, *click the Knowledge Base Article ID Number Search link under the Search the Knowledge Base link, and enter the article number in the box. In case this page changes, you should be able to find instructions on the support page.*

Microsoft's Knowledge Base as well as other companies' knowledge bases are full of articles about hardware devices identified by brand and model number, or by chipsets, that have problems when used with certain versions of Windows or programs. If the problem could be related to hardware, it is a good idea to identify the device in the search dialog.

Searching for Error Messages

Perhaps the most important category of items to search for is the error message. Often, error messages are identified by numbers, but provide either cryptic descriptions or no descriptions at all. Therefore, the only way to find out what they mean is by searching the Internet or a particular site's knowledge base. Try searching on the manufacturer's Web site first, and try in different ways until you get a useful response. For example, if you get the message "Internal error 46," you could try searching for the full message text or just the number. You could also try searching for "error" or "error messages," and hopefully you'll get a list of error messages or a place to search for the specific message. Sometimes you won't find any information, but often you will. If you find nothing, search for the full text of the message on a search engine such as Google (*google.com*). It is usually helpful to use the search engine's advanced search function and select to search for the exact phrase. If you do, however, it is crucial not to make any typos; if you make even one typo, you might not get any hits.

TIP

To make it easier to copy the exact text of error messages, as long as the computer is booted to Windows and is still running, you can use the <Print Screen> key. This key does not print directly; see Chapter 9 for instructions on its use.

To search for Microsoft error messages, go to *support.microsoft.com*, click *Advanced Search and Help*, select the product, or select *All Microsoft products* if you're not sure, enter the message verbatim (unfortunately, you probably won't be able to copy and paste the message), select the exact phrase search type, and then click the arrow. Also follow these guidelines if you get a "blue screen of death," officially known as a stop error. For more information on stop errors, see Chapter 2.

Tips for Obtaining Personalized Assistance

It will be extremely helpful to follow these simple guidelines to get effective assistance.

- Before you seek assistance, write down everything you want to ask.
- Call the support desk if you can. Although fewer and fewer companies offer free telephone support, especially out of warranty, some companies still do. However, it is rarely a good idea to pay for telephone support because the rates are often between $35 and $200 per problem.
- Have access to the system when you call.
- Be polite. Whether or not you think support personnel know what they're talking about, let them think you think they do. They will be more willing to help and escalate the problem to supervisors if necessary.

- Always provide as much information as possible, especially when e-mailing. For example, writing "My sound doesn't work" isn't particularly helpful. Identify your exact OS version, your hardware (such as computer or motherboard model number, processor speed, amount of memory, and model of hardware that pertains to your question), and any other piece of information you think might be pertinent. Also include information about what happened when the problem first occurred, what changes you made, if any, before the problem occurred, the steps you have taken to resolve the problem, and so forth. Many times, you'll have to fill out a Web form with this information. Even if the form asks for information that you're sure couldn't possibly pertain to your problem, answer these anyway, because leaving out the information will only delay the answer.
- Expect to answer questions you've already answered. Support personnel always seem to ask you for information that you provided earlier. Just tell them again. Don't make an issue about it; doing so will only delay assistance.

Information-sharing Groups

These often take the form of *Usenet newsgroups*, or other similar forums on Web pages. Some, such as Microsoft's public newsgroups, are monitored by experts, and some aren't. There is no guarantee that anyone will respond to a particular post, and there is also no guarantee that information provided will be accurate or useful. Despite these limitations, however, you can often get the help you need from these groups.

There are many Web pages with articles and forums that are searchable from Web search pages such as Google. Frame your topic as succinctly as possible and click the Search button. Very often, you'll find some useful information.

ON THE CD

See the Industry Contacts document on the accompanying CD-ROM.

BOOT FLOPPIES

When a computer can't boot, a boot floppy is often the only way to get access to the hard drive to troubleshoot and repair the system. Boot disks for 9x allow you only to get to DOS, but you'll have access to any FAT or FAT 32 hard drive on the system. Boot disks for XP/2000 can be used only to boot to Windows.

9x/DOS Boot Disks

When you install Windows 9x, you are prompted to create a boot floppy. If you don't have one, find a 9x computer that works and create one. With a blank floppy in the drive, go to Control Panel > Add/Remove Programs, and click the Windows

Setup tab. Then, click the boot disk tab. Follow the simple instructions for making a disk.

You can also make a disk using DOS, but it won't have all the features that a Windows boot disk has. For Windows 98SE and previous versions, you can format a floppy using the option to copy system files. Alternatively, from a DOS prompt you can use the command *format a:/s*. This is useful anytime you need a bootable floppy with extra room for other programs or drivers.

You should have one for each version of 9x, but a different version's disk will often work in a pinch. The exception to this is that boot disks for 95 might not be able to access FAT 32 hard drives.

NOTE *Although you will be able to start up any PC with a Windows 9x boot disk, you won't be able to access an NTFS-formatted hard drive partition. Therefore, unless you have a 2000 or XP computer with a FAT 16 or FAT 32 partition you need to access, a 9x boot disk isn't going to do you much good on these systems.*

XP/2000 Boot Disks

Boot disks for XP and 2000 are different. There is no provision in 2000 or XP to create a boot disk. A boot disk will work only if Windows system files are intact. The most common reasons you might need to make a boot disk are if something happens to the Master Boot Record (MBR), or the disk configuration has been changed. In the latter situation, the problem is that one of the files, Boot.ini, points to the wrong partition for the boot files. In this case, you'll have to edit another boot.ini file to make the boot disk work, and then you'll need to edit the boot.ini file on the computer to correct the problem and enable Windows to boot normally. See the note after the tutorial for more information. You can make a boot disk on any XP or 2000 computer, or even a Windows NT 4.0 system. Tutorial 11.1 provides instructions for making an XP/2000 boot floppy.

TUTORIAL 11.1 MAKING AN XP/2000 BOOT FLOPPY

1. On any 2000, XP, or Windows NT 4.0 computer, format a floppy disk. Do this by inserting the disk, opening My Computer, right-clicking the floppy drive icon, and clicking Format from the menu that appears. Do not select the Quick Format check box.
2. Double-click to open the disk partition where the boot files are stored, the C: drive by default.
3. If hidden files aren't already showing, click the Tools menu and then Folder Options from the menu that appears. Click the View tab.

4. Look for and select the Show Hidden Files and Folders option button. In addition, make sure the "Hide protected operating system files (Recommended)" check box is cleared. It is also helpful to clear the "Hide file extensions for known file types" check box.
5. Locate the following files and copy them to the floppy disk: boot.ini, ntldr, and ntdetect.com. To copy the files, right-click each, click "Send to" from the menu that appears, and then click 3½ Floppy (A).

NOTE

This boot disk will work only if the disk configuration of the computer you're making the boot disk on is the same as the computer you need to start; for example, if there is only one disk partition on each machine. If the disk configurations are different, you'll have to edit the boot.ini file in Notepad. That exercise is beyond the scope of Part I of this book. Search the Internet for editing boot.ini. A good selection of useful boot disk files can be found at bootdisk.com. There is also a Web site, http://www.nu2.nu/bootdisk/ntboot/index.php, where you can copy or even download a boot.ini file that is purported to be all-purpose. We find that it sometimes works. If the name of the folder with the Windows files is different than the one in the boot.ini file, you'll have to change it. The two default possibilities are "Windows" and "Winnt."

BASIC REPAIRS THAT MIGHT HELP (AND COULDN'T HURT)

There are certain simple things to try with a malfunctioning computer that can save a great deal of time if they work:

- Check for power.
- Reboot (after removing the floppy).
- If the computer is locked up, you'll have to turn off the power, wait 30 seconds, and turn it back on. On ATX systems, which have a soft power switch, holding down the power button for at least four seconds will almost always shut the computer off.
- Boot from a boot floppy.
- Reinstall or roll back a device driver.
- Reseat expansion cards.
- Disconnect and reconnect connections.
- Clean adapter card contacts with a pencil eraser.
- Replace the power supply.
- Run ScanDisk and Defrag.
- Check Windows Device Manager.
- Check for a software patch or update.

DIAGNOSING SYSTEM CRASHES AND LOCKUPS

Virtually all PCs lock up at one time or another, 9x more than 2000 and XP. Also unpleasantly common is the "near lockup," in which the mouse pointer still moves, but nothing else works. If the mouse and keyboard are of the PS/2 variety, check to make sure they are connected to the correct ports and that no pins are bent. Make sure the heat sink and fan are properly mounted on the CPU. Check the air intake and other fans, and the operating temperature. Use a laser thermometer such as the Raytek to check the processor temperature, and/or a hard drive temperature-monitoring program such as SIGuardian™ (*siguardian.com*). Check the system resource use as discussed in Chapter 2. If there are too many programs running, close them and see if the system runs better. If it does, follow the instructions in Chapter 2 to resolve the problem. Also, scan for viruses and malware. Run ScanDisk & Defrag. If Windows or applications have been recently upgraded, consider adding memory.

Shorted out parts can also cause lockups. If all other attempts fail, you can use a program such as Micro-Scope to diagnose the problem, or you might have to remove all expansion cards and then add one at a time until the computer locks up. Cables can also short, so check the cables and power supply. If you don't have a tester, you'll have to swap all the cables and power supply for known good units.

REMOTE TROUBLESHOOTING

You might find yourself in the position of having to troubleshoot a computer but traveling to it is impractical or impossible. Remote Desktop and Remote Assistance are two features that can make remote troubleshooting possible by actually placing another desktop on your own either through the Internet or a private network. PCAnywhere™ from *Symantec.com* is an excellent program for this purpose and is much more reliable than the Windows features. Another nice feature is that it can be configured to work from behind a firewall if one or both users have a router or firewall set up. Remote Desktop is a program that comes with XP. You can install it on other Windows computers by using the XP installation CD-ROM. When the main page appears, click Perform additional tasks, then Set up Remote Desktop connection, and follow the prompts.

Remote Assistance, which is basically the same, is available on Windows Messenger (XP only), or on NetMeeting™ (in any version with NetMeeting installed, type "conf" in the Run dialog). Search the Windows Help files for more information. NetMeeting, however, is often unreliable.

Some tips on troubleshooting:

- Any time troubleshooting becomes too time-consuming, or if the problem resists all efforts to solve it, it is best to back up the data, format the hard drive, reinstall Windows and the programs, and then restore the data.
- If you run a virus scan and find any Klez or Elkern viruses in the System and/or System32 folders, chances are the system is damaged beyond repair. Reinstall the system as described previously. However, Panda Software (*pandasoftware.com*) has repair utilities available that might help so the system can be repaired instead of redone.
- If you intend to format the hard drive and reinstall the system from scratch, and you don't have driver disks for all the hardware, it is a good idea to run an information-gathering utility that lists hardware, as discussed earlier in this chapter, and print a report. This way, if Windows doesn't recognize some of the installed hardware, you'll have a much easier time finding drivers.
- If you are upgrading Windows, instead of running the upgrade disc from within the previous version, it often is a better idea to back up the data, format the hard drive, and run a clean install from the upgrade disk. This is especially advisable if you're upgrading Windows Me. While installing Windows, you'll be prompted to insert the disk from the version of Windows that was previously installed on the computer. Make sure you have it handy.

TROUBLESHOOTING PRINTING PROBLEMS

Printing problems are very common, yet the fixes are usually not difficult. The main applet in Windows to configure a printer is called the Printers folder, except in XP where it's called "Printers and Faxes." Access the Printers folder by clicking it in My Computer, if it's there; in Start > Settings > Printers in most versions; in Control Panel in all versions; and in Start > Printers and Faxes in XP without the classic Start menu. You should see a folder containing an icon for each installed printer and fax program. Figure 11.3 shows a sample from Windows 2000.

If you double-click the icon for a specific printer, you'll call up the print queue for that printer. A *print queue* is a queue of all documents waiting to be printed by that printer. Figure 11.4 shows a sample print queue.

The Printer and Document menus contain some useful commands, notably Pause Printing and Cancel All Documents in the Printer menu, and Pause, Resume, Restart, and Cancel in the Document menu. To use the Document menu commands, you must highlight the document in the print queue.

TIP

On 9x, attempts to pause or cancel printing usually take a long time to work, and are not worthwhile to use unless the document has many pages to go. If you try this and it says Deleting in the Status column, but nothing changes, you'll just have to wait for it. Don't turn off the power to the printer; you'll just cause more problems.

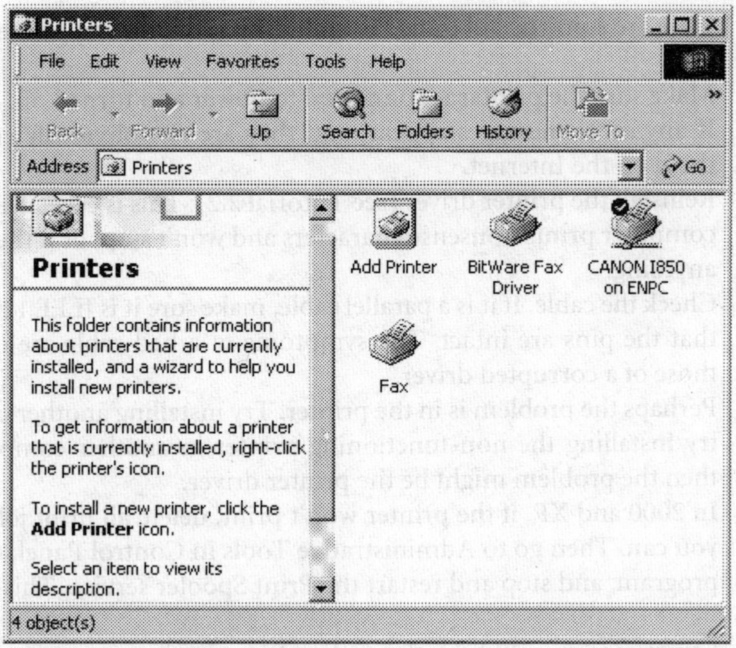

FIGURE 11.3 The Printers folder.

The other important location is Printer Properties, accessible by clicking the Properties command in the print queue's Printer menu, or by right-clicking the printer icon in the Printers folder and clicking Properties from the menu that appears. Use the Print Test Page button for a good test as to whether the printer is working. Other pages in the printer's properties vary based on the specific model of printer installed.

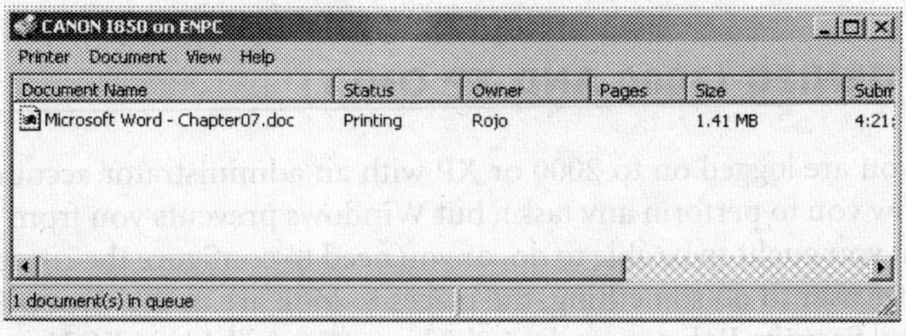

FIGURE 11.4 A print queue.

Here are some useful things to check if you are having printer problems:

- Make sure the printer is connected to power and turned on.
- If any error messages appear, and they are not obviously correct, search for them on the Internet.
- Reinstall the printer driver (see Tutorial 2.2). This is especially applicable if the computer prints nonsense characters and won't stop, or if the printer won't do anything.
- Check the cable. If it is a parallel cable, make sure it is IEEE 1284 compliant and that the pins are intact. The symptoms of a bad cable are often the same as those of a corrupted driver.
- Perhaps the problem is in the printer. Try installing another one. If that works, try installing the non-functioning printer in another computer. If it works, then the problem might be the printer driver.
- In 2000 and XP, if the printer won't print, delete all print jobs in the queue if you can. Then go to Administrative Tools in Control Panel, open the Services program, and stop and restart the Print Spooler service. This usually works.

Sometimes, a problem with another driver on the system causes the printer not to work. This seems to happen occasionally when USB devices are installed on certain laptops. Check to see if any new hardware devices have been installed. Try uninstalling the drivers of the new device and then attempting to print. Make sure that any program that is part of the new hardware is uninstalled, or at least not running. If printing resumes, you'll have to troubleshoot the problem related to the new hardware.

TIP

Printer inkjet cartridges should be replaced only if the printing becomes faint, if colors are missing, or if the printer software reports low ink. Consider carefully whether you want to replace ink cartridges in old printers to get them to work. If the printer still doesn't work and you decide on a new one, you won't be able to return the open cartridges.

ACCESS DENIED (2000 AND XP ONLY)

If you are logged on to 2000 or XP with an administrator account (which should allow you to perform any task), but Windows prevents you from doing something that you ought to be able to do, or you need to configure the computer to allow another user to do something, the places to look are in the Group Policy Editor and Local Security Policy consoles (which are not available in XP Home), in addition to the security settings for users, groups, folders, and files. It often requires entire books or courses for users to learn these tools completely, but you should be able to view these and make basic changes without all that studying. Search the help files for these items, or consult an appropriate *Microsoft Certified Systems Engineer* (*MCSE*) certification book.

To open the Group Policy Editor, type "gpedit.msc" in the Run dialog. Access the Local Security Policy console from Administrative Tools in Control Panel.

NOTE *If there is nothing in either local policy or group policy prohibiting an activity but the activity is still being prevented, you might have to consult Microsoft support. For example, after one laptop was upgraded from 98 to 2000, even the administrator was prevented from creating new Internet connections. None of the policies prevented this, but some arcane setting in the registry that only a Microsoft support technician could find, did.*

THE WINDOWS REGISTRY

The *registry* is a database that stores every changeable piece of information related to Windows, including hardware and software configuration. In 9x, it is stored in two files, system.dat and user.dat. In 2000 and XP, the registry is stored in a series of files. Every change that a user or a program makes is stored in the registry. For this reason, the registry is delicate. Make one wrong move and your computer can become unbootable. Microsoft warns you over and over again that they bear no responsibility for a registry-editing mistake, even if they tell you what changes to make. They insist that every change can be made in a safer place, such as Control Panel. This is absolutely not true. If you search Microsoft's Web site for solutions to problems, you'll find that often, the registry is the only place to make certain changes and to correct certain problems. If the registry never needed to be modified directly, Microsoft wouldn't provide a registry editor with every installation, which, of course, they do.

Backing Up the Registry

It is highly advisable to back up the registry before editing so that incorrect changes can be undone. The registry is automatically backed up every time the system is booted, but you can't always depend on this being successful. Instructions are provided here and later in this chapter. It is possible to back up portions or the entire registry.

Windows 9x Registry Backups

There are a few different ways to back up the registry in 9x. One way starts with booting into DOS. You might recall that you can do this in 95/98 by selecting to reboot into DOS in the shutdown menu. You can also use a boot floppy (this is the only way to do this in Me). The same procedure can also be done by booting into Safe Mode, Command Prompt Only, which you do by pressing F8 at the beginning of booting and making the appropriate selection. Once you get a command prompt, navigate to the Windows folder if you're not already there. (If you get a C:\> prompt, type "CD Windows" and then press <Enter>. If you get an A:\> prompt, type "C:\", press <Enter>, and then type "CD Windows" and then press <Enter> again.) Once you have reached the C:\>WINDOWS prompt, type the following, pressing <Enter> after each line:

```
attrib -r -h -s system.dat
attrib -r -h -s user.dat
copy system.dat *bu
copy user.dat *.bu
```

Then, restart the computer. See Chapter 13, "Command-Line Tutorial," for a tutorial on using commands in MS-DOS. The *attrib* command changes the attributes of the file. The minus sign turns off each attribute; *r* represents the read only attribute; *h*, the hidden; and *s* means system. This is necessary in order to do anything with these files. The copy command is self-explanatory—these commands are making copies of the two files and naming them System.bu and User.bu.

NOTE

Windows names the automatically backed up registry files System.da0 and User.da0. These final characters are zeros.

To restore these backups, get to the C:\>WINDOWS prompt as described in the backup instructions and type the following, again pressing <Enter> at the end of each line:

```
attrib -r -h -s system.dat
attrib -r -h -s system.da0
attrib -r -s -h user.dat
attrib -r -s -h user.da0
ren system.dat system.daa
ren system.da0 system.da1
ren user.dat user.daa
ren user.da0 user.da1
copy system.bu system.dat
copy user.bu user.dat
```

Then, restart the computer (*ren* is the rename command). If you need to restore the automatic backup in 95 (it *should* be handled automatically by 98 and Me), type the following, pressing <Enter> after each line:

```
attrib -h -r -s system.dat
attrib -h -r -s system.da0
attrib -h -r -s user.dat
attrib -h -r -s user.da0
copy system.da0 system.dat
copy user.da0 user.dat
```

Then, restart the computer.

There are utilities you can use to back up the registry. On the Windows 95 installation disc is a utility called ERU in the Other\Misc\ERU folder. Run the program from the CD-ROM and follow the prompts. For more information, search the Microsoft Knowledge Base for Article 139437 entitled "Windows 95 Emergency Recovery Utility."

Windows 98 and Me have a utility called the Registry Checker. This is actually a combination of two program files. Scanreg.exe runs only in DOS, while Scanregw.exe runs in both DOS and Windows. Registry Checker runs automatically and, if it discovers no registry problems, makes a new backup of the registry every day in which the computer is successfully booted. If it finds problems, it will attempt to restore the backup automatically, and if that proves unsuccessful, Registry Checker will attempt to repair the registry. You can run scanregw in either the Run dialog or from a command prompt. For more information on Registry Checker and other information about the 9x registry, search the Microsoft Knowledge Base for "Chapter 31—Windows 98 Registry."

Instructions on backing up and restoring the entire registry in 2000 and XP appear later in this chapter. Because backing up portions of the registry is done with the registry editor, we'll discuss partial backups with the editor next.

The Registry Editor: Regedit.exe (All Versions)

Regedit is available only by typing "regedit" in the Run dialog or at a Windows command prompt. Open the editor and take a look. You'll see that the registry has five keys: *HKEY_CLASSES_ROOT, HKEY_CURRENT_USER, HKEY_LOCAL_MACHINE, HKEY_USERS*, and *HKEY_CURRENT_CONFIG*, shown in Figure 11.5.

A *key* is like a *root folder* in Windows. It is the highest item in the hierarchy. Click the plus sign next to any of the keys and the next level of the hierarchy becomes visible (see Figure 11.5). These are called *subkeys*, just as folders inside other folders are called subfolders. The last subkeys in the hierarchy have values (called *Name* in the editor), and some of the values have data, as you can see in Figure 11.6.

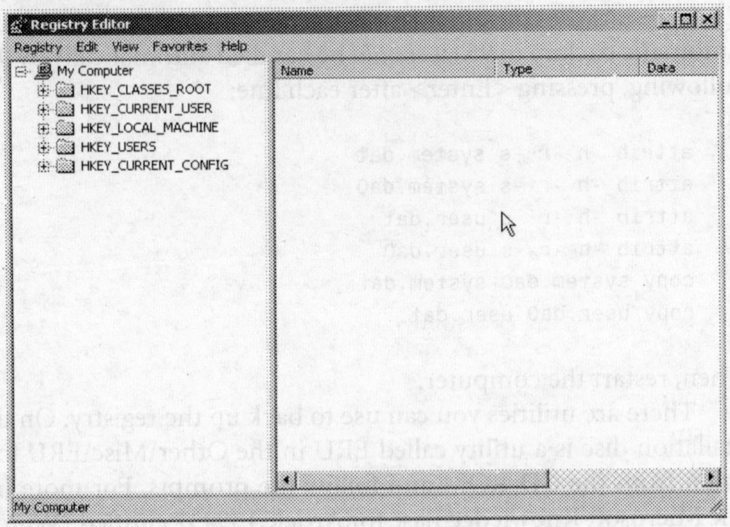

FIGURE 11.5 The registry has five keys.

The other column, labeled *Type*, refers to the type of data (REG_SZ,REG_DWORD, etc.). Data types aren't important for this discussion. Now, look at the bottom of Figure 11.6. This displays the full path to the last subkey you are on.

Editing the registry is very similar to editing any text document. The Edit menu contains straightforward commands, as shown in Figure 11.7. Especially helpful are the Find and Find Next commands. In addition, the basic keyboard shortcuts such

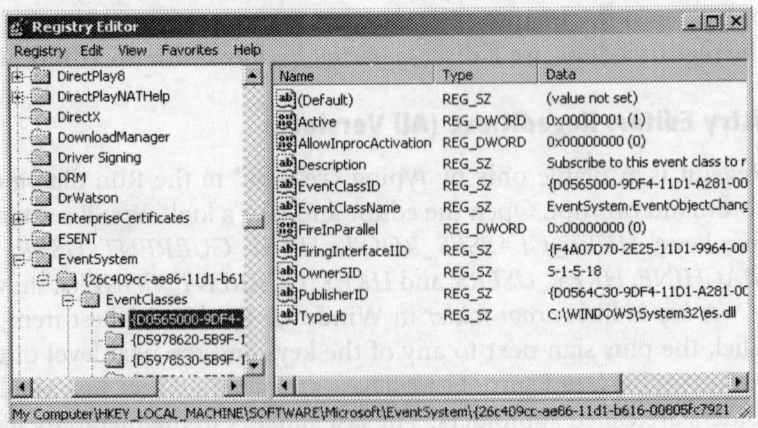

FIGURE 11.6 Keys, values, and data.

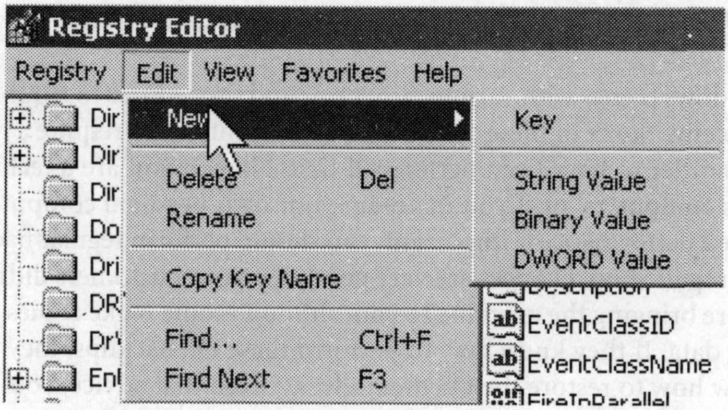

FIGURE 11.7 Regedit's Edit menu.

as <Ctrl> + <C> for copying the selected item work in the registry. For more information, search for "keyboard shortcuts" in Windows Help.

Backing Up and Restoring Registry Keys

Regedit's File menu has two commands for backing up and restoring keys and subkeys. These are the Import Registry File and Export Registry File commands. With a key selected, click the Export command. You can then give the file a name and save it anywhere on the system. Make sure to keep a record of the file's name and location. If you need to restore the file, click the Import command and browse for the file, and click Open when you find it. These commands also give you the opportunity to back up and save the entire registry by selecting the All option button at the bottom of the Export dialog box.

TIP

Unless and until you become experienced with editing the registry, it is recommended to limit editing to exact instructions by Microsoft support personnel and documents.

If you do make a serious mistake editing the registry in 2000 or XP, and you have not backed it up first, you can still restore the registry using the Last Known Good boot option, discussed later in this chapter.

Windows 2000 also has a registry editor called Regedt32.exe (type regedt32 at the Run dialog or command prompt). This looks much like the Sysedit.exe program covered in Chapter 2. It has some important capabilities that regedit doesn't have, although it lacks a Find command. Microsoft recommends using Regedt32 for editing in Windows 2000. For more information on Regedt32, search Windows 2000 Help or the Microsoft Knowledge Base.

WINDOWS REPAIR UTILITIES AND PROCEDURES

Windows comes with various programs and procedures to troubleshoot and repair problems. Some of these can be used at will, but others require a backup of one type or another to have been performed first. Now, if you are a technician who maintains computers, or if you maintain your own personal computers and their continued performance is important, you should perform regular backups. If you work in a repair shop, chances are very good that your customers didn't back up the OS before bringing the machine to you, although some make copies of their important user data. If they knew how to perform these OS backups, they would most likely know how to restore the OS themselves. Given that advice, you'll be able to determine which of the following procedures are most useful to you.

Safe Mode Boot (All Versions)

In the event that Windows is loading some program or device driver that is causing a problem, you can boot into Safe Mode (the system might force you to) and try to fix the problem. Safe Mode loads only essential drivers and programs. In standard Safe Mode, you won't be able to print, get on a network, hear sounds other than beeps, and so forth, but you will be able to make changes in Device Manager, .ini files, and other places. Press <F8> as early in the boot process as possible to get the boot menu from which you can select Safe Mode. In 95/98 you can hold the <Ctrl> key when booting, or you can press <F5> to go directly into Safe Mode in most versions. If you get the boot menu and select Safe Mode with networking support (Me, 2000, and XP only) you can get on the Internet and perform some network functions. This will allow you to copy data to or from the computer or download drivers or other important files from the Internet.

System File Checker (98, 2000, and XP Only)

Microsoft developed this utility for Windows 98, put a different version in 2000 and XP, but inexplicably left it out of Windows Me. System File Checker scans the system files for corruption or unauthorized replacement by rogue programs, and retrieves a correct version from either a special system folder or the Windows installation CD-ROM.

System File Checker (SFC) in Windows 98

In the Run dialog from the Start menu, type "SFC." This invokes the program, as shown in Figure 11.8.

You can go into settings by clicking the button, but the default settings are generally the best. You'll want to be prompted to replace each corrupted file so that if

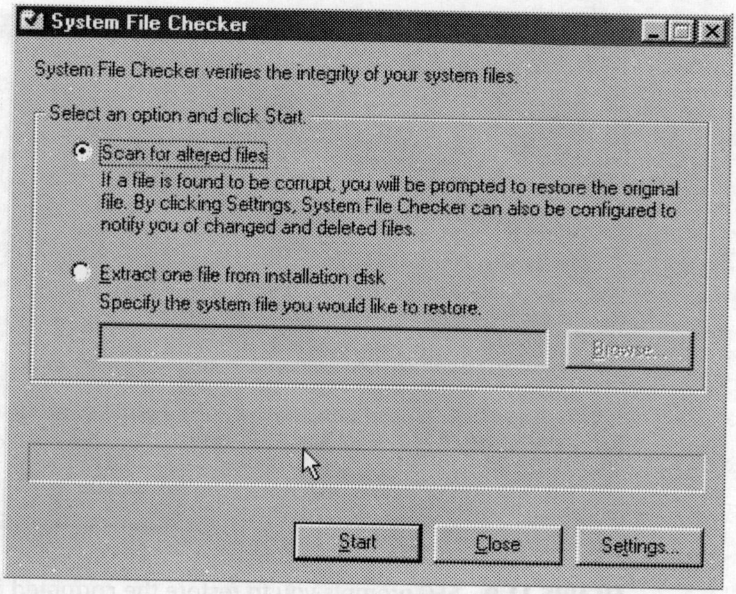

FIGURE 11.8 Windows 98 System File Checker.

the problem appears to be solved, you'll be able to tie the problem to the corruption. Figure 11.9 shows such a prompt.

It is a good idea to run SFC every time you install Windows 98, and any time you have a problem that is not easily corrected. One new Windows 98 computer had a sound problem. The sound either sounded terrible or it didn't work at all. Replacing the sound driver didn't help, but a run of SFC found nine corrupted files. Replacing these files solved the problem permanently.

In most installations of 98 (and 95 as well), there is a system folder whose default path is C:\Windows\Options\Cabs (it is usually C:\Windows\options\install in Me). These contain all of Windows' installation files in a highly compressed state. You might need to navigate to this folder using the Browse button to help SFC find the files to restore. If this folder doesn't exist, you'll have to browse to the Windows 98 folder on the Windows installation CD-ROM.

NOTE

When SFC finds a corrupted file and prompts you to replace it, you will be prompted to make a backup of the original system file. Write down the location where SFC is going to place the backup of the file. You should also limit your folder names to eight characters or fewer here so you can find them in DOS in the event that you must restore the file in a no-boot situation. We suggest you accept the default path offered by SFC to keep things consistent.

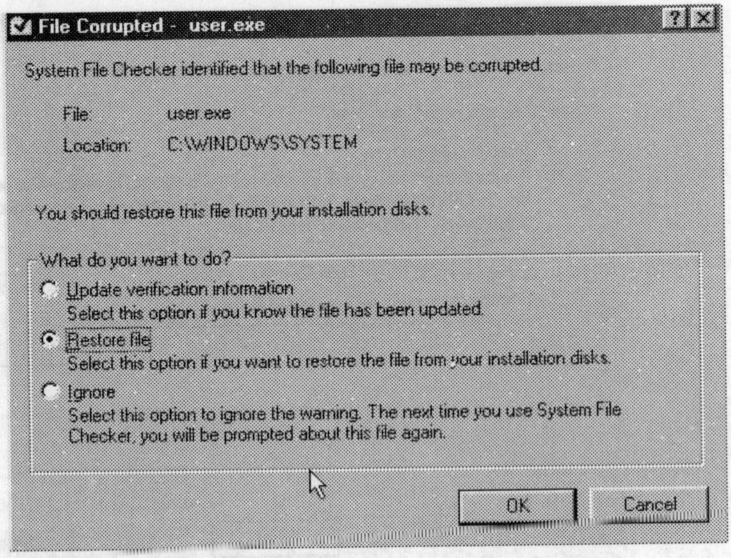

FIGURE 11.9 SFC prompts you to restore the corrupted file.

Extraction of System Files (98 and Me)

Windows Me does have one of the functions of SFC: system file extraction. When you suspect that a particular system file is the cause of a problem, you can use Msconfig in Windows Me to extract the file. When you first open Msconfig (see Chapter 2) you will see the Extract File button near the lower right-hand corner of the window. By clicking here, you can follow the dialog boxes just as you would in Windows 98 SFC. Be sure to make a backup and write down the location of the files just in case the system is unable to boot after you attempt to restart the system.

You can use SFC in Windows 98 without running the file check portion of the program if you know ahead of time just what file you need to replace. You might know this because of a message at boot, or if you get a dialog box or error message when Windows starts indicating that a particular file is not found or is corrupted. Or, you might have been told by a support representative from a component manufacturer to replace a particular file. If this is the case, do so and follow the same steps as you would if you had run SFC and it had found a corrupt file.

Windows 2000 and XP System File Checker

SFC in these versions is a command-line program. It is much less likely to be needed in these systems as compared to 98. Open a command prompt and type "SFC." This will give you the list of command switches shown in Figure 11.10.

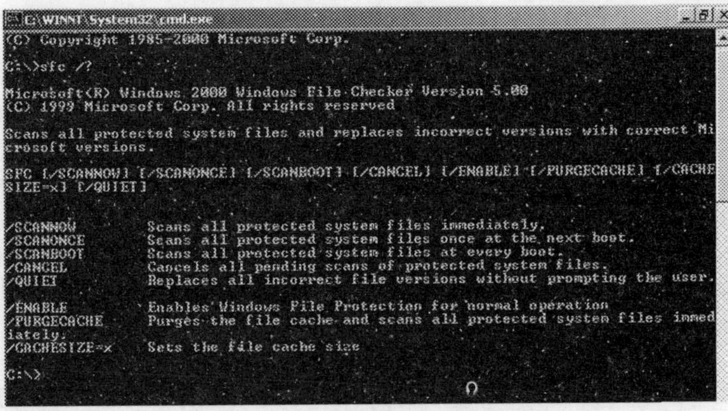

FIGURE 11.10 2000/XP SFC command switches.

Let's say you want to run it now. At the following prompt, type the following:

```
SFC /scannow
```

If you are prompted for the installation CD-ROM, insert it. Then, wait for SFC to work.

Last Known Good Configuration (2000 and XP only)

Each time Windows 2000 and XP boots successfully, it stores a profile of the system in a system folder. If a computer won't boot or develops a serious problem after a change has been made, the next time you attempt to boot, press <F8> and select *Last Known Good Configuration* (*LKG*). If the problem was caused by a change made since the last successful boot, LKG will undo it, along with all other changes made since then.

NOTE *Any time the computer boots successfully, the LKG is reset to the system's current configuration. If you experience a problem after a change, try not to boot the computer again before you invoke LKG. In case the computer boots successfully but the problem is still not solved, the new LKG will include the problem, causing LKG to cease being an effective tool for that problem.*

Windows 9x Registry Repairs

See the Windows 9x Registry section, earlier in this chapter.

Emergency Repair Process (2000 Only)

This process can be especially helpful if you can't boot your computer, as long as your hard drive hasn't failed, in which case the repair process is useless. It is much more useful if you have a very recent *Emergency Repair Disk* (*ERD*) made on the computer in question. Chances are excellent that if you are fixing someone else's computer, you will not have such a recent ERD to use. If you start the Windows Backup program (Start > Programs > Accessories > System Tools > Backup, or by typing "ntbackup" in the Run dialog), and you start in the Welcome screen, you'll see an option for making an ERD. Simply follow the prompts.

To repair the system using the ERD, you'll have to boot either from the four Windows 2000 installation floppies, or from the installation CD-ROM. It is easier to boot from the CD-ROM, as long as the computer supports it. You might have to go into the BIOS to move CD-ROM up in the boot order. If you cannot boot from the CD-ROM and you don't have the installation floppies, you'll have to create the floppies from the CD-ROM. Tutorial 11.2 tells you how.

TUTORIAL 11.2 Creating 2000 Setup Boot Floppies from the CD-ROM

1. Obtain four floppy disks and label each "Windows 2000 Setup Boot Disk." Number them from 1 through 4.
2. Insert the Windows 2000 installation CD-ROM in any Windows computer.
3. The disc will probably start up automatically. If it does, close it. Go to My Computer, right-click the disc, and click Explore from the menu that appears. A Windows Explorer window should appear.
4. Locate and open the Bootdisk folder, usually by double-clicking.
5. If the computer you're using to make the floppies runs Windows 9x, run (usually by double-clicking) the MAKEBOOT program. If you are on 2000 or XP, run the MAKEBT32.exe program.
6. Follow the prompts.

TIP

Installation floppies can be obtained for XP only by download. For information, see Microsoft Knowledge Base Article number 310994.

To use the ERD, boot the computer using either the CD-ROM or the floppies. Go through Setup as if you are installing Windows 2000. Eventually, you'll get to a prompt to set up or repair Windows. Choose R to repair, and follow the prompts, which will include one to insert the ERD. You will be prompted to select manual or fast repair. Manual repair gives you three options:

Inspect Startup Environment: This applies only if the system is a *dual-* or *multiple-boot* system, meaning that you get a choice of different OSs when you boot the computer.

Verify Windows 2000 System Files: Inspects files needed for Windows to boot and run and replaces them if necessary.

Inspect Boot Sector: Inspects and repairs boot sector problems.

Manual repair doesn't give the option to repair the registry, but fast repair does.

Fast repair automatically performs all repair functions, including checking the registry for corruption. If it does find registry corruption, it copies portions from the %systemroot%\Repair\Regback folder (assuming that folder is accessible), where the system keeps the backup registry (*%systemroot%* refers to the main system folder, be it Winnt\System32, or Windows\System32). This registry backup is made automatically when the ERD is made.

If you don't have an ERD, instead of choosing to repair the system, choose to set up Windows. Follow the prompts and you will soon get another prompt to set up or repair. At this point, choose R to repair the system. This will reinstall Windows over the existing installation, hopefully fixing the problems in the process. Have the product key ready in the event you are prompted for it. Most existing settings, and all non-OS files should remain intact.

Reinstalling Windows 9x over an Existing Installation

In the discussion about system file checker, we referred to the folder C:\Windows\Options\Cabs (C:\Windows\Options\Install in Me), which is present in most 9x installations. This folder has another purpose. If you are unable to fix a problem with 9x, navigate to it and locate Setup.exe. Note that the default setting for Windows is not to show known file extensions. You can change this setting by going to Tools: >Folder Options in any Windows folder, clicking the View tab, and clearing the Hide extensions for known file types check box. If you don't want to change the setting, look for the word *Setup* followed by an icon that has a picture of a computer with an open box of disks in front of it (see Figure 11.11).

It is important to know whether the system you are working on was ever upgraded from an earlier version of Windows. If that were the case, then the setup files found in the C:\Windows\Options\Cabs folder might attempt to install an older version of Windows and cause the installation to fail.

Once you have found Setup.exe, run it (usually by double-clicking) and follow the prompts. You might need to input the product key and other information, so

FIGURE 11.11 C:\Windows\Options\Cabs\Setup.exe from Windows 98.

have it ready. It can take anywhere from about 20 minutes to sometimes well over an hour to install Windows depending on the performance of the system. When you are finished, your settings and non-OS files should be intact.

TIP *Make sure the Windows CD-ROM that you use to reinstall Windows is exactly the same version as what is installed in the system. Otherwise, you might get errors or Windows might not allow the installation to continue.*

If your system doesn't have a Cabs or Install folder, you can still reinstall Windows from the installation disc. Insert the disc and follow the prompts to install, or open the disc in My Computer and run Setup.exe. When you are prompted to select the folder directory for the installation, selecting the original, usually C:\Windows, will install Windows over the old version, leaving all your settings intact. If you select a different directory, assuming you have enough disk space, you will cause the original Windows installation to be unusable, and your settings will not be kept. Then, you can delete the folder that contains the original installation.

TIP *It is a very good idea to back up important data files before reinstalling Windows, even when you use procedures that normally leave your files intact.*

If reinstalling the system doesn't solve the problem, you might need to back up the data and downloaded program installation files (not actual program files), format the hard drive, reinstall Windows from scratch, reinstall the programs, and restore the data. If you get to a situation in which diagnosing and correcting problems will take an extraordinary amount of time, or when a computer has significant virus infection, this is usually your best bet. Just make certain not to restore any virus-infected data.

System Restore (Me and XP Only)

System Restore allows you to undo system changes made since the last restore point was created. A *restore point* is a point at which all of Windows' settings are recorded. Multiple restore points can be stored simultaneously. If System Restore is enabled, Windows sets restore points daily and when certain changes are made to the system. The user can also set restore points manually; it is a good idea to do this before installing new hardware or software, or making other significant changes. You would use System Restore to undo changes that you suspect caused problems. This can cause other problems. For example, if you restore to a point before a new program was installed, the program will probably not work correctly or at all afterward, even though all the program's files would be left intact. This is because System Restore removed all the registry entries related to the program. Of course, the new program might have been causing the problem you are using System Restore to fix. The best thing about System Restore is that you can undo a restore. The worst thing about it is that the folder System Restore uses to store the restore point data, entitled "_Restore," can be a receptacle for viruses. The folder is hidden by default, and it is very difficult to delete an individual file in this folder. It is for this reason that some users disable System Restore. See Chapter 2 for advice on deleting infected files from the _Restore folder.

Enabling/Disabling and Accessing System Restore

System Restore is enabled by default. To enable or disable it in Me, go to System Properties (right-click My Computer and select Properties or open the System applet in Control Panel), click the Performance tab, the File System button, and then the Advanced tab, and select or clear the Enable System Restore check box. In XP, go to System Properties and click the System Restore tab. Select or clear the check box. You can also use the slider on this page to set the maximum size of the _Restore folder on this page. Leave it at its maximum setting unless disk space is an issue.

To access System Restore, go to Start: >Programs (or All Programs) > Accessories > System Tools > System Restore. From here, you can set a restore point, restore the system, or undo a restore.

Recovery Console (2000 and XP Only)

The Recovery Console is a command-based system, similar to DOS, but has fewer commands. You can use it to access only the root folder, the Winnt or Windows folder, the Cmdcons folder, and removable media sources such as floppies or CD-ROMs. The Recovery Console is good for replacing missing files, stopping or starting services, formatting drives, and other tasks.

There are two ways to run the Recovery Console.

A. **Run Recovery Console from the Windows Installation CD-ROM:** Boot the computer from the Windows installation CD-ROM, or the 2000 setup boot floppies. At the "Welcome to Setup" screen, press <F10> or press <R>. In XP, you can start the console. In 2000, you'll have to press <C>. Make sure to have the administrator password handy (if one exists).

B. **Install Recovery Console so that it becomes a choice of OSs available at boot:** Insert the Windows Installation CD in the drive, click Start: >Run, and type the following in the box (Substitute the CD-ROM drive letter for D if applicable):

```
D:\i386\winnt32.exe /cmdcons
```

Click OK, and then follow the prompts. Chances are good that installation will fail, but you'll be given a prompt to try it again. Do so, and it will probably work the second time. Reboot the computer and select the number for Recovery Console from the list of OSs.

Once you have started the Recovery Console, you'll be prompted to select the OS to which you want to boot, assuming you have a dual- or multi-boot system, and then you'll be prompted for the administrator password.

Using the Recovery Console

For a helpful tutorial on using Recovery Console commands, see the Recovery Console Commands section in Chapter 13. You can also type "HELP" at the prompt and then press <Enter> for a complete list of commands. You can enter any individual command followed by a space and /? (such as DISABLE /?) to view a brief explanation plus the command's syntax and parameters. Additional helpful information is available in Windows' Help (search for Recovery Console Commands), and on the Microsoft Knowledge Base. The article numbers are 229716 for 2000 and 314058 for XP.

Restoration of System State Data (2000 and XP Only)

System State data consists of the registry files and many OS files. A recent System State data backup on a Windows 2000 machine created a 241MB file. Back up System State data by using Windows Backup (Start: > Run > ntbackup, or Start > Programs (or All Programs) > Accessories > System Tools > Backup). If you use the Backup Wizard, you have the option of backing up the entire or parts of the system, or only the System State data.

NOTE *Windows XP Home Edition does not have the Backup program; however, if you have a retail or OEM copy of XP Home (not a brand name recovery disk), you can install Backup from the disc. Navigate to the VALUEADD\MSFT\NTBACKUP folder on the CD-ROM and double-click the Ntbackup.msi file on the disc to install Backup.*

If there is a recent backup of System State data, restoring it is the next step to take if using the ERD fails. If Windows is still running, open Backup and follow the instructions to restore the System State data. If not, you'll have to reinstall Windows, perhaps on a new hard drive, and then perform the restore.

Automated System Restore (XP Professional Only)

Automated System Restore (ASR) is XP Pro's system for backing up the entire OS, including the System State data. It is done through the Backup program, covered earlier.

NOTE *If Backup is installed on XP Home Edition as described in the previous note, ASR appears to be available. However, it won't work.*

The ASR Wizard re-creates every disk partition on which there are Windows OS components. For this reason, ASR will back up user data on those partitions, even though Microsoft insists that ASR won't back up user data. In a system with one disk partition and XP Pro, ASR should be a valid method for backing up and restoring the entire computer. However, because of Microsoft's warnings, you will probably want to back up user data separately.

The ASR Wizard also creates a floppy that is needed for an ASR restore. An ASR backup includes System State data. Microsoft considers an ASR a last resort.

To create a backup for an ASR, open Backup as described earlier, make sure to be in the Advanced mode, not the Wizard mode, and select the ASR option button. You will need one blank floppy and media for the backup.

ASR Restore

To restore from an ASR backup, boot from an XP Pro CD-ROM as described in the section on the Emergency Repair procedure. When prompted, press <F2> to start the restore process, and follow the prompts. You will be prompted to insert the floppy made during the ASR backup, and the backup media. The restore wizard will format the hard drive before restoring the system.

Backup of All Information on the Computer (XP Pro Only)

If you run Backup in Wizard Mode and run through the wizard, there is a choice to back up "All information on this computer." This is actually a combination of ASR and a full data backup. Just follow the prompts in the wizard. Restore by running Setup from the Windows XP disc and following the prompts to do a restore.

NOTE *Neither the "All information on this computer" nor the ASR backup will work on XP Home. To accomplish a backup and recovery in XP Home, you'll have to install Backup from the Windows disk and do a regular full backup. Then, you'll have to reinstall Windows anew and then restore the backup.*

RESCUING A WET LAPTOP

It is unfortunately common for liquid to be spilled on laptops. Rescuing such a laptop is a dicey proposition. Success depends on a number of factors, such as the type and quantity of liquid spilled, the steps taken after the spill, and how fast those steps were taken. The proper steps to take are immediately disconnecting the power, removing the battery, and turning the machine over. Never try to power on the machine until it has been serviced—doing so will almost guarantee that the computer will be ruined.

To rescue the laptop, disassemble it. There are some instructions for doing this in Chapter 9, but because there is such variation in laptops, you'll probably want to consult the manufacturer's Web page for instructions. You'll find that some manufacturers provide better instructions than others do. IBM and Dell tend to provide detailed disassembly/reassembly instructions. Soak up any remaining liquid with an absorbent material such as paper towels, hold the computer at an angle, and spray liberally with an electronic contact cleaner that is safe for plastics, such as Blow Off Contact Cleaner (*blowoff.com*). Spray every nook and cranny in the machine except inside disk drives. Allow the unit to dry, and then reassemble. Then, reconnect power and attempt to boot. If it doesn't work, it is probably wise to give up, although you should try to connect the hard drive to another machine to back up the data (see Chapter 6, "Magnetic Disk Drives," for more information).

A FINAL COMMENT

Sometimes, all the hardware can be in working order and all the software configured correctly, yet something still doesn't work correctly. It is as if you've fixed everything but Windows doesn't quite realize it. Occasionally in these cases, the problem might go away spontaneously. The point here is that despite all the advancements, computers are still far from perfect. As we said earlier, if diagnosing and fixing a problem is taking more time than it's worth, it is usually best to back up the user data, format the hard drive, and start over again.

PRACTICAL TROUBLESHOOTING TABLES

Tables 11.1 through 11.14 contain common problems and possible solutions.

TABLE 11.1 Dead Computer

Symptom	Check and/or Try
Dead computer (nothing happens when you press the power button).	• Check to make sure the power cable is connected, the outlet strip is plugged in and turned on, and the wall outlet is live. • If there is a UPS with a soft power switch, press it to turn the UPS on. • Check the rear power switch on the power supply if present. • Check the voltage switch on the power supply. Never attempt to power on the computer if the voltage switch is set incorrectly. • Check internal connections. • Check the computer's power switch to make sure it isn't broken.

TABLE 11.2 System Powers On but Won't Boot Properly or at All

Boot Error Messages	Check and/or Try
ntldr missing or non-system disk or disk error, or similar message.	• Remove any removable disks from their drives and restart. • Use a POST card. • Run a diagnostic utility. • Check the BIOS for boot order. • 2000/XP only: In case of recent disk configuration changes, boot with the boot disk. The boot.ini file might need to be edited.
OS not found.	• Check the boot order in BIOS. • The hard drive might be bad. Test with diagnostic utility, hard drive utility, FDISK, Partition Magic Drive Information, Disk Management on a separate 2000 or XP computer or hardware-based hard drive tester.
Computer locks up while booting.	• Check the BIOS to see if Plug and Play is enabled. • A driver might be incompatible with the OS, especially 2000/XP. Boot to Safe Mode and check Device Manager for problems, or use Last Known Good Configuration or System Restore. • A hardware device might be malfunctioning. Check with a POST card or diagnostic utility, or remove all peripherals and replace them one at a time.
Computer boots directly to Safe Mode.	• Attempt to boot to Normal Mode. It might work. • After boot to Safe Mode, check Device Manager for hardware problems and resource conflicts. • Use a POST card. • Run a diagnostic utility.

TABLE 11.3 Bad Performance/Erratic Behavior

Symptom	Check and/or Try
Windows won't shut down properly.	• Install Windows updates. • Search Microsoft Knowledge Base for shutdown problem, specifying the Windows version and using the "Any of the words" and 150 articles options. There are many articles for each version.
Compaq Presario won't shut down properly.	• Check the Startup tab of msconfig or the registry at HKEY_LOCAL_MACHINE\SOFTWARE\Microsoft\Windows\CurrentVersion\Run for the file SXGDSENU.exe. This file needs to start with Windows in order for Presarios to shut down.
Computer runs badly; might lock up, give random error messages, etc.	• Scan computer for viruses and malware. • Check temperatures, fan performance, and that the heat sink is properly seated on the CPU. • Run System File Checker. • Run a registry-cleaning program. • Use a diagnostic utility. • Run the 2000 emergency repair process or reinstall Windows over the existing installation. • You might have Windows Me. Back up and do a clean install of Windows XP.

TABLE 11.4 Software Installation Problems

Symptom	Check and/or Try
Windows won't install.	• Make sure the computer *exceeds* the system requirements of the Windows version. • Search for an error message. • Test the hard drive. Use the hard drive manufacturer's utility to set up the drive. • Run EZ BIOS to see if it's installed; if it is, try uninstalling it.
2000 or XP installation hangs during hardware detection phase.	• Check for incompatible hardware. See Hardware Compatibility Lists (Microsoft Knowledge Base article 131303 for 2000, or 314062 for XP). Attempt to identify problem hardware. If non-essential, remove it or disable it in BIOS. Windows should install successfully. Then, search for an appropriate driver and reinstall device.
Windows 98 error message: Windows Setup requires 'largest executable program size' to be at least 442368 bytes to run.	• From a command prompt, run setup /im. This skips the memory check that allows the problem to occur.
Program won't install.	• Check the program documentation. • Make sure the program is compatible with Windows version; 16-bit programs (for DOS or Windows 3.x) that need to access hardware directly will not work in 2000 or XP. Newer versions of a program might not run on older versions of Windows. • Make sure the computer meets the system requirements of the program. • Copy setup files to the hard drive before running the installation program (usually setup.exe).

TABLE 11.4 Software Installation Problems *(continued)*

Symptom	Check and/or Try
Driver installation unsuccessful.	• Make sure the driver being installed is designed for the installed Windows version. • Make sure the hardware is compatible with the Windows version and with other hardware. See Hardware Compatibility Lists (Microsoft Knowledge Base article 131303 for 2000, or 314062 for XP). • Make sure the computer meets the system requirements of the hardware (usually printed on the box and in the documentation). • The device might be malfunctioning. Try the questionable device in another computer or another device in the same computer.
Hardware not detected when installation is attempted.	• Make sure the device is seated or otherwise connected properly. • Make sure Plug and Play is enabled in BIOS. • Test the device in another machine to make sure it's not defective or broken.

TABLE 11.5 Heat Problems

Symptom	Check and/or Try
Computer runs hot.	• Check the fan operation. • Vacuum and use air spray inside the computer. • Make sure the vents aren't blocked. • Cover openings such as unused expansion card slots and drive bays. • Make sure the computer isn't near a heat source. • Check for a BIOS update. Some BIOS updates allow a computer to run cooler, especially laptops.

TABLE 11.6 Video Problems

Symptom	Check and/or Try
No video.	• Make sure the monitor is powered on, connected to the computer, and that the brightness control is not turned all the way down. If the power indicator is blinking or glows orange, that means there is no video signal coming from the computer. Try another monitor, or connect the dark monitor to a different computer. • If there is no video at boot, listen for the POST beep code and/or use a POST card (this chapter contains information on POST beep codes and POST cards). • Try removing the hard drive and scanning for viruses. • Try installing a known good video adapter.

(continues)

TABLE 11.6 Video Problems *(continued)*

Symptom	Check and/or Try
Video at low resolution with splotchy colors.	• Try to adjust the settings from 640 x 480 resolution and 16 colors. • The video driver might be corrupted. Update or reinstall the driver. Try installing a known good video adapter.
Artifacts (parts or shapes of windows continue to appear on screen after the window is closed), other unwanted spots appear on screen.	• Reinstall or upgrade the video driver. • Scan for viruses.
Line appears on screen.	• Swap the monitor with a known good monitor. Reinstall or update the video driver.
One or more colors missing.	• Check the VGA connector pins. If the monitor cable is replaceable, swap with a known good cable. If not, swap with a known good monitor.
Problems with video and display settings. No choices in either resolution or color depth, or both.	• Certain LCD screens can display video at only one preset resolution. • Design limitation of the video adapter or monitor. • The computer is in Safe Mode. • There is a problem with the adapter or its driver.
One parameter decreases as the other one is increased.	• Lack of sufficient video memory to support high resolutions and large color palettes simultaneously.
The image is odd-shaped.	• The aspect ratio of the selected screen resolution does not match that of the screen (4x3 for standard computer monitors).
The page displays unusable or poor quality video.	• The settings exceed the capability of the video adapter or monitor.

TABLE 11.7 Sound Problems

Symptom	Check and/or Try
No sound.	• Make sure the speakers are connected, powered, and turned up. • Make sure the volume is up and not muted in the Windows volume control and Windows sound mixer. • Make sure sounds are enabled in the Multimedia/Sounds applet in Control Panel. • Check the audio connectors. Make sure they are in the right jacks and free from damage. • Run SFC. • Check Device Manager for an installed sound card. • Install or reinstall the sound driver. • Try a known good sound card.
Bad sound.	• Check the audio connectors. Make sure they are in the right jacks and free from damage. • Run SFC. • Enable or disable digital sound playback in the sound card properties in Device Manager. • Check to see if the sound card is next to the video card. If so, try separating them. • Reinstall the sound driver.

TABLE 11.8 Printing Problems

Symptom	Check and/or Try
Printer won't print.	• Make sure the printer is connected to power and turned on. • If any error messages appear, and they are not obviously correct, search for them on the Internet. • Reinstall the printer driver. • Check the cable. If it is a parallel cable, make sure it is IEEE 1284 compliant and that the pins are intact. • Try a known good printer and/or cable. • Test the non-functioning printer in another computer. • If the computer is a laptop, uninstall any recently installed USB devices. • Try to print a test page in Printer Properties. • 2000/XP only: Check the print queue. If documents seem to be stuck in the queue, go to Administrative Tools > Services and stop and restart the spooler service.
Print quality is bad. Printer prints nonsense characters and/or prints on every page without stopping.	• Reinstall the printer driver. • Check the cable. If it is a parallel cable, make sure it is IEEE 1284 compliant and that the pins are intact.
One or more colors missing. Printed documents have streaks. Printer prints too light.	• Reinstall the printer driver. • Check the ink cartridges. • Follow the manufacturer's directions for cleaning the printer.

TABLE 11.9 Lost Data/I Can't Open My Files/I Can't Find My Files

Symptom	Check and/or Try
Certain files won't open.	• Make sure you have a program that will open that type of file. • The file could be corrupted. Replace the file if possible. • Scan the system for viruses and malware. • On 2000 and XP, make sure you have permissions to open these files. • Check the hard drive for damage such as bad sectors.
Entire folders won't open.	• On 2000 and XP, make sure you have permission to open these files. • The folder could be corrupted. Replace the files in the folder if possible. • Scan the system for viruses and malware. • Check the hard drive for damage such as bad sectors.
Disk drive not recognized.	• Make sure the drive is connected and jumpered properly. • Make sure the file format is recognized by Windows (9x won't recognize NTFS). • Check the drive with FDISK, Partition-Magic, Windows Disk Management (2000 or XP only), or a diagnostic utility. • Run EZ BIOS; install or uninstall as needed.
Files open, but nonsense characters appear.	• The program used to open the file is not the correct program for that type of file. For example, a Microsoft Word file opened in Notepad will show nonsense characters. • The file could be corrupted. Check the hard drive for damage and scan the system for viruses and malware.

TABLE 11.9 Lost Data/I Can't Open My Files/I Can't Find My Files *(continued)*

Symptom	Check and/or Try
Entire partitions or drives don't open.	• Check the hard drive for damage. • Scan the system for viruses and malware. • Run hard drive restoration programs. If data is critical, send to data recovery company such as OnTrack.

TABLE 11.10 Problems With Hardware Peripherals

Symptom	Check and/or Try
Expansion cards don't work or work poorly.	• Check in Device Manager to see if there is a problem. If there is, reinstall the driver. • Reseat the card in its slot. • Run a diagnostic utility. • Try a known good card with the same function.
External devices don't work or work poorly.	• Make sure the device is powered (unless power is provided through a USB or FireWire port). • Make sure all cables are intact—swap with known good cables. • Check in Device Manager for a problem with the device or the port. • Swap the device with a known good model. • If the device connects via infrared, make sure the infrared receiver/emitter is enabled in the BIOS.

TABLE 11.11 Floppy Drives/Optical Drives Don't Work

Symptom	Check and/or Try
Floppy drive can't open files.	• The disk might be bad. Check the floppy disk in a known good drive. • The drive might be the problem. Spray compressed air in the drive or replace the drive.
Floppy drive can't write files or format disk.	• The disk might have its write protect tab moved into place. Move the tab back to the other position or use another disk. • The disk might be bad. Try another disk. • The drive might be the problem. Spray with compressed air or replace the drive. • Make sure the BIOS isn't set to prevent writing to or formatting a floppy.
The A drive is not recognized on the system.	• Make sure the drive is enabled in the BIOS. • Check the drive cables and connections. Reattach the drive and/or replace the cable if necessary. • Replace the drive with a known good drive.
Optical drive can't read files.	• The disk might be in a format unrecognized by the drive, or it might have not been finalized after it was burned. Try a newer drive. • The disk might be damaged. Inspect the disk for damage and use a repair kit if necessary. • The drive might be broken. Try the disk in another drive.

TABLE 11.11 Floppy Drives/Optical Drives Don't Work *(continued)*

Symptom	Check and/or Try
Writable optical drive can't write files. You get a buffer underrun error message when attempting to burn a disk.	• The disk might not be writable, or it might have been writable but not rewritable and have already been written to. Try another disk. • The drive might be defective. Try another drive. • Copy the files to the hard drive before attempting to burn the disk.
Optical drive not recognized in system.	• Check in BIOS to make sure the drive is enabled. • Check all cables and jumpers. Reattach and replace cables if necessary.

TABLE 11.12 Hard Drive Problems

Symptom	Check and/or Try
System reports bad sectors.	• Run a diagnostic utility. • Run thorough ScanDisk. • Copy data and replace the hard drive.
Hard drive crashes.	• If data is critical, send the drive to data recovery company such as OnTrack.

TABLE 11.13 Unusual Noise

Symptom	Check and/or Try
Change in fan noise.	• Check all fans in the system, plus the power supply.
Strange noises coming from speakers.	• Follow the instructions in Sound Problems. • The system might be running badly. Reboot. • Scan the system for viruses and malware.

TABLE 11.14 Internet and Modem Problems

Symptom	Check and/or Try
You cannot connect to the ISP—dial-up or broadband.	• Check all the cables and connections. • Call the ISP to see if there is an outage. • Make sure the telephone line works (dial-up or DSL). Make sure the television cable is working (cable). • Check the configuration of the computer and any other connection devices. • Check all the connection hardware devices for power and proper operation. • Reinstall the ISP software. • If you have Windows XP, stop using the ISP software and create a broadband connection in Windows. If dial-up, configure manually with any Windows version. • Make sure the correct modem or network adapter is selected. Detect the new device or delete and reinstall the connection. • Make sure the firewall, if used, is configured correctly. • Make sure there aren't multiple firewalls running on the system. • Make sure the username and password are correct and in the correct format. • Make sure Caps Lock isn't changing the case of the password. • Make sure the modem is dialing the correct telephone number with all necessary codes. • If the telephone line does not have Call Waiting, make sure the modem isn't dialing the code to disable it.

TABLE 11.14 Internet And Modem Problems *(continued)*

Symptom	Check and/or Try
	• Scan for viruses and malware. • If the line has voicemail, make sure a pulsed dial tone isn't interfering with the modem. Either listen to the messages before connecting, or add three commas to the beginning of the dial-up telephone number.
You can connect to an ISP, but no Web pages appear.	• Call the ISP to see if there is an outage. • Make sure the firewall, if used, is configured correctly. • Make sure there aren't multiple firewalls running on the system. • Check the configuration in Internet Options. Make sure Security, Privacy, and Content settings aren't blocking Web pages. • Scan for viruses and malware. • Call the ISP to see if there is a problem with the Internet and request technical support if needed.
Your home page changed.	• Change it back in the Internet Options, General page. • Scan for viruses and malware.
The wrong e-mail program or Web browser appears when you connect to the Internet.	• Change the settings in Internet Options, Programs page. • 2000 and XP: Change the settings in Set Program Access and Defaults from the Start menu.
Data transfer speed is slow.	• Try another ISP to see if the first ISP's modems are slow. • Call your ISP to see if there's a slowdown in the system. • Upgrade to a 56Kbps modem. • If you're connecting through a hotel telephone line, this might be normal.

TABLE 11.14 Internet And Modem Problems *(continued)*

Symptom	Check and/or Try
	• Check the quality of the telephone line. • Scan for viruses and malware.
The connection gets dropped frequently.	• Make sure to disable Call Waiting if you have it. • Check the quality of the telephone line. • Scan for viruses and malware.
You can't get your e-mail.	• Make sure the username and password are correct and in the required format. • Make sure all configuration information is the same as required by the ISP. • Make sure the computer is connected to the Internet.
You can't download attachments.	• Check your security settings.

12 Things *Not* to Do with a Computer

Many of us have heard of how the PC user called in to say his cup holder was not working on his computer only to find out he was referring to his CD drive. Well, that's obviously a silly thing to do, but following are some less obvious but also not-so-wise things to do with your computer.

The switch on the back of the power supply that says *115/230* is not to be used to see if there is a problem with the power by switching it back and forth.

No matter how much you think you know, make it a rule never to plug in a new USB device until you read the manual. In most cases, the software has to be installed first or in a specific manner, and by skipping the proper steps, you might waste a lot of time trying to get the device to work correctly.

We are constantly getting laptop computers in the shop for repair due to all types of liquids spilling on the keyboard that were kept right next to it. We just bought a laptop for parts that was less than a year old. The owner was very careful with her laptop, but her cat was not and knocked a glass of Chablis right into the keyboard instantly ruining it. Unlike a desktop computer where the keyboard is a separate and usually inexpensive peripheral, the notebook keyboard is directly over the circuitry of the computer, and the liquid will wick its way into every crevice and corrode and short out the system. Don't do as the user in Figure 12.1; keep your drinks and food away from electronics.

Speaking of spilling liquids on the laptop, customers often turn on their laptops after only wiping the outside of it right after the spill. Basic science tells us that will only ensure more, and most likely permanent and possibly fatal, damage. We try to tell all of our customers that if a spill ever occurs to immediately remove the battery, unplug the laptop, turn it upside down to minimize migration of the liquid into the components, and bring it to a qualified technician right away to be cleaned out. Never let your curiosity force you to turn it back on.

A customer recently walked into the shop and asked if we could test his Pentium 4 processor. When asked if he had it with him, he retrieved it from his pocket and held it up proudly by the corners. Another time a customer asked if we could

FIGURE 12.1 Don't try this at home.

test his memory module. He took it out of his shirt pocket (it wasn't in any type of container) and dropped it on the floor. The items might have been working before they brought them in, but their chances started decreasing when they handled them that way. *Do not ever* handle a static-sensitive component (processor, memory, add-in card, etc.) with your bare hands unless you are wearing a wrist strap and using precautions to ground yourself and prevent static discharge.

Another customer brought in his server because it was dead. We checked it out and discovered a ¼-inch gap between the processor and its heat sink. We removed the heat sink and found globs of thermal transfer compound—so much that the heat sink didn't make good contact with the processor—and there was a thermal pad as well. Now, the ironic thing is that this customer is obsessed with cooling. There were two fans on the processor and various case fans. However, his failure to follow directions (see Chapter 3, "Motherboards and Their Components") caused his CPU to overheat and fail. The rule: use either a thermal pad or a small amount of thermal transfer compound, and make sure that the heat sink is flush against the processor.

One time a customer called and frantically explained that his video disappeared, and he needed his computer for business right away. He was willing to buy a new monitor. We told him to bring in his computer and monitor. When we checked out the monitor, we found that the brightness had been turned all the way down. The lesson here is to always check the simplest, most obvious things first.

Often, when a PC comes in to the shop it has loose wires hanging inside even though the original system builder took the time to tie the wires. The problem was that they used rubber bands, and the rubber bands had rotted away from age and the heat within a computer. Another thing we have seen is short-circuited wiring from twist ties. When the paper on a twist ties dries up and goes away, all that is left is a thin metal wire that can wear through insulation and short out connections. When you tie up all the wires inside your computer to make them look neat and to help increase the airflow for cooling, use nylon zip ties or nylon wire restraints and clips designed for the purpose. They are easier to work with and will last much longer.

Up in the cooler climates, we occasionally have PCs come in for freeze-ups or damage that cannot be immediately explained, until we find out that the computer is kept right next to a radiator or heating vent.

One of the frequent causes of problems in PCs we see is viruses. Most name brand computers come with some form of virus protection. Usually, it is good for one year or is a three-month trial version. When we ask the customers if they have virus protection, they say yes. When we ask them if it is up to date, they usually assume that you install it and forget it and you are protected forever. After they get the bill to clean out the virus and save the data on the computer, they rarely forget to stay up to date.

On that note, many people out there cannot believe they got a virus because they do not open attachments or open e-mails only from people they know. They forget or do not know that the virus can come from an e-mail sent from their friend's or family member's PC without their knowledge. Additionally, viruses can come over the Web, even if there is no browser open. In fact, my virus detection software detected and cleaned a virus while I was researching links on a Web site while writing this chapter.

Another less technical but important issue is the choice of cabinets for computers. While many computers are getting smaller all the time, we constantly see customers choosing a computer desk or cabinet that does not fit the case. I recently installed a pair of computer systems at a home and the new furniture had arrived and was installed. The so-called computer desks looked great, but the first thing I noticed was that the shelf for the PC had a door and only one small hole for the cables in the back. There was no consideration of ventilation, or cabling, and you had to open the door just to insert a CD, DVD, or floppy disk. Things worked out after I opened the backs and installed small bumpers on the doors so they would allow some ventilation. Often, the problem is size, and there is no room for the computer once it is in place with all the cables attached. It sometimes seems as if the designers of computer office furniture forget that they have to accommodate machines with cables attached and the need for ventilation.

Many times, I have been called upon to work with a small business with two or more PCs it purchased at a big box store or online, and now the company wants to be able to take advantage of networking or need a server to accommodate its needs and growth. The assumption of many of these customers is that a computer is a computer, and one for home is the same as one for business, and the only difference is the work they are doing on them. That cannot be further from the truth. The difference between a professional versus home version of Windows when purchasing a new PC is usually $60 to $90 dollars versus approximately $180 dollars to upgrade later. Most home PCs come with a home suite of programs to keep the cost of the PC lower and more attractive to the buyers. However, Microsoft Office Professional or a similar office suite at the time of purchase will cost you about $300 now, or you can buy the full product later for about $600. The point here is that consulting an expert first will probably save you time and money in the long term.

13 Command-Line Tutorial: MS-DOS and 32-Bit Commands: A Practical Tutorial and Reference

In This Chapter

- Overview
- Using Command
- Command List

OVERVIEW

In this chapter, we will discuss only those commands, switches, and parameters likely to be helpful to those repairing a computer. Because general networking is beyond the scope of Part I of this book, networking commands are excluded. In most command references, there is so much punctuation to indicate variables that until you become experienced with the commands, you might have trouble determining which punctuation is for variables and which is part of the syntax of the command. Therefore, we attempted to show these commands with a minimum of punctuation.

The most basic information is how to access commands. Commands can be accessed from the following locations:

MS-DOS Prompt in 9x: Start > Programs > MS-DOS Prompt in 95/98, Start > Programs > Accessories > MS-DOS Prompt in Me. Alternatively, you can type "command" in the Run dialog (Start > Run).

Run dialog (all versions): Start > Run. Many commands are accessible from here.

32-bit Command Prompt (2000/XP): Start > Programs (or All Programs) > Command Prompt or type "cmd" in the Run dialog (Start > Run).

MS-DOS Command Prompt (all versions): Type "command" in the Run dialog (Start > Run).

MS-DOS Prompt from boot (95/98): After booting you'll automatically get a prompt.

MS-DOS Prompt from boot floppy (all versions): After booting you'll automatically get a prompt.

Safe Mode Command Prompt Only (Me/2000/XP): After powering on the computer, press <F8> and select Safe Mode Command Prompt only from the boot menu.

Recovery Console (2000/XP): See the instructions in Chapter 11, "Troubleshooting." The Recovery Console has its own set of commands, most of which are covered in the final section in this chapter.

Not all commands are available in all these places.

USING COMMANDS

Before we get to actual commands, we will provide information that will make it easier to use them. Tutorial 13.1 shows how to select and copy text in a command prompt window.

TUTORIAL 13.1 SELECTING AND COPYING TEXT FROM A COMMAND PROMPT WINDOW

1. Click the icon in the upper left-hand corner of the bar on top of the window, point to Edit in the menu that appears, and click Mark.
2. Click at the beginning of the text you want to copy.
3. Press and hold down the <SHIFT> key, and then click at the end of the text you want to copy.
4. Click the icon again, click Edit, and then click Copy.

5. Paste the text into a document by holding the <Ctrl> key and pressing <C>, or by selecting Paste from the Edit menu. If you want to paste the text back into the command prompt window, click the icon again, point to Edit, and click Paste.

Using Wildcard Characters

Wildcard characters can be used when using Windows Search or Find, and to represent multiple files or folders when using a command prompt. Wildcard characters are as follows:

Asterisk (*): Acts as a substitute for zero or more characters. For example, to search for or make a change to any .txt file that starts with G, enter *G*.txt.* If you want any file that has an extension starting with *.tif*, enter **.tif*. For all files in a particular folder, enter *.*.

Question mark (?): Acts as a substitute for any single character. For example, to search for or make changes to all .doc files that start with *Karen* followed by a single character, enter *karen?.doc*. This would find or change *karen1.doc*, *karen2.doc*, and so forth, but would ignore *karen10.doc* because the number *10* has two characters.

Comment Indicators

When directly editing the MS-DOS configuration files Autoexec.bat and Config.sys, or their XP/2000 counterparts, Config.nt and Autoexec.nt, the safest way to stop a line of text from being implemented is to "comment it out." In these files, you do this by typing REM at the beginning of a line. This tells the system to ignore that line. The advantage to using these indicators as opposed to simply deleting the line is that it's very easy to reverse if you discover that you erroneously commented out an important line.

For .ini files such as Win.ini and System.ini, comment out lines using a semicolon.

Command Notes

- For information on commands not listed here, 2000's and XP's Help files have lists of all available prompts. Search 2000's Help for "Command Reference Main Page," or XP's for "Command-line Reference." For 9x's commands, search the Internet. You can also search Windows' Help for individual commands.
- Not all commands are available in all versions. Additionally, certain MS-DOS commands won't be available in 2000 or XP if you access the 32-bit command

prompt (Start > Programs (or All Programs) > Accessories > Command Prompt), or by typing "cmd" in the Run dialog. However, if you type "command" in the Run dialog, you'll be able to run some MS-DOS commands that would normally not be available in that version of Windows. Finally, not all commands work as described in Microsoft's documentation.

- For a description and syntax of each command, plus a complete list of switches and parameters, enter the command followed by a space and "/?". For example, for information about the CD command, type:

```
CD /?
```

- Because folders were originally called *directories*, Microsoft uses the term whenever writing about commands. The two terms (*folders* and *directories*) are interchangeable.
- Most of these commands can be used either by entering the full path of the file or folder being acted upon after the command name, or by navigating to that folder first. In our experience, it is usually easier to navigate to the folder first, eliminating any chance of typos invalidating the command and requiring the command to be retyped. For instructions on navigating to the correct folder, see the description of the CD (CHDIR) command.
- In addition to the 8.3 limitation of file and folder names in MS-DOS (see Chapter 2, "System Configuration and Computer Hygiene"), there cannot be spaces in MS-DOS file and folder names. When referring to file and folder names containing spaces when using an MS-DOS prompt on Windows, you might need to use quotation marks around the folder or filename. Otherwise, the system might interpret only the first word as the name and anything after that as invalid parameters or switches. This is however, by no means a universal rule, especially in 2000 and XP.
- Commands, parameters, and switches are not case sensitive.
- All switches must be preceded by a space character when typed as part of a single command line. The only time you would omit the space is when you are responding to a prompt, such as is possible in the CHKDSK command.
- Press <Enter> after each command to start it.
- A great trick that you can use with these commands is use of the < and > keys. < inputs the text from a text file into a command, and > sends the output from a command to a text file. For example, if you use the DIR command with the /p switch and want the output to go to a file in the current folder that you want to name output.txt, type "DIR /p > output.txt".
- If you want to import text from a file into a command, use the < key after the command and switches, followed by the name of the file.

- If you find that commands you want to use are not available, running the PATH command might help. This tells the system where to find commands.

COMMAND LIST

The following commands are not all available in all versions and in all locations.

ATTRIB

In Windows, files and folders have certain properties (called *attributes)* that can be configured. If you right-click on the file or folder's icon, you'll see some check boxes that allow you to change these attributes. The ATTRIB command allows you to do this when the Windows GUI is not available. The possible attributes, which vary based on Windows version and other factors, are as follows:

Read only: When set, this allows the file to be opened and viewed, but not changed or deleted.

Archive: This attribute affects whether the file will be backed up in certain backup schemes using a backup program, or whether running the XCOPY command will copy that particular file. For more information, see Windows Backup help files.

System: This indicates that the file is necessary for some Windows process.

Hidden: Windows hides certain files by default; however, any file can be hidden or displayed by changing this attribute. In 2000 and XP, when the user has enabled the showing of hidden files (in any Windows folder in Tools > Folder Options > View tab), icons for hidden folders and files appear translucent.

The most common repair use for the ATTRIB command is to replace corrupted registry files in 9x (see Chapter 11 for more information).

When run without switches, ATTRIB shows the attributes of each file in the current folder.

ATTRIB displays, sets, or removes the read-only, archive, system, and hidden attributes assigned to files or folders. Used without parameters, ATTRIB displays attributes of all files in the current folder.

Use

ATTRIB uses the plus sign (+) to turn on an attribute, and the minus sign (–) to turn off an attribute. To use ATTRIB, navigate to the folder where the desired file is located (see the CD command description later in this appendix), and type the command followed by the filename (with or without wildcards) and the desired parameters and switches.

Parameters

- **+r:** Sets the read-only file attribute
- **-r:** Clears the read-only file attribute
- **+a:** Sets the archive file attribute
- **-a:** Clears the archive file attribute
- **+s:** Sets the system file attribute
- **-s:** Clears the system file attribute
- **+h:** Sets the hidden file attribute
- **-h:** Clears the hidden file attribute

Switches

- **/s:** Applies the command to matching files in the current folder and all its subfolders.
- **/d:** Applies the command to the entire folder.

Note

To apply a change to a group of files using wildcard characters, files with their system and/or hidden attributes will not be affected unless you turn off the hidden and system attributes first.

Examples

To display the attributes of a file named *chapter07.doc*, navigate to the folder and enter:

```
ATTRIB chapter07.doc
```

To assign the read-only attribute to the file, enter:

```
ATTRIB +r chapter07.doc
```

To remove the read-only, hidden, and system attributes from all .reg files on the C: drive, including in all subfolders, navigate to the C: drive and enter:

```
ATTRIB -r -h -s *.reg /s
```

CD OR CHDIR

This refers to *Change Directory*, and is used to change the current folder. When directions for another command say, "navigate to the xxx folder," this is the command that you would use to do that.

Use

When narrowing down to a subfolder within the current folder, type "CD", followed by the subfolder name. For example, if the current folder is C:\WINDOWS, and you want to navigate to C:\WINDOWS\DESKTOP, type:

```
CD Desktop
```

To change the current folder to a root level (a drive letter without any additional folders) (e.g., C:\Documents and Settings to C:), make sure to enter the backslash (\) after the drive letter. For example, if the prompt says *C:\Documents and Settings:* and you want to navigate to the C drive, enter:

```
CD C:\.
```

Switch

.. : This navigates to the higher level folder. For example, if the current folder is C:\Documents and Settings\All Users, running CD with this switch will take you to C:\Documents and Settings. Note that there is a space before the two periods.

CHKDSK (PRESENT IN ALL VERSIONS, USEFUL IN 2000 AND XP ONLY)

CHKDSK is a program used for checking the status of magnetic drives/disks, fixing certain errors, and even recovering readable data from bad disk sectors. It isn't particularly useful in 9x, except for obtaining a report on files on the disk. To correct any disk errors on 9x, run ScanDisk. In 2000, and XP, CHKDSK replaces 9x's ScanDisk. In 2000 and XP, it is easier to run CHKDSK from Windows, so you might as well save the command-line version for when the computer is booted into Safe Mode, Command prompt only. When invoked with the /f and/or /r switches to run on a disk in use, CHKDSK will prompt you to run at the next boot. See Chapter 2 for more information on CHKDSK and ScanDisk.

Use

Type "CHKDSK" followed by the drive letter and colon (:), followed by any switches (each switch must be preceded by a space character).

Switches

/c: Use with NTFS-formatted drives only. Skips folder structure cycle checking, resulting in a faster completion.

/f: Fixes file system errors on the disk. If run on a disk currently in use, /f causes CHKDSK to be run on the next boot.

/i: Use with NTFS-formatted drives only. Performs a less exhaustive check of index entries, resulting in a faster completion.

/r: Recovers readable information from bad disk sectors. If run on a disk currently in use, /r causes CHKDSK to be run on the next boot. See the listing for the RECOVER command for another tool that can recover lost data.

/v: Displays the name of each file in every folder as the disk is checked.

/x: Use with NTFS-formatted drives only. Makes all necessary changes to any network-mapped drives in order for CHKDSK to work on them. /x also includes the functionality of the /r switch.

Notes

- Running CHKDSK without the /f, /r, and/or /x switches is usually pointless and might report false disk errors.
- If you are prompted to convert lost chains (unidentified file fragments) to files, do so by typing <Y>. You can then find the files in the root folder (C:\ in the C: drive). The files are named File****.chk (the asterisks stand for any character). If the files don't contain any data you need, you can delete them. If you type "<N>" (answer no) to the prompt, the fragments will be deleted automatically.
- If you use the /f or /x switch on a very large disk such as 80GB, or one with huge numbers of files (e.g., millions of files), CHKDSK might take several days to complete. CHKDSK cannot be stopped while it is running, so the computer will not be available for this time.

CLS

CLS removes all text except the main heading and prompt from the command prompt window. CLS stands for *Clear Screen.*

Use

Type "CLS".

CMD (2000 AND XP ONLY)

Although this command can be used in a command prompt window, its most common use is to be entered in the Run dialog for the purpose of opening a new 32-bit command prompt window in 2000 and XP.

Use

Type "CMD" in the Run dialog and click OK or press <Enter>.

COMMAND

Although this command can be used in a command prompt window, its most common use is to be entered in the Run dialog for opening an MS-DOS prompt window in all versions.

Use

Type "COMMAND" in the Run dialog and press <Enter>.

COMP (2000 AND XP ONLY)

Compares the data in two files or sets of files byte by byte. The two files or sets can be on the same or different drives or folders.

Use

Type "COMP" and press <Enter>. You'll be prompted for the first file to compare. Enter the full path and press <Enter>. You'll then be prompted for the second file to compare. Enter the full path and press <Enter>. You'll then be prompted for any switches. If you want to use no switches, press <Enter>. If you do want to use a switch, enter the first desired switch with any applicable parameters, if any, and press <Enter>. Every time you enter a switch, you'll be prompted to enter another after you press <Enter>. After you press <Enter> after having entered no switches, COMP will proceed to make the comparison.

Alternatively, you can type "COMP" followed by the first file path, the second file path, and any switches and other parameters desired. For example, using the 32-bit command prompt in 2000 or XP, compare two files designating the output to be noted in characters:

```
COMP C:\Documents and Settings\Rojo\My Documents\Chapter05.doc D:\Book
Chapters\Chapter05KJI.doc /a
```

Switches

/a: Displays differences as characters.

/c: Performs a comparison that is not case sensitive.

/d: Displays differences in decimal format. (The default format is hexadecimal.)

/l: Displays the number of the line on which a difference occurs, instead of displaying the byte offset.

/n=*number*: Compares the first *number* of lines of both files, even if the files are different sizes.

Notes

- Use wildcard characters to compare groups of files.
- COMP displays the results in memory addresses, so it's useful only to indicate that the files are different, not to display the differences.
- Files must be the same size, or the only result will be that the files aren't the same size. The exception to this is if the /n=number switch is used. In place of the word *number*, enter the number of lines of data to be compared. If you enter, for example, 10, the first 10 lines of each file will be compared.
- This command is extraordinarily particular; even a change in case somewhere in the path might cause COMP to report that it cannot open the file. If you use it in an MS-DOS prompt, you might have to convert folder names or filenames to the 8.3 standard. Look up 8.3 filename standard on the Internet if you need help.

CONVERT (XP AND 2000 ONLY)

Converts hard drive partitions formatted as FAT and FAT32 to NTFS. CONVERT cannot convert a partition to any file system other than NTFS.

Use

Type "CONVERT" followed by the drive letter and colon, and then /fs:ntfs followed by any switches. If you were converting drive C to NTFS in the verbose mode (see the switch listings), you would type:

```
CONVERT C: /fs:ntfs /v
```

and then press <Enter>.

Switches

/fs:ntfs: CONVERT won't work without this switch following the drive letter. fs means file system.

f/nosecurity: Specifies that files and folders already on the drive are accessible to everyone who uses the computer.

/v: Verbose mode. All possible information will be displayed while the conversion is taking place.

/x: Performs all changes to network-mapped drives necessary for the conversion to take place.

Note

Any drive in use will be converted at the next boot.

COPY

Copies one or more files. XCOPY provides much more flexibility than does COPY.

Use

Type "COPY" followed by general switches, then type the path of the file(s) to be copied followed by any switches that apply to the source files, then the path of the destination, if desired, followed by any switches that apply to the destination. The source can be a path to a drive, folder, or file. If it is a drive or folder, it will copy all the files in that folder to the destination, but it will not copy subfolders or any files within subfolders. Wildcards can be used in a source. Two or more files or folders can be specified in the source by using the plus sign (+) followed by a space character before each file after the first one listed, as in:

```
COPY /v D:\Backup\*.dll + D:\Backup\Example.txt C:\Windows\System32
```

This example would copy all .dll files in the Backup folder on the D drive, but no files in subfolders of Backup, plus the file Example.txt to the C:\Windows\System32 folder. The /v switch verifies that each file is copied properly.

The destination can also be a path to a drive, folder, or file. If the destination is a path to a drive or folder, the copy will keep the name of the original file. If the destination is a file with a name different from the original, the copy will have the new filename. If the destination is not specified, the copy will be placed in the current folder, as long as the current folder isn't the same as the source folder; in which case no copying will occur.

If two or more source files are specified but only one destination file is specified, the files will be combined into a single file, assuming the file formats are compatible with each other and can handle such a change. Text files (.txt), for example, can be combined.

Switches

/d: If any of the source files are encrypted, this switch removes the encryption attribute on the copies.

/n: Causes the filename to be converted to one that complies with the DOS 8.3 filename convention.

/v: Verifies that new files are copied correctly. It is advisable to use when copying critical files. It does cause the copying to take more time than without /v.

/y: By default, Windows prompts you to confirm that you want to overwrite an existing destination file of the same name in the same folder; /y stops these prompts.

/-y: Turns off the /y switch. Restores prompts to confirm that you want to overwrite an existing destination file of the same name in the same folder.

/z: In case copies are being made over a network and the network connection is lost, or one of the computers goes off line, /z sets the copy operation to automatically resume from where it left off after the connection is reestablished.

/a: Indicates an ASCII text file (see Windows' Help for more information).

/b: Indicates a binary file (see Windows' Help for more information).

Note

You might have to surround folder names or filenames containing spaces with quotation marks, or use the 8.3 standard filenames when using this command.

DEL OR ERASE

Deletes specified files.

Use

Navigate to the folder that contains the file, and type "DEL" or "ERASE" followed by the filename and by any desired switches. You can also enter the entire path at the prompt rather than navigating to the folder. Multiple filenames can be entered separated by spaces, commas, or semicolons, or wildcards can be used. If only a folder name is entered, DEL or ERASE will delete only the files in the root of the folder. Subfolders and files within subfolders will not be affected unless the /s switch is used.

Switches

/f: Normally, files with the read-only attribute will not be deleted. /f overrides this and forces deletion.

/p: Prompts you to confirm that you want the file to be deleted.

/q: Prevents Windows from prompting you to confirm that you want the file to be deleted.

/s: Deletes specified files from the current folder and all subfolders. Displays each filename as the file is deleted.

Note

Once you delete a file using the DEL or ERASE command, that file does not appear in the Recycle Bin and is considered irretrievable without some third-party recovery program.

DIR

Displays a list of the subfolders and files in a folder or drive with some information such as total file size, the last date and time each file was modified, and the amount of free disk space on the disk.

Use

Navigate to the desired folder and type "DIR" followed by any desired switches. Does not show hidden or system files unless you use the /a switch.

Switches

/p: Displays one screen at a time. To continue, press any key on the keyboard.

/q: Displays the owner of each file, if applicable.

/a: Displays all files, including files with the hidden and system attributes.

/a followed by attribute codes: displays only files or other items with attributes you specify.

Attribute Codes

a: Files ready for archiving only

d: Folders only

h: Hidden files and folders only

r: Read-only files only

s: System files and folders only

Each of these codes can be inversed by preceding it with a minus sign (–). For example, –r displays only files with the read-only attribute. In addition, using multiple attribute codes, Windows will display only files with *all* of the attributes indicated by the codes. Don't leave a space between codes when using multiple codes. For example, to display only files that are *both* read only and hidden, type:

```
DIR /arh
```

/s: Lists every occurrence, in the specified folder and all its subfolders, of the specified filename.

/x: Displays both long filenames and 8.3 filenames.

Note

DIR has several more switches. Consult Windows' Help or run DIR with the /? switch for more information.

EDIT (LIMITED USE IN 2000 AND XP)

Starts the MS-DOS Editor, which creates and changes ASCII text files. EDIT is an antiquated text editor that works without benefit of a mouse. It can be essential to use if you boot into DOS and need to edit a text file such as autoexec.bat or config.sys. Access menu commands by pressing and holding the <Alt> key while typing the first letter of the menu and the highlighted letter of each command. Once you have accessed a menu, the arrow keys can be used to navigate the menus. Another way to invoke a menu command is to highlight it by using the arrow keys, and then press <Enter>.

Use

Type "EDIT" followed by the full path to the file you want to open or create, followed by any desired switches.

EXIT

Closes a DOS prompt and many DOS programs. If you click the X to close the window in a DOS program, you'll get a message indicating that closing the program this way will cause any unsaved data to be lost. While you'll rarely have any unsaved data, it is probably easier to use this command to avoid the prompt.

Use

Type "EXIT".

EXPAND (2000 AND XP ONLY)

Expands one or more compressed files. This command is used to retrieve compressed files from distribution disks such as Windows installation disks, often designated with an underscore as the final character in the file extension, or found in 9x in the \Windows\Options\Cabs or \Windows\Options\Install folder.

Use

Type "EXPAND" followed by the path of the source file and the path of the destination file. If you are expanding a file within a cabinet file, navigate to the cab file's folder and type "EXPAND" followed by the cab filename and then the -f: switch, followed, without a space, by the individual files within the cab file. For example, navigate to C:\Windows\Options\Cabs (found in many Windows 9x installations) and type:

```
EXPAND net10.cab -f:snip.vxd C:\Windows
```

This will expand the snip.vxd file into the C:\Windows folder.

Switch

/f: -f followed, without a space, by filenames of files within cab files.

FDISK (DOS AND 9X ONLY)

Opens a program that allows creation and deletion of partitions, and the viewing of partition information. Once the program is open, it is no longer a command-line program, but instead is menu based.

Use

While booted into DOS, type "FDISK" to open the program. Two switches will also perform functions without opening the menu-based program.

Switches

/mbr: This will replace the master boot record (MBR). The MBR is the first sector on the hard disk. There is a small program in the MBR that tells the system which partition is bootable. You cannot boot without the MBR being intact. Use this switch to replace a damaged MBR. This can occur if there is a boot-sector virus, or for other reasons. Try using this if you can't boot and you can't determine another cause. Using this switch does not open the menu-based program.

/status: This will display information about the partition. Using this switch does not open the menu-based program.

/x: Ignores extended disk partition support. If you receive a disk access or stack overflow error, use this switch; /x can be used with /status, but if used by itself, the menu-based program does open.

FORMAT

Formats magnetic disks and partitions in specified file formats (FAT, FAT32, NTFS). Works with floppy and hard disks.

Use

Type "FORMAT" followed by the drive letter and a colon, a space, then /fs: and the name of the file system (FAT, FAT32, or NTFS). For example, to format drive E: as FAT32, you would type:

```
FORMAT E: /fs:FAT32
```

Floppy disks can be formatted only as FAT. FAT is the designation for FAT16. If you omit the /fs switch, the system will use the default.

Switches

/fs: followed by the desired file system: This switch determines the file system, but if you leave it out, Windows will use the default. For example, floppies will automatically be formatted as FAT.

/q: Quick format. Skips a sector-by-sector surface scan of the disk. Use only with a disk known not to have any bad sectors.

/c: Compress newly added files. Works only with NTFS partitions.

/s: (95, 98, and DOS only) Formats a floppy and copies the three DOS files (Command.com, IO.sys, MSDOS.sys) onto it. This switch will work in 95 and 98, and any time the computer is booted into MS-DOS.

Note

Formatting a disk erases all data on the disk, regardless of the method used to format.

MD OR MKDIR

Stands for "Make Directory." Creates a folder or subfolder.

Use

Type "MD" followed by the full path of the new folder, including the name of the new folder. Alternatively, you can navigate to the drive or folder one level above that of the new folder, and type "MD" followed only by the desired name of the new folder.

MMC (2000 AND XP ONLY)

Opens a Microsoft Management Console (MMC). It is normally run from the Run dialog rather than the command prompt. If you have created or saved an MMC console, this command is an easy way to open it. MMC is beyond the scope of Part I of this book, but you might be instructed to use it by a Microsoft support technician. For more information on MMCs, search Windows 2000's or XP's Help for MMC.

Use

Type "MMC" in the Run dialog. If opening a saved console, navigate (browse) to the location of the saved console file, and then type "MMC" followed by a space and the filename.

Switch

/a: Opens a saved console in author mode. This switch is necessary to make changes to saved consoles.

MORE

Allows the viewing of files and the output of other commands one screen at a time. This command is commonly used to view long files. When the window is full, you will get the MORE prompt. There are several options for how you want to view the remaining output.

Use

To use MORE by itself, navigate to the folder that contains the files you want to view, type "MORE" followed by any desired switches, and then the path to the file. If you want to view multiple files, you can enter all the filenames separated by space characters. You can even view files in different folders by entering the full path for each. For example, to view files in 2000 or XP in the root folder of the C: drive, My Documents, and in a folder on a CD-ROM, clearing the screen before displaying the next page, navigate to My Documents, and type:

```
MORE /c test1.txt C:\test2.txt D:\"text files"\test3.txt
```

This will display one screen of test1.txt and allow you to view the remainder of the file using commands that will be described later. Once the entire test1 file has been displayed, test2 will be displayed, followed by test3.

To use MORE with another command, type the command followed by any desired switches for the command, a space, the pipe character (|) (see the note at the end of this listing), MORE, any desired switches pertaining to the MORE command, and then the path to the file or files you want to view. For example, to use the MEM /P command with MORE, clearing the screen after each page, type:

```
MEM /p | MORE /c
```

Switches

/c: Clears each screen before you use a command to view the next screen

/s: Reduces a series of blank lines to a single blank line.

Responses to the—More—Prompt

<spacebar>: Displays next page
<Enter>: Displays next line
<F>: Skips to next file
<Q>: Quits
<?>: Displays available responses to - More - prompt

<=>: Displays line number

<P> followed by a space and a number: Displays the specified number of lines

<S> followed by a space and a number: Skips the specified number of lines

Note

To type the pipe character, hold <Shift> and press the backslash (\) key.

MOVE

Moves files or folders from one drive or folder to another. Similar to COPY, except that MOVE deletes the source file.

Use

Type "MOVE" followed by a switch, if desired, then the source folder or file name, and then the destination folder or file name. If moving more than one file, the destination must be a folder.

Switches

/y: Normally, you would be prompted to confirm if you want to overwrite an existing destination file or folder of the same name; /y turns off this prompt. It is not necessary to use unless there actually is such a destination file or folder and you want to suppress the prompt.

/-y: Turns on the prompt to confirm that you want to overwrite a destination file or folder of the same name, if present.

Note

MOVE will not move encrypted files or folders to a drive that doesn't support the Encrypting File System (EFS). EFS is supported on NTFS drives in 2000, XP, or Windows Server 2003 only. Non-upgraded NTFS drives on systems that were upgraded from Windows NT do not support EFS, but that scenario is rare. To move these files, decrypt them first.

PATH

Although "path" has a more general meaning, "the path" refers to the path to all of these commands. In 9x, some of these are in the root folder of the boot drive (usually C:\), some are in the Windows folder (usually C:\Windows), and some are in the Command folder (usually C:\Windows\Command). In 2000 and XP, commands can be found in the Windows folder (usually C:\Windows or C:\Winnt), and in the System32 folder (usually C:\Windows\System32). There also might be a Command folder (usually C:\Windows\Command or C:\Winnt\Command). The PATH command sets the computer to recognize the locations of these commands. That is how Windows can find each command simply from the user entering commands at the command prompt or in the Run dialog. Run by itself, PATH displays the current path.

Use

Type "PATH" followed by the path that contains commands. You can enter multiple command paths by separating them with semicolons (;).

Parameter

;: Separates the different paths that are to make up "the path." If you use this by itself, the existing command path will be deleted.

Example

In 9x, if you find you don't have access to all commands that should be available, type:

```
PATH C:\;C:\Windows;C:\Windows\Command
```

You can add any other paths you want, separated by semicolons. This can be especially useful if you boot a 9x machine with a startup (MS-DOS) floppy.

RECOVER

Recovers readable data from a damaged or defective disk.

Use

Type "RECOVER" followed by the path to the file you want to rescue. RECOVER requires that the disk not be in use, so it cannot be used on the Windows boot partition while the computer is booted to Windows.

Note

RECOVER reads a file sector by sector and recovers data from the good sectors. Data in bad sectors is lost. It is common practice to open the file after recovery and attempt to re-enter missing data manually.

REN OR RENAME

Changes the name of a file or folder.

Use

Navigate to the folder that contains the file you want to rename, or to the parent folder of the subfolder you want to rename. Type "REN" followed by the existing file or folder name, a space, and then the new file or folder name. REN cannot be used to move files or folders, so you cannot enter a new path for the file.

Notes

- You can use wildcards in either or both the existing and the new filenames, with the caveat that the wildcard characters will stand for the same real characters in both names. For example, let's say that the current folder has three files named test1.doc, test2.doc, and test3.doc. You enter test*.doc as the existing filename and sample*.doc as the new filename. Test1.doc will become sample1.doc, test2.doc will become sample2.doc, and so on.
- If you try to rename a file to a filename in use in the same folder, you'll get an error message and the renaming operation will not proceed.

REPLACE

Replaces files in the destination folder with files in the source folder that have the same name. It also can be used to add files to the destination folder that don't already exist there. For example, if you need to make sure that all files on an optical disc have been copied to a folder on the hard drive, you could use another method to copy them again, and then get the prompt to overwrite existing files. Using REPLACE with the /a switch automatically copies only files that don't exist on the destination folder while ignoring those files that do exist there.

Use

To replace files or folders, type "REPLACE" followed by the path to the source files or folders, then the destination files or folders, followed by any appropriate switches. You can also navigate to the source folder before running the command. If you specify neither a source nor a destination folder, the current folder is used.

Switches

/a: Adds only files to the destination folder that aren't there already; /a cannot be used at the same time as the /s or /u switches.

/p: Prompts you for confirmation before replacing or adding a file or folder.

/r: Replaces read-only, hidden, or system files or folders. Files or folders in the destination folder with these attributes normally would cause the operation to stop.

/w: Waits for you to insert a disk before searching for source files or folders. Without this switch, REPLACE attempts to replace or add files immediately after the user presses <ENTER>.

/s: Includes subfolders of the destination folder (not the source folder); /s cannot be used at the same time as the /a switch.

/u: Replaces only those files in the destination folder that are older than those with the same names in the source folder; /u cannot be used at the same time as the /a switch, nor can it be used to update hidden or system files. You'll have to remove these attributes first, using the ATTRIB command or the Windows interface.

RD OR RMDIR

Deletes a folder. RD stands for "Remove Directory."

Use

Type "RD" followed by the path to the folder you want to delete, followed by any desired switches. Make sure to enter the full path, starting with the drive letter. Do not navigate first to the folder you want to delete; RD won't work if you do. Additionally, RD won't work if the folder to be deleted is a subfolder of the current folder.

Switches

/s: Includes all subfolders and their contents.

/q: Quiet mode. Normally, a confirmation is given after the deletion is complete; /q turns off this confirmation.

Note

You cannot delete a folder with hidden or system files without removing these attributes first. See DIR to locate these files and ATTRIB to remove these attributes.

SCANREG AND SCANREGW (9X ONLY)

See Chapter 11.

SFC (98, 2000 AND XP ONLY)

See Chapter 11.

SHUTDOWN (XP ONLY)

Allows you to shut down, restart, or log a user off the computer. Used without switches, SHUTDOWN will log off the current user.

Use

Type "SHUTDOWN" followed by any desired switches.

Switches

-s: Shuts down the computer.

-r: Reboots the computer.

-f: Forces any running programs to close.

-t followed by a space and a number of seconds: This sets the timer for system shutdown in the specified number of seconds. The default is 20 seconds.

-a: Aborts shutdown. If you run shutdown and then change your mind, during the timed interval before the machine shuts down you can abort the shutdown by running SHUTDOWN -a.

SYS (DOS AND 9X ONLY)

Copies the DOS system files, COMMAND.COM, IO.SYS, and MS DOS.SYS, to a disk.

Use

Navigate to the drive and folder you want to copy the DOS system files to and type "SYS". *Never* run SYS on an NTFS drive.

SYSTEMINFO (XP ONLY)

Displays detailed configuration information about a computer and Windows, including operating system (OS) configuration, security information, product ID, and hardware properties, such as memory, disk space, and network adapters.

Use

Type "SYSTEMINFO". If you want to configure the format of the output, use the /fo switch. SYSTEMINFO is an ideal command to be accompanied by the MORE command.

Switches

/fo followed by one of the three possibilities: TABLE, LIST, or CSV (Comma Separated Value). LIST is the default.

Note

You might get the error message indicating that a required file, framedyn.dll, is missing. If this is the case, you'll need to find the file framedyn.dl_ on the XP installation disk in the I386 folder. Copy this file to Windows\System32. Then, use the EXPAND command to expand it and then REN or the Windows interface to rename it framedyn.dll.

TASKKILL (XP ONLY)

Terminates one or more programs or processes. Processes can be called by their process ID or by their name. View running processes by using the TASKLIST command.

Use

Run TASKLIST or Windows' Task Manager (type "<Ctrl> + <Alt> + <Delete>"). Once you've determined which processes to terminate, type "TASKKILL" followed by the appropriate switches and parameters.

Switches and Parameters

/pid followed by the process ID: Specifies the process ID of the process to be terminated.

/im followed by the process name: Specifies the process name (called *image name*) of the process to be terminated. TASKKILL will terminate all instances of a process.

/f: Terminates the process(es) by force, if necessary. Some processes will ordinarily not be terminated without this switch. Most of these are crucial to the operation of Windows, so don't be surprised if Windows shuts down if you end the wrong process.

/t: Terminates all "child processes" of the specified process.

TASKLIST (XP ONLY)

Displays a list of programs and processes with their Process ID (PID) for all tasks running on the computer. Useful to compile data for the TASKKILL command.

Use

Type "TASKLIST" followed by any desired switches.

Switches and Parameters

/fo followed by the type of output desired: Possible output types are TABLE, LIST, and CSV. CSV stands for Comma Separated Value. The default is TABLE.

/m followed by the module name: A module is a program that uses DLL files. *DLL* stands for *Dynamic Link Library*. Files with this extension are used by programs, and are often used by more than one program. For example, different card games might all use the same Cards.dll file to provide a deck of cards. If you run TASKLIST with this switch and specify a module, the output will show all the DLL files that could be used for that module. If you use the /m switch without a module name, all modules will be listed. The /m switch is incompatible with the /svc and /v switches.

/svc: Lists complete service information for each process. This switch will work only if the output is set to TABLE, the default (see the /fo switch). /svc is incompatible with the /m and /v switches.

/v: Verbose mode. All information will be displayed. /v is incompatible with the /svc and /m switches.

TYPE

Displays the text in a text file.

Use

Navigate to the text file's folder and type "TYPE", or type "TYPE" followed by the path to the file or files to view. To view multiple files, separate them with spaces.

This is a command in which it is very helpful to use the MORE command.

VER

Displays the Windows version and number.

Use

Type "VER".

WINNT32 (2000 AND XP ONLY)

Performs an installation of or upgrade to Windows 2000 or XP. WINNT32 is not in the usual command path. It is available when the current folder is an installation source such as a Windows 2000 or XP CD.

Use

Insert the 2000 or XP installation disk or connect to another installation source. Close the installation program after it opens. Open a command prompt and navigate to the installation folder, which will probably be I386. Type "WINNT32" followed by any desired switches.

Switches

/checkupgradeonly: Checks your current version of Windows to determine if it's eligible to be upgraded to the new version, and checks your hardware to make sure its compatible with the new version. If you use this option with /unattend, you will not be prompted for any input. If you don't use /unattend, the output is displayed, and you are prompted to save it in a file. The default filename is Upgrade.txt, and its default location is in the System32 folder, usually C:\Windows\System32 or C:\Winnt\System32.

/cmdcons: Use this switch on a system that already has Windows 2000 or XP installed to install the Recovery Console as a startup option. For more information on the Recovery Console, see Chapter 11 and the last section in this chapter.

/unattend: Upgrades existing 98, Me, 2000, or XP in a mode that requires no user input. All information that is normally requested during setup is taken from the existing installation.

Note

There are a great many other switches for WINNT32 that are beyond the scope of this book. They are of use primarily to network administrators and others responsible for installing Windows on many machines simultaneously.

XCOPY

Copies files, folders, and subfolders. XCOPY offers great flexibility over any other way to copy, be it by command line or using the Windows graphical interface.

Use

Type "XCOPY" followed by the path to the source file or folder, then the destination file or folder, and then any desired switches.

Switches

/w: Prompts you to press a key before copying commences.

/p: Prompts you to confirm that you want to create each destination file.

/c: Continues copying regardless of errors.

/q: Quiet mode. XCOPY messages are not displayed.

/f: Displays filenames while copying.

/l: Displays the names of all the files that are set to be copied.

/g: Specifies that destination files not be encrypted (2000 and XP only).

/d followed by a colon and the date in the mm-dd-yyyy format: Copies only those source files that had been modified on or after the specified date. If you do not include a date, all source files newer than the existing destination files of the same name are copied. The purpose of this command is to update files with newer versions. For example, to copy only .doc files newer than March 5, 2006 from a CD to a folder, you would type:

```
XCOPY D:\*.doc c:\folder /d:03-05-2006
```

/u: Copies only those source files with the same names as those already in the destination folder.

/i: If you have specified a folder or a file name with wildcards as the source and the destination folder doesn't already exist, /i causes XCOPY to create the new folder. The default is for XCOPY to prompt you to specify whether the destination is a folder or file.

/s: Copies folders and subfolders as long as there are files inside them.

/e: Copies all subfolders, regardless of whether there are files inside them.

/t: Copies the entire folder tree, but none of the files. Add the /e switch to copy empty folders.

/k: (2000 and XP) Causes the copied files to retain the read-only attribute if the source files had it. By default, copied files do not have the read-only attribute.

/k: (9x) Causes all attributes to be copied with the files.

/r: Copies files with the read-only attribute, but is not supposed to copy the attribute. However, it might actually copy the attribute in some cases.

/h: Copies files with hidden and system attributes. The default is for system and hidden files not to be copied.

/a: Copies only files with the archive attributes.

/m: Copies only files with the archive attributes, but removes the archive attribute from the *source* file.

/n: Applies 8.3 file and/or folder names to the copies. Necessary when copying files with long filenames to systems that can handle only 8.3 filenames. See Chapter 2 for more information.

/y: Normally, XCOPY prompts you to confirm that you want to overwrite a destination file of the same name as the one being copied; /y turns off this prompting.

/-y: Restores prompting to overwrite existing files of the same name as the one being copied.

/z: (2000 and XP only) If you are copying over a network and the network connection is lost for whatever reason, if you used /z, copying can pick up where it left off once the connection is restored; /z saves you from having to start over again; /z also displays the copying progress for each file.

Notes

- If you attempt to copy encrypted files onto a drive that doesn't support the Encrypted File System (EFS), there will be an error and copying will not continue.
- If you don't specify a destination, XCOPY uses the current folder.
- By default, unless you use the /m switch, XCOPY's file copies all have the archive attribute set, regardless of whether it was set in the source files.

RECOVERY CONSOLE COMMANDS (2000 AND XP ONLY)

The Recovery Console is discussed in Chapter 11. The Recovery Console has a limited number of commands. Many of the commands are the same, but most of these have different switches and parameters. Additionally, there are other commands that are unique to the Recovery Console. Because the functions of the shared commands are very similar or the same as in the standard commands, only the differences, if any, will be noted. Moreover, only selected commands and switches will be presented here. For a complete list, search Windows' Help for "Recovery Console."

There are a few rules to be concerned with when using the Recovery Console:

- Except where indicated, wildcard characters don't work.
- Type quotation marks around folder and file names containing spaces.
- Only certain folders can be accessed (attempts to access other folders will cause an "Access Denied" message):
  - The root folder of any hard drive partition.
  - The Windows or Winnt folder and its subfolders.
  - The Cmdcons folder, which is the folder, usually in the root folder of the C:\ drive, that contains the Recovery Console. It is hidden by default.
  - Removable media, but only to read and copy files. Files on removable media cannot be modified using the Recovery Console.
  - The Windows installation media.
- The /? switch for help works with all Recovery Console commands.

ATTRIB

Switches

+r: Sets the read-only attribute.

-r: Clears the read-only attribute.

+s: Sets the system attribute.

-s: Clears the system attribute.

+h: Sets the hidden attribute.

-h: Clears the hidden attribute.

+c: Sets the compressed attribute.

-c: Clears the compressed attribute.

CD OR CHDIR

This is the same as the command-prompt version, except that you always have to use quotation marks around folder names containing spaces.

CHKDSK

Switches

/p: Normally, a disk that doesn't indicate problems will not be checked exhaustively. Use /p to override this indication and run the exhaustive check anyway. CHKDSK does not make any changes to the drive when run only with /p.
/r: Locates bad sectors and recovers any readable data. /r automatically includes /p.

Note
CHKDSK requires the file Autochk.exe in order to work. If it cannot find it in the system folder (usually \Winnt\System32 or \Windows\System32), it will look for it on the Windows Installation CD.

CLS

This command is the same as the command-prompt version.

COPY

Copies a single file only to another location. COPY will not copy a folder.

Note
When copying a compressed file from the Windows installation CD, the file is automatically decompressed.

DEL OR DELETE

Deletes a single file only. DEL will not delete a folder.

DIR

Lists the volume (drive) label, serial number, and contents, along with codes indicating what each item is and what attributes are set in each.

Parameter

/ followed by a folder name, filename or group of filenames: DIR can limit itself to showing just those folder or file names you select, along with everything within a folder. *Wildcard characters can be used with this parameter*. Multiple filenames can be used by using wildcards or separating file names with spaces, commas, or semicolons.

Notes

The /p switch is not available with DIR in the Recovery Console because the command runs as if used with the MORE command prompt command.

DIR's output includes the volume (drive) label, serial number, total number of files, the total size of all displayed items, and the amount of free disk space remaining (in bytes). Other information in the output includes time of last modification, file extension, individual file size, file attributes, and whether the item is a file or directory (folder). The last two items use the codes shown in Table 13.1.

TABLE 13.1

Code	Meaning
d	Directory (folder)
h	Hidden
s	System
e	Encrypted
r	Read-only
a	Archive
c	Compressed
p	Reparse point

DISABLE

Disables a device driver or service. The opposite command is ENABLE.

Use

Type "DISABLE" followed by the service or driver name. You can use the LISTSVC command for a list of services and drivers on the computer.

Parameters

Service name: Type "DISABLE" followed by a service name, as shown:

```
DISABLE Messenger
```

This causes the messenger service to be disabled the next time the computer is booted to Windows. The previous state of the service is displayed as well.

Device driver name: Type "DISABLE" followed by the driver name. The driver will be disabled for the next boot to Windows. The previous state of the service is displayed as well.

DISKPART

Allows management of disk partitions.

Use

Type "DISKPART" followed by the appropriate switches and parameters. Run without switches and parameters, DISKPART starts the Windows Setup partitioning program. You'll recognize the program if you have installed NT 4.0, 2000, or XP.

Switches and Parameters

/add followed by the device name and the desired size, in MB, of the partition: Creates a new partition. For example, to add a 10-MB partition, type:

```
DISKPART /add \Device\HardDisk0 10
```

Device name is defined after the /delete switch.

/delete followed by the drive letter, partition name, or device name: Deletes an existing partition.

Device name and *partition name* are defined here:

Device name: An identifier for the hard drive that uses a direct naming convention. This precludes the confusion that can come about due to drive letters than can change. To get this, run the MAP Recovery Console command with no switch and ignore the partition portion of the output. A typical device name is \Device\Harddisk0. The device name is valid only with both the /add and /delete switches.

Partition name: This uses the same naming convention as the device name, but has the added partition number at the end. A typical partition name is \Device\Harddisk0\Partition1. The partition name is valid only with the /delete switch.

Deletion Examples

```
DISKPART /delete \Device\HardDisk0\Partition2
DISKPART /delete E:
```

ENABLE

Enables a service or device driver.

Use

Type "ENABLE" followed by the service name or device driver name and the startup type. The possible startup types are SERVICE_BOOT_START, SERVICE_SYSTEM START, SERVICE_AUTO_START, and SERVICE_DEMAND_START. For example, to enable the Messenger service to start automatically, type:

```
ENABLE Messenger SERVICE_AUTO_START
```

When the ENABLE is run with a device driver name or service name but no start type, the current start type is displayed. Write this down if you need to keep a record of it.

You can use the LISTSVC command for a list of services and drivers on the computer.

Parameter

Startup type: The possible startup types are defined in Table 13.2.

TABLE 13.2

Startup Type	Definition	Applies Primarily To
SERVICE_BOOT_START	Starts with Windows	Device drivers
SERVICE_SYSTEM_START	Starts with the computer	Device drivers
SERVICE_AUTO_START	Starts with Windows	Services
SERVICE_DEMAND_START	Starts manually by a program or user	Services

EXIT

Exits the Recovery Console and restarts the computer.

EXPAND

Use

Type "EXPAND" followed by the source file and then the destination folder. If you want to select an individual file to extract from a cab file, type "EXPAND" followed by the cab filename, /F: followed without a space by the name of the file within the cab file, the destination folder, and then the /y switch if desired. The source cannot use wildcards, but the name of a file within a cab file can use wildcards. If you do not specify a destination folder, the current folder is used.

For example, to expand the Drvspace.bin file from within the C:\Windows\-Options\Cabs\Base4.cab file to the root directory (realizing that this file is from Windows 98 and wouldn't actually be expanded using the Recovery Console), from the C:\ prompt type:

```
EXPAND \Windows\Options\Cabs\Base4.cab /F:drivespace.bin C:\
```

Entering the destination was optional because the command was run from the C:\ prompt. Recall that EXPAND uses the current folder if the destination folder isn't specified.

Switches and Parameters

/d: Lists the files within the cabinet file. /d performs no action on the file. It is not recommended for use on folders with large number of files.

/y: Normally, you are prompted to confirm that you want to overwrite files in the destination; /y turns off these prompts.

FIXBOOT

Creates a new boot sector on the system partition. It is useful if the boot sector has been damaged.

Use

Type "FIXBOOT". This will create a new boot sector on the partition that you are logged onto. If you want to create a boot sector on a different drive, enter the drive letter followed by a colon after FIXBOOT and a space. For example, to create a new boot sector on the E: drive, type:

```
FIXBOOT E:
```

FIXMBR

Creates a new MBR on a hard drive. The MBR is the first sector on a hard drive. A small program on the MBR contains information about the partitions, indicating which one is bootable in case there are more than one.

Use

Type "FIXMBR". This will create a new MBR on the existing boot disk drive. To select another drive, enter the device name after FIXMBR. Run the MAP command to find the device name. For example, to replace the MBR on the first drive on the system, you can type:

```
FIXMBR \Device\HardDisk\0
```

Note

Use FIXMBR with caution. Never run FIXMBR unless you are having trouble accessing the drive or booting the computer and you cannot determine another reason. In certain cases, you can damage your partition. It is recommended not to use FIXMBR unless directed to do so by Microsoft support personnel or unless you are well versed in its use.

FORMAT

Use

Type "FORMAT" followed by the drive letter, fs:, the desired file system, and any desired switch. This version of FORMAT does not work with floppy disks, only hard drives.

Switches and Parameters

/q: Normally, FORMAT scans the disk for bad sectors. The /q switch causes FORMAT to skip this step, so it should be used only if the drive is known to be good and has been formatted before.

/fs: followed, without a space, by the name of the file system (NTFS, FAT, or FAT32): Specifies the file system. If you don't specify a file system, FORMAT uses the existing file system, if there is one.

LISTSVC

Lists the services and drivers available on the computer along with the startup type and description for each. The output appears one page at a time as if the MORE command prompt command were used.

LOGON

Logs you onto a particular installation of Windows. Useful on dual- or multi-boot systems when each OS is compatible with Recovery Console (NT 4.0, 2000, XP, Windows Server 2003). You will be able to select from a list of all Windows installations the Recovery Console can find. You will be prompted for the administrator password. If you get the password wrong three times, the Recovery Console will quit and the computer will automatically reboot.

MAP

Displays the assignment of drive letters to physical partitions. The output is useful if you want to run DISKPART, FIXBOOT, or FIXMBR.

Use

Type "MAP", followed by the arc switch, if desired.

Switch

arc: Causes the output to use the ARC format rather than the device name format. The arc switch is preceded only by a space, not by a slash or any other punctuation mark, as shown:

```
MAP arc
```

Note

The ARC name looks like the following: multi(0)disk(0)rdisk(0)partition(1)

The device name for the same drive and partition is \Device\HardDisk0\Partition1. For more information on device names and the ARC naming convention, search the Web.

MD OR MKDIR

Wildcard characters will not work.

MORE

Displays the text in a text file.

Use

Type "MORE" followed by the path to the text file you want to read. Use quotation marks or asterisks around filenames with spaces. MORE displays one page at a time and prompts for input on how to view the next part of the text file.

Note

In the Recovery Console, MORE is identical to the TYPE command.

REN OR RENAME

Renames a single file. Wildcards will not work.

RD OR RMDIR

RD will not delete a folder unless it is empty.

SYSTEMROOT

Makes the system root folder (almost always \Windows or \Winnt) the current folder.

TYPE

See the MORE Recovery Console command.

Chapters 9–13 A+ Certification Review Questions

The following A+ Certification Review Questions are related to the general topics introduced in Part I, Chapters 9 through 13, of this book. The answers and supporting references are provided after the review questions. All of the answer references specify chapters that are located in Part II of this book: The A+ Certification Exams.

1. Of the following choices, which is a hand-held pen-shaped device that is commonly used as a pointing or writing instrument to input text into a system such as a PDA?

- ○ A. Optomechanical pencil
- ○ B. Stylus
- ○ C. MIDI pen
- ○ D. Joystick
- ○ E. None of the above

2. If you are trying to connect to an ISP through a dial-up connection and you keep getting the error message "Server cannot negotiate an appropriate protocol," what is most likely the problem?

- ○ A. You have IPX/SPX bound to your Network Interface Card.
- ○ B. Your Internet Service Provider has run out of available connections.
- ○ C. Your modem driver is corrupt.
- ○ D. You have an improperly configured or corrupt TCP/IP configuration.

3. What action would you take first if your mouse pointer were not responding correctly?

- ○ A. Check DMA channel 2.
- ○ B. Check the mouse ball for debris.
- ○ C. Check COM2 settings.
- ○ D. Cascade IRQ2 to IRQ9.

4. **Which motherboard form factors used a 5-pin DIN connector for keyboard connections? (Choose Two)**
   - □ A. ATA
   - □ B. ATX
   - □ C. AT
   - □ D. XT

5. **You are attempting to connect a USB mouse, a USB keyboard, and USB digital camera to your new USB 2.0-compatible laptop system. How many system resources (IRQs) will you need?**
   - o A. 1.
   - o B. 3.
   - o C. 1,024.
   - o D. You cannot use USB 2.0 devices on a laptop.

6. **You are having trouble displaying entire Web pages in your Web browser. You want to view entire pages without having to use the left to right scroll bars. What should you modify?**
   - o A. Use the screen size buttons on your monitor.
   - o B. Select the Advanced tab under Display Properties Settings and change the Font Size.
   - o C. With your mouse, move the Screen Area Bar from 640 by 480 to 800 by 600 or more.
   - o D. Select the Advanced tab under Display Properties Settings and select big screen.

7. **You need more hard drive space to install a really big game in Windows 9x. You notice a large amount of unnecessary Temporary Internet Files. How do you get rid of them? (Choose Three)**
   - □ A. C:\DELTREE.
   - □ B. The Disk Cleanup Tool.
   - □ C. Internet Explorer Tools > Internet Options > Delete Files.
   - □ D. Control Panel > Internet Options > Delete files.
   - □ E. Internet Explorer Tools > Advanced > Restore Defaults.
   - □ F. Drag the Internet Explorer Icon to the Recycle Bin.

8. **You can receive e-mail messages without any problems. Unfortunately, you cannot send e-mail. What settings should you check?**
   - o A. IMAP
   - o B. MAPI
   - o C. POP
   - o D. SMTP
   - o E. None of the above

9. **Which utilities can be used to determine the IP address of known Internet domain names? (Choose Three)**
   - □ A. NetBEUI
   - □ B. PING
   - □ C. TRACERT
   - □ D. NetBIOS
   - □ E. NSLOOKUP
   - □ F. PONG
   - □ G. All of the above

10. **A customer informs you that he keeps getting paper jam error messages on his printer. You observe that there isn't any paper in the paper feed tray. What would you observe next to fix this issue?**
    - o A. The daisy wheel
    - o B. The printer's I/O memory address
    - o C. The printer's paper feed sensors
    - o D. The printer rollers

11. **You are running Windows 9x. How can you direct a print job straight to the printer instead of the print spooler?**
    - o A. Select Start > Settings > Control Panel > Disable Spooler.
    - o B. In the Spool Settings dialog box, select "Print directly to the printer."
    - o C. In the Spool Settings dialog box, select "Disable printer spooling."
    - o D. Specify Full-Duplex printing.

12. **What command can you use to get an important system file of executable file from the Windows 9x installation CD?**
    - o A. EXTRACT
    - o B. COPY D:\FILENAME C:\WINDOWS\SYSTEM
    - o C. RESTORE
    - o D. IMPORT

13. You are experiencing strange things in Windows 9x. Your task bar is missing and you cannot load certain programs. What is most likely the cause?

- o A. The AUTOEXEC.BAT file is corrupt.
- o B. You have experienced a total hard drive crash.
- o C. The Windows 9x registry is corrupt.
- o D. The WIN.INI and SYSTEM.INI files are corrupt.

14. Automated System Recovery (ASR) is available in which Windows NT-based operating system?

- o A. Windows XP Home
- o B. Windows XP Professional
- o C. Windows NT 4.0
- o D. All of the above

15. How many setup floppy disks can be created from the Windows XP (Home or Professional) CD-ROM?

- o A. Three
- o B. Four
- o C. Six
- o D. None of the above

16. Which of the following versions of Windows can be upgraded to Windows XP Professional? (Choose Two)

- □ A. Windows 95
- □ B. Windows 98/SE
- □ C. Windows 3.1
- □ D. Windows XP Home

17. Which of the following operating systems could be upgraded to Windows Me? (Choose Two)

- □ A. Windows 98SE
- □ B. Windows XP
- □ C. Windows 2000
- □ D. Windows 98

18. Which file executes when you restart your computer in MS-DOS mode?

- o A. DOSSTART.BAT
- o B. DEFRAG.EXE
- o C. WINSTART.BAT
- o D. DOSBOOT.EXE

19. A customer is trying to print very large documents to a laser printer and consistently receives memory overflow error messages. How can you resolve this issue? (Choose Three)

- ☐ A. Decrease the print resolution.
- ☐ B. Increase the size of the toner cartridge.
- ☐ C. Add more memory to the printer.
- ☐ D. Use a SCSI cable connector.
- ☐ E. Press Ctrl+Alt+Delete twice.
- ☐ F. Decrease the Resolution Enhancement Technology.

20. What type of printing technology has become very popular based on the growth of digital camera use?

- ○ A. Dye sublimation
- ○ B. CAD/CAM
- ○ C. Ink dispersion
- ○ D. Saddle stitch and fold
- ○ E. Ozone filtering

BONUS A+ CERTIFICATION PRACTICE QUESTIONS!

The following A+ Certification Practice Questions are in place to get you ready for Part II of the book. It is likely that you have not seen this material yet. If you can correctly answer the following questions, you have a very good chance of passing the current A+ exams. Good luck.

21. System Monitor in Windows 9x can be used to monitor which information? (Choose Three)

- ☐ A. RAID configurations
- ☐ B. Virtual memory
- ☐ C. Network client resources (on local computer)
- ☐ D. Network server memory (on local computer)
- ☐ E. Differential backup scenarios
- ☐ F. Windows NT audit trails

22. The Dr. Watson utility offers two ways to view information that it has logged. What are they?

- o A. Diagnostic View and Report View
- o B. Standard View and Advanced View
- o C. Standard View and Graphics View
- o D. Text View and GUI View

23. Which devices can be shared on a network using Windows 98? (Choose Three)

- □ A. Monitor
- □ B. Printer
- □ C. Modem
- □ D. CD-ROM
- □ E. Mouse
- □ F. Keyboard

24. Which protocols can be used to share printers in Windows 9x? (Choose Three)

- □ A. NetBEUI
- □ B. TCP/IP
- □ C. IPX/SPX
- □ D. NetBIOS
- □ E. TCP/IPRINT
- □ F. PTPTPC

25. Which TCP/IP utility command would you use from a Windows NT command prompt to see your workstation's IP address, subnet mask, and default gateway?

- o A. IPCONFIG
- o B. WINIPCFG
- o C. PING
- o D. TRACERT

26. Which TCP/IP utility command would you use from a Windows NT command prompt to test a connection that includes several computers and routers between you and a destination computer?

- o A. NETSTAT
- o B. WINIPCFG
- o C. PING
- o D. TRACERT

27. What does Dr. Watson do?

- ○ A. Provides access to "the Blue Screen of Death"
- ○ B. Takes a picture or "snapshot" of a system during an error state or fault
- ○ C. Automatically resets the Event Log files when run from a command prompt
- ○ D. Does a full system and registry scan for spyware

28. Where in Windows NT would you go to join a workgroup or a domain?

- ○ A. Control Panel > System > Network > Change
- ○ B. Right click on Network Neighborhood > Select Properties > Under the Identification tab select Change...
- ○ C. Start > Run > Command > Join
- ○ D. Right click on My Computer > Properties > Advanced > Environment

29. What protocol is used to communicate with Macintosh systems?

- ○ A. TCP/IP
- ○ B. AppleTalk
- ○ C. IPX/SPX
- ○ D. SMTP
- ○ E. None of the above

30. Which of the following are built-in power schemes available from the drop-down menu in the Power Options Properties/Power Schemes window in Windows 2000? (Choose Six)

- □ A. Home/Office Desk
- □ B. Portable/Laptop
- □ C. Presentation
- □ D. Always On
- □ E. Minimal Power Management
- □ F. Max Battery
- □ G. Always Off
- □ H. Car/Air port

31. An unattended installation of Windows XP requires which kind of file?

- ○ A. Question
- ○ B. INI
- ○ C. UDF
- ○ D. Answer

32. Which kind of file do you use to override specific settings created for an unattended installation?

- o A. Question
- o B. INI
- o C. UDF
- o D. Answer

33. A hardware abstraction layer (HAL) provides secured, restrictive access to which of the following? (Choose Two)

- □ A. The registry
- □ B. Software
- □ C. IRQ
- □ D. I/O addresses

34. When upgrading to Windows Me, you are prompted to save your system files. Should you not choose to save these files, you will be unable to:

- o A. Revert back to your previous operating system once Windows Me is installed.
- o B. Continue the upgrade installation.
- o C. Use programs associated with the older operating system you are installing over.
- o D. Use REGEDIT to update your registry once Windows Me has been installed.

35. Which of the following operating systems are considered a part of the Windows 9x family? (Choose Two)

- □ A. Windows 98SE
- □ B. Windows CE
- □ C. Windows XP
- □ D. Windows Me

36. What component of a dot matrix printer strikes a ribbon and leaves a character, number, or symbol on the paper?

- o A. A print hammer
- o B. A toner impaction device
- o C. A pin
- o D. A ribbon presser

37. You have collected several used laser printer toner cartridges. What is a standard procedure for disposal of such items?

- o A. Place them in the dumpster out back.
- o B. Send them back to the manufacturer.
- o C. Do not dispose of them. Shake the cartridges to free up loose toner. Toner is very expensive.
- o D. Empty toner into a half-used cartridge. Place the empty toner cartridge into a recycle bin.

38. How many pins does a dot matrix print head typically have?

- o A. 9 or 24
- o B. 27 or 16
- o C. 14 or 7
- o D. 1 or 4

39. What are the stages of the laser printing process collectively known as?

- o A. Electric Photo Magnetic Process
- o B. Electronic Laser Photographic Process
- o C. Electro Photographic Process
- o D. ELO Imaging Process

40. Which of the following are considered to be valid parallel port standards? (Choose Three)

- □ A. Bi-directional
- □ B. ECP
- □ C. Encapsulated Postscript
- □ D. Reverse DNS lookup
- □ E. EPP
- □ F. Serial

41. At what stage of the laser printing process is an image melted onto the paper?

- o A. Writing
- o B. Developing
- o C. Conditioning
- o D. Fusing

42. When working on the inside of a laser printer, what should you never touch based on its extremely high temperatures?

○ A. A toner cartridge

○ B. The print head

○ C. The fuser

○ D. The power supply

43. What is the minimum category cable type that can be used to support 100BaseTX?

○ A. Category6

○ B. Category43

○ C. Category4

○ D. Category5

44. What technological communication method is most popular with PDAs today?

○ A. USB

○ B. 10BaseT

○ C. The fourth OSI layer

○ D. Infrared technology

45. What types of connectors are used with coaxial cable? (Choose Two)

□ A. BNC

□ B. RJ-45

□ C. RJ-11

□ D. BNC T

46. Name three characteristics of a peer-to-peer network. (Choose Three)

□ A. Password protected shares.

□ B. 10 or fewer workstations.

□ C. Individual workstations can act as both client and server.

□ D. A user must authenticate with a security accounts manager database.

47. What device would you use to extend the length of your 10base2 bus segment?

○ A. A gateway

○ B. A bridge

○ C. A hub

○ D. A repeater

48. A star typology typically uses which type of cable to connect workstations?

- ○ A. Token Ring cable
- ○ B. FDDI cable
- ○ C. Twisted pair
- ○ D. Fiber optic

49. A 10Base2 would be implemented in which type of network typology?

- ○ A. Ring
- ○ B. Bus
- ○ C. Star
- ○ D. FDDI

50. What type of network would be implemented if users must be authenticated before they could access resources?

- ○ A. Peer-to-peer
- ○ B. Stand alone
- ○ C. Server based
- ○ D. Share level permission

51. Which of the following is usually posted in a hazardous area?

- ○ A. ESD wrist strap
- ○ B. APW Hose
- ○ C. Uninterruptible Power Supply
- ○ D. Halon gas warning
- ○ E. MSDS

52. What is a common name used to describe a single device that combines printing, scanning, copying, and faxing capabilities?

- ○ A. PSCAF (Printing, Scan, Copy, and Fax)
- ○ B. MFD (Multifunction Device)
- ○ C. Hub
- ○ D. Sublimation Device
- ○ E. None of the above

53. What is WEP?

- ○ A. A wireless transceiver that transmits and receives RF signals.
- ○ B. WEP is a standard for Windows Enterprise Programming.
- ○ C. Wireless security protocol specified under the IEEE 802.11b.2.
- ○ D. Windows Standard for Encapsulated Post Script.
- ○ E. None of the above.

54. Which of the following is a non-routable, small, efficient, Transport layer protocol meant for use in small networks with 1–200 workstations?

- o A. NetBEUI
- o B. TCP/IP
- o C. IPX/SPX
- o D. LDAP
- o E. WEP
- o F. All of the above

55. What does a DNS server do?

- o A. Allows Web pages to be formatted with graphics and symbols other than plain text
- o B. Converts fully qualified domain names to IP addresses
- o C. Offers developers and designers more flexibility in creating Web pages through the use of call tags
- o D. Connects different network typologies together, such as Token Ring and Ethernet
- o F. None of the above

A+ CERTIFICATION REVIEW ANSWERS AND REFERENCES

Answer Key	References Taken from Part II: The A+ Certification Exams
1. B	Chapter 18, "Mice and Pointing Devices"
2. D	Chapter 24, "Diagnosing and Troubleshooting Test Tips"
3. B	Chapter 18, "Mice and Pointing Devices"
4. C and D	Chapter 21, "Keyboard and Mouse Connectors"
5. A	Chapter 21, "USB Connections"
6. C	Chapter 24, "Utilities and Settings"
7. B, C, and D	Chapter 24, "Utilities and Settings"
8. D	Chapter 26, "Windows 2000 Networking and the Internet"
9. B, C, and E	Chapter 25, "Diagnosing and Troubleshooting Test Tips"
10. C	Chapter 19, "Dot Matrix and Ink-jet Printers"
11. B	Chapter 24, "Printers"
12. A	Chapter 24, "Diagnosing and Troubleshooting Test Tips"
13. C	Chapter 24, "The Windows 9x Registry"
14. B	Chapter 28, "Windows XP Installation Process"
15. D	Chapter 28, "Windows XP Installation Process"
16. B and D	Chapter 28, "Windows XP Upgrade Procedures"
17. A and D	Chapter 27, "Windows Me Installation Process"
18. A	Chapter 24, "Diagnosing and Troubleshooting Test Tips"
19. A, C, and F	Chapter 19, "Laser Printers"
20. A	Chapter 19, "Laser Printers"
21. B, C, and D	Chapter 24, "Utilities and Settings"
22. B	Chapter 24, "Utilities and Settings"
23. B, C, and D	Chapter 24, "Printers"
24. A, B, and C	Chapter 24, "Windows 9x Networking"
25. A	Chapter 25, "Utilities and Settings"
26. D	Chapter 25, "Utilities and Settings"
27. B	Chapter 25, "Diagnosing and Troubleshooting Test Tips"
28. B	Chapter 25, "Diagnosing and Troubleshooting Test Tips"
29. B	Chapter 26, "Diagnosing and Troubleshooting Test Tips"
30. A, B, C, D, E, and F	Chapter 26, "Windows 2000 Tools and Utilities"
31. D	Chapter 28, "Windows XP Installation Process"
32. C	Chapter 28, "Windows XP Installation Process"

A+ CERTIFICATION REVIEW ANSWERS AND REFERENCES *(continued)*

Answer Key	References Taken from Part II: The A+ Certification Exams
33. C and D	Chapter 28, "Windows XP Start-up Process"
34. A	Chapter 27, "Windows Me Installation Process"
35. A and D	Chapter 27, "Windows Me Introduction"
36. C	Chapter 19, "Dot Matrix and Ink-jet Printers"
37. B	Chapter 19, "Laser Printers"
38. A	Chapter 19, "Dot Matrix and Inkjet Printers"
39. C	Chapter 19, "Laser Printers"
40. A, B, and E	Chapter 19, "Parallel Port Standards"
41. D	Chapter 19, "Laser Printers"
42. C	Chapter 19, "Laser Printers"
43. D	Chapter 21, "Networking Connectors and Cables"
44. D	Chapter 21, "Wireless Connectivity"
45. A and D	Chapter 21, "Networking Connectors and Cables"
46. A, B, and C	Chapter 22, "Network Categories"
47. D	Chapter 22, "Network Topology"
48. C	Chapter 22, "Network Topology"
49. B	Chapter 22, "Network Topology"
50. C	Chapter 22, "Network Categories"
51. E	Chapter 15, "Preventive Maintenance and Safety"
52. B	Chapter 19, "Laser Printers"
53. C	Chapter 21, "Wireless Connectivity"
54. A	Chapter 22, "Protocols"
55. B	Chapter 22, "The Internet and Viruses"

Part II

The A+ Certification Exams

14 Introduction to the A+ Certification Exams

In This Chapter

- The CompTIA A+ Certification 2003 Exam Objectives
- Registering for the A+ Tests
- Test Site Requirements and a Little Advice
- How Computerized Testing Works
- Your State of Mind
- Useful Tools, Tips, and Study Techniques
- Book Structure and Sample Review Questions
- Chapter Summary
- References

Welcome to the very best available tool to help you prepare for and pass the current A+ Certification exams! In the next several pages you will learn the importance of A+ certification and how it can affect your career goals. You will learn why you should use this particular book to prepare for the current A+ exams and future certification exams. You will gain insight into the process of scheduling an exam and what to expect when you get to the test site.

If you are interested in gainful employment in the technology industry, you should be certified. The majority of businesses today require applicants to provide proof of certification. If you are applying for a position as a PC technician, network administrator, systems engineer, software engineer, developer or programmer, A+ certification is normally a minimum requirement. If you are already employed and wish to enhance your technical job opportunities, as well as your income, A+ certification is for you. Many businesses today require their entire IT staff to be A+ certified.

THE COMPTIA A+ CERTIFICATION 2003 EXAM OBJECTIVES

There are two tests you must pass to become A+ certified: the A+ Core Hardware Service Technician test (220-301) and the A+ Operating System Technologies test (220-302). Both A+ tests are currently in conventional format, which is addressed later in detail in this chapter. These new tests are offered in English, Japanese, French, Spanish, and German.

The A+ Core Hardware Service Technician test focuses on computer hardware, including motherboards, processors, peripherals, memory, cables and connectors, electronics, and basic networking. The A+ Operating System Technologies test focuses primarily on the most popular operating systems in use, including Windows® 95 operating system, Windows® 98 operating system, Windows NT® operating system, Windows® 2000 operating system, Windows® Me operating system, and Windows® XP operating system. It also includes test questions focusing on memory utilization, printing, hard drive partitioning, and basic networking. For those wondering about Linux, there are no Linux-based questions on this test. CompTIA has a separate certification called Linux+.

It is important to note that CompTIA recommends at least 500 hours of hands-on lab or field experience before taking these tests. The author of this book recommends an A+ based training class, six months of hands-on (real world) experience, and the mastering of all questions included in this book and its accompanying CD-ROM.

The CompTIA domains, concepts, and modules are public knowledge, and are provided in PDF (Portable Document Format) for download at the following CompTIA Web site: *http://www.comptia.org/certification/A/upgrade.asp.*

A Brief History and Exam Upgrade

In the fourth quarter of 2003, CompTIA changed both the A+ Hardware Core Service Technician test and the A+ Operating System Technologies test from adaptive-based testing to conventional-based testing. Although the current tests are both given in conventional format, it is important for your future certification goals that you also have a basic understanding of how adaptive testing works. Both of these testing formats will be described in detail shortly.

The current A+ tests contain questions that draw upon knowledge based on CompTIA's 2003 domain objectives. In a nutshell, CompTIA has recently changed the format of their A+ exams from adaptive to conventional testing and created new test questions based on their 2003 A+ exam objectives.

CompTIA states the following information on their A+ Web site regarding the 2003 A+ tests; "Changes incorporated in the 2003 Upgrade are not major. The certification content continues to validate that the successful candidate has important knowledge and skills necessary to competently install, build, configure, upgrade, troubleshoot and repair personal computer compatible hardware and PC operating systems, including troubleshooting basic network and Internet connectivity, dial-up, DSL, and cable. In addition, the 2003 Upgrade covers the latest memory, bus, peripherals, operating systems (Me and XP), and wireless."

The A+ Core Hardware (2003) Examination Objectives

The specific questions on the A+ Core Hardware Service Technician exam will be drawn from subject matter related to the following six domains, concepts, and modules created and publicly posted by CompTIA. For your convenience and easy reference, a complete list of both (2003) examination objectives is provided in Table 14.1. You will find that all of the CompTIA domains are covered in detail in this book.

TABLE 14.1

Domain	Percent of Examination
1. Installation, Configuration, and Upgrading	35%
2. Diagnosing and Troubleshooting	21%
3. PC Preventive Maintenance, Safety, and Environmental Issues	5%
4. Motherboards/Processors/Memory	11%
5. Printers	9%
6. Basic Networking	19%
	Total 100%

Domain 1: Installation, Configuration, and Upgrading

1.1 Identify the names, purpose, and characteristics of system modules. Recognize these modules by sight or definition.

Examples of concepts and modules are:

- Motherboard
- Firmware
- Power supply
- Processor/CPU
- Memory
- Storage devices

- Display devices
- Adapter cards
- Ports
- Cases
- Riser cards

1.2 Identify basic procedures for adding and removing field-replaceable modules for desktop systems. Given a replacement scenario, choose the appropriate sequence.

Desktop components:

- Motherboard
- Storage device
  - FDD
  - HDD
  - CD/CDRW
  - DVD/DVDRW
  - Tape drive
  - Removable storage
- Power supply
  - AC adapter
  - AT/ATX
- Cooling systems
  - Fans
  - Heat sinks
  - Liquid cooling
- Processor/CPU
- Memory
- Display device
- Input devices
  - Keyboard
  - Mouse/Pointer devices
  - Touch screen
- Adapters
  - Network Interface Cards (NIC)
  - Sound card
  - Video card
  - Modem
  - SCSI

    - IEEE 1394/FireWire
    - USB
    - Wireless

1.3 Identify basic procedures for adding and removing field-replaceable modules for portable systems. Given a replacement scenario, choose the appropriate sequences.

Portable components:

- Storage devices
    - FDD
    - HDD
    - CD/CDRW
    - DVD/DVDRW
    - Removable storage
- Power sources
    - AC adapter
    - DC adapter
    - Battery
    - Memory
    - Input devices
    - Keyboard
    - Mouse/Pointer devices
    - Touch screen
- PCMCIA/Mini-PCI adapters
    - Network Interface Card (NIC)
    - Modem
    - SCSI
    - IEEE 1394/FireWire
    - USB
    - Storage (memory and hard drive)
- Docking station/Port replicators
- LCD panel
- Wireless
    - Adapter/Controller
    - Antenna

1.4 Identify typical IRQs, DMAs, and I/O addresses, and procedures for altering these settings when installing and configuring devices. Choose the appropriate installation or configuration steps in a given scenario.

Content may include the following:

- Legacy devices (e.g., ISA sound card)
- Specialized devices (e.g., CAD/CAM)
- Internal modems
- Floppy drive controllers
- Hard drive controllers
- Multimedia devices
- NICs
- I/O ports
    - Serial
    - Parallel
    - USB ports
    - IEEE 1394/FireWire
    - Infrared

1.5 Identify the names, purposes, and performance characteristics of standardized/common peripheral ports, associated cabling, and their connectors. Recognize ports, cabling, and connectors by sight.

Content may include the following:

- Port types
    - Serial
    - Parallel
    - USB ports
    - IEEE 1394/FireWire
    - Infrared
- Cable types
    - Serial (straight through versus null modem)
    - Parallel
    - USB
- Connector types
    - Serial
        - DB-9
        - DB-25
        - RJ-11
        - RJ-45

- Parallel
  - DB-25
- Centronics (mini, 36)
  - PS2/MINI-DIN
  - USB
  - IEEE 1394

1.6 Identify proper procedures for installing and configuring common IDE devices. Choose the appropriate installation or configuration sequences in given scenarios. Recognize the associated cables.

Content may include the following:

- IDE interface types
  - EIDE
  - ATA/ATAPI
  - Serial ATA
  - PIO
- RAID (0, 1, and 5)
- Master/Slave/Cable select
- Devices per channel
- Primary/Secondary
- Cable orientation/requirements

1.7 Identify proper procedures for installing and configuring common SCSI devices. Choose the appropriate installation or configuration sequences in given scenarios. Recognize the associated cables.

Content may include the following:

- SCSI interface types
  - Narrow
  - Fast
  - Wide
  - Ultra-wide
  - LVD
  - HVD
- Internal versus external
- SCSI IDs
  - Jumper block/DIP switch settings (binary equivalents)
  - Resolving ID conflicts
- RAID (0, 1, and 5)

- Cabling
  - Length
  - Type
  - Termination requirements (active, passive, auto)

1.8 Identify proper procedures for installing and configuring common peripheral devices. Choose the appropriate installation or configuration sequences in given scenarios.

Content may include the following:

- Modems and transceivers (dial-up, cable, DSL, ISDN)
- External storage
- Digital cameras
- PDAs
- Wireless access points
- Infrared devices
- Printers
- UPSs and suppressors
- Monitors

1.9 Identify procedures to optimize PC operations in specific situations. Predict the effects of specific procedures under given scenarios.

Topics may include:

- Cooling systems
  - Liquid
  - Air
  - Heat sink
  - Thermal compound
- Disk subsystem enhancements
  - Hard drives
  - Controller cards (e.g., RAID, ATA-100, etc.)
  - Cables
- NICs
- Specialized video cards
- Memory
- Additional processors

1.10 Determine the issues that must be considered when upgrading a PC. In a given scenario, determine when and how to upgrade system components.

Issues may include:

- Drivers for legacy devices
- Bus types and characteristics
- Cache in relationship to motherboards
- Memory capacity and characteristics
- Processor speed and compatibility
- Hard drive capacity and characteristics
- System/Firmware limitations
- Power supply output capacity

Components may include the following:

- Motherboards
- Memory
- Hard drives
- CPU
- BIOS
- Adapter cards
- Laptop power sources
  - Lithium ion
  - NiMH
  - Fuel cell
- PCMCIA Type I, II, III cards

Domain 2: Diagnosing and Troubleshooting

2.1 Recognize common problems associated with each module and their symptoms, and identify steps to isolate and troubleshoot the problems. Given a problem situation, interpret the symptoms and infer the most likely cause.

Content may include the following:

- I/O ports and cables
  - Serial
  - Parallel
  - USB ports
  - IEEE 1394/FireWire
  - Infrared
  - SCSI

- Motherboards
  - CMOS/ BIOS settings
  - POST audible/visual error codes
- Peripherals
- Computer case
  - Power supply
  - Slot covers
  - Front cover alignment
- Storage devices and cables
  - FDD
  - HDD
  - CD/CDRW
  - DVD/DVDRW
  - Tape drive
  - Removable storage
- Cooling systems
  - Fans
  - Heating sinks
  - Liquid cooling
  - Temperature sensors
- Processor/CPU
- Memory
- Display device
- Input devices
  - Keyboard
  - Mouse/Pointer devices
  - Touch screen
- Adapters
  - Network Interface Card (NIC)
  - Sound card
  - Video card
  - Modem
  - SCSI
  - IEEE 1394/FireWire
  - USB
- Portable Systems
  - PCMCIA
  - Batteries
  - Docking stations/Port replicators
  - Portable unique storage

2.2 Identify basic troubleshooting procedures and tools, and how to elicit problem symptoms from customers. Justify asking particular questions in a given scenario.

Content may include the following:

- Troubleshooting/Isolation/Problem determination procedures
- Determining whether it is a hardware or software problem
- Gathering information from the user
  - Customer environment
  - Symptoms/Error codes
  - Situation when the problem occurred

Domain 3: PC Preventive Maintenance, Safety, and Environmental Issues

3.1 Identify the various types of preventive maintenance measures, products, and procedures, and when/how to use them.

Content may include the following:

- Liquid cleaning compounds
- Types of materials to clean contacts and connections
- Nonstatic vacuums (e.g., for chassis, power supplies, fans)
- Cleaning monitors
- Cleaning removable media devices
- Ventilation, dust, and moisture control on the PC hardware interior
- Hard disk maintenance (defragging, scan disk, CHKDSK)
- Verifying UPS (Uninterruptible Power Supply) and suppressors

3.2 Identify various safety measures and procedures, and when/how to use them.

Content may include the following:

- ESD (Electrostatic Discharge) precautions and procedures
  - What ESD can do, and how it might be apparent or hidden
  - Common ESD protection devices
  - Situations that could present a danger or hazard
- Potential hazards and proper safety procedures relating to
  - High-voltage equipment
  - Power supply
  - CRTs

3.3 Identify environmental protection measures and procedures, and when/how to use them.

Content may include the following:

- Special disposal procedures that comply with environmental guidelines
- Batteries
- CRTs
- Chemical solvents and cans
- MSDS (Material Safety Data Sheet)

Domain 4: Motherboard/Processors/Memory

4.1 Distinguish between the popular CPU chips in terms of their basic characteristics.

Content may include the following:

- Popular CPU chips (Pentium-class compatible)
- Voltage
- Speeds (actual versus advertised)
- Cache Levels 1, 2, 3
- Socket/Slots
- VRM(s)

4.2 Identify the types of RAM (Random Access Memory), form factors, and operational characteristics. Determine banking and speed requirements under given scenarios.

Content may include the following:

- Types
  - EDO RAM (Extended Data Output RAM)
  - DRAM (Dynamic Random Access Memory)
  - SRAM (Static RAM)
  - VRAM (Video RAM)
  - SDRAM (Synchronous Dynamic RAM)
  - DDR (Double Data Rate)
  - RAMBUS
- Form factors (including pin count)
  - SIMM (Single In-line Memory Module)
  - DIMM (Dual In-line Memory Module)
  - SoDIMM (Small outline DIMM)
  - MicroDIMM
  - RIMM (Rambus Inline Memory Module)

- Operational characteristics
  - Memory chips (8 bit, 16 bit, and 32 bit)
  - Parity chips versus nonparity chips
  - ECC versus non-ECC
  - Single sided versus double sided

4.3 Identify the most popular types of motherboards, their components, and their architectures (bus structures).

Content may include the following:

- Types of motherboards
  - AT
  - ATX
- Components
  - Communication ports
  - Serial
  - USB
  - Parallel
  - IEEE 1394/FireWire
  - Infrared
- Memory
  - SIMM
  - DIMM
  - RIMM
  - SoDIMM
  - MicroDIMM
- Processor sockets
  - Slot 1
  - Slot 2
  - Slot A
  - Socket A
  - Socket 7
  - Socket 8
  - Socket 423
  - Socket 478
  - Socket 370
- External cache memory (Level 2)
- Bus architecture
- ISA
- PCI
  - PCI 32 bit
  - PCI 64 bit

- AGP
  - 2x
  - 4x
  - 8x (Pro)
- USB
- AMR (Audio Modem Riser) slots
- CNR (Communication Network Riser) slots
- Basic compatibility guidelines
- IDE (ATA, ATAPI, ultra-DMA, EIDE)
- SCSI (narrow, wide, fast, ultra, HVD, LVD [Low Voltage Differential])
- Chipsets

4.4 Identify the purpose of CMOS (Complementary Metal-Oxide Semiconductor) memory, what it contains, and how and when to change its parameters. Given a scenario involving CMOS, choose the appropriate course of action.

CMOS settings:

- Default settings
- CPU settings
- Printer parallel port—uni-/bi-directional, disable/enable, ECP, EPP
- COM/serial port—memory address, interrupt request, disable
- Floppy drive—enable/disable drive or boot, speed, density
- Hard drive—size and drive type
- Memory—speed, parity, nonparity
- Boot sequence
- Date/Time
- Passwords
- Plug-and-Play BIOS
- Disabling onboard devices
- Disabling virus protection
- Power management
- Infrared

Domain 5: Printers

5.1 Identify printer technologies, interfaces, and options/upgrades.

Technologies include:

- Laser
- Ink dispersion
- Dot matrix

- Solid ink
- Thermal
- Dye sublimation

Interfaces include:

- Parallel
- Network
- SCSI
- USB
- Infrared
- Serial
- IEEE 1394/FireWire
- Wireless

Options/Upgrades include:

- Memory
- Hard drives
- NICs
- Trays and feeders
- Finishers (e.g., stapling, etc.)
- Scanners/Fax/Copier

5.2 Recognize common printer problems and techniques used to resolve them.

Content may include the following:

- Printer drivers
- Firmware updates
- Paper feed and output
- Calibrations
- Printing test pages
- Errors (printed or displayed)
- Memory
- Configuration
- Network connections
- Connections
- Paper jam
- Print quality
- Safety precautions
- Preventive maintenance
- Consumables
- Environment

Domain 6: Basic Networking

6.1 Identify the common types of network cables, their characteristics, and connectors.

Cable types include:

- Coaxial
  - RG6
  - RG8
  - RG58
  - RG59
- Plenum/PVC
- UTP
  - CAT3
  - CAT5/e
  - CAT6
- STP
- Fiber
  - Single mode
  - Multimode

Connector types include:

- BNC
- RJ-45
- AUI
- ST/SC
- IDC/UDC

6.2 Identify basic networking concepts, including how a network works.

Concepts include:

- Installing and configuring network cards
- Addressing
- Bandwidth
- Status indicators
- Protocols
  - TCP/IP
  - IPX/SPX (NWLINK)
  - AppleTalk
  - NetBEUI/NetBIOS

- Full duplex, half duplex
- Cabling—twisted pair, coaxial, fiber optic, RS-232
- Networking models
  - Peer to peer
  - Client/Server
- Infrared
- Wireless

6.3 Identify common technologies available for establishing Internet connectivity and their characteristics.

Technologies include:

- LAN
- DSL
- Cable
- ISDN
- Dial-up
- Satellite
- Wireless

Characteristics include:

- Definition
- Speed
- Connections

The A+ Operating System Technologies (2003) Examination Objectives

The specific questions on the A+ Operating Systems Technologies exam will be drawn from subject matter related to the following four domains, concepts, and modules that are listed in Table 14.2.

TABLE 14.2

Domain	Percent of Examination
1. Operating System Fundamentals	28%
2. Installation, Configuration, and Upgrading	31%
3. Diagnosing and Troubleshooting	25%
4. Networks	16%
	Total 100%

Domain 1: Operating System Fundamentals

1.1 Identify the major desktop components and interfaces, and their functions. Differentiate the characteristics of Windows 9x/Me, Windows NT 4.0 Workstation, Windows 2000 Professional, and Windows XP.

Content may include the following:

- Contrasts between Windows 9x/Me, Windows NT 4.0 Workstation, Windows 2000 Professional, and Windows XP
- Major operating system components
  - Registry
  - Virtual memory
  - File system
- Major operating system interfaces
  - Windows Explorer
  - My Computer
  - Control Panel
  - Computer management console
  - Accessories/System tools
  - Command line
  - Network Neighborhood/My Network Places
  - Task bar/Systray
  - Start Menu
  - Device Manager

1.2 Identify the names, locations, purposes, and contents of major system files.

Content may include the following:

- Windows 9x specific files
  - IO.SYS
  - MSDOS.SYS
  - AUTOEXEC.BAT
  - COMMAND.COM
  - CONFIG.SYS
  - HIMEM.SYS
  - EMM386.exe
  - WIN.COM
  - SYSTEM.INI

- Registry data files
- SYSTEM.DAT
- USER.DAT
- Windows NT-based specific files
  - BOOT.INI
  - NTLDR
  - NTDETECT.COM
  - NTBOOTDD.SYS
  - NTUSER.DAT
  - Registry data files

1.3 Demonstrates the ability to use command-line functions and utilities to manage the operating system, including the proper syntax and switches.

Command-line functions and utilities include:

- Command/CMD
- DIR
- ATTRIB
- VER
- MEM
- SCANDISK
- DEFRAG
- EDIT
- XCOPY
- COPY
- FORMAT
- FDISK
- SETVER
- SCANREG
- MD/CD/RD
- Delete/Rename
- DELTREE
- TYPE
- ECHO
- SET
- PING

1.4 Identify basic concepts and procedures for creating, viewing, and managing disks, directories, and files. This includes procedures for changing file attributes and the ramifications of those changes (e.g., security issues).

Content may include the following:

- Disks
  - Partitions
    - Active partition
    - Primary partition
    - Extended partition
    - Logical partition
  - Files systems
    - FAT16
    - FAT32
    - NTFS4
    - NTFS5.x
- Directory structures (root directory, subdirectories, etc.)
  - Create folders
  - Navigate the directory structure
  - Maximum depth
- Files
  - Creating files
  - File naming conventions (most common extensions, 8.3, maximum length)
  - File attributes—read only, hidden, system, and archive attributes
  - File compression
  - File encryption
  - File permissions
  - File types (text versus binary file)

1.5 Identify the major operating system utilities, their purposes, location, and available switches.

- Disk management tools
  - DEFRAG.EXE
  - FDISK.EXE
  - Backup/Restore utility (MS Backup, NT Backup, etc.)
  - ScanDisk
  - CHKDSK
  - Disk cleanup
  - Format

- System management tools
  - Device manager
  - System manager
  - Computer manager
  - MSCONFIG.EXE
  - REGEDIT.EXE (view information/backup registry)
  - REGEDT32.EXE
  - SYSEDIT.EXE
  - SCANREG
  - COMMAND/CMD
  - Event viewer
  - Task manager
- File management tools
  - ATTRIB.EXE
  - EXTRACT.EXE
  - Edit.com
  - Windows Explorer

Domain 2: Installation, Configuration, and Upgrading

2.1 Identify the procedures for installing Windows 9x/Me, Windows NT 4.0 Workstation, Windows 2000 Professional, and Windows XP, and bringing the operating system to a basic operational level.

Content may include the following:

- Verify hardware compatibility and minimum requirements.
- Determine OS installation options.
  - Installation type (typical, custom, other)
  - Network configuration
  - File system type
  - Dual boot support
- Disk preparation order (conceptual disk preparation)
  - Start the installation
  - Partition
  - Format drive
- Run appropriate set-up utility
  - Setup
  - Winnt
- Installation methods
  - Bootable CD-ROM
  - Boot floppy

- Network installation
- Drive imaging
- Device driver configuration
  - Load default drivers
  - Find updated drivers
- Restore user data files (if applicable)
- Identify common symptoms and problems

2.2 Identify steps to perform an operating system upgrade from Windows 9x/Me, Windows NT 4.0 Workstation, Windows 2000 Professional, or Windows XP. Given an upgrade scenario, choose the appropriate next steps.

Content may include the following:

- Upgrade paths available
- Determine correct upgrade start-up utility (e.g., WINNT32 versus WINNT)
- Verify hardware compatibility and minimum requirements
- Verify application compatibility
- Apply OS service packs, patches, and updates
- Install additional Windows components

2.3 Identify the basic system boot sequences and boot methods, including the steps to create an emergency boot disk with utilities installed for Windows 9x/Me, Windows NT 4.0 Workstation, Windows 2000 Professional, or Windows XP.

Content may include the following:

- Boot sequence
  - Files required to boot
  - Boot steps (Windows 9x/NT based)
- Alternative boot methods
  - Using a start-up disk
  - Safe/VGA-only mode
  - Last known good configuration
  - Command prompt mode
  - Booting to a system-restore point
  - Recovery console
  - Boot.ini switches
  - Dual boot

- Creating emergency disks with OS utilities
- Creating an Emergency Repair Disk (ERD)

2.4 Identify procedures for installing/adding a device, including loading, adding, and configuring device drivers and required software.

Content may include the following:

- Device driver installation
  - Plug-and-Play (PnP) and non-PnP devices
  - Install and configure device drivers
  - Install different device drivers
  - Manually install a device driver
  - Search the Internet for updated device drivers
  - Using unsigned drivers (driver signing)
- Install additional Windows components
- Determine if permissions are adequate for performing the task

2.5 Identify the procedures necessary to optimize the operating system and major operating system subsystems.

Content may include the following:

- Virtual memory management
- Disk Defragmentation
- Files and Buffers
- Caches
- Temporary file management

Domain 3: Diagnosing and Troubleshooting

3.1 Recognize and interpret the meaning of common error codes and start-up messages from the boot sequence, and identify steps to correct the problems.

Content may include the following:

- Common error messages and codes
  - Boot failure and errors
- Invalid boot disk
- Inaccessible boot device
- Missing NTLDR
- Bad or missing command interpreter
  - Start-up messages

- Error in CONFIG.SYS line XX
- Himem.sys not loaded
- Missing or corrupt Himem.sys
- Device/Service has failed to start
  - A device referenced in SYSTEM.INI, WIN.INI, Registry is not found
  - Event Viewer—event log is full
  - Failure to start GUI
  - Windows Protection Error
  - User-modified settings cause improper operation at start-up
  - Registry corruption
- Using the correct utilities
  - Dr. Watson
  - Boot Disk
  - Event Viewer

3.2 Recognize when to use common diagnostic utilities and tools. Given a diagnostic scenario involving one of these utilities or tools, select the appropriate steps needed to resolve the problem.

Utilities and tools may include the following:

- Start-up disks
  - Required files for a boot disk
  - Boot disk with CD-ROM support
- Startup Modes
  - Safe mode
  - Safe mode with command prompt
  - Safe mode with networking
  - Step-by-step/Single-step mode
  - Automatic skip driver (ASD.exe)
- Diagnostic tools, utilities, and resources
  - User/Installation manuals
  - Internet/Web resources
  - Training materials
  - Task Manager
  - Dr. Watson
  - Boot disk
  - Event Viewer
  - Device Manager
  - WinMSD
  - MSD

    - Recovery CD-ROM
    - CONFIGSAFE
- Eliciting problem symptoms from customers
- Having the customer reproduce error as part of the diagnostic process
- Identifying recent changes to the computer environment from the user

3.3 Recognize common operational and usability problems, and determine how to resolve them.

Content may include the following:

- Troubleshooting Windows-specific printing problems
    - Print spool is stalled
    - Incorrect/incompatible driver for printer
    - Incorrect parameter
- Other common problems
    - General Protection Faults
    - Bluescreen error (BSOD)
    - Illegal operation
    - Invalid working directory
    - System lockup
    - Option (sound card, modem, input device) or will not function
    - Application will not start or load
    - Cannot log on to network (option-NIC not functioning)
    - Applications don't install
    - Network connections
- Viruses and virus types
    - What they are
    - TSR (Terminate Stay Resident) programs and virus
    - Sources (floppy, e-mails, etc.)
    - How to determine presence

Domain 4: Networks

4.1 Identify the networking capabilities of Windows. Given configuration parameters, configure the operating system to connect to a network.

Content may include the following:

- Configure protocols
    - TCP/IP
- Gateway
- Subnet mask

- DNS (and domain suffix)
- WINS
- Static address assignment
- Automatic address assignment (APIPA, DHCP)
    - IPX/SPX (NWLink)
    - AppleTalk
    - NetBEUI/NetBIOS
- Configure client options
    - Microsoft
    - Novell
- Verify the configuration
- Understand the use of the following tools
    - IPCONFIG.EXE
    - WINIPCFG.EXE
    - PING
    - TRACERT.EXE
    - NSLOOKUP.EXE
- Share resources (understand the capabilities/limitations with each OS version)
- Setting permissions to shared resources
- Network type and network card

4.2 Identify the basic Internet protocols and terminologies. Identify procedures for establishing Internet connectivity. In a given scenario, configure the operating system to connect to, and use Internet resources.

Content may include the following:

- Protocols and terminologies
    - ISP
    - TCP/IP
    - E-mail (POP, SMTP, IMAP)
    - HTML
    - HTTP
    - HTTPS
    - SSL
    - Telnet
    - FTP
    - DNS
- Connectivity technologies
    - Dial-up networking
    - DSL networking

    - ISDN networking
    - Cable
    - Satellite
    - Wireless
    - LAN
- Installing and configuring browsers
    - Enable/Disable script support
    - Configure proxy settings
    - Configure security settings
- Firewall protection under Windows XP

REGISTERING FOR THE A+ TESTS

This book has you and your certification status in mind. You (the examinee) must reduce the stress levels involved with preparing and scheduling for the tests in order to focus your energy on your goal: getting A+ certified for life. The *A+ Exams Guide (2003 Objectives)* is your best resource.

In the United States and Canada, there are two companies to register with to take the A+ certification tests (as well as other certification tests): Pearson VUE and Prometric. You can register online or call either company. To register with Pearson VUE, visit *http://www.vue.com,* or call 1-877-551-PLUS (7587). To register with Prometric, visit *http://www.2test.com,* or call 1-800-776-4276.

You are required to register at least 12 hours before you take the test. If you decide to cancel after registering, you must call 12 hours before your scheduled test time to cancel, or you will forfeit your money. Your best bet is to pick a target date for taking the tests, give yourself at least 30 days to study this book, and answer all questions correctly on the included test-preparation CD-ROM. Register at least three days ahead of the date and time you wish to sit for the exams. Ask the registration person for the nearest test center location.

ON THE CD

Currently, the cost of each test is approximately $145 (U.S.). You do not get your money back if you fail. That's around $300 to get certified (not including this book), so don't fail! You can take each test separately or take them together. For complete CompTIA exam pricing by country, please visit: *http://www.comptia.org/certification/general_information/test_pricing.asp?type=certification.*

If you pass one test, you will get credit for that test only. You must pass both tests to become A+ certified. In other words, if you pass one test and fail the other, you must re-register for the test you failed and pass it to complete the certification objectives. If you pass both tests, you are instantly A+ certified. A welcome kit will be sent to you within four to six weeks, depending on shipping and other factors.

Information you need to have ready before you register:

- Your name, company name, and your mailing address.
- The exam name and number you wish to take—in this case, A+ Core Hardware Service Technician exam 220-301 and/or A+ Operating Systems Technologies exam 220-302.
- Your method of payment. For quick registration and getting the testing date and time slot that fits your schedule, pay with a valid credit card. Other forms of payment must be received by the registration center before the tests can be scheduled.

TEST SITE REQUIREMENTS AND A LITTLE ADVICE

It is advised that you arrive at the test site one hour before your exam. Take a little time to get comfortable with the surroundings at the test site, sign in at the registration desk, and take the time to study any charts and details that you feel are your weak points. Depending on the schedule of tests at the test site, you can generally take care of the paperwork, find a quiet area to do some last-minute cramming, and then go take the tests. If no one is scheduled before you, it may be possible to take the tests before your scheduled time. You will be asked to provide two forms of identification at the testing site. A valid driver's license and a credit card are sufficient. One form of identification must be a photo ID. When you are ready to enter the testing room, you will be given a blank sheet of paper and a marker or pencil. You cannot take any other books or notes with you. Cell phones are usually not allowed. If you are taking both A+ exams together, you will be allowed a quick break after the first one.

After you have signed in at the testing center, a testing coordinator will direct you to a computer that will have your test ready to go. You may be required to enter a security ID before you start the test. This ID is normally your Social Security number. The testing coordinator will inform you of any special procedures for the particular testing center.

The CompTIA Certification Program has been changed recently to produce a more valuable and desired certification. This book is up to date with the current exams. For more information about the CompTIA A+ Certification Program and other CompTIA certifications, visit the CompTIA Web site at *http://www.comptia.org*.

HOW COMPUTERIZED TESTING WORKS

The majority of computerized certification tests offered today are given in either conventional or adaptive format. Because you are studying A+, which is considered an entry-level certification, it is likely that this will be one of your first computerized testing experiences. For that reason, it is important that you understand the basics regarding each of these testing techniques. It's kind of like having a home field advantage if you fully understand how the test (your opponent) 'thinks' and 'reacts.' As a general rule, you should always educate yourself on the particular testing format in which the tests you choose to take will be presented. Next, we will discuss the basics of conventional and adaptive testing.

Conventional Testing

A conventional computerized test is a test that is fixed in length. It has a set number of questions that you must answer in a certain amount of time. You will often find conventional tests referred to as fixed length, traditional, or linear.

Both of the A+ Certification 2003 Objectives tests are in conventional format. You will be allotted 90 minutes to complete each 80-question test. You must answer all 80 questions in order to finish each exam. A timer in the upper-right-hand corner of the test screen displays the amount of time you have remaining to complete the test.

Again, you will be required to answer all multiple-choice questions. Be careful—some questions require more than one answer. If there are circles next to your choices, you must choose only one answer. However, if you see squares next to your choices, you will have the option to select one or more answers. Read the questions carefully; they usually say, "Choose Two" or "Choose Three." If a question asks you to "Choose Two" and you select only one answer, the test will prompt you to choose two before you can proceed. The same is true for "Choose Three" and so on.

There will be questions that require you to click a graphic radio button to display a diagram or image. Be careful when viewing graphics; some are notorious for being unclear. Make sure you know what you are selecting on the images. It is likely that you'll be asked to select the correct answer or best choice from the displayed diagram or image. Some diagrams require you to select or identify several choices. You will be allowed to refer back to the diagram to make your selections. This is a good place to use scratch paper to keep your thoughts straight.

As with most conventional exams, you will have the option to 'mark' a question for later review. In other words, you will have the ability to review previously answered questions by going backward.

You will encounter many situational questions on these new exams. To be more specific, you will be presented with a problem situation. You will have to choose which troubleshooting method or approach is best to resolve that particular situation. Some of the more difficult questions may ask in what order certain steps should be taken to isolate and ultimately resolve a problem.

When you have finished the last question on the test, your final score will be tabulated, and your test results will be instantly presented to you. You will know then and there whether you have passed or failed the test.

Each exam will be graded on a scale from 100 to 900.

Adaptive Testing

Many certification exams are given in Computerized Adaptive Testing (CAT) format. Traditionally, CompTIA has released its new exams in conventional testing format and then eventually converted them to adaptive format. As stated earlier in this chapter, the current exams are in conventional format. But again, it is better for you to have a clear understanding early in your test-taking career of how adaptive tests work. It is very likely that you will encounter them once you have passed A+. For that reason, the following information on adaptive testing is provided.

The adaptive testing software engine will evaluate your most recently answered question. If you answered the question correctly, the next question is generated from a group of more difficult questions, until the testing software is satisfied that you have met the required level of knowledge on that subject matter. If you answered the question incorrectly, a less difficult question is generated. This process continues as the testing engine accurately keeps track of your knowledge level. Picture a graph running behind the scenes, keeping track of your answers. The more questions you answer correctly, the higher above the passing line you move. The more you answer incorrectly, the farther you fall below the passing line. If you are approaching question number 20 (on a typical 30-question adaptive exam), and you have answered most of the questions correctly, the testing software will determine that you know the subject matter and may end the test. However, if you are answering the questions inconsistently and riding the pass/fail line on the graph, you may be required to answer up to 30 questions until the software determines whether you pass or fail.

YOUR STATE OF MIND

It is important to focus when studying for and taking a certification test. Make sure that you give yourself time daily to study this book and its accompanying practice test CD-ROM without any distraction. It is not a good practice to study when you are tired and unable to retain the required information. You should be well rested and in a good frame of mind when you take these tests. Don't stay up all night before taking the exams, trying to cram 15 years of technical information into your head.

Confidence, along with good study habits, plays a very big role in this process and increases your chances of success. When preparing to take a certification exam, not only should you prepare to pass, but you should also prepare to score as close to 100% as possible.

The A+ exams are usually the first certification tests taken by people interested in the technologies industry. Make sure this is a positive experience to set the stage for your future certification testing goals. Learn to develop good study habits early on in your certification career. This book is based on information, tools, and techniques that have springboarded thousands of students and professionals to A+ certification success and beyond. Many of the people who have used these study techniques to master A+ have gone on to successfully take and pass such certification exams as CompTIA's Network+, Server+, Security+, Microsoft's MCSA (Microsoft Certified Systems Administrator), and MCSE (Microsoft Certified Systems Engineer).

USEFUL TOOLS, TIPS, AND STUDY TECHNIQUES

Many test takers prepare for certification exams by focusing only on certain areas of subject matter they assume will be on the exam. In the author's opinion, this is a huge mistake. The current A+ exams cover a broad range of information. In order to increase your chances of passing, it is important that you spread your focus of study across all identified areas of content in this book, based on the domains specified by CompTIA.

It seems that most certification preparation guides are geared to have you figure out some sort of magical strategy to answer questions correctly and ultimately pass the tests. Anyone who has come before you and passed these exams will tell you that it's really quite simple. Prepare yourself well with proper study, and choose the right answer to each question on the exam.

The book you are holding in your hands will help you become A+ certified. Read the entire book twice. It has been crafted with your certification success in mind.

ON THE CD

The practice tests included on the CD-ROM are very accurate and are good simulations of the real tests. Take the practice tests repeatedly until you score 100% every time. When you take a test, whether it is a practice test or a real test, read each question carefully and go with your initial choice. Try not to read too much into the questions. Certification developers are great at making the wrong answers look good. They include key words in the questions to confuse you. The longer you sit there staring at the screen, the more likely you are to pick the wrong answer. Here is another useful tip: do not worry about the questions you have already answered. If you are not sure of a particular question you have answered, mark it for later review when you have answered all questions. Only focus on the questions in front of you, and try not to think of anything else. Learn to prepare yourself well, and always remember that the difference between pass and fail can be one question.

Test takers who have gone before you post 'brain dumps' on many Internet sites. These are usually questions that they remember seeing on the test. Be very careful if you study these postings—many of them contain incorrect answers and information. These brain dumps may be helpful by identifying certain topics or material that may show up the test, but you should really know the material.

If you study this book, take the suggestions, and do the groundwork, you should do very well on the real tests.

BOOK STRUCTURE AND SAMPLE REVIEW QUESTIONS

This section of the book is divided into two parts—Part II A: A+ Core Service Technician Study (220-301) and Part II B: A+ Operating Systems Technologies Study (220-302).

Several chapters in this book contain a References section at the very end of the chapter. These contain specific Web site addresses that have been picked out of the chapter to help you expand your knowledge of a particular subject. It is advised that you make good use of them in order optimize your success rate on the real exams.

You will notice "Note" icons throughout Part II. These Note icons are used to warn you of important information that has been identified as a CompTIA 2003 Objective upgrade. In other words, information in this section that is targeted by a Note icon is likely to be on the exam.

At the end of each chapter in this book, you will be able to test your knowledge by answering several chapter content-related review questions. You may see questions relative to earlier chapters as you move forward. This design is in place to help you build on your skill sets as you move through the book. Use a piece of paper to cover the answers provided underneath the questions (don't cheat). If you do not understand the question or the answer, you may have to go back and do some review work. Pay very close attention; you may see similar questions on the actual tests.

Notice the circles next to your choices in question 1. You will select one answer.

1. **You are starting up your PC. The floppy diskette drive light stays on. What is most likely the problem?**
   - o A. The floppy drive is defective.
   - o B. The data cable is defective.
   - o C. The data cable is on backwards.
   - o D. The CMOS battery is bad.

   Correct Answer = C

   (Notice the squares next to your choices in questions 2 and 3. You will select one or more answers.)

2. **You want to improve hard disk access time in Windows 9x. Which utility should you use?**
   - □ A. Task Manager
   - □ B. System Monitor
   - □ C. Control Panel
   - □ D. Disk Defragmenter

   Correct Answer = D

3. **Which of the following represent types of video RAM? (Choose Three)**
   - □ A. SGRAM
   - □ B. VRAM
   - □ C. MRAM
   - □ D. WRAM

   Correct Answers = A, B, and D

CHAPTER SUMMARY

Chapter 14 introduced you to the CompTIA A+ certification tests and testing formats, which included conventional and adaptive testing. It provided you with a breakdown of the test structure and what you should expect to see from the start of the test to the finish. You were introduced to the exact CompTIA A+ domain objectives, concepts, and modules from which your knowledge will be tested. You learned useful tips and study techniques that you should develop early on in your certification test preparation days (and nights) to save you time, money, and disappointment in the long run. Finally, you were introduced to review questions and their format. The best practice and preparation for any certification exam includes a combination of confidence and practice with relative practice questions.

Great lengths have been taken in this chapter to answer as many of your questions as possible regarding A+ certification preparation in general. If you have more general questions regarding A+ certification, they are most likely asked and answered at the following CompTIA Web site: *http://www.comptia.org/certification/A/faqs.asp*.

REFERENCES

http://www.comptia.org/certification/A/upgrade.asp. The CompTIA A+ Certification 2003 Exam Objectives can be downloaded in PDF format from this Web site.

http://www.vue.com/. You can easily register for your A+, as well other certification exams, at this Pearson VUE Web site.

http://www.2test.com/. You can easily register for your A+, as well other certification exams, at this Thompson/Prometric Web site.

http://www.comptia.org/. The CompTIA homepage.

http://www.comptia.org/certification/general_information/test_pricing.asp?type=certification. You can find CompTIA's exam pricing schedules listed by country at this Web site.

http://www.comptia.org/certification/A/faqs.asp. The CompTIA Web site answers the most commonly asked A+ certification questions.

Part II

A

A+ Core Hardware Service Technician Study (Exam 220-301)

15 Motherboards, Power, BIOS, and Expansion Buses

In This Chapter

- Motherboards and Form Factors
- Slots and Sockets
- Electricity and the Power Supply
- Preventive Maintenance and Safety
- Complementary Metal Oxide Semiconductor (CMOS)
- The System Basic Input/Output Services
- Plug and Play
- Power-On Self-Test (POST) and Error Codes
- Expansion Bus Architecture
- PCMCIA (PC Cards)
- Chapter Summary
- Review Questions
- References

MOTHERBOARDS AND FORM FACTORS

The motherboard, sometimes referred to as the planar or system board, is the central part of a computer that brings together all devices attached to the computer. The main components on the motherboard are the CPU (Central Processing Unit) and CPU chipset, expansion bus, I/O (Input/Output) interface, disk drive controllers, and Random Access Memory (RAM). The motherboard's main function is to distribute power and data to all devices attached to it.

Motherboards have different form factors. A form factor is simply the physical size and layout of the motherboard and its components. Several form factors and their features are described below.

Advanced Technology (AT) and Baby AT

Until 1997, the Advanced Technology (AT) and baby AT form factors were the most popular types of motherboards on the market. The main difference between the two is the width of the motherboards, themselves. The AT motherboard is 12 inches wide by 13 inches long. The baby AT is 9 inches wide by 10 inches long. See Figure 15.1 for the baby AT and its components.

The AT and baby AT form factors have the processor and memory socket locations toward the front of the motherboard. Very long expansion cards were designed to extend over them, which made removing the processor difficult. One had to take the expansion cards out first to remove the processor or to get to the memory. It is important to note that an AT power supply gives an output of 12V and 5V to the motherboard. Additional regulators are needed on the motherboard if 3.3V cards (peripheral component interface, or PCI) or processors are used.

This design was acceptable when clearance and cooling were not issues. With the advent of faster Pentium-class processors, which required more cooling and memory sockets that extended off the motherboards, a better motherboard design was needed.

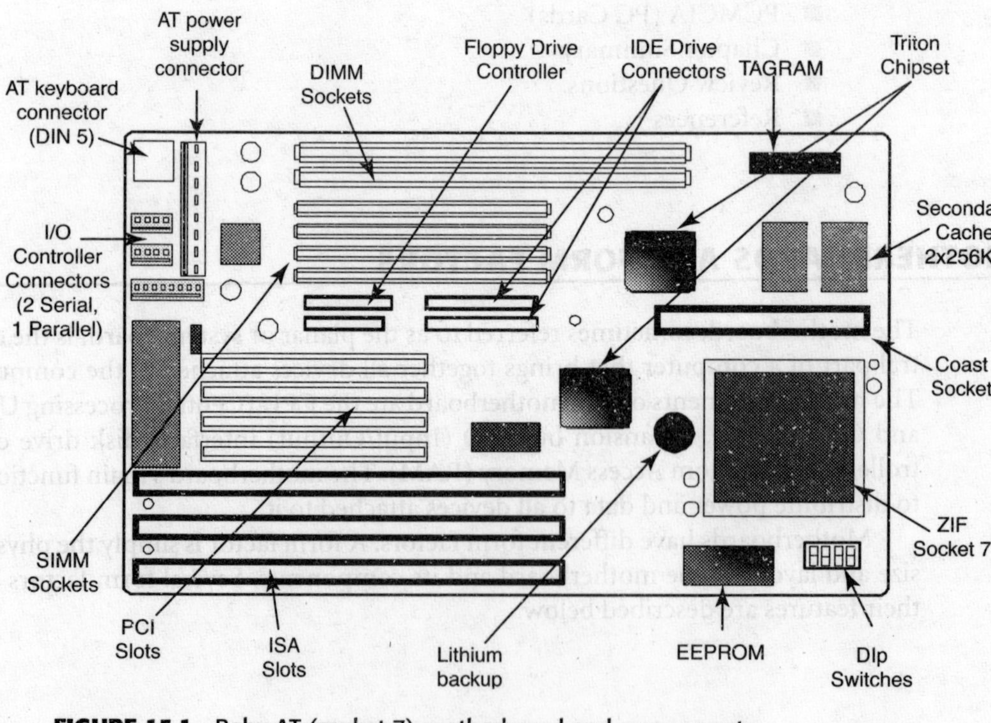

FIGURE 15.1 Baby AT (socket 7) motherboard and components.

Study the motherboard diagrams very closely. The A+ Core Test may show you a similar graphic representation that requires you to identify individual motherboard components.

LPX

In 1987, Western Digital introduced the Low Profile Extensions (LPX) motherboard form factor. This form factor was developed to meet the need for a slimmer desktop. This goal was accomplished based on the implementation of a riser card that extended from the motherboard and allowed expansion cards to be installed parallel to the motherboard.

NLX

As the need for more expansion slots and easier access to components increased, the LPX form factor was redesigned by Intel and named the NLX (InteLex) form factor. The NLX form factor moved the riser card from the center of the motherboard to the outside edge.

ATX

The ATX form factor was developed to solve the problems associated with the baby AT form factor design (Figure 15.2). This new design had many advantages that affected not only the motherboard, but the system unit and power supply, as well. The dimensions of the ATX form factor are 12 inches wide by 9.6 inches long. A mini ATX is typically 11.2 inches wide by 8.2 inches long.

The ATX design provides the following advantages:

Integrated I/O port connection: Baby AT motherboards have cables connecting them to the physical serial and parallel ports mounted on the system unit. With the ATX form factor, this connection is integrated into the motherboard. The ATX form factor uses a 20-pin plastic power supply connector. This is called a *keyed connector*, and it can be plugged into the motherboard in one direction only.

Integrated PS/2 mouse connector: ATX motherboards have PS/2 mouse ports integrated into the motherboard. Most baby AT motherboards do not have a PS/2 mouse port. Older-style AT motherboards required a serial mouse. (The serial interface is covered in Chapter 8.)

Easier access to components: The ATX motherboard was designed with functionality and accessibility in mind. It provides much easier access to components than the baby AT form factor and offers more room in general for additional components.

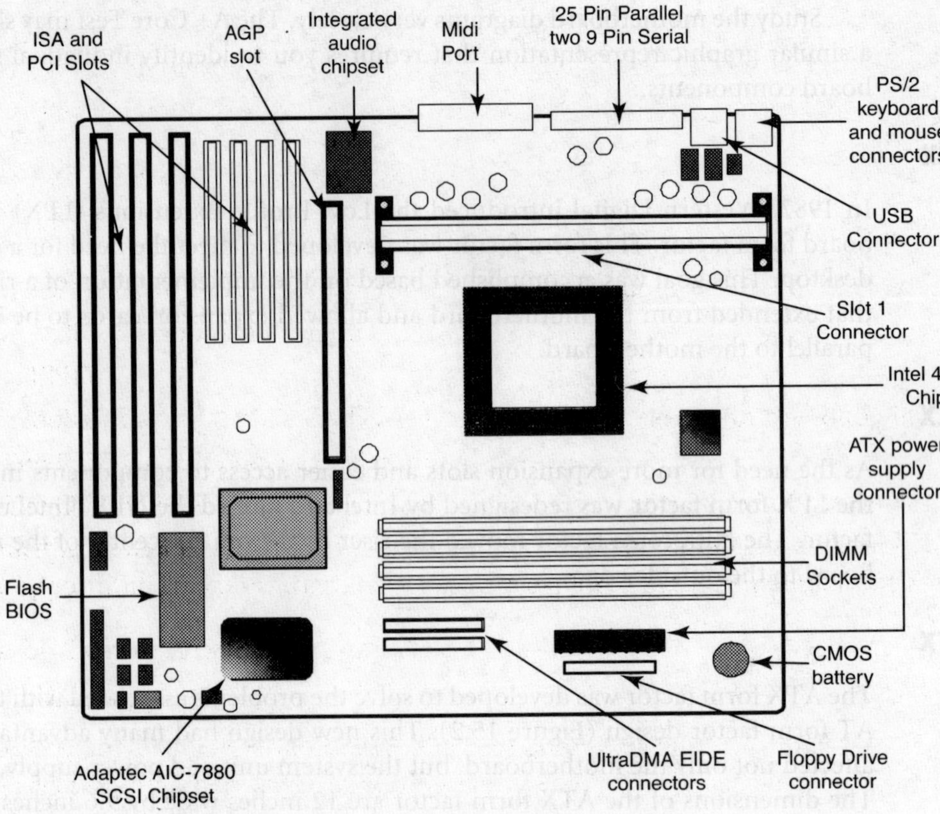

FIGURE 15.2 ATX (Slot 1) motherboard and its components.

Improved power supply connection: The new ATX form factor incorporated a single 20-pin connector in place of the pair of 6-pin connectors used on the baby AT motherboard.

Support for 3.3V: The ATX motherboard supports 3.3V power from the ATX power supply. This voltage is used by most newer processors.

"Soft switch" power support: The ATX power supply uses a signal from the motherboard to turn itself off. This feature enables you to use the power management utilities offered with newer operating systems to shut down a computer, as opposed to physically turning it off with the power button.

Better airflow: With the ATX form factor, the processor is moved closer to the power supply, providing it with better air circulation and cooling. For proper air circulation, it is also important to replace any slot covers on the back of a computer that may be missing as a result of removed expansion cards.

Some very important facts to remember for the exam: most AT-style motherboards use a five-pin DIN keyboard connector. The ATX motherboard uses the smaller, six-pin mini-DIN keyboard connector, which is more commonly referred to as a *PS/2 connector*. The keyboard PS/2 connector is identical to the mouse PS/2 connector. In addition, motherboards use "jumpers" to configure or adjust certain onboard settings, such as the motherboard's clock speed (which is measured in megahertz, or MHz). Older motherboards used Dual In-line Package (DIP) switches to perform this function.

Micro-ATX

The micro-ATX form factor was developed to meet the need for a smaller and less expensive motherboard. The micro-ATX design offers all of the functionality of the traditional ATX, and is also backward compatible. The micro-ATX form factor is not listed in the CompTIA 2003 Objectives. But, because it is better to be safe than sorry, it is mentioned here. If you are interested in educating yourself further about this technology, the First International Computer, Inc. Web site offers some information: *http://www.fic.com.tw/support/motherboard/faq.aspx?type=microatx#qid470.*

SLOTS AND SOCKETS

There are two major ways that a CPU or processor can be installed on the motherboard: socket design and slot design. The socket design is square and is made for a Pin Grid Array (PGA) or Staggered Pin Grid Array (SPGA) chip package. The socket itself is made up of many tiny holes that correspond to pins on the bottom side of the CPU. This socket is known as a Zero Insertion Force (ZIF) socket. Socket design is also referred to as flat architecture (see Table 15.1).

Slot technology is implemented when a CPU that is already attached to an Integrated Circuit (IC) board is plugged into a slot on the motherboard. This slot is typically known as Slot 1. Slot technology is pretty much the standard today. There are variations of slot and socket technologies designed to support specific CPUs (see Table 15.2).

NOTE

It is important that you pay close attention to the tables in this chapter. The A+ Core Hardware 2003 Objectives are sure to test your knowledge regarding the newer slots, sockets and CPUs. Know them well.

TABLE 15.1 Major Sockets, Slots, and the CPUs They Support

Socket or Slot	CPU
Socket 7	Pentium (75MHz), MMX, X86, Cyrix MLL, AMD K-5, K-6
Socket 8	Pentium Pro
Socket 370	Pentium III PGA, Celeron PGA
Socket 423	First-generation Pentium 4 (423-pin Willamette)
Socket 478	Second-generation Pentium 4 (478-pin Northwood) Celeron Family (478-pin Northwood)
Socket A	AMD Athlon PGA, AMD Duron, and Athlon XP
Slot 1	Pentium II, Pentium III SEC, and Celeron SEP
Slot A	AMD Athlon SEC
Slot 2	Pentium II Xeon, Pentium III Xeon

TABLE 15.2 Details of Major Slots and Sockets

Socket or Slot	CPU
Socket 7	321 pinholes (19x19), SPGA ZIF socket
Socket 8	387 pinholes (24x26), MSPGA ZIF socket
Socket A	453 pinholes (19x19), SPGA ZIF socket
Slot 1	242 leads, SEC slot
Slot A	242 leads, SEC slot
Slot 2	330 leads, SEC slot
Socket 423	423 pinholes, PPGA
Socket 478	478 pinholes, PPGA FC-PGA2

ELECTRICITY AND THE POWER SUPPLY

The flow of electrons is known as electricity. When electricity flows in only one direction, it is called *Direct Current* (DC). When electricity flows in two directions or in a bi-directional fashion, it is called *Alternating Current* (AC). To understand the flow of electricity through a computer system and troubleshoot electrical issues in a computer system, you should be familiar with the following electrical terms:

- *Current* is the amount of electricity moving across a wire. Current is measured in milliamperes or amperes (amps).
- *Resistance* is a measure of how much an object resists or holds back the flow of current. When electrical resistance is increased, the amount of current is decreased. Resistance is measured in ohms.
- *Voltage* is a measure of the pressure on electrons as they are being pushed through a medium. Voltage is measured in volts.
- *Wattage* is the amount of work that electrical current is capable of performing. Wattage is measured in watts. You should be very concerned about wattage and its effects when changing or repairing a power supply. A common practice is to simply replace a power supply that is defective.

The main function of your computer's power supply is to convert AC to DC. Current that enters the power supply from an electrical outlet in the wall is typically at 110V or 115V AC.

The power supply converts AC to the +5V, –5V, +12V, or –12V DC current that the motherboard and its components require. A useful tool to test power (voltage) coming from the power supply and going to the motherboard is a digital multimeter. The wires that extend from the typical power supply have different colors, and each represents a different voltage: red = +5V, white = –5V, yellow = +12V, and blue = –12V. Older motherboard form factors (e.g., AT) accept the P8 and P9 Molex-type connectors from the power supply. These connectors plug into the motherboard side by side. When plugging the P8 and P9 connectors into the AT motherboard, you must remember to keep the black ground wires next to each other. If you don't, you might cause electrical damage to the board. The ATX form factor introduced a single 'keyed' power connector that eliminated the risk of plugging the P8 and P9 connectors into the wrong power sockets on the motherboard (see Figure 15.3).

If you are troubleshooting a 'dead' computer, first verify that there is electricity coming from the AC wall outlet. Next, use a digital multimeter to measure the voltage going from the power supply to the motherboard. There are fuses in a computer system that can also be tested with a multimeter. A good fuse measures a resistance of zero ohms. If the fuse is bad, the multimeter registers a resistance of infinity ohms. If your system continuously reboots on its own, it may not be receiving enough power from the power supply.

Uninterruptible Power Supply

To protect your computer and data, your computer should be connected to an Uninterruptible Power Supply (UPS), also known as a battery backup. If it is not connected to a UPS, your computer may be subject to a power surge. If your computer

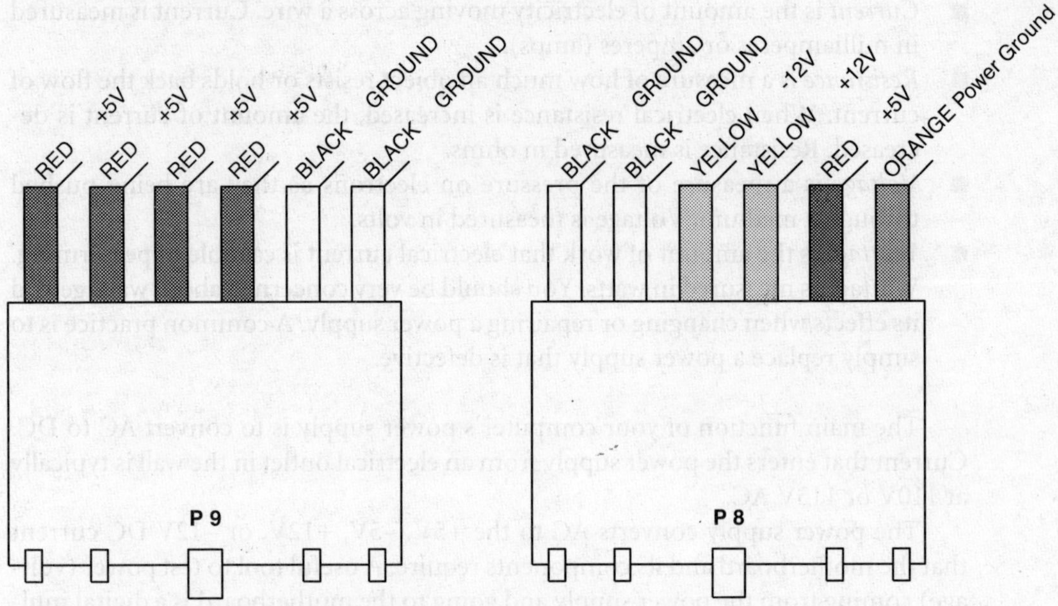

FIGURE 15.3 P9 and P8 power supply connector wiring.

screen is flickering, you may be experiencing simple power sag. The UPS (if properly maintained) provides power to the computer in the event of a power failure; it is not meant to be a long-term power-providing solution. There are three types of UPS: online, standby, and line-interactive. In an online UPS, the battery is contained in a circuit. In a standby UPS, the battery is not contained in the circuit. A line-interactive UPS has the best characteristics of the online and standby UPSs.

A laser printer should never be plugged into a UPS. A laser printer draws a large amount of electricity. It should be placed on its own electrical circuit, separate from the system unit and other electrical devices.

Surge Suppressors

A surge suppressor is a device used to protect electronic equipment, such as computer systems, printers, modems, and monitors, from transient voltage or 'spikes' that occur in the flow of electricity. In America, the average or 'effective' AC power voltage is around 110V to 120V. Spikes, which can be caused by lightning or other electrical conditions, can cause electrical surges of hundreds or even thousands of volts. A surge suppressor or 'protector' can stop AC voltage from going above or below a certain amount of voltage. A typical surge protector has several outlets that equipment can be plugged into, a main power switch, and a three-pronged plug that plugs into a power outlet.

PREVENTIVE MAINTENANCE AND SAFETY

An important acronym to be familiar with is *Electrostatic Discharge* (ESD). ESD is a phenomenon that occurs when electricity builds up (usually in a person's body) and is passed on to the computer and its components. ESD can cause serious damage to your computer and components. You should always wear a protective ESD wrist strap, which contains a resistor, when handling the components inside the system unit. Expansion cards, such as a Network Interface Card (NIC) or video adapter card, have onboard memory and Read-Only Memory (ROM) chips that can be damaged by ESD. Always wear a protective wrist strap when installing these components. Never use a piece of wire to ground yourself if you are using an ESD wrist strap. Instead, use a grounded ESD mat to absorb and discharge electricity. In addition, you should never wear an ESD wrist strap when working on a monitor. A monitor can store high levels of voltage (about 15,000V), which can cause serious bodily harm when interacting with a resistor in an ESD strap. Warm and dry environments are a breeding ground for static electricity buildup. Place any spare electronic components, such as motherboards, hard drives, memory modules, and processors, in reusable ESD protective bags and store them in a cool and dry environment. When cleaning the inside of your computer, be sure to use a special-purpose vacuum that is designed to not create ESD.

Use the following guidelines for keeping your system clean:

ROM media: Dip media in a diluted cleaning solution and let air dry.

Inside of computer: Spray with a can of condensed air. Use a small brush for the system unit itself.

Airflow: Use two internal fans to keep the air cool and circulating inside your system. This prevents too much dust from settling between components.

Circuit boards: Clean with a contact cleaning solution.

Electromagnetic Interference (EMI): This is caused when electrical wires are placed too close to each other, or when the wires cross each other. This can cause havoc with computer signals traveling down a wire.

Another consideration in an electronic environment is fire safety. You should have a plan in case of fire, and have the proper equipment available and ready to use in case of fire. To extinguish an electrical fire, use a Type C or multipurpose-Type ABC extinguisher. In an environment with a built-in preventive sprinkler system, consider having protective plastic drop cloths available to cover your most important computer systems. If a fire detection sprinkler system is in place, and fire is detected, you could lose electronic assets to water damage.

There are four types of handheld fire extinguishers you should be familiar with. They are:

Air Pressurized Water (APW): An APW fire extinguisher is a large, silver, handheld extinguisher that is filled with a combination of air and water. It should never be used to put out a chemical or electrical fire. This is an older type of extinguisher that is used primarily to take the heat element away from a fire.

Dry Chemical (ABC and BC): These types of handheld extinguishers are very effective at putting out various types of fire. Dry chemical extinguishers smother a fire with a phosphorous chemical that separates the oxygen and fuel within a fire. ABC-type extinguishers can be used to put out chemical, electrical, or wood/paper burning fires. You can identify whether the extinguisher is an ABC or a BC extinguisher by the pictures and labels on the extinguisher itself. Caution: never use a BC extinguisher on a Class A fire. Class BC fires are electrical and chemical, only. Class A fires are paper/wood burning fires. Simply put, educate yourself on the type of extinguishers available at your facility. Chances are that you have ABC-type fire extinguishers in your building.

NOTE

Computer-related electrical fires should be extinguished with an extinguisher that is rated for Class C fires. For the exam question, "Your company's main server computer is on fire!" use a Class BC or C extinguisher.

Carbon Dioxide (CO_2): This type of extinguisher uses carbon dioxide gas to remove or displace the oxygen in a burning fire. It can easily be identified by a hard black 'horn' or spout, which is used to spray the chemical. Carbon dioxide handheld fire extinguishers are designed to put out BC-type fires.

Halon: Halon extinguishers are filled with a gas instead of a chemical powder. This gas is more effective at putting out ABC-type fires than an ABC-type extinguisher. Besides providing better fire suppression than the previously mentioned extinguisher types, a Halon extinguisher will not ruin the electrical devices that you have just saved from fire destruction. The chemicals in an ABC-type extinguisher will ruin electrical wires, computers, or anything else you use them on. Although Halon works well at putting out fires, Halon extinguishers are banned in many places. It has been scientifically proven that Halon gas depletes the ozone layer, and Halon is considered very dangerous to humans. A good substitute for Halon is FM-200. FM-200 is a widely accepted, chemical-based fire suppressor that extinguishes fire by cooling or removing the heat from the flames.

Material Safety Data Sheet (MSDS)

A Material Safety Data Sheet (MSDS) is a document created and posted for workers, emergency personnel, and officials, which specifies a set of guidelines regarding the proper handling, transporting, storage, and disposal of a hazardous substance or chemical. Most MSDSs also contain information regarding first-aid treatment, should exposure to danger occur. They are usually prominently displayed for easy reference in areas where a danger exists. In an emergency, such as exposure to a toxic chemical, the proper actions can be taken to treat the situation based on the information posted on the MSDS. The failure of a company or organization to create and post MSDSs in required (hazardous) areas might result in serious consequences to a business, such as a fine or loss of their business license.

NOTE

It is likely that the exam will question your basic knowledge of MSDSs. Make sure you know what they are and what they are used for.

COMPLEMENTARY METAL OXIDE SEMICONDUCTOR (CMOS)

A *Complementary Metal Oxide Semiconductor* (CMOS) is a battery-backed bank of flash memory chips on the motherboard. The information and settings stored in CMOS can be *flashed*, meaning that they can be changed. The information stored in the CMOS is read by the system basic input/output service on startup. A lithium battery on the motherboard provides power to hold the CMOS system settings when the computer is off. If the CMOS battery begins to lose some of its battery charge, a CMOS checksum error may appear when the computer starts up. If the battery loses its charge completely, chances are some or all of your system settings will be lost, including date and time, hard drive settings, and system password.

Knowing that the system settings will be lost if the CMOS battery loses its charge or is removed from the motherboard can prove useful. If you don't know the password to enter the system setup, you can remove the CMOS battery, wait about three minutes, and then put the battery back into the motherboard. This process clears the system settings, including the setup password that is locking you out. After clearing the CMOS settings and re-entering setup, you should first check to see if the system date and time are correct. Second, check the major hard drive settings for accuracy, including heads, sectors, and cylinders. Another way to clear the system settings is to short out the CMOS jumper on the motherboard. In other words, locate the CMOS jumper on the motherboard and close, or 'short' the circuit with a plastic jumper. Consult the motherboard manufacturer's instructions for the location of the CMOS jumper and instructions for this process.

You can modify your system settings by selecting F2 or Delete during system booting. Depending on what type of BIOS is installed on your computer, here are some settings that you can change in the system setup: system setup password, system date and time, boot sequence, parallel port settings, com/serial ports, hard drive type and size, memory, floppy drive, and plug-and-play options.

If the user plans to upgrade the CPU chip, the CMOS chip may have to be changed or upgraded as well. In addition, if a CMOS checksum error ever appears during the system startup, the BIOS may need upgrading.

THE SYSTEM BASIC INPUT/OUTPUT SERVICES

The system Basic Input/Output Service (BIOS) is made up of a group of tiny programs that control input and output services to devices internal to the computer. The BIOS itself is usually stored on a ROM chip that is usually soldered onto the motherboard. Newer BIOSs come in the form of *flash ROM*, which is ROM that can be changed. The major manufacturers of BIOS are Phoenix™, Award™, and AMI™. You may have seen one of their names flash by on the computer screen as the BIOS carries out instructions during boot. From time to time, a user may want to upgrade, or flash, the current version of BIOS with software updates from the manufacturer. It is important to know the make and model of the motherboard for BIOS updates, and it is also very important to document system configuration settings before upgrading the BIOS.

When a computer is booted, instructions are first available to the system from the ROM BIOS. The main functions of the BIOS are to carry out boot operations and to act as an intermediary between peripheral devices, software applications, and operating systems. As mentioned earlier, the BIOS is permanently stored on ROM chips. The next section describes some types of BIOS chips.

Programmable Read-Only Memory (PROM) Chips

A Programmable ROM (PROM) is a BIOS chip that cannot be changed. Data can only be stored on it once. A device known as a ROM burner is used to record information into the chip. If the PROM chip goes bad or loses its information, there is no way to reprogram it. The user has no choice but to get another chip from the manufacturer.

Erasable Programmable Read-Only Memory (EPROM) Chips

Erasable PROM (EPROM) BIOS chips look almost identical to PROM chips, with the exception of a little window that is used to shine an ultraviolet light through to erase their contents. Many BIOS chips in the past were EPROM chips. This was great for upgrading the BIOS if you had a tool to erase the chip's contents. They were easily identified on the motherboard by the shiny label on the top of the chip that usually contained the manufacturer's name and the version of the chip.

Electronically Erasable Programmable Read-Only Memory (EEPROM)

By applying a higher voltage to one of the pins on the Electronically Erasable PROM (EEPROM) chip, the program on the chip is erased. A new program or set of instructions can then be electronically written to the chip. EEPROM is also known as flash ROM.

PLUG AND PLAY

Plug and Play (PnP) was introduced with Windows 95. It was meant to auto-detect devices that were connected to the computer. This worked well if the devices were plug-and-play compliant. Unfortunately, not all devices meet this standard; those that do not must be configured manually. Three requirements must be met in order to meet the industry-standard definition for plug and play: PnP hardware, PnP BIOS, and PnP operating system.

A plug-and-play BIOS can auto-detect devices connected to the computer and automatically assign resources to them. If a new PnP device is added to a system, the BIOS will check an ESCD (Extended System Configuration Data) database (a running list of active system resources assigned) stored on the CMOS chip to see what resources are unavailable and can be assigned to the new device. In modern computers, the plug-and-play settings are configured in the BIOS under the advanced settings option. Legacy or non-PnP devices are normally configured first; plug-and-play devices are configured next. The following operating systems are considered PnP compliant: Windows 9x, Windows Me, Windows 2000, and Windows XP. For an operating system to use plug-and-play features and recognize new devices, the plug-and-play option in the system BIOS settings must be enabled.

POWER-ON SELF-TEST (POST) AND ERROR CODES

The Power-On Self-Test (POST) is a self-diagnostic program that runs a test on RAM, I/O devices, and the CPU on system startup. The POST is stored in the ROM BIOS and requires at least a processor, memory, and video adapter to complete its diagnostic tests. The POST recognizes errors related to BIOS configuration settings and I/O connectivity, such as a stuck keyboard. Be forewarned: you may be asked to identify errors the POST might not recognize. Table 15.3 lists some examples of

POST numeric error codes that you may encounter while using a computer. There is a good chance you may also encounter one or two POST numeric error code questions on the test.

There are also sounds or beep codes associated with POST operations and system startup to alert you in the event of an error. BIOS manufacturers, such as IBM, Phoenix, and Award, each provide their own distinct set of beep codes. A list of IBM's common beep codes is provided in Table 15.4. It is likely that the test will focus on numeric error codes. If you are interested in learning more about beep codes specific to BIOS manufacturers that are not listed, you should consult that manufacturer's Web site.

TABLE 15.3 Common Post Error Codes

Error Code	Error Associated with Code
1XX	System board error
201	Memory error
301	Keyboard error
5XX	Monitor error
601	Floppy drive/adapter error
1101	Serial card error
1701	Hard drive controller error

TABLE 15.4 Common IBM Beep Codes

Beep Description	Error Associated with Beep
No beep	Motherboard or power failure
One short beep	All POST operations completed successfully
Two short beeps	POST error
One long beep, one short beep	Motherboard error
One long beep, two short beeps	Video adapter failed
One long beep, three short beeps	Video adapter error
Three long beeps	Keyboard failure

EXPANSION BUS ARCHITECTURE

Electronic signals need a medium to travel on from one location to another. The motherboard is really a circuit board composed of little electronic data paths that allow all those zeroes and ones to travel from one location to another. These little 'highways' are known as the motherboard's bus or I/O bus. The motherboard's I/O bus leads to expansion buses. The expansion buses are narrow slots on the motherboard, and these buses have different architectures that accept integrated circuit boards, otherwise known as cards. These circuit boards, or cards, are used to communicate with devices, such as monitors, printers, modems, and CD-ROM writers.

There are different buses for memory, processors, addresses, and expansion slots. Each of these buses may have different bus widths or number data paths associated with their architecture. In simple terms, if you are looking at an older motherboard that will only accept 8 bits of information at a time and a 16-bit processor to connect to that motherboard, a bottleneck will occur. The motherboard cannot utilize the full 16 bits of information from the processor.

Table 15.5 lists the most popular expansion slots. An important note for the test: most modern motherboards utilize Accelerated Graphics Port (AGP), Peripheral Component Interconnect (PCI), and Industry-Standard Architecture (ISA) slots.

TABLE 15.5 Popular Expansion Slots

Bus/Slot	Bits	Comments
ISA	8 or 16 bits	Operates at 8MHz or 8.33MHz.
EISA	32 bits	Supports PnP and bus mastering. ISA slot compatible.
VL-Bus	32 bits	Supports bus mastering. Compatible with ISA.
MCA	16 or 32 bits	Supports PnP and bus mastering. Older, proprietary architecture.
PCI	32 bits	Supports PnP, bus mastering, and burst mode. Utilizes a host bridge to communicate with other expansion slots.
PCI-2	64 bits	Supports PnP and bus mastering. PCI slot compatible.
AGP	32 or 64 bits	Designed for accelerated graphics and video processing.

PCI 32 bit/64 bit

Currently, PCI is by far the most commonly used bus standard for NICs, sound cards, and modems. An expansion bus technology created by Intel, the PCI bus is designed to sync up with the clock speed of the system's CPU.

There are two main PCI bus implementations: PCI 32-bit bus and PCI 64-bit bus. Most of the motherboards on the market today implement a PCI 32-bit bus that runs at 33MHz. The PCI 32-bit bus is able to access up to 4GB of memory.

A PCI 64-bit bus runs at clock speeds of 33MHz and 66MHz, and has a throughput rate of up to 133Mbps. It uses double 32-bit PCI cycles, called Dual Address Cycles (DAC), which allows a 64-bit PCI bus to access up to 17 billion gigabytes of memory space. What does this mean in simple terms? PCI 64-bit running at 66MHz speed offers greater bandwidth and throughput, which in turn provides better performance for such technologies as Ethernet or graphics. PCI technology is designed to transmit data at 32 bits at a time with a 124-pin connection, and 64 bits at a time using a 188-pin connection.

Accelerated Graphics Port (AGP)

The Accelerated Graphics Port (AGP) specification was designed to offer faster and clearer display of graphical images, such as 3D images and video. Developed by Intel, AGP is based on PCI technology. However, unlike PCI, AGP works on its own point-to-point dedicated channel and allows a graphics controller to directly access a computer system's RAM in order to provide the faster production of images to the monitor. AGP technology uses memory dynamically. When the memory is not being used by AGP for such things as rendering, texturing, alpha blending, z-buffering, or the general production of images, it is restored to the Operating System (OS) for other purposes.

AGP 2x, 4x, and 8x

AGP technology comes in several specifications. To the end consumer or user, these specifications are better known as acceleration speeds. In simple terms, one can purchase an AGP video card at various rates of acceleration. The higher the acceleration rate, the better the card.

There are two main Intel specifications for AGP that you should be aware of. They are:

AGP Specification Revision 2.0: This specification defines interfaces supporting AGP 1x and 2x.

AGP Specification 3.0: This specification defines AGP 4x and 8x technology. With AGP 8x, it is possible to deliver over 2.1GB. This specification was developed to handle today's bandwidth-hungry applications and those of the near future.

Universal Serial Bus (USB)

Universal Serial Bus (USB) is a fairly new plug-and-play architecture that uses the PCI bus to communicate between the CPU and memory, and utilizes a 12 million bits per second (Mbps) data transfer rate. USB allows one to attach many low-speed devices to a computer without the need for an expansion card. Devices such as mice, keyboards, printers, and CD-ROMs have been designed with their own built-in controllers that accept the USB standard. You can connect up to 127 peripheral devices to a system with the use of one USB port. In other words, let's say you want to connect a USB keyboard and a USB mouse to your system. These two USB devices together will only require one system resource Interrupt Request (IRQ).

For the exam, make sure you are able to identify USB ports if presented with a picture of a motherboard or system unit. If you require more information regarding USB, the following HowStuffWorks Web site does a great job explaining how USB ports work: *http://computer.howstuffworks.com/usb3.htm*.

Riser Cards

As computer systems have evolved and the need for more internal system unit space has increased, PCI riser cards have become a welcome solution in the battle for motherboard extension and overall space savings inside a computer system. When a riser card is plugged into a motherboard, it forms a 'right angle' with the motherboard as opposed to lying flat above the motherboard. This allows for more technology to be plugged into the motherboard and provides more space overall. PCI riser cards also provide additional slots for both 64-bit or 32-bit adapter cards.

Riser cards allow for faster production of new technologies. For example, in the past, developers and manufactures of technologies had to go through lengthy certification processes to get their technologies certified for 'on-the-motherboard integration.' Riser cards allow for technologies to be developed faster by placing them above the motherboard on a riser card. A perfect example of this will be seen shortly in the discussion of the Audio Modem Riser (AMR) slots.

There are many types of riser cards on the market today. Some of the most popular include riser cards for memory modules such as Dual Inline Memory Module (DIMM), RIMM, and Small-Outline Dual Inline Memory Module (SODIMM). (Memory modules will be discussed in Chapter 17.) There are other popular riser cards, such as the Slot 1 riser cards used for Pentium II processors and Slot 2 riser cards used for XEON processors. (Processors will be discussed in more detail in

Chapter 16.) There are also riser cards for other technologies, such as audio, modem, Local Area Network (LAN), and USB. If you look closely at the CompTIA A+ 2003 Objectives, you will notice that AMR and Communication Network Riser (CNR) are targeted. For that very reason, we will discuss them next.

Audio Modem Riser (AMR)

Intel created the Audio Modem Riser (AMR) specification. This specification for motherboard architecture allows analog I/O functions to be separate from the motherboard by placing them on a riser card that contains a codec (Compressor/Decompressor) chip. In simple terms, separating analog I/O functions from the motherboard allows designers to develop newer and better technology faster without having to go through the grueling time-consuming certification process for motherboard manufacturer approval and integration. Another extremely important benefit to this riser card technology is the high quality of audio that can be produced as a result of this process.

Communication Network Riser (CNR)

The Communication and Network Riser (CNR) is an Intel-created standard that applies to riser cards. A CNR card is an ATX-compatible PCI riser card that offers logic support for such technologies as audio, modem, LAN, and USB. The whole idea here is to enable developers to better integrate and compact these technologies into a smaller, more scaleable hardware device that makes better use of motherboard resources and system unit space.

The following Adex Electronics, Inc. Web site provides a superb display and explanation of various riser cards: *http://www.adexelec.com/riser.htm*.

And the following reference is available on the Web in Portable Document Format (PDF). It explains many technical details associated with the ATX form factor riser card specification. Pay special attention to the PCI slot assignments on ATX form factor boards with ATX riser support. *http://www.formfactors.org/developer/specs/atx/ATX_Spec_V1_0.pdf*.

NOTE

Both AMR and CNR riser technologies have been identified as targets for the CompTIA A+ 2003 Objectives exam. Make sure you know what they are.

North and South Bridges

PCI architecture is based on the concept of bridging. A PCI bus has a north bridge and a south bridge. The north bridge communicates with the CPU and is used to send signals to devices that run at higher speeds, such as memory and high-speed graphics ports. The south bridge communicates with a super I/O chip and is used to send signals to slower devices, such as ISA slots, COM ports, and LPT ports.

PCMCIA (PC CARDS)

This section is designed to get you up to speed with the most popular laptop computer expansion card technologies. The two major expansion card technologies for laptop systems that are targeted by CompTIA A+ 2003 Objectives are PCMCIA (PC Cards), which is a 16-bit expansion card technology, and mini-PCI, which is a 32-bit bus technology.

In the early 1990s, the Personal Computer Memory Card International Association (PCMCIA) standard was developed for laptop computer expansion cards. It was and still is a 16-bit standard offered in the form of three various card types that all use the same type of 68-pin connector. The major differences between the three card types are in their sizes and functions. The three types of PC cards that you need to be familiar with for the exam are as follows:

- Type I is used for memory and is 3.3mm thick.
- Type II is used for network interface cards or modems and is 5mm thick.
- Type III is 10.5mm thick and is used for hard drives.

MINI-PCI

The need for faster connection speeds and overall throughput spawned the need for a faster, wider bus that would support newer technologies, such as wireless and bandwidth-hungry media adapters. Thus, the mini-PCI form factor was born. Inspired by the PCI Special Interest Group (SIG), the mini-PCI is a 32-bit, 33Mhz technology that is based on the PCI form factor, which is found in most modern-day desktop systems. Keep in mind that the mini-PCI cards are internal cards, or 'modules,' that are typically installed by the laptop/system manufacturer. Mini-PCI comes in three different form factors. The main differences in these form factors are the way in which they connect to the system board and other I/O connectors. The three types of mini-PCI form factors are:

Type I: This card form factor connects via a twisted-pair cable to the phone (RJ11) or network (RJ45) connectors inside a laptop or system. It connects to the system board with a 100-pin stacking connector. This card can be positioned away from the edge of the system board or docking station chassis because the RJ45 or RJ11 jacks do not reside on the card.

Type II: Based on their design, Type II cards must be located at the edge of the system board or docking station chassis in order to connect the cards' built-in RJ11 and/or RJ45 I/O connectors directly to the mounted external RJ11 and RJ45 ports. Like the Type I mini-PCI form factor, Type II connects to the system board with a 100-pin stacking connector.

Type III: These have the flexibility of connection to external I/O (RJ11 and RJ45) ports via the same cable connection type as is used with a Type I card. Type III differs from Type I and Type II mini-PCI cards in the way they connect to the system board. Type III uses a 124-pin card-edge connector that is similar to the connector used by Small-Outline, Dual In-Line Memory Modules (SODIMMs) to connect to the system board. Type III mini-PCI cards have a lower profile, which allows manufactures to create smaller laptops.

CHAPTER SUMMARY

In this chapter, you were introduced to motherboards and their form factors, slots and sockets, expansion board architecture, power, POST, BIOS, and other important information. On the test, be prepared to list the major motherboard components by form factor, answer basic power-related troubleshooting questions, and know whether slot or socket technology is implemented. Many questions on the A+ Core Hardware Test are likely to be related to topics that were discussed in this chapter.

REVIEW QUESTIONS

1. **Your computer will not start. There are no lights whatsoever. What would you do first to troubleshoot this problem?**

   o A. Buy a new hard drive.

   o B. Change the CMOS battery.

   o C. Test the power supply.

   o D. Verify that the AC wall outlet has power.

   Correct Answer = D

   If you are troubleshooting a "dead" computer, first verify that there is electricity coming from the AC wall outlet.

2. Which of the following devices are compatible with an AGP slot?

○ A. Type II PC card

○ B. Parallel port

○ C. Serial port

○ D. Video card

Correct Answer = D

The AGP slot was designed for accelerated graphics and video processing.

3. You have replaced a bad CMOS battery. What should you check next?

○ A. COM port settings

○ B. Hard drive settings

○ C. Date and time

○ D. BIOS version

Correct Answer = C

After clearing the CMOS settings and re-entering setup, you should first check to see if the system date and time are correct.

4. You have experienced a floppy drive failure. What error code will your POST most likely display?

○ A. 301

○ B. 161

○ C. 601

○ D. 1701

Correct Answer = C

Table 15.3 identifies common POST error codes. Error code 601 identifies a Floppy Drive/Adapter Error.

5. A computer is continuously rebooting on its own. What is most likely the problem?

○ A. There is a ghost in the machine.

○ B. The CMOS battery is losing its charge.

○ C. You are experiencing ESD.

○ D. The system is not getting enough power.

Correct Answer = D

If your system continuously reboots on its own, it may not be receiving enough power from the power supply.

6. **You cannot remember your password to get into the system settings on boot-up. How can you address this? (Choose Two)**
   - □ A. Remove the CMOS battery.
   - □ B. Use a multimeter.
   - □ C. "Short" the CMOS jumper.
   - □ D. Press Ctrl+Alt+Del.

   Correct Answers = A and C

   Removing the CMOS battery or "short" the CMOS jumper will clear the CMOS settings, which include a previously stored password. This will allow you to reenter CMOS and change the system settings.
7. **Label all of the components specified on the diagram in Figure 15.4.**
   Answers: see Figure 15.1.
8. **Label all of the components specified on the diagram in Figure 15.5.**
   Answers: see Figure 15.2.

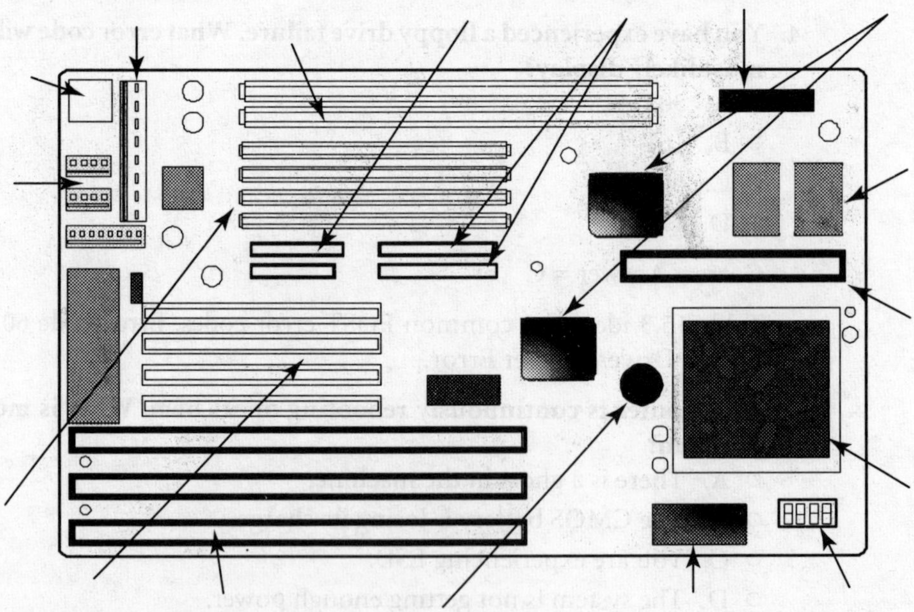

FIGURE 15.4 Baby AT motherboard.

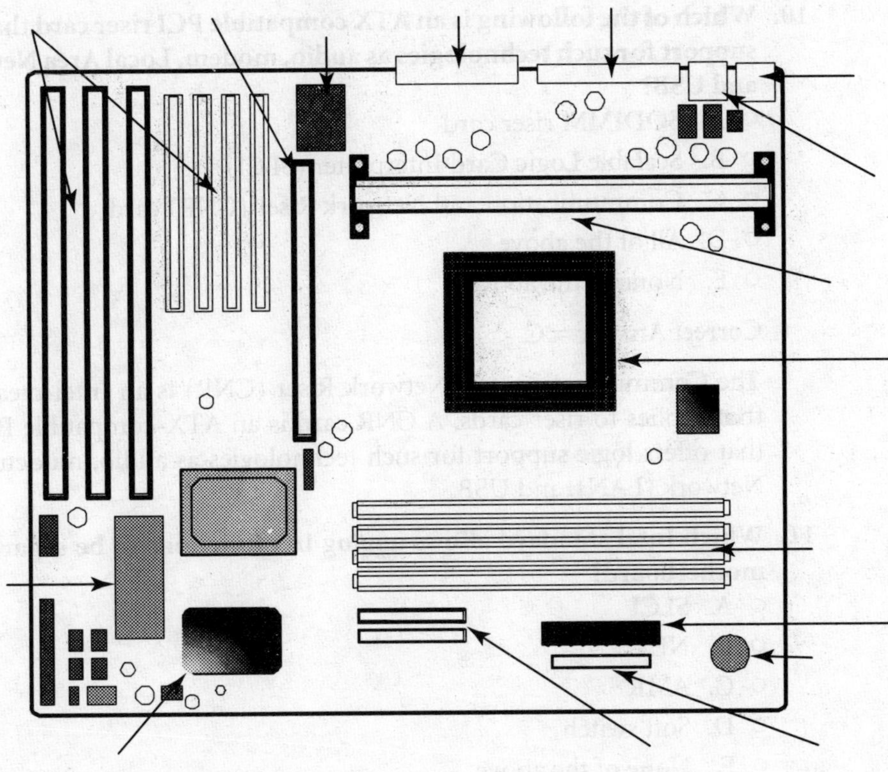

FIGURE 15.5 ATX motherboard.

9. What information is usually found in a MSDS? (Choose Four)

- □ A. Microsoft Systems Development Software
- □ B. Disposal instructions
- □ C. First aid instructions
- □ D. Hazardous material handling information
- □ E. Transportation instructions

Correct Answers = B, C, D, and E

A Material Safety Data Sheet (MSDS) contains information regarding the proper handling, disposal, and transportation of hazardous material. It also contains first aid instructions should an emergency or exposure to a hazard occur.

10. Which of the following is an ATX compatible PCI riser card that offers logic support for such technologies as audio, modem, Local Area Network (LAN), and USB?

- o A. SODIMM riser card
- o B. Scalable Logic Card Interpreter (SLCI)
- o C. Communication and Network Riser (CNR) card
- o D. All of the above
- o E. None of the above

Correct Answer = C

The Communication and Network Riser (CNR) is an Intel-created standard that applies to riser cards. A CNR card is an ATX-compatible PCI riser card that offers logic support for such technologies as audio, modem, Local Area Network (LAN), and USB.

11. Which Intel standard allows analog I/O functions to be separate from the motherboard?

- o A. SLCI
- o B. NLX
- o C. AMR
- o D. Soft switch
- o E. None of the above

Correct Answer = C

This Audio Modem Riser (AMR) specification for motherboard architecture allows analog I/O functions to be separate from the motherboard by placing them on a riser card that contains a codec (compressor/decompressor) chip. Intel developed the AMR standard.

12. Of the following devices, which is used to protect electronic equipment from transient voltage or "spikes"?

- o A. Multimeter
- o B. Surge suppressor
- o C. Integrated I/O port
- o D. An AC compressor/decompressor
- o E. None of the above

Correct Answer = B

A surge suppressor is a device used to protect electronic equipment, such as computer systems, printers, modems, and monitors, from transient voltage or "spikes" that occur in the flow of electricity.

13. An educated remote user calls you and states that he needs you to send a replacement modem card for his laptop computer. What type of PCMCIA card will you be sending him?

- o A. Type I
- o B. Type II
- o C. Type III
- o D. Type IX
- o E. None of the above

Correct Answer = B

Type II PCMCIA cards are used for network interface cards or modems and are 5mm thick.

14. Your company's main server computer is on fire! What type of extinguisher should you use?

- o A. Type I
- o B. Type II
- o C. Class "A" rated
- o D. Class "C" rated
- o E. All of the above

Correct Answer = D

Computer-related electrical fires should be extinguished with an extinguisher that is rated for class "C" fires.

15. Which type of Mini-PCI card must be located at the edge of the system board or docking station chassis in order to connect the card's built-in RJ-11 and/or RJ-45 I/O connectors directly to the mounted external RJ-11 and RJ-45 ports?

- o A. Type I
- o B. Type II
- o C. Type III
- o D. Type IX
- o E. None of the above

Correct Answer = B

Based on their design, Type II cards must be located at the edge of the system board or docking station chassis in order to connect the card's built-in RJ-11 and/or RJ-45 I/O connectors directly to the mounted external RJ-11 and RJ-45 ports.

REFERENCES

http://www.fic.com.tw/support/motherboard/faq.aspx?type=microatx#qid470. This First International Computer, Inc. Web site offers information regarding the micro-ATX motherboard form factor.

http://computer.howstuffworks.com/usb3.htm. This HowStuffWorks Web site provides great information regarding USB technology and USB ports.

http://www.adexelec.com/riser.htm. This Adex Electronics, Inc. Web site provides a superb display and explanation of various riser cards.

http://www.formfactors.org/developer/specs/atx/ATX_Spec_V1_0.pdf. This desktop form factors Web site provides an excellent education on motherboard form factors in general, and in this case provides an excellent explanation of the ATX form factor specification for riser cards.

16 Processors and Cache

In This Chapter

- CPU Defined
- Clock and Bus Speeds
- Cache Levels 1, 2, and 3
- Chipsets and Controllers
- SEC and SEP
- PGA and SPGA
- Processors and Modes
- Cooling Fans and Heat Sinks
- Liquid Cooling
- Thermal Compounds
- VRM (Voltage Regulator Module)
- Chapter Summary
- Review Questions
- References

CPU DEFINED

The CPU, also known as the microprocessor, is the core or central intelligence of a computer system. The CPU accepts data input, processes the data, and carries out instructions. The CPU handles logical and mathematical functions. It is important to have as fast a CPU as possible for quick calculation and manipulation of data. The speed of the CPU (measured in megahertz) and the motherboard (clock speed) determine the amount of time it takes to complete a desired function or task.

A motherboard and its components (including the CPU) are always in danger from ESD. As mentioned in Chapter 15, ESD can damage the circuitry on a motherboard and destroy a CPU. Always transport components in an antistatic ESD-protective bag and wear a protective ESD wrist strap when upgrading a CPU.

The new A+ Core Hardware Service Technician exam will likely test your knowledge of newer microprocessors; their motherboard speeds; the slot or socket technology they are associated with; Levels 1, 2, and 3 caches; and basic processor troubleshooting.

CLOCK AND BUS SPEEDS

The motherboard contains an oscillating system crystal, or oscillator. This built-in timer or clock controls the speed at which the CPU can transfer information to and from memory, and communicate with peripheral devices. Clock speed is normally expressed in megahertz (MHz). For example, if you have a 550MHz Pentium III processor, the clock speed is 550MHz. One megahertz is equal to 1 million cycles per second of the oscillating clock. The clock speed on the motherboard can be configured with little plastic jumpers located on the motherboard itself. Most motherboards are designed to run at multiple clock speeds. It is important to set the CPU and other motherboard components to run at the maximum clock speed of the motherboard; the wrong settings can result in an overheated processor. Also, if a processor fan on top of your processor is being used for cooling purposes, every so often you should verify that it is working properly. If it has failed, the system may lock up, and the processor may suffer irreversible damage due to overheating.

Looking at a motherboard, you can see little pathways that lead from component to component. These pathways are actually tiny wires that carry information from place to place. These wires make up the system bus. Bus speed is measured by the width of the bus. The width of the bus is calculated by the number of bits of information the bus can move at a given time. The actual speed of the bus is provided in the form of megahertz. Typical bus widths are 16, 32, and 64 bits. Most systems today have 64-bit-wide buses that run at 100MHz. There are newer chipsets on the market that run at 133MHz.

The External Data Bus

The external data bus is made up of tiny wires integrated into the motherboard that the CPU uses as a means to communicate with peripheral devices.

The Address Bus

The CPU uses the address bus, which is also made up of tiny wires integrated into the motherboard, to access areas of memory by the Memory Controller Chip (MCC). The address bus keeps track of locations in memory called memory addresses. The number of memory addresses in a system is based on the size, or 'width,' of the address bus.

CACHE LEVELS 1, 2, AND 3

The processing and calculation of information takes place inside the processor itself. When the processor needs quick, predetermined information, it relies on cached memory. *Cached memory* is a special set of memory chips that are internal or external to the processor itself. Cached memory is physically closer to the CPU than RAM and is therefore much faster. Cache memory is designed for quick access by the processor.

Level 1 cache, otherwise known as internal or primary cache, is internal to the processor. It is not part of any other memory and is not restricted by the system clock. It is fast memory that the CPU uses first for quick storage and calculation. Unfortunately, Level 1 cache is not very large in storage capacity. Its storage capability ranges from 8K to 64K. Level 2 cache, otherwise known as external or secondary cache, is external to the processor. It is slower than Level 1 cache, but can provide more than 512K of storage space. Performance gains are mostly realized from the storage capacity of the Level 2 cache.

Technology advances again! Recently, manufacturers such as Intel have developed technology that brings an additional 1MB (512K) Level 3 (L3) cache onto the CPU chip. This Level 3 cache addition has dramatically increased the speed at which a processor or dual processors can access stored information. This in turn provides better processor support for overall application access speed and system support.

To educate yourself further on cache, processors, and other newer components, you should check out the specifications listed at the following Intel Web site: *http://program.intel.com/SHARED/products/servers/index.htm.*

NOTE: *You will be tested on cache Levels 1, 2, and 3. Make sure you know their differences.*

CHIPSETS AND CONTROLLERS

CPUs are generally faster than the devices they communicate with. So that smooth communication can take place between CPUs and peripheral devices, interfaces known as chipsets have been developed to handle this transition or *buffering* of information. Early computers used separate chips to control the transition of data for specific tasks. Some of the early chips and notable controller interfaces were:

The bus controller chip: Handles or 'supervises' the flow of information on the different motherboard buses.

The Direct Memory Address (DMA) controller: The DMA controller allows devices to utilize addressed memory without interacting with the CPU.

Math coprocessor: Supervises the flow of information between the math coprocessor and the CPU.

Super I/O Controller

The super I/O controller was a great advancement. It combined the functions of older, separate controller chips into one 'smart chip.' The super I/O controller chip became a welcomed standard. Some of the major functions controlled by the super I/O include control of serial port Universal Asynchronous Receiver/Transceiver (UART), control and support for floppy disk and tape drives, and control functions related to parallel ports and their enhanced capabilities.

Chipset Controllers (Built-In)

Chipsets are designed to support specific devices, motherboards, CPUs, and computers that they will control. Several built-in devices and controllers included with common chipsets are worth mentioning.

Enhanced Integrated Drive Electronics (EIDE) controller: The EIDE (or IDE) controller is used to communicate and support devices such as hard disk drives, floppy disk drives, CD-ROMs, and other storage devices. Most computers today have chipset support for two EIDE onboard controllers.

Memory controller: The memory controller controls the flow of data in and out of memory. Devices that need access to the system memory or RAM must first pass through this controller.

PCI bridge: As mentioned in Chapter 15, PCI bridging, or north and south bridge, is used to connect the PCI interface on the motherboard with older devices, such as ISA.

DMA controller: This manages the availability and support for ISA and AT Attachment (ATA) devices. (ATA is a set of rules or specifications that apply to the IDE controller. Both are described in Chapter 20.)

SCSI adapters, network interface cards, and sound cards: All of these use DMA channels to move data in and out of system memory without assistance from a CPU. This controller provides the ability for the previously mentioned devices to access the system memory. SCSI adapters are discussed in Chapter 21.

Real-Time Clock (RTC): Controller support is provided for the RTC. The RTC controls system date and time.

PS/2 mouse: This controller provides a direct interface between the PS/2 mouse and the processor.

Keyboard controller: Controls functions between the keyboard and the CPU.

IRDA (Infrared Data Association) controller: Infrared controller packaged with most laptop computers.

RISC vs. CISC

There are two important terms that apply to the programming and instruction sets of chipsets: Reduced Instruction Set Computer (RISC) and Complex Instruction Set Computing (CISC).

RISC is a technology used in high-end computing systems. It uses a limited number of instructions and fewer transistors than CISC does. The result is a less expensive chipset. Most Sun computing systems incorporate RISC technology.

Most conventional computing systems utilize CISC. CISC architecture is capable of supporting many more instructions than RISC. Pentium systems utilize CISC technology.

SEC AND SEP

In Chapter 15, you became familiar with slot and socket technology. *Slot technology* integrates the processor onto a circuit board or IC board. The circuit board is then plugged into a motherboard slot. The actual edge of the circuit board that is plugged into the motherboard comes in two forms: Single Edge Connector (SEC) or Single Edge Processor (SEP). Most modern processors, including the Celeron, AMD Athlon, Pentium II, and Pentium III, use either SEC or SEP packaging and employ slot technology. Intel's SEC design contains both a CPU and a Level 2 cache.

PGA AND SPGA

Socket technology typically uses a ZIF socket on the motherboard that awaits a processor with many tiny pins extending from the bottom side of the square processor. The configuration of these pins is called a PGA package. A second design of the PGA standard is SPGA, in which the tiny pins underneath the processor are staggered, thereby allowing the processor to be smaller.

PROCESSORS AND MODES

In 1978, the Intel 8086 processor was introduced. Recently, many of the processors on the market have been based on the characteristics of the 8086 processor. Several modes and advancements in early processors designed to maintain backward compatibility with the original 8086 processor are worth mentioning.

Real Mode

Provided by the 8086 (XT) processor, real-mode processing offers the processor access to the limited memory space or environment of 1MB (1024K of memory addresses). Real mode uses a 16-bit data path and has a direct access path to RAM.

Protected Mode

Introduced with the 80286 processor, protected mode allows the processor to access memory above 1MB (1024K) and up to 16MB. Protected mode allows programs to use a 32-bit data path.

Virtual Real (Protected) Mode

Introduced with the 80386 processor, virtual real (protected) mode allows multiple programs to run at the same time in their own protected separate memory addresses or Virtual Machines (VMs). If one of these programs or VMs fails, the other programs are not affected.

386DX

Made of CMOS material, the 386DX provides 32-bit processing power and can run in virtual real mode. A 386 operates at +5V, is capable of addressing up to 4GB of memory, and has an internal cache. The clock speeds for 386DX range from 16MHz to 33MHz.

386SX

Released in 1988, the 386SX is a scaled-down version of the 386DX. It has a smaller, 16-bit external bus and a 24-bit memory address bus that addresses 16MB of RAM. This makes the 386SX less expensive than the 386DX. It was available from 16MHz to 33MHz.

386SL

In 1990, the 386SL was introduced to meet the demand for a smaller processor with lower power consumption. This need came from the desire for laptop computing systems that required smaller components. The 386SL is basically the 386SX designed for laptops and their power management capabilities. The 386SL was offered with a 25MHz clock speed.

486DX

The 486DX featured 32-bit internal and external memory address buses. It offered internal Level 1 cache at 8K. This processor introduced burst mode memory and had a coprocessor or Floating-Point Unit (FPU) integrated into the CPU chip.

486SX

The 486SX is a scaled-down version of the 486DX processor. The math coprocessor was disabled by the manufacturer and sold as a lower-cost alternative to the DX model.

486DX2

The 486DX2 was designed to run at double the speed (with the exception of the external bus) of its predecessor, the 486DX. The 486DX2 processor operates at +3.3V.

AMD 5X86 (K5)

The AMD K5 was offered as a 75MHz to 133MHz processor, released by AMD. It was produced to be competitive with early Pentium CPUs. It offered 50, 60, and 66 bus speeds, and an internal (primary) cache of 24K. The AMD K5 uses Socket 7 technology. The K5 has a Level 1 cache of 24K.

CYRIX 5X86

A Socket 7-type CPU released to compete with early Pentiums.

The Early Pentiums (60MHz To 200MHz)

The first Pentium processor, which became known as the classic Pentium I, was offered in 1992, and it was backward compatible with previous Intel processors. The early Pentiums operated with a data bus of 64 bits, an address bus of 32 bits, and a 64-bit memory bus. It offered 16K of Level 1 cache. The Pentium I introduced the single-cycle instruction technology known as dual pipelining.

Pentium Pro

The Pentium Pro offered onboard Level 1 cache at 16K and Level 2 cache at 256K, 512K, or 1MB, which answered the need for large amounts of cached memory. It introduced the concept of quad pipelining and dynamic processing. The Pentium Pro worked well for a program-intensive workstation or server. Unfortunately, it did not handle 16-bit (DOS) application code well.

AMD K6

The K6 was developed as competition for the Pentium Pro. Speeds available were 166MHz, 200MHz, 233MHz, 266MHz, and a Super Socket 7 version designed to run at 100MHz motherboard bus speed and higher clock speeds. The AMD K6 has an internal cache size of 64K.

Cyrix 6X86MX

In order to compete with the Pentiums, AMD and Cyrix developed a Processor Rating (PR) system designed to match up equivalent competitor clock speeds. The Cyrix 6x86MX processors ranged from PR-166 to PR-366. The 6x86 had an external bus speed of 75MHz.

Celeron

Introduced as a lower-end Pentium II, the Intel Celeron processor came to the market to answer the need for less-expensive chips that could keep pace with the Pentiums. Depending on its version, the Celeron could be purchased in PII- or PIII-comparable speeds. Celeron packages came in PGA or FC-PGA format and required a 66MHz motherboard. The Celeron is compatible with Multimedia Extensions (MMX). It has a Level 1 cache of 32K.

In May of 2002, Intel introduced a new Celeron based on the same technologies used to produce the Willamette Pentium 4. This Socket 478 processor came in speeds of 1.7GHz and 1.8GHz. It offered 128k of L2 cache (as opposed to the Pentium 4's 256K), ran at 1.75V, and had a 400MHz front side bus (100MHz quad pumped effective at 400MHz). In November of 2002, Intel would release a newer, updated Celeron model based on the Pentium 4 Northwood Core. It was offered as a 2.0GHz product (Socket 478) running at 1.5V, with 128k of L2 cache, and a 400MHz front side bus (100MHz quad pumped effective at 400MHz).

Xeon

The Xeon processor succeeded the Pentium Pro. It was meant to be a server computer processor, primarily because of its choices of Level 2 cache, which was available at 512K, 1MB, or 2MB. It was also noted for its ability to support up to eight processors in one computer and up to 64GB of memory.

Pentium II

The Pentium II processor is available in 233MHz, 266MHz, 300MHz, 333MHz, 350MHz, 400MHz, and 450MHz clock speeds. This processor is designed to take full advantage of MMX technology. MMX introduced new hardware technology processing that is integrated into the system for better calculation and acceleration of multimedia. The Pentium II provides a larger pipeline cache size than its predecessor, the Pentium I. It has a Level 1 cache of 32K and a Level 2 cache of 512K. The Pentium II uses Slot 1 technology. In Table 16.1, you can see a comparison of Pentium II processor speeds to their corresponding motherboard clock speeds.

Pentium III

Pentium III offers 32K of Level 1 cache and fully supports Level 2 cache at 512K. It is offered with clock speeds that range from 450MHz to 1.4GHz. It is available in a second-generation SEC package known as SECC2. Remember, the Pentium III utilizes both Slot 1 and Socket 370 technologies.

AMD Athlon and Duron

A processor available through AMD is the AMD 1GHz Athlon processor. It replaces the AMD K-6 series. It is available in both Slot A and Socket A formats, and boasts a 200MHz to 400MHz Alpha EV-6 bus.

The AMD Duron, released to the public in 2000, was meant to be the Celeron's major competitor. The AMD Duron was developed for the mid-range workstation market. The Duron processor clock speeds range from 600MHz through 1.3GHz. The Duron used either Slot A or Socket A technology, and has the Level 2 cache internal to the processor (unlike the Athlon, which has the Level 2 cache external to the processor), and is rated at a motherboard speed of 100MHz.

TABLE 16.1 Pentium II Processor and Motherboard Speed Comparison

Pentium II Processor Speed	Motherboard
233MHz	66MHz
266MHz	66MHz
300MHz	66MHz
333MHz	66MHz
350MHz	100MHz
400MHz	100MHz
450MHz	100MHz

Athlon XP

The Athlon XP was introduced in November of 2001 by AMD as a follow-up to the very successful Athlon line of processors. Athlon XPs range in speed from 1.33GHz to 2.167GHz, but you won't find them listed anywhere with those clock speeds. AMD decided, in an interesting public relations move, to rename the processors according to how they compared to previous Athlon processors. For example, an Athlon 1500+ (clocked at 1.3GHz) is comparable with the previous Athlon model clocked at 1.5GHz (had they gone over 1.4GHz with the classic Athlon). The difference in performance was attributed to "Quantispeed Architecture," which (in simplified terms) means that the processor is handling more operations per clock cycle—not new technology, just a catchy new name.

The original XPs, based on the Palomino core, came clocked at 1.33GHz (XP 1500+) through 1.60GHz (XP 1900+). These processors were soon replaced with a processor revision dubbed the Thoroughbred, which reduced the core size utilizing the 0.13-micron process. The advantage to the revised line with the smaller core was that lower core voltages could be utilized for lower clocked processors. Voltage requirements scaled with processor speed, so a 1.47GHz (1700+) would only require 1.50V, while the higher-clocked processor at, say, 1.80GHz (2200+) required 1.65V. (Lower voltage consumption rates meant less heat, which made it more attractive to consumers at large.) Both Thoroughbred and Palomino Athlon XPs utilized a 266MHz front side bus (133MHz double data rate effective at 266MHz), with 256K of L2 cache. *All* of the processors in the Athlon XP line use Socket A technology, with DDR-SDRAM memory options in chipsets being the memory configuration of choice.

Only recently has the XP line of processors again been revised. The newly released Barton core boasts not only a larger L2 cache (512K), but also a faster front side bus, effectively at 333MHz. Bartons are currently being offered in variable speeds, all the way up to 2.167GHz (Athlon XP 3000+).

Pentium 4

Originally introduced July 2, 2001, the Pentium 4 ranges in speed from 1.3GHz to 3.06GHz. It is important to realize, however, that the Pentium 4 has undergone some serious changes throughout its life span.

When the Pentium 4 was introduced in mid-2001, it was available as a Socket 423 and (in later processor models) Socket 478 processor. Dubbed the Willamette, it came with a 400MHz (100MHz quad pumped effectively 400MHz) front side bus and 256K of L2 cache. In this form, it was available in speeds that ranged from 1.3GHz to 2.0GHz. These processors were only used with costly RDRAM (Rambus), and generally were regarded as "fast but too expensive."

In early 2002, however, the current iteration of the Pentium 4 was introduced: the Northwood. The Northwood is based solely on Socket 478 technology, and out of the gate offered 512K L2 cache. The extra 256K of L2 cache offered a 10% performance increase for similarly clocked processors (as there was overlap of processor speeds between the Willamette and the Northwood). It is also important to note that the physical size of the silicon core had been reduced from 217mm^2 to 146mm^2. The decrease in core size also benefits the new Northwood in terms of voltage requirements, as the requirement dropped from 1.75V (for Willamette) to 1.5V. With these processors came the several different chipsets supporting several different memory types, from SDRAM, DDR SDRAM, and, of course, the original RDRAM.

The Northwood core, itself, has undergone changes since its inception. The 533MHz (133MHz quad pumped effective at 533MHz) front side bus versions of the processor were released in May of 2002. And only just recently, the 800MHz (200MHz quad pumped effective at 800MHz) front side bus version has been released.

The test is likely to present you with questions that test your knowledge of processor/motherboard compatibility and speed. For example, you should know that early Pentiums, such as the 75MHz Pentium, were designed to run at a 66MHz motherboard bus speed. The original Pentium through the Pentium II 333MHz processors were designed to run at 66MHz motherboard bus speed. The Pentium II 350MHz through the Pentium III series processors are intended to run at 100MHz motherboard bus speed.

COOLING FANS AND HEAT SINKS

All the components inside the system unit can generate heat. This heat can be very dangerous to your processor. The processor, itself, is one of the main heat-generating components inside the system unit. When a system is on for a while, the processor, expansion cards, and memory chips heat up. When the system is turned off, these components cool down. Such continual changes in temperature can result in expansion and contraction of the mentioned components. Over time, these components can work their way out of their sockets and slots. This phenomenon is known as *thermal card* or *chip creep*. It is very important to maintain proper temperatures in the system unit to protect the components.

Most computers today incorporate the use of processor cooling fans and heat sinks to maintain a temperature between 90°F and 110°F. The cooling fan usually sits on top of the processor, drawing heat from it, and pushing the heat out and away from the motherboard, where it can be drawn out of the system unit by the power supply fan. Some CPUs need more than a cooling fan. In these cases, a heat sink can be placed between the processor and the cooling fan to assist with the extraction of heat from the processor.

LIQUID COOLING

Liquid cooling is used to super-cool processors far past the limits of standard heat sink/fan combinations. There are many different types of liquid cooling apparatuses, but most work under the same basic premise: they cool water with a radiator, pump that water over the CPU to absorb heat, and then pump the water back to the radiator to recool and dissipate that heat.

All liquid cooling devices have the same basic parts: a radiator (with fan to help dissipate heat from the radiator), tubing, water reservoir, a water block (which acts as a sort of heat sink for the processor) that water flows through (this is where the heat transfer takes place), and a pump.

To simplify your understanding of liquid cooling devices, please refer to the diagram in Figure 16.1.

It is important to realize that while water can be used, many other substances that are more thermally conductive are being used in different types of systems. At

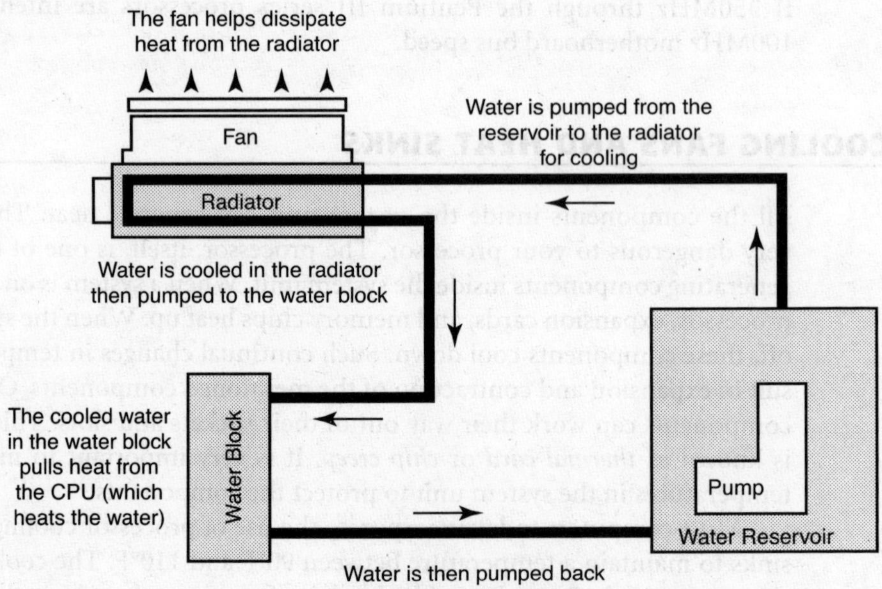

FIGURE 16.1 Processor liquid cooling process.

the very least, even in the case of a system using only water, distilled water (only pure H_2O) is used in combination with a coolant substance that helps reduce algae and mineral deposits.

Liquid cooling systems are primarily utilized by people seeking to over-clock their processors past stock operating speeds. Liquid cooling systems require a great deal of setup and maintenance to ensure that there is no leakage, which could be devastating to the hardware. Routine cleanings and water/coolant changes are necessary to avoid mineral and algae buildup, and constant monitoring of system temperatures is necessary to ensure that water is being properly pumped and cooled throughout the system. While only CPU cooling has been discussed, there are several variations that facilitate the cooling of other devices (e.g., video card gpu/ memory and system memory).

THERMAL COMPOUNDS

A thermal compound is defined as a semi-fluidic grease that conducts heat several times more efficiently than air. Why is this important? To the naked eye, the mating surfaces of a heat sink and CPU are smooth and flat; but on a microscopic level, they are anything but smooth, with peaks and valleys on both surfaces. And in fact, when the two surfaces are mated, less than one percent of the surface of each entity (the peaks on both the heat sink and CPU) touches the other surface. The result is a great deal of air left between the processor and the heat sink. Air is an extremely poor thermal conductor, and the end result is a CPU that runs hot (causing damage). Thermal compound is used to fill the space between the mating surfaces and help transfer heat from the CPU to the heat sink.

VRM (VOLTAGE REGULATOR MODULE)

A VRM (Voltage Regulator Module) is a motherboard-installable module that regulates the electrical voltage that is fed to the system's microprocessor. Most motherboards today have a built-in voltage regulator or a VRM. Its function is to protect the processor by detecting and correcting any changes in voltage. Various processors require different amount of voltage for basic I/O functions and core operations. If you are considering upgrading your processor, it is a must that you consult both the processor and motherboard manufacturers' instructions regarding the specific voltage requirements for your new processor's core and I/O functions. You may need to add a VRM, depending on the voltage requirement of your new processor.

NOTE *It is likely that the A+ Hardware Core exam will expect you to know that a VRM is a motherboard-installable module that regulates the electrical voltage that is fed to the system's microprocessor.*

CHAPTER SUMMARY

As you have learned in this chapter, the CPU is the core of a computing system. Supporting components and technology that enhance its features surround the CPU. Bus architecture and cache play a major role in the overall performance of a processor. In this chapter, you were guided through a general history of the processor, from the early 8086 to the new Pentium 4 processors. As you have seen, competition has clearly kept the manufacturers continually striving to make a better, faster, more affordable CPU.

As mentioned earlier in this chapter, the new A+ Hardware Service Technician core test is likely to focus on newer processors and bus speeds. You will probably be tested on basic processor troubleshooting and maintenance. Let's get serious and focus: your future as a skilled technician may depend on it. Imagine that you just paid $150 to take the next practice test. One wrong question, and you lose your money and your shot at getting certified.

REVIEW QUESTIONS

1. Which of the following are valid AMD processors? (Choose Two)

☐ A. Athlon

☐ B. Celeron

☐ C. K6

☐ D. K9

Correct Answers = A and C

The AMD Athlon and the AMD K6 are valid AMD processors. Intel developed the Celeron processor. K9 is used as a description for police dogs.

2. Which of the following processors runs at 66MHz motherboard speed?

- o A. Pentium III 500
- o B. Pentium IV
- o C. Pentium II 300
- o D. 80386

Correct Answer = C

The Intel Pentium II 300 runs at 66MHz motherboard speed. See Table 16.1 for a Pentium II processor and motherboard speed comparison.

3. Which of the following processors runs at 100MHz motherboard speed?

- o A. Pentium III 500
- o B. XT
- o C. Pentium I
- o D. 80386

Correct Answer = A

The Pentium II 350MHz through the Pentium III series processors are intended to run at 100MHz motherboard bus speed.

4. Your processor fan has malfunctioned. What result might you expect? (Choose Two)

- □ A. Serial port errors
- □ B. Processor damage
- □ C. 601 POST error
- □ D. System halts

Correct Answers = B and D

If your processor fan has failed or malfunctioned, your system may lock up or "halt" and your processor may suffer irreversible damage due to overheating.

5. The AMD Duron processor was developed with what type of workstation in mind?

- o A. Low end
- o B. Midrange
- o C. High end
- o D. MSCDEX

Correct Answer = B

The AMD Duron processor was developed for midrange workstations.

6. **What should you always put your processor and other components in when storing or transporting it?**

   o A. An EMI bag

   o B. An FDISK bag

   o C. A grocery bag

   o D. An antistatic ESD bag

   Correct Answer = D

   An antistatic ESD bag will protect your processor as well as other electronic computer components from electrostatic discharge.

7. **You are considering upgrading your processor. What must you also consider for this upgrade?**

   o A. An NLM

   o B. A permanent swap file

   o C. An MPV

   o D. A VRM

   o E. Your jealous friend's feelings

   o F. None of the above

   Correct Answer = D

   If you are considering upgrading your processor, it is a must that you consult both the processor and motherboard manufacturer's instructions regarding the specific voltage requirements for your new processor's core and I/O functions. You may need to add a VRM depending upon the voltage requirement of your new processor.

8. **To provide faster access to memory and to provide better overall application and system support, CPU manufacturers have added this to newer processors. What is it?**

   o A. ESD protection

   o B. VLM

   o C. L6 cache

   o D. L3 cache

   o E. Seal of approval

   o F. None of the above

   Correct Answer = D

The L3 cache addition to newer processors has dramatically increased the speed at which a processor, or dual processors, can access stored information. This, in turn, provides better processor support for overall application access speed and system support.

9. Which of the following processor lines have products that utilize socket 478 technology? (Choose Two)

□ A. Pentium 4 (Northwood)

□ B. Celeron

□ C. Duron

□ D. Pentium 3

Correct Answers = A and B

Both Pentium 4 and Celeron's latest incarnation use socket 478. The Duron uses both Socket A and Slot A technology, and the Pentium 3 uses either Slot 1 or Socket 370 technology.

10. A first series of Pentium 4 processors had how much L2 cache?

o A. 128K.

o B. 256K.

o C. 512K.

o D. The first model of Pentium 4 had no L2 cache.

Correct Answer = B

The first Pentium 4s were enabled with 256K of L2 cache, which has since been updated to 512K.

11. Which of these are necessary in a liquid cooling system? (Choose Two)

□ A. Radiator/fan

□ B. Heat sink/fan combination for processor

□ C. Water block

□ D. A water filter

Correct Answers = A and C

A liquid cooling system requires a radiator (with fan to help dissipate heat from the radiator), tubing, water reservoir, and a water block (which acts as a sort of heat sink for the processor, that water flows through a radiator/fan and a water block). The water block as the primary cooling device replaces a heat sink/fan combination for the CPU in a liquid cooling setup. While a water filter sounds good in theory, the water/coolant must be changed out routinely to avoid algae/mineral deposits.

REFERENCES

http://program.intel.com/SHARED/products/servers/index.htm. This Intel Web site can be used as an excellent resource to educate yourself on the latest specifications for server and workstation components.

17 Understanding Memory

In This Chapter

- Memory Defined
- Random Access Memory
- Memory Types and Characteristics
- Popular DRAM Advances and Technologies
- Memory Packaging
- Memory Parity and ECC
- Logical Memory
- Chapter Summary
- Review Questions
- References

MEMORY DEFINED

Memory is where the computer temporarily stores electronic instructions and data. Computing systems have different types of memory, which produce different results. For example, when a processor needs to store and retrieve information quickly in order to carry out a specified function or calculation, it stores and retrieves data from cache memory that is internal to the processor. If access to information isn't needed as quickly, the data or instructions may be stored in RAM (main memory).

There are many different types of physical and logical memory to suit specific operational needs. The memory types addressed in this chapter are those you need to be familiar with to successfully prepare for the CompTIA A+ exams.

RANDOM ACCESS MEMORY

RAM, also known as primary storage or main memory, is where the CPU and applications store information and instructions for future use. RAM is considered volatile memory. Volatile memory loses all its stored information when it is disconnected from its power source. In other words, when you turn off the computer, you lose all the information stored in RAM. For example, if you are entering data into a document and suddenly experience loss of power to the system, you will lose the information you have entered into the document unless it has been saved to a permanent storage location, such as the hard disk, CD-ROM, Zip disk, or floppy disk.

The CPU uses unique locations of RAM, called memory addresses, to store information. Memory addresses vary in size depending on how much RAM is available in the system. The CPU can store and retrieve information from specific memory addresses in a random or direct fashion.

RAM Speed

RAM access speed is measured in nanoseconds (ns, or billionths of a second). Older computers operated with RAM access speeds that ranged from 80ns to 120ns. Today it is common to find RAM access speeds of 50ns and faster. Memory speeds can vary greatly, depending on the type of memory being used. In fact, memory such as Synchronous Dynamic Random Access Memory (SDRAM) is measured in megahertz, not nanoseconds. You can determine the access speed of memory by looking at the last printed number on most DRAM chips; for example, BAC4G302H-05 means the access speed is 50ns. An important consideration when installing new memory in a system is to match the speed of the memory to the speed of the motherboard's bus.

NOTE

For the test, it is important to remember that the RAM speed is faster in nanoseconds as the number decreases—that is, 6ns is faster than 10ns.

RAM Size

The smallest unit of information measured in a computer system is a bit. A bit is represented in electronic computer terms as a (binary) 0 or 1. There are 8 bits in 1 byte. (See Chapter 18 for more information on binary conversion.)

RAM size and storage capacity are measured in multiples of bytes known as megabytes, gigabytes, and terabytes. Table 17.1 will assist you with RAM units of measure.

Some important considerations when purchasing memory or a new computer are what type of memory and how much memory will be needed. Specific types of

TABLE 17.1 RAM Units and Sizes

Unit Measured	Size of Unit
Bit	Binary digit equal to 0 or 1
Byte	8 bits
Kilobyte	1024 bytes
Megabyte	1,048,576 bytes
Gigabyte	1,073,741,824 bytes
Terabyte	1,099,511,627,776 bytes

memory serve different functions (memory types are discussed later in this chapter). For most home and office workstations, 128MB of RAM should be sufficient to support most of today's memory-hungry applications. High-end server computers require more memory to process, calculate, and serve applications to workstations. Server computers today generally have at least 1GB of RAM installed.

MEMORY TYPES AND CHARACTERISTICS

Many forms of memory have been available since the first computer was introduced. Table 17.2 provides a quick reference to the conceptual aspects of memory that you should be aware of before taking the A+ core test.

Read-Only Memory

You should recall from Chapter 15 that ROM contains small programs installed at the factory. ROM is installed on the motherboard and on some types of expansion boards. ROM chips contain the system BIOS, whose main function is to carry out boot operations by communicating with I/O devices and programs.

Dynamic Random Access Memory (DRAM)

DRAM is the most common type of memory in use today. It is considered affordable, and it is the memory most often used by modern CPUs. DRAM is volatile memory that will lose all its stored information if it is disconnected from the power source. A DRAM chip is made up of little storage units called cells. Each cell contains a *capacitor*. A capacitor is an electronic device that can hold an electrical charge that can be positive or negative. If the charge is positive, the capacitor registers a binary

TABLE 17.2 Memory Concepts

Memory Type	Packaging	Volatile	Nonvolatile
Main DRAM	DIP	X	
Main SDRAM	DIMM	X	
Main DDRAM	DIMM	X	
Main RDRAM	RIMM	X	
Main VRAM	Adapter	X	
Cache Level 1	IC Card	X	
Cache Level 2	IC Card	X	
Cache Level 3	IC Card	X	
ROM BIOS	Chip		X
Virtual memory	Swap file on hard drive		X

digit value of 1. If the charge is negative, the capacitor registers a binary digit value of 0. The capacitors in DRAM must be electronically refreshed continuously in order to hold their information. DRAM is considered a very slow type of memory, with speeds of approximately 50ns. Originally, DRAM chips were mounted on the motherboard using Dual Inline Packages (DIPs). DIPs are long chips with flimsy pins that are very difficult to install on the motherboard. DIPs tended to heat up quickly due to thermal cycling and often caused the DRAM chips to creep out of their sockets. This creeping effect is known as chip creep. Today, DRAM chips are soldered onto integrated circuit boards that are inserted into the motherboard more securely.

Static Random Access Memory

SRAM or static RAM is memory that also holds data as long as there is power available to the chip. Power is provided to the SRAM chip by the system battery. SRAM does not require the use of capacitors and does not need to be constantly refreshed, as does DRAM. Instead, SRAM uses a flip-flop method of regenerating its contents by means of transistors.

Through the use of its own internal clock, SRAM is synchronized with the motherboard's bus speed, thereby helping SRAM achieve higher speeds than DRAM.

Level 2 memory cache (fast memory frequently accessed by the processor) is stored on SRAM chips. SRAM typically comes in sizes of 128MB to 4MB and is more expensive than DRAM.

POPULAR DRAM ADVANCES AND TECHNOLOGIES

Many technological improvements have been made to DRAM in order to create a faster type of memory. The following section describes some of these improvements.

Fast Page Mode (FPM) DRAM

FPM DRAM is faster than DRAM, but is relatively slow compared to other enhancements. With FPM, the memory controller knows ahead of time to look in the pages of addressed memory after the CPU's read or write requests. This reduces the amount of time the memory controller has to wait to take instructions from the CPU and read from or write to memory. FPM DRAM is not suitable for motherboard bus speeds greater than 60MHz.

Extended Data Output (EDO) DRAM

EDO DRAM was the first memory introduced with the ability to hold several pieces of information at a time without having to be refreshed. In other words, if the CPU needs to access the same information several times, the information can wait in EDO memory until the CPU is through accessing it. The information does not have to be continuously reloaded or reregistered into memory. EDO was intended to run with Pentium systems rated between 60MHz and 75MHz.

EDO is faster than FPM memory. EDO memory was advertised to increase system performance by 60%. True benchmarks of EDO showed a 10% to 15% increase in performance.

Burst EDO (BEDO) DRAM

Burst EDO memory is a form of EDO DRAM that can process multiple (up to four) memory addresses at a time in small bursts. Burst EDO did not have great success because it could not retain its synchronization with the processor for long periods.

Synchronous Dynamic Random Access Memory

SDRAM is similar to DRAM. What distinguishes SDRAM is that it uses an internal clock to synchronize input and output operations with the CPU. The synchronization between the memory and CPU results in enhanced performance. SDRAM uses burst mode (automatic retrieval of data before it is requested) for read and write operations. SDRAM sends data in high-speed bursts by utilizing burst mode. It is important to note that SDRAM speed is not measured in nanoseconds. It is measured in megahertz.

Double Data Rate SDRAM (DDR SDRAM)

DDR SDRAM is a type of synchronous dynamic random access memory that dramatically increases memory throughput by allowing data to be transferred on both the rising and falling edges of the system clock as opposed to just the rising edge. What does this mean in English? Data throughput is (approximately) doubled on a memory chip that implements DDR SDRAM technology. It is important to note that the DDR SDRAM is very effective for laptop computer systems because it draws less power. It is also sometimes referred to as SDRAM II. DDR SDRAM can be easily purchased in 128MB, 256MB, and 512MB increments. It is very important to note that DDR SDRAM has a bus clock speed of 100MHz and a transfer of data rate equal to 200MHz. It comes packaged on a 184-pin DIMM.

RDRAM (RAMBUS) DRAM

Rambus RDRAM is proprietary memory from Rambus, Inc. RDRAM improves on memory latency by transferring data in and out of memory at about 600MHz. RDRAM can achieve this speed by synchronizing directly with the memory bus instead of the motherboard bus. Rambus memory uses a narrow bus width and comes on proprietary memory modules called RIMMs. Rambus RDRAM is being used in conjunction with the newer Pentium 4s offered by Intel.

The following Advanced Horizons, Inc. Web site offers excellent insight regarding various RAM specifications. Pay special attention to the "Evolution of Memory" table located at this site: *http://www.ahinc.com/hhmemory.htm*.

Video Memory

The need for high-speed graphics acceleration, higher resolution, and faster video refresh rates has spawned a growing need for better engineered video memory. For the A+ core test, you need to be familiar with the following three types of video memory.

Video Random Access Memory (VRAM)

A computer screen is made up of many tiny dots called pixels. The bit depth is the number of bits assigned through VRAM to each pixel. The more VRAM that can be assigned to each pixel, the greater the bit depth will be. This results in better resolution and color scale. The larger the monitor, the more pixels there are to fill, and thus there is a greater need for video memory.

VRAM is memory specifically designed for video. VRAM acts as a buffer between the CPU and the monitor. It is designed with two access paths (or dual ports), which provide separate passages to the same area of memory or memory address. This means that two devices can access VRAM at the same time. With this design, the video adapter chip, known as RAMDAC (RAM Digital-Analog Converter), can convert the digital signals to analog, to be displayed on the screen; and at the same time, the video controller (processor) can bring more data into VRAM. VRAM does not need to be refreshed as often as DRAM.

Windows Random Access Memory (WRAM)

Do not be confused—WRAM does not mean Microsoft Windows™ memory. WRAM is similar to VRAM, with the exception that WRAM makes better use of the dual ports available through VRAM. WRAM can take advantage of more memory address storage space, resulting in better color depth and video resolution (1600 × 1200). WRAM is faster than VRAM.

Synchronous Graphics RAM (SGRAM)

SGRAM is a form of DRAM that uses a single port. SGRAM uses its own program instructions, called masked write and block write commands, to provide better throughput for graphic-intensive applications. SGRAM is synchronized with the CPU clock speed and can support up to 100MHz. If you ever receive a nonmaskable interrupt error, you are probably experiencing defective RAM or SGRAM.

Cached Memory

As mentioned in Chapter 16, cached memory is memory the processor uses for very fast access to information. It is very important to remember that Level 1 cache is considered primary cache and is internal or built into the processor itself. Level 2 cache is secondary cache that is external to the processor. Level 3 cache adds 1MB (512K) on to the CPU chip. With memory caching, a memory cache controller anticipates (about 90% correctly) what the processor is going to require from memory. This method eliminates the processor's constant need to access the slower DRAM.

Virtual Memory (Swap File)

Today's popular operating systems are typically installed with a predetermined amount of hard drive space set aside to act as a memory buffer area for main memory (RAM). This area of hard drive space is referred to as *virtual memory, swap file*, or *page file*. (The different names refer to the same area of hard drive space.) Data is temporarily moved, or *swapped* between memory and the hard drive. Moving data out of main memory and placing it into a swap file frees up valuable space in main memory for other purposes. The swap file size can vary depending on the amount of free space available on the hard drive. You can manually configure the swap file size or let the operating system take care of its configuration.

If you are running an application that uses up all the current RAM, the extra memory needed to run the application can be provided automatically from virtual memory. This memory area is managed differently than main memory. As you may recall, data is stored in memory addresses within RAM. These addresses are known as *real memory addresses.* With virtual memory, the operating system logically divides the set-aside hard drive space into memory pages that contain virtual memory addresses. These virtual memory pages can typically hold more memory addresses than RAM can. The process by which these virtual memory addresses are converted into real memory is called *memory mapping.* In order for virtual memory to be utilized, the operating system must be able to run in protected mode. Disk Operating System (DOS) was only able to run in real mode. Microsoft Windows 3x introduced 386 enhanced mode, which paved the way for virtual memory utilization.

MEMORY PACKAGING

We have discussed memory types and how they function. Now we will focus on how memory is packaged together and attached to the motherboard.

A DRAM chip is considered one unit or a single chip. When several DRAM chips are soldered onto a circuit board, a bank of chips is formed. The combination of DRAM chips soldered onto the circuit board makes up a memory module or memory package. The memory modules are inserted into the motherboard to form rows of memory banks. There are several types of memory modules, each of which has its own characteristics and design.

Pay very close attention to the packaging methods discussed in this chapter. The A+ Core Hardware Service Technician test is very likely to test your knowledge on memory modules, including SIMMs, DIMMs, RIMMs, SODIMMs, and MicroDIMMs. You will likely be shown a graphic and be asked to describe the memory module being displayed. See Table 17.3 for a quick reference on memory modules.

Gold and Tin Edge Connectors

SIMMs and DIMMs both have edge connecters (or leads) that are pushed into the motherboard's memory slots. These edge connectors come in two distinct forms: tin (silver colored) and gold colored. There is not much of a difference between the two forms, but it is very important that the color of the connector match the color of the inside of the motherboard's memory slot. The inside of the motherboard's memory slot is either gold or tin. In short, match the gold-edged SIMM or DIMM connector to the gold memory slot on the motherboard. Match the tin (silver-colored) edge connector to the silver-colored memory slot on the motherboard. The two different metal forms have different chemical compositions; a mismatch in

TABLE 17.3 Memory Module Quick Reference

Module Type	Number of Pins	Memory Bus Width
SIMM	30 pins	8 bits
SIMM	72 pins	32 bits
DIMM	168 pins	64 bits
RIMM	184 pins	16 bits (or 2 bytes wide)
SODIMM	72 pins	32 bits
SODIMM	144 pins	64 bits
MicroDIMM	144 pins	64 bits

color may result in corrosion and eventually cause the system to fail or become unbootable.

Single Inline Memory Module (SIMM)

A SIMM is a memory module that has either a 30-pin or 72-pin edge connector that inserts into the motherboard memory sockets at a 45° angle. A 30-pin SIMM (Figure 17.1) has DRAM chips soldered onto one side of its circuit board. Older, 30-pin SIMMs used FPM technology and generally came in sizes of 256K to 4MB, with an 8-bit memory bus width. The newer 72-pin SIMMs use EDO technology and come in sizes ranging from 1MB to 128MB, with a 32-bit bus width. A 72-pin SIMM (Figure 17.2) can have DRAM chips soldered on one or both sides of the circuit board. As you learned earlier in this chapter, memory speed is measured in nanoseconds. Most SIMMs run at 60ns, 70ns, or 80ns.

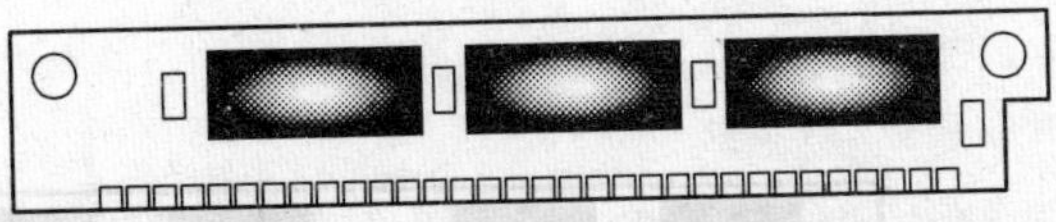

FIGURE 17.1 A 30-pin SIMM (memory module).

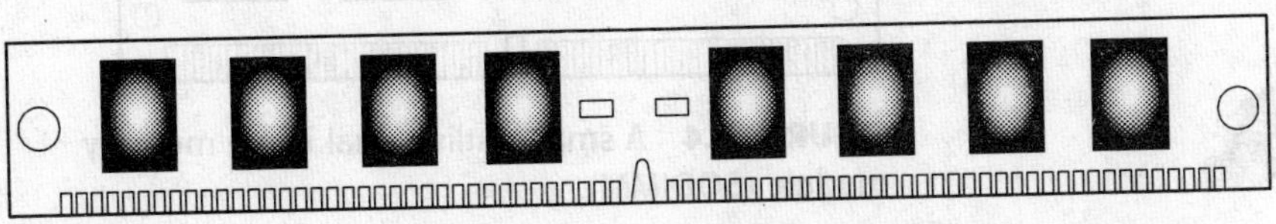

FIGURE 17.2 A 72-pin SIMM (memory module).

Dual Inline Memory Module (DIMM)

Systems that provided 64-bit or wider memory buses opened the door for the DIMM. Most modern computers provide memory slots on the motherboard that support the 168-pin DIMM memory module (Figure 17.3). A DIMM is larger than a SIMM and has an additional set of leads that make it impossible to install the DIMM improperly. DIMMs come in different voltages (3.3V and 5.0V) and are available in buffered or unbuffered form. When purchasing new DIMMs, you should consult the motherboard manufacturer's guide.

Small-Outline Dual Inline Memory Module (SODIMM)

A SODIMM is a smaller DIMM that was specifically designed for laptop computers. There are two major types of SODIMMs. They come on a module that has 72 pins with a transfer rate of 32 bits or a module with 144 pins at a transfer rate of 64 bits (Figure 17.4).

The following Crucial Technologies Web site has a great PDF document that explains how to properly install a SODIMM in a laptop computer system: *http://images.crucial.com/pdf/sodimm_install.pdf.*

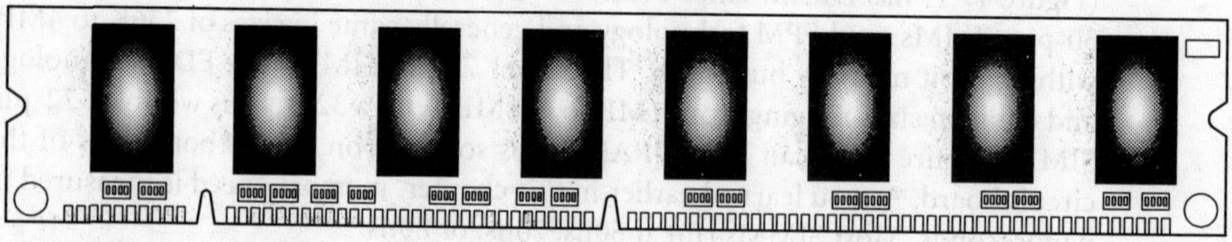

FIGURE 17.3 A 168-pin DIMM (memory module).

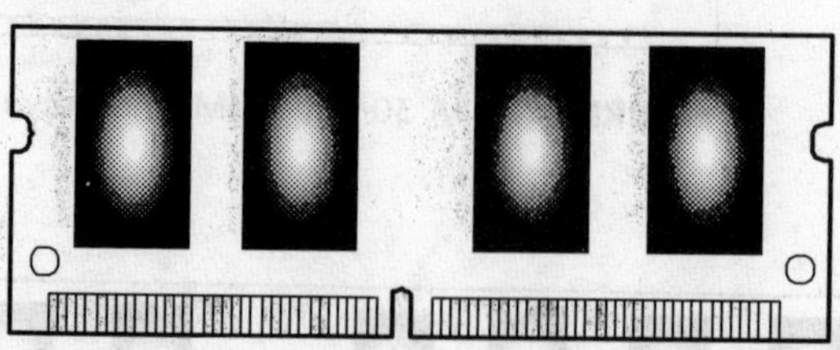

FIGURE 17.4 A small-outline dual inline memory module (SODIMM).

Micro Dual Inline Memory Module (MICRODIMM)

MicroDIMMs are memory modules that are often used in subnotebook computers. They have 144 pins and provide a 64-bit data path (Figure 17.5).

The following TransmetaZone Web site provides a great demonstration regarding the installation of a 128MB, 144-pin MicroDIMM. *http://www.transmetazone.com/articleview.cfm?articleid=1195&page=4.*

RIMM

Trademarked by Kingston Technology Corp., a RIMM is a memory module that uses RDRAM chips. A RIMM uses a special circle-like technology that rotates data in a unidirectional, looped system between the RIMM modules and special blank memory banks called continuity RIMMs (C-RIMMs) that must be placed between RIMMs. This looping system eliminated the bottleneck that resulted from DRAM and its bidirectional bus, which caused data to wait before being sent down a row of memory modules. A RIMM is physically smaller than a DIMM and uses a different pin configuration. Noticeably, a RIMM uses a 184-pin connector (Figure 17.6).

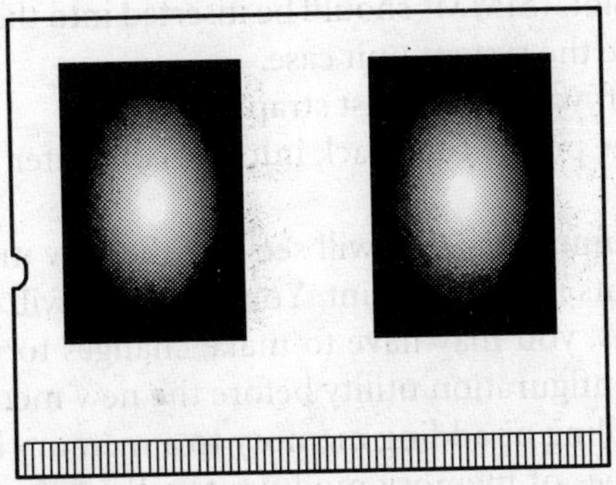

FIGURE 17.5 A micro dual inline memory module (MicroDIMM).

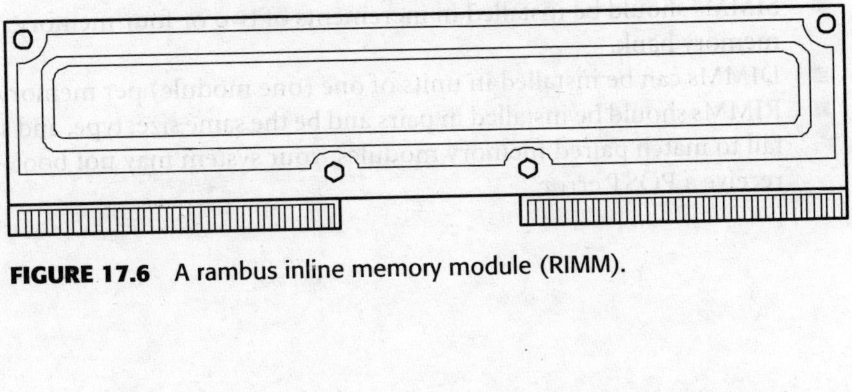

FIGURE 17.6 A rambus inline memory module (RIMM).

If you want to know more about RIMM technology, visit the Kingston Technology Web site at: *http://www.kingston.com/newtech/rambusarch.asp*.

Installing SIMMS, DIMMS, and RIMMS

There was a time when installing memory modules into a computer could be very painful on your fingers. Older motherboards did not have the clip and spring features supported by today's motherboard memory slots, which allow the memory modules to be easily pushed into place.

Here are the basic steps for installing SIMMs, DIMMs, and RIMMs into your computer.

1. Unplug power to the computer.
2. Remove the system unit case cover.
3. Make sure you are wearing an ESD wrist strap.
4. Identify the SIMM or DIMM slots.
5. With both hands, line up the SIMM, DIMM, or RIMM with the open motherboard memory slot.
6. Push firmly on both sides of the SIMM, DIMM, or RIMM until it is seated in the slot. (SIMMs should be inserted into the motherboard at a 45° angle.)
7. Replace the system unit case.
8. Take off your ESD wrist strap.
9. Plug the power cord back into the computer and turn the computer on.

In newer computers, you will see that the new memory has been added when the POST runs its memory count. Your memory will be automatically configured. In older systems, you may have to make changes to your memory settings in the system BIOS configuration utility before the new memory is recognized.

When installing or adding memory to a memory bank, you should avoid mixing different types of memory modules together. You can mix different speeds of memory within the same memory bank. However, the speed of the slowest module within a bank of RAM will become the speed used by the system.

- SIMMs should be installed in increments of two or four memory modules per memory bank.
- DIMMs can be installed in units of one (one module) per memory bank.
- RIMMs should be installed in pairs and be the same size, type, and speed. If you fail to match paired memory modules, your system may not boot, or you may receive a POST error.

NOTE *It is very likely that the exam will present you with a graphic display of a memory module and ask you to identify it by name. You should know what all the memory modules mentioned in this chapter physically look like, or there is a good chance you will find yourself counting pins on the test display screen!*

CompactFlash

CompactFlash is a type of memory card that depends on flash memory. CompactFlash is commonly used in devices such as PDAs, pocket PCs, and digital cameras. They are smaller than a regular PC card and can be easily used with a special adapter in Type I and Type II PC card slots.

CompactFlash technology has also become very popular in the wireless world. In fact, 11Mbps wireless CompactFlash network cards are available everywhere, and connecting your PDA, pocket PC, or other devices to a network is now easy and hassle free.

MEMORY PARITY AND ECC

The integrity of memory and its contents are crucial to the successful operation of a computing system. There are two logical diagnostic memory tools that serve as a system of checks and balances for the contents of DRAM. These two forms of memory checking are called "parity" and "error correction code," or Error Checking and Correction (ECC).

Parity

As you may recall, there are 8 bits in 1 byte. Parity checking adds another bit, called a parity bit (ninth bit), to each byte of information that is stored in memory to verify its integrity. In other words, an even or odd parity bit is added to every byte of information (8 bits). The parity bit for each byte of information is made to force all bits or units to have either an odd or even number of bits. Later, when the byte of information is needed, the computer checks to verify the even or odd state of the byte; if it does not match its original assignment of even or odd parity, a memory parity error occurs, and the system may halt. Some parity errors may show up on the computer screen if the parity check fails. A parity error 1 indicates that the parity error or check has failed on the motherboard. A parity error 2 indicates that the error has most likely occurred on a memory expansion board. An important fact to remember is that parity is a tool used only to detect errors in memory—parity does not fix memory problems.

Calculating the number of parity bits associated with memory is fairly simple. If one parity bit is assigned to every byte (8 bits) of data, we can calculate that 16 bits have 2 parity bits, 32 bits have 4 parity bits, and 64 bits have 8 parity checking bits.

Less expensive memory modules are available that provide fake parity. Fake parity does not provide a valid test of data stored in memory; it simply fools the system into believing that any results from memory are acceptable.

Another way of manufacturing a less expensive memory module or chip is to disable parity altogether.

Inexpensive or used memory is often to blame for parity errors and General Protection Faults (GPFs). Generally, GPFs occur when more than one application or program attempts to access or write to an area of memory already assigned to another application.

Error Correction Code or Error Checking and Correction

ECC works in conjunction with the memory controller to not only detect errors found in data as it passes out of memory, but also to fix single-bit errors with its built-in logic. ECC adds a special bit to data, called an error correction code bit, which is decoded by the memory controller for accuracy.

Some SDRAM chips support ECC. DIMMs (which normally have eight chips on a circuit board) that have a ninth chip show the presence of ECC. You can look in the BIOS configuration to see if ECC is enabled. ECC is worth the extra money it costs, because of its reliability.

LOGICAL MEMORY

Chances are that the current A+ exams will not test you on the use of logical memory, as did previous tests. The current exams are likely to test your knowledge of loading device drivers and configuration files that support more current operating systems. (See Part II B, A+ Operating Systems Technologies Study, of this book for information on operating systems.) However, newer operating systems must remain backward compatible to support older applications, so it is a good idea for you to understand the concepts of logical memory.

Operating systems and software divide areas of memory into logical sections in which applications and programs can run. Today's popular operating systems, such as Windows NT, Windows 9x, Windows 2000, Windows Me, and Windows XP, automatically divide and maintain logical memory areas. Older operating systems, such as DOS, PC DOS, and Windows 3x, required manual configuration of logical memory areas by skilled technicians who were very familiar with the configurations of DOS and logical memory management software tools.

Logical memory is divided into four basic divisions, as shown in Table 17.4.

TABLE 17.4 Logical Memory Divisions

Memory Area	Memory Description
Conventional memory	The first 640K of system memory addresses are used to load and run device drivers, programs, and applications. This is also referred to as lower memory area.
Upper memory area (UMA)	The first 384K of memory above conventional memory are used for device drivers, video RAM, and ROM BIOS. This is also referred to as expanded or reserved memory.
High memory area (HMA)	The first 64K of extended memory, minus 16 bytes, provide 'real-mode' support to operating system.
Extended memory (XMS)	All memory addresses above 1MB and up to 4GB. This area is used primarily for programs and applications.

Conventional Memory

In the early days of personal computing, the original PC and software developers created 640K of addressable memory space and named it *conventional memory*. At the time, it was assumed that 640K would be more than enough memory to store the entire operating system, software device drivers, and applications. This amount of memory was acceptable in the early 1980s, when operating systems were small and applications ran one at a time. As time progressed, the need for addressable memory space increased greatly. Today's computing systems require very large amounts of memory for operating systems, Graphical User Interfaces (GUIs), and multitasking applications.

Upper Memory Area (UMA)

The upper memory area, also referred to as reserved memory, is the first 384K of memory addresses directly above conventional memory. The first section of upper memory addresses is reserved for video RAM and ROM. The top section of memory addresses in upper memory is reserved for the system BIOS. (You may have heard the term *shadowing* before. In computer terms, shadowing refers to moving ROM BIOS information into the reserved area of memory.) BIOS programs for expansion boards other than video are located or 'mapped' to the memory addresses between video RAM and the system BIOS. Table 17.5 lists the areas in reserved

TABLE 17.5 Reserved (Upper) Memory Map

Reserved Memory Area	Assigned Memory Address Range (Hexadecimal)
System BIOS	F000-FFFFF
Optional BIOS area	C8000-EFFFF
Video BIOS	C0000-C7FFF
Color text	B8000-BFFFF
Mono text	B0000-B7FFF
VGA/EGA	A0000-AFFFF

memory with associated computer hexadecimal memory addresses. Unused memory addresses in upper memory are referred to as Upper Memory Blocks (UMBs).

As applications grew more sophisticated, the need for more conventional memory space increased. To meet this demand, developers redesigned the UMA into expanded memory. Special DOS memory management programs and device drivers, such as EMM386.exe, Memmaker, and Himem.sys, were developed to move device drivers out of conventional memory and into expanded memory, freeing up space for the operating system and applications.

- EMM386.EXE uses Limulation (conversion of extended memory to expanded memory) to open access to the UMBs. This makes it possible to load programs and device drivers into memory using the AUTOEXEC.BAT and CONFIG.SYS files of DOS.
- Memmaker was introduced with DOS 6.0. It is a utility that allows you to free up conventional memory by loading device drivers and terminate-and-stay-resident programs (TSRs) into UMBs.
- Himem.sys is a memory device driver that also opens the HMA and directs programs to memory addresses in extended memory. Himem.sys must be loaded in the config.sys file for access to extended memory.

High Memory Area (HMA)

The high memory area is the first 64K of extended memory minus 16 bytes. This area of memory is controlled by Himem.sys and is the only area of extended memory available to a processor running in real mode.

Extended Memory (XMS)

Extended memory includes all addressable memory above reserved memory (above 1MB) and up to 4GB. You must have at least a 286 processor to take advantage of extended memory.

If you are interested in learning more about logical memory and its divisions, you may find the following PCGuide.com Web site informative: *http://www.pcguide.com/ref/ram/logic-c.html.*

CHAPTER SUMMARY

This chapter introduced you to computer memory types and characteristics. At this point, you should be able to physically identify the types of RAM packages discussed. You should also be able to describe the three main types of video memory, have a basic understanding of memory error detection and correction, and have conceptual knowledge of logical memory. For the exam, you should focus on valid memory acronyms and physical RAM packages. The following review questions will help you to familiarize yourself further with these concepts.

REVIEW QUESTIONS

1. **Which of the following are valid types of memory modules used in a computer? (Choose Three)**

   □ A. ZIMM
   □ B. SwapSIM
   □ C. RIMM
   □ D. DIMM
   □ E. ZDRIMM
   □ F. SIMM

   Correct Answers = C, D, and F

   RIMM, DIMM, and SIMM are valid memory modules. All others listed are not.

2. **Of the following types of RAM, which is the fastest?**

   o A. Page Fault RAM
   o B. FPM DRAM
   o C. EDO RAM
   o D. Swap File RAM

Correct Answer = C

EDO is faster than FPM memory. Page Fault RAM and Swap File RAM are made-up names intended to trick you.

3. **Which type of memory is internal to the processor?**
   - o A. Level 1 cache
   - o B. Bus RAM
   - o C. BEDO RAM
   - o D. EDO RAM
   - o E. Parity with ECC

Correct Answer = A

Level 1 cache is considered primary cache and is internal or built into the processor itself.

4. **Which type of memory uses burst mode to send data?**
   - o A. CD-RW RAM
   - o B. SDRAM
   - o C. High-speed RAM
   - o D. Coast RAM

Correct Answer = B

SDRAM uses burst mode (automatic retrieval of data before it is requested) for read and write operations. SDRAM sends data in high-speed bursts by utilizing burst mode.

5. **What type of memory module is displayed below?**

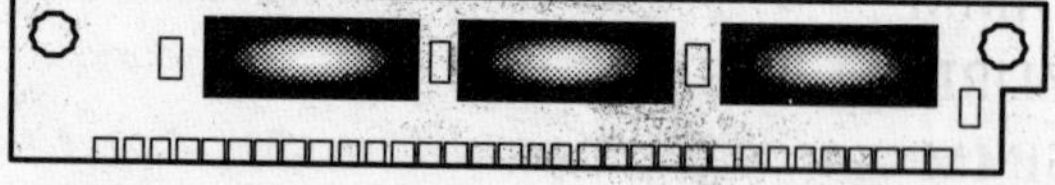

FIGURE 17.7 A memory module.

   - o A. 168-pin DIMM
   - o B. 72-pin SIMM
   - o C. RIMM
   - o D. 30-pin SIMM

Correct Answer = D

6. **What type of memory module is displayed below?**

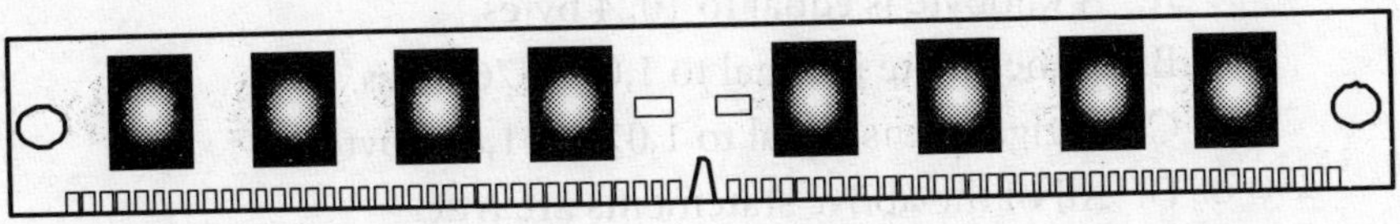

FIGURE 17.8 A memory module.

- o A. 168-pin DIMM
- o B. 72-pin SIMM
- o C. RIMM
- o D. 30-pin SIMM

Correct Answer = B

7. **What type of memory module is displayed below?**

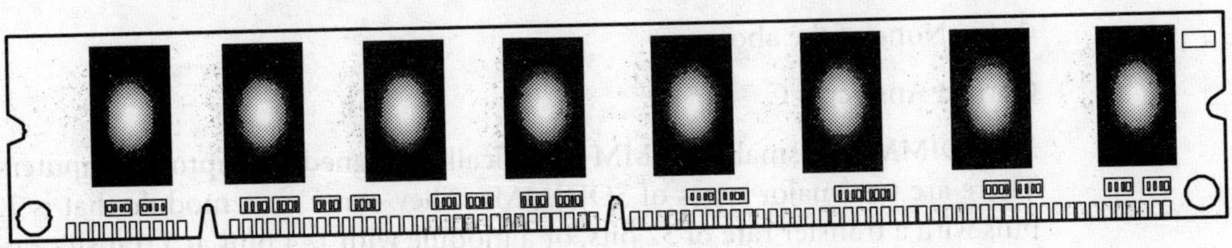

FIGURE 17.9 A memory module.

- o A. 30-pin SIMM
- o B. 72-pin SIMM
- o C. SGRAM
- o D. 168-pin DIMM

Correct Answer = D

8. **How many DIMMS are required per memory bank on a motherboard?**

- o A. 2
- o B. 1
- o C. 1,073,741,824
- o D. 8

Correct Answer = B

DIMMS can be installed in units of 1 (one module) per memory bank. In other words, you can install one DIMM on a motherboard if you so choose.

9. **Which of the following statements is not true?**
   - o A. A kilobyte is equal to 1024 bytes.
   - o B. A megabyte is equal to 1,048,576 bytes.
   - o C. A gigabyte is equal to 1,073,741,824 bytes.
   - o D. All of the above statements are true.

   Correct Answer = D

   The correct answer to this question is D. All statements are, in fact, true. Please reference Table 17.1, RAM Units and Size.

10. **Which of the following memory modules are specifically designed for laptop computers?**
    - o A. FSO RAM
    - o B. SOSORIMM
    - o C. SODIMM
    - o D. SDIMM
    - o E. None of the above

    Correct Answer = C

    A SODIMM is a smaller DIMM specifically designed for laptop computers. There are two major types of SODIMMs. They come on a module that is 72 pins with a transfer rate of 32 bits, or a module with 144 pins at a transfer rate of 64 bits.

11. **What would a technician use WRAM for?**
    - o A. Video
    - o B. Audio
    - o C. Windows memory
    - o D. L3 cache acceleration
    - o E. None of the above

    Correct Answer = A

    WRAM is used for video.

12. **What type of memory module is displayed below?**

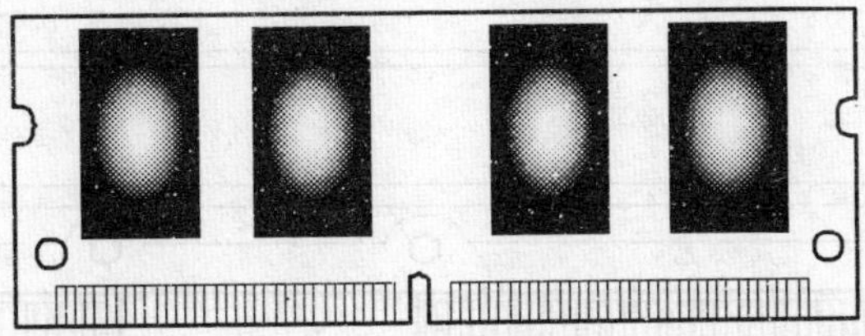

FIGURE 17.10 A memory module.

- o A. 30-pin SIMM
- o B. Small-outline dual inline memory module (SODIMM)
- o C. SGRAM
- o D. 168-pin DIMM

Correct Answer = B

13. **What type of memory module is displayed below?**

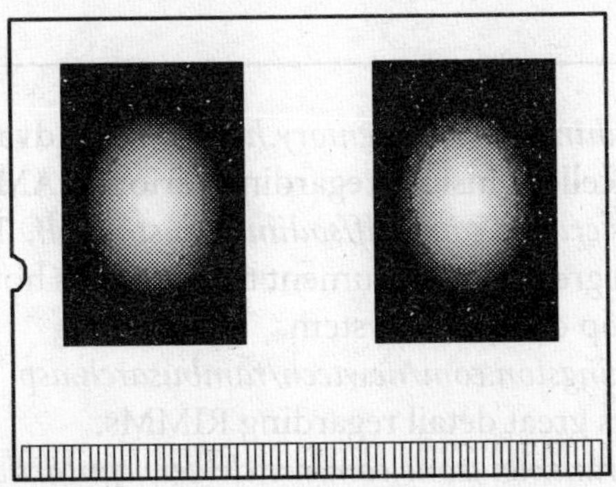

FIGURE 17.11 A memory module.

- o A. 30-pin SIMM
- o B. Small-outline dual inline memory module (SODIMM)
- o C. Micro dual inline memory module (MicroDIMM)
- o D. 168-pin DIMM

Correct Answer = C

14. What type of memory module is displayed below?

FIGURE 17.12 A memory module.

- ○ A. 30-pin SIMM
- ○ B. Micro dual inline memory module (MicroDIMM)
- ○ C. SGRAM
- ○ D. Rambus inline memory module (RIMM)

Correct Answer = D

REFERENCES

http://www.ahinc.com/hhmemory.htm. This Advanced Horizons, Inc. Web site offers excellent insight regarding various RAM specifications.

http://images.crucial.com/pdf/sodimm_install.pdf. This Crucial Technologies Web site has a great PDF document that explains how to properly install a SODIMM in a laptop computer system.

http://www.kingston.com/newtech/rambusarch.asp. This Kingston Technology Web site offers great detail regarding RIMMs.

http://www.transmetazone.com/articleview.cfm?articleid=1195&page=4. This TransmetaZone Web site will show you how to install a 144-pin MicroDIMM into a laptop computer.

http://www.pcguide.com/ref/ram/logic-c.html. This PC Guide Web site provides some very interesting details regarding logical memory.

18 System Resources and Input Devices

In This Chapter

- Binary
- Hexadecimal
- Overview of System Resources
- Interrupt Requests (IRQs)
- Direct Memory Access Channels (DMAs)
- Input/Output Addresses (I/Os)
- Input Defined
- Keyboards
- Mice and Pointing Devices
- Touch Screen
- Modems
- Scanners
- Sound Cards
- Digital Cameras
- PDAs
- Laptops
- Batteries and Power
- Chapter Summary
- Review Questions
- References

BINARY

Humans use a base 10 numbering system. Computers operate using a base 2 numbering system called binary. Binary works well with computers because there are only two values, or digits, that a computer recognizes: 0 and 1.

As you may recall from Chapter 17, the smallest unit of measure in a computer is a negative or positive electrical charge held in a cell within a capacitor. If an electrical charge is negative, a 0 digit is represented. If the charge is positive, a 1 is represented. A 0 or a 1 represents a single bit. There are 8 bits (combinations of 0s and 1s) in 1 byte. In human terms, a computer uses 1 byte of information to determine a single character, symbol, space, number, or letter. A group of bytes together form a word.

There are two ways to convert a binary number to a decimal number, or a decimal number to binary. The simplest way is to use a scientific calculator. The default software calculator installed by most versions of Windows is handy for this task. Click Start >Programs >Accessories >Calculator, and change the view to scientific. Enter a number in decimal and click the radio button Bin; the decimal number will be converted to binary. Click the radio button Dec to convert the binary number back to a decimal number. The Windows calculator can also be used to convert decimal numbers to hexadecimal format. (Hexadecimal notation is discussed later in this chapter.) Use the Hex radio button for this purpose.

Manually converting a binary number to decimal is a little more difficult. Figure 18.1 represents an 8-bit byte, 00101101. The top row of numbers in the figure represents base 2 increments (increasing powers of 2, from right to left). To convert the binary number 00101101 to a decimal number, simply multiply the 0s and 1s by their corresponding power of 2. Add the eight results together and you will have the decimal equivalent to 00101101. You can replace the binary number 00101101 in Figure 18.1 with any combination of bits to calculate a different binary number's decimal equivalent. See Table 18.1 for examples of other binary numbers and their decimal equivalents.

Use Figure 18.1 to calculate the decimal equivalent of 00101101 by multiplying the 0s and 1s by their corresponding power of 2.

$0 \times 128 = 0$

$0 \times 64 = 0$

$1 \times 32 = 32$

$0 \times 16 = 0$

$1 \times 8 = 8$

$1 \times 4 = 4$

$0 \times 2 = 0$

$1 \times 1 = 1$

Add the eight results together

$0 + 0 + 32 + 0 + 8 + 4 + 0 + 1 = 45$ (the decimal equivalent of 00101101)

128	64	32	16	8	4	2	1
0	0	1	0	1	1	0	1

FIGURE 18.1 Eight-bit byte and base 2 increments.

TABLE 18.1 Binary Numbers and Their Decimal Equivalents

Binary Number	Decimal Equivalent
00000000	0
00000001	1
00000010	2
00000011	3
00000100	4
00001010	10

HEXADECIMAL

Hexadecimal is a base 16 numbering system associated with memory and other addresses in a computer. The hexadecimal numbering system consists of the following 16 numbers and letters: 0, 1, 2, 3, 4, 5, 6, 7, 8, 9, and A, B, C, D, E, and F. The letter A represents a decimal equivalent of 10, B = 11, C = 12, D = 13, E = 14, and F = 15. Hexadecimal numbers use an *h* suffix to identify the address as a hexadecimal number—for example, 10*h*. Hexadecimal is easier to read because it is based on groups of four bits (known as nybbles), unlike binary, which uses groups of eight bits.

Table 18.2 displays decimal, binary, and hexadecimal equivalents.

TABLE 18.2 Decimal, Binary, and Hexadecimal Equivalents

Decimal	Binary	Hexadecimal
0	0000	0
1	0001	1
2	0010	2
3	0011	3

TABLE 18.2 Decimal, Binary, and Hexadecimal Equivalents *(continued)*

Decimal	Binary	Hexadecimal
4	0100	4
5	0101	5
6	0110	6
7	0111	7
8	1000	8
9	1001	9
10	1011	B
12	1100	C
13	1101	D
14	1110	E
15	1111	F

OVERVIEW OF SYSTEM RESOURCES

There are many devices inside or attached to a computer system that require communication with the system's processor and memory in order to send and receive data and instructions. There are three built-in mechanisms that allow this communication to take place: Interrupt Requests (IRQs), Direct Memory Access (DMA) channels, and I/Os.

INTERRUPT REQUESTS (IRQs)

An IRQ is a wire incorporated into the motherboard's bus that is used by a device, such as a printer or a keyboard, as a mechanism to capture the attention of the CPU for a request of service.

The default IRQ assignment for a standard 101 keyboard is IRQ 1. When you enter data using the keyboard, you are requesting the CPU to stop what it is doing and take notice of your request to input data. Your request is sent to the CPU by the use of IRQ 1.

There are 16 IRQ assignments in a computer system. (Refer to Table 18.3 for typical system default IRQ settings.) Early computers had eight IRQs. As the need for more devices increased, another eight IRQs were added.

TABLE 18.3 Typical System Default IRQ Assignments

IRQ	Device Assigned
0	System timer
1	Standard 101/102 keyboard
2	Interrupt controller (cascaded to IRQ 9)
3	COM2 and COM4 (serial ports 2 and 4)
4	COM1 and COM3 (serial ports 1 and 3)
5	LPT2 (extra printer or sound card)
6	Floppy drive controller
7	LPT1 (parallel port)
8	Real-Time Clock (RTC)
9	Cascaded to IRQ 2
10	Available (advanced audio)
11	Available (SCSI or VGA card)
12	PS/2 mouse
13	Math coprocessor
14	Primary hard drive controller (IDE)
15	Secondary hard drive controller

For the exam, remember that the system reserves IRQ 2 to connect the two sets of eight IRQs. In other words, IRQ 2 is 'cascaded' to IRQ 9, which provides the usage of IRQs 9 through 15. Of the 15 IRQs available, 10 are used for I/O devices and 5 are reserved for system devices.

An IRQ is connected to every port, slot, and device on the motherboard. The IRQ assignments are typically handled by the system BIOS settings on start-up. Some expansion cards and peripheral devices (usually legacy, non-plug-and-play devices) are configured manually through the use of jumpers on the motherboard or on the device. A Network Interface Card (NIC), for example, may allow you to change the memory address and IRQ settings with the use of plastic jumpers on the card. It is important to note that an IRQ can only be assigned to one active device at a time. Multiple devices can be assigned to the same IRQ. If two devices attempt to use the same IRQ at the same time, an IRQ conflict may occur. IRQ conflicts typically occur when new devices, such as sound cards, modems, and NICs, are added to a system with their manufacturer's default settings. For example, suppose a sound card is installed that is assigned to IRQ 5. Then you install a NIC that has a preassigned manufacturer's setting of IRQ 5. You reboot the system and notice that the new NIC is not recognized or won't function. Chances are that the sound card is currently using IRQ 5, and a conflict has occurred. You will have to manually assign the NIC to an open IRQ.

To check for any device conflicts on a system (assuming use of Windows 2000), click Start > Settings > Control Panel > System > Hardware > Device Manager. If you see a yellow diamond containing a black exclamation point, you have a device conflict.

IRQ 14 is reserved for the primary IDE or ATA controller (hard drive controller). Two devices can be attached to the primary IDE controller. The first device is the *master*, or primary hard drive. The second device attached to your primary IDE/ATA controller is the *slave*, or secondary device. This secondary device is typically another hard drive, CD-ROM, DVD-ROM, or DVD-R. If you wanted to add a third and fourth drive, you would need to use the secondary IDE controller and IRQ 15, which also allow two more devices to be attached. Refer to Figure 18.2 for a typical Windows 2000 display of IRQ assignments.

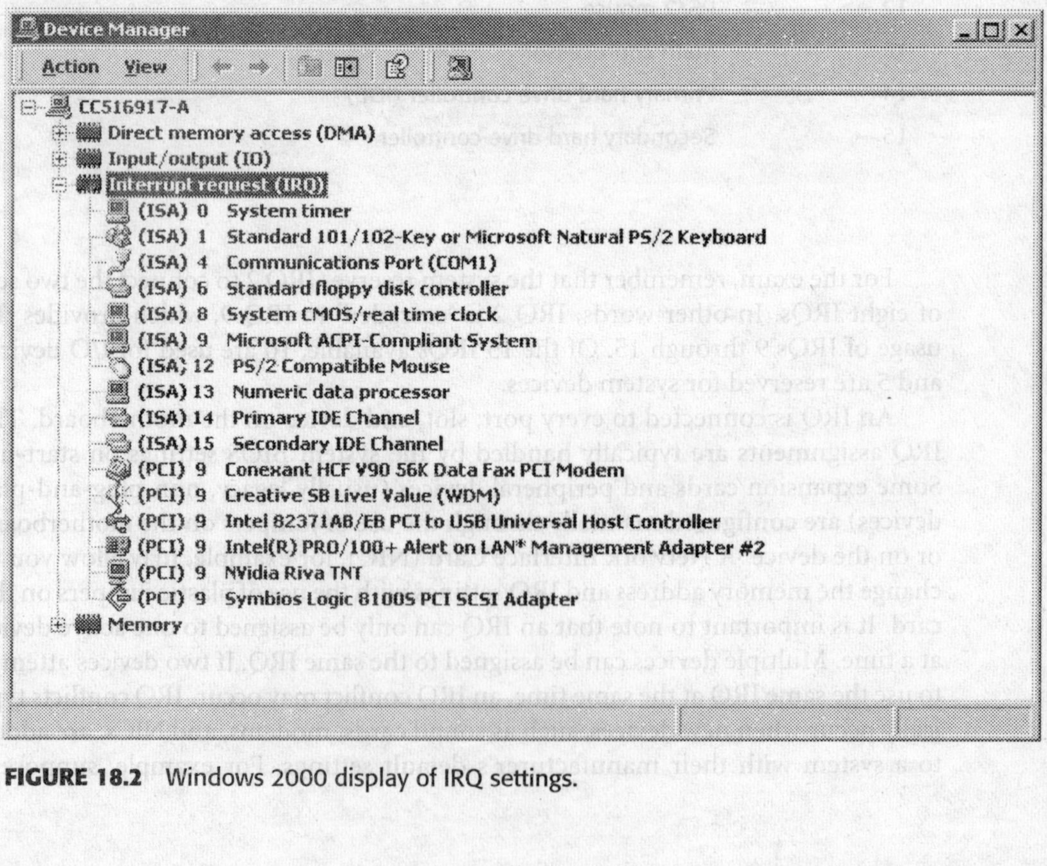

FIGURE 18.2 Windows 2000 display of IRQ settings.

The old A+ Hardware core exam asked simple IRQ questions such as, "What is IRQ 2 used for?" The current A+ Hardware core test will likely have you resolve at least one basic IRQ conflict. The review questions at the end of this chapter will help you to sharpen your IRQ conflict-resolution skills.

DIRECT MEMORY ACCESS CHANNELS (DMAs)

DMA is a memory controller with a straight path to memory. DMA channels, unlike IRQs, allow DMA devices to access memory directly, without interrupting the CPU. This allows the CPU to carry out more important functions and the DMA devices themselves to process requests faster.

DMA controller chips are integrated into the motherboard and control the DMA channels. DMA devices, such as ISA (non-plug-and-play) cards and IDE/ATA controller interfaces, have access to DMA services. DMA does not support PCI or AGP technology.

Early computing systems, such as the AT-class computer, provided only one DMA controller with only four DMA channels, which supported 8-bit and 16-bit cards. Today's computers are equipped with two DMA controllers and eight DMA channels, DMA 0 to DMA 7. Table 18.4 shows standard DMA channel device assignments. Refer to Figure 18.3 for a Windows 2000 display of DMA channels. You need to be familiar with DMA channel assignments 2 and 4 for the test. You may also be asked to identify which DMA channels are available by default for use with peripheral devices.

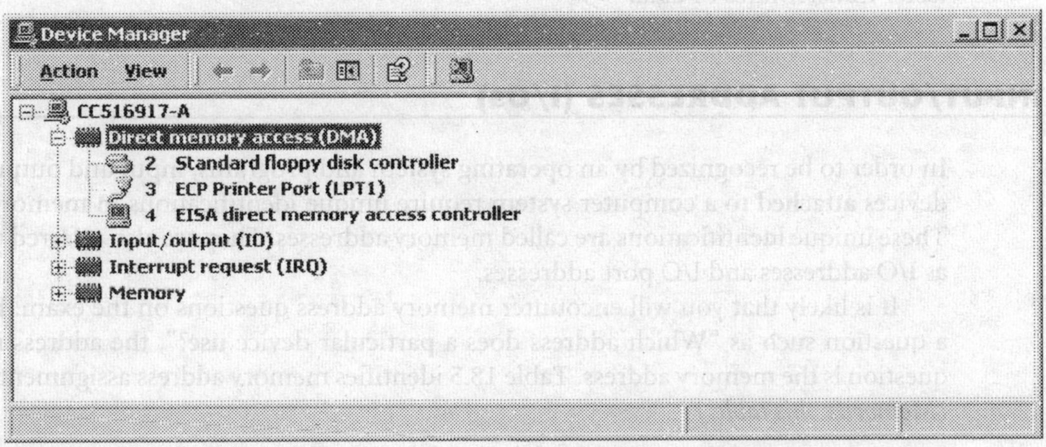

FIGURE 18.3 Windows 2000 direct memory access (DMA) assignments.

TABLE 18.4 DMA Channel Device Assignments

DMA Channel	Device Attached
0	Available
1	Available
2	Floppy drive (possible tape drive)
3	Available
4	Second DMA controller (cascades to DMA channels 0-3)
5	Available
6	Available
7	Available

As with IRQs, there can only be one active device using a DMA channel at a time. If more than one device attempts to access a DMA channel already in use, a DMA conflict will occur.

Different forms of DMA technology are available. Third-party DMA is the original implementation of the DMA. The DMA controller chip resides on the motherboard and is designed for supporting ISA devices. Newer, first-party DMA is very popular. With first-party DMA, the DMA controller resides on the peripheral device. This allows the peripheral to actually take control of the system bus to handle the transfer of data in and out of memory. This process is referred to as *bus mastering.* Newer DMA modes are available, such as ultra DMA, offering even faster transfer rates of data.

INPUT/OUTPUT ADDRESSES (I/Os)

In order to be recognized by an operating system and programs, input and output devices attached to a computer system require unique identifications in memory. These unique identifications are called memory addresses. They are also referred to as I/O addresses and I/O port addresses.

It is likely that you will encounter memory address questions on the exam. In a question such as "Which address does a particular device use?", the address in question is the memory address. Table 18.5 identifies memory address assignments. *(Memorize this table.)*

TABLE 18.5 Base Memory Address Assignments

Memory Address	Device
00F0	Math coprocessor
060h	Keyboard controller
170h	Secondary IDE hard drive controller
1F0h	Primary IDE hard drive controller
220h	Sound card
300h	NIC
330h	SCSI adapter
3F2h	Floppy drive controller
3F8h	COM1
2F8h	COM2
3E8h	COM3
2E8h	COM4
378h	LPT1
278h	LPT2
C000-C7FFF	Video adapter (memory address)

Devices attached to the motherboard perform I/O operations by accepting instructions sent to them by operating systems and programs. The instruction sets are first sent to preassigned unique memory addresses or memory address ranges that represent each attached device. Devices require different amounts of memory for processing. The size of memory allocated to a device's memory address can vary. The average device in a system uses 4, 8, or 32 bytes of memory address space. A video card, which requires significant amounts of memory to process output, may need more memory space assigned to its I/O address than a mouse would. The bus architecture of a device is the determining factor for the amount of memory space allocated to it.

Many memory addresses are available in a typical computer system. However, an I/O memory address conflict may occur if a device attempts to use the same memory address space already assigned to another device. It is possible to change a device's I/O address by a process called *memory-mapped I/O*. Once a device is mapped to a legitimate I/O address, the CPU can recognize it.

INPUT DEFINED

Input is defined as anything that goes into a computer in the form of data, graphics, commands, or sounds. Devices used to place or feed information into a computer, such as a keyboard or a mouse, are called input devices. Many devices can serve as both input and output devices, including hard disks, diskettes, and writable CD-ROMs. The main input devices used today and addressed on the CompTIA A+ core test are described below.

KEYBOARDS

The keyboard is the one of the most widely used peripheral input devices. It allows manual entering of characters, numbers, punctuation, and symbols that represent data and commands into a computer system. Keyboards are available in many different forms, shapes, and sizes. Most are manufactured to meet the English standard computer keyboard layout known as QWERTY. QWERTY is the first line of character keys on the top left side of the keyboard. The keyboard keys are laid out into three main groups: alphanumeric, punctuation, and special function keys. You can configure a keyboard's setting through the use of the keyboard applet in most Windows-based operating systems.

There are actually three types of keyboards: the original PC keyboard with 84 keys, the AT-style keyboard (which also has 84 keys), and the enhanced keyboard with 101 keys. The main differences between the three designs are the layout and placement of the special function keys. Today's keyboards are designed with interchangeable connectors that allow them to be used with different systems. A 6-pin mini-din (PS/2) connector is most commonly used today to connect a keyboard to a computer. (See Chapter 21 for more on keyboard connectors.)

Keyboard Technologies

There are two main keyboard technologies: switch technology, which is mechanical, and capacitive technology, which is nonmechanical. Each technology has its own specific design and usefulness.

Switch Technology

When you enter data using a keyboard, you are actually pushing on a keycap that is attached to a key switch. The key switch closes a circuit, which creates a signal. This electronic signal is converted to a digital scan code by the keyboard's processor, and is manipulated until it is finally readable by an application in American Standard Code for Information Interchange (ASCII) format.

There are two contact key switches worth mentioning:

Foam element and foil key switch: This key switch is a combination of stem, foam element, foil, and spring. When a key is pressed, the stem pushes on the foam, foil, and spring combination, which eventually touches copper contacts on the keyboard's circuit board to create a signal. The spring pushes the stem back up to its original position and awaits the next keystroke.

Rubber dome key switch: This key switch technology uses a rounded rubber dome with carbon material on its underside. When a key cap is pressed, a stem pushes on the rubber dome, which in turn pushes the carbon material onto the circuit board, thus completing the circuit.

Capacitive Technology

Capacitive technology, the nonmechanical keyboard technology, uses a switch housing that contains two conductive plates and a stem. When a key is pressed, the stem pushes the top plate toward the bottom plate, causing a change in capacitance within the switch housing. The keyboard controller recognizes the change in capacitance, and a signal is created. This technology is expensive, and with good reason: it lasts longer than switch technology and has a good level of tactile feedback.

Keyboard Troubleshooting and Maintenance

Keyboards are considered Field-Replaceable Units (FRUs). FRUs are computer parts or components that a technician can easily replace while troubleshooting computer systems in a work area or on a job site. The best way to fix a broken or defective keyboard is to replace it. Keyboards are inexpensive components. Like a computer monitor, it can cost more to have a keyboard repaired than replaced.

The keyboard is connected to a port that is connected to the motherboard. If you think you have a bad keyboard, you should verify that the problem exists with the keyboard itself and not with the motherboard. Follow these simple steps to verify if your keyboard is bad:

1. Turn the computer off.
2. Carefully unplug the keyboard connector from the back of the system.
3. Plug a known working keyboard with a similar keyboard connector into the system.
4. Turn the computer on.

If the known working keyboard is functional, the original keyboard or its connector is bad. If the known working keyboard is not functional, you most likely have a motherboard-related issue.

Keyboard problems are rare. Common keyboard issues are typically related to stuck keys or loose keyboard connectors, and are most likely detected by the POST at system boot with a 301 error (refer to POST error codes in Chapter 15).

Keeping a keyboard in good working order requires regular cleaning. To clean a keyboard, follow these basic steps:

1. Turn the computer off.
2. Carefully unplug the keyboard connector from the back of the system.
3. Turn the keyboard upside down and shake it until any foreign material is dislodged.
4. Use a can of compressed air to spray out dust and other particles.
5. Use a very dilute combination of soap and water applied with a nonabrasive cloth to remove stains from the keycaps. Alternatively, soak the keyboard in distilled, demineralized water.
6. Carefully plug the keyboard back into the system. (Verify that the keyboard is completely dry before doing so.)
7. Turn the computer on.

If a keyboard has been subjected to a major soda, coffee, or other chemical spill, you can rinse it off with water or run it through the rinse cycle in a dishwasher (no-heat cycle; this is recommended only for mechanical keyboards, not capacitive). For best results, replace the keyboard.

MICE AND POINTING DEVICES

The PC mouse was developed as an ergonomic device that allows its user to select data, menus, and adjust the location of an insertion point (cursor). The invention of the GUI, such as Windows, spawned the demand for the mouse. Today, if you notice a computer without a mouse attached, it probably has a touch-screen video display for inputting data and selecting menus. Many types of mice are available today. The main types of mice you should be familiar with for the exam are as follows:

Mechanical: This is the most common type of mouse in use. A mechanical mouse contains a hard rubber ball, wheels, and sensors. When the mouse unit is moved, the rubber ball moves in the same direction, which makes the wheels supporting the ball spin. The mouse's built-in sensors detect the movement of the wheels. The sensors send the detected signal to the computer. If your mouse pointer does not respond correctly as you move about the screen, you may need to inspect the rubber ball inside the mouse unit for foreign particles.

Optical: There are no moving parts inside the optical mouse. This type of mouse uses an optical system with a sensor to calculate the *x* and *y* coordinates of the screen's cursor.

Optomechanical: This is a combination of the mechanical and optical mouse. A rubber ball is used in conjunction with a photo-interrupter disk. Light-emitting diodes are used to detect mouse movements.

Serial Mouse

Almost every computer has at least one serial (COM) port. A serial mouse's female DB-9 connector attaches to the computer's male DB-9 (9-pin) serial port. (See Chapter 21 for more information on connectors.) Before connecting a serial mouse to a serial port, you should check your BIOS configuration settings to verify that a COM port is available for the serial mouse to use. Remember, IRQs are assigned to COM ports. If the COM port you want to use has already been assigned to a modem, the serial mouse may not work.

A serial mouse can be connected to a PS/2 mouse port with a serial-to-mini-DIN adapter.

PS/2 Mouse

Today, it is standard for new PCs to come with PS/2 mouse and keyboard ports. The PS/2 mouse is a PnP device that uses IRQ 12 by default. This default IRQ assignment frees up a COM port that was previously needed to support a serial mouse.

It is important that you do not unplug a PS/2 mouse when the system is turned on. Unplugging an 'active' mouse can cause serious damage to your system and your mouse.

USB Mouse

A Universal Serial Bus (USB) mouse is a hot-swappable PnP device. This means it can be plugged into an already powered-up system and will automatically be detected by the operating system. With most new operating systems, the USB mouse drivers (software used to support the mouse) are automatically installed.

Trackballs

A trackball is a mouse with a plastic ball housed on its topside that uses less desk space than a traditional mouse. A thumb or finger is used to maneuver the ball. Trackballs use optomechanical technology and are connected to a system with a PS/2 or USB connection.

Infrared Wireless Mouse

The wireless mouse uses Infrared (IR) technology. A beam of infrared light goes from a receiver, which gets its power from a serial or PS/2 port, to the mouse. There must be a clear path from the mouse to the receiver in order for the mouse to work properly. This is called line-of-site infrared technology.

Touchpads

A touchpad is a small pad that is sensitive to the touch. It is used as a pointing device with most laptop computers. You direct the mouse pointer on your computer screen by sliding your finger across a square or rectangular pad. Programs can be started and objects selected by tapping on the pad. A touchpad does everything a mouse can do and eliminates the need for a mouse tail (wire).

Joysticks

Joysticks are used mostly for computer games and Computer-Aided Design (CAD) programs. A joystick is a pointing device that is attached to a sound or video card's Musical Instrument Digital Interface (MIDI) port, also known as a game port. The exam might ask you to identify the MIDI (game) port on a sound card. Do not confuse this port with a 15-pin video connection (see Chapter 21 for information on connectors). Like a mouse, a joystick can move the screen pointer in all directions.

Stylus

A stylus is a handheld pen-shaped device that is commonly used as a pointing or writing instrument to input text and interact with a computer. A stylus, which uses an electronic tip or head instead of ink, is used to input text or small pictures into computer devices such as PDAs (Personal Data Assistants) or touch screens. PDAs and touch screens typically use a digitized electronic tablet to accept responses from a stylus.

TOUCH SCREEN

A touch screen is a computer display device that reacts to human touch. It can be classified as both an input or output device because it 'inputs' signals through a controller to a processor and then 'outputs' or 'presents' information through a display screen. Touch screens are most often used in such places as kiosks, restaurants, and in some training facilities where the use of a pointing device such as a mouse or a keyboard might prove cumbersome or awkward. Touch screens are typically connected to computer systems through external USB or serial ports.

There are three different types of touch screen technology used today. They are:

Surface wave: This touch screen technology is by far the most advanced. It uses ultrasonic waves that run across the touch screen. When a particular area of the touch screen is pushed with a finger or touched with a pointing device, such as a stylus, that area is 'absorbed,' and a signal representing that area is sent to a controller. One drawback to this technology is that it is highly sensitive to outside conditions, such as inclement weather.

Resistive: This technology uses a metallic layer that is electrically conductive and resistive. When an area on the screen is touched with a finger or stylus, a change occurs in the electrical current present within that area. This electrical change is registered, and an event is passed to the controller for further processing. Resistive technology touch screens are much more affordable than surface wave touch screens, and they are not affected by normal outside weather conditions, such as water. The drawbacks are that resistive displays are substantially less clear to the sight than surface wave or capacitive technology.

Capacitive: Capacitive technology employs a screen that is covered with a substance or material that stores electrical charges. Electrical sensors (circuits) are located at the corners of the screen. These sensors recognize when an area on the screen has been touched by human contact. They in turn gather the electrical charges registered and forward the collected information to a controller for processing. Capacitive technology provides a good deal of clarity. It is not affected by normal outside conditions, such as dust and weather.

MODEMS

The current A+ Core Hardware exam is likely to target your knowledge of analog dial-up modem commands and troubleshooting customer-related modem issues.

There are many types of modems on the market today. Popular modem types include cable, wireless, Digital Subscriber Line (DSL), and analog dial-up modems. For the purpose of the A+ Core Hardware Service Technician exam, we will focus on analog dial-up modems.

Modem is an acronym for Modulate Demodulate. A computer sends data from the CPU to a modem in digital format. The modem (modulator) converts digital data to analog format, which can be sent over a Plain Old Telephone Service (POTS) line. When the analog signal reaches the receiving modem, it is converted back to digital format, which can be understood by the receiving computer.

Typical 56Kbps analog modems are connected to a system internally or externally. An internal modem is inserted into an expansion slot on the motherboard. An external modem is connected to an RS-232c standard serial port with a 9-pin or

25-pin modem cable, or a USB port with a USB cable connector. After an analog modem has been connected to the computer system, either internally or externally, it can then be connected to a traditional phone jack with an RJ11 connector.

As discussed earlier in this chapter, a computer works with data in units of 8 bits, called a byte. A serial port transmits data only one bit at a time. A Universal Asynchronous Receiver Transmitter (UART) chip is used to break down incoming bytes into bits that can be transmitted serially (one bit at a time) out of the serial port. There are three types of UART chips:

8250: The first UART chip. Used in XT and AT computers. It has a 1-byte buffer.

16450: Introduced in the AT with a 2-byte buffer.

16550A: Introduced with the 486 computers. Common in Pentiums. Uses 16-byte, First-In First-Out (FIFO) buffering.

A modem, like any other device attached to a computer, requires a software driver in order to be recognized by the operating system. If a modem software driver is outdated, the user may experience intermittent problems with the connection to the Internet or another modem. Another consideration is that if your dial-up connection to the Internet is unusually slow or unstable, you should first contact your local phone company and have them clear the noise on the phone line.

You can test the ability of an analog modem to send and receive signals properly with an analog loopback adapter or a loopback plug.

At Modem Commands

The Hayes Microcomputer Products Company developed some of the earliest modems. Many modems are compatible with the modem standards set forth by Hayes (*Hayes compatible*). Hayes developed a set of modem commands that can be used to control modems manually. Today, the control and configuration of modems is generally handled by the operating system. Table 18.6 identifies some of the basic Hayes-compatible AT modem commands that you should be familiar with for the A+ Core Hardware exam.

Modem Flow Control (Handshaking)

When using dial-up communications, it is typical for a sending device to deliver data faster than a receiving device can accept it. *Flow control*, or *handshaking*, is a verification process that two communication devices use to verify that proper communication is taking place. Several flow-control protocols are available to assist with the smooth transmission of data from a Data Terminal Equipment (DTE) device, such as a serial port, to a Data Communication Equipment (DCE) device, such as a modem, and vice versa. These protocols are as follows:

TABLE 18.6 AT Modem Commands

AT Command	Command Action
ATA or A0	Answer call
ATD or ATDT	Dial the number specified
ATE	Echo (show) command on screen
ATH and ATH0	Hang up or disconnect modem
ATZ	Reset the modem
XON/XOFF	Modem flow control

XON/XOFF: This software flow control mixes control characters in with the data to perform handshaking between devices. When the receiving device's buffer is full, it sends a request, or XOFF message, to the sending device. When the buffer on the receiving device is ready to accept more data, an XON message is sent to the sending device, and transmission resumes. This is a commonly used type of flow control, although it does have a high margin of error.

RTS/CTS (Request To Send/Clear To Send): A dependable, commonly used form of hardware flow control between a computer and a modem, the RTS signal represents a computer, and the CTS signal represents a modem. If a computer is not ready to receive data, it drops its RTS signal. Its attached modem in turn drops its CTS signal and refuses to accept incoming data. When the computer is ready to receive data, it raises its RTS signal, which in turn raises its attached modem's CTS signal, and data acknowledgment can resume.

XMODEM: An error-checking method used to verify that data is not corrupted or lost, XMODEM sends data in 128-byte blocks.

YMODEM: Data is sent in 1024-byte blocks over a dial-up connection. YMODEM error-checking protocol is faster than XMODEM and is less reliable than ZMODEM.

ZMODEM: This method also sends data in 1024-byte blocks. ZMODEM protocol is faster than XMODEM. ZMODEM can resume or restart a file transfer at the point it previously failed.

SCANNERS

A scanner is an input device that captures analog images in the form of text, photographs, or drawings and converts them to digital information (0s and 1s) that can be recognized by a computer system and supporting scanner software. A scanner uses a sensor to capture the reflection of light from a desired object to create a digitized image. Scanner software or supporting applications can be used to modify the digital image to suit the needs of the user. Finally, the image can be duplicated, printed, saved as a file, or sent as an e-mail attachment.

Optical scanners and digital cameras use Charge-Coupled Devices (CCDs) to sense variations in light reflected off an image. These tiny CCDs are lined up in rows or arrays.

A CCD represents a pixel. A pixel (picture element) is an area in a graphic image. Computer monitors, for example, are split into sections that are represented by millions of pixels. The more pixels there are to an area, the sharper the graphic image or monitor resolution. Scanner resolution is measured in optical dots per inch (dpi). In simple terms, a CCD in a scanner represents one dot on a graphic image. The more CCDs there are per area in a scanner, the sharper the final image will be.

Scanners are available in various forms and offer different delivery methods:

Flatbed scanner: The most common type of scanner, larger flatbed scanners that bind documents together are often seen in business environments. With a flatbed scanner, a document or image is placed on a flat glass surface. A light source and an array of sensors (CCDs) pass below the document.

Single sheet-fed scanner: Smaller, single-feed flatbed scanners can be purchased at reasonable prices for home use. This type of scanner uses a set of rollers to feed the image to be scanned past the light source and sensors. This is not a useful scanner for large amounts of information to be scanned.

Handheld scanner: A handheld scanner is a flexible device that allows you to scan stationary objects or images. It is also a useful tool for gathering inventory information; for example, a bar code scanner can be used to gather stock information at a grocery store or warehouse.

There are several ways to interface a scanner to your computer system, including parallel, SCSI, and USB connections. These types of connectors are discussed in detail in Chapter 21.

SOUND CARDS

A sound card can act as an input or output device. It combines all the technology needed to convert audio signals to digital, and digital signals to audio, through the use of Digital-to-Analog Converters (DACs) and Analog-to-Digital Converters (ADCs).

A sound card can be integrated into the motherboard, or it can be an expansion card that is connected to the motherboard through a PCI or ISA expansion slot. As is the case with every peripheral device attached to the motherboard, a sound card requires the use of system resources, such as an IRQ, a DMA channel, and an I/O address. PCI sound cards are fairly easy to install. If the system has a plug-and-play operating system and BIOS, you just install the card into an open PCI slot and the BIOS takes care of the system resources and configuration for you. The majority of ISA sound cards on the market are preconfigured with a set of onboard jumpers that specify the use of IRQ 5. This can cause an IRQ conflict if you already have an LPT2 (a second printer port) or another device, such as a NIC, already configured to use IRQ 5. Some sound cards use special software drivers that are installed into system files, such as DOS's AUTOEXEC.BAT and CONFIG.SYS. These system files run when the computer is started and tell the operating system to recognize that there are sound-related devices attached to the computer.

Most sounds cards are connected to a CD-ROM by a wire known as a CD audio cable that comes standard with a CD-ROM device. This allows the sound card to act as an input device between your CD-ROM and the computer system. If you are using your CD-ROM as a music device and there is no sound coming from your PC speaker or attached sound system speakers, you should verify that the wire is connected between the sound card and the CD-ROM.

Sound cards are a combination of components that allow audio to be manipulated and transferred in and out of a computer system. Some of the important components that make up a sound card are these:

- An *ADC*, which is a circuit used to convert infinite analog wave signals in the form of human voice, music, or camera, to digital signals (0s and 1s) that can be understood, manipulated, and stored by a computer system.
- A *DAC* is a circuit used to convert stored digital data back to infinite analog wave signals that are outputted to audio devices, such as a microphone or speakers.
- *Analog inputs* are sound cards designed with input jacks that accept low-level voltage input from devices such as musical instruments, CD players, and microphones.
- *Analog outputs* are designed to support sound card output to speakers. There are normally two analog outputs found on a sound card. For novices, this is where you plug in your PC speakers.
- A *MIDI/game port* is a sound card port that provides support for a joystick (external game device attachment). It also provides support for musical instruments and synthesizers. The MIDI/game port is often mistaken for a video card connector on the back of a computer. It is possible that on the core exam you will see a graphic of a sound card, and you may be asked to identify the joystick/MIDI port or speaker output jacks.

- Many newer sound cards have a *synthesizer chip* built onto the sound card. This chip is used to support external MIDI devices and uses a technology known as wave-table synthesis.

DIGITAL CAMERAS

Digital cameras have taken the world by storm. They are considered an input device used to capture images that can be downloaded to a computer system. Once downloaded, the digital images can be fine-tuned and manipulated with graphical software applications to suit the needs of the end user. The final result can then be stored, e-mailed, or printed.

Like scanners, most digital cameras use CCDs to capture images. Most digital cameras are connected to a computer system using a USB port or serial port that is IEEE 1394 compliant. They can use infrared technology to download images to a system. Most digital cameras have two ways in which to store images: internal storage, which typically has to be erased after a maximum number of images have been taken; or removable or 'external' storage, which is comparable to conventional camera film. The four most popular technologies employed for storing images externally are:

- PC cards
- CompactFlash
- SSFDC (Solid State Floppy Disk Card)
- Miniature card

Digital cameras have become so popular these days that operating systems such as Windows Me, Windows 2000, and Windows XP all have Control Panel applets called "Scanners and Cameras," which can be used to easily add, configure, and troubleshoot these devices.

The following digital camera resource page Web site provides a wealth of information regarding new digital camera technology products and reviews: *http://www.dcresource.com/*.

PDAs (PERSONAL DATA ASSISTANTS)

A PDA is a small, mobile, handheld computing device that includes features such as fax, phone, networking, and Internet. Most PDAs in use today can accept input through the use of a stylus (mentioned earlier in this chapter), a small keyboard, and possibly voice input through voice recognition technologies. A very interesting development for PDAs was the implementation of the Graffiti handwriting recognition system. This allows one to write text to the operating system directly through the PDAs display screen with a stylus. The information written on the display screen is actually converted from input to text. The text can then be manipulated, stored, or e-mailed.

NOTE *The most popular operating systems installed on most PDAs today are Microsoft Windows CE, PalmOS, and EPOC.*

Synchronization

After data is inputted into a PDA system, it is often necessary to transfer or synchronize this data to a desktop computer system, laptop, or another PDA on a regular basis. Most PDAs come with a cradle that conveniently connects to a desktop with a serial (most commonly USB) cable. When the laptop is in the cradle, information can be transmitted or synced to the desktop system. Most cradles also provide power recharge capabilities while the PDA rests in the cradle. Data can be transferred through the serial connection from the PDA to a connected system and vice versa. In simple terms, the PDA's cradle is to a PDA what a docking station is to a laptop computer. (Docking stations will be discussed later in this chapter.) The most common methods used today to transfer information from one PDA to another PDA are through IR/IRDA (Infrared/Infrared Data Association) or Bluetooth (wireless specification standard). It is very important to note that PDAs can easily connect with each other, home computers, business systems, and phones using today's popular wireless standards, such as Bluetooth. Infrared and wireless connectivity will be explained in greater detail in Chapter 21.

NOTE *The A+ Core Hardware exam is likely to question you on how data is transferred from PDA to desktop and from PDA to PDA.*

Technological advances, which allow most PDAs to do everything that a regular desktop can do, have made PDAs a 'must have' in today's hectic mobile electronic business world. You can use a PDA to remotely work with such things as databases, spreadsheets, documents, e-mail, games, and calendars.

LAPTOPS

A laptop is a battery- or AC-powered mobile computer system that typically weighs between two to five pounds. Its compactness makes it ideal for mobile users who are on the go and need to work or access data, whether in or out of the office. Great strides have been made over the past few years to improve the effectiveness and ease of using laptop systems. Technological improvements regarding such things as battery power, docking stations, port replicators, wireless accessibility, USB, form factors, and overall general size have contributed to the growth in laptop use.

Docking Stations

A docking station is basically a housing or frame, if you will, that allows a laptop computer to act as a desktop system when it is inserted or 'plugged in' to the docking station. Docking stations contain electronic interfaces that allow laptops to connect with peripheral devices, such as monitors and printers. Docking stations allow the flexibility of using larger keyboards and monitors when a laptop is inserted into a docking station. They are typically equipped with bays and slots for extra storage media and additional expansion cards.

A laptop system has its own configuration or 'personality.' To be more descriptive, it has its own set configuration of software services as well as hardware device drivers for such things as video and networking. This is called a *hardware profile.* Most operating systems installed on laptop systems today allow the use of hardware profiles. When most operating systems are installed, a default hardware profile is created. A separated hardware profile can be set up and used for drivers loaded when a laptop is 'docked' in a docking station. If more than one hardware profile is present on a laptop system, the user is prompted to choose the profile they wish to use. The choices are usually "docked" or "undocked" profile. You can rename these profiles from within the OS to anything you wish—for example, "At Work" or "At Home."

One of the most common mistakes made by laptop users is choosing the wrong hardware profile when a system is booted. If you choose a docked profile when the laptop is undocked, or vice versa, it is likely that the wrong device drivers will be loaded for video, mouse, keyboard, network, printing, or sound. Make sure you pick the right profile. Rebooting and selecting the proper hardware profile can quickly resolve issues resulting from this common mistake.

Port Replicators

A port replicator replicates laptop ports. It is basically a docking station without slots for storage or extra expansion card usability. Similar to docking stations, port replicators provide things such as parallel and serial ports. When a laptop is attached to a port replicator, easy access can be accomplished to stationary devices such as large monitors, printers, joysticks, MIDI devices, and full-size keyboards. It should be noted that there are no real industry standards for docking stations and port replicators. These devices are usually proprietary to a particular laptop manufacturer. In other words, when you purchase a particular laptop computer, you will have to buy the docking station or port replicator made by the laptop's manufacturer.

BATTERIES AND POWER

Charging and keeping charged the batteries that keep today's portable electronic devices alive has become a very popular topic, and CompTIA will no doubt target this topic on the A+ Core exam. There are several types of rechargeable chemical batteries available today, and each has its own characteristics. You do not have to focus on the detailed science of batteries. However, you do need to be able to identify the following battery types that CompTIA has included in their 2003 Core objectives:

NiCad (Nickel-Cadmium)

NiCad batteries are rechargeable batteries that lose their strength after only a few hours of use. Earlier NiCad batteries suffered from a phenomenon known as memory effect. If these battery types were recharged before most of their power was used up, they would lose their ability to become fully charged.

NiMH (Nickel Metal Hydride)

A NiMH battery is a rechargeable battery that was designed to provide long-lasting power and overall battery savings for such devices as energy-hungry PDAs and digital cameras. NiMH batteries are considered inexpensive at around $2.50 a battery. NiMH batteries do not suffer from the phenomenon of memory effect, as did early NiCad batteries, and they can store up to 50% more power. The average AAA NiMH battery has a standard rating of 1.2V. Traditional alkaline batteries carry a rating of 1.5V.

Lithium Ion

A lithium ion battery contains lithium derived from chemicals. Lithium is the lightest metal available. It is ideal for electrochemical potential. Lithium rechargeable batteries offer twice the power life of NiCad.

Lithium batteries are the most commonly used battery types for mobile systems. They are lightweight, safe, efficient, and do not suffer from memory effect. They are, of course, more expensive than the previously mentioned battery types.

Fuel Cell

The fuel cell is the latest and greatest power invention introduced in the struggle to efficiently deliver more power to laptops and mobile systems. A fuel cell produces hydrogen that is converted from methanol or alcohol. It is proposed that fuel cell technology will replace the popular lithium ion batteries that are used in most laptops today. Fuel cells can last up to 10 hours and may eliminate the need for rechargeable batteries.

CHAPTER SUMMARY

In this chapter, you learned how a computer converts digital information to a readable format that humans can understand. This chapter also addressed important input devices and the system resources they utilize to communicate with the computer's main components. To be a proficient computer technician, it is essential that you are aware of how computer resources work together. So that you can properly install, upgrade, diagnose, and troubleshoot a system, it is imperative that you understand IRQs, DMA channels, and base I/O memory addresses. It is a safe bet that the A+ Core Hardware exam is going to focus on these areas.

REVIEW QUESTIONS

1. The default address used by the primary IDE controller is?

o A. C000-C7FFF
o B. 1F0h
o C. 378h
o D. 3F8h

Correct Answer = B

C000-C7FFF is used for the video adapter memory address. 378h is the memory address reserved for LPT1. 3F8h is the memory address reserved for COM1.

2. The default address used by the secondary IDE controller is?

o A. 170h
o B. 1F0h
o C. 378h
o D. 3F8h

Correct Answer = A

1F0h is the memory address reserved for the primary IDE controller. 3F8h is the memory address reserved for COM1. 378h is the memory address reserved for LPT1.

3. The default I/O address for COM2 is?

- A. 170h
- B. 1F0h
- C. 378h
- D. 2F8h

Correct Answer = D

170h is reserved for the secondary IDE controller. 1F0h is the memory address reserved for the primary IDE controller. 378h is the memory address reserved for LPT1.

4. The floppy drive controller uses which DMA channel?

- A. 1
- B. 2
- C. 4
- D. 7

Correct Answer = B

DMA channel 2 is used for a floppy drive or a possible tape drive unit. DMA channels 1 and 7 are available. DMA channel 4 is used for the second DMA controller (cascades to DMA channels 0–3).

5. How many devices can you attach (chain) to a single IDE controller or channel?

- A. 1
- B. 2
- C. 4
- D. 127

Correct Answer = B

Two devices can be attached to a single IDE controller. For example, the first device attached to the primary IDE controller would be your "master" or primary hard drive. The second device attached to your primary IDE/ATA controller is your "slave" or secondary device.

6. **Which IRQ is reserved for the system timer?**

   ○ A. 0
   ○ B. 1
   ○ C. 2
   ○ D. 9

   Correct Answer = A

   IRQ 1 is reserved for a standard 101/102 keyboard. IRQ 2 is an interrupt controller (cascaded to IRQ 9). IRQ 9 is cascaded to IRQ 2.

7. **Which of the following are valid touch screen technologies? (Choose Three)**

   □ A. Capacitive.
   □ B. Conducive.
   □ C. Resistive.
   □ D. Surface wave.
   □ E. Switch.
   □ F. All are valid touch screen technologies.

   Correct Answers = A, C, and D

   Common touch screen technologies include capacitive, resistive, and surface wave technologies.

8. **What is the most common way to transfer information between two PDAs?**

   ○ A. IR
   ○ B. USB
   ○ C. SCSI
   ○ D. LPT
   ○ E. RS232
   ○ F. IEEE 1284
   ○ G. None of the above

   Correct Answer = A

   The most common methods used today to transfer information from a one PDA to another PDA are through IR (Infrared)/IrDA (Infrared Data Association) or Bluetooth (wireless specification standard).

9. Which of the following ports are most often used when connecting a digital camera to a computer system? (Choose Two)

□ A. SCSI port

□ B. Port 25

□ C. USB port

□ D. Parallel port

□ E. IEEE 1394-compliant port

□ F. Port 1099

Correct Answers = C and E

Most digital cameras are connected to a computer system using a USB port or serial port that is IEEE 1394 compliant.

10. A laptop user who uses a docking station while at work calls you and states he cannot connect to the network and his LCD screen is "all messed up." What is most likely the problem?

o A. The NIC card's video driver is corrupt.

o B. Wrong user profile.

o C. Wrong hardware profile.

o D. The network is malfunctioning.

o E. The ports on the laptop are not IEEE 1284 compliant.

o F. None of the above.

Correct Answer = C

One of the most common mistakes made by laptop users is choosing the wrong hardware profile when a system is booted. If you choose a docked profile when the laptop is undocked or vice versa, it is likely that the wrong device drivers will be loaded for video, mouse, keyboard, network, printing, or sound.

11. Which of the following devices is similar to a docking station with the exception that it doesn't provide extra slots for storage and expansion cards?

o A. A port replicator

o B. A port sniffer

o C. A hardware profile

o D. An AC/DC converter

o E. None of the above

Correct Answer = A

A port replicator is similar to a docking station except it does not have slots for storage or expansion cards.

12. Which of the following battery types suffer from the phenomenon known as memory effect?

o A. Lithium ion

o B. NiMH

o C. NiCad

o D. Copper tip

o E. Silver bunny battery

o F. All of the above

Correct Answer = C

Earlier NiCad batteries suffered from a phenomenon known as memory effect. For example, if these battery types are recharged before most of their power is used up, they will lose their ability to become fully charged.

13. Which of the following produces hydrogen that is converted from methanol or alcohol and may replace the lithium ion batteries used today?

o A. Lithium ion

o B. NiMH

o C. NiCad

o D. Copper tip

o E. Fuel cell

o F. None of the above

Correct Answer = E

A fuel cell produces hydrogen that is converted from methanol or alcohol. It is proposed that fuel cell may replace the popular lithium ion batteries used in most laptops. A fuel cell lasts up to 10 hours without a need to recharge.

REFERENCES

http://www.dcresource.com/. This digital camera resource page provides a wealth of information regarding new digital camera technology products and reviews.

19 Basic Output Devices

In This Chapter

OUTPUT TYPES AND DEVICES

Output is defined as data or information that is sent out of a computer system, program, or device. Output can take many forms, including electronic characters, numbers, symbols, signals, sounds, paper, and/or graphics.

Output is generally categorized into two main types: transient and final. *Transient output* is temporary output that is produced in the form of electronic signals or data moving from one location to the next, to be used for only a short period. An example of transient output is an electronic request from one device to another to carry out a specific function, such as an operating system sending a request or message to a printer to print. The request to print is temporary. Transient output can be in the form of information stored in RAM or a temporary swap file on a hard drive. It exists to serve a temporary purpose. In other words, transient output is output that is not stored or saved.

Final output is more permanent. It is data or information that can be saved, recorded, or physically held on to. Some examples of final output are a printed report, an image displayed on a video display monitor, a sound that comes from computer speakers, or a file stored in a permanent location, such as a hard drive, floppy disk, writable CD-ROM, or DVD.

An output device is any machine or peripheral device that is capable of producing information from binary data that it receives from the CPU. Typical output devices are printers, plotters, video displays, computer speakers, and synthesizers. To list all the various output devices available on the market is beyond the scope of this book. However, this chapter will prepare you well for the A+ Core Hardware exam topics that relate to output devices and their functions.

VIDEO DISPLAY DEVICES

The computer monitor is by far the most common computer output device in use today. It is the window to the electronic world. Think about it: how many people around the world are staring at a computer screen at this very moment?

A computer monitor is a vehicle by which information that has been processed is presented to the end user. The components involved in producing a final image from a computer system are a video adapter (or video card) and a monitor. The computer monitor has had many names since its inception. In the early (DOS) days of computing, the monitor was called a console, or CON for short. It has also been called a CRT, which is an acronym for Cathode Ray Tube.

Computer monitors are categorized into two main groups: CRTs and Liquid Crystal Displays (LCDs).

Before we continue, here are a few important tips for the test. A computer monitor uses a DB-15 pin-style male connector to attach to the 15-pin female connector on the back of a computer. If one of these pins is bent or broken, the display screen may flicker, turn many strange colors, or show nothing at all. In addition, it is essential to know that most of today's video adapters contain their own BIOS chip, which interacts between the video card and the system processor.

CATHODE RAY TUBE (CRT)

A CRT is based on the same technology used in a television set. An electronic beam is directed by a glass vacuum tube that uses an electron gun to the back of a glass screen that has a phosphorus coating. When the beam of electrons hits the phosphorus material, moving from the top of the slightly curved glass to the bottom, the phosphors combine to form pixels, and visible light representing a viewable image is displayed.

There are two types of CRTs: monochrome (single color, plus background) and color (multiple colors). A monochrome monitor uses two colors—a solid color (usually black or grayscale) that represents the background, and either amber, green, or white for the foreground. A single beam from the electron gun illuminates the foreground area with a single color.

Color monitors use three electron gun beams to represent each of the three colors of light from the basic primary colors of Red, Green, and Blue (RGB). These are the primary colors from which all other colors are derived. Solid colors are derived from the three primary colors to form the colors Cyan, Magenta, and Yellow (CMY). If you take a look at a typical desktop color printer's ink cartridge, you will see the CMY solid colors. The combination of the three electron beams projected from the electron gun form a triangular representation of the three primary colors. This is called a triad picture element, or pixel (Figure 19.1). The final image displayed on the CRT screen is a combination of many pixels with different intensities. The more pixels or dots that can be grouped together, the greater the color depth (i.e., number of possible colors).

Here are some important CRT terms that you should be familiar with.

Shadow mask: A thin metal sheet that the electron gun beams must pass through. The shadow mask ensures that the electron beam hits the correct phosphor.

Degauss: Degaussing is a method used to remove any magnetic fields that may cause the shadow mask to become magnetized. For example, placing a magnetic speaker too close to a CRT can cause the visual image to become distorted. Degauss normally runs when you turn your monitor on. Most modern CRTs have a manual degauss button.

Dot Pitch, Resolution, and Color Depth

A pixel is basically a dot on a CRT or LCD display. As previously stated, the more pixels that can be grouped together, the more defined the final image will be. Dot pitch, which is measured in millimeters (mm), is the distance between pixels. For example, a 0.28 dot pitch measurement means that the pixels are 0.28mm apart from each other on the display. When purchasing a monitor, it is important to get as low a dot pitch measurement as possible for a clear, well-defined image.

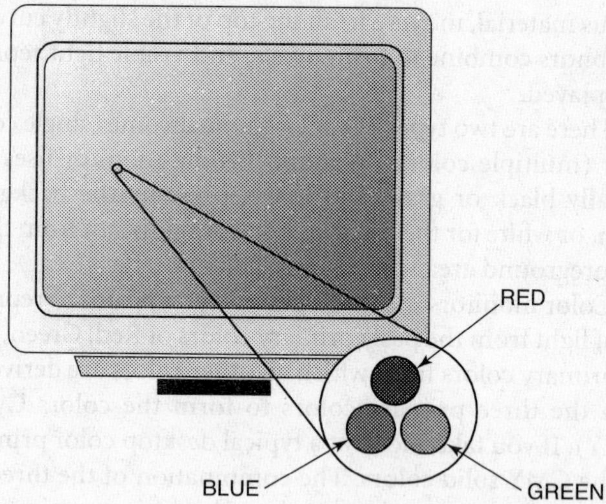

FIGURE 19.1 Representation of a triad pixel element.

Popular dot pitch measurements are 0.31mm, 0.28mm, 0.27mm, 0.26mm, and 0.25mm. Resolution is the total number of pixels that can be displayed on a screen at one time. To calculate resolution, you multiply the number of pixels per horizontal row by the number of vertical rows of pixels. For example, standard VGA resolution is 640×480, which equates to 307,200 pixels. Color depth is the total amount of pixels that a screen or monitor can display. To be more specific, the total number of bits used to represent a pixel stored in video memory is referred to as *color depth*. Commonly used color depths are 32 bit, 24 bit, 16 bit, and 8 bit. Early computing systems used 8-bit color. Each pixel uses 1 byte of video memory. Each pixel can select one of 256 colors. The software that creates the image using either 18 bits or 24 bits per pixel defines these colors; therefore, 256 colors can be displayed on the monitor, selected from a palette of 262,144 or 16,777,216 colors. Table 19.1 shows video color depths.

You will not have to do pixel calculations on the A+ Core Hardware exam. You may be required to know video adapter types, their resolutions, and the number of colors they represent. Table 19.2 shows an overview of video adapters and their corresponding resolutions and colors.

Refresh Rates

The tiny phosphors inside a CRT lose their illumination very quickly. They must be refreshed many times per second so that the image displayed on the screen does not fade or flicker. The electron gun inside the CRT must redraw the image continuously in order to keep the phosphors active. This process is called a CRT's *refresh rate*.

TABLE 19.1 Video Color Depths

Color Name	Available Colors	Color Depth (Measured in Bits)
Monochrome	2	1
VGA	16	4
256 (colors)	256	8
High color	65,536	16
LCD color	262,144	18
True color	16,777,216	24
True color	4,294,967,296	32

Table 19.2 Video Standards, Resolution, and Colors

Video Adapter	Resolution	Colors
MDA (monochrome display adapter)	720×3500	2 (text only)
CGA (color graphics adapter)	320×2000	4 (text only)
	640×2000	2 (text only)
EGA (enhanced graphics adapter)	640×3500	16 (text only)
VGA (video graphics adapter)	640×4800	16 (text only)
	320×2000	256 (text only)
SVGA (super video graphics adapter)	800×6000	16 (text only)
	1024×7680	256 (text only)
	1280×1024	256 (text only)
	1600×1200	256 (text only)

A CRT's refresh rate is measured in hertz. The higher the number of hertz (Hz), the faster the CRT's refresh rate. Common video refresh rates run from 60Hz all the way through 120Hz (depending on the quality of the monitor). An 80Hz refresh rate, for example, means that a screen will be redrawn, or 'refreshed,' 80 times per second. Something else to remember is that the higher the resolution, the fewer hertz options you will have to choose from. (Typically, at 1600×1200, you are limited to only 7580Hz; while at 1280×1024, you might have an option to go as high, as say, 100Hz.)

Have you ever been watching television and noticed that when a monitor is displayed, a horizontal line traveling vertically can be seen? That's because typically, a television set's refresh rate (around 30Hz) is significantly lower than a standard PC monitor's. If the monitor is set even at the bare minimum 60Hz, the television would only be displaying the screen half as fast as the monitor. The result is a horizontal line is drawn (that typically runs from bottom to top), because the television can't keep up with the monitor. The higher the refresh rate is set on the monitor, the faster the horizontal line will travel. Monitor refresh rate is something that will definitely have an impact on your PC experience (especially as time passes). Most people find that 60Hz is far too low a refresh rate, and it can even cause some people to experience headaches after prolonged use of a monitor at that setting. Most people who work on computers for extended periods of time tend to use 75Hz, as it is a bit easier on the eyes.

NOTE

It is very important that you don't set your refresh rate (in an operating system's display panel settings) faster than the recommended refresh rate stated by the monitor's manufacturer. This may cause your monitor to go blank.

Two scan rates are used to determine the ultimate speed of the refresh rate. The horizontal scan rate is the speed at which the phosphors are refreshed from left to right. The vertical scan rate is the speed at which the entire screen is refreshed.

Interlacing is a refresh process in which every other row of pixels (even or odd) is refreshed by the electron gun in order to increase monitor resolution. The electron gun refreshes the odd number of rows in a display and then returns to refresh the even rows. Although interlacing helps to increase resolution, it also causes the display to jitter or flicker.

Noninterlacing is when every row of pixels is refreshed consecutively. This reduces jitter and screen flicker, and generally provides for a better viewing experience. When purchasing a monitor, it is a good idea to buy a noninterlaced display.

High resolution requires video memory, or VRAM. The higher you set your display resolution and the more colors you choose to support, the more VRAM your system will require. The A+ Core Hardware test may ask you to identify the amount of memory needed to support a particular resolution with a defined number of colors.

For example, how much memory is needed to support a resolution of 1024×768 using 24-bit, true color? The answer is 4MB. Table 19.3 provides the answer to this question, along with other video resolutions and VRAM requirements.

NOTE

You can also use the following mathematical formula to assist you with calculating VRAM requirements: memory requirement = horizontal pixels × vertical pixels × color depth.

TABLE 19.3 Video Resolution and VRAM Requirements

Video Resolution	8 Bits 256 Colors	16 Bits 65,000 Colors	24-Bit True Color 16.7 Million Colors
640×480	512K	1MB	1MB
800×600	512K	1MB	2MB
1024×768	1MB	2MB	4MB
1280×1024	2MB	4MB	6MB
1600×1200	4MB	8MB	8MB

VIDEO DISPLAY STANDARDS

The very first video adapter was an MDA (Monochrome Display Adapter). MDA has a resolution of 720×350 pixels and is capable of supporting text, but not graphics or color. CGA (Color Graphics Adapter) and EGA (Enhanced Graphics Adapter) were the early display standards for monitors. CGA was capable of producing just two colors with a resolution of 640×200. EGA could produce 16 colors with a resolution of 640×350. These video technologies were used in the early to mid-1980s. If you worked for extended periods using these technologies in the 1980s, your eyesight might be the worse for it now.

Video Graphics Array (VGA)

VGA is the standard for all graphic devices, such as monitors and video cards. It has a resolution of 640×480 with a color depth of 16 colors, or 320×200 with 256 colors. VGA uses analog signals, as opposed to the digital signals used by its predecessors, CGA and EGA. The original implementation of the VGA standard introduced the following video subsystem standards to assist with processing and ultimately produce a better image:

Frame buffer: The frame buffer is a memory buffer used to store data before it is displayed. The amount of information stored before it is sent to the display is called a *frame.*

Graphics command language: With VGA, the CPU manages all the work of producing an image. Graphics command language introduced a set of simple commands that alleviated some of the CPU's video-related tasks.

CRT controller: The CRT controller produces signals that control and reset the electron guns inside the monitor.

Sequencer: The sequencer is basically a timer on the video adapter. It loads display addresses into memory and operates with a 16-bit internal counter.

Serializer: The serializer is used to serialize data held in video memory before it is sent to an attribute controller.

Attribute controller: This houses a color template that determines the *value*, or color, of a pixel.

Display memory: A bank of 256KB DRAM separated into four 64KB color planes, its function is to store screen-displayed information.

Graphics controller: The graphics controller carries out logical functions and calculations on data being placed in display memory.

VGA introduced many advantages, including these subsystems. Unfortunately, it didn't use resources fast enough to support the demands of GUIs and applications that were hungry for new standards. VGA circuitry is directly tied to the processor. It relies on the processor to do most of its work, which takes a toll on the processor's performance.

8514/A

The IBM standard of 8514/A was introduced at the same time as the VGA standard. It provided three new graphics modes that enabled higher resolution and color, and was well suited for IBM's proprietary Micro Channel Bus. The 8514/A standard provided some processing capabilities. It supported a resolution of 1024×768 and 256 colors in graphics mode.

Extended Graphics Adapter

Extended Graphics Adapter (XGA) cards were introduced in later IBM PS/2 model computers. The XGA adapters use either 512K or 1MB of VRAM and are capable of bus mastering using IBM's Micro Channel Architecture (MCA). Using 1MB of VRAM, XGA supports a graphics resolution of 1024×768 and 256 colors, or 640×480 using high color (16 bits). This standard would be followed by SXGA (Super Extended Graphics Adapter, capable of 1280×1024) and UXGA (Ultra Extended Graphics Adapter, capable of 1600×1200).

Super VGA and Ultra VGA

Today's video cards are called Super VGA (SVGA) cards. Technically, SVGA and Ultra VGA (UVGA) are not distinct video standards; they are words that describe a video card's capability to achieve higher resolution and colors. Manufacturers of SVGA and UVGA video cards each provide their own sets of instructions and software drivers to maximize the performance of the cards they produce. A group of graphic and video card manufacturers known as the Video Electronics Standards Association (VESA) has standardized video rules. SVGA was originally developed by VESA as competition to IBM's proprietary 8514/A and XGA technologies. (XGA was introduced by IBM in 1990 as a replacement for their old 8514/A video standard, capable of displaying 640×480–1024×768.) All varieties of SVGA support a palette of 16 million colors. The basic SVGA resolutions are 800×600, 1024×768, 1280×1024, and 1600×1200.

MONITOR SHAPES AND SIZES

Today, monitors are available in many shapes, sizes, and colors. Monitor size is calculated in inches. Popular monitors are available in the following sizes: 15, 17, 19, and 21 inches. The size of a monitor screen is measured diagonally from the bottom right corner to the top left corner; this is known as the monitor's *nominal size* The actual viewable size of the display is typically at least an inch smaller than the advertised nominal size of the monitor. For example, a 19-inch monitor (nominal size) actually has a viewable size area of less than 18 inches. A 17-inch monitor has a viewable display area of 15.6 inches. The monitor's *bezel*, which is the black plastic boundary that supports and surrounds the edge of the glass screen, reduces the viewable size of the display area.

Smaller monitors (generally 15 inches and smaller) have trouble displaying higher resolutions because they cannot support very small pixels. Typically, monitors that are 15 inches or smaller can only display up to 1024×768, 17-inch monitors can display up to 1280×1024, and 19-inch and larger monitors can display 1600×1200. A larger monitor that supports smaller pixels is handy for higher resolution settings and fitting in more icons on the desktop. If you increase the resolution settings in the Windows 2000 Display Properties window, the icons on the desktop become smaller (Figure 19.2).

NOTE

If you change your monitor's resolution, video card drivers, or NIC drivers, and then cannot re-enter the Windows GUI, you can enter the operating system through the use of Safe Mode. Safe Mode loads only the drivers needed to enter the operating system for troubleshooting purposes. Higher resolution changes and other drivers are not loaded when you enter Safe Mode.

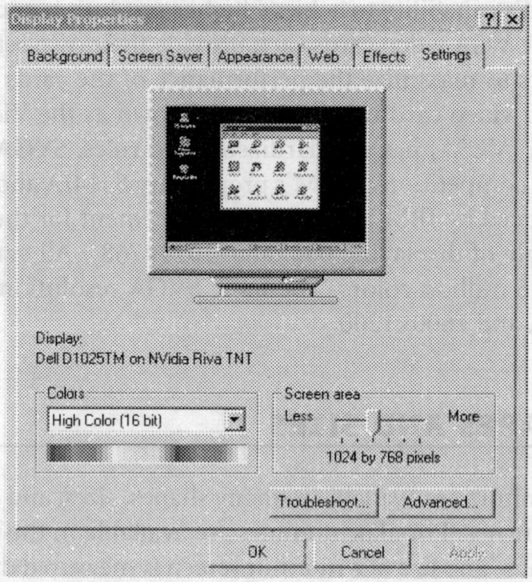

FIGURE 19.2 Windows 2000 Display Properties window.

Graphics

Two technical drawing methods are used to draw an image on a video screen: raster graphics and vector graphics.

Raster graphics: Raster images are digital images that are created from a grid of *x* (horizontal) and *y* (vertical) coordinates. The *x* and *y* coordinates represent the locations of pixels on a display screen. Raster is the most common method used to produce an image. Some of the more common types of raster formats are JPEG, BMP, and TIFF images. These raster image types are produced from software graphics applications such as Microsoft Paint. Most monitors and printers produce information in raster format and are considered raster output devices.

Vector graphics: Vector graphics programs produce a sharper image than raster. Vector is based on mathematical equations that define where and how an image is to be drawn or sized on a display. Vector graphics programs, such as Corel Draw®, Microsoft Visio™, and Adobe® Illustrator®, are used to create scalable, detailed drawings. Two- and three-dimensional graphic animations are created using vector graphics technology and software.

LIQUID CRYSTAL DISPLAY

Liquid Crystal Display (LCD) is a flat-panel display technology that is used in most laptop computers. LCD technology can also be used for other display devices, such as car radio displays, clocks, desktop computers, and any other display devices that can take advantage of flat-panel technology. The biggest advantages of LCD flat screens are that they reduce physical space requirements, they are lightweight and portable, and they require less energy to operate. (Laptop LCDs are powered by low-voltage DC.) Traditional CRTs take up more desktop space than LCDs and require more energy to operate. With an LCD display, what you see is basically what you get. Unlike CRTs, in which the nominal size is less than the described measurement of the monitor, the measurement of an LCD screen is accurate. In other words, if you purchase a 15-inch LCD, you get a 15-inch display. LCD monitors are now available in all sizes, from 15 inches through 23 inches. Please note that while LCD monitors are great space savers, they are far more expensive that standard (and even flat-panel) CRT monitors.

LCD technology uses two panels of a polarizing substance, with a liquid crystal solution between the two panels. An electric charge is sent through the crystals, causing them to form a shield from light. The crystals either allow or disallow the passage of light, and eventually form an image.

Different types of LCDs serve different purposes and provide various levels of display quality. Some of the more common types are as follows.

Passive matrix LCD: A passive matrix display uses LCD elements, electrical current, and a grid of wires to control the passage of light. It has a fixed resolution of pixels.

Active matrix LCD: This LCD type is based on Thin Film Transistor (TFT) technology. It constantly refreshes each pixel, providing a consistently sharp image. This technology provides better visual quality than passive matrix and is more expensive.

Dual scan: With dual scan, the LCD screen is divided in two. Each half of the screen is refreshed separately. This process increases the resolution rate, but decreases the brightness (contrast) level of the LCD.

Monitor Power Management

A monitor uses a tremendous amount of AC. The Environmental Protection Agency (EPA) came up with a program and a set of standards, known as Energy Star™, to reduce the amount of energy used by monitors and PC-related equipment. To see if a monitor is Energy Star compliant, click Start > Settings > Control Panel > Display > Screen Saver. If the monitor is compliant, you will see the Energy Star logo and "Energy saving features of monitor" (Figure 19.3).

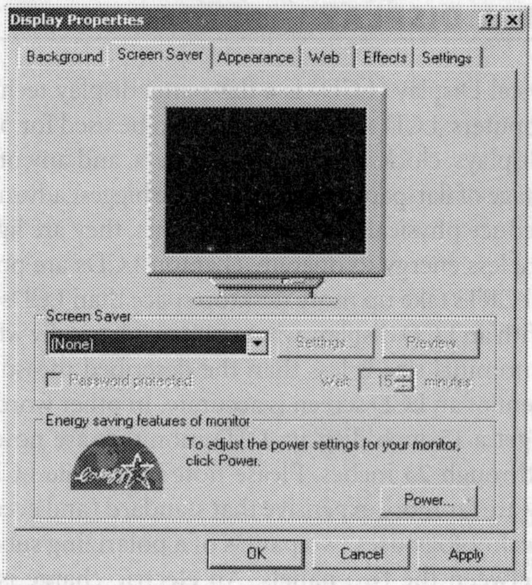

FIGURE 19.3 Windows Energy Star Compliance logo.

Important Monitor/Video-related Information and Test Tips

The following important monitor/video-related information and test tips are included to give you an extra boost in the exam room. Pay close attention here; this information may help you in the field as well:

- ✓ Using a video resolution of 800×600 is equivalent to using SVGA video mode.
- ✓ Video cards are most often designed for AGP slots.
- ✓ If your monitor goes blank after changing your video resolution from say 640×480 (16 Colors) to 800×600, (16-bit high color) it is likely that your refresh rate has been set too fast for your monitor to handle.
- ✓ The amount of time required for CRT's electron beam to draw or "paint" a screen is called refresh rate.
- ✓ 4MB of video random access memory (VRAM) would be required to display 1024×768 at 24-bit color.
- ✓ If you have a monitor that is displaying abnormal odd colors such as green or orange, there is a high probability that your monitor is either defective or you have a bad or bent pin on your monitor's cable connector.
- ✓ WRAM is used for and on many video cards today.

- ✓ If you find yourself browsing the Internet and you can't see entire pages displayed on your monitor, the first thing you should do is adjust your video resolution settings.
- ✓ Always unplug the power from your system when installing video cards.
- ✓ In order for a system's POST (Power-On Self-Test) to complete at boot up, it must recognize video support.
- ✓ If you change your monitor's refresh rate and nothing will display on your monitor, the first step you should take is to restart the computer and enter Safe Mode. Safe Mode will load the basic video drivers and setting, which will further allow you to troubleshoot.
- ✓ A VGA connector has 15 pins.
- ✓ If a signal to an Energy Star Compliant monitor does not vary or change, it can change or "switch" to a lower power status.

PRINTERS

A printer is an output device that accepts information from a computing system and produces output, usually text and graphics, to the end user in paper form. Many printing devices and printing technologies are available today. For the purpose of studying for the exam and its printer troubleshooting questions, we will focus on the current printer port standards, dot matrix, ink-jet, and laser printer technologies.

Printers can be categorized into groups based on the way they apply an image or text to a consumable product, such as paper. The three most popular printer groups are impact printers, thermal ink printers, and laser printers.

Impact printers: Impact printers include dot matrix and daisy wheel printers. They typically use a print head (which can get very hot) with pins to strike against an ink ribbon to create a character, number, or symbol. They are very noisy and are considered old-fashioned technology. Their main purpose in today's world is for printing multipart, carbon-copy forms.

Thermal ink printers: Thermal ink printers include the very popular ink-jet and bubble-jet printers. Small nozzles are used to disperse ink onto paper to form an image. These printers are considered affordable and are commonly used in households across the world.

Laser printers: Laser printers use an electrophotographic process to place an image on paper. This more-expensive technology is well worth the price for the speed at which it can print, as well as the quality it can produce. Laser printer speed is measured by the number of Pages Per Minute (PPM) that the printer can produce. Laser printers can be found in most business environments.

PARALLEL PORT STANDARDS

Printers can be connected to a computer using several methods as well as special connectors. (Connectors are discussed in detail in Chapter 21.) Currently, the fastest available connection for a printer is realized through a USB connection. Older printers were and still are connected to a computer system's DB-9 male serial port connector, which is capable of transmitting only 1 bit of information at a time in a half-duplex manner (i.e., it is incapable of sending and receiving information at the same time).

Today, most printers are connected to a computer system using a Data Bus (DB) 25-pin male connector that inserts into a DB 25-pin female connector on the back of the system. This is known as an LPT/parallel port connection (or LPT1). Parallel transmission of data is bidirectional, meaning that the parallel port can communicate with the CPU during transmission. Parallel communication transfer rates are 8 bits at a time. The opposite end of the DB 25-pin male connector cable is connected to a printer with a Centronics 36-pin connector.

The Institute of Electrical and Electronics Engineers (IEEE) has developed a set of parallel port communication standards that control the flow of data between computer systems and print devices. These standards (protocols) are known as IEEE 1284.

NOTE *Questions on the test may refer to printer cables and the IEEE standard they represent. Remember that the IEEE 1284 is a standard for parallel communication and printer cables.*

There are five modes (IEEE standards) of parallel communication that you need to know for the test. Keep in mind that bidirectional is considered a standard.

Compatibility mode: This is an obsolete, unidirectional, parallel communication, forward-only mode implemented with the original 36-pin Centronics connector.

Nibble mode: Also obsolete, nibble mode is used to reverse the communication between a printer and a host by two 4-bit pieces of information at a time. Nibble mode complements compatibility mode and is also considered bidirectional.

Byte mode (SPP): Byte mode is a very common mode of parallel reverse communication that sends 8 bits of information at a time, side by side. Picture a typical parallel cable with eight separate 'highways' next to each other. One bit of information travels down each 'highway' at the same time.

Extended Capabilities Port (ECP) mode: ECP mode is the fastest form of bidirectional printer-to-host, parallel port transmission standard available. It

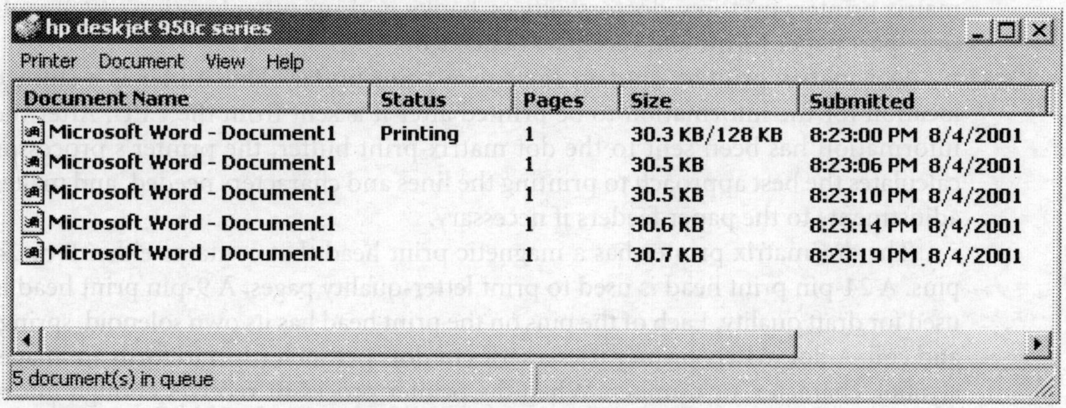

FIGURE 19.4 Windows print queue with print jobs waiting to print.

uses both forward and reverse transmission techniques, and sends data 8-bit wide at a time. ECP also supports handshaking and compression.

Enhanced Parallel Port (EPP) mode: EPP mode is similar to ECP in its ability to support forward and reverse communication, and 8-bit-wide transmission of data. EPP does not support handshaking.

Print Queues and the Spooler Service

Before a print request is sent to a physical printer, it is typically held temporarily in a print queue (buffer) in the operating system. If you send multiple print jobs to a printer, they wait in the print queue until the previous print job completes. If a print job errors out or gets stalled in the print queue, all jobs waiting to print in the queue will not print until the stalled or 'hung' print job is deleted or canceled. Figure 19.4 shows a Windows print queue display with print jobs waiting to print. Most current operating systems run a system service known as the spooler service. The spooler service controls the print queue. If simply canceling or deleting the stalled print job does not allow waiting print jobs to print, you may have to stop and start the spooler service.

DOT MATRIX AND INK-JET PRINTERS

A dot matrix printer is a form of impact printer whose technology closely resembles that of a typewriter. They have survived based on their ability to print multiple-part forms and because of their paper-feeding capabilities. It is common to find dot matrix printers in stores, doctors' offices, banks, and any other location where multiple-part paper forms and receipts are needed.

Dot matrix printers contain their own print buffer. This buffer is a storage location for the information to be printed after it is sent from the CPU. After the information has been sent to the dot matrix print buffer, the printer's processor calculates the best approach to printing the lines and characters needed, and makes adjustments to the paper feeders if necessary.

The dot matrix printer has a magnetic print head that contains either 9 or 24 pins. A 24-pin print head is used to print letter-quality pages. A 9-pin print head is used for draft quality. Each of the pins on the print head has its own solenoid, spring, and coil. A dot matrix printer uses a series of dots per inch (dpi) to form an image, symbol, character, or number. When the printer processor receives enough information from the print buffer to begin printing, a signal is sent to the magnetic print head. A combination of events takes place, and the pins attached to the print head hit an ink ribbon, which is held in place by a platen, that is between the pins and the paper. After the pin has applied its dot, it is pulled back, and the next pin applies its dot. This process repeats until a character is complete. All of this happens very quickly. The friction caused by the constant movement of the print head can make it get extremely hot. When working on a dot matrix printer, never touch the print head until it has time to cool down. Dot matrix printer speeds are measured in printed Characters Per Second (cps). Characters-per-second speeds differ based on print quality and manufacturer. Dot matrix printers are capable of up to 500 cps.

Dot matrix printers use either a pressure roller or tractor-feed method of pulling continuous-form paper through the printer one line at a time. The continuous use of a dot matrix printer without proper maintenance can cause the tractor-feed rollers and platen to become misaligned. This commonly results in ink fading as it is applied from left to right or uneven lines of output across the paper. Lack of proper maintenance can also result in constant paper jams. Use a can of compressed air regularly to spray out any loose particles around the tractor rollers. Rubber-cleaning solutions should be used to clean the tractor belts and rollers.

Ink-jet printers are a very popular type of printer, and are used in many homes and small businesses. Ink-jet technology is typically faster than dot matrix, but not as fast as the average laser printer. Its main benefits are its affordability and ease of maintenance compared to laser printer technology.

Ink-jet printers use a type of print head that houses many tiny nozzles, sometimes referred to as jets. These jets spray or drop fast-drying ink into a condensed area to form the tiny dots that make up a character. A thermal resistor actually heats up the ink until it expands and is eventually forced out of the print nozzle in the form of a bubble or droplet. The ink bubble is then sprayed or dropped onto paper. The ink droplets can tend to smear or splatter when they hit the paper, which causes the dot created on the paper to become somewhat distorted. To refine this process, the thermal resistor bubble-creation process was replaced with piezoelectric crystal. The piezoelectric process uses crystals that react to electric charge. When charged, a crystal draws or pulls ink from an ink storage unit held above the crystal. In simple terms, the piezoelectric process can cut or refine the exact amount of ink needed to refine the dot placed on paper. This reduces the smudging effect of traditional ink-jet technology and provides better printer resolution. In fact, this process allows resolutions greater than 1440 dpi.

Ink-jet printers accept paper one sheet at a time. This process, called *single-sheet form feed*, involves pulling paper into the printer with rollers. The paper is aligned under a print mechanism that moves across the paper to apply an image.

If sheets of paper connected into one long sheet are placed in printer guides with plastic teeth, the printer is said to be a continuous form-feed printer. Ink-jet printers use single-sheet form feed technology. Dot matrix printers use the continuous form-feed process.

LASER PRINTERS

The previous A+ Core Hardware Service Technician exams used to bombard the examinee with questions relating to minute details of the stages of the laser printing electrophotographic process. The current exam may also address some of these details. It is very important that you understand this process and its intricacies, as well as the laser printer paper-feeding process. Equally important, however, is to focus your study on printer troubleshooting and maintenance in general. The current A+ Core test laser printer questions seem to be headed in the direction of the overall use of the technology. For example, you may know that a uniform charge of -600V is applied to the laser printer's photosensitive drum by the primary corona wire during the conditioning phase of the EP process, but that knowledge will not help you on the test if you can't answer a question asking you how to dispose of a toner cartridge properly.

A laser printer is a popular type of nonimpact printer that is capable of producing resolutions of 1400 dpi or greater, with a usual minimum requirement of 600 dpi. Laser printers use technology similar to that of photocopiers.

A laser printer also puts many dots on paper that eventually form an image. Unlike the previously mentioned printing technologies, however, the laser printing process uses plastic toner particles that bond to an electrophotosensitive drum to create an image. These toner particles are actually a combination of organic material, plastic, and iron. A toner cartridge houses the powder toner and is inserted into the laser printer itself. A used toner cartridge should be sent back to the toner cartridge manufacturer for proper disposal or possible refilling. Note for the exam that the toner, paper, and disposable ribbons are considered printer-consumable items.

If laser-printed output begins to appear wavy or inconsistent, the problem may be an empty or malfunctioning toner cartridge.

The laser printing process begins after you send a document or image from your computer to the laser printer. After the image is accepted by the laser printer, a laser beam and a mirror are used to write an electrostatic representation of the image to a photosensitive drum. The electronically charged drum then rolls through the toner, which adheres to the drum to form an image. At this stage of the process, a sheet of paper is fed into the printer, where it receives an electrostatic charge. The paper is then rolled over to the drum, and the toner image is transferred to the paper. In the next process, the toner is heated and fused to the paper. The final output is directed out of the printer, and the printer awaits the next document or image. This process is repeated every time a page of information is sent to the printer.

Printer Quality Types

Printer quality type standards refer to the quality of the printed dots produced, mainly by dot matrix printers. Printer quality types can also apply to other printing technologies, such as laser printing. You should be familiar with the following printer type qualities for the A+ Core Hardware Service Technician test.

Letter Quality (LQ): LQ is the standard for printing today; it is the best quality type available and requires a device that can support a minimum of 300 dpi. LQ produces characters that are crisp and clear. There are no noticeable spaces between the dots printed on the paper. LQ is used mostly in higher end dot matrix and laser printers.

Near Letter Quality (NLQ): Dot matrix and ink-jet printers that produce output at 150 dpi utilize NLQ. The dots that make up a character, number, or symbol are printed over twice, which gives them a better look than draft quality. Unfortunately, the tiny printed dots are still somewhat noticeable.

Draft quality: Draft output is a very low-grade print quality. All the dots that make up a printed image are noticeable.

Raster Image Processing

A raster is a rectangular area or grid of the monitor's display area used for images or for the mathematically created vector drawing processes. The size of the raster area depends on the resolution of the display area. Monitors use auto sizing to calculate the raster grid size of a display area. A *Raster Image Processor* (RIP) is used to translate complicated raster images and vector drawings sent to a laser printer. The RIP requires memory to store large images before they are processed. If there is not enough memory in the printer to support the image to be stored, it is more than likely that you will get a "Memory Overflow" error message. Resolution Enhancement Technology (RET) allows a printer to print raster images at a higher resolution than the printer is technically capable of. RET uses a combination of technologies to fill in the spaces between dots on an image for better visual quality. Decreasing the printer's resolution and decreasing the RET can also help to reduce the frequency of "Memory Overflow" error messages.

Laser Technologies

Laser printer manufacturers utilize different laser printing technologies and processes to attain the same result of producing a high-quality image on final output. For the A+ Core test, we are focusing on the Electrophotographic (EP) process. There are three important laser-printing processes that you should be familiar with.

LCD process: The LCD process technology replaces the laser used in the EP process with an LCD panel or grid to write an image to the photosensitive drum.

Light-Emitting Diode (LED) process: LEDs are used in this technology in place of a laser beam to provide a light source to the photosensitive drum.

Electrophotographic process: The EP process is by far the most common printing process in use today. A laser beam, mirror, toner, and EP drum are used to produce a final image.

The EP Laser Printing Process

The stages of the EP laser printing process that you need to be familiar with for the A+ Core exam are listed below. Figure 19.5 shows a diagram of the EP laser printing process.

1. **Cleaning:** The EP drum must be cleaned, erased, and desensitized of any electronic charge it may have as a result of a previous process. A rubber blade is used to remove any toner or particles from the drum. The used toner is disposed of into a cleaning unit or bucket. A fluorescent lamp is used to remove any electronic charge retained by the EP drum from a previous process. This preparation stage is vital; the drum must be properly prepared in order to produce a sharp image. Think about it: if your camera lens is dirty, you are probably not going to get a clear picture.
2. **Conditioning:** At this point, the EP drum cannot hold an image; it needs to be conditioned to do so. This is accomplished with a charge of –600V applied to the EP drum by the primary corona wire. The charge is evenly distributed across the entire drum, creating an electronic field. This process enables the drum to become photoconductive and prepares it for the writing phase.

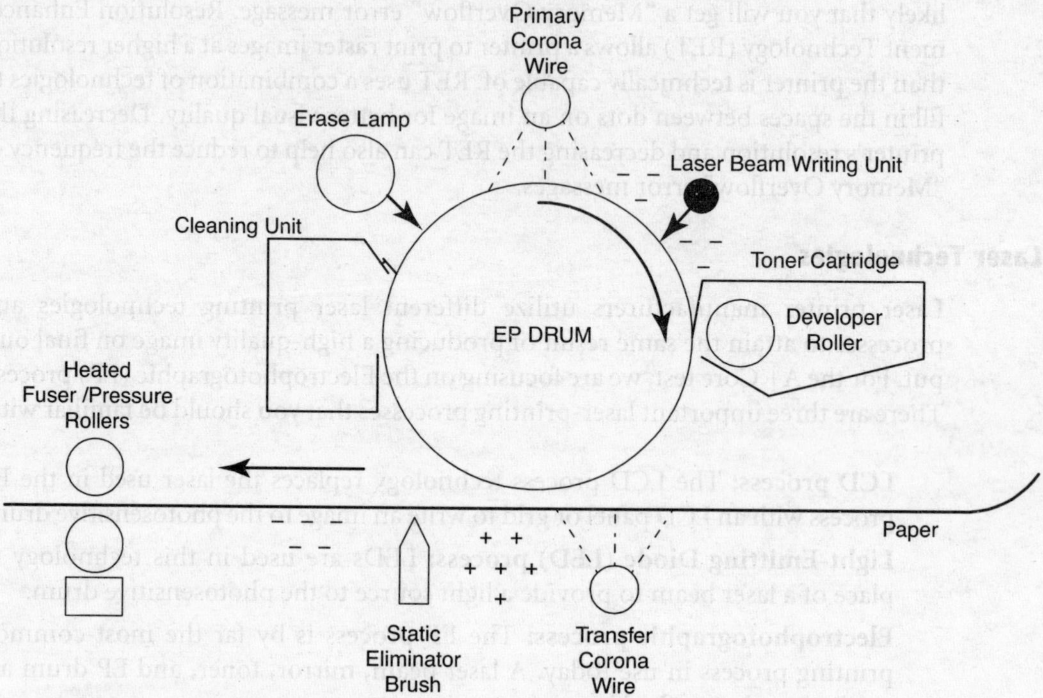

FIGURE 19.5 The electrophotographic (EP) laser printing process.

3. **Writing:** At this stage of the process, the printer's laser beam writing unit and a series of mirrors are used to draw tiny dots on the EP drum, which represent the final image to be produced. The area of the drum that the laser beam comes in contact with loses some of its negative charge (by approximately –100V) and becomes relatively more positive (the charge is still considered negative, just not as negative as the areas not hit by the laser beam). When the laser beam has finished creating the image on the relatively positive EP drum, the printer's controller starts the paper sheet-feed process by pulling a sheet of paper into the printer. The paper stands ready at the printer's registration rollers until the controller directs it farther into the printer.

NOTE

Paper-feed rollers have sensors to control the proper flow of paper out of the paper tray. It is a common occurrence to receive a "paper jam" error on the printer LED display—but on investigation, you find that there is no paper in the tray. Chances are that there is a particle of foreign matter in the way, or the sensor is dirty. While troubleshooting, always check the paper-feed sensors first in this situation.

4. **Developing:** At this point in the process, the EP drum is ready to accept toner on the areas or dots that have a more positive charge. The toner cartridge houses a toner-developing roller that is magnetized and constantly turning. The magnetized roller attracts the toner particles located near it and dispenses the toner to the positively charged areas (dots) on the rotating EP drum. The EP drum now has a 'picture,' or mirror duplicate of the image, to be placed on the paper.
5. **Transferring:** It's time to get the image, drawn in toner, from the EP drum to the paper. Keep in mind that the toner is being held on the EP drum with a relative negative charge. At this point, the paper has been pulled into the printer. The paper passes by the transfer corona wire, or in some printers a transfer roller, where it receives a highly positive charge on its back side. The paper then passes under the negatively charged EP drum, and the toner is transferred onto the highly charged paper. A static charge eliminator, otherwise known as an eliminator comb, is used to keep the paper from wrapping itself around the EP drum.
6. **Fusing:** The toner must now be fused, or bonded onto the paper. A fuser assembly, which is a quartz heating lamp inside a roller tube, is situated above a rubber roller pressure assembly. The paper and its toner are fed between the two devices. The toner is heated (melted) by the fuser assembly and pressed onto the paper permanently by the pressure rollers. It is important to note that there is a built-in temperature sensor on the heated rollers. If the temperature during this process rises above 180°F, the sensor will shut down the printer.

NOTE

Silicon oil is used to lubricate the fusing rollers during the fusing process to keep the paper from sticking to the rollers.

7. **End of cycle:** A cleaning pad is used to remove excess toner and residue from the heated rollers. The paper containing the final image is rolled out of the printer.

The following alphasupply.com Web site has an excellent laser printing troubleshooting page that lists detailed laser printing problems and solutions in step-by-step detail. This page is definitely worth a look: *http://alphasupply.com/printer_problems.htm*.

Ink Dispersion

Dispersion can be defined as the act of dispersing, which means to separate, distribute, or scatter in different directions. Most printer inks are made up of a combination of ingredients, including pigments, resins, solvents, and varnishes. For a printed document or photo to be clear and precise, it is important that printer ink pigments are dispersed free of lumps and other particles, in a smooth and even manner. Scientifically speaking, ink dispersion has to do with the ink manufacturing and production processes involved with how pigments are separated or broken down from other material. For the A+ exam it is important to note that if ink is improperly dispersed, or if there is a problem with an ink dispersion nozzle (used with most ink-jet printers), printing may become faded or unclear.

Dye Sublimation

Dye sublimation technology and dye sublimation printers have brought clear, crisp, photo-quality printing home. With a dye sublimation printer, a heat-sensitive print head moves over a ribbon of transparent film that contains heat-activated inks or sections that represent the four primary printing colors of cyan, magenta, yellow, and black. (CMYK). These solid inks are vaporized and sublimate (adsorb) onto special polymer-coated gloss paper.

Here are some important highlights regarding dye sublimation:

- It produces smooth, clear prints, making digital pictures look very realistic.
- The final print is less susceptible to fading over time.
- It offers very fast printing.
- Dye sublimation printers are more expensive than ink-jet printers.
- Special "gloss" paper is used.

In conclusion, the process of dye sublimation produces a smooth, photographic-quality image.

NOTE

Dye sublimation technology and dye sublimation printers have become very popular with the heavy use of digital cameras in today's society. CompTIA recognizes this and will most likely ask you about this technology on the exam.

Print, Copy, Fax, and Scan

In the past, the average home or small office required separate devices for such tasks as printing, copying, faxing and scanning. This required enormous amounts of desk/office space, as well as a high cost of ownership and maintenance. Enter the MFD (Multifunction Device)! An MFD is a device that combines the functionality of a printer, a copier, a scanner, and a fax machine into one unit. An MFD has only one warranty, so you don't need a separate warranty for each of your devices. An MFD is usually connected to a computer system with one cable (usually parallel or USB) and possibly an RJ11 patch for a phone line. An MFD typically requires only one power cord. A networked MFD is typically connected to a switch or router and can be accessed by many users if set up to do so. Most MFDs come with easily installed software packages that allow you set up all of the MFD's software drivers and functions with minutes. The popularity of MFDs has pretty much flattened the market for single, stand-alone devices. The most popular versions of MFDs offer ink-jet or laser jet technology.

NOTE *MFDs have been identified by CompTIA as part of the 2003 A+ objectives. Make sure you are familiar with these combination devices that are used to print, copy, fax, and scan.*

Finishers (Stapling, Etc.)

Most high-end printers allow the use of optional units called multifunction finishers. A multifunction finisher is simply a printer-attachable unit that allows some or all of the following options and features:

- Ability to stack multiple sheets of letter- or ledger-size paper
- Ability to offset multiple print jobs
- Ability to stack sheets into booklets
- Ability to staple sheets of letter- or ledger-size paper
- Ability to fold single pages
- Ability to saddle stitch and fold booklets

Most finishers have interfaces that are proprietary to the printer manufacturer, meaning they are not interchangeable between printers. The jamming of staples or paper causes the majority of problems that occur with most finishers. Every manufacturer has its own set of procedures for dealing with these jams. It is advised that you follow the finisher's manufacturer instructions for finisher-related jams.

Important Printer Information and Test Tips

The following printer-related information and test tips are included to ensure that you are well prepared for the many printer-focused questions that may come your way on the real exam:

- ✓ A dot matrix's printer pins strike or "hit" paper to create a final image.
- ✓ Concerning the laser printing process: If the printer drum has an image on it, but the printer is just printing blank pages out, there is most likely a Transfer Corona failure or problem.
- ✓ If you experience printed lines of miscellaneous characters, text, or code followed by blank sheets of paper after installing a new printer, it is likely that

you have installed the wrong printer driver or it is possible that you have a loose printer cable.

- ✓ With an inkjet printing, ink is sprayed onto the paper with a nozzle.
- ✓ Such things as ribbons and paper are considered to be printer consumables.
- ✓ By no means should a laser printer ever be plugged into a UPS.
- ✓ Centronix, DB25, and USB represent possible printer connections.
- ✓ Humidity, worn rollers, or bad feeder separator pads and bad media are all very common causes for more than one sheet of paper being fed into a printer at a time.
- ✓ Laser printers have ozone filters that are used to protect the environment. It is very important that a laser printer's ozone filter be vacuumed or replaced during routine printer maintenance.
- ✓ If you send a print job to a printer and nothing is printed at all except blank pages you should verify that your toner cartridge is not empty and in good condition. You should also verify that you have removed the manufacturer's tape from the toner cartridge if it is new.

CAD/CAM

CAD/CAM (Computer-Aided Design/Computer-Aided Manufacturing) is a specialized program or graphics software package that works in conjunction with specialized hardware to help architects and manufacturers create and design such things as computers, buildings, and office layouts. CAD/CAM helps with the designing of special-purpose machines for automation. With CAD/CAM, a designer can create, view, and change two-dimensional (2D) and three-dimensional (3D) drawings. The CAD software allows the designer to zoom in, select, and modify particular parts of a design.

Several years ago, CAD required specially built computer systems. Today, CAD/CAM software packages are designed to run on multipurpose/multifunctional workstations and servers. The software does, however, have minimum and recommended system requirements. They are:

Minimum system requirements:

- Intel Pentium 233 (minimum)
  - Pentium 450 or higher (recommended)
- Windows NT 4.0 with Service Pack 5.0
- Windows 98

- Windows Me (Millennium Edition)
- Windows 2000
- Windows XP Professional Only
- 128MB RAM
- 1024×768 video card
- 125MB-225MB of free hard drive space

Recommended system requirements:

- Intel Pentium or AMD 1600MHz or greater
- Windows NT 4.0 with Service Pack 5.0
- Windows 2000
- 512MB DDR physical RAM
- 64MB DDR AGP video card (resolution set to 1152×864 or higher, 16 bits)

To be useful and effective, CAD/CAM programs also depend on specialized input and output devices, such as high-end computer monitors, specialized printers, plotters, digitized tablets, and light pens.

For the A+ Core Hardware exam, you do not have to demonstrate that you can create automation equipment using CAD/CAM. What is important is that you understand that CAD/CAM is very graphics intensive and requires as much computer horsepower as you can get your hands on in order to use it effectively.

CHAPTER SUMMARY

This chapter introduced some of the most common types of output devices in use today. You should have paid close attention to monitor types and their associated resolutions, colors, and technologies. At this point, you should also have a good understanding of dot matrix and laser printing technology, including the EP laser printing process. If you have trouble answering the review questions at the end of this chapter, go back and read the chapter again. If you want to pass the A+ Core test, you are going to have to master questions very similar to these questions relating to output devices.

REVIEW QUESTIONS

1. A video adapter resolution of 800×600 would represent which video standard?

- ○ A. CGA
- ○ B. VGA
- ○ C. SVGA
- ○ D. Monochrome

Correct Answer = C

As displayed in Table 19.2, a resolution of 800×600 is supported by SVGA. CGA supports 320×200 and 640×200. VGA supports 640×480 and320×200. Monochrome supports 720×350.

2. You should not use this while working on a monitor. However, you should use this when installing a video adapter card. What is it?

- ○ A. An electron gun
- ○ B. Anti-phosphorous beam
- ○ C. A multimeter
- ○ D. An ESD wrist strap

Correct Answer = D

You should never wear an ESD wrist strap while working with the components inside of a monitor. An electronic reaction that can be deadly may occur. You should, however, wear a protective wrist strap while installing adapter cards in your system to protect them from ESD. An electron gun is used in a monitor to direct an electronic beam to the back of a glass screen that has a phosphorous coating. A multimeter is a device used to measure wattage.

3. Which of the following are printer consumable items? (Choose Three)

- □ A. Platen
- □ B. Print buffer
- □ C. Toner cartridges
- □ D. Printer drivers
- □ E. Printer paper
- □ F. Printer ribbons

Correct Answers = C, E, and F

Toner cartridges, paper, and disposable ribbons are considered printer consumable items.

4. Several users have been trying to print reports to a networked printer. The users complain that their reports are not printing. What would you do to solve this issue?

- o A. Press the reset button on the printer.
- o B. Go into Safe Mode and remove the print driver.
- o C. Realign the platen.
- o D. Delete the reports from the printer queue (buffer). Then, stop and start the print spooler service.

Correct Answer = D

With a networked printer, print jobs are typically queued in a printer buffer that is managed by the print spooler service. If print jobs are not printing to a networked printer, this process will clear the print queue and allow print jobs to be resubmitted and printed.

5. Your printed output appears to be fading from left to right. What is causing this problem?

- o A. The printer ribbon is old.
- o B. Your print driver is outdated.
- o C. The platen is out of alignment.
- o D. The print head is wearing out.

Correct Answer = C

A misaligned platen commonly results in a faded level of ink application to the paper as it is applied from left to right or may result in uneven lines of output across the paper.

6. A laser printer is producing inconsistent, wavy output. What is a very common cause associated with this problem?

- o A. The rollers are broken.
- o B. The fuser is damaged.
- o C. The platen is out of alignment.
- o D. The toner cartridge is empty.

Correct Answer = D

If your laser printed output begins to appear wavy or inconsistent in print, you may have an empty or malfunctioning toner cartridge.

7. Of the following choices, which uses a heat sensitive print head that moves over a ribbon of transparent colored film?

o A. Color impact

o B. Dye sublimation

o C. Laser transformation

o D. Ink dispersion

Correct Answer = B

With a dye sublimation printer, a heat sensitive print head moves over a ribbon of transparent film that contains heat-activated inks.

8. Dye sublimation uses a heat sensitive ribbon or film that is made up of the primary printing colors. What are the four primary printing colors?

o A. Magenta, black, yellow, and blue

o B. Yellow, blue, black, and red

o C. Cyan, magenta, yellow, and black

o D. Red, white, blue, and magenta

Correct Answer = C

With a dye sublimation printer, a heat sensitive print head moves over a ribbon of transparent film that contains heat-activated inks or sections that represent the four primary printing colors of cyan, magenta, yellow, and black (CMYK). All other choices are invalid.

9. Which of the following is considered the newest and fastest form of connectivity for printers?

o A. Serial

o B. USB

o C. Parallel

o D. ECP

o E. ECC

Correct Answer = B

Currently, the fastest available connection for a printer is realized through USB technology and a USB connection.

10. **What should you check first if a printer has no paper, but there is an error code on a printer LED that states there is a paper jam?**

o A. Paper-feed sensors
o B. USB port
o C. Drum
o D. Platen
o E. Ink cartridge

Correct Answer = A

Paper-feed rollers have sensors to control the proper flow of paper out of the paper tray. It is a common occurrence to receive a "paper jam" error on the printer LED display but on investigation, you find that there is no paper in the tray.

11. **What acronym describes a multifunction device that is used to print, scan, copy, and fax?**

o A. CMYK
o B. NLD
o C. CMY
o D. NLQ
o E. MFD

Correct Answer = E

An MFD is a device that combines functionality of a printer, a copier, a scanner, and a fax machine into one unit.

12. **Which of the following are common features of a multifunctional finisher?**

o A. Ability to stack multiple sheets of letter or ledger-sized paper
o B. Ability to fold single pages
o C. Ability to stack sheets into booklets
o D. Ability to staple sheets of letter or ledger-sized paper
o E. All of the above

Correct Answer = E

All of the items listed are common features of a multifunctional finisher.

13. **What is the smallest monitor (in terms of size) that can be used to display 1600×1200?**
    - o A. 15-inch CRT
    - o B. 17-inch CRT
    - o C. 19-inch CRT
    - o D. 17-inch LCD

    Correct Answer = C

    The 15-inch CRT can typically only display up to 1024×768, the 17-inch CRT and LCD can only do 1280×1024 (just because the screen is a true 17-inch screen, you are still limited to 1280×1024).

14. **Which one of these statements is true? (Assuming that the refresh rate listed is the max the monitor could handle at the given resolution).**
    - o A. A 15-inch monitor, running at 1024×768 at a refresh rate of 65Hz, is capable of displaying 1280×1024 at 60Hz.
    - o B. A 17-inch monitor that can handle 1280×1024 at 80Hz, is more than likely capable of handling 1024×768 at approx. 95–100Hz.
    - o C. A 19-inch monitor that displays 1024×768 at 80Hz, is more than likely capable of handling 1600×1200 at 85Hz.
    - o D. None of the above.
    - o E. All of the above.

    Correct Answer = B

    A 15-inch monitor is not capable of 1280×1024 (the smallest monitor capable of 1280×1024 is a 17-inch one). The 19-inch monitor running 1024×768 at 80Hz could probably display 1600×1200—but not at a higher refresh rate than running at 1024×768!

REFERENCES

http://alphasupply.com/printer_problems.htm. This alphasupply.com Web site has an excellent laser printing troubleshooting page that lists detailed laser printing problems and solutions in step-by-step detail.

20 Storage Devices and Interfaces

In This Chapter

In Chapter 17 we discussed RAM, which is temporary or primary storage. In this chapter, we discuss forms of permanent or secondary storage devices, such as hard drives, floppy drives, Zip drives, tape devices, and optical storage. Permanent storage devices are sometimes referred to as mass storage or auxiliary storage devices. We also explore the interfaces and technologies used to connect storage devices to a computing system. Some of the more common interfaces are IDE/ATA, serial ATA and SCSI.

The core exam is likely to test your knowledge of the proper methods of configuring, connecting, and troubleshooting storage. It seems that the recent A+ Core Hardware exam focused heavily on storage devices. The current test will probably concentrate on your ability to install and configure multiple hard drives, and dwell on the details of SCSI configurations and priorities. Pay close attention to the topics discussed in this chapter; they may make the difference on whether you pass or fail the core exam.

THE FLOPPY DRIVE

A *floppy drive* is an internal device that reads or writes information to and from magnetic floppy disks, and communicates with the system's CPU. The floppy drive is typically mounted into an available drive bay inside the system unit. A floppy drive adapter kit may be necessary if you are installing a floppy drive unit into a large drive bay. Older computing systems used 5.25-inch floppy drives that required a larger bay. Today, most computing systems come with a standard 3.5-inch floppy drive installed. Similar to a hard drive, a floppy disk stores information on magnetic media. A hard drive's storage medium is called a platter. A floppy drive's storage medium is called a floppy disk. The major advantage of a floppy disk is that it is portable. You can store files on a floppy disk and take it wherever you go. The major disadvantages of floppy disks are that they are slow to access and cannot store as much information as a hard disk.

A floppy disk must receive both a low-level format and a high-level format before it can be considered useful.

A *low-level format* prepares the floppy disk with an organized structure by creating sectors, tracks, and clusters on the floppy disk. A *high-level format* prepares the floppy disk with a File Allocation Table (FAT) and adds a root directory to it. You can format a floppy from a DOS command prompt or through the use of an operating system GUI, such as Windows. Preformatted floppy disks can be purchased just about anywhere computer supplies are sold.

To format a floppy disk from a DOS prompt, simply place the disk in the floppy drive "A" and type "format a:". A low-level format as well as a high-level format will be carried out on the disk. When the format process is complete, the floppy will be ready to have files saved to it. (See the section "The Hard Drive" later in this chapter for more information on the formatting process.)

There are two basic forms of floppy disk media available:

5.25-inch: This style of floppy disk was popular in the1980s. The 5.25-inch floppy came with two common data storage capacities: 360K and 1.2MB. The 5.25-inch floppy disk used a 5.25-inch floppy drive that is now considered obsolete.

3.5-inch: This floppy drive is found in most computers today. The 3.5-inch floppy disk can store 720K (double density) or 1.44MB (high density) of data.

Floppy Drive Components

A floppy drive's components are similar to that of a hard drive. The basic components that make up floppy drives include the read/write heads, which read and write data onto the floppy media and work in tandem with an erase tunnel mechanism to erase information if requested by the floppy drive's controller. The head actuator, sometimes referred to as a stepping motor, is controlled by the floppy disk controller; it moves the drive's read/write heads in and out of place. A spindle motor, driven by a belt system, makes the floppy disk spin or rotate at the desired speed. The speed at which the floppy disk spins is measured in revolutions per minute. A floppy drive uses a circuit board, also known as a logic board, which controls all of the floppy drive's components and communicates with the computer system. Finally, there are two floppy drive connectors. One is used to connect the floppy drive to the system's power supply, and the other is used to connect the floppy drive to the motherboard's floppy drive controller.

Floppy Drive Configuration and Troubleshooting

A floppy drive is connected to a floppy drive controller on the motherboard with a data cable. The data cable has a red stripe that runs down its right side. The red stripe represents pin 1 on the data cable. When plugging the data cable connector into the floppy drive controller on the motherboard, you must match pin 1 on the data cable connector to pin 1 on the controller. The same is true when connecting the other end of the data cable to the floppy drive itself. If you plug the floppy drive's data cable in backward, the LED light on the front of the floppy drive unit will stay lit, and you will not be able to access the floppy drive.

A computer system reserves certain letter designations for its components. The primary hard drive gets the letter designation of C by default. The letters A and B are reserved by the system for assignment to the floppy drives. A typical 3.5-inch floppy drive is attached to the far end of a ribbon data cable (after the twist in the ribbon cable) and gets the letter A assignment. If you have a second floppy drive, such as a 5.25-inch floppy drive, it should be attached to the middle connector on the floppy data cable, and it gets the letter B assignment.

Over time, floppy drives and floppy disks can get dirty and warped. This can cause them to fail mechanically or render them incapable of data storage and retrieval. If you attempt to access your floppy drive and receive an error message such as "Drive A is not ready, Abort, Retry or Fail," either your floppy disk is bad or your floppy drive needs cleaning and/or maintenance.

There are times when you may need to boot up your computer with a bootable floppy disk installed in the A drive. This is frequently done for troubleshooting purposes, maintenance, or operating system installation. If you are unable to boot from your bootable floppy disk, check your boot sequence settings in the BIOS configuration and verify that your system is set to boot from the A drive before the C or D drive. Otherwise, the system will not look for your bootable floppy at start-up.

One of the most common mistakes people make is to leave a nonbootable floppy disk in a floppy drive when restarting the system. This can cause the error message "Nonsystem disk or disk error; replace and strike any key to continue."

Ejecting the nonbootable floppy from the drive and pressing any key on your keyboard will bypass this error message, and your system will continue to load. (By the way, there is no such thing as an "any" key.)

Exchanging floppy disks with others and using them in your system without proper virus protection poses a serious virus threat to your computer. The two most common sources of virus attack come from floppy disks and the Internet. Always scan your floppy media for viruses.

THE HARD DRIVE

There have been many names associated with the hard drive since its inception. It has been called the hard disk, the fixed disk, Direct Access Storage Device (DASD), and the C drive. For the purposes of our A+ Core Hardware test study focus, we will use the terminologies *hard drive* and *hard disk*.

The hard drive is a component attached to a computer system unit in a fixed manner. It is usually installed in a drive bay that is inaccessible from the front of the system unit. When purchasing a computer, it is important to consider a system unit that has enough drive bays available to support multiple hard drives. You may wish to expand your storage capabilities in the future.

The hard drive is used as a mass storage device for data and programs. The hard drive is made up of metal platters, a spindle motor, an actuator arm, and a set of read/write heads. Hard drive space is measured in kilobytes, megabytes, and gigabytes. Today's hard drives generally have a storage capacity between 10GB and 40GB, and rotation speeds between 5200 and 7400 Revolutions Per Minute (rpm).

In order for data to be stored, organized, and retrieved from a hard drive in a timely, organized fashion, the hard drive's media (platters) must be divided into separate tracks, sectors, cylinders, and clusters. The sizes of these separations are collectively known as a hard drive's geometry.

As mentioned earlier, a hard drive's components are similar to a floppy drive's. Some of the main components and organizational units that make up a hard drive are listed below.

Platter: A hard drive has many platters. A platter is a circular, magnetized disk that holds information and programs. The platters that make up a hard drive are stacked on top of each other with head actuators and read/write heads between them. Platters can store information on both sides.

Landing zone: Older hard drives used the landing zone as a place to position the read/write heads of a hard drive when they were not in use. The landing zone is an area of the hard disk that does not have data stored. The landing zone is now obsolete.

Read/Write heads: Hard drives and floppy drives have read/write heads that read and write data to the hard drive's platters. Most hard drives have two heads for each platter. One head is used to read and write data to the top of the platter, the other is used to read from and write to the bottom side of the platter. Six platters (or magnetic disks) have a total of 12 heads.

NOTE

If you hear a grinding noise coming from inside your computer, your read/write heads may be 'crashing' onto the hard drive's platter. This will most likely result in a hard drive failure.

Tracks: A hard drive platter is divided into many tracks. Picture a horse racing track with separate lanes all lined up next to each other, forming a circle. The platter is the entire race track. The tracks are separate lanes running parallel to each other in a circle. The tracks are numbered consecutively for organizational purposes. The first track is track 0. It is located closest to the outside edge of the platter. Floppy disks also have tracks. The average floppy has 80 tracks.

Sectors: The smallest measurable area on a hard drive is a sector. A sector can hold a maximum of 512 bytes of information. A sector is a section of a track. Picture the race track again. A single lane is broken down into smaller units called sectors. A platter on a typical hard drive contains approximately 63 sectors per track (this number can vary depending on your system's BIOS settings). Figure 20.1 illustrates the single side of a platter and identifies a sector within a track. A group of sectors is called a cluster.

Cylinders: Cylinders are a logical grouping of similarly numbered tracks on all the platters combined. For example, if you have six platters, you would have a total of 12 surfaces, or sides. Each side of the platter would have its own track 4. Remember, the tracks are numbered starting with track 0 from the outside edge of the platter. If you combine the four tracks on the 12 surfaces, you will have a logical cylinder 28. Typical BIOS configuration settings allow for a total of 1024 cylinders.

NOTE

When your computer is powered on, the system BIOS looks for the boot sector, or Master Boot Record (MBR), on a hard drive for operating system load instructions. The boot sector is assigned to head 0, cylinder 0, track 0, and sector 0 on the first platter of a hard drive. If your boot sector becomes damaged or corrupted, you will most likely receive a "Bad or missing operating system" error message. This is a really good time to be happy about the daily backups you have been performing on your system. You may need to restore data back to the hard drive after you repartition and reformat the damaged disk. Read on for more information about partitioning and formatting.

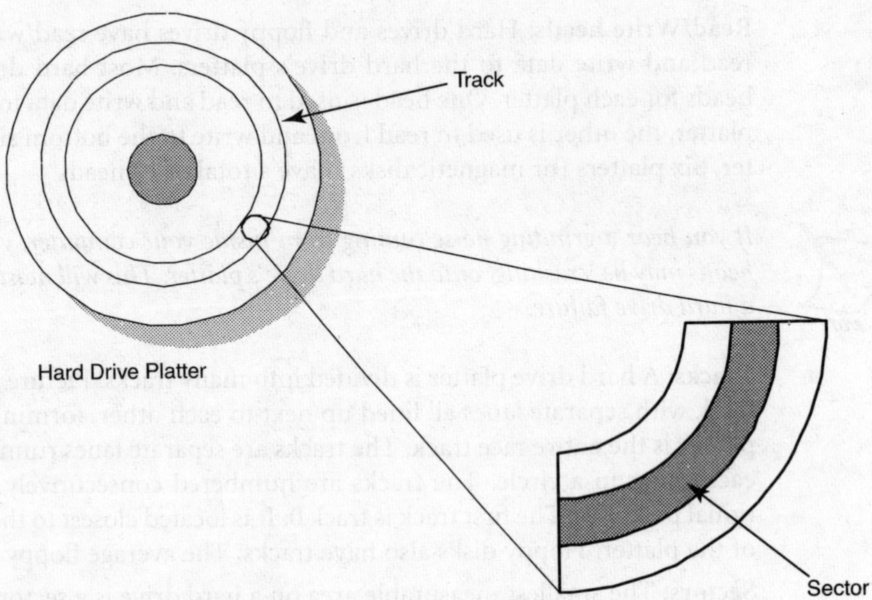

FIGURE 20.1 A single side of a platter sector and track.

Hard Drive Partitioning and Formatting

Two primary methods are used to prepare hard drives for supporting operating systems and applications: partitioning and formatting. Without being partitioned and formatted with an organized, logical file structure, a hard drive would be nothing more than a large metal paperweight. A hard drive must have the following processes done to it in order to be useful.

Partitioning

A hard drive normally receives a low-level format and is partitioned at the factory. If you receive or purchase a hard drive without a preinstalled operating system, you will need to partition and format the drive yourself.

Partitioning is the process of dividing one physical hard drive into separate areas of storage. In other words, you can create several logical hard drives out of one physical hard drive. This is useful for file storage purposes, installing multiple operating systems, and supporting multiple file system structures, such as FAT32 and NTFS (NT File System). Two partition types can be created on a hard drive: primary partitions and extended partitions:

Primary partitions: A primary partition is a partition that contains an active, bootable operating system, such as DOS or Windows. It is the partition that provides the system files necessary to boot into the operating system. A hard drive can be divided into four primary partitions, but only one of the four primary partitions can be set as the active partition. The active partition is specifically designated as the boot partition. It contains the MBR. The system BIOS looks to the active partition for boot-up commands. This partition is always labeled "C:."

Extended partitions: Extended partitions can be separated into units called logical partitions. There can be up to 23 logical partitions on one hard drive. Each logical partition receives a different alphabetic assignment, such as D, E, or F. These partitions are used mostly for file and applications storage. Any partition other than the primary partition is considered an extended partition.

DOS, Windows 3x, and the early versions of Windows 95 are FAT16 operating systems, and will allow you to create only a single partition size up to 2GB. If you want to use more than 2GB of hard drive space with these operating systems, you will need to create multiple partitions of 2GB. If you want to use more than 2GB for a single partition on a single hard drive, you will need to use a newer operating system that supports FAT32 or NTFS file systems. Windows 98, Windows 2000, and Microsoft Me allow you to create a single partition of up to 4TB (terabytes).

FDISK

FDISK is a common DOS utility program that enables the partitioning of a hard drive. FDISK is located on a DOS bootable disk and is run from the command prompt.

To use FDISK, simply enter "FDISK" at a command prompt. If your hard drive is larger than 512MB, a menu appears that asks if you would like to enable large disk support. You have the option of replying "Y" for yes or "N" for no. Pressing "Y" accepts the default of yes, and you are presented with the FDISK Options menu. At the FDISK Options menu, you can create one large partition for the whole hard drive. However, if you plan on dividing your hard drive into primary and extended partitions, you will need to use options 1, 2, and 3 to partition the disk accordingly. If you create more than one primary partition, you will need to set one of them as the active, bootable partition. After creating partitions with FDISK and formatting partitions for operating systems and files, you can always use FDISK again to create new partitions. The FDISK Options menu has an option for displaying partition information, which can be a useful tool to assist you with making the right partition choices to suit your needs.

Third-party partitioning programs that will allow you to partition a hard drive through the use of a GUI can be purchased.

For the test, you can use FDISK to divide a hard drive into three primary partitions and one extended partition. The extended partition can be divided into 23 logical partitions. If you are installing a new hard drive and receive an "Invalid Media Type" error message after booting the computer, you will need to use the FDISK utility to repartition the drive and set the active partition. If you run FDISK after installing a large hard drive, and the entire space available on the new drive is not recognized, chances are your BIOS did not recognize the hard drive changes or was not updated before you ran FDISK.

It is important to note that FDISK has an undocumented switch called /MBR. This switch causes FDISK to write the master boot record to the hard disk without altering partition table information. If you use the command FDISK /MBR, you will replace a systems boot loader with a generic boot loader. This is typically done if the originally installed system boot loader has become corrupted. Many viruses are written to infect a system's master boot record. Running the FDISK /MBR will also help remove these MBR infector viruses.

Formatting

Before an operating system or application can be installed on a partitioned hard drive, the drive must be formatted. Formatting is a two-level process that prepares a partition on a hard drive to accept an operating system, along with files and programs.

Two levels of formatting are implemented before the operating system is installed:

- **Low-level format:** A low-level format is usually done at the factory before the hard drive is shipped. A low-level format is a type of physical formatting process that erases all information and prepares the hard drive for a logical structure. This type of format also looks for bad areas on the drive and marks them so that they are not used as potential storage locations. A low-level format creates tracks and sectors on the hard drive platters, and determines what type of disk controller will be able to access the hard drive; the controller may be IDE/ATA, EIDE, or SCSI. A low-level format takes place before the hard disk is partitioned.
- **High-level format:** High-level formatting is often referred to as "formatting a hard drive." A high-level format creates a FAT and root directory on the hard drive. This is the process that actually prepares the drive for an operating sys-

tem. The FAT is a logical structure that keeps track of which sectors certain files are stored in on the hard drive. The FAT has the ability to identify good and bad sectors on a hard drive. When you install a newer operating system or upgrade your current operating system to a newer version, the formatting process is normally done for you automatically. A high-level format takes place after the hard drive has been partitioned.

FORMAT.COM is a DOS utility program that is also run from the DOS command prompt. The FORMAT command will allow you to format the hard drive in preparation for an operating system. You can also format the hard drive from within an operating system, such as Windows, if the operating system supports FORMAT.

From a DOS command prompt, type

```
FORMAT D:
```

You can replace D: in this example with the letter of any drive you wish to format.

ScanDisk and Defrag

Over time, the constant use of your hard drive can cause the sectors to get worn out or damaged. Utility programs such as ScanDisk, Norton Utilities, and Check It are available to help you identify bad sectors on a hard drive. If you are developing bad sectors on your hard drive, it is a good idea to run ScanDisk and select the "Thorough" option in the ScanDisk settings options. This runs a complete scan of your hard drive and attempts to fix any bad sectors it finds.

When files are written to a hard drive, they are not stored in contiguous order (one file written directly after another file). Files are stored in a noncontiguous order (anywhere there are available blocks of space). After a while, this can cause the clusters on your drive to become fragmented. It takes time for the CPU to request a file from the hard drive, and it takes even more time if the files are not in any order. Windows offers a built-in utility program called Disk Defragmenter that will help put clusters of files into a contiguous, structured order. Running Disk Defragmenter, or defrag, can increase the disk access time and the overall performance of your system. If a customer complains that his or her system is getting slower over time, running the defragmenter utility will most likely assist you with restoring the customer's disk access time. It is important to note that Windows 9x, Windows Me, and Windows 2000 offer a built-in defragmenter utility. Windows NT does not. This is discussed in more detail in Part II B of this book.

DRIVE CONTROLLERS AND INTERFACES

A hard drive uses its own internal controller board and processor to manage the interaction of read/write operations. The controller board also provides support for interfaces such as IDE/ATA, EIDE, or SCSI.

Before we continue with interface specifications, it is important for you to understand the basic connectors located on a typical hard drive (Figure 20.2). Two main connectors and a set of jumpers are usually located at the rear of the hard drive. The first connector is a 5-pin power connector that receives 5V and 12V DC power from the system's power supply. The 5V power is the 'dangerous power' used by the hard drive's circuit board. If the 5V power fluctuates, your hard drive's circuit board and components may be in danger. The 12V power is used to power the hard drive's motor and actuator heads. The second connector is an IDE 40-pin data connector or an SCSI connector. This connector is used to transmit and receive information and instructions from the computer's processor.

Plastic jumpers are used with IDE interfaces to set the configuration of the hard drive as either a master or a slave drive, along with the use of a data cable that supports multiple or shared interfaces. SCSI devices use plastic jumper blocks to uniquely identify SCSI drives or controller cards.

A hard drive communicates with a computer system through the use of an interface. Several communication transfer interfaces and standards ensure that a hard drive will be compatible with a system's motherboard and processor. These standards are in place to assist manufacturers with a common set of electronic rules for interfaces.

ST506 Interface

Now obsolete, the ST506 was the first standard interface developed in 1980 by Seagate Technologies (ST). This interface required the installer to modify the CMOS configuration manually, provide a low-level format, partition the drive manually,

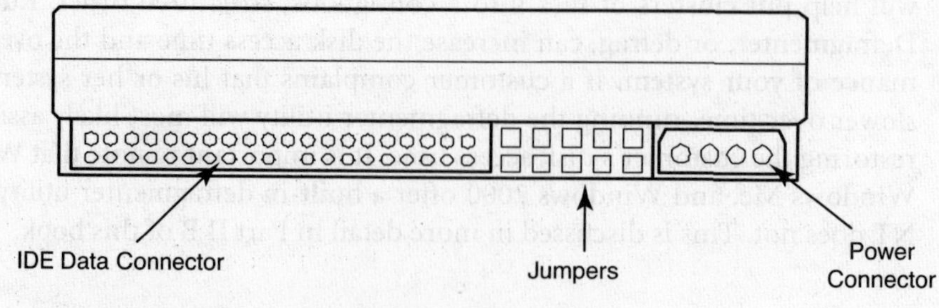

FIGURE 20.2 A hard drive with built-in connectors.

and finally, provide a high-level format. This standard was universally accepted based on its ability to attach to a standard interface data cable.

ESDI Interface

Introduced in 1983, the Enhanced System Device Interface (ESDI) standard for hard drives was the first interface standard to have a controller actually reside on the hard drive itself. It required a compatible ESDI controller installed on the motherboard. ESDI technology was several times faster than ST506 and was much more expensive as a result.

IDE/ATA Interface

The IDE/ATA is currently the most widely accepted interface standard. The IDE is an interface controller built into the hard drive. ATA is actually a set of rules or specifications that apply to the IDE controller. The ATA standard is a 16-bit, parallel connection. ATA allows you to have a master drive (drive 0) and a slave drive (drive 1). ATA also provides a way for multiple hard drives to communicate with the same system bus. If your motherboard does not have an IDE/ATA interface, or your system only has one IDE controller, you can purchase an IDE add-on expansion card, such as a PCI card that supports this technology. This will allow you to have up to four devices.

One of the major advantages of IDE is that it can provide sector translation. This allows you to change the drive's properties in CMOS configuration settings. It also allows computer systems to recognize hard drives larger than 528MB by utilizing Logical Block Addressing (LBA) support. LBA is considered a type of IDE transaction. You can enable LBA support, if available, in your BIOS configurations settings for your hard drive.

There are two common transfer methods or protocols used to communicate information between memory and an IDE/ATA hard drive controller:

Programmable Input/Output (PIO): PIO is a standard whereby the transfer of information between memory and the drive is controlled by the system's processor. PIO is measured in megabytes per second. Most versions of IDE/ATA can utilize PIO modes 0 and 1. Table 20.1 shows PIO modes and transfer rates per second. IORDY is a CMOS configuration that controls the speed of a disk head as it moves across a platter. IORDY is used with PIO modes 3 and 4.

Direct Memory Access (DMA): All IDE/ATA hard drives support DMA. As mentioned in Chapter 18 DMA is used to transfer information from memory directly to a peripheral, such as a hard drive, without interrupting the processor.

TABLE 20.1 PIO Modes and Transfer Rates Per Second

PIO Mode	Transfer Rate per Second	Standard
0	3.3MB	ATA
1	5.2MB	ATA
2	8.3MB	ATA
3	11.1MB	ATA-2
4	16.7MB	ATA-2/ATA-3

Several improvements have been made to the original implementation of the ATA standard interface. These improvements allow more devices to be attached to an ATA interface and increase the speed at which data can pass between an ATA interface and a device. Some of the ATA standards that you should be familiar with are listed below.

ATA: Traditional ATA, also known as IDE, provides support for up to two hard drives per controller. ATA has a 16-bit interface and utilizes PIO modes 0, 1, and 2.

ATA-2: ATA-2 provided support for LBA (drives larger than 504MB) and is sometimes referred to as Fast ATA. ATA-2 provides support for PIO modes 3 and 4. ATA-2 is basically the same technology as EIDE (which is discussed in the next section). It is an improvement on the original IDE/ATA standard that allows for up to four devices to be connected to one motherboard interface controller, for a total of eight devices in a typical system.

ATA-3: ATA-3 is the latest revision to the ATA standard. ATA-3 features enhanced security, better power management, support for PIO mode 4, and a new feature called *Self-Monitoring Analysis and Report Technology* (S.M.A.R.T.), which will warn you of certain failures.

Ultra-ATA: Known as Ultra-DMA, ATA-33, or UDMA/-33, Ultra-ATA provides support for multiword DMA mode 3 running at 33Mbps. The technology assists with keeping the CPU synchronized with faster hard drives.

Ultra-ATA/66: ATA/66 is an ATA version that doubles the traditional ATA throughput to 66Mbps. An ATA/66 data cable is different from an ATA/33 cable. You can differentiate the two by the number of wires in each data cable.

Ultra-ATA/100: ATA/100 is an ATA implementation that improves upon the bottlenecks caused by the ATA/66 version of ATA. The most significant difference between ATA/100 and ATA/66 is in the increased transfer rate and error-checking capabilities included with ATA/100. ATA/100 has a clock period of 20ns and a data transfer rate of 100Mbps. In order for a system to run in Ultra-ATA/100 mode, the following requirements must be met:

- You must have an Ultra-ATA/100-capable system board and BIOS.
- You must use an Ultra-ATA-capable 40-pin, 80-conductor cable.
- You must use an operating system that can handle DMA transfers. Windows 95 (OSR2), Windows 98, Windows Me, Windows 2000, and Windows XP are all capable of this.
- You must have an Ultra-ATA/100-compatible device, such as an ATA/100 hard drive.

Ultra ATA/133: As hard drive manufacturers continue to develop faster drives, the need for faster throughput between the host system and the hard drive is needed. To satisfy the bottleneck caused by the ATA/100, the faster ATA/133 was developed. ATA/133 has a clock period of 15ns and a data transfer rate of 133Mbps. Here are some features to remember regarding Ultra-ATA/133:

- ATA/133 maintains backward compatibility with ATA/100, ATA/66, and ATA/33.
- ATA/133 uses an 80 conductor cable with a 40-pin connector.
- The ATA/133 solution addresses large hard drive accessibility issues, and ATA/133 allows the use of hard drives larger than 137.4GB.

EIDE (Similar To Ata-2) Interface

Enhanced IDE (EIDE) technology is the same technology as IDE/ATA. It improves on the original IDE standards by allowing ATA drives to utilize PIO modes 3 and 4. An EIDE interface can support up to four drives on the same interface, including CD-ROMs and tape drive units. EIDE uses Advanced Technology Attachment Packet Interface (ATAPI) standards to allow a controller to communicate with CD and tape drive devices.

Serial ATA (S-ATA)

Just about everything in the computer electronics world eventually evolves into something smaller, faster, and more efficient. This includes the standards for ATA. The Serial ATA (S-ATA) specification is a serial link point-to-point disk-interface connection standard that was developed by the Serial ATA Working Group to overcome some of the limitations of the earlier mentioned ATA (parallel) specifications. Serial ATA is a point-to-point connection that uses a special S-ATA serial cable, which makes use of a minimum of four wires for sending and receiving data. Figure 20.3 displays a Serial ATA cable and connector. Serial is faster than parallel. The clock rate of Serial ATA is a whopping 1.5GHz (150Mbps).

Here are some very important points to remember regarding the new Serial ATA specification:

- It uses a minimum of four wires with pairs for transmitting and receiving.
- It is a point-to-point connection.
- It has a maximum cable length of 3 feet.
- The increased (3-foot) cable allows the use of external S-ATA compatible drives (drive arrays).
- It will eliminate the need for master/slave jumper settings in the future.
- S-ATA compatible devices are hot swappable.
- Most newer computer systems support a maximum of two Serial ATA connections.
- S-ATAs connect through PCI adapters or chips.
- S-ATA uses a 7-pin connector that is much more compact than a traditional ATA connector.
- Serial ATA is most often used in high-end servers with NAS (Network Attached Storage) units.
- A Serial ATA controller is typically located on the motherboard or implemented as an add-in, RAID card.
- With better pin efficiency, Serial ATA uses only 4 signal pins; parallel ATA uses 26 signal pins.
- Serial ATA, which has lower voltage than parallel ATA, reduces input signaling voltages to approximately 250 millivolts, while parallel ATA signaling voltages can reach as high as 5V.

FIGURE 20.3 A Serial ATA cable.

Serial ATA (S-ATA) has been identified as a CompTIA 2003 Objective. It is very likely that the A+ Core exam will ask you to identify Serial ATA connections on a motherboard. Pay close attention to Figure 20.4. Be familiar with this figure for the exam!

Make sure that you are familiar with the important points mentioned in this section. It is very likely that you will run across them in the exam room.

If you are interested in obtaining more information regarding Serial ATA, the following Tom's Guides Publishing site has an excellent description of Serial ATA: *http://www4.tomshardware.com/storage/20020812/*.

The Serial ATA Working Group page is also quite informative: *http://www.serialata.org/*.

SCSI Interface

If you need more than four devices and want the fastest throughput available for storage devices, then an SCSI chain is what you want. An *SCSI chain* is a group of

FIGURE 20.4 Serial ATA motherboard connections.

SCSI devices attached together with a centralized SCSI controller that requires only one IRQ for the entire chain of devices. SCSI is not technically defined as an interface; it is really an I/O bus in itself.

SCSI technology supports peripheral devices such as hard drives, hard disk arrays, tape units, and CD-ROMs.

If you want to attach a tape drive unit to an SCSI interface, you must enable INT 13h support on the SCSI controller card.

SCSI devices have unique SCSI ID numbers associated with them. These ID numbers are typically set with a jumper block on the SCSI device that includes three switches. Each switch setting represents a series of binary numbers that set a unique ID for each device. Each number represents the device's position on the SCSI chain; these numbers are 0 through 7 for an SCSI-1 chain. The highest ID that can be assigned on a three-jumper SCSI-1 device is 7. A typical SCSI-1 chain can have up to eight devices (numbered 0 to 7) attached to it. An SCSI controller card is considered a device and uses SCSI ID number 7. That leaves seven SCSI IDs (0 to 6) available for peripheral devices.

A SCSI controller card, otherwise known as an SCSI adapter card, can be plugged into any available PCI, VESA Local (VL-Bus), EISA, or ISA expansion slot.

SCSI priorities are applied from the highest ID number on the SCSI chain to the lowest number. For example, on an SCSI-1 chain, the controller with the unique SCSI ID of 7 has the highest priority. The priority decreases as you move down the SCSI chain to device 0. The same is true for the more popular SCSI-2 chain, which allows for 16 devices numbered 0 to 15. Device 15 would have the highest priority on the chain; device 0 would have the lowest priority.

An SCSI chain must be terminated at both ends. Most SCSI devices come with a built-in terminator (*terminator* is another word for *resistor*). A terminator absorbs a signal so that the signal is not sent back to where it came from, causing a signal collision to occur. If you have an SCSI chain with a hard drive and a CD-ROM, you will need to terminate both ends of the SCSI chain for proper signal transmission to occur. In this case, you would terminate the SCSI hard drive and the SCSI CD-ROM.

There have been several improvements made to SCSI technology since its original implementation. The following list stresses the important facts in reference to SCSI advances.

SCSI-1: The original implementation of SCSI technology, SCSI-1 implements an 8-bit data bus and supports 4Mbps data transmission rates. It requires a host adapter and can support up to seven other devices. SCSI-1 uses a 25-pin DB connector.

SCSI-2: Similar to SCSI-1, except that SCSI-2 uses a 50-pin Centronics connector, SCSI-2 is the most common implementation of SCSI. It supports up to 16 devices, including the controller card. SCSI-2 introduced the concepts of bus mastering and command queuing to SCSI. These improvements increased transfer rates and allowed SCSI devices to handle multiple instruction sets.

SCSI-3: Also referred to as Fast/Wide SCSI, SCSI-3 is a combination of SCSI specifications. SCSI-3 utilizes a 16-bit bus and supports data transfer rates to 40Mbps. SCSI-3 includes three subsets that are known as SCSI parallel interface or SPI specifications. These specifications are SPI-1 (Ultra-SCSI), SPI-2 (Ultra 2 SCSI), and SPI-3 (Ultra 3 SCSI). Each specification adds to the functionality and throughput capabilities of SCSI-3. For the A+ test, 16-bit Fast/Wide SCSI is the most common implementation of SCSI.

SCSI Termination

Both ends of an SCSI bus must be terminated. The use of terminators prevents a signal from becoming distorted and prevents reflection that can cause severe data errors. There are two distinct types of SCSI termination used for a single-ended SCSI bus. They are known as active termination and passive termination:

- *Active termination* uses what is called a voltage regulator to control the impedance at both ends of an SCSI bus. More stable than passive termination, active termination actually maintains a certain amount of impedance. Active termination was developed for a Fast SCSI-2 bus.
- *Passive termination* uses what is called a terminating resistor at the end of an SCSI bus to reduce the amount of reflection. It does not regulate power between a device and a controller; instead it converts power (usually +5V) to an expected level of impedance. The main purpose of leveling out impedance is to prevent these reflections. This impedance level is typically close to that of the impedance level for the SCSI cable being used. Passive termination was designed for SCSI-1 or SCSI-2, and is less popular than active termination.

If you are interested in learning more details regarding SCSI and SCSI termination, it is suggested that you visit the STA (SCSI Trade Association) Web site at: *http://www.scsita.org/aboutscsi/SCSI_Termination_Tutorial.html#top.*

High-Voltage Differential (HVD)

The original SCSI standard for SCSI interfaces was named single-ended (SE) SCSI, or SCSI-1. This specification for SCSI devices, which used a 50-pin connector, proved very susceptible to noise and did not offer long SCSI cable lengths. The HVD SCSI specification was introduced to overcome the noise and short cable length issues present in the original (SE) SCSI specification.

High-voltage differential is a method by which an SCSI interface places data signals on SCSI cable. HVD SCSI interfaces utilize dual lines for each SCSI data signal. HVD SCSI is less susceptible to noise than SE and has a maximum cable length of 25 meters (approximately 82 feet). HVD SCSI interfaces can provide 20Mbps data transfer rates for narrow SCSI devices and 40Mbps transfers for wide SCSI. HVD SCSI uses +5V logic and terminators that run on 5V DC power.

Low-Voltage Differential (LVD)

Low-voltage differential is the newer data transmission standard for SCSI devices. LVD uses much less power than HVD and is less expensive. It is backward compatible with earlier single-ended SCSI (SCSI-1 and SCSI-2) and can automatically sense which type of SCSI you have. In other words, when your device is first powered up, LVD can distinguish whether your SCSI device is LVD compatible or single-ended. This auto-sensing LVD feature is called multimode operation. LVD device standards are defined (fall under) the Ultra 2 SCSI/SCSI-3 standards.

Here are some of the benefits included with the LVD standard:

- Low-voltage differential uses 3.3V or 1.5V, which replaces the standard +5V used by HVD devices. It is highly advisable that you do not mix LVD and HVD on SCSI cable (BUS). They are not electronically compatible, and damage to your LVD-compatible device may result.
- LVD uses a dual wire system (uses two wires for each signal) and filters noise more effectively than HVD.
- The reduction in noise reflections allows for higher transmission rates, which in turn allows for the use of longer data cables. In simple terms, the data signals can travel farther.

NOTE

HVD and LVD SCSI transmission standards have been identified as new A+ Core Hardware Objectives. Make sure you can identify their differences for the exam. Pay particular attention to the benefits of using LVD.

DEVICE INSTALLATION, CONFIGURATION, AND TROUBLESHOOTING

A typical IDE/ATA interface supports two devices per motherboard controller. Most systems today have two separate motherboard controllers, allowing for a total of four devices to be attached. An EIDE interface can support up to four devices per controller, for a total of eight devices. EIDE is the same as ATA-2. ATA-2 is an improvement on IDE/ATA that also allows for up to four devices per controller, which equates to eight total devices.

For the purposes of the A+ Core Hardware exam, we will focus on the traditional IDE/ATA standard interface that allows for two devices to be attached to each of the two motherboard controllers. This allows us to have a total of four devices—for example, two hard drives, a CD-ROM, and a tape drive unit.

IDE hard drives, CD-ROMs, floppy drives, and other storage devices have jumper settings that determine the role they will play on an IDE interface. A jumper is a plastic and metal clip that is placed on two or more pins. These pins protrude from a device or a motherboard to close a circuit. With these jumpers, you can set the hard drive to be a master or slave drive, or choose cable-select settings.

NOTE *If you want to specify a certain connector on an IDE data cable, set your jumpers for cable select.*

A motherboard typically has a built-in primary and secondary controller (interface). A ribbon cable with a red stripe that represents pin 1 connects the hard drive and an optional device, such as a second hard drive or CD-ROM, to the motherboard's primary IDE controller. Your primary master hard drive should be attached to the connector at the far end of the ribbon cable. When connecting the data cable to the hard drive, make sure that you match pin 1 on the adapter to pin 1 on the hard drive. The slave device should be connected to the middle connector. And finally, attach the other end of the data cable to the motherboard's controller, verifying again that pin 1 on the cable matches pin 1 on the controller. The secondary controller can be used to connect two more devices to the motherboard. If you are only using the primary controller to connect devices, you can disable the secondary controller in the BIOS to free up IRQ 15 for other peripheral devices. The first device attached to the secondary controller is known as the secondary master. The second device attached is called the secondary slave.

NOTE *If you install a second device to an IDE interface, such as a hard drive, and the operating system is plug and play, the operating system will automatically assign a letter designation to the new device.*

If you are installing two new hard drives on the same IDE channel, you need to configure one to be the master drive and one to be the slave drive. If you reboot and the slave drive is not recognized by the system BIOS, you should test the slave drive by configuring it to be the master drive, remove the original master, and reboot the system. This will tell you if you have an incompatible or bad drive.

NOTE *If you notice that a hard drive's LED light indicator is constantly lit or pulsing, this is a sign that you need to install more memory.*

Following are the basic steps to installing a hard drive:

1. Unplug the power cord that is connected to the back of the computer. Put on your antistatic wrist protector.
2. Remove the screws or clips that attach the computer's case to the system unit itself.
3. Determine whether the hard drive will be installed as a master or a slave device and make the necessary jumper changes on both drives to reflect your decision.
4. Plug one end of the data cable into the hard drive. Ensure that pin 1 on the data cable matches pin 1 on the drive. Plug the center connector into the slave drive if required. Plug the other end of the ribbon cable into the motherboard, also matching pin 1 of the cable to pin 1 on the motherboard's controller.
5. Connect an available system power connector into the hard drive's power socket. Do the same for the slave drive if using a slave drive.
6. Anchor the hard drive or drives into an open drive bay with screws.
7. Replace the system unit's cover. Take your wrist strap off. Plug the computer's power cord back into the system. Power the computer on.
8. If the CMOS hard drive settings are set to auto-detect, the hard drive or drives should be detected for you. If not, you will have to manually set the drive's geometry, including the number of cylinders, sectors, and heads, in the CMOS settings.
9. Partition and format the drive or drives if no operating system is present.

RAID (REDUNDANT ARRAY OF INDEPENDENT DISKS)

Although the A+ Core exam is not likely to nail you with high-level questions regarding the various types of RAID (Redundant Array of Independent Disks) implementations, it is important for you to understand the basic implementations of RAID. Besides, anyone pursuing a career in the computing industry needs to understand fault-tolerance basics and RAID.

RAID is one of the most popular means of providing fault-tolerant systems in use today. Through a process known as disk or "data" striping, RAID divides data into separate units and distributes the data across two or more hard disks. There are many variations of RAID available; the most popular are:

RAID level 0: This level of RAID is not considered fault tolerant. It spreads data in blocks across multiple disks, but provides no data redundancy. This level of RAID only produces better performance. If one disk fails with this configuration, all data is lost.

RAID level 1: This level is also known as "disk mirroring." With RAID level 1, all data is duplicated or 'written to' a second hard disk. If one of the disks fails, the information is still available on the second disk. This level of RAID is fault tolerant, although its performance is not rated as well as RAID level 5.

RAID level 3: This level also spreads data units across several disks, but it also uses a dedicated disk for parity information, which is used for error-correction purposes. In simple terms, it provides a basic level of fault tolerance.

RAID level 5: Level 5 provides excellent fault tolerance and good performance. It stores parity information across all disks in the disk array and provides concurrent disk reads and writes. It is the most popular RAID implementation.

With all that being said about RAID, it is important that you know that RAID requires fast controllers/interfaces to be effective. All that reading and writing to multiple hard disks can quickly hamper a workstation's or server's ability to properly store and process data.

OPTICAL STORAGE DEVICES

Optical storage devices and the usefulness of optical storage media, such as the Compact Disk Read-Only-Memory (CD-ROM), Compact Disk Recordable (CD-R), Compact Disk Rewritable (CD-RW), and Digital Versatile Disk (DVD), have taken the computer industry by storm. Optical media were originally intended as a replacement for recordable cassette tapes in the music industry; but as we know, optical media offer many advantages to the data storage world and have put the beloved 1.44MB floppy disk to shame. Although optical storage devices have a much slower access time than hard drive technologies, they offer many benefits. We can store books, music, pictures, and files on optical storage media. We can watch movies with DVD technology. The possibilities are almost endless, at least until the next form of storage media comes around.

CD-ROM

A CD-ROM is an optical storage disk capable of storing large amounts of data. A typical CD-ROM can hold 600MB to 800MB of information. This is equal to the storage capacity of about 700 1.44MB floppy disks. CD-ROMs are well suited for storing graphics files, movies, and music. A CD-ROM is typically written to, or 'burned,' once with information provided by the manufacturers of the CD-ROM. Optical media such as CD-ROMs have information burned into them by a laser beam. Actually, the term *burned* is used quite loosely here. For information to be written to a CD-ROM, the actual process involves changing the reflective properties of an organic dye that covers a CD-ROM by using a laser. The data can only be written to a disk one time. Reading the data on a CD-ROM requires the use of a CD-ROM device or player.

CD-ROM players and writers can be installed internally or connected externally to a computer system. Most computers today come with an internal CD-ROM player installed. An internal CD-ROM device is typically installed as a slave device on either the primary or secondary IDE controller. An external CD-ROM device is connected to an SCSI, parallel, or USB port.

MSCDEX.EXE (Microsoft CD-ROM Extension) is a file that contains a 16-bit software driver, which enables older operating systems, such as DOS and Windows 3x, to interact with and control CD-ROM players. MSCDEX was later replaced in Windows 95 by the 32-bit CD-ROM File System (CDFS), which offered better performance.

CD-R

A CD-R is an optical form of media that allows information to be written to the CD-ROM one time and read many times by the end user. It is sometimes referred to as Write-Once, Read-Many (WORM). To create CD-ROMs using CD-R technology, you need a compact-disk recordable drive and a CD-R software program installed in your system.

CD-R technology is excellent for storing personal data and providing data backup capabilities. When purchasing such a unit and software, make sure that it has the capabilities for multisession recording. This is the ability to add files to a section of the CD-ROM that has not yet been written to. CD-R technology has become more affordable and is now commonplace.

CD-RW

CD-RW is the most popular CD technology at the present time. A CD-RW disk, with the use of a CD-ROM writing device, allows you to write information to the entire disk many times (approximately 25 times). CD-RW disks are more expensive than CD-R, but are well worth the price for the capabilities they offer. CD-RW technology will most likely be replaced by DVD technology when DVD storage advances become somewhat affordable.

DVD

DVD is quickly becoming the optical player and storage technology of choice. It has the capability to store up to 17GB of data, which is many times that of a CD-ROM, and can support several full-length motion pictures on one disk. DVD uses Motion Pictures Expert Group (MPEG) compression standards to provide its tremendous storage capabilities. Another great feature of DVD technology is that it is backward compatible with CD-R and CD-RW. This means that DVD can read CD-ROMs that you have created with CD-R or CD-RW technology.

Several types of DVD technology are available today:

DVD-ROM: This is the DVD drive installed in your computer.

DVD-R: Similar to CD-R technology, the DVD-R disk can record, or be 'written-to' one time. It is capable of recording up to 3.95GB of information.

DVD-RW: A DVD-based technology, this disk has the ability to be 'written-to' many times. It can store data on either side of the disk.

DVD-RAM: Similar to CD-RW, a DVD-RAM disk can be written to many times (approximately 100,000 times). However, a double-sided DVD-RAM can store up to 9.4GB, dwarfing the storage capacity of CD-RW and DVD-RW. DVD-RAM drives are most often backward compatible and can read most variations of both CD and DVD technologies.

Test-related Tips For Optical Devices

- ✓ If a CD or DVD unit has become inoperative and you need to open the tray that holds the CD or DVD media, you can insert a pin or paper clip into the tiny hole on the front of the unit. This forces it to open the tray.
- ✓ If you have inserted a music CD into your CD device and no sound is coming from the PC or connected stereo speakers, verify that the CD or DVD's audio cable is connected to an installed sound card.
- ✓ If you install a new CD-ROM, CD-RW, or DVD device into a computer and it doesn't work after the installation, the first troubleshooting step should be to verify that the jumper settings on the device are configured properly.

SUPERDISKS AND ZIP DRIVES

SuperDisks and Zip drives are used to store substantial amounts of information, which can help you free up hard disk space. They are an excellent portable storage alternative when you need more storage capability than a 1.44MB floppy can provide.

The average SuperDisk can store 120MB of data, while remaining compatible with the average 1.44MB floppy disk. SuperDrive technology supports IDE, PCMCIA, USB, and parallel connectivity.

Zip disks resemble floppy disks, but are about twice as thick. Zip disks can store either 100MB or 250MB, which is convenient for storing graphics or any other large files or programs for archival purposes, as well as for exchanging large amounts of information. Zip drive technology supports a parallel or SCSI connection. The Zip drive can be external or internal to the system unit.

CHAPTER SUMMARY

This chapter covered very important material in relation to the current A+ Core Hardware exam and its heavy focus on storage devices and their interfaces. We covered the installation, configuration, and troubleshooting of the major storage devices and their components. There are many Internet sites available that go into far more detail on storage device engineering than is required for the goal and scope of this book. In order to be a proficient computer technician, you need hands-on practice installing and troubleshooting storage devices and computer-related equipment.

REVIEW QUESTIONS

1. **A technician installs a 2GB hard drive and proceeds to run the FDISK utility. FDISK only shows a 540MB hard drive. What action did not take place?**

   o A. FDISK will only recognize 540MB by default.
   o B. The version of FDISK was not updated.
   o C. The BIOS was never updated.
   o D. The technician should have run Defrag.

   Correct Answer = C

   When you're installing a new hard drive, it is important to verify that your hard drive settings have been updated in the system BIOS settings. If your BIOS settings for your hard drive are set to AUTO (Auto Detect), the full capacity of your hard drive should be recognized.

2. **What is the maximum number of devices, not including the SCSI controller card, that can be attached to a fast-wide SCSI-2 bus?**

   o A. 1
   o B. 7
   o C. 10
   o D. 15

   Correct Answer = D

   A fast-wide SCSI-2 bus can support 15 devices not including the SCSI controller card. SCSI-1 can support seven devices.

3. Which numbers display the SCSI priorities for devices on a SCSI chain from lowest to highest?

- ○ A. 1–8
- ○ B. 7–1
- ○ C. 0–15
- ○ D. 2–14

Correct Answer = C

On a SCSI-1 chain, the controller with the unique SCSI ID of 7 has the highest priority. The priority decreases until you move down the SCSI chain to device 0. The same is true for the more popular SCSI 2 chain, which allows for 16 devices numbered 0–15. Device 15 would have the highest priority on the chain; device 0 would have the lowest priority.

4. Your computer made a grinding noise and then the screen went blank. What is the most probable cause?

- ○ A. The Read/Write heads crashed onto the hard drive's platter.
- ○ B. A virus caused your resolution to exceed itself.
- ○ C. Your computer went into Hibernation Mode.
- ○ D. You installed your hard drive cable backwards, resulting in a crash.

Correct Answer = A

If you hear a grinding noise coming from inside your computer, your Read/Write heads may be "crashing" onto the hard drive's platter. This will most likely result in a hard drive failure.

5. You have noticed that your system is running slower over time and you also notice several bad sectors. What two utilities would you run to rectify this situation?

- ○ A. FDISK and FORMAT from the command prompt.
- ○ B. COMMAND.COM and DEFRAG.
- ○ C. Create 23 logical partitions and make one active.
- ○ D. ScanDisk with the "thorough" option and Defrag.

Correct Answer = D

If you are developing bad sectors on your hard drive, it is a good idea to run ScanDisk and select the "thorough" option in the ScanDisk settings options. Running a defragmenter utility will place the files stored on your hard drive in contiguous order, resulting in better file access performance.

6. You want to add a second IDE hard drive to your system. You only have one IDE controller on your motherboard. The controller is already connected to a hard drive and a CD-ROM. What would you do?

- o A. Install an IDE add-on card.
- o B. Use a hard drive on the network.
- o C. Unplug the CD-ROM and attach the second hard drive when you want to use it.
- o D. Connect the second hard drive to a floppy drive controller.

Correct Answer = A

If your motherboard does not have an IDE/ATA interface, or your system only has one IDE controller, you can purchase an IDE add-on expansion card, such as a PCI card that supports this technology. This will allow you to have up to four devices.

7. You install a 5¼ floppy drive. When you power the computer on, the floppy drive light stays on. Where did you go wrong?

- o A. You plugged the floppy drive cable in backwards.
- o B. You have an incompatible slave drive configuration.
- o C. You dislodged the onboard video card.
- o D. You didn't update the BIOS.

Correct Answer = A

If you plug the floppy drive's data cable in backwards, the led (light emitting diode) light on the front of the floppy drive unit will stay lit, and you will not be able to access the floppy drive.

8. You power your computer on and receive a "Bad or missing operating system" message. What is most likely the cause of this message?

- o A. Your memory is corrupt.
- o B. You have an incompatible slave drive configuration.
- o C. You have a missing or corrupt boot sector.
- o D. Your SCSI controller card has a priority of 15.

Correct Answer = C

If your boot sector becomes damaged or corrupt, you will most likely receive a "Bad or missing operating system" error message.

9. A SCSI adapter card can be used with which available expansion slots? (Choose Three)

- □ A. PCI
- □ B. VL-Bus
- □ C. EISA
- □ D. USB
- □ E. AGP

Correct Answers = A, B, and C

A SCSI adapter card can be plugged into any available PCI, VESA local (VL-Bus), EISA, or ISA expansion slots.

10. A technician installs a brand new hard drive and attempts to format the drive. Unfortunately, the technician receives a message stating, "Invalid Media Type." What should the technician do?

- o A. Purchase another brand new hard drive.
- o B. Schedule ScanDisk and reboot.
- o C. Run Defrag.
- o D. Run antivirus software immediately.
- o E. Use the FDISK utility.

Correct Answer = E

If you are installing a new hard drive and receive an "Invalid Media Type" error message after booting the computer, you will need to use the FDISK utility to repartition the drive and set the active partition.

11. Which of the following hard drive settings are stored in CMOS?

- o A. RMA, HDD, LBA
- o B. Manufacturer, ship date, RMA
- o C. Cylinders, heads, and sectors
- o D. Jumper settings, HDD backup
- o E. HDD, LVD, and HVD
- o F. All of the above

Correct Answer = C

If the CMOS hard drive settings are set to auto-detect, the hard drive or drives should be detected for you. If not, you will have to manually set the drive's geometry, including the number of cylinders, sectors, and heads in the CMOS settings.

12. This serial standard is faster than parallel ATA. It is a hot-swappable, point-to-point standard that offers a maximum cable length of three feet. What is the standard being described?

- o A. USB-ATA
- o B. Fast/Wide-ATA
- o C. ESDI
- o D. S-ATA
- o E. Ultra-ATA
- o F. None of the above

Correct Answer = D

The Serial ATA (S-ATA) specification is a serial link point-to-point disk-interface connection standard that was developed by the Serial ATA Working Group to overcome some of the limitations of ATA (parallel) specifications. Serial ATA is a point-to-point connection that uses a special S-ATA serial cable.

13. What type of a connector does Serial ATA use?

- o A. 26-pin
- o B. 40-pin
- o C. 7-pin
- o D. 15-pin
- o E. No pins
- o F. None of the above

Correct Answer = C

S-ATA uses a 7-pin connector that is much more compact than a traditional ATA connector.

14. What do you need in order to run in Ultra ATA/100 mode?

- o A. An operating system that can handle DMA transfers
- o B. An Ultra ATA-capable 40 pin, 80-conductor cable
- o C. An Ultra ATA/100-compatible device
- o D. An Ultra ATA/100-capable system board and BIOS
- o E. All of the above
- o F. None of the above

Correct Answer = E

In order for a system to run in Ultra ATA /100 mode, you need an Ultra ATA/100-capable system board and BIOS, an Ultra ATA-capable 40 pin, 80-conductor cable, an operating system that can handle DMA transfers.

Windows 95 (OSR2), Windows 98, Windows Me, Windows 2000, and Windows XP are all capable of this. You also need an Ultra ATA/100-compatible device such as an ATA/100 hard drive.

15. Low Voltage Differential (LVD) is the new data transmission standard for SCSI devices. Which of the following choices describe LVD?

o A. LVD uses 3.3 volts or 1.5 volts, which replaces the standard +5 volts.

o B. LVD uses a dual wire system and filters noise more effectively.

o C. LVD allows for the use of longer data cables.

o D. LVD's auto sensing feature is called multimode operation.

o E. All of the above.

Correct Answer = E

Low-Voltage Differential uses 3.3 volts or 1.5 volts, which replaces the standard +5 volts used by HVD. LVD uses a dual wire system (uses two wires for each signal) and filters noise more effectively than HVD. Data signals can travel farther, allowing for the use of longer data cables. LVD's auto sensing feature, called multimode operation, can distinguish whether your SCSI device is LVD compatible or single-ended.

16. What does Active Termination use to control the impedance of a data signal at both ends of an SCSI bus?

o A. Voltage regulator

o B. MSCDEX

o C. Terminating resistor

o D. 7-pin connector

o E. A dongle

Correct Answer = A

Active termination uses what is called a voltage regulator to control the impedance at both ends of an SCSI bus. More stable than passive termination, active termination actually maintains a certain amount of impedance.

17. What does Passive Termination use at the end of an SCSI bus to reduce reflection?

o A. Voltage regulator

o B. Voltmeter

o C. Terminating resistor

o D. Voltage resistor

o E. Terminating regulator

Correct Answer = C

Passive termination uses what is called a terminating resistor at the end of an SCSI bus to reduce the amount of reflection.

18. What was the original standard for SCSI interfaces called?

- ○ A. GOSCSI
- ○ B. SE
- ○ C. HVD
- ○ D. LVD
- ○ E. Differential

Correct Answer = B

The original SCSI standard for SCSI interfaces was named single ended (SE) SCSI. This specification for SCSI devices proved very susceptible to noise and did not offer long SCSI cable lengths.

19. Which RAID level provides the best level of fault tolerance and performance?

- ○ A. RAID 32
- ○ B. RAID 0
- ○ C. RAID
- ○ D. RAID 5
- ○ E. None of the above

Correct Answer = D

RAID level 5 places parity information across all disks in an array. It provides the best combination of fault tolerance and performance of the popular RAID implementations.

REFERENCES

http://www4.tomshardware.com/storage/20020812/. This Tom's Guides Publishing site has an excellent description of Serial ATA.

http://www.serialata.org/. This site is home of the Serial ATA Working Group. Serial ATA interface standards information is available at this site.

http://www.scsita.org/aboutscsi/SCSI_Termination_Tutorial.html#top. This SCSI Trade Association Web site has an easy-to-understand paper regarding SCSI and SCSI termination.

21 Cables, Connectors, and Ports

In This Chapter

Computing systems and other electronic devices use cables, connectors, and ports as a means to connect to and communicate with other devices. A cable is used to connect two devices. On each end of a cable is a connector; connectors are characterized as male or female. A cable's male connector plugs into a female port, which may reside on a computer system or peripheral device. A female connector is connected to a male port, which may also be located on a system or peripheral device. Ports can be classified as internal or external to a system. Internal ports reside inside the system unit and connect components and devices directly to the motherboard. External ports are an extension of the motherboard or a peripheral device's circuit board that protrudes from the system or device. A port on the back of a system unit is often referred to as a connector. It is important for the purposes of the test that you realize the term *port* can be used interchangeably with the term *connector*. As you go through this chapter, you will be introduced to some of the finer details related to cables and connectors. It is important to keep in mind that the exam will focus on the DB 25-pin and 36-pin Centronics D-shell parallel connector, 9-pin serial (COM) connector, DB 15-pin video connector, game/MIDI port connector, and 50-pin SCSI cable connector.

EXTERNAL PORTS

On the back of a computer system you will find ports that are an extension of the motherboard's form factor. You may find port extensions for devices such as NICs, AGP cards, modems, or sound cards. The expansion cards that these ports are attached to are inserted into the motherboard's form factor. Most motherboards today are based on the ATX form factor, as described in Chapter 15, and include external connections for a parallel port, two serial ports, USB or FireWire (IEEE 1394) ports, a game controller port with microphone and speaker jacks, and a video port. Figure 21.1 shows the external ports associated with the ATX form factor. Pay special attention to the keyboard and mouse PS/2 connectors; the exam may focus on your ability to identify these in a graphic.

The central focus of this chapter is these ports and the connectors associated with them. Before we continue with the fine details of ports and connectors, it is important to understand the transmission methods that many devices are capable of using.

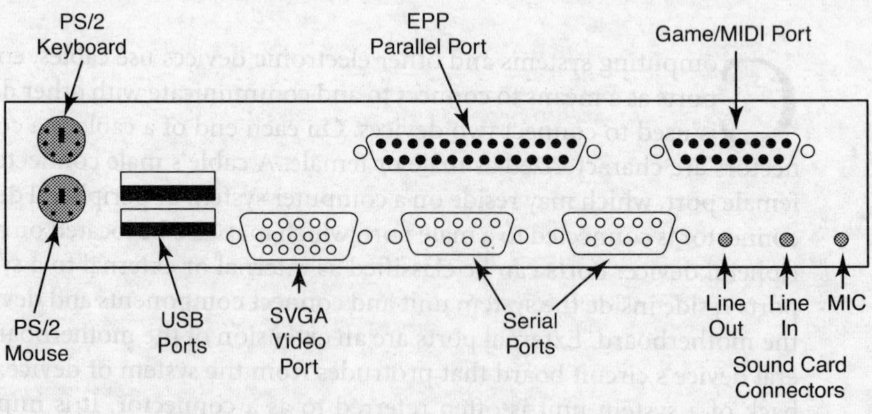

FIGURE 21.1 ATX form factor and external ports.

ASYNCHRONOUS AND SYNCHRONOUS TRANSMISSION

Most peripheral devices, such as printers, scanners, and modems, utilize asynchronous transmission methods. With asynchronous transmission, data is not synchronized. Unlike synchronous transmission, data is not sent as a steady stream in a predetermined fashion. Instead, a start bit and a stop bit are placed between each piece, or 'packet' of information. Asynchronous transmission methods are typically used for devices attached to parallel or serial ports.

Unlike asynchronous transmissions, synchronous transmissions are steady streams of data that are predetermined by a clock or counter. The CPU communicates with internal devices synchronously, basing the transmission of data and instructions on its own internal clock.

Transmission Modes

When two devices connect to each other, they establish and utilize a transmission mode. The transmission mode established between the two devices depends on the technology and configuration of the devices. Three general transmission modes are available that determine whether the transmission of data between two devices will occur only one way, one way at a time, or both ways at the same time. These transmission modes are simplex, half-duplex, and full-duplex.

Simplex: The simplex form of data transmission goes only one way; data or information can be transmitted in only one direction. A radio and speakers are examples of devices that utilize simplex communication.

Half-duplex: With half-duplex data transmission, data can be transmitted in both directions, but can only be transmitted in one direction at a time. An example of this transmission method is walkie-talkie: both parties can speak, but only one party can speak at a time.

NOTE

If two devices are set up so that they cannot send and receive data at the same time, they are utilizing half-duplex data transmission.

Full-duplex: In full-duplex transmission, or simultaneous transmission, data or voice can be transmitted and received at the exactly the same time. Human speech during a regular phone conversation is an example of full-duplex transmission that doesn't work well. Two parties can speak at the same time, although they might not understand each other.

PARALLEL PORTS AND CONNECTORS

A parallel port, otherwise referred to as LPT1 or LPT2, is an external interface associated with the IEEE 1284 standard that is used to connect a computer to peripheral devices such as printers, CD-ROM players, scanners, or tape unit devices. Figure 21.1 shows a standard parallel port on the back of a system unit. A parallel port uses parallel transmission methods to transmit or send data one byte at a time to a peripheral device. A parallel cable has eight internal wires, and each wire is capable of sending one bit of information at a time. (Remember, there are eight bits in one byte.) Information is transmitted eight bits across all at once, for a total of one byte, in only one direction at a time using parallel transmission.

It is important to note for the core exam that parallel transmission methods are faster than serial transmissions. Serial transmission methods will be discussed shortly.

A parallel port on the back of a computer system is a female DB-25 connector that accepts a DB 25-pin male connector on one end of a parallel cable. The other end of a parallel cable has a 36-pin male Centronics D-shell connector that connects to a Centronics connector located on the back of a printer or device. Figure 21.2 shows the connectors on both ends of a typical parallel printer cable. Printer and scanner Centronics connectors typically use two clips to secure the connector to the port located on the back of the device. In addition, it is important to note that a parallel cable can also be used to connect or network two computers together.

To ensure that the signals traveling down a parallel wire do not become distorted, the length of a parallel cable should not exceed 10 feet. Remember for the core exam that parallel transmission occurs 1 byte at a time.

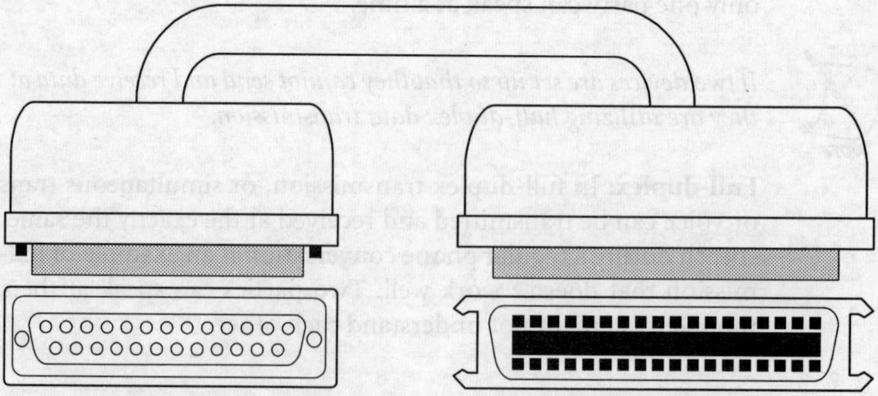

FIGURE 21.2 A parallel printer cable.

The newest addition to the IEEE 1284 standard for bidirectional communications and printing is the Type C-Mini 36-pin parallel connector. Also known as "Half Pitch Centronics 36 connectors," these compact-size parallel connectors are often used with laptops and some newer printers. The Type C-Mini 36-pin parallel connector also provides support for Enhanced Parallel Port (EPP) applications.

NOTE *The Type C-Mini 36-pin connector has been identified as one of the A+ 2003 Objective additions. Make sure that you are aware that this is an IEEE 1284 Mini 36-pin parallel connector with clip latches, which provides support for EPP applications.*

In concluding our discussion of parallel cables and connectors, there are three types of parallel connections that you should be familiar with. They are:

Type A: This is a DB-25 male or female connector that uses thumbscrews.

Type B: This is the standard Centronics 36-pin ribbon connector plug.

Type C: This is the Mini 36-pin Centronics connector plug with clip latches.

The following RAM Electronics Industries, Inc. Web site offers some very good images of the three main parallel connector types as well as many of the other connectors mentioned in this chapter: *http://www.ramelectronics.net/html/connecters.html.*

SERIAL PORTS AND CONNECTORS

Today's computers typically come equipped with one or two RS232C-compliant serial ports that are also located on the back of a computer system. (Refer to Figure 21.1 for a standard serial port.) A serial port transmits data one bit at a time. To transmit a byte (eight bits) serially, eight separate bits are transmitted one at a time, one after another. For example, try to picture pouring eight marbles into a funnel all at the same time. Only one of the marbles can exit the funnel at a time. All the other marbles will follow the first marble until the funnel is empty. Serial transmission is much slower than any of the parallel transmission techniques.

An operating system identifies serial ports in the BIOS setup program and references the serial ports as COM ports. The first serial port is referenced as COM1, the second serial port is referenced as COM2, and so on for COM3 and COM4.

Serial ports can come in the form of a DB 9-pin or older style DB 25-pin male connector. Most systems today have one DB 9-pin (male) serial port that is used for a serial mouse or a communications device, such as a modem.

Two basic serial cables are available that are used to connect a device to a serial port. The most common serial cable in use today has a DB 9-pin female adapter on one end of the cable that plugs into the DB 9-pin male serial port on the system unit. The other end of the cable has a DB 25-pin male connector, which is connected to a DB 25-pin female connector on the external device. An older-style serial cable is the DB 25-pin female to DB 25-pin male, which can connect two devices that have DB 25-pin serial ports. Yes, serial cables can network two computers together, but you should expect very slow transmission rates. Regardless of which serial cable is in use, the maximum length of a serial cable should not exceed 25 feet. Figure 21.3 displays the pin array configurations for male and female DB 9-pin and DB 25-pin serial connectors.

KEYBOARD AND MOUSE CONNECTORS

There are three main types of connectors used for keyboards and mice: the 5-pin Deutsche Industrie Norm (DIN) connector, the 6-pin mini-DIN (PS/2) connector, and USB mouse and keyboard connectors. Modern ATX form factor motherboards use PS/2 connectors for both the mouse and the keyboard. Older AT systems typically used a 5-pin DIN connector for the keyboard and a serial mouse. Figure 21.4 shows a 5-pin DIN and a 6-pin mini DIN (PS/2) connector.

The 5-pin DIN keyboard connector was used in AT- and XT-class computers for a keyboard connection. It is much larger than a 6-pin mini-DIN connector and requires its own 5-pin port. The more popular 6-pin mini-DIN, otherwise known as a PS/2 connector, is the standard connector in use today for mice and keyboards. Nearly all systems today support PS/2 connections for mice and key-

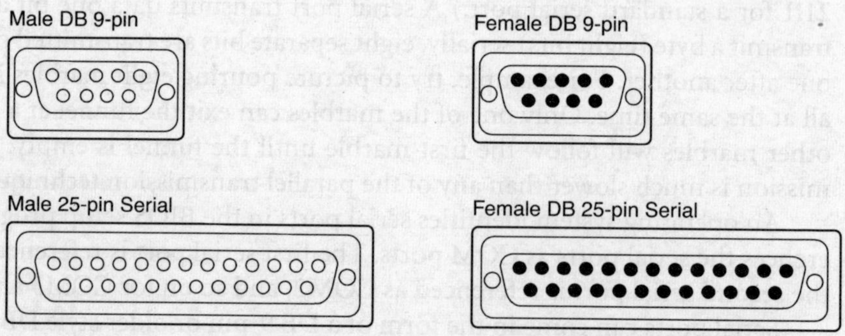

FIGURE 21.3 Male and female DB 9-pin and DB 25-pin serial connectors.

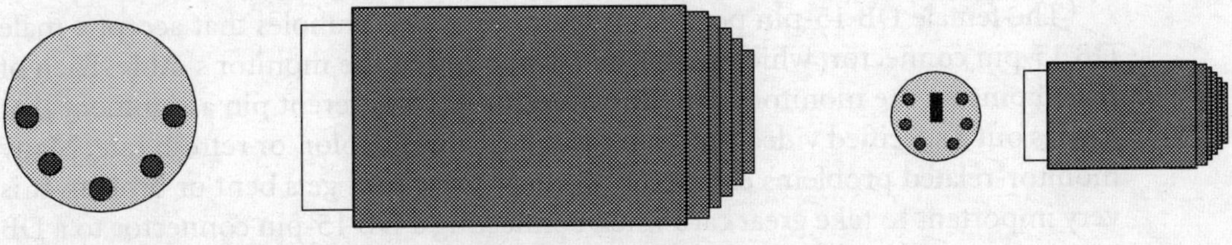

FIGURE 21.4 A 5-pin DIN and 6-pin mini-DIN connector.

boards. (See Figure 21.1 for PS/2 mouse and keyboard ports on the back of a system using the ATX form factor.)

Newer systems support USB mice and keyboard connections, which are very easy to install, support, and use. USB connectors will be discussed shortly.

Older systems use a serial port DB-9 connector for what is commonly referred to as a bus mouse. A bus mouse requires the use of a free COM port and IRQ.

Following are some very important facts to remember about mice and keyboards for the Core exam. The most important feature to look for when replacing a mouse or keyboard is the connectors associated with the device.

- A PS/2 mouse and an ATX-style keyboard connector look identical. It is easy to make the mistake of plugging the keyboard connector into the mouse port, or vice versa.

NOTE

You should only connect a PS/2 mouse or keyboard to a system unit if the system is powered off. If the system is on when you make a keyboard or mouse swap, it is possible that the mouse or keyboard may not be recognized.

- USB mice and keyboards can be replaced, or 'hot-swapped' while a system is running.

VIDEO CONNECTORS

All computer monitors have at least one thing in common: they all connect to a female DB 15-pin port on the back of a computer system. (Figure 21.1 shows a standard female DB 15-pin video port on the back of a system unit.) The DB 15-pin port may be attached directly to the motherboard, or it may be located on a video expansion card.

The female DB 15-pin port has three rows of five pinholes that accept a male DB 15-pin connector, which is attached to the end of the monitor's cable. Each of the 15 pins on the monitor's DB-15 connector has a different pin assignment that carries out a specified video function related to power, color, or refresh rate. Many monitor-related problems can occur if one of these pins gets bent or broken. It is very important to take great care when connecting a DB 15-pin connector to a DB 15-pin port on the back of your system. Table 21.1 displays the functionality of each of the 15 pins on a DB 15-pin video connector.

The A+ Core exam is likely to present you with a question or diagram that tests your knowledge of the difference between a DB 15-pin video connector and a game/MIDI port, otherwise known as a joystick/MIDI port on a sound card. (See Figure 21.1 for the location of a game/MIDI port on a system unit.)

NOTE *Remember for the exam that a female DB 15-pin video port has three rows of five pinholes. A joystick/MIDI port on a sound card has two rows of pinholes: one row of eight pinholes and one row of seven pinholes.*

TABLE 21.1 Individual Pin Assignments for a DB 15-Pin Video Connector

Pin Number	Video Function
1	Red video
2	Green video
3	Blue video
4	Monitor identification 2
5	Ground pin/unused
6	Red video return
7	Green video return
8	Blue video return
9	Unused
10	Ground
11	Monitor identification 0
12	Monitor identification 1
13	Horizontal synchronization
14	Vertical synchronization
15	Unused

USB CONNECTIONS

As mentioned in Chapter 15, USB is a fairly new technology that supports mice, keyboards, scanners, printers, and digital cameras. USB is an external serial bus that supports both low-speed and high-speed devices, and offers data transfer rates of up to 12Mbps. Some of the advantages that USB technology has to offer are listed here.

- USB can support up to 127 devices with the use of one system resource.
- USB is plug-and-play compliant; USB devices are automatically recognized and configured by the operating system.
- USB supports hot plugging.
- The cables and connectors that are used to attach USB devices to a system are standardized.

USB devices can be 'hot-swapped' while an operating system is up and running. This means that you can attach or detach a USB mouse or keyboard when a computer is powered on.

NOTE

It is likely that the exam will display several adapter images. Be prepared to identify a USB connector.

There are two types of USB connectors in use today. Type A USB connectors have one of their connectors permanently attached to a device, such as a keyboard or a mouse. Type B USB connectors are totally detachable from both a device and a port. Figure 21.5 displays a typical Type A USB connector.

One end of a Type A connector is actually built into the peripheral device. The other end of a Type A connector connects to a Type A port located on a host or USB hub. A Type A connector is flat and rectangular. Type B USB connectors are square and plug into a Type B USB port on both the device and the host. (See Figure 21.1 for the location of USB ports on a system unit.)

USB 2.0

The newest version of USB is called USB 2.0. USB 2.0 is sometimes referred to as Hi-Speed USB and supports transmission rates of up to 480Mbps. It is fully backward

FIGURE 21.5 A typical Type A USB connector.

compatible with the early version of USB (USB 1.1). In a nutshell, USB version 2.0 uses the same exact connector cables and ports as the first version of USB. This USB specification was developed to meet the bandwidth-hungry needs of new devices and their technologies.

Here are some USB tips for the exam:

- ✓ The newest type of serial bus architecture is USB.
- ✓ A USB port can supply power for most USB devices.
- ✓ Digitals devices such as cameras most often use USB ports.
- ✓ USB supports hot plugging of devices such as mice and keyboards. You can connect or disconnect them when a computer system is powered up.
- ✓ Windows 95 requires special drivers and operating system "supplements" before it will recognize USB devices.
- ✓ One system resource (IRQ) will support up to 127 USB devices!

The exam will ensure that you know that USB is RS232 compliant. In plain English (and on the CompTIA exam), this means that USB, RS232, and serial connections are all basically the same thing. For example, you might see something similar to this: "What is a very popular connection method for camcorders or digital cameras?" The possible choice of answers may include USB, RS232, or serial connection. You'd better choose them all!

FIREWIRE (IEEE 1394)

FireWire is associated with Apple Computer Company's original implementation of the IEEE standard 1394. The IEEE 1394 standard references high-speed serial transmissions of up to 400Mbps (in version 1394a) and 800Mbps (in version 1394b). FireWire is plug-and-play compatible and hot swappable; it also allows up to 63 devices to be connected to one port. A plug-and-play system will use the process known as "enumeration" to assign an address and auto-detect any FireWire-connected devices.

A FireWire connector is somewhat similar in shape to a USB connector. The main difference is that a FireWire connector is larger and squarer than a typical USB connector. Figure 21.6 displays a FireWire connector.

FireWire technology and other forms of the IEEE 1394 standard are expected to replace most serial and parallel connections in the future. For now, the IEEE 1394 standard is well suited for devices that require high speeds and large real-time throughput, such as video equipment. FireWire is much faster than USB, supporting data transfer rates of 100Mbps to 800Mbps. As a result, FireWire is also much more expensive than USB.

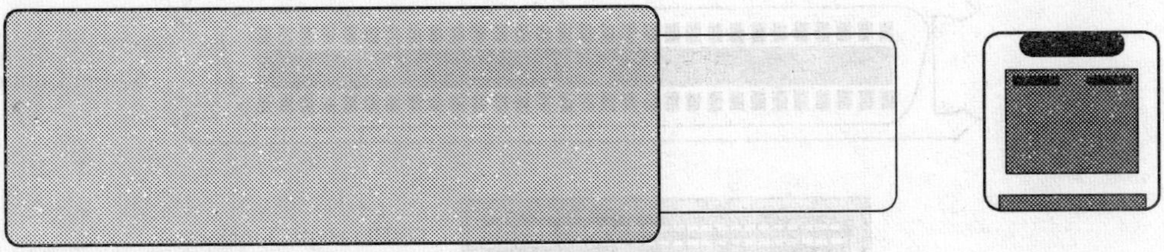

FIGURE 21.6 A FireWire connector.

NOTE *The A+ Core exam may ask, "Which technology is faster, IEEE 1394 or USB?" Make sure that you are prepared to identify technologies by their IEEE association. You may know all there is to know about connecting devices together, but if you can't identify technologies and standards, you will not be able to pass the Core exam.*

If you wish to learn more regarding FireWire, the following HowStuffWorks, Inc., Web site offers a superb explanation of FireWire basics: *http://computer.howstuffworks.com/firewire1.htm.*

SCSI CONNECTORS

As mentioned in Chapter 20, SCSI interfaces can be attached internally or externally to a computer system. For example, an SCSI hard drive can be attached to an internal SCSI controller on the motherboard. A device such as an SCSI printer or SCSI CD-ROM can be connected to an external SCSI controller card that extends out of the back of a computer. The devices that attach to SCSI controller cards have SCSI interfaces built onto them. There are internal and external SCSI connectors that reflect the SCSI standard being implemented on the device or controller. The most common SCSI interface connectors in use today are 50-pin and 68-pin SCSI internal and external SCSI connectors, as well as the 80-pin internal SCSI SCA connector. Devices such as printers and CD-ROMs utilize an SCSI 50-pin or 68-pin cable and connectors. SCSI SCA 80-pin connectors are used for hot-swappable hard drives, most commonly with internal RAID (Redundant Array of Independent Disks, or Redundant Array of Inexpensive Disks) configurations. The SCA SCSI adapter card includes a built-in power connection to support its special voltage requirements. Figure 21.7 shows the basic SCSI connectors and SCSI pin configurations. Remember, the exam will most likely focus on the 50-pin or 68-pin SCSI cable.

NOTE *SCSI technology offers the fastest available printing capabilities.*

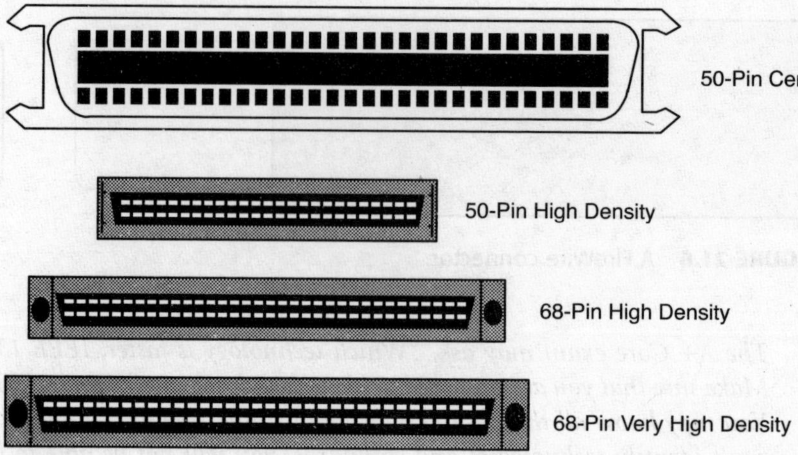

FIGURE 21.7 Basic SCSI connectors and their pin configurations.

Here are several useful tips to remember about SCSI technology and interfaces:

- Most SCSI cables are 50-pin.
- SCSI Wide refers to a 68-pin parallel interface cable.
- SCSI-3 is considered ultra-wide and can support up to 16 devices, including the controller card.
- SCSI-3 is backward compatible with previous forms of SCSI technology.
- Each SCSI device must have a unique SCSI ID.
- A SCSI chain must be terminated at both ends.
- You cannot network two computers together with an SCSI cable.

NETWORKING CONNECTORS AND CABLES

There are more than 2,500 types of cable in use for connecting computers and peripherals. The majority of computers today still use some type of wire or cable to transmit data from one system to another. There are three main types of network cables in use that you need to be familiar with for the Core exam: coaxial, twisted pair, and fiber optic. Each of these cable types has characteristics that set it apart from the others, such as cost, distance limitations, data transfer methods, data transfer rates, and installation methods used. The exam will focus on your ability to identify which technology is used by a certain cable category, and which cable medium should be used to connect two or more specific devices.

Coaxial Cable

Coaxial cable is a type of copper cabling that is often times used for Ethernet local area network and cable TV connections. There are two common types of coaxial cable, they are thicknet and thinnet which are described next.

Thicknet

Thicknet coaxial cable, also known as 10Base5, is approximately half an inch thick; it is a heavy type of cable with a copper core, which was used with early mainframe computers and early networks. Thicknet coaxial still exists, but it is very limited in its ability to achieve the high data transfer rates that are needed to support today's bandwidth-hungry computers and applications.

Thicknet coaxial cable has the ability to carry 10Mb (megabits) of data a total distance of 500 meters, or approximately 1,500 feet. Thus, the naming convention scheme of 10Base5 has been established for coaxial cable. In other words, 10Base5 means that 10Mb of information can travel over a baseband medium, or base, a total of 500 meters (the naming convention drops the last two zeros): 5 × 100 = 1,500 feet; the true measurement is closer to 1,640 feet.

Thicknet coaxial cable was and sometimes still is used as a backbone connection that connects to a small thinnet cable by use of a vampire tap and an Attachment Unit Interface (AUI) connector.

Thinnet

Thinnet coaxial cable, also known as 10Base2, is approximately a quarter-inch thick. It is a thinner, more flexible type of coaxial cable that is usually connected directly to an NIC with a BNC or BNC T-connector. Figure 21.8 displays a BNC and BNC T-connector. Thinnet is much easier to install and work with than thicknet,

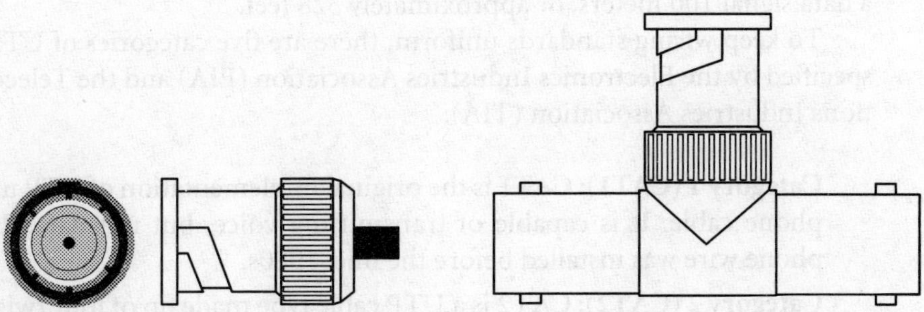

FIGURE 21.8 A BNC and BNC T-connector.

but thinnet only carries a data signal the distance of 185 meters, or approximately 607 feet.

Both thicknet and thinnet coaxial can make up a network referred to as a bus network. (Bus networks are described in Chapter 22.) A bus network must be terminated at both ends of a cable, or the bus network will fail. Thus, thicknet and thinnet both require terminators at both cable ends.

Twisted-Pair Cable

Twisted-Pair (TP) cable arose from the need to replace the distance and other limitations associated with coaxial-type cable. TP is referred to as 10BaseT. Once again, the 10 refers to the transmission rate of data, Base refers to a baseband media type, and the T refers to the twisted pair, or wiring twists in the cable itself.

There are two types of twisted-pair wiring: Shielded Twisted Pair (STP) and Unshielded Twisted Pair (UTP).

Shielded Twisted Pair

STP is basically the same type of wire as UTP, with the exception that STP uses a woven copper braided shielding and foil wrapping that protect the twisted wire pairs from outside interference, such as Electromagnetic Interference (EMI). This shielding makes an STP wire less susceptible to cross-talk from other wires. STP is more expensive than unshielded twisted pair, based on its extra protection and ability to transmit a data signal over a greater distance than UTP.

Unshielded Twisted Pair

UTP is also a 10Mbps baseband cable. UTP, generally referred to as 10BaseT, is the most common type of Ethernet cable in use today and is found mostly in what is called a star typology network. (Star typology networks are discussed in detail in Chapter 22.) UTP in its simplest form is two insulated copper wires that can carry a data signal 100 meters, or approximately 328 feet.

To keep wiring standards uniform, there are five categories of UTP wiring, as specified by the Electronics Industries Association (EIA) and the Telecommunications Industries Association (TIA):

Category 1 (CAT1): CAT1 is the original implementation of UTP used for telephone cable. It is capable of transmitting voice, but not data. This type of phone wire was installed before the mid-1980s.

Category 2 (CAT2): CAT2 is a UTP cable type made up of four twisted pairs of wires. It supports transmission rates up to 4Mbps.

Category 3 (CAT3): CAT3 can transmit data up to 10Mbps. It has four twisted pairs that are twisted three times per foot.

Category 4 (CAT4): CAT4 cable is capable of data transmissions up to 16Mbps. It has four twisted pairs of wire.

Category 5 (CAT5): CAT5 cable is capable of data transmission rates of up to 100Mbps. It is also made of four twisted pairs of wire. CAT5 UTP is also referred to as 100BaseT or 100BaseTX. It carries a data signal 100 meters, or approximately 328 feet.

Category 5e (CAT5e): Otherwise known as "Enhanced" CAT 5 cable, CAT5e is capable of data transmission rates of up to 350Mbps. Like CAT5, CAT5e can carry a data signal up to 100 meters, or 328 feet, without a bridge or other form of amplification. Also like CAT5, CAT5e is made of four twisted pairs of wire. The difference here is that CAT5e was created to support high-speed gigabit Ethernet devices and technology, such as ATM (Asynchronous Transfer Mode). CAT5e has better performance, resistance, and suffers less from attenuation than traditional CAT5.

- ✓ CAT5 and CAT5e both have 100-ohm impedance and are terminated with RJ45 connectors.
- ✓ CAT5e is backward compatible with traditional CAT5.
- ✓ CAT5e is built using a 24-gauge conducting wire
- ✓ The "enhanced" electrical technology built into CAT5e makes it possible for CAT5e cable to support additional bandwidth needed for such technology as gigabit Ethernet.

Category 6 (CAT6): The CAT6 cabling standard is rated up to 550M or 1000Mbps.

- ✓ CAT6 cabling is built using 23-gauge conductor wire.
- ✓ CAT6 has a better performance rating than CAT5e and suffers less from cross talk and noise.
- ✓ CAT6 is more expensive to install support than CAT5 or CAT5e.

NOTE

CAT5 UTP is the most popular UTP cable in use today and will most likely be the focus of UTP category questions on the Core exam. However, CAT5e and CAT6 are newer specifications, and are identified as 2003 A+ Objectives. Be prepared to answer basic CAT5e and CAT6 questions, as well.

To keep you sharp for the exam, here are the updated IEEE standard requirements for UTP cabling:

10BaseT: IEEE standard for requirements of sending data at 10Mbps over unshielded twisted-pair cable.

100BaseT: IEEE standard for requirements of sending data at 100Mbps over unshielded twisted-pair cable.

1000BaseT (also known as gigabit Ethernet): IEEE standard for requirements of sending data at 1,000Mbps over unshielded twisted-pair cable.

Twisted-Pair Connectors

There are two types of UTP connectors you need to know about for the test: RJ-11 connectors and RJ-45 connectors.

An RJ-11 phone connector was used for early categories of UTP to connect a modem to a typical phone jack, or your phone to a phone jack. In technical circles, an RJ-11 wire is a simple phone wire that houses four wires or connections. See Figure 21.9 for an RJ-11 connector.

An RJ-45 connector is the most common type of TP data cable connector in use. It houses eight wire traces. The RJ-45 connector on one end of a TP wire plugs into an NIC that is installed into a system. The RJ-45 connector on the other end of the TP cable plugs into a network hub, router, or RJ-45 wall jack. Figure 21.10 shows an RJ-45 connector.

Crossover Cable

A crossover cable is a type of Ethernet TP cable that is commonly used to connect two computers in a peer-to-peer fashion. The crossover cable switches the transmit and receive lines of the cable, which allows two computers to communicate directly with each other without the use of a hub or router. If you want an inexpensive alternative to purchasing a hub, a crossover cable is the way to go to connect two computers.

A null modem cable can also be used as a crossover cable to network two computers. A null modem cable is serial cable that is connected to the serial ports of two system units.

Fiber-Optic Cable

Fiber-optic cable, otherwise known as 10BaseFL, is the network wire of choice. It is capable of extremely fast transmission rates over long distances, without interference.

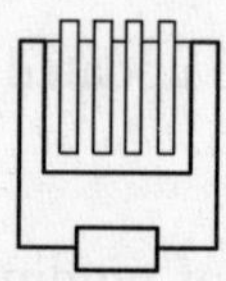

FIGURE 21.9 An RJ-11 connector.

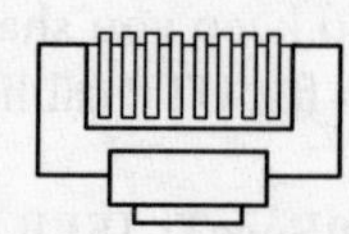

FIGURE 21.10 An RJ-45 connector.

A fiber-optic cable has a core that is composed of plastic or glass. A glass cladding or sheath covers the core. Finally, a Kevlar fiber jacket surrounds the entire wire. Data can be transmitted through a fiber-optic cable with a laser or LED at a rate of 2GBps or higher. The data signal on a fiber-optic wire can travel up to a distance of 100 kilometers (about 60 miles), depending on which technology is being implemented with the fiber and if a repeater is used. Fiber-optic cables use special ST- and SC-type connectors to attach to NICs and fiber-optic ports. These connectors are precisely crafted and specially designed to suit fiber-optic cable connection requirements.

Fiber-optic cable needs great care and consideration when being installed. Specially trained, certified fiber installers are usually employed to carry out this task. Because of its high transmission speeds and specialized installation methods, fiber-optic technology is quite expensive.

Next we will discuss the two fiber-optic cable mode technologies that you will need to be familiar with for the exam.

Single-Mode (SM)

Single-mode fiber optic, also referred to as monomode fiber, is a fiber technology meant for very long distance data transmissions. With single-mode fiber, a laser is used to generate a single pulse of light, or 'mode of light,' into the fiber media. This light is used as a data transmission carrier for a very long distance. Photodiodes are used to receive the transmission sent over the fiber-optic media.

Multi-Mode (MM)

Multi-mode fiber uses LEDs (Light Emitting Diodes) to generate signals of light into the core fibers for transmission over fiber media. This mode of fiber is designed to carry many light signal rays, or 'modes,' at the same time over a shorter distance than single mode. If the light rays, or 'modes of light,' have to travel too far with this mode, modal dispersion occurs and transmission fails. The core of the fiber media used with multi-mode is larger than with single mode; thus, the accepting photodiodes have a much larger circumference.

Here are some key points:

- ✓ The core of single-mode fiber is much smaller than the core used multi-mode type fiber.
- ✓ Single mode fiber has greater distance and bandwidth capabilities than multi-mode.
- ✓ Single-mode fiber is more expensive than multi-mode.
- ✓ It is much more difficult to repair breaks in single-mode fiber optic media.
- ✓ Multi-mode fiber uses LEDs (light emitting diodes) to generate signals of light.

✓ With single-mode fiber a laser is used to generate a single pulse of light
✓ Bridged media connectors (converters) are available, which enable Ethernet connections to be converted to fiber and fiber connections to be converted to Ethernet. Multi-mode fiber converters can support distances up to 2 Km. Single-mode fiber converters support distances of up to 60 Km.

NOTE *You should remember the key points regarding single-mode versus multi-mode fiber for the exam. These two modes have been identified as CompTIA 2003 Objectives and are likely to appear on the exam.*

Refer to Table 21.2 for a comparison chart of the major networking cables described in this chapter.

IDC (Insulation Displacement Connector)

An insulation displacement connector is a connector that is used in various different types of network termination media or connection equipment. An IDC connector removes the insulation on a cable or wire when a connection is made. It works by piercing, or 'crimping' the insulation around the cable's wires with a special tool called an IDC crimper. This technique is used to push or 'force' a single wire between two pieces of plastic, or 'blades,' that are part of a connector, such as an RJ-45 patch. An IDC assists with the process of timely termination and makes for an effective and reliable connection.

WIRELESS CONNECTIVITY

All those messy, dangling computer wires and connectors will soon be a thing of the past. Wireless technology has become very popular and affordable. In fact, you can

TABLE 21.2 Cable Comparison Chart

Cable Type	Transmission Speed	Distance
10BaseT	10Mbps	100M/328ft
10Base2	10Mbps	185M/607ft
10Base5	10Mbps	500M/1500ft
100BaseT	100Mbps	100M/328ft
Fiber optic	100Mbps to 2GBps	100K/60 miles

set up a small wireless network at home for about $400. All you really need to set up a wireless network is a couple of transmitters, receivers, and a pair of wireless NICs. The operating system configuration for a wireless network is another story in itself.

There are two main forms of wireless technologies in use for connecting computers together: Radio Frequency (RF) and Infrared (IR).

Radio Frequency (RF)

Many computer peripheral devices today utilize RF technology. With RF, a wireless mouse, keyboard, or modem can communicate with a host system as long as the distance between the peripheral and host does not exceed a specified distance. RF devices use transmitters, receivers, or transceivers (or a combination of these devices) to communicate back and forth. A typical RF mouse or keyboard transmits data through a built-in transmitter to a waiting receiver, which is attached to a system unit through a PS/2 or serial connection. RF devices are designed to meet the IEEE 802.11 standards that apply to wireless networking.

Infrared (IR)

Infrared transmission is a wireless form of transmission that also uses a transmitter and receiver. Instead of sending information with radio signals, however, infrared uses a beam of light that is not visible to the human eye to transmit data between two devices. Line-of-sight is a very popular type of infrared technology used to connect wireless devices, such as a mouse or keyboard, to a host system. The Infrared Data Association (IRDA) is the organization that is responsible for infrared transmission standards. Infrared technology has become very popular with laptop computers, PDAs, and digital cameras. With the infrared IRDA Standard 1.1, the maximum transmission rate is 4Mbps with a data size of 2048 bytes.

Some of the common uses available for infrared transmission are these:

- Messages can be sent between PDAs or between laptop computers.
- Faxes can be sent from any device utilizing IR technology.
- Pictures or images from a digital camera can be sent to a desktop or laptop computer.
- Letters or documents can be sent from a desktop or laptop computer to a printer.

The majority of infrared transmissions occur between two computers or a single computer and an infrared-enabled device, such as a printer or PDA. The sending host or device uses an infrared transmitter or 'emitter,' which sends pulses of infrared light to the receiving host or device that accepts the pulses with an infrared receiver. In order for the transmission of this signal to occur, there must be a direct line of sight between communicating systems or devices, as well as a protocol and a computer name resolution.

Infrared was originally designed for point-to-point bidirectional transmissions via an RS232C serial port. Today, most modern systems come equipped with an IRDA-standard port that can interface directly with an IR transmitter/receiver. IR connections can also be made through the use of a parallel or USB port.

In conclusion to our infrared discussion, keep in mind that IR is sometimes called the "one-to-one" technology. You can only send to or receive from one device at a time. In other words, while you are transmitting or receiving information between your desktop computer and your PDA, you cannot transmit or receive data from your laptop and at the same time use infrared.

Popular operating systems such as Microsoft Windows 95, 98, NT, 2000, XP and Windows Me offer support for adding IR devices. Early versions of Windows 95 required a special IRDA Software Patch that could be downloaded from Microsoft.com to enable IR support. In order for your system to use IR, support must be enabled in your system's BIOS.

Wireless Networking And Security

Wireless transmission is defined as the sending of signals over electromagnetic 'radio' waves. Wireless networks have become very widespread. In some cases, wireless networks have replaced the need for tradition wiring. But in larger networks, wireless technology is typically used as an extension or addition to a wired network. Wireless networks offer the ability for computing in places that would be otherwise hard to reach with a wire or cable. The use of wireless technology has been widely accepted by the military, hospitals, businesses, cell-phone companies, Global Positioning System (GPS) customers, museums, and home users alike. The IEEE has developed standards for wireless technologies. These standards are a set of rules that provide a sort of instruction map of guidelines for technology developers to follow when creating new technologies or adding to existing technologies. The IEEE standards that apply to wireless networking are: 802.11, 802.11a, 802.11b, and 802.11g. In its simplest of forms, a wireless network, or WLAN (Wireless Local Area Network), is displayed connected to a 'wired' LAN in Figure 21.11. Basic wirelesses networks typically have a wireless client, an authentication server, or 'host,' and an access point.

The need to secure the use of wireless technologies and remote wireless user access has become paramount. Not too long ago, wireless connections were thought to be somewhat secure. Recently, these thoughts have changes, based on security holes found in the technology. Next we will discuss 802.1X standards and basic wireless protocols.

802.1X

The use and support of wireless networking, equipment, security, and protocols are on the rise. Although the fine details regarding 802.1X will most likely not be

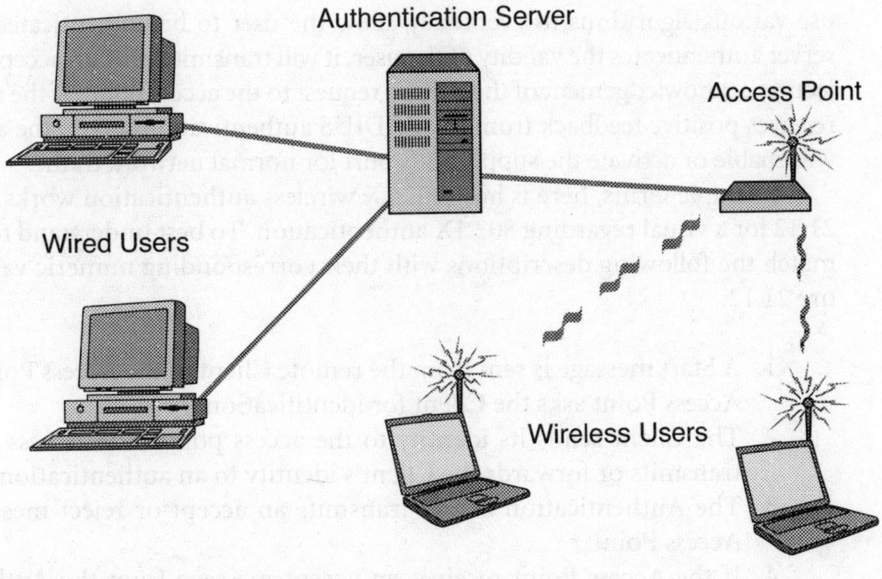

FIGURE 21.11 A basic wireless network.

addressed on the exam, the following information will give you a very good understanding of wireless concepts.

802.1X is an IEEE standard for wireless connectivity that uses port-based access control. It falls under the influence of the initial IEEE standard 802.11 for WLANs. The IEEE and the standards that apply to networking technologies in general are explained in Chapter 22. In this chapter, we will discuss all of the IEEE 802.11 standards for wireless networking. The 802.1X standard is designed to provide a better framework that supports improved security for users of wireless networks by the implementation of centralized authentication. Standard 802.1X uses the Extensible Authentication Protocol (EAP), which enables the technology to work with wireless, Ethernet, and Token Ring networks.

With 802.1X authentication, a wireless client who wishes to connect to and be authenticated on the network is called a supplicant. The supplicant must first request access from an access point, which is also known as an authenticator. If the access point detects the request for access from the supplicant, the access point will enable the supplicant's port and only let 802.1X traffic be transmitted. This allows the client to transmit a start-up message, known as an EAP start message; the supplicant's identity and credentials are then provided to the access point. The access point then transmits the information to an authentication server, which is typically a server that runs RADIUS (Remote Authentication Dial-In User Service). The authentication server can use various algorithms to eventually allow the user to be authenticated. Once the server authenticates the validity of the user, it will transmit either an acceptance or rejection acknowledgement of the client's request to the access point. If the access point receives positive feedback from the RADIUS authentication server, the access point will enable or activate the supplicant's port for normal network traffic.

In simple terms, here is how 802.1X wireless authentication works. See Figure 21.12 for a visual regarding 802.1X authentication. To best understand this process, match the following descriptions with their corresponding numeric values in Figure 21.12:

1. A Start message is sent from the remote Client to the Access Point, and the Access Point asks the Client for identification.
2. The Client sends its identity to the access point. The Access Point then transmits or forwards the Client's identity to an authentication server.
3. The Authentication Server transmits an accept or reject message to the Access Point.
4. If the Access Point receives an accept message from the Authentication Server, the Client's port activates, and the Client is allowed to communicate with the Server.

The 802.1X standard is fairly new and it is not likely that CompTIA will target it extensively on the exam. However, you should be aware of the basics concepts. Microsoft does a great job explaining this technology. If you are interested in learning more about 802.1X you may find the following site very informative: *http://www.microsoft.com/windowsxp/pro/techinfo/planning/wirelesslan/solutions.asp.*

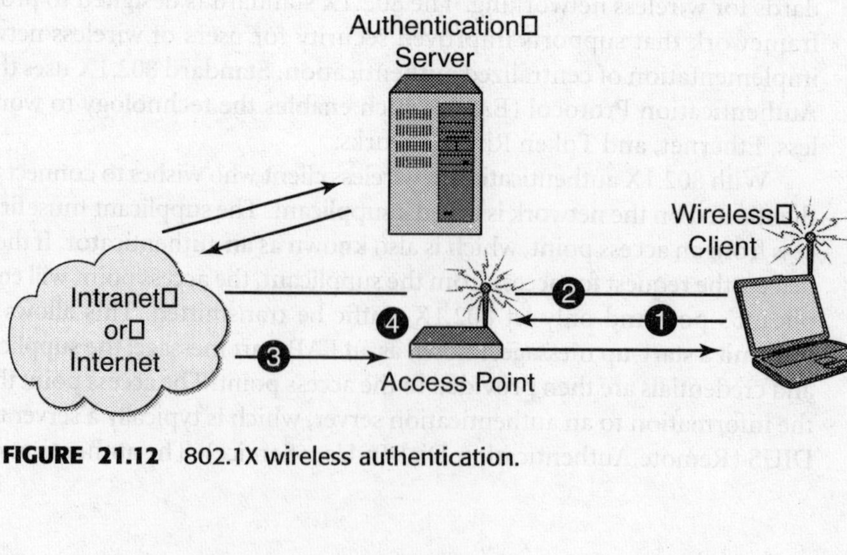

FIGURE 21.12 802.1X wireless authentication.

WAP

WAP (Wireless Application Protocol) is a wireless standard that applies to wireless communication protocols and devices. There are several standards that are used by various wireless device service manufacturers. WAP is positioned to allow interoperability between them.

WAP has its own built-in security. It uses WTLS (Wireless Transport Layer Security), which uses secure certificates and a client/server verification/authentication process.

WEP

WEP (Wired Equivalent Privacy) is wireless security protocol specified under the IEEE 802.11b. WEP is intended to provide a WLAN with a similar security level as the protection that can be found in traditional LANs. WEP attempts to secure the obvious security hole that exists between a wireless client and an access point by encrypting the data that is transmitted. Once the data has been safely transmitted, it is thought that conventional network security measures (e.g., VLANS, antivirus, tunneling, and authentication solutions) can be implemented for security purposes.

NOTE

The exam is likely to ask you very basic questions relating to wireless networking; for example, What technology does WEP have to do with? Or, what does WAP do? For this exam, it is sufficient to know that they wireless standards that apply to wireless communication protocols and devices.

Wireless Access Points

Wireless access points are used in WLANs as central points of communication between wireless users. They are sometimes referred to as transceivers because they have the ability to transmit and receive RF signals. They are the 'hub' of wireless networks. Access points can also serve as a connection point between wireless users and a wired LAN, as depicted in Figure 21.11.

Access points allow wireless users to roam in a generally predefined area called a "cell." This cell is actually the area in which the RF signals can be successfully transmitted from the access point to the roaming, or 'wireless,' user and back again. In a small business environment, this area is typically around 100 feet, depending upon many outside physical and electrical conditions. In many businesses today, it is very common to find multiple access points strategically positioned around the business environment. When a mobile user moves outside the transmission area of one particular cell, they enter another cell area without losing the RF signal to the entire WLAN. Much larger cell areas are used for broadcasting such things as cellular phone 'wireless' radio waves. These cell areas can be as small as a city block or carry radio waves several hundred miles.

Wireless Antennas

In wireless networking, an antenna is used to propagate, or 'radiate' RF signals to wireless users and access points in a wireless network. There are various antennas for wireless networking, and each has its own physical characteristics and specialized features. The two main types of wireless antennas that we need to be concerned about are:

Directional antenna: A directional antenna has the ability to direct an RF signal farther than an omnidirectional antenna. It focuses its power in a single direction, which minimizes RF interference. Directional antennas are well suited for long-distance transmissions and work well for transmitting RF signals between buildings or other locations where a direct line of site can be established.

Omnidirectional antenna: An omnidirectional antenna transmits its signals in many different directions, usually in a 360° radius. They are ideal for home, classroom, or small business. A good 802.11b omnidirectional antenna will evenly blanket your WLAN. Most omnidirectional antennas are either snap-on or dipole antennas. A snap-on is typically connected to a radio card located within a mobile or portable access point. A dipole antenna, the simplest form of antenna, is a mobile antenna that connects to a radio card with a relatively short cable.

Ad-Hoc

If a wireless network is set up using a peer-to-peer mode where wireless stations communicate directly with each other without the use of an access point, the wireless network is said to be using ad-hoc mode. An ad-hoc mode is usually implemented for temporary wireless transmission purposes.

Site Surveys

Before you install a wireless network solution into an existing building or between existing buildings (building to building), you should first have a professional site survey conducted by certified RF engineers. These engineers can properly recommend and assist you with an integration plan, as well as keep you in line with federal, state, and local regulations as they apply to wireless networks.

With traditional network installations, it is much easier to plan out a network topology and possibly foresee obstacles that will need to be addressed. However, with wireless networks that implement the use of radio transmission techniques, it is very difficult to plan for and determine how a network will react to the surrounding conditions. Obstacles such as asbestos-lined walls, trees, and other physical impediments can severely impact the effectiveness of wireless communication. The interference with other RF bands in busy airways can severely hamper your performance and ability to communicate between access points. Certified site survey technicians can detect potential interference between RF bands with a tool called a spectrum analyzer.

A good site survey should provide you with the most suitable wireless equipment options to integrate with your current topology and applications. It should also provide you with a wireless standard that is in line with your required transmission speeds and, ultimately, your budget.

NOTE *If you are interested in getting a wireless network solution, the first step is to have a site survey performed.*

CHAPTER SUMMARY

This chapter introduced you to several of the many types of cables and connectors used to attach devices together. There are literally thousands of connectors, wire types, and media used to make connections and data transfer possible between devices. The Internet is a great tool to utilize if you are interested in finding out more details on the subject matter discussed in this chapter. By now, you should have a good basic understanding of cables and connectors.

REVIEW QUESTIONS

1. Which of the following can connect or "network" two computers together? (Choose Three)

☐ A. A 6-pin mini-DIN

☐ B. A serial cable

☐ C. 10Base2

☐ D. A parallel cable

Correct Answers = B, C, and D

You can connect two computers together with a serial cable, an Ethernet thinnet 10Base2 cable, or a parallel cable. A 6-pin mini-DIN connector is used to connect a PS/2 mouse or keyboard to a computer.

2. **How does a parallel port transmit data to a device?**
   - o A. 1 bit at a time
   - o B. 1 byte at a time
   - o C. Serially
   - o D. By use of a parallelogram

   Correct Answer = B

   A parallel port uses parallel transmission methods to transmit or send data 1 byte at a time to a peripheral device. A serial port transmits data one bit at a time.

3. **If two devices cannot send and receive data and information simultaneously, they are using which form of data transmission?**
   - o A. Full Duplex
   - o B. Quarter Duplex
   - o C. Half Duplex
   - o D. Half Simplex

   Correct Answer = C

   With Half Duplex transmission, data can be transmitted in both directions but can only be transmitted in one direction at a time. Full Duplex is simultaneous transmission where data or voice can be transmitted at exactly the same time.

4. **A parallel printer cable has a different connectors on each end. Name the two types of connectors on a parallel printer cable. (Choose Two)**
   - □ A. DB25-pin male connector
   - □ B. DB9-pin connector
   - □ C. An RS232c compliant cable
   - □ D. 36-pin Centronics connector

   Correct Answers = A and D

   A parallel port on the back of a computer system is a female DB25 connector that accepts a DB25-pin male connector on one end of a parallel cable. The other end of a parallel cable has a 36-pin male Centronics D-shell connector that connects to a Centronics connector located on the back of a printer or device. A DB9-pin connection is used for connecting a modem or serial mouse to the back of a system. RS232C is a serial port standard.

5. A connector that has two levels of 15 total pins is which type of cable?

- o A. Monitor cable
- o B. Modem cable
- o C. Serial port
- o D. Game port

Correct Answer = D

A game or MIDI female port on the back of system has two levels of 15 total pins that accept a male connector with two levels of 15 total pins.

6. Which is the fastest technology available for printers?

- o A. SCSI
- o B. Parallel
- o C. USB
- o D. Serial

Correct Answer = A

The fastest technology available for printers today is SCSI.

7. Which technology has the fastest data transfer rates?

- o A. IEEE 1394
- o B. Parallel
- o C. USB
- o D. A fast crossover cable

Correct Answer = A

FireWire is much faster than USB or parallel; it supports data transfer rates of 100Mbps to 400Mbps.

8. Name the minimum category cable type that can be used to support 100BaseT.

- o A. Category 2
- o B. Category 3
- o C. Category 4
- o D. Category 5

Correct Answer = D

Category 5 UTP supports 100BaseT or 100BaseTX. Category 2, 3, and 4 cable types do not support 100BaseT.

9. Name the minimum category cable type that can be used to support 10BaseT.

- o A. Category 3
- o B. RJ-11
- o C. Category 4
- o D. Category 5

Correct Answer = A

The minimum cable type needed to support 10BaseT is Category 3. An RJ-11 phone connector is used for earlier categories of UTP to connect a modem or your phone to a typical phone jack.

10. Which of the following is an IEEE standard for parallel type C?

- o A. Standard Centronics 36-pin
- o B. Mini 36-pin Centronics connector
- o C. FireWire (IEEE 1394)
- o D. DB25 male

Correct Answer = B

The newest addition to the IEEE 1284 standard for bi-directional communications and printing is the Type C Mini 36-pin parallel connector.

11. Which of the following are associated with parallel printer ports? (Choose Three)

- □ A. Bi-directional
- □ B. IEEE 1284
- □ C. EPP
- □ D. USB
- □ E. Omnidirectional

Correct Answers = A, B, and C

Parallel printer ports support bi-directional as well as Enhanced Parallel Port (EPP) application data transmissions. They are associated with the IEEE 1284 parallel standard that is used to connect a computer to peripheral devices such as printers.

12. Which of the following IEEE standards addresses FireWire?

- o A. IEEE 802.11
- o B. IEEE 1284
- o C. IEEE 1234
- o D. IEEE 1394
- o E. None of the above

Correct Answer = D

The IEEE 1394 standard references FireWire high-speed serial transmissions of up to 400Mbps (in version 1394a) and 800Mbps (in version 1394b). You better know the difference between IEEE 802.11, IEEE 1284, IEEE 1394, and RS232 for the real exam!

13. What process will a Plug-and-Play system use to detect connected FireWire-compatible devices?

- o A. FireWire-N-Play
- o B. Enumeration
- o C. Collaboration
- o D. IrDa standard 1.1
- o E. None of the above

Correct Answer = B

FireWire is Plug-and-Play-compatible and hot swappable. It also allows up to 63 devices to be connected to one port. A Plug-and-Play system will use the process known as enumeration to assign an address and auto detect any FireWire-connected devices.

14. A network interface card that supports SC or ST connections is an example of which type of technology?

- o A. FireWire
- o B. Ethernet
- o C. Fiber optic
- o D. IR or IrDa
- o E. None of the above

Correct Answer = C

Fiber-optic cables use special ST and SC type connectors to attach to NICs and fiber-optic ports. These connectors are precisely crafted and specially designed to suit fiber-optic cable connection requirements.

15. When a sending host or device uses a transmitter or "emitter" to send pulses of light to a receiving host or device, which technology is being implemented?

o A. FireWire

o B. Ethernet

o C. Fiber optic

o D. IR

o E. RF

o F. None of the above

Correct Answer = D

The majority of infrared (IR) transmissions occur between two computers or a single computer and an infrared-enabled device such as a printer or PDA. The sending host or device uses an infrared transmitter or "emitter," which sends pulses of infrared light to the receiving host or device, which accepts with an infrared receiver.

16. You want to use an IR keyboard with your new desktop system. What must be enabled in order for you to do this?

o A. Simplex transmission

o B. COM4

o C. ECC

o D. IR support in your system's BIOS

o E. None of the above

Correct Answer = D

In order for your system to use Infrared, IR, or IrDa (same thing), support must be enabled in your system's BIOS.

17. What is considered the "hub" in a wireless network?

o A. Ad-hoc

o B. Access point

o C. WLAN

o D. Receiver

o E. None of the above

Correct Answer = B

Wireless access points are sometimes referred to as transceivers because they can transmit and receive RF signals. They are the "hub" of wireless networks.

18. Your boss has asked you to implement a wireless network solution for your company. What is the first step you should take before implementing this solution?

o A. Do a site survey.

o B. Purchase access point and wireless NICs.

o C. Convert all Ethernet to fiber.

o D. Activate 128-bit encryption.

o E. None of the above.

Correct Answer = A

Before you install a wireless network solution into an existing building or between existing buildings (building to building) you should first have a professional site survey conducted by certified RF (Radio Frequency) engineers.

19. Your boss has asked you to implement a fiber-optic solution for your corporate enterprise. You need a solution for fast data transmission over a very long distance. What fiber-optic solution will you recommend?

o A. Double-mode (DM)

o B. Single-mode (SM)

o C. Multi-mode (MM)

o D. Multi-homed (MH)

Correct Answer = B

Single-mode fiber optic, also referred to as monomode fiber, is a fiber technology meant for very long-distance data transmissions.

20. What does multi-mode (MM) fiber use to generate signals of light rays or "modes"?

o A. Laser

o B. Phaser

o C. Core illuminator

o D. LED

o E. None of the above

Correct Answer = D

Multi-mode fiber uses LEDs (light emitting diodes) to generate signals of light into the core fibers for transmission over fiber media. This mode of fiber is designed to carry many light signal rays or "modes" at the same time over a shorter distance than single-mode.

21. Which category of UTP uses a 23-gauge conductor wire and is rated for speeds up to 550M or 1000M?

o A. CAT5

o B. CAT6

o C. CAT5e

o D. CAT4b

o E. CAT6g

Correct Answer = B

CAT6 cabling is built using 23-gauge conductor wire. The CAT6 cabling standard is rated up to 550M or 1000M.

REFERENCES

http://www.ramelectronics.net/html/connecters.html. This RAM Electronics Industries, Inc., Web site offers some very good images of the three main parallel connector types, as well as many of the other connectors mentioned in this chapter.

http://computer.howstuffworks.com/firewire1.htm. This HowStuffWorks, Inc., Web site offers a superb explanation of FireWire basics.

http://www.microsoft.com/windowsxp/pro/techinfo/planning/wirelesslan/solutions.asp. This Microsoft Web site explains wireless LAN technology in good detail.

22 Basic Networking

In This Chapter

- IEEE 802 Specifications
- OSI Reference Model
- Network Categories
- Network Topology
- Protocols
- Bridges, Routers, Switches, and Hubs
- Network Interface Cards
- The Internet and Viruses
- Cable, ISDN, DSL, and Satellite
- Firewalls
- Troubleshooting and Basic Networking Test Tips
- Chapter Summary
- Review Questions
- References

In Chapter 21, you were introduced to some of the important cables and connectors that are used to link computers and peripherals; many of the topics discussed were intended to prepare you for basic networking. In Chapter 22, we will focus on the various types of networks—the communication methods computers use to talk to each other—and some of the important hardware used in various network typologies. We will also focus on troubleshooting network-related connectivity issues, as well as harmful threats that may come in the form of an uneducated user or a computer virus.

It is very important for anyone studying networking architecture and concepts to be familiar with the IEEE 802 specifications for networking components and the Open Systems Interconnect (OSI) reference model, which provides a set of standards for computers to communicate with each other. These two topics are the foundation on which networks are based. However, it is unlikely that the A+ Core exam will tax you with detailed questions on these two topics. The IEEE 802 standards that you may need to know for the exam will be identified.

IEEE 802 SPECIFICATIONS

The IEEE is a technical organization that develops standards for Local Area Networks (LANs) and Wide Area Networks (WANs). The IEEE 802 project standards were developed in the 1970s as a set of specifications, or rules, that manufacturers and users can use as a sort of road map for understanding and developing networks and network-related devices. The IEEE specifications are associated with certain networking layers of the OSI networking model, which is discussed in this chapter.

Throughout this book, you have been introduced to many of the IEEE standards and the particular technologies to which they apply. For example, in Chapter 21, you were introduced to the IEEE standard 1394, which applies to high-speed serial transmission, as well as the IEEE 1284 standard, which applies to parallel transmission. Project 802 was developed to address standards for NICs, network cables, and WANs. There have been many additions and addendums added to the IEEE 802 standards as technology has progressed.

The 12 categories of the 802 specifications and their associations are as follows:

- 802.1—Internetworking
- 802.2—The Logical Link Control (LLC) sublayer of the OSI networking model
- 802.3—Carrier Sense Multiple Access/Collision Detection (CSMA/CD) LANs (Ethernet)
- 802.4—Token bus LAN
- 802.5—Token Ring LAN
- 802.6—Metropolitan Area Network (MAN)
- 802.7—Broadband Technical Advisory Group
- 802.8—Fiber Optic Technical Advisory Group
- 802.9—Integrated voice and data networks
- 802.10—Network Security Technical Advisory Group
- 802.11—Wireless networking
  - 802.11a—Applies to 5GHz wireless technology, commonly at 6Mbps, 12Mbps, or 24Mbps transmission rates.
  - 802.11b—Applies to 2.4GHz wireless technology at 11Mbps per second transmission rate.
  - 802.11g—Also applies to 2.4GHz wireless technology range and offers wireless transmission rates up to 54Mbps.
- 802.12—Demand priority access LAN 100BaseVG, any LAN

The three IEEE 802 standards that are most important for A+ study purposes are: 802.3, which represents Ethernet; 802.5, which refers to Token Ring or token passing; and 802.11, which refers to wireless networking. Later in this chapter, we will discuss topologies, such as bus, star, and ring. It is important to remember that the 802.3 Ethernet standards apply to bus and star networks that utilize CSMA/CD access methods, whereas Token Ring topologies utilize token-passing methods to place a data signal on a wire.

As mentioned earlier, the IEEE 802 standards apply mostly to the physical aspects of networking components. For example, they have to do with how a NIC is connected to a network or what types of media transmission methods are used to carry a signal down a physical wire.

Just about every networking component manufactured today is designed to meet one of the above-mentioned IEEE standards. If you purchase a hub, cable/DSL router, NIC, or wireless network component, take a look at the specifications on the package or in the advertisement. You will see that the product was manufactured to meet one of the standards set forth by the IEEE.

For more information regarding the IEEE standards and updates to these standards, please visit the IEEE home page located at: *http://www.ieee.org/portal/index.jsp*.

OSI REFERENCE MODEL

As networking became more popular in the world, a well-organized, logical framework for connecting networks and developing applications was needed. In the late 1970s, the International Standards Organization (ISO) developed the OSI networking reference model.

The OSI reference model is a seven-layer logical approach to network communication that includes specifications for the actual hardware connection to the network at the bottom layers, and rules for applications and more complicated functions at the higher layers. Networking rules for communication, also known as *protocols*, exist at almost every layer of the OSI model. The more complicated the protocol, the higher up on the model it resides. Network transmission, security, session connection information, and hardware are each associated with a particular layer.

Picture yourself sitting at your computer, working on a Microsoft Word document. You are actually utilizing functions that reside at the top layer of the OSI reference model, known as the application layer, or layer 7. You decide to attach the Word document to an e-mail message and send it to a co-worker. The message, or signal that you are sending is directed from the application layer (layer 7) down to the physical layer (layer 1), where it is placed in converted format (0s and 1s) on a network medium, such as a wire, and transmitted to your co-worker. Your co-worker on the receiving end accepts the message through his or her physical layer (layer 1). The message is converted back to a readable format from 0s and 1s, and is presented to your co-worker's application layer (layer 7).

Here are the seven layers of the OSI reference model, starting with layer 7.

7. **Application Layer:** Applications, e-mail, FTP, user authentication, and any other major services that the end user directly interacts with are associated with this high-level layer. Network access and forms of error recovery are handled at this layer. High-level devices, such as gateways, are present at this layer. Application-specific protocols, such as X.500, SMTP, SNMP, Telnet, and SMB, reside at this layer, as well as the presentation and session layers.
6. **Presentation Layer:** Data on the sending computer is converted to a format that can be transmitted over media to another computer. On the receiving end, data is converted into a format that the end user or application layer can understand. Encryption and data translation occur at this level. The network redirector operates at this level.
5. **Session Layer:** The session layer establishes, holds, and controls sessions or connections between two applications. It provides checkpoint and synchronization service between two communication sessions. Security is handled at this layer.
4. **Transport Layer:** The transport layer's primary concern is flow control and data handling. Large forms of data are broken down into manageable packets that can be presented to the higher layers on the receiving end. The successful transmission of data is acknowledged at this layer. If the transfer of information is incomplete or interrupted, this layer is responsible for requesting the information to be retransmitted by the sending application or session. Transfer protocols such as TCP, NetBEUI, NWLink, and SPX reside at this layer.
3. **Network Layer:** The network layer is responsible for the routing of information to the correct network, device, or computer. Logical names are converted to physical names at this layer. In other words, computer Internet Protocol (IP) addresses are converted to their Media Access Control (MAC) equivalents. Priority of connection and quality of service are also handled at this layer. A network router and switch reside at this layer, as do network protocols, such as IP and IPX.
2. **Data Link Layer:** Data frames received from the network layer are converted into bits (0s and 1s) at the data link layer in preparation for the physical layer. On the receiving end, bits are packaged together into frames that can be understood by the higher layers. Frame synchronization, flow control, and error handling are addressed at this level. The data link layer has two

sublayers, known as the Logical Link Control (LLC) and MAC layers. The LLC sublayer is associated with IEEE standards 802.1 and 802.2, and is responsible for the implementation and placement of Service Access Points (SAPs). The MAC sublayer is associated with IEEE standards 802.3, 802.4, 802.5, and 802.12. The MAC sublayer communicates directly with an NIC. It is responsible for error-free communication between network interfaces. Devices called *bridges*, which segment network traffic, operate at this layer.

1. **Physical Layer:** The physical layer is the physical adapter or connection to the network wire or medium. It is where bits of information are prepared to go across the network medium. Incoming bits of information are organized and prepared to move through the higher layers.

If you are interested in pursuing a career in networking, it is very important that you understand the theory behind the OSI reference model. You will also need a solid understanding of the OSI reference model and the IEEE specifications if you are interested in passing CompTIA's Network+ certification examination. However, that is another story altogether—or is it? This book has been designed as a springboard to your computer certification future. You will already have a great start toward CompTIA's Network+, Security+, and Server+ certification examinations when you complete this book.

If you are interested in viewing one of the very best charts available regarding the OSI Reference Model, please visit the following Geocities Web site: *http://www.geocities.com/SiliconValley/Monitor/3131/ne/osimodel.html.*

NETWORK CATEGORIES

A *network* is defined as two or more computers attached to each other that share information. Networks can be formed to make up an LAN or a WAN. An LAN is a network that resides in one physical location, such as a building. It usually has a limited number of computers attached to it and is designated a certain scope or range of computer IP numeric addresses. A WAN is a larger network that usually combines two or more LANs together over a larger physical distance. For example, a business may have two LANs in different buildings or different cities. The two LANs can be connected to form a WAN. A WAN typically has a larger range of computer IP addresses and is used to control communication between LANs. Access to a WAN is usually accomplished through use of a leased or dedicated T1 line, or a dial-up modem connection using ISDN, cable, or DSL.

There are two basic types of networks in use today: peer-to-peer and server-based. Each of the two network categories has its own set of built-in characteristics that differentiate it from the other.

Peer-To-Peer Networks

A *peer-to-peer network* is a small network, usually of 10 or fewer computer systems, connected without the use of a larger specialized server computer. In peer-to-peer networks, a workstation can function as both a client and a server computer. In other words, a single computer can share information or devices attached to it or act as its own entity to carry out day-to-day workstation functions.

A peer-to-peer network does not require a high-end server computer to provide login authentication or a highly trained staff to secure and administer network resources. A peer-to-peer network uses password-protected shares that utilize share-level security at the workstation level. The user of the workstation decides who will be able to read, write, execute, or delete files that exist. Windows 3.11, 95, 98, Me, NT, 2000 and Windows XP operating systems can all provide peer-to-peer capabilities.

Many small businesses and home enthusiasts implement peer-to-peer networks. They are a less expensive alternative to server-based networks and are fairly easy to maintain, as long as you remember all the passwords that may be associated with all the files, folders, and devices.

Server-Based Networks

A *server-based network* is typically implemented for networks that have more than 10 computers and that require quick access to services that specialized high-end servers can provide. A server-based network is designed to centralize the control and administration of network access (security) and resources. When a user logs on to a server-based network, a specialized server that controls network access authenticates the user by utilizing user-level security. A network administrator or manager is typically empowered in a server-based network to control, monitor, and carry out the daily network maintenance associated with this type of network. Some examples of operating systems that can provide server-based functionality are Microsoft Windows NT Server, Windows 2000 Server, Windows Server 2003, Novell Netware, and Unix.

Server computers are designed to provide specific services to client computers. Some of the different types of server computers are listed in Table 22.1.

Network Redirector

The network redirector is software that is built into the code of a network operating system. The redirector intercepts requests made by the system's processor and decides whether the request should be forwarded to another system on the network or remain local to the system. If a request is made from a client workstation for a particular instruction, such as printing to a network printer, the redirector grabs

TABLE 22.1 Types of Network Server Computers

Server Type	Server Function
Authentication Server	Centralized location of security accounts database used to allow users access to the network—for example, Windows NT Primary Domain Controller. (PDC)
Database Server	Houses the common database. Is responsible for storage and management of data warehouse services—for example, Microsoft SQL Server.
Application Server	Handles high-end operations to take load off of client computers. Application software is installed on a server. Client computers request services from the application server.
Print Server	Handles all client side requests for network printing. Manages network printers and print queues.
Communications Server	Responsible for e-mail, fax, Internet access and dial-up modem connections. Microsoft Exchange Server is an example of a communications server application.
Web Server	Serves up Internet or intranet Web pages—for example, a server that runs Microsoft Internet Information Services (IIS) or Samba.

the request and sees that it is forwarded to the network so that print operations can commence.

Universal Naming Convention

A Universal Naming Convention (UNC) name is used to access a particular share on a particular workstation or server on a network. If you want to access a resource, such as a printer or folder that has been shared on the network, you can gain access to it by typing in the UNC name from the Start > Run option in Windows. A UNC name always follows the format \\Servername\sharename. For example, suppose you want to access a folder on the network named "Certified." The Certified folder resides on a server named "Bigserver." You would go to Start > Run and type in \\Bigserver\Certified. If you have rights to the Certified folder, you can have access to it.

NETWORK TOPOLOGY

A network's topology is the actual physical layout of the network. The topology of a network is based on factors such as the number of workstations and servers required, the communication methods that will be implemented, and the cables and specialized equipment that are available.

The three standard network topologies are bus, star, and ring. Be sure that you can identify the three main topologies and the cable type associated with each. The core exam is likely to present you with a topology diagram similar to the three figures you will see in this chapter, or to ask which cable type is associated with each topology. For example, 10Base2 is associated with a bus topology network.

The three topologies and their associated characteristics form the framework from which most networks are based. All three topologies are described next.

Bus

An Ethernet bus topology, otherwise known as a linear bus, is a topology designed for a limited number of computers that are typically attached to a single wire, or trunk, in a straight line. As more workstations are added to a bus topology, performance decreases. Figure 22.1 displays a typical bus topology.

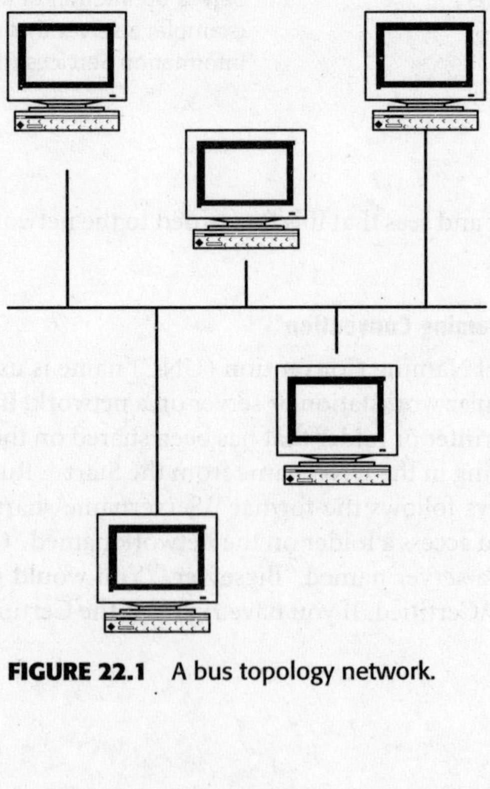

FIGURE 22.1 A bus topology network.

The main type of cable implemented in a bus topology network is 10Base2 (which was described more fully in Chapter 21). Devices called terminators must be placed on both ends of a bus network or wire to keep the data signal that is placed on the wire from bouncing back and forth, a phenomenon referred to as *signal bounce.* All computers on the bus listen for the data signals. If the signal is addressed to a particular workstation, the workstation accepts the signal. If the physical wire or connection that makes up the bus topology is damaged or breaks, the individual computers on the bus will still be able to operate independently, but will not be able to accept data signals and communicate with other computers on the bus network.

Bus and star networks utilize CSMA/CD media access control methods to place a signal on a wire. CSMA/CD is an Ethernet error-detection method used to ensure proper data handling on a wire.

BNC (Bayonet Nut Connector) and BNC barrel connectors are used to attach a bus cable to a device or connect one piece of the bus cable to another. A device called a repeater is used to boost or regenerate the signals placed on a 10Base2 or bus network. Adding a repeater to a bus can extend the length of the entire bus network. For distances associated with a bus network, refer to Chapter 21 and 10Base2 distance capabilities.

Star

A star topology physically looks like a star. Figure 22.2 shows a simple star topology network. A star topology utilizes a central device, which can be a hub, a router,

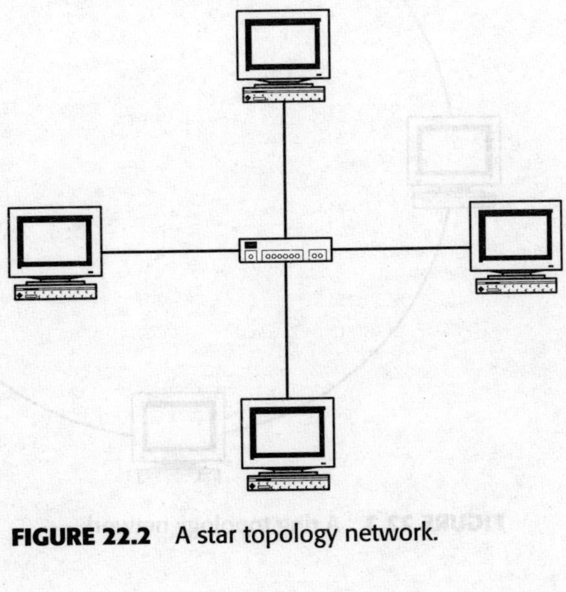

FIGURE 22.2 A star topology network.

or a switch. We will refer to a simple hub for the central connection point in a star network.

All devices in a star topology network are typically connected to a hub with twisted pair, otherwise known as 10BaseT cable. A star topology network is known to require large amounts of cable for larger networks. The hub provides a central location at which the network can be managed and tested. If one computer fails on a star network, the other computers connected to the hub can still function and communicate with one another. If the hub fails, however, all communication between devices will cease.

Ring

A ring topology network is best understood by picturing an actual circle of cable. Workstations and servers are all connected to the circle of cable. Each computer attached to the circle regenerates the data signal sent in the form of a token. The circling of the token to each of the servers and workstations on the ring is known as *token passing*. If the wire that makes up the ring is damaged, all network activity on the ring ceases. Keep in mind that IEEE 802.5 is a standard that applies to token-passing technology. Figure 22.3 displays a simple Token Ring topology.

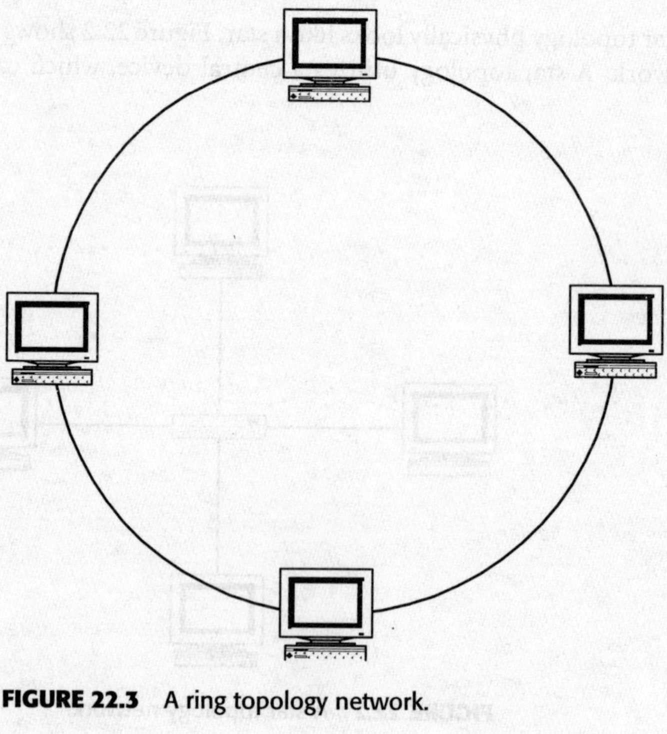

FIGURE 22.3 A ring topology network.

PROTOCOLS

As mentioned earlier in this chapter, network protocols are a common language or set of rules that computers use to communicate with one another. Protocols come in packages known as protocol stacks. Individual protocols reside at each layer of the OSI reference model in order to carry out specified functions. If the Core exam tests you on protocols, it will most likely focus on the TCP/IP and IPX/SPX protocol stacks. There are many network protocols in use. We will focus on the protocols you need to know for the Core exam.

TCP/IP

Transmission Control Protocol/Internet Protocol (TCP/IP) is the most popular protocol in use today. It is the protocol of choice for the Internet. TCP/IP is commonly used with Ethernet, Token Ring, and Internet or network dial-up connections. Every computer on a TCP/IP network uses an IP address as a unique numeric identification. An IP address is a 32-bit numeric combination of four period-delimited octets, each of which can be a number from 0 to 255. An IP address can be up to 12 digits long.

An example of an IP address is 209.15.176.206. This IP address is associated with the domain name address that is provided by a domain name system (DNS) server of the publisher of this book, charlesriver.com. From a DOS prompt, you can use the TCP/IP ping utility to test a connection to the Charles River Media, Inc. Web site. Try it. Using Windows 2000, navigate to the DOS prompt. At the DOS prompt, type "Ping charlesriver.com." You should receive an associated IP address of the Web site as well as four echo replies. Another popular TCP/IP utility is the tracert command. The tracert will tell the route you are using to establish a connection with a destination computer. In other words, it gives you all the TCP/IP addresses and domain names of the computers you are using to reach your final destination. Try the tracert command from the DOS prompt. Type "tracert charlesriver.com." You will receive the IP addresses and domain names of the computers you are hitting to get to the Charles River Media, Inc. Web site. The time it takes for your request to go from each destination's IP address is measured in units of time called *hops*. A subnet mask is used to specify which particular network a TCP/IP address belongs to.

You can check the IP configuration of your computer using two popular commands. If you are using Windows 95 or 98, type "winipcfg" at the DOS prompt. If you are using Windows NT, Me, 2000, or XP, type "ipconfig" or "ipconfig/all" at the DOS prompt. Your computer's IP address, subnet mask, and default gateway settings will be displayed.

If your computer is unable to communicate with other computers on the network and all the other computers are functioning correctly, you should first check your computer's IP address configuration settings. They may not be properly configured. If this is the case, your computer can only access itself.

IPX/SPX

Internetwork Packet Exchange/Sequenced Packet Exchange (IPX/SPX) is a protocol stack used in Novell networks that supports routing. There are several versions of Novell operating systems in use today. When connecting a system to a Novell network, it is often necessary to bind a specific frame type to your NIC for connection to various Novell operating system versions. Frame type specifications are beyond our study focus; just remember that if you are having trouble connecting to a Novell network, you should first verify that the proper frame type is bound to your NIC.

NetBIOS

NetBIOS (Network Basic Input/Output System) is a program or API (Application Programming Interface) that allows application programs on separate computers to recognize and talk to each other. NetBIOS operates at both the session and transport layers of the OSI reference model. Operating systems such as DOS and Windows use a message format called SMB (Server Message Block) to assist with the sharing of folders, files, devices, and other tasks/tools. NetBIOS relies on and uses SMB format.

NetBIOS was originally created by IBM, and was later adopted and changed for use in operating systems that were created by Microsoft and Novell.

NetBIOS is not routable. This means that it, alone, does not allow communication between systems or programs that exist on separate networks (usually separated by routers). In other words, NetBIOS works well in LANs, not WANs. For WAN communication, you need TCP/IP.

NetBEUI

NetBEUI (NetBIOS Extended User Interface) is a nonroutable, small, efficient transport layer protocol meant for use in small networks with 1–200 workstations. NetBEUI does not have the overhead associated with larger protocols and is very efficient for workgroups or peer-to-peer networks.

In a nutshell, if you have a small workgroup that includes operating systems such as Windows 95, 98, Me, 2000, XP, or NT, installing NetBEUI will allow them to efficiently communicate with each other. According to Microsoft, the only configuration requirement needed for installing the NetBEUI protocol is a valid computer name.

> *NetBIOS and NetBEUI are specific CompTIA 2003 Upgrade Objectives. Know them well; it is likely that they will show up on the new A+ Core Hardware exam.*

BRIDGES, ROUTERS, SWITCHES, AND HUBS

Network devices such as routers, switches, bridges, and hubs connect computing systems and networks together. They are responsible for productive network functionality, backbone support, and the proper forwarding of information to other networks. In short, without them, there would be little or no network connectivity and minimal network security at best.

As the number of computers or nodes on a network increases, a network requires specialized equipment to expand its length, direct its flow of traffic, and provide a centralized location for troubleshooting and maintenance. Next, we will discuss the functionality of each of these devices.

Bridges

Bridges are hardware devices that operate at the MAC sublayer of the OSI reference model's data link layer. Bridges are used to segment or separate LANs. Separating a larger network into smaller, more manageable segments can improve network performance and provide a way to isolate network bottlenecks.

A bridge reads the MAC hardware address that is stored in the NIC card of every computer or node installed on either side of the bridge. The bridge knows where all the computers are on the network and can forward information to a particular computer by the use of its NIC MAC address. Let's say you are sitting at a computer that resides on network segment number 1. You want to send Brian, whose computer is located on network segment number 2, a Word document. There is a bridge that separates you on network segment number 1 from Brian on network segment number 2. The bridge can identify both of your computers by their respective NIC's MAC addresses. Therefore, when you send a Word document to Brian, it is forwarded to his network segment by the use of the bridge.

Bridges can provide the following services:

- Reduce network traffic that results from too many computers being attached to a network.
- Connect different types of media connections, such as coaxial cable and twisted-pair cable.
- Expand the length of a network segment.
- Connect different network typologies together, such as Token Ring and Ethernet.

Although bridges serve their primary purpose, they are limited in their capabilities. If a destination's MAC address is not found in a bridge's internal table, the bridge will proliferate, or broadcast (pass traffic) to all network segments. This can result in a broadcast storm that can slow or take down a network.

As networks grew larger, the demand increased for a more intelligent device that could handle an increasing number of attached computer nodes and direct network traffic in a more efficient manner. The router was technology's answer to this demand.

Routers

A *router* is another device that connects different network segments; but unlike a bridge, a router does not use a computer's MAC address to forward information. Instead, a router operates at the network layer of the OSI reference model and has the ability to forward information based on a network or an individual computer's TCP/IP address. This allows a router to connect entirely separate networks and to filter information to the proper network or network segment. In other words, a router has the ability to send a request to a specific location without broadcasting to all the other computer nodes on a network or network segment.

Routers are very intelligent. They hold sophisticated routing tables and have the ability to remember previous connections that were used as pathways from one computer node to another. Routers can actually decide which path is most efficient for a packet of information to take in order to reach its final destination.

Routers are primarily used for the following tasks:

- Provide filtering of packets and reduce broadcast storms.
- Segment networks into smaller, more manageable pieces.
- Provide a network security layer between separate networks (a firewall).

Routers use specialized protocols, such as Internet Control Message Protocol (ICMP), Open Shortest Path First (OSPF), and Routing Information Protocol (RIP), to communicate with each other and carry out their advanced functions.

Switches

A *switch* is a network device similar to a router; it chooses certain paths or routes in a network on which to send data. A switch is not a router, although a switch can contain router functionality. Most modern switches can operate at both the data link and network layers of the OSI reference model. A switch that has the ability to operate at the network layer is known as a layer 3 or IP switch. Switches can connect networks and subnetworks comprised of the same or different cable types. They can send units of data (packets) faster than most routers based on digital packet-switching technology. Switches typically connect LAN segments that use the same protocol.

Hubs

A *hub* is a network device that acts as a central point used to connect computers together. In network terms, a hub is a simple connection device that sends all data packets to all connected systems. A basic hub operates at the physical layer of the OSI reference model. Generally speaking, in a basic networking set-up, if the hub goes down or becomes dysfunctional, all systems connected to the hub will be unable to communicate with each other.

NETWORK INTERFACE CARDS

A NIC is a circuit board that is inserted into an available bus expansion slot on a computer system's motherboard. It allows a computer to connect to and communicate with other computers on a network or LAN.

A NIC operates at the MAC sublayer of the OSI reference model's data link layer and has a 10-digit unique MAC address stored on its ROM chip. As mentioned earlier, a device such as a bridge can identify a computer on the network by its MAC address.

ROM chips, such as EEPROM on an NIC, store vital information, such as the NIC's I/O address, IRQ, and MAC address.

On a 10BaseT Ethernet network, a twisted-pair wire with an RJ-45 connector is plugged into the back of a typical 10/100Mbps PCI-bus NIC. If the NIC has been properly attached to the network, the green and amber LEDs on the back of the NIC will flicker on and off.

NIC cards are typically available at network access speeds of 10Mbps, or both 10Mbps and 100Mbps. If your network can support transmission speeds of higher than 10Mbps, and you are only using a 10Mbps NIC, you will not be able to take full advantage of your network's bandwidth. Your NIC will cause what is known as a bottleneck.

NICs are fairly easy to install if you have purchased a popular brand name and are utilizing a plug-and-play operating system. Most newer operating systems have fully compliant software drivers built in that support newer NICs. However, if you are using an ancient, legacy NIC, or your operating system does not support plug and play, it will be necessary to use the software driver that came with the NIC. If you do not have the installation software or drivers for the NIC, you should consult the NIC manufacturer's Web site for a possible free driver download.

There are several ways that settings on NICs can be configured. Older, legacy NICs were configured with the use of jumpers or DIP switches on the card itself. Today, most NIC settings are configured with the use of software provided by the manufacturer, or simply by letting plug and play make the necessary setting automatically if your NIC card is plug and play.

NICs and their connections are notorious for causing network-related trouble if they are malfunctioning or improperly connected. If you or a customer cannot connect to your network, first verify that the NIC and the patch cable connected to it are in working order. If all the hardware is intact and you see flashing lights on the back of the NIC, you may want to try typing in the correct password to access your network resources.

THE INTERNET AND VIRUSES

The Internet is a huge network that connects millions of host computers with unique IP addresses, all over the world. It is the largest source of information available. The Internet offers a vast array of services: you can buy almost anything, see just about anywhere, and talk or chat with anyone who is connected.

Here are some important Internet-related terms that you should be familiar with for both of the A+ exams:

Uniform Resource Locator (URL): The URL is the line typically located at the top of the browser, such as *http://www.charlesriver.com*. The first part of the line is the Internet protocol to be used—for example, http:. The second part of the URL line is used for the Internet address you are trying to access. It can be an IP address or a domain name, such as charlesriver.com.

DNS (Domain Name System) server: This server or service converts fully qualified domain names to IP addresses and makes it possible for you to enter "charlesriver.com" into your Web browser instead of entering the 12-digit IP address.

Hypertext Transfer Protocol (HTTP): Internet protocol used to transmit instructions to the World Wide Web from a Web browser.

Hypertext Markup Language (HTML): HTML allows Web pages to be formatted with graphics and symbols other than plain text. HTML provides the Web page with a set of instructions pertaining to how the page should be displayed to the end user.

Extensible Markup Language (XML): XML is similar to HTML, but XML offers developers and designers more flexibility in creating Web pages through the use of call tags.

Viruses

A *virus* is a program or specific piece of code that is designed, when executed, to duplicate itself and/or spread itself to other areas of a system or other systems in a networked environment. In general terms, a virus will replicate itself until it uses up all available system resources, such as memory or hard drive space. The result of an undetected virus that has infected a system and has been successful at achieving its goal is a system that simply will not function. In most cases, this makes the system unavailable to other systems or results in a denial of service.

NOTE *Never open an e-mail attachment if you are not sure of the identity of its sender. That "Incredibly Interesting and Free Offer" may make you reformat your hard drive.*

The Internet also offers a vast array of threats to you and your computer. You can lose your good credit standing if certain personal information is obtained and used for illegal purposes. Computers are vulnerable to computer viruses, as well as full-scale marketing attacks.

The Internet is swarming with many unfriendly computer viruses. A computer virus is a program or piece of code that is typically designed to store itself in your computer's memory or on your hard drive. Most viruses make copies or duplicate themselves over and over until your memory or hard drive become inoperable. If you are interested in protecting the integrity of your stored data or the business you may be responsible for, it is very important to utilize a good virus protection program and update your antivirus .DAT files (definitions) on a regular basis. .DAT is the file extension used for a file or program that contains a list of the most current viruses. If you are running an enterprise network, you should incorporate a good enterprise antivirus solution. The top manufactures of antivirus software offer single-user or multi-user versions of their antivirus software programs. It is important to remember that computer viruses are most commonly obtained from the Internet and floppy disks.

Worms

A *worm* is a type of virus that gets its name from its inherent ability to spread itself to other networked systems, remain resident in memory, and keep in contact with other segmented pieces of itself until triggered by a certain event to duplicate and spread itself.

Most worm viruses reside in memory, unattached to files, and when triggered, will reproduce themselves until available resources are exhausted. A worm is a self-contained unit or program that is typically spread through e-mail attachments and network connections, such as drive mappings.

A worm is a type of virus that can replicate itself; however, worms do not attach to other programs. In other words, worms are not carried by or attached to hosting files.

Trojan Horses

A *Trojan horse* is a program that appears on the outside to be harmless. It masquerades itself as an apparently nondestructive, harmless, and innocent application, program, or message. Trojan horses can carry very dangerous payloads that are highly destructive to networks and systems.

Most Trojan horses are hidden in Internet attachments that oftentimes are distributed with e-mail in the form of jokes, love letters, and misguiding advertisements. One of the most important facts to understand about Trojan horses is that they do not replicate or copy themselves. They require actions by the user to activate and deliver their dangerous contents, such as the opening of an attachment or the running of an application. Worms and viruses duplicate themselves. Trojans do not.

Antivirus Practices

A combination of education, training, and management practices, along with the use of strong antivirus products, are essential to the survival and welfare of computer systems and networks.

There are some basic guidelines that should be followed when using and managing antivirus software at home or in a business enterprise:

- Install, update, and maintain reputable, quality antivirus software in servers and workstations. This includes setting up daily antivirus definition updates, enabling real-time protection, setting up scheduled scans of all system drives, and enabling e-mail and attachment scanning.

NOTE

If you are unable to install new software programs or device drivers on your system, your virus protection software or firewall may be blocking your install abilities. You may have to disable real-time protection or disable your entire antivirus suite altogether before installing new software. You should consult your antivirus manufacturer's manual for protection and new installation instructions.

- All users of computer systems (at home or in the workplace) should be educated/alerted when virus attacks occur or are expected to occur. Symantec Corporation does a great job at updating their Web site when virus threats are anticipated. This information can prove invaluable to administrators who need to apply particular patches or make updates in preparation for new or anticipated variations of viruses.

- Educate all users (at home or in the workplace) that opening e-mail attachments as well as instant messaging attachments may be detrimental to your system's life span.
- In a business environment, ensure that your corporate antivirus business policy is up to date and accurate. Ensure that new and existing employees sign an addendum that states they are familiar with the company's policy regarding computer usage as well as virus policy and procedures.

CABLE, ISDN, DSL, AND SATELLITE

Most connections to the Internet are accessed through an Internet Service Provider (ISP). A local or national ISP provides an IP address that can be used to gain access to the Internet. Although many individuals and businesses still use a 56Kbps analog dial-up connection to access the Internet, broadband services, such as cable, ISDN, and DSL, are becoming increasingly popular (and somewhat more affordable) based on their high transmission speeds and instant accessibility. See Table 22.2 for a quick reference of Internet technology connection types and associated speeds.

Cable

Broadband cable modem connections seem to be the Internet connectivity tool of choice for today's home users. All you really need for this technology is a cable modem, an NIC, RJ-45 cable, a coaxial cable, and an ISP. This technology allows Internet access speeds of around 1.5Mbps. It provides a connection similar to that of cable television. The signal is always at the end of the cable wire, waiting to be accessed; in other words, the connection is always available. There is no need to reconnect to the ISP every time you want to access the Internet.

TABLE 22.2 Internet Connection Types and Speeds

Connection Type	Average Connection Speed
Telephone modem	14.4–56Kbps
Cable modem	1–2Mbps
ISDN	128Kbps
DSL	1.5Mbps and higher
Satellite	400Kbps
T1 line	1.544Mbps

A traditional cable modem uses two connections. It connects to a wall-mounted incoming cable connection with a coaxial cable and connects to a computer system, hub, or router using a standard 10BaseT Ethernet cable with an RJ-45 connector.

The previously mentioned cable connection speed of approximately 1.5Mbps is much faster than that of a 56Kbps telephone modem. Cable is also faster than ISDN, which has a speed of approximately 128Kbps and currently competes with speeds by DSL.

Integrated Services Digital Network (ISDN)

ISDN is a baseband transmission technology that is well suited for the transmission of audio and video at rates of up to 128Kbps. ISDN utilizes an adapter that is included with an ISDN router in place of a standard analog modem.

There are two types of ISDN services typically available by ISPs or local phone carriers: basic rate interface and primary rate interface.

Basic Rate Interface (BRI): BRI is an ISDN technology made up of two 64Kbps B channels that carry data and voice and a 16Kbps D channel that is responsible for control information. BRI implementations are common for small-business and home use.

Primary Rate Interface (PRI): PRI is an ISDN technology that is used with larger businesses, such as ISPs and telecommunication companies. PRI is made up of 23 B channels and one D channel. PRI typically utilizes the bandwidth capabilities of a T1 connection.

ISDN has for the most part been replaced with DSL technology, which is described next.

Digital Subscriber Line (DSL)

DSL is a connection technology that uses regular copper wire telephone lines, or Plain Old Telephone Service (POTS), to bring access speeds of up to 6.1Mbps to homes or businesses. In actuality, DSL offers upload speeds of up to 128Kbps and download speeds of 1.5Mbps for individual connections. DSL utilizes a modem for a highly sophisticated modulation process and is well suited for high-speed transmission of audio and video.

DSL has provided major competition to the cable modem and is commonly used in locations that cable service or access is not offered.

Unlike using less secure cable modem services, DSL is not a shared service connection. To be more specific, you do not share your DSL connection with your neighbors, as cable subscribers do.

DSL implements two types of speeds. An upload speed, or 'upstream speed,' and a download speed, or 'downstream speed.' The upload speed represents how fast you can transmit information to other locations or computers connected to the Internet. The download speed represents how fast you can download such things as files, programs, or music to your system from other systems on the Internet.

As well as these two types of speeds, there are two separate forms of DSL technology available that can offer different speeds. They are ADSL (Asymmetric DSL) and SDSL (Symmetric DSL), which are described next.

NOTE *DSL is a connection technology that uses existing POTS wires. It requires a special modem and typically requires that a signal splitter be installed in the home or office. DSL is a technology that can be remotely activated.*

ADSL (Asymmetric DSL)

ADSL is by far the most commonly used form of DSL today. ADSL works simultaneously with voice over existing telephone lines. It works asymmetrically, meaning that the speed used for downstream receiving transmissions is far greater than the speed used for upstream sending. ADSL was developed with the home and small-business user in mind. The ADSL conceptual theory is based on the fact that the typical end user will download far more information than they will be sending.

It supports receiving data rates (downstream rate) from 1.5–9.0Mbps and sending data rates (upstream rates) from 16–640Kbps.

Remember for the exam, asymmetric means that transmission rates are not the same in both directions.

SDSL (Symmetric DSL)

SDSL is well suited for business applications and programs that require and depend on the same speed for sending and receiving data. In other words, with SDSL, your upstream speed is identical to your downstream speed. SDSL can support data rates up to 3Mbps.

SDSL operates on the same phone wires that are used for normal voice communication. But because SDSL technology works at higher frequencies than that of normal voice, it can exist on the same media without interfering.

Remember for the exam, symmetric means that transmission rates are the same in both directions.

SATELLITE

A satellite is a wireless communications device that orbits the earth, acting as a receiver/transmitter for such things as Internet connectivity and GPS (Global

Positioning Systems). A satellite Internet connection is similar to a satellite TV connection in that a satellite signal is transmitted to a receiver and the signal is decoded on the satellite subscriber's end. Most satellite Internet connections are considered asynchronous, with upstream speeds for a single system averaging 50–150Kbps and up to 1,200Kbps for downloads or 'downstreaming.'

Satellite connections are ideal for those who are located out of the range of cable and DSL service providers. In order to use a satellite Internet connection, you will need a satellite dish antenna, a transceiver (for transmitting and receiving), and a two-way satellite Internet service provider.

In general terms, here's how it works:

- The satellite dish antenna is mounted on or near your home or business.
- The satellite dish antenna is connected to a satellite modem (transceiver) with a coaxial cable.
- The satellite modem communicates with your PC through an Ethernet or USB connection.
- Information is transmitted to and received from a two-way geosynchronous satellite that orbits approximately 22,300 miles above the equator.
- The geosynchronous satellite communicates with a provider facility that is connected to the Internet.

Using an Internet satellite connection is not always perfect or guaranteed; it is not uncommon that such things as solar interference and periods of rain fade (signal loss caused by inclement weather) cause signal degradation or loss of connection.

FIREWALLS

A firewall is an implementation of software, hardware, or a combination of both, specifically designed to keep unauthorized users, programs, and other threats from entering a computer system or network. A typical firewall analyzes every packet of information that attempts to enter or exit a network or computer system. If the packet does not meet the specifications implemented by the firewall, the packet or connection is denied access. Several implementations of firewall techniques are provided through the use of a packet filter, a proxy server, an application, or a circuit gateway. For our test study focus, you should be aware that a software firewall is installed or located on a hard drive. For more protection from outside influences, you should also consider the use of data encryption.

There are many types of firewalls that can be implemented to protect inside information from outside sources. Some of the most common types of firewalls are:

Dual Homed Host: A dual homed host, sometimes referred to as multihomed, is a system with two NIC cards. One NIC card supports access to a private network, and one supports access to a public network. This acts as a filter, and is also known as a multihomed bastion host.

Packet Filter: Packet sniffing programs and network monitors can capture and analyze network packets coming into or going out of a network. A packet filtering firewall identifies good from bad packet information. The main fallback with most of the packet filtering programs available today is their inability to identify whether the packets were sent by a normal, innocent user or a threatening, vicious source.

Circuit Gateway: A circuit gateway operates at the session layer of the OSI reference model. It is essentially a packet filter that relays packets from one host to another based on protocol and IP address. A circuit gateway forms a sort of 'tunnel' through a firewall, allowing two specified hosts to interact.

Stateful Inspection Firewall: This type of firewall has the ability to remember detailed information about packets that have previously passed through them. Then, they are able to compare and analyze this information and decide whether to let certain packets through the firewall. In other words, a stateful firewall can compare incoming requests to outbound messages and see if there is a relationship between the two. If not, the firewall can block the incoming request. Stateful firewalls provide better overall analysis than most other firewall types, such as packet filters.

TROUBLESHOOTING AND BASIC NETWORKING TEST TIPS

The troubleshooting and basic networking test tips that are provided next have been included to give you a taste of the various types of networking topics and questions that may come your way on the real exam.

Pay very close attention to the following test tips. They just might be what you need to secure a passing score on the networking portion of the Core exam:

- If you have a workstation physically connected to your network, but you cannot PING or communicate with other systems on your network, you should first verify the link status on your network interface card and see if it is blinking.
- If you are connected to the Internet using a 56k modem, but your connection speed is only 28k, it is likely that there is noise on your phone line connection or your ISP is only handing out 28k connections.
- The easiest way to connect two computers that both have NIC cards in a peer-to-peer style network fashion is to use a crossover cable.

- A device called a repeater can be used to extend the length of a 10base2 network.
- If you keep receiving the message "This page cannot be displayed" while attempting to access a particular Web site, it is very likely that the host computer, which provides the resource you are trying to access, is having issues or is down.
- If you are using a dial-up connection and your mouse pointer freezes on your screen when you attempt to access the Internet, it is more than likely that you are experiencing an IRQ conflict. Check this first and then get cable or DSL!
- ISDN (Integrated Service Digital Network)—Carries data and voice over traditional telephone networks.
- DSL (Digital Subscriber Line)—Considered a better and faster replacement for ISDN, DSL is a technology that can provide considerable bandwidth capabilities to small business and homeowners alike. DSL uses traditional existing twisted pair telephone lines.
- Cable Modem—Considered the most insecure technology based on the fact that a default installation does not provide firewall or any other sort of packet filtering. With a default installation method, users share a single Coax cable connection.
- Wireless Technologies—Fastest growing area for connectivity.
- Dial-up (Asynchronous)—Traditional connection method that uses an ISP and an analog phone line to connect to the Internet.
- When assessing a network or computer related issue over the phone, you should only ask users or clients troubleshooting questions that are directly relate to gaining information that will assist with fixing the issue at hand. Questions such as, "When did this issue first start happening?" or "What were you specifically doing when the issue began?" are purposeful, structured questions that are directly focused on gaining helpful troubleshooting information. Questions such as, "What color is your mom's computer?" or "What kind of system would you buy if you won the lottery?" are useless when attempting to gain information that will directly affect the time it takes to resolve a system or network related issue. Yes, you may actually experience customer service related questions like this on the real exam.

CHAPTER SUMMARY

The primary focus of this chapter was to get you up to speed on the basic concepts of networking. At this point, you should be familiar with the basic network categories and topologies, and the media access methods used for networks. You should also have a basic understanding of TCP/IP and be able to troubleshoot simple network connectivity issues.

This chapter was designed to help you handle just about any networking questions the A+ Core exam may ask. Once again, however, there is no substitute for hands-on training. As a final important note and warning regarding your A+ Core Hardware Service Technician study, CompTIA seems to be putting more operating systems and set-up related questions into the Core Hardware exam. For example, the exam may ask you something like, "Where is regedit.exe found or stored?" For this reason, it is highly recommended that you complete the Operating Systems Study (Part II B) of this book to better increase your chances of passing the Core Hardware exam.

REVIEW QUESTIONS

1. A computer on your network is unable to communicate with other computers. What would you check first?

o A. That other computers are working

o B. That your Internet connection is functional

o C. The computer's IP address configuration

o D. The IP address configuration of the network file server

Correct Answer = C

If a single computer on your network cannot communicate with other systems on the same network, it is probable that its IP address is invalid or the system has not received an IP address from a DHCP server, which hands out IP addresses randomly on the network.

2. In order for two computers to communicate with each other, they must have a common language. What is this common language called?

o A. Binary conversion

o B. Data translation

o C. IPCONFIG /ALL

o D. Protocol

Correct Answer = D

In order for two computers to communicate, they must have a common language or set of rules known as a protocol. Binary conversion is a process used to convert binary numbers to decimal numbers to binary. IPCONFIG /ALL is a TCP/IP command used to display TCP/IP configuration settings.

3. What are two tools you can use to test a modem? (Choose Two)

□ A. A loopback plug
□ B. A digital multimeter
□ C. An analog loopback adapter
□ D. A small brush and compressed air

Correct Answers = A and C

A loopback plug or analog loopback adapter can be used to test the integrity of a modem. A digital multimeter is used to troubleshoot system power-related issues. A small brush and compressed air are used to clean a system unit.

4. You want to connect a new computer to your Ethernet network. What device must you install to do so?

o A. An internal modem
o B. A switch
o C. An IP converser
o D. A NIC card

Correct Answer = D

In order to communicate with your Ethernet network, you would need to install and configure a NIC card with associated software drivers.

5. Ten users on your network have all downloaded a fancy game from the same Internet site. Unfortunately, not one of the ten computers will work anymore. What question would ask each of the ten users?

o A. Is the game really worth it?
o B. Did you do this on company time?
o C. Did you virus scan the game's executable program before running?
o D. What version of BIOS is installed on your computer?

Correct Answer = C

If you get this question wrong, please start reading this book from page one again. ALWAYS VIRUS SCAN ANY PROGRAMS YOU DOWNLOAD FROM THE INTERNET!

6. Where do most computer viruses come from? (Choose Two)

□ A. A borrowed floppy disk

□ B. A mosquito

□ C. The Internet

□ D. Software provided by the manufacturer

□ E. A big wooden horse from Greek mythology

Correct Answers = A and C

Most computer viruses arrive through a borrowed floppy or other removable media disk or the Internet.

7. A customer cannot log into the network. Others on the network segment can log in without an issue. You are logged into the network using your computer and the customer's ID and password without an issue. What is most likely causing the login issue at the customer's workstation? (Choose Three)

□ A. The customer is entering the wrong password at his workstation.

□ B. The NIC card in the customer's workstation is malfunctioning.

□ C. The patch cable that attaches the customer's workstation to the network is bad.

□ D. The entire network is experiencing RFI (Radio Frequency Interference).

□ E. The switch that both you and the customer are attached to has been powered off.

Correct Answers = A, B, and C

Answers A, B, and C are valid choices. If the entire network were affected by RFI, you would have problems with more than one user. A network hub or switch is used to connect several computers together on a network. If the hub or switches were powered off, all users on that particular network would be affected.

8. What type of connections can be used with TCP/IP? (Choose Three)

□ A. Ethernet

□ B. Token Ring

□ C. Can and string

□ D. Analog modem dial-up connection

Correct Answers = A, B, and D

Ethernet, Token Ring, and modem connections can all be configured to use TCP/IP.

9. How can configuration settings on a network interface card be changed? (Choose Three)

□ A. Jumpers

□ B. Wire traces

□ C. Configuration software

□ D. Operating system's Plug-and-Play features

Correct Answers = A, C, and D

You can configure your NIC settings with onboard jumpers or NIC configuration software usually provided by the manufacturer. If you are using a Plug-and-Play operating system, your NIC setting can be configured automatically in most cases.

10. Which of the following represent peer-to-peer networks? (Choose Two)

□ A. Centralized administration and security

□ B. Limited number of computers (usually fewer than 10)

□ C. One computer can act as a client and a server

□ D. Requires a high-end server computer to provide login authentication and resources

Correct Answers = B and C

A peer-to-peer network is a small network, usually of 10 or fewer computer systems, connected without the use of a larger specialized server computer. In peer-to-peer networks, a workstation can function as both a client and a server computer.

11. You have a network interface card that doesn't have jumpers and is not Plug-and-Play-compliant. How will you configure it to be used with your system?

○ A. Purchase add-on jumpers.

○ B. Install IPX/SPX.

○ C. The operating system will detect it.

○ D. Use the manufacturer's configuration software.

○ E. None of the above.

Correct Answer = D

Legacy NICs were configured with the use of jumpers or DIP switches on the card itself. Today, most NIC settings are configured with the use of software provided by the manufacturer or simply by letting Plug and Play make the necessary settings automatically.

12. You are attempting to install a 64-bit video card driver for a newly purchase video card. When you try to install the driver, nothing happens. What could be the problem?

- o A. Most newer computer operating systems require P.A. (Parents Approval) before the installation of new video card drivers.
- o B. Your antiviral software of a firewall may be blocking your install abilities.
- o C. You forgot to enter the EULA (End User License Agreement) code for the video card software.
- o D. Your ISP does not allow 64-bit video cards to be used on connected systems.
- o E. All of the above.

Correct Answer = B

If you are unable to install new software programs or device drivers on your system, your virus protection software or firewall may be blocking your install abilities. You may have to disable real-time protection or disable your entire antivirus suite altogether before installing new software.

13. Which are considered to have the least amount of overhead and are meant for efficient communications in small networks or LANs?

- o A. TCP/IP and IPX/SPX
- o B. TCP/IP and NetBIOS
- o C. NetBEUI and TCP/IP
- o D. NetBIOS and NetBEUI
- o E. None of the above

Correct Answer = D

NetBIOS is not routable. NetBIOS works well in LANs not WANs. For WAN communication you need TCP/P. NetBEUI is a non-routable small efficient transport-layer protocol meant for use in small networks with 1–200 workstations.

14. With which type of DSL is the data rate considered the same in both directions?

- o A. ADSL (Asymmetric DSL).
- o B. SDSL (Symmetric DSL).
- o C. BiDSL (Bi-directional DSL).
- o D. DDRDSL (Dual Data Rate DSL).
- o E. All of the above transmit and receive data at the same data rate.

Correct Answer = B

SDSL (Symmetric DSL) is well suited for business applications and programs that require and depend on the same speed for sending and receiving data. With SDSL, your upstream speed is the same as your downstream speed.

15. Which statement is not true regarding DSL?

- o A. DSL most often uses exiting POTS lines.
- o B. ADSL and SDSL are DSL transmission types.
- o C. DSL most often requires a special DSL modem and splitter.
- o D. DSL is less secure than a cable modem Internet connection because a single DSL is shared.
- o E. All of the above statements are true.

Correct Answer = D

Unlike when you use less secure cable modem services, DSL is not a shared service connection. To be more specific, you do not share your DSL connection with your neighbors as cable subscribers do.

16. Which statement is not true regarding satellite Internet connectivity?

- o A. Satellite modems communicate with your PC through an Ethernet or USB connection.
- o B. A two-way geosynchronous satellite is used.
- o C. Satellite connections are ideal for those located outside the range of cable and DSL services.
- o D. In order to use a satellite Internet connection, you need a satellite dish antenna.
- o E. All of the above statements are true.

Correct Answer = E

All of the statements are true of satellite Internet connectivity.

REFERENCES

http://www.ieee.org/portal/index.jsp. This site is the home of the IEEE standards. The IEEE standards, as well as updates to these standards, can be viewed at this Web site.

http://www.geocities.com/SiliconValley/Monitor/3131/ne/osimodel.html. This Geocities.com site has an OSI reference model chart that describes each OSI layer, as well as associated protocols and network components. It is simply fantastic for basic networking study.

Part II

B

A+ Operating Systems Technologies Study (Exam 220-302)

23 Operating System Fundamentals and DOS

In This Chapter

- Operating System Fundamentals
- Introduction to DOS
- DOS System and Configuration Files
- DOS File Name Structure
- DOS Commands, Switches, and Wildcards
- DOS Windows Utilities
- Memory Management Utilities
- Windows Initialization Files
- Operating System Fundamentals Test Tips
- Chapter Summary
- Review Questions
- References

Welcome to the first chapter of our CompTIA A+ Operating Systems Technologies study guide. You may have noticed that the chapters in Part II B of this book are titled by individual operating systems, as opposed to the CompTIA domain structure titles. This structure is in place to not confuse the reader by going back and forth between operating systems within the same chapter, as many other books do. It is very important for you to learn and retain the concepts and functionality of each operating system individually. We will refer to and compare some of the functions in different operating systems within the same chapter, but the intention is to keep your focus on the particular operating system at hand.

CompTIA states that you should have at least six months of hands-on experience with the operating systems you will be tested on. These include DOS, Windows 9x, Windows NT, Windows Me, Windows 2000, and Windows XP. Be forewarned, however, that two years of hands-on experience with these operating systems is not enough to pass the tough CompTIA examination if you do not focus on the specific concepts and theories required to answer the test questions correctly.

Please keep in mind that this section of the book is designed to prepare you to take and pass the CompTIA A+ Operating Systems Technologies exam. It is not a substitute for hands-on experience, nor does it explain the entire history and every detail of all the operating systems covered.

The A+ Operating System Technologies exam will ensure that you are knowledgeable about the underlying command prompt (or line) functions associated with Windows 9x, Windows Me, Windows NT, Windows 2000, and Windows XP. Many of the DOS commands and command line utilities you will learn about in this chapter can be utilized through the command prompt provided with newer operating systems. It is therefore highly recommended that you pay close attention to the details and concepts in this chapter so that you are prepared for the command line functions and utilities discussed in the chapters that follow.

In this chapter, we focus on DOS (Disk Operating System) commands, procedures, and utilities. We also address system configuration files and DOS memory management.

Before we begin our focus on DOS, it is important for you to understand the basic functions of an operating system.

OPERATING SYSTEM FUNDAMENTALS

To run applications and interact with input and output devices, every functional computer system must have an operating system. An operating system is the core software platform of a computer system. It is the underlying program or set of programs on top of which applications reside.

Some of the more popular operating systems in use today are DOS, Windows, Novell Netware, OS/2, Unix, Linux, and Mac OS.

An operating system controls computer access, processing, and provides a user interface through which human beings interact with the computer system and its resources. Operating systems such as DOS and Unix provide a text-based user interface or environment. With a text-based interface, letters, numbers, and symbols are entered on a command line to communicate with the OS, whereas other OSs, such as Windows 9x, Windows Me, Windows NT, Windows 2000, and Windows XP provide a GUI (Graphical User Interface) environment.

In a GUI environment, graphic representations of commands, such as icons and menu bars, are used to interact with the OS. What about Windows 3x? For the record, Windows 3x is a GUI that sits on top of DOS. It is not technically considered an operating system. Windows 9x is a true multitasking GUI operating system that consists of three basic core files. They are GDI.EXE, KRL386.EXE, and USER.EXE.

An operating system is primarily responsible for the following:

- Providing a user interface used to store and manage data and programs.
- Providing a platform on which applications and commands can be run.
- Acting as a mediator for input and output devices.

The major Microsoft operating systems are:

- MS-DOS
- Microsoft Windows 3x
- Microsoft Windows 95 OEM Release, Win95A (OSR1), Win95B (OSR2), Win95C (OSR2) (Windows 9x refers to all versions of Windows 95)
- Microsoft Windows 98
- Microsoft Windows 98 Second Edition (SE)
- Microsoft Windows Millennium Edition (Me)
- Microsoft Windows NT 3.51
- Microsoft Windows NT 4.0 (Workstation and Server)
- Microsoft Windows 2000 (Professional and Server)
- Microsoft Windows XP (Home and Professional)
- Microsoft Windows 2003 (Server)

Before we move forward, it is important for you to understand the level of detail involved with the operating system test questions. The exam poses very specific questions that compare various operating system concepts and technologies. A good example of the comparison between operating system technologies is shown by the following sample question:

1. **You have one connection to the Internet that you want to share with other systems. Which operating systems will allow you to do this? (Choose Four)**

   □ A. Windows 2000

   □ B. Windows NT 4.0

   □ C. Windows 98

   □ D. Windows 98 SE

   □ E. Windows Me

   □ F. Windows XP

   □ G. Windows 95

   Correct Answers = A, D, E, and F

The question refers to Internet Connection Sharing (ICS), which is available in Windows 98 SE, and Windows 2000, Me, and XP. This type of detail is what makes the test so tough. You may know one or two operating systems inside and out, but you must remember the details of all the major systems in order to pass this test.

Keep in mind the following concepts of each operating system as we proceed:

- The file system structure of each operating system
- The minimum hardware requirements needed to install the operating system
- The boot or start-up file sequence for each operating system
- The emergency repair operations and procedures for each operating system (e.g., creating an emergency boot disk)
- The ability of an operating system to support new applications and APIs (Application Programming Interfaces)
- The methods used by each operating system to access, move, delete, copy, and rename files, as well as methods used to access certain hidden system files
- The methods used by each operating system to change and configure display, printer, modem, and Internet connection options and settings

Checking the Operating System Version

Operating systems are packaged in different releases and versions, each of which has its own set of characteristics and updates. Our study of operating systems focuses on the popular versions of MS-DOS, Windows 9x, Windows Me, Windows NT 4.0, Windows 2000, and Windows XP.

The exam will most likely test your ability to display an operating system's version by using the Control Panel in Windows or entering the VER (version) command at the command prompt.

To determine which operating system version of Windows 95/98, Windows Me, Windows NT, Windows 2000, or Windows XP is currently running on a computer, follow these steps:

1. Click the Start button, select Settings, and click Control Panel.
2. Double-click the System icon in the Control Panel.
3. Verify that the General tab is selected.
4. Look under the System heading for the operating system, version, and any service packs applied. You should also notice the total memory installed under the Computer heading. Figure 23.1 shows the Windows 2000 System Properties window of the installed operating system, version, service pack, and memory.

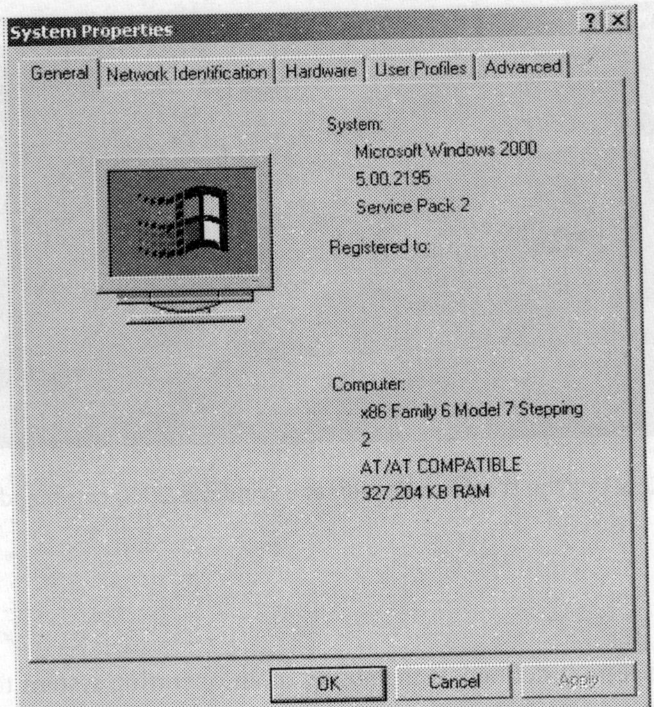

FIGURE 23.1 Checking the version of Windows in System Properties.

To determine which operating system version of DOS or Windows you are running from a command prompt, use the VER command. In a true DOS environment, type the VER command at the DOS command prompt (as follows) and press Enter:

```
C:\VER
```

The version of DOS will be displayed.

In a Windows 2000 environment, navigate to the command prompt by selecting Start > Programs > Accessories > Command Prompt, and type VER on the command line. Press Enter, and the version of Windows will be displayed. Figure 23.2 displays the VER command and the version of Windows at a Windows 2000 command prompt.

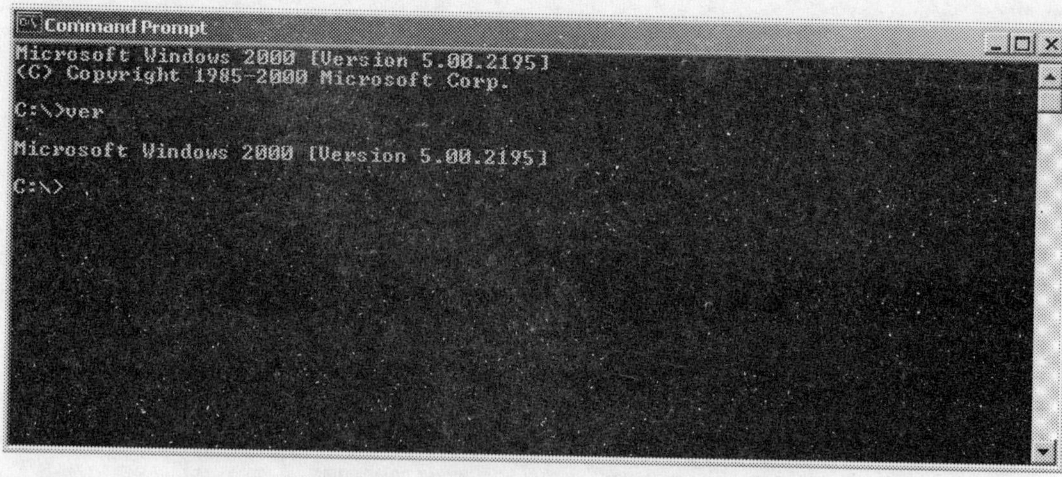

FIGURE 23.2 Checking the Windows Version at a Windows 2000 command prompt.

Multitasking

Multitasking is defined as the ability of an operating system to handle more than one function or carry out more than one task at the same time. Older operating systems, such as DOS, were designed to handle only one task at a time. Newer operating systems can handle many tasks at once. If you are using a relatively new OS, you can download MP3 files, run an application program, and take the A+ practice tests on the CD-ROM included with this book, all at once. There are two types of multitasking you should be familiar with:

Cooperative multitasking: With cooperative multitasking, the application or task is in control of the CPU until it is finished with processing. Cooperative multitasking is not considered true multitasking. Although more than one task at a time appears to be running, only one task actually gets the CPU cycle at a time. Windows 3x utilizes cooperative multitasking techniques.

Preemptive multitasking: With preemptive multitasking, the operating system hands out CPU time slices to applications or programs. The operating system is in control of how much time the application can have. When the period allotted expires, the OS stops the processing cycle and allots time to another application. Newer versions of Windows, such as Windows 9x/Me, NT, 2000, and Windows XP, as well as Unix, utilize preemptive multitasking techniques.

INTRODUCTION TO DOS

DOS is a 16-bit (FAT16), command line driven, text-based operating system. Microsoft's version of DOS is called MS-DOS. IBM's version of DOS is called PC-DOS. Our study and the current CompTIA exam focus on MS-DOS, which we refer to from now on simply as DOS. Microsoft has introduced 12 versions of pure DOS since the original 1.0 version. There is no need for you to study or memorize the fine details of each separate DOS version for this exam. However, it is important for you to understand how a 'pure DOS' environment works in order to understand how and why we still use the command prompt in newer releases of Windows. It is also important to note that not all DOS commands and functions are interchangeable between DOS versions and operating systems.

Windows 3x and Windows 9x require DOS and DOS system files in order to boot and function properly. These operating systems are basically GUIs that sit on top of DOS. Windows 95 attempted to separate from 'pure DOS' with its implementation of DOS version 7.0. Windows Me, 2000, NT 4.0, and Windows XP include specialized system files that allow them to boot and function without the necessity of DOS.

Command Interpreter

All Windows operating systems use a command interpreter. The command interpreter, also called a command processor, is a program built into an operating system that has the ability to interpret entries and make decisions based on the data entered with a mouse, keyboard, or other input device.

DOS, Windows 3x, Windows 9x, and Windows Me use the DOS file COMMAND.COM as the *shell*, or command interpreter. COMMAND.COM basically waits for instructions to be entered at a command prompt. It then makes a decision on whether to pass the instructions on to a program or display, such as an error message to the screen.

Unlike the version of DOS used with Windows 3x and Windows 9x, a file named CMD.EXE actually carries out the instructions entered at the Windows NT, 2000, and XP command line. In other words, CMD is the command interpreter for Windows NT, 2000, and XP.

The DOS file COMMAND.COM is actually a utility program that contains internal DOS commands, such as the DIR and COPY commands.

NOTE

CMD.EXE is a 32-bit command line interpreter in Windows NT, 2000, and XP.

DOS SYSTEM AND CONFIGURATION FILES

Three files make up the core of DOS: IO.SYS, MSDOS.SYS (which are hidden system files), and COMMAND.COM (which is a visible file). All three of these files are located on the primary active boot partition and are stored at the root of drive C:. All three files are required to successfully boot a system into DOS. They are also the minimum files required for booting Windows 9x to a DOS prompt. If one of these files is corrupt or missing, the message "Missing or unknown operating system" will be displayed.

Although these three system files meet the minimum requirements to boot to DOS on a Windows 9x OS, the complete DOS boot order is as follows.

1. IO.SYS—Interacts with the BIOS to determine the hardware environment.
2. MSDOS.SYS—Houses the DOS kernel and interacts with programs and devices.
3. CONFIG.SYS—Used primarily to load device drivers.
4. COMMAND.COM—Translator or interpreter of commands entered.
5. AUTOEXEC.BAT—Used to configure specific user settings.

NOTE

The exam may ask for the overall system starting order, regardless of what operating system you are running. The overall system start order is ***POST, BIOS, Boot Sector****, and* ***GUI****. See The Windows 9x Start-Up Process in Chapter 24 for further details.*

The major functions of the DOS system and configurations files, as well as their relationships with newer operating systems, are explained next.

IO.SYS

IO.SYS is a binary (uneditable) executable hidden file that is loaded first when a computer system is booted. IO.SYS works with the systems BIOS to determine what hardware is to be used by the operating system. IO.SYS is like a scout that discovers the physical layout of a system by looking at the CONFIG.SYS file, which is used to load hardware drivers and control DOS memory. Keep in mind that Windows 9x comes with a newer version of IO.SYS that replaces the old IO.SYS and MSDOS.SYS utilized in 'pure DOS.' The new version of IO.SYS eliminates the need for use of the AUTOEXEC.BAT and CONFIG.SYS files in newer operating systems. Newer operating systems still allow the use of AUTOEXEC.BAT and CONFIG.SYS to maintain backward compatibility with legacy programs and hardware.

NOTE

Binary files consist of 0s and 1s, and are basically unreadable without being interpreted. Text files contain readable characters that can be understood by the average human being.

MSDOS.SYS

MSDOS.SYS is a hidden system text file that contains the DOS kernel. The kernel is the core software code of an OS that is retained in memory to control all processes.

NOTE

The kernel that resides in the MSDOS.SYS file and the kernel used in newer operating systems are two totally separate things.

MSDOS.SYS is loaded after IO.SYS and is responsible for the interaction of software applications and hardware settings. MSDOS.SYS controls whether the computer will be booted into a DOS, Windows 3x, Windows 9x, or Windows Me GUI environment. If you want to set up Windows 9x or Windows Me for dual booting purposes, you can modify the BootGUI=0 to BootGUI=1 entry under [Options] in the MSDOS.SYS file.

NOTE

The BOOT.INI file is modified in Windows NT 4.0, Windows 2000, and Windows XP for dual booting purposes.

CONFIG.SYS

The CONFIG.SYS file is the first editable DOS configuration text file that you can modify at system start-up. Its primary function is to load 16-bit real mode device and memory management drivers for a DOS environment. At system start-up, MSDOS.SYS loads the device drivers and instructions specified in the CONFIG.SYS file before continuing on to AUTOEXEC.BAT.

In DOS, typing "EDIT CONFIG.SYS" or "EDIT AUTOEXEC.BAT" and pressing Enter at the DOS command prompt opens the DOS utility editor known as EDIT.COM. You can use EDIT.COM to view and make changes to the CONFIG.SYS and AUTOEXEC.BAT files. This can be very useful for troubleshooting if you encounter errors on start-up with settings in either of these files.

The CONFIG.SYS is available in Windows 9x and Windows Me for backward compatibility with legacy devices. It can be edited by running the SYSEDIT program at the Start > Run line in Windows 9x. Simply click Start > Run, then type in "SYSEDIT", and press Enter. Windows NT 4.0, Windows 2000, and Windows XP have basically replaced the CONFIG.SYS file with the file CONFIG.NT. You can also edit either of these files by using any available text editor in Windows, such as Notepad.

Next, we look at a typical CONFIG.SYS file that is used to configure hardware- and memory-related settings for a DOS Windows environment. Each of the lines in the following CONFIG.SYS file are described.

```
DEVICE=C:\WINDOWS\HIMEM.SYS
DEVICE=C:\WINDOWS\EMM386.EXE NOEMS
DEVICE=C:\DOS\SETVER.EXE
FILES=40
STACKS=9,256
BUFFERS=10
FCBS=16,0
DOS=HIGH,UMB
SHELL=C:\DOS\COMMAND.COM C:\DOS /P /E:1024
DEVICE=C:\WINDOWS\IFSHLP.SYS
DEVICEHIGH=C:\WINDOWS\COMMAND\ANSI.SYS
DEVICEHIGH=C:\MTMCDAI.SYS /D:MSCD0001
LASTDRIVE=Z
```

DEVICE=C:\WINDOWS\HIMEM.SYS: HIMEM.SYS is a memory device driver that allows device drivers to be loaded into the upper memory area. It is necessary for a Windows 3x operating system load.

DEVICE=C:\WINDOWS\EMM386.EXE NOEMS: This loads the EMM386 memory manager that manages the extended memory area.

DEVICE=C:\DOS\SETVER.EXE: This line loads the SETVER program that is used to instruct whichever DOS program is being run to recognize the MS-DOS version table that is currently loaded into system memory.

FILES=40: This sets the number of files that can be opened by DOS at one time. In this case, DOS can open or access 40 files.

STACKS=9,256: STACKS is a rarely used line-handled access to hardware interrupts. It was sometimes necessary to increase or decrease the STACKS value when receiving "Stack overflow" or "Internal stack failure" error messages.

BUFFERS=10: This line allows disk buffers to be loaded into memory for Windows to utilize.

FCBS=16,0: The number of File Control Blocks (FCB) that windows can have open and share at any one time is specified. FCBS can be set from 1 to 255. Today's programs rarely require the use of FCBS.

DOS=HIGH,UMB: This line should always be placed after the HIMEM.SYS line. It is used to load DOS into the upper memory block in the high memory area.

SHELL=C:\DOS\COMMAND.COM C:\DOS /P /E:1024: The SHELL command specifies the location and particular command interpreter that you wish

DOS to use. In this case, the SHELL command is telling the system to use the COMMAND.COM interpreter that is located in the C:\DOS directory.

DEVICE=C:\WINDOWS\IFSHLP.SYS: Otherwise known as the Installable File System (IFS) manager, this is a driver that assists with the integration of 32-bit APIs.

DEVICEHIGH=C:\WINDOWS\COMMAND\ANSI.SYS: ANSI.SYS is a driver that configures color, cursor, and keystroke settings in a DOS environment.

DEVICEHIGH=C:\MTMCDAI.SYS /D:MSCD0001: This line is used to load the real mode CD-ROM driver that will be used for the operating system. The CD-ROM driver in this statement must match the CD-ROM driver specified in AUTOEXEC.BAT.

LASTDRIVE=Z: The LASTDRIVE statement is used to specify the last drive letter that can be addressed by the system. If you are using this command, the letter assignment must be equal to at least the number of drives in your system. For example, if you have A, B, C, and D drives, the minimum setting for the LASTDRIVE= statement would be LASTDRIVE=D.

COMMAND.COM

As previously mentioned in this chapter, COMMAND.COM is responsible for translating what you input into the computer into information that the OS can understand. COMMAND.COM processes information entered and passes it back to MSDOS.SYS, where the operating system's kernel resides.

In DOS, COMMAND.COM is responsible for providing a user interface, such as the DOSSHELL or command prompt. With a default installation of DOS, Windows 3x, Windows 9x, or Windows Me, COMMAND.COM is stored in the root directory of the C: drive. Windows 9x and Windows Me also store a backup copy of COMMAND.COM in the C:\Windows directory. The AUTOEXEC.BAT file uses the SET COMSPEC= command to place COMMAND.COM in a location other than the root directory of C:. With Windows NT, Windows 2000, and Windows XP, COMMAND.COM is stored in the C:\WINNT\SYSTEM32 directory.

It is important to note that the DOS COMMAND.COM file should be from the same version of DOS installation as the IO.SYS and MSDOS.SYS files. If it is not, you may receive the error message "Incorrect DOS version" at system start-up.

AUTOEXEC.BAT

The AUTOEXEC.BAT (automatically executed batch) file is the second editable DOS batch file that is used at start-up to create an environment for the operating system. The AUTOEXEC.BAT file sets the stage for programs to run. It holds Terminate and Stay Resident (TSR) programs, such as DOSKEY and MOUSE.COM, which are held in RAM, and can be quickly accessed and easily loaded by the system. The AUTOEXEC.BAT sets environment variables with the PATH= statement, which is used to tell the system where to look for files and executable programs. The AUTOEXEC.BAT file is the last program that is run in the DOS boot sequence. It is important to remember that any command that is in the AUTOEXEC.BAT file can be run from the command prompt.

Now we will look at a typical AUTOEXEC.BAT file that is used to configure user-related and environment settings for a DOS Windows environment.

Each of the lines in the following AUTOEXEC.BAT file is described following the file listing.

```
@ECHO OFF
SET COMSPEC=C:\DOS\COMMAND.COM
SET TEMP=C:\TEMP
PROMPT $P$G
PATH=C:\;C:\WINDOWS;C:\DOS
REM LH C:\WINDOWS\COMMAND\MSCDEX.EXE /D:MSCD0001
DOSKEY
CLS
LH C:\MOUSE\MOUSE.EXE
WIN
```

@ECHO OFF: This line instructs DOS to turn ECHO off, which disables the display of DOS batch file messages on the screen when a batch file is executed.

SET COMSPEC=C:\DOS\COMMAND.COM: The SET command is used to specify or set environmental variables each time the AUTOEXEC.BAT is run. This SET statement sets a variable for the command interpreter.

SET TEMP=C:\TEMP: This statement sets a variable for the location of temporary files.

PROMPT PG: This line configures how the DOS prompt will display on screen. For example, PG displays C:\. You can change the prompt line to display the date, time, and DOS version, to name a just few possibilities.

PATH=C:\;C:\WINDOWS;C:\DOS: Please remember for the exam that the PATH= statement, or 'line,' is located in the AUTOEXEC.BAT file. This statement sets an environment variable that simply finds the location of a program. For example, if you are in the C:\Windows directory and want to run a program that is located in another directory, such as C:\DOS, that program can be executed from the C:\Windows directory as long as the C:\DOS directory is specified in the AUTOEXEC.BAT. You can tell the system where to look for a program on the fly by simply typing "PATH=(name of directory where file is located)" at a DOS prompt and pressing Enter.

REM LH C:\WINDOWS\COMMAND\MSCDEX.EXE /D:MSCD0001: Notice the REM statement at the beginning of this line; REM means remark. Any statements contained in the AUTOEXEC.BAT or CONFIG.SYS files that begin with the REM statement will not be processed when the file is loaded at system start-up. The statement that is being remarked out here contains the file MSCDEX.EXE. This file contains the driver necessary for DOS and Windows 3x to recognize and run a CD-ROM device. Remember for the test that Windows 9x has replaced the 16-bit MSCDEX.EXE with the 32-bit CD-ROM File System (CDFS).

DOSKEY: DOSKEY is a TSR program used to remember commands that you have entered at the DOS command line. It keeps a history of what you have entered. If DOSKEY is loaded into memory, you can use the up arrow or down arrow keys on your keyboard to scroll through recently entered commands.

CLS: This is a DOS command used to clear the screen. Only the DOS command prompt is left on the screen after the CLS command has been entered.

LH C:\MOUSE\MOUSE.EXE: This line loads the mouse executable program into upper memory, which will make more conventional memory available for other programs to run. Remember Chapter 17 and memory utilization? For the test, remember that LH statements are used in the AUTOEXEC.BAT file. DEVICEHIGH statements are used in the CONFIG.SYS file.

WIN: This command calls on the file WIN.COM. WIN.COM is used to configure the system automatically to boot directly into the Windows 3x GUI. If the WIN statement is not in AUTOEXEC.BAT, the system will boot to a DOS prompt. Four switches can be added to the WIN command; each switch starts Windows 3x in a different mode. The four switches used with the WIN command are /R, which starts Windows 3x in Real Mode; /S, which starts the OS in Standard Mode; /3, which starts Windows 3x in Enhanced Mode; and /B, which is used to keep a log file of Windows 3x start-up problems.

NOTE

WIN.COM is built into Windows 9x.

DOS FILE NAME STRUCTURE

DOS files are stored in directories or subdirectories. In today's Windows world, directories are called *folders.* In DOS, specific rules apply to creating and naming files and directories.

DOS uses what is called an 8.3 file-naming structure, otherwise known as *eight dot three.* This simply means that a file name can be up to eight characters long and have a three-character extension representing the file type. A period is used to separate the file name from the extension. The total length of the DOS file name, plus the extension, cannot exceed 11 characters. The file extension is not necessary unless the file is associated with a particular function. Table 23.1 displays a list of common DOS Windows file extensions with their associations.

Let's use the DOS file name AUTOEXEC.BAT as an example. The AUTOEXEC segment is the DOS file name. The .BAT extension specifies that the file is a batch file. The same is true for the CONFIG.SYS file. CONFIG is the name of the file, and the .SYS extension identifies the file as a system file.

Following are rules that apply to DOS file and directory name creation:

- A file or directory name can be no more than eight characters long.
- An extension can be no more than three characters long.
- No spaces can be included in the file name, the extension, or the directory name.
- Certain characters (? * , ; = + #### >| [ ] / \) are illegal and cannot be used.

TABLE 23.1 DOS/Windows Common File Extensions

File Extension	Association
.BAK	DOS backup file
.BAT	DOS file housing a sequence of commands
.BMP	Windows bit-mapped graphics file
.CAB	Windows 9x cabinet file
.COM	DOS command program file
.DLL	Windows dynamic link library file
.DOC	Text document file (usually Microsoft Word)
.EXE	DOS executable program
.GRP	Windows 3x program group file
.HTM	Hypertext markup language file
.ICO	Windows 3x icon file
.INI	DOS Windows initialization file
.SYS	DOS system driver/hardware configuration file
.TMP	Temporary file
.TXT	Text file created by DOS or the Windows text editor
.VXD	Virtual device driver file

Long File Names (LFNS)

Windows 9x, NT, 2000, Me, and Windows XP support long file names (LFNs). LFNs can be up to 255 characters in length. Although these newer operating systems support LFNs, they still allow for backward compatibility with the 8.3 naming structure associated with DOS by creating an associated 8.3 file name for every new file created. LFNs are broken into 12-byte sections that allow the use of up to 255 characters, as in the following:

```
LFN = BEST CERTIFICATIONBOOK.DOC
8.3 associated file name = BESTCE~1.DOC
```

Notice that the space after BEST is eliminated in the 8.3 associated file name. Windows automatically removes any spaces or invalid characters and truncates the file name.

It is important to note that the Windows 9x root directory (C:\) can hold only 255 files. The truncation of LFNs to 8.3 names can quickly fill up this 255-file storage limitation and cause your system to halt. For this reason and others, it is good practice to avoid storing files in the root directory of any operating system.

The following PC Guide Web site has a great page that describes LFNs: *http://www.pcguide.com/ref/hdd/file/fatLong-c.html.*

File Attributes

System files in DOS and Windows, such as IO.SYS and MSDOS.SYS, are hidden, read-only system files. This means that they cannot be viewed or deleted unless their file attributes are modified. Four major attributes can be assigned to DOS and Windows files: R (read-only), A (archive), H (hidden), and S (system).

In DOS, the ATTRIB command can be used to modify the attributes of a file at the command line. For example, to change the attributes for the system file MSDOS.SYS from a read-only/hidden file, enter the following command at a DOS prompt:

```
C:\ATTRIB -R -H MSDOS.SYS
```

This command removes the read-only and hidden attributes associated with the file. You will then be able to read and delete the file. Please don't delete MSDOS.SYS until you are certified. You can add the attributes back to MSDOS.SYS by issuing the following command at the DOS prompt:

```
C:\ATTRIB +R +H MSDOS.SYS
```

In Windows 9x, Me, NT, 2000, and Windows XP, the attributes of a file can be viewed and changed (if the currently logged on user has permissions to do so) by simply right-clicking a file in Windows Explorer and either checking or unchecking the appropriate file attribute.

To locate the file MSDOS.SYS in Windows 9x, right-click the Start button. Left-click Explore, then left-click View (located on the top menu bar). Left-click Folder Options, then left-click View. Under the Files and Folders/Hidden Files section, left-click "Show all files," then left-click Apply and left-click OK. Close the Folder Options window. The MSDOS.SYS file, along with other system files, will now be visible on the right side of screen. Find the MSDOS.SYS file and right-click it. Left-click Properties. You should now see a window similar to the one shown in Figure 23.3. You can remove the selected file attributes by removing the check marks, or you can add desired attributes by adding check marks. Keep in mind that folders as well as files also have attributes.

NOTE

Many important operating system files are hidden with a typical default operating system installation for the protection of the average user. You should always remember to "Show all files" or "Show hidden files and folders" under Folder Options before troubleshooting.

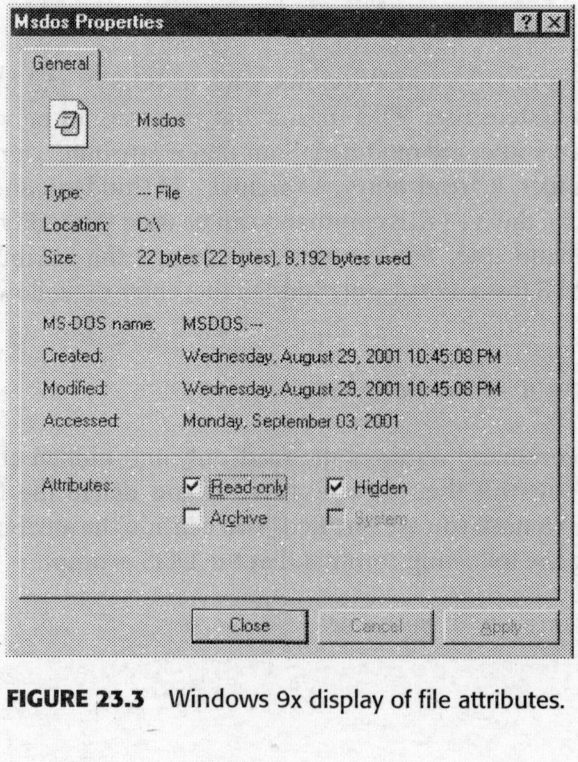

FIGURE 23.3 Windows 9x display of file attributes.

DOS COMMANDS, SWITCHES, AND WILDCARDS

DOS has its own set of commands that are entered at a DOS command prompt to instruct the operating system to carry out specific instructions or tasks. DOS commands are defined as internal or external.

- Internal DOS commands reside in the DOS file COMMAND.COM. They are the most commonly used DOS commands implemented at the DOS command prompt. Some examples of internal DOS commands are COPY, DIR, DEL, RD, and CLS.
- External DOS commands are typically located in the C:\DOS directory. They are usually associated with running a program or a task. External DOS commands are most often associated with file extensions such as .COM, .BAT, and .EXE. External DOS commands are often implemented by more advanced users. Some examples of external DOS commands are DELTREE, ATTRIB, EDIT, and MEM.

You should be familiar with the important DOS commands and switches displayed in Table 23.2. Practice using these DOS commands.

Switches

Switches are symbols used in conjunction with DOS commands that instruct DOS to carry out specific functions, such as displaying a screen in wide view or pausing a screen after a certain number of lines have been displayed.

The most common switch is the forward slash (/). It is often used in conjunction with the DIR command. For example, if you enter "DIR /P" switch at a DOS or Windows command prompt, 23 lines will be displayed at a time. You can then press Enter for the next 23 lines to display, and so on. This lets you read what is listed one page at a time instead of watching many pages scroll by. If you enter the "DIR /W" switch, a wide view of the files in the current directory will be displayed to the screen.

A very useful switch to utilize in a DOS or Windows environment is the forward slash question mark switch (/?). When this switch is entered in combination with a DOS command, you are presented with a screen that displays all the switches that can be used with that DOS command, as well as the function of each. Figure 23.4 displays the DIR /? switch and its results at a Windows 2000 command prompt.

Wildcards

Two wildcards used in DOS and Windows allow you to find or display multiple occurrences of similar file name associations. In other words, wildcards are used to

TABLE 23.2 DOS Commands and Switches

Command	Function	Switches Used
ATTRIB	Displays or sets the attributes of a file	+R/-R,+A/-A,+S/-S,+H/-H
CD	Changes to another directory	\ Takes you to the root
CD..	Back up one directory level	
COPY	Copies the files and directories	
XCOPY	Copies file directories and subdirectories	/H Copies hidden files /S Copies subdirectories /V Verifies each file copied
DISKCOPY	Copies the entire disk	
DEL	Deletes a file	
DELTREE	Deletes the directory, subdirectory, and files	
TREE	Displays directory and subdirectory structure	| more View one screen
DIR	Displays all files in current directory	/P Pauses each screen /W Displays wide view
MEM	Displays memory used and available	/C Detail memory list
MD	Creates or makes a directory	
MOVE	Moves a file	
RD	Removes a directory or subdirectory	
REN	Renames a file	
SETVER	Updates the current DOS version table	
SYS	Makes a drive bootable by copying the three main system files to it; used to create bootable DOS disks	
VER	Displays the version of DOS installed	

find or identify common directories and files. DOS reserves the question mark (?) and the asterisk (*) to be used as wildcards. These wildcards can also be used through a Windows GUI at the command prompt or in Windows 2000 by selecting Start > Search > For Files or Folders, and then entering the required criteria in the Search for files or folders named selection box.

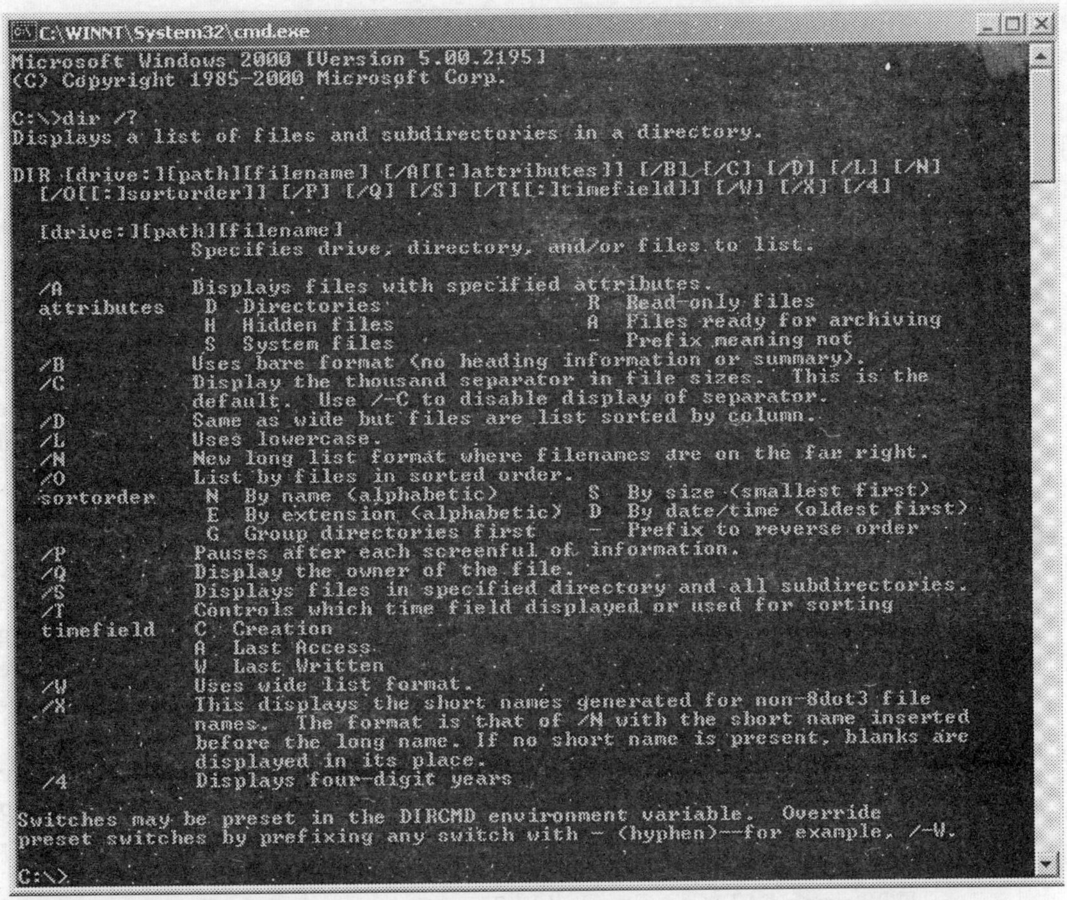

FIGURE 23.4 The /? switch results displayed at a Windows 2000 command prompt.

Asterisk (*): The asterisk symbol replaces the characters to the right of itself and finds all instances of the specified criteria. For example, if you enter "DIR *.*" at the C: prompt in DOS, all the files in the ROOT directory of C:\ are displayed. If you are in the C:\Windows directory and enter "DIR *.INI" all the .INI files in the C:\Windows directory are displayed.

Question mark (?): The question mark wildcard is similar to the asterisk, except that the question mark can represent only one character at a time for each question mark specified. For example, if you wanted to find all of the .INI files stored in the C:\Windows directory from a command prompt, you would enter the following:

```
C:\WINDOWS\DIR *.INI
```

To display the .INI files with up to three characters in the file name, enter the following:

```
C:\WINDOWS\DIR ???.INI
```

DOS WINDOWS UTILITIES

Several DOS command prompt utilities can be very useful to a computer technician for memory configuration and hard drive or floppy disk preparation. A few of the more useful DOS utilities are described next, with an emphasis on how some of them are used through the GUIs of newer operating systems.

FDISK and FORMAT

The two DOS command line utilities FDISK and FORMAT were described in detail in Chapter 20. It is important to remember that FDISK is a disk-partitioning utility used to separate one physical hard drive into 24 logical partitions for more efficient use of storage. FDISK also makes it possible for you to install multiple operating systems on one physical drive.

Before you run FDISK, consider which operating system or systems you are going to install and how much space you need to allocate for each partition. Keep in mind that different BIOS settings can affect the size of the partitions you can create, and that various file systems require different cluster sizes.

DOS uses a FAT16 partition table. The maximum size of a FAT16 partition is 2.1GB. Windows 95 B/C and Windows 98 use a FAT32 partition table that allows for a single partition to reach 2TB (terabytes) in size.

Following are some important notes about FDISK.

- You can use the FDISK command FDISK/MBR from a DOS prompt to construct a new Master Boot Record (MBR) if yours has become corrupt or infected by a virus.
- You can partition a disk in Windows 2000 using disk management (this is discussed in Chapter 26).
- FDISK is accessible from a bootable floppy disk, which can be useful for troubleshooting undetected hard drive issues. For example, suppose you have a desktop or laptop system that does not detect a hard drive when booted. You can boot to a bootable floppy disk and run the FDISK utility on the undetected hard drive to see if the drive is configured properly.

The FORMAT utility is used to prepare a hard disk or floppy for a file system. Remember, FORMAT.COM creates the FAT (File Allocation Table) and the root directory on a hard disk or floppy disk.

The syntax for formatting a floppy disk from a DOS or Windows command prompt is as follows.

```
C:\FORMAT A: /S
```

The /S option copies the three system files necessary to make the disk bootable.

To format a floppy disk in Windows 9x or Windows 2000, simply insert a blank floppy disk into your 3.5-inch floppy drive, navigate to Windows Explorer, and right-click the 3½ Floppy (A:) icon (drive A:). Next, left-click Format. The Format A: window appears. Click Start to begin the formatting process.

SYS

As mentioned above, SYS is really a DOS command. It is used to copy the three main DOS system files (IO.SYS, COMMAND.COM, and MSDOS.SYS) to a disk. The proper syntax for using the SYS command is C:\SYS A:. The message "System transferred" appears after the command has been entered.

This is an easy way to transfer the system files to a disk without going through the whole format routine. If you are missing the important system files on your hard drive, you can also use the SYS command to SYS C: from a floppy.

CHKDSK and SCANDISK

CHKDSK is an old DOS utility that was used to search out bad clusters and lost allocation units on a hard drive. It was common to implement the CHKDSK /F command to attempt to repair bad clusters. The CHKDSK utility has been, for the most part, replaced by the ScanDisk utility. ScanDisk is a Microsoft disk analysis and repair utility that is used to recover and repair lost or bad clusters on a disk. Windows 9x and Windows Me utilize a GUI version of ScanDisk that can be accessed and run by selecting Start > Programs > Accessories > System Tools > ScanDisk. You can use the GUI version of ScanDisk to scan your floppy or hard disk. You will have the option of running a standard scan, which checks files and folders for errors, or a thorough scan, which also scans the disk surface for errors. For best results, make sure that you select the thorough option and place a check mark in the "Automatically Fix Errors" box before you start the scan.

To check a disk for errors in Windows NT, Windows 2000, and Windows XP, open My Computer and right-click on the drive you wish to check. Select Properties > Tools, and under Error-checking, select Check Now...; a Check Disk message box will open, and you will have the options to "Automatically fix file system errors" and "Scan for and attempt recovery of bad sectors." You should then select both options and click Start. If you are checking your system drive, you will receive a message stating that the disk check could not performed because the check utility needs exclusive access to the drive. In the same message box, you are asked if you would like to schedule the check on the next restart of your computer. If you select "Yes" the check utility will run the next time your computer is restarted.

Defrag

Defrag is a DOS and Windows utility that improves system performance by placing files that are fragmented into a contiguous order on a hard or floppy disk. In the Windows world, the program is actually called Disk Defragmenter. This tool can be run from Windows 9x, Me, 2000, or Windows XP by selecting Start > Programs > Accessories > System Tools > Disk Defragmenter. Alternately, you can open My Computer, right-click the C: drive, left-click Properties, select Tools, and select Defragment now. Windows NT does not come with a built-in defrag utility.

Keep in mind that there are usually at least three ways to accomplish the same task in a typical Windows GUI. You must practice these concepts and explore others if you want to become a well-rounded technician. See if you can find a third way to use the defragmenter utility in Windows 9x. Here is a hint: Start > Run > ...

SMARTDRV.EXE

SMARTDRV.EXE and SMARTDRV.SYS make up a 16-bit disk caching utility that is used to improve the access speed to data stored on a hard drive in a DOS or Windows 3x environment. The SMARTDRV line is only used in the AUTOEXEC.BAT file. Windows 9x uses a 32-bit program known as VCACHE in place of SMARTDRV. VCACHE can automatically adjust the hard drive's cache size based on the needs of the operating system and programs.

MSD.EXE

MSD.EXE is a DOS-based utility that is executed at the command prompt. It is used to view information on the system configuration, including devices, memory, video display, mouse, disks, ports, and TSR programs. In the old DOS days, MSD was a very useful program that provided vital information for troubleshooting. Although MSD.EXE is included on the Windows 9x installation CD-ROM, most people prefer to use the Device Manager in Windows 9x for troubleshooting purposes.

POWER.EXE

POWER.EXE is an optional program that is loaded in CONFIG.SYS. If your computer supports Advanced Power Management (APM), the POWER.EXE driver can be loaded to reduce the amount of power a system uses when it is idle.

The syntax for loading the POWER.EXE device driver in the CONFIG.SYS file is as follows:

```
DEVICE=[drive:] [path] POWER.EXE
```

POWER.EXE has proven to be a very useful tool for conserving battery life in laptop computers.

LABEL.EXE

The LABEL.EXE utility is used to create, change, or remove the name of a disk. The LABEL command can be used in DOS, Windows 9x, Me, NT, 2000, or Windows XP to create a volume name of up to 11 characters, including spaces. Use the following syntax to label a floppy disk:

```
C:\LABEL A: [Enter a label name up to 11 characters in DOS.]
```

DEBUG.EXE

DEBUG.EXE is simply a DOS program that is used to debug or test programs. Changes made to programs using DEBUG.EXE cannot be undone; therefore, only advanced users should use it.

MEMORY MANAGEMENT UTILITIES

In Chapter 17, you were introduced to the basic DOS memory model and concepts. You should recall that conventional memory is used primarily for programs and applications. *Conventional memory* encompasses the first 640K of memory used in the DOS memory structure. *Expanded Memory Specification* (EMS) is extended or reserved memory that emulates conventional memory. It ranges from the top of the 640K barrier to 1024K. The High Memory Area (HMA) utilizes the top 384K of expanded memory in the DOS memory model. The *Extended Memory Specification* (XMS) is above the HMA. It includes all the memory addresses over 1088K. If you need more information about this structure, refer to Chapter 17 for a refresher.

Several DOS memory management utilities and software drivers organize and make better use of available memory.

- MEMMAKER is a DOS memory utility program that is run from a DOS command line. It loads device drivers and TSRs into Upper Memory Blocks (UMBs). This helps to free up conventional memory space for programs.
- HIMEM.SYS is a DOS device driver loaded in the CONFIG.SYS that allows applications to run in extended memory. HIMEM.SYS is also present in Windows 9.x. In fact, both Windows 3x and Windows 9x require HIMEM.SYS for booting up.
- EMM386.EXE is a DOS memory management utility that opens the door to UMBs so that software drivers and programs can be loaded. EMM386.EXE uses limulation. *Limulation* is a technique used to translate or change extended memory to expanded memory.

Virtual Memory and Swap Files

A portion of a hard disk that is set aside for a certain range of memory address is referred to as virtual memory. This space on the hard drive acts as a sort of overflow buffer for RAM, or 'real memory' as more memory is needed. A process called memory paging is used to create and swap memory addresses in and out of the hard drive's allocated virtual memory space. The main purpose of virtual memory is to allow the CPU to use hard drive space as memory. The virtual memory manager controls virtual memory. If the virtual memory manager cannot allocate memory requested by a specific application in Windows 9x, a page fault will occur.

Virtual memory space is allocated on a hard drive in two ways: as a temporary swap file and as a permanent swap file.

- A *temporary swap file* is hard drive space that is used temporarily for memory overflow. If the computer is powered off, all information in the temporary swap file is lost. In other words, a temporary swap file is considered volatile memory. The original temporary swap file was named WIN386.SWP in Windows 3x.
- A *permanent swap file* doesn't go away when the computer system is turned off. It handles the memory paging process faster than a temporary swap file. The permanent swap file was called 386PART.PAR in Windows 3x.

The procedures for changing virtual memory settings in Windows 9x, Me, NT, 2000, and Windows XP are discussed in their respective chapters (i.e., Chapters 24, 25, 26, 27, and 28).

The Virtual Machine

When you start a DOS session or go to the command prompt from within Windows, the OS actually creates a separate memory space for your session to run in. This is called a Virtual Machine (VM). It was evident in Windows 3x that multitasking was occurring, because the user could open several 'DOS windows' or VMs at once.

The most important thing to realize about VMs is that they run in their own protected memory space. This means that if one program running in its own VM fails, other programs running in separate VMs are not affected. In other words, you can open multiple DOS or command prompt sessions. If one of the sessions fails, the other sessions will not be affected. This explains why the core components of an operating system, such as KERNEL.EXE, GDI.EXE, and USER.EXE, are designed to run in a protected memory space—so that they are protected from other programs that may fail.

In Windows 3x, we used Program Information Files (PIFs) to allocate specific amounts of memory to our separate DOS VMs. In newer operating systems, you can still create PIF files and assign properties to VMs.

To display the assigned properties of the MS-DOS prompt in Windows 95, click Start > Programs, right-click the MS-DOS prompt, and left-click Properties. You will see the following tabs: General, Program, Font, Memory, Screen, and Misc. If you click the Memory tab, you will see the conventional, expanded, and extended memory assigned to the DOS VM. If you click the Program tab and select Advanced, the window shown in Figure 23.5 will display. If you are trying to run a DOS application in a Windows 95 environment and receive the message "This Program cannot be run in Windows," you should make sure that the "Prevent

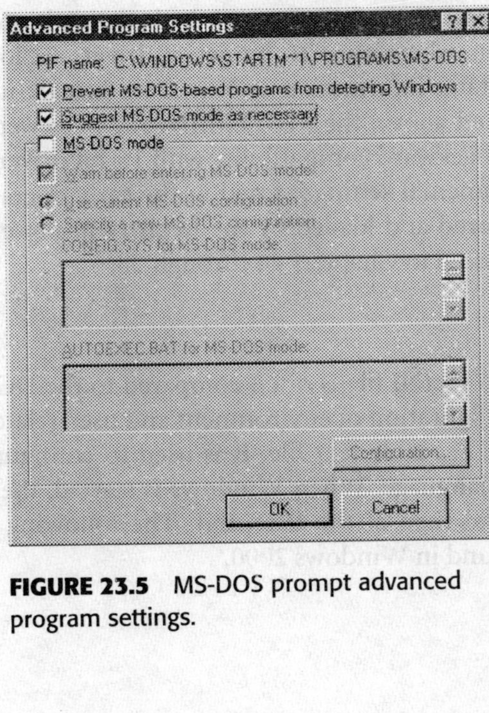

FIGURE 23.5 MS-DOS prompt advanced program settings.

MS-DOS-based programs from detecting Windows" box (also shown in Figure 23.5) is checked for the advanced properties of the DOS prompt properties associated with the application. Click OK twice and run your DOS application again.

WINDOWS INITIALIZATION FILES

Initialization files are Windows plain ASCII configuration text files that have an .INI extension. Windows 3x used the SYSTEM.INI, WIN.INI, PROGRAM.INI, and PROTOCOL.INI files to configure almost all its settings and device drivers. Operating systems such as Windows 9x, Me, 2000, and Windows XP still make use of .INI files, such as the SYSTEM.INI, to load old 16-bit drivers for backward compatibility. However, the newer operating systems do not need these files to boot up, as did Windows 3x.

The main Windows initialization files and the text editors used to view and modify them are described next.

The SYSTEM.INI

The SYSTEM.INI file got its start in Windows 3x. It is a configuration file that is used to load 32-bit VxDs (Virtual Device Drivers) and 16-bit device drivers. It is often said that the SYSTEM.INI is the Windows version of the DOS file CONFIG.SYS, because it deals mostly with device settings and drivers.

The SYSTEM.INI file in Windows 3x is divided into two main sections: the [386Enh] section, where most 16-bit device drivers are loaded; and the [boot] section, which contains information on Windows 3x start-up operations.

As mentioned above, the SYSTEM.INI file in newer versions of Windows is maintained for backward compatibility with 16-bit drivers. Most of the device drives and environmental settings stored in the early operating system initialization files are now stored and loaded by the Registry in newer operating systems. The Registry is discussed in Chapters 24 through 28.

The WIN.INI

The Windows WIN.INI file is often compared to the DOS file AUTOEXEC.BAT, based on its configuration of environment and user-related settings. The WIN.INI is also an ASCII readable text file. It is used to configure settings such as fonts, date, time, and language. When Windows is started, the system looks first at the SYSTEM.INI and then at the WIN.INI. The following lines are from a typical WIN.INI file found in Windows 2000.

```
; For 16-bit app support
[fonts]
[extensions]
[mci extensions]
[files]
[Mail]
MAPI=1
CMC=1
CMCDLLNAME=mapi.dll
CMCDLLNAME32=mapi32.dll
MAPIX=1
MAPIXVER=1.0.0.1
OLEMessaging=1
[MCI Extensions.BAK]
```

There are two items here that are important to note. Notice the first line of the WIN.INI file:

```
; For 16-bit app support
```

The semicolon (;) is used to remark out the line. This line is being used for informational purposes only. The semicolon can also be used in the SYSTEM.INI to exclude a line from being processed.

NOTE

The semicolon is used in .INI files to remark out information. In AUTOEXEC.BAT and CONFIG.SYS files, the REM statement is used to remark out information.

Text Editors

Text editors such as SYSEDIT.EXE, Notepad, and WordPad can be used in Windows to view and edit the SYSTEM.INI, WIN.INI, CONFIG.SYS, and AUTOEXEC.BAT files. The SYSEDIT utility in particular can be used in any of the major operating systems for this purpose. For example, in Windows 9x, NT, AND 2000, click Start > Run, enter "SYSEDIT" on the Open: line, and click OK. The SYSTEM.INI, WIN.INI, CONFIG.SYS, and AUTOEXEC.BAT files will open as displayed in Figure 23.6.

NOTE

The SYSTEM.INI, WIN.INI, CONFIG.SYS, and AUTOEXEC.BAT files display different results on different systems. The display depends on which operating system you are running and what else you have installed on your system.

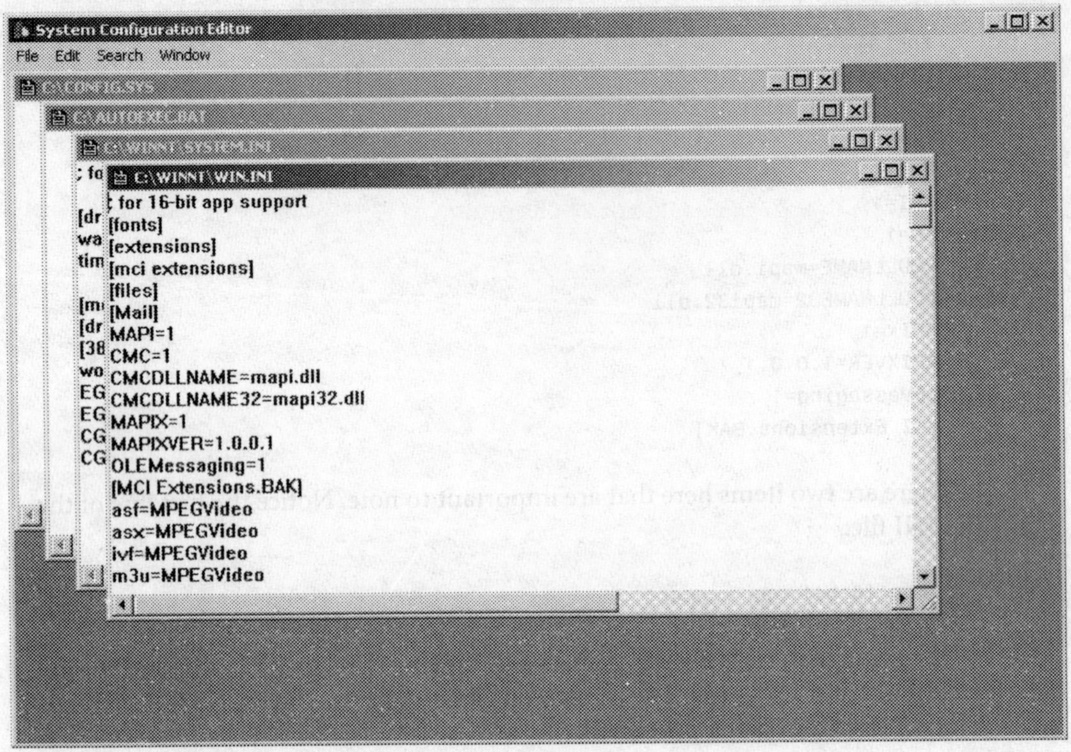

FIGURE 23.6 The results of SYSEDIT in Windows 2000.

OPERATING SYSTEM FUNDAMENTALS TEST TIPS

The following operating system fundamentals test tips will assist you with your final test preparation. Although some of these tips are not explained in detail in this chapter, they are important facts that may prove valuable to you in the exam room. Remember them.

- ✓ A corrupt or very old version of the file command.com can lead to the error message "bad or missing command.com." To correct this issue, you can boot to an emergency repair disk and use the SYS.COM to correct this error.
- ✓ In Windows 95, a duplicate copy of COMMAND.COM can be found in C:\WINDOWS.
- ✓ The operating system Windows 3x used a utility called file manager to manage folders and files. Early versions of Windows 9x used this File Manager instead of "Explore" which is found in newer versions of Windows. It

should be noted that File Manager does not support long file name structures. File manager will truncate long file names to 8.3 names.

- ✓ If you are installing a program and it cannot make changes to files such as AUTOEXEC.BAT or CONFIG.SYS, you should verify that their attributes are not set to read only. From a DOS prompt type ATTRIB -R and the file name. Or right-click the File:Select Properties and uncheck the read only box in Windows Explorer.
- ✓ To hide a file while at a DOS command prompt enter: ATTRIB +H (FILENAME).
- ✓ If you receive error messages that state there is not enough disk space while trying to install old DOS legacy programs (FAT16) on newer Operating Systems (FAT32), it is likely that the old DOS programs do not recognize the FAT32 file system. The maximum size of a FAT16 logical drive is 2GB. FAT32 has a 2TB limit.
- ✓ In most Windows Operating Systems, you can type SYSEDIT or REGEDIT in at the Start:Run command line to troubleshoot SYSTEM.INI, WIN.INI, AUTOEXEC.BAT, CONFIG.SYS or Windows Registry related issues.
- ✓ If you ever receive the message "sector 0 bad, disk not usable" while formatting a hard drive, it is very likely that you have a bad or defective hard drive.
- ✓ The tool EDIT.COM can easily be used to edit text files from a command prompt.
- ✓ To easily display the current running operating system in Windows, right-click on the My Computer icon, then select Properties.
- ✓ FDISK/MBR will repair a master boot record.
- ✓ The proper syntax for formatting a floppy disk from a command prompt would be FORMAT A:
- ✓ If you want to edit MSDOS.SYS from a command prompt, you must first enter ATTRIB -S -H -R MSDOS.SYS.
- ✓ With protected mode memory, the operating system manages memory resources and controls application access to memory.
- ✓ Disk Defragmenter is used to improve hard disk access time, which results in faster data transfers.
- ✓ The command line utility SCANREG can be used to restore a backed up copy of a Registry if the Registry has become damaged or corrupt.
- ✓ If your system's BIOS is set to boot to a floppy and you boot with an unformatted floppy disk inserted in your floppy drive, you will receive the error message "No operating system found."
- ✓ Using the /? Switch after a particular DOS command will list the possible switches available for the DOS command as well as their functions.

✓ If you want to check your "C" drive for surface disk errors before Windows 9x starts, you can enter SCANDISK C:/SURFACE from a command prompt. Also remember, SCANDISK fixes cross-linked files.
✓ To truly be considered Plug and Play, an environment requires a Plug-and-Play operating system, BIOS, device drivers, and peripheral devices.

CHAPTER SUMMARY

This chapter has given you a solid foundation in operating system basics, DOS, and command prompt functionality in Windows. It is meant to prepare you for the chapters that follow. In fact, this entire book has been preparing you for the study of Windows 9x, Windows NT 4.0, Windows 2000, Windows Me, and Windows XP operating systems.

In this chapter, you should have gained an understanding of the underlying files and command line utilities that were used to create and maintain the operation of early operating systems. Although many DOS and Windows 3x details were not covered in this chapter, the concepts needed to prepare you for the core operating systems components of the test have been well defined.

You will really need to focus over the next few chapters. The Operating Systems Technologies exam is much more difficult that the Core Hardware Service Technician exam.

REVIEW QUESTIONS

1. The ability for an operating system to control and delegate the processor's time to different tasks is called?

o A. Preemptive multitasking
o B. Time slice
o C. Cooperative multitasking
o D. Multi-process collaboration

Correct Answer = A

With preemptive multitasking, the operating system hands out CPU time slices to applications or programs. The operating system is in control of how much time the application can have. With cooperative multitasking, the application or task is in control of the CPU until it is finished with processing.

2. Which entry is not found in the CONFIG.SYS file?

- o A. Buffers=
- o B. Device=
- o C. Files=
- o D. C:\path

Correct Answer = D

The C:\path entry is found in the AUTOEXEC.BAT file. All other entries listed can be located in the CONFIG.SYS file.

3. The DIR and COPY commands are considered internal DOS commands. Where do internal DOS commands reside?

- o A. C:\Windows\Command
- o B. C:\Winnt\System32\Drivers\ETC
- o C. C:\Windows\System\Command
- o D. COMMAND.COM

Correct Answer = D

Internal DOS commands are considered part of COMMAND.COM. External DOS commands are typically located in the C:\DOS directory although their location can be modified.

4. What file should you change to set up your Windows 9x operating system to dual boot?

- o A. COMMAND.COM
- o B. IO.SYS
- o C. MSDOS.SYS
- o D. BOOT.INI

Correct Answer = C

The file MSDOS.SYS in Windows 9x can be modified for dual booting purposes. The BOOT.INI file is used for similar purposes in Windows NT. COMMAND.COM is a utility program that contains internal DOS commands such as the DIR and COPY commands. IO.SYS interacts with the BIOS to determine the hardware environment.

5. Your computer has Windows 9x installed. You want to boot your computer to a DOS prompt. What are the three files necessary to do this? (Choose Three)

□ A. IO.SYS

□ B. MSDOS.SYS

□ C. CONFIG.SYS

□ D. COMMAND.COM

□ E. AUTOEXEC.BAT

Correct Answers = A, B, and D

IO.SYS, MSDOS.SYS, and COMMAND.COM are all located on the primary active boot partition and are stored at the root of C:\. All three of these files are required to successfully boot a system into DOS. The files CONFIG.SYS and AUTOEXEC.BAT are not required.

6. You have received a message on boot-up stating that a line in your CONFIG.SYS is incorrect. What DOS command-line tool can you use to correct this issue?

○ A. AUTOEXEC.BAT

○ B. SYSEDIT

○ C. EDIT.COM

○ D. CONFIG.EDITOR

Correct Answer = C

You can use DOS utility EDIT.COM to view and make changes to the CONFIG.SYS and AUTOEXEC.BAT files. This can be very useful for troubleshooting if you encounter errors on boot-up with settings in either of these files. SYSEDIT is a GUI text editor that can be used to edit these files from within an OS. CONFIG.EDITOR is invalid.

7. Which line can be found in the CONFIG.SYS file?

○ A. PATH=C:\WINDOWS

○ B. PROMPT PG

○ C. SET TEMP=C:\TEMP

○ D. DEVICE=C:\WINDOWS\HIMEM.SYS

Correct Answer = D

The DEVICE=C:\WINDOWS\HIMEM.SYS is used to load HIMEM.SYS from within the CONFIG.SYS file. All other choices are located in the AUTOEXEC.BAT file.

8. You have accidentally deleted COMMAND.COM while using Windows 95. Where can you get a backup copy of COMMAND.COM that will be compatible with your particular operating system?

o A. C:\DOS.

o B. C:\Windows.

o C. C:\Winnt\System32.

o D. Just go to the COMMAND.COM Web site and download your version.

Correct Answer = B

Windows 9x stores a backup copy of COMMAND.COM in the C:\WINDOWS directory.

9. What file should you change to set up your Windows 2000 operating system to dual boot?

o A. COMMAND.COM

o B. IO.SYS

o C. MSDOS.SYS

o D. BOOT.INI

Correct Answer = D

The BOOT.INI file is used in Windows NT, Windows 2000, and Windows XP to configure a system for dual booting. MSDOS.SYS is used for dual booting in Windows 9x and Windows Me.

10. DOS uses COMMAND.COM as its command-line interpreter. What does Windows 2000 use as a command-line interpreter?

o A. COMMAND.COM

o B. A bilingual expert

o C. CMD.EXE

o D. The Windows 2000 HAL

Correct Answer = C

The command interpreter for Windows 2000, NT, and XP is CMD.EXE. The command interpreter for DOS, Windows 9x, and Windows Me is COMMAND.COM.

11. After a typical installation, what do you need to do in order to view an important operating system file such as MSDOS.SYS?

○ A. Modify the BootGUI=0 to BootGUI=1 entry under [Options] in the MSDOS.SYS file.

○ B. Show all files or Show hidden files and folders.

○ C. Reinstall the operating system.

○ D. Reinstall a noncorrupt command interpreter.

Correct Answer = B

MSDOS.SYS is an important hidden system file by default. You should always remember to "Show all files or Show Hidden files and folders" under Folder Options before troubleshooting. All other choices are invalid.

REFERENCES

http://www.pcguide.com/ref/hdd/file/fatLong-c.html. This PC Guide Web site describes LFNs in great detail.

24 Windows 9x

In This Chapter

OVERVIEW OF WINDOWS 9X

In this chapter we will focus on the Windows 9x family of operating systems. As stated in Chapter 23, by *Windows 9x* we generally mean Windows 95 and Windows 98. Windows 95 and Windows 98 are considered true 32-bit operating systems that are backward compatible with Windows 3.x and DOS. Windows 95 had two major release versions: Windows 95A (OSR1) and Windows 95B (OSR2). Windows 98 also had two release versions: Windows 98 and Windows 98 Second Edition (SE).

Windows 95B (OSR2) and both versions of Windows 98 come packaged with the ability to provide hard drive partitions above the 2GB barrier that was a limitation of Windows 95A (OSR1).

The Windows 9x family as a whole has introduced many major improvements to the computing world, including the following:

- Plug-and-Play (PnP) support
- Preemptive multitasking abilities
- Improved network capabilities and Internet sharing
- Better support for multimedia devices and applications
- Dynamic support for 32-bit applications and supporting devices
- Long file name support (up to 255 characters)
- Support for Protected Mode versus Real Mode device drivers
- Installation and support Wizards to assist with installation and operating system administration
- The implementation of a Windows Registry that is used to support environments and devices in place of initialization files

These are just a few of the important improvements that were introduced by the operating system that changed the world. We will discuss these improvements as well as other operating system characteristics specific to Windows 9x throughout this chapter.

INSTALLATION AND UPGRADING

Manufacturers of operating systems provide minimum and recommended hardware specifications that should be considered before installing or upgrading an OS.

The current A+ Operating Systems Technologies exam is not likely to focus on specific questions about the amount of memory or hard disk space required to install a particular OS. Instead, it will most likely focus on operating system installation processes and the techniques used to troubleshoot or debug failed installations.

Before You Start

The following steps should be considered in preparation for a full Windows 9x installation or an upgrade from a previous version of DOS or Windows.

First, you should always check the manufacturer's recommended hardware requirements for a Windows operating system installation. Do not count on study guides or books for this information. For some reason, all operating systems seem to have their own special set of specifications.

Second, verify that you are using the correct CD-ROM for your choice of operating system installation or upgrade. Windows 9x is available in many versions, as stated in Chapter 23. A full Windows 9x installation can be performed on a blank hard drive without a previously installed OS, but an upgrade requires the presence of a previously installed Windows version. OEM operating system releases, such as the Windows 95 OEM release, are designed for specific systems and do not work as a full installation on all systems.

NOTE *The test may get tricky and ask you why a Windows 95 installation keeps failing for no apparent reason. Remember: using the nonbootable OEM Windows 95 release CD-ROM that is not intended for the system you are installing it on could cause this problem.*

Next, consult the Microsoft Hardware Compatibility List (HCL) at: *http://www.microsoft.com/whdc/hcl/search.mspx* to see if your hardware is supported by the Windows operating system you want to install.

Finally, you should consider the type of file system that will be used to support the OS.

If you are going to do a full installation or an upgrade to Windows 95B or Windows 98, you should consider configuring your hard disk as FAT32 in order to take advantage of its many benefits. Some of the benefits of FAT32 include 4K cluster sizes that make better use of the hard disk's space. Smaller 4K cluster sizes increase the overall storage efficiency and file-access speed of the disk. FAT32 makes better use of system resources than FAT16, which in turn provides better use of storage. FAT32 also allows for the ability to support more than 65,535 files with fewer resources.

If you plan to install Windows 9x, it is best to install Windows 98 SE. It has many advantages over its predecessors, Windows 95 and Windows 98. It can handle larger hard drives and support newer technologies, such as USB, FireWire, and Internet connection sharing.

If you need to maintain backward compatibility with older versions of DOS and Windows, you need to configure for dual booting scenarios; or if you plan on installing the original version of Windows 95 that doesn't support FAT32, you should configure your system for FAT16. However, if you configure a partition using FAT16, you will not be able to take advantage of features such as encryption and disk quotas that are offered in newer operating systems.

Windows 98 comes with a powerful FAT32 drive conversion utility program called Drive Converter, which has the ability to convert an already formatted FAT16 partition into a FAT32 or NTFS partition. The only caveat here is that it is said to be impossible to go back to FAT16 once the Drive Converter program has been run and the partition has been converted. (With a partitioning tool like Power Quest Partition Magic 7.0, you can convert back to FAT16 if you like.) Keep in mind that the correct order of preparing a hard disk before a Windows 9x installation is to partition with FDISK, format the drive, and finally reboot the system.

Installation or Upgrade Process

The processes for installing Windows 9x to a blank hard drive or upgrading from an earlier version of Windows 9x are almost the same. The only exceptions are in the early stages of the installation or upgrade processes. Installing a full version of Windows 9x requires you to first format and partition the drive. After you have prepared the hard drive for a new operating system, all you have to do is run the SETUP.EXE program from the Windows 9x installation CD-ROM. You may need a boot disk that contains your particular CD-ROM drivers in order to support the CD-ROM device. For the test, remember that the minimum files required on a boot disk to support a CD-ROM device are AUTOEXEC.BAT, COMMAND.COM, and MSCDEX.EXE. It is also recommended that you have the following files on a high-density 1.44MB boot disk for troubleshooting and diagnostic purposes:

- IO.SYS
- MSDOS.SYS
- SYS.COM
- EDIT.COM
- ATTRIB.EXE
- REGEDIT.EXE
- CHKDSK.EXE
- SCANDISK.EXE
- UNINSTAL.EXE
- FDISK.EXE
- FORMAT.EXE
- EDB.SYS

If you are performing an upgrade of Windows, simply place the Windows 9x upgrade CD-ROM into the CD-ROM drive under the current version of Windows. You will be presented with the Windows 9x upgrade prompt. Here is where it all comes together. At this point, the install or upgrade processes are basically identical. Both methods check the system for the minimum set of requirements necessary for the installation or upgrade to continue. After a restart, you are presented with the Windows Setup Wizard Setup Options menu, which gives you the option of choosing a Typical, Portable, Compact, or Custom setup type. After you choose the setup type you want, you are prompted with the Windows Product Key screen. Enter the Product Key, excluding any dashes, and click the next radio button.

Next, you are prompted to select a directory in which Windows is to be installed. By default, the C:\WINDOWS directory is selected for you. If you are upgrading from Windows 95 to Windows 98, you must install Windows 98 to the same directory that contained your previous Windows 95 files; otherwise, Windows

98 installs itself without consideration of the existing settings and applications, leaving them useless. Now you are asked if you wish to create a start-up disk. This step can be bypassed; a start-up disk can be created from the Add/Remove Software option in the Control Panel after the installation is complete.

From there, you go on to network options, starting with the option to configure the NIC. In practice, it is probably better to bypass this option and configure the NIC and network settings after the Windows 98 upgrade has been completed. At this point, a huge copying phase takes place, followed by the hardware detection phase. The Windows 98, PnP features make this phase quite painless. After all that, the point you will need to remember for the exam is that the upgrade from Windows 95 to Windows 98 is considered the easiest of all upgrades.

Installation Log Files

Windows 9x keeps track of problems that may arise with the setup process in a group of log files stored in the root directory. These log files keep track of devices detected during the installation process, as well as successes and failures associated with the various stages of the installation process. The main installation log files are the following:

SETUPLOG.TXT: A log of the entire setup process, it tracks all successes and failures that occur during installation. It is a good tool for finding the last process that may have failed and caused the system to halt.

DETLOG.TXT: This log file keeps a record of all hardware detected. It is a viewable version of DETCRASH.LOG.

DETCRASH.LOG: This is an unreadable log file that is created if setup fails during the hardware-detection phase. If the entire setup process completes without error, this file is removed from the system.

BOOTLOG.TXT: This logs all device drivers and programs during the installation.

NETLOG.TXT: This log file is used to track the network portion of setup.

THE WINDOWS 9X START-UP PROCESS

The overall system starting order for a typical system is covered in Chapter 23. As you may recall, the exam may look for POST, BIOS, boot sector, and GUI as the overall system starting order. To reveal what happens behind the scenes when a computer system is turned on and booted into Windows 9x, we will break down the start order into the POST/BIOS, Real Mode load, Protected Mode load, and GUI load.

POST/BIOS

When the system is first powered up, the POST is loaded by the ROM BIOS. Next, the MBR is read by the Bootstrap loader, which determines the operating system that is loaded into the system's memory.

Real Mode Load

After the system BIOS has run and the OS is loaded into memory, 16-bit Real Mode drivers are loaded. This is how Windows 9x maintains backward compatibility with DOS and Windows 3x. In this sequence of the start-up process, IO.SYS, MSDOS.SYS, CONFIG.SYS, COMMAND.COM, and AUTOEXEC.BAT are processed.

NOTE *As mentioned in Chapter 23, Windows 9x uses its 32-bit drivers in place of the AUTOEXEC.BAT and CONFIG.SYS files. These files are not needed by Windows 9x; they are there simply to maintain backward compatibility.*

Protected Mode Load

In this phase of the Windows 9x start-up process, WIN.COM is used to start up Windows 9x. Next, VMM32.VXD, which contains an entire package of Windows 9x 32-bit virtual device drivers, loads necessary drivers (VxDs) into memory.

NOTE *The VMM that was used to load 16-bit and 32-bit device drivers for Windows 3.x is replaced in Windows 9x with VMM32.VXD.*

Finally, the SYSTEM.INI file is processed for any device drivers it may contain that need to be loaded.

GUI Load

In the final phase of the Windows 9x start-up process, the KERNEL32.DLL, KRNL386.EXE, GDI.EXE, GDI32.EXE, USER.EXE, and USER32.EXE are loaded, and the user is finally presented with the Windows interface screen known as Explorer.

Start-up Menu And Options

If the operating system cannot boot into Windows 9x successfully, the Windows 9x Startup Menu will most likely appear. The Startup Menu interacts with MSDOS.SYS (which should have a minimum size of 1024K for a stable OS environment) and is used to isolate and troubleshoot problems related to system start-up. You can access the Startup Menu manually by pressing the F8 function key just before the Windows 9x splash screen appears on your display. The Startup Menu offers eight configuration options for various diagnostic and configuration purposes. The Startup Menu and its eight options are explained next:

1. **Normal:** This option is used to simply boot the system up normally. No special drivers are added or removed with this configuration.
2. **Logged (BOOTLOG.TXT):** This option is similar to the Normal option. The only exception is that the steps of the start-up process are written to the file BOOTLOG.TXT.
3. **Safe Mode (Press F5):** This is considered the most useful mode for troubleshooting purposes. Safe Mode loads a generic VGA driver for basic video, a keyboard driver, and HIMEM.SYS (which manages extended memory). Safe Mode does not load the configuration files AUTOEXEC.BAT and CONFIG.SYS. It does not load NIC, modem, and other specialized drivers. Safe Mode is an excellent tool for troubleshooting drivers that do not work properly with the operating system. For example, if, after installing a new advanced video driver, you can no longer view the screen, simply reboot the computer and enter Safe Mode. Safe Mode loads a basic set of drivers that allow you to remove the new video driver from the system and reboot normally.

NOTE

You can also enter Safe Mode directly by pressing the F5 function key before the Windows 9x splash screen is displayed.

4. **Safe Mode with Network Support (Press F6):** This option also allows you to enter Safe Mode and loads support for networking devices and connections. By pressing the F6 function key before the Windows 9x splash screen is displayed, you can directly enter Safe Mode with network support.
5. **Step-by-step configuration (Press Shift+F8):** When this option is used, you are prompted as to which configuration files and file lines will be executed on start-up. For example, if you press the Shift+F8 keys before the Windows 9x splash screen is displayed, you will be asked if you would like to process such files as the CONFIG.SYS and AUTOEXE.BAT. If you enter "Y" for yes, you will be asked if you would like to process each line of each of these files. This is an excellent way to troubleshoot individual devices and settings that are loaded by each file, one line at a time.
6. **Command prompt only (Press Shift+F5):** This option is used to start up the system in MS-DOS. It is often used for troubleshooting purposes if Safe Mode doesn't work.

7. **Safe Mode command prompt only:** This option is used to start DOS without network support. The major configuration files are bypassed, and you are directed to a command prompt.
8. **Previous version of DOS (Press F4):** This option is available if a previous version of DOS is installed on your system. Pressing the F4 function key before the Windows splash screen appears will get you there.

THE WINDOWS 9X REGISTRY

The Windows 9x Registry, as well as the registries implemented in Windows NT and Windows 2000, are hierarchical databases made up of special Registry Keys that hold most of the operating system's software, hardware, and application settings. The Windows 9x Registry was developed with the intention of replacing the dependency on the WIN.INI, SYSTEM.INI, AUTOEXEC.BAT, and CONFIG.SYS files for loading system initialization, device, and user environment settings.

The Windows Registry is a sort of common ground that is used to link applications, programs, objects, and settings. Windows 3x utilized the Object Linking and Embedding (OLE) functionality of a binary file called REG.DAT. *Object linking* is a method whereby a program or application can use an object or part of a program that is created by another program.

The Windows 9x Registry is made up of two important files called USER.DAT and SYSTEM.DAT. These files are stored as hidden, read-only system files in the C:\WINDOWS directory. The USER.DAT file stores user-related Registry settings, such as user preferences and desktop settings. The SYSTEM.DAT file is used to store device settings. Every time Windows 9x is started, the system looks for USER.DAT and SYSTEM.DAT to create and load the operating system's environment and related device settings. If these two files are not found, the system automatically looks for the files USER.DA0 and SYSTEM.DA0, which are backup copies of the two main Registry files maintained by the operating system.

NOTE *It is very important to note that system files are purposefully hidden by default as a security precaution.*

Viewing and Modifying the Registry

Warning! Great care should be taken when entering or making changes to the Windows 9x Registry—or any Registry, for that matter. Making improper changes to the binary values stored in the Registry or installing certain software that can cause Registry corruption may leave you with a system that is unstable at best. If your users or customers observe strange happenings, such as a missing taskbar, blank icons, or programs that won't load, they are most likely experiencing a corrupt Registry or virus activity. You should always manually back up the Registry before making any changes to it. Windows 98 comes with an excellent tool called Registry Checker that works well for this purpose. If your Registry becomes corrupted, you can use the SCANREG utility from a DOS prompt to restore a backup copy of the Registry. The command used for restoring a Registry from a DOS prompt is SCANREG/RESTORE.

Using the Windows 9x Device Manager and Control Panel options to change settings and devices is considered the safest way for most users to make edits to the Registry. It is more common for advanced users to edit the Registry in Windows 9x with the REGEDIT.EXE program stored in C:\WINDOWS in Windows 9x by default. To enter the Windows 95 Registry, simply click Start > Run, and then type in "REGEDIT" on the Open command line. The window shown in Figure 24.1 will appear.

The six major Registry keys are displayed in Figure 24.1. Each of these keys and their subkeys are responsible for holding system and device settings and information. The current A+ Operating Systems Technologies exam will expect you to be familiar with the techniques used to edit, backup, and restore the Windows 9x Registry. For the exam's purposes, you should know the functionality associated with HKEY_LOCAL_MACHINE.

The functions of each of the six major Registry HKEYs are as follows:

HKEY_CLASSES_ROOT: Stores file extensions and OLE information.

HKEY_CURRENT_USER: Stores all information as it pertains to the specific user who is currently logged into the local system.

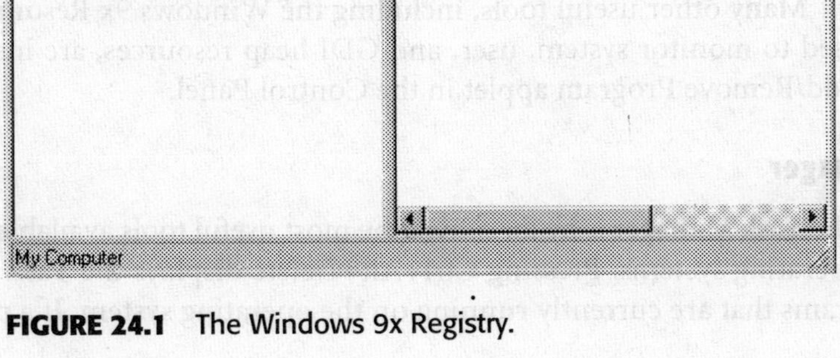

FIGURE 24.1 The Windows 9x Registry.

- **HKEY_LOCAL_MACHINE:** Stores all the software, hardware, and operating system settings of all configurations used on the system.
- **HKEY_USERS:** Stores all user preferences for each separate user with a profile located on the local system.
- **HKEY_CURRENT_CONFIG:** Stores the current hardware profile for peripheral devices, such as monitors and printers.
- **HKEY_DYN_DATA:** Stores all current performance data, such as the results of running System Monitor.

UTILITIES AND SETTINGS

Windows 9x has many useful utilities for managing and maintaining the integrity of the operating system. This section is dedicated to the many utilities, configuration options, and settings that are available in Windows 9x. Pay close attention to the details listed in this section—it is very likely that they will appear on the exam.

System Monitor and System Resource Meter

System Monitor is an excellent troubleshooting tool used to monitor the system's performance in a real-time graphics snapshot. It can be used to view the system's CPU, virtual memory, and network client/server resources used (only on the local system), just to name a few. If System Monitor is not installed on your system, you can install it by navigating to Start > Settings > Control Panel > Add/Remove Programs > Windows Setup > System Tools > System Monitor. Select the OK button and you will be prompted to insert the Windows installation CD-ROM. After System Monitor is installed, you can locate and run it from Start > Programs > Accessories > System Tools. Figure 24.2 displays a snapshot of System Monitor.

NOTE

Remember that System Monitor is not used to monitor the network utilization of other client and server computers.

Many other useful tools, including the Windows 9x Resource Meter, which is used to monitor system, user, and GDI heap resources, are installed through the Add/Remove Program applet in the Control Panel.

Task Manager

The Task Manager is by far one of the most useful tools available in most Microsoft operating systems. Pressing Ctrl+Alt+Delete displays the Task Manager and programs that are currently running on the operating system. If a process or program

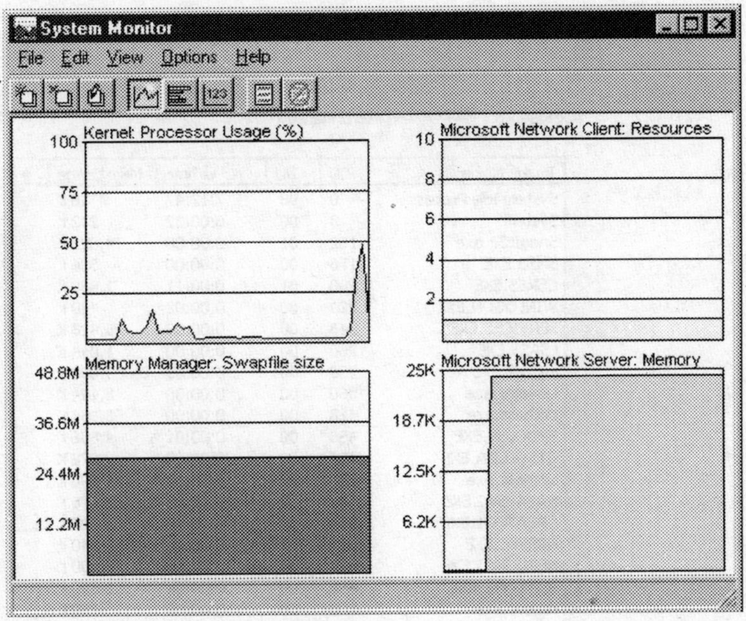

FIGURE 24.2 System Monitor.

is stalled or not responding, you can select the program and press the End Task radio button to remove it. Pressing Ctrl+Alt+Delete twice restarts the system. Figure 24.3 displays some of the many system processes in the Task Manager of Windows 2000.

Dr. Watson

Dr. Watson™ is a program error debugger tool used in Windows 9x, NT, and 2000 to detect and log critical error information pertaining to system halts. Dr. Watson also attempts to point you in the right direction by offering possible tips for problem and error resolution. The question at hand does not seem to be "Dr. Watson, I presume?" Instead, the question seems to be, "Dr. Watson, where are you storing your log files?" The Dr. Watson tool stores its information in log files located in various places. In Windows 9x, the Dr. Watson log file is called WATSONXXX.WLG and is stored in C:\WINDOWS\DRWATSON. In Windows NT, Dr. Watson creates two log files named DRWTSN32.LOG and USER.DMP that are stored in C:\WINNT. When Dr. Watson intercepts a program fault in Windows 2000, the file DRWTSN32.LOG is produced and is stored in the C:\DOCUMENTS AND SETTINGS\ALL USERS\DOCUMENTS\DRWATSON. Dr. Watson offers a standard view and an advanced view for diagnostic reporting purposes.

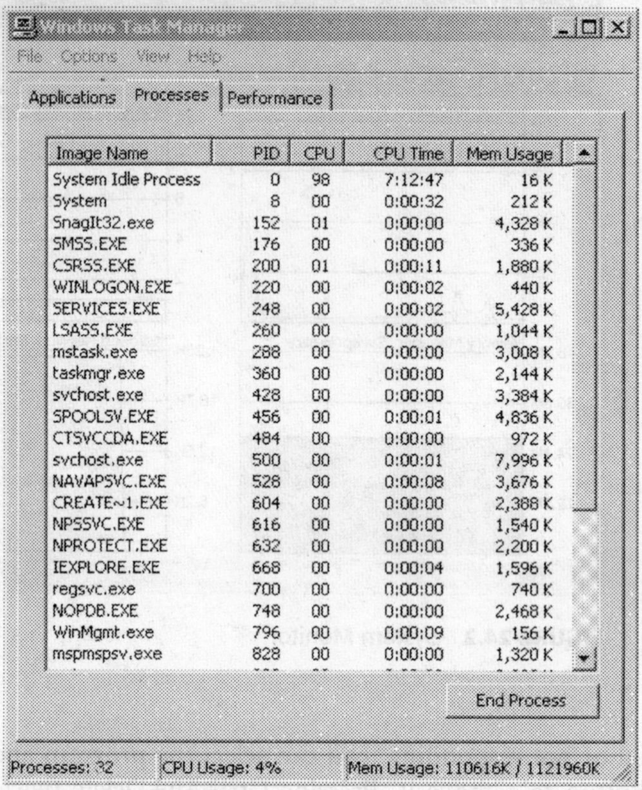

FIGURE 24.3 Windows Task Manager.

Device Manager

The Device Manager is probably the most useful utility ever created for viewing, troubleshooting, and installing devices that are attached to a computer system. As mentioned earlier in this book, the Device Manager can be used to view or change system resources, such as IRQs, I/Os, and DMAs. The Device Manager is available in Windows 9x and Windows 2000. It is not available in Windows NT.

There are two easy ways to navigate to the Device Manager utility in Windows 9x. A quick way to access it is to right-click the Desktop icon My Computer, select Properties, and choose Device Manager. You can also access Device Manager by clicking Start > Settings > Control Panel, double-clicking the System icon, and choosing the Device Manager tab. The Device Manager opens, and you see a display similar to that shown in Figure 24.4.

The Properties button depicted in Figure 24.4 allows you to view more information about the device that you select. If you click Computer and select Proper-

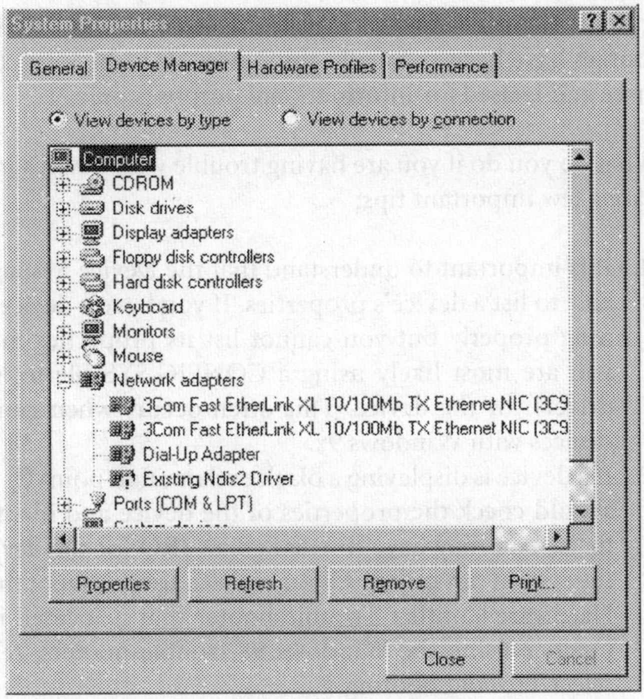

FIGURE 24.4 Windows 9x Device Manager.

ties, you can view information regarding the IRQs, DMAs, I/Os, and memory of your particular system. The Refresh button forces the system to refresh the device through a process called enumeration. This means the system will simply start the plug-and-play process for the device. The Remove button forces the device to be deleted from the operating system's Registry. The Print button prints out a report based on the devices listed in Device Manager. You can expand and view more information for a particular device by clicking on the plus (+) sign that is located to the right of it.

The Device Manager places specific symbols on its list of devices to notify you if a particular device is having a problem or has been disabled. The most common Device Manager symbols and their meanings are as follows:

- A black exclamation point (!) in a yellow circle represents a device in a problem state. The device in question may still be operational; the error may be related to the system's ability to detect the device, or it may be a device driver issue.
- A red "X" means that the device in question has been disabled by the system. A resource conflict or a damaged device usually causes this error.

- A blue "I" on a white background is used to show that a device's system resources have been manually configured. It is the least common symbol of the three and is used for informational purposes only.

What do you do if you are having trouble with devices in the Device Manager? Here are a few important tips:

1. It is important to understand that the Device Manager may not always be able to list a device's properties. If you have a device that seems to be running properly but you cannot list its properties in the Device Manager, you are most likely using a CONFIG.SYS file to load older Real Mode drivers for the device. This often occurs when running older CD-ROM devices with Windows 9x.
2. If a device is displaying a black exclamation point (!) on a yellow circle, you should check the properties of the device and identify any resource conflicts. You may have to reassign an IRQ for the device in question before the system can utilize it. You can also troubleshoot this error by starting the Hardware Conflict Troubleshooter that is located in Windows Help. To practice using the Windows 98 troubleshooters, select Start > Help and select Troubleshooting.

NOTE

The Device Manager should always be your first-choice utility to view and modify device resources.

The Windows 95 installation CD-ROM contains several useful hardware diagnostic tools, such as MSD.EXE and HWDIAG.EXE. MSD.EXE is based on the old DOS diagnostic reporting tool. HWDIAG.EXE is a more robust diagnostic tool that will provide detailed information about hardware devices. Neither of these tools loads by default; your best bet is to use the Device Manager.

Windows Update

All current versions of Windows operating systems include the Windows update feature known as Windows Update Manager. This utility is used to keep your operating system up to date with current patches, fixes, security updates, service releases, and other information offered by Microsoft. Simply select Start > Windows Update. You will be directed to *http://windowsupdate.microsoft.com/*. Follow the instructions on this site to bring your operating system up to date.

Here are some important notes regarding Windows Update:

- It is recommended that you view the Web pages on the Windows Update site at an 800 × 600 or higher screen resolution.
- When you enter the Microsoft Windows update site, ActiveX controls are downloaded to your system. These controls are used to check your system for specific updates that your system may require. After checking your system, Windows update provides you with a list of updates, software, and drivers that are suggested in order to keep your system up to date.
- If you reinstall windows or upgrade you system, it is recommended that you re-install any components you had previously installed using Windows Update.

Display Settings

When you experience display-related problems, start by navigating to the Windows 9x Display Properties Window. Select Start > Settings > Control Panel, and double-click on the Display icon. The Display Properties Settings Window should appear by default (Figure 24.5). You can also get to this window by right-clicking the Windows Desktop, selecting Properties, and clicking the Settings tab.

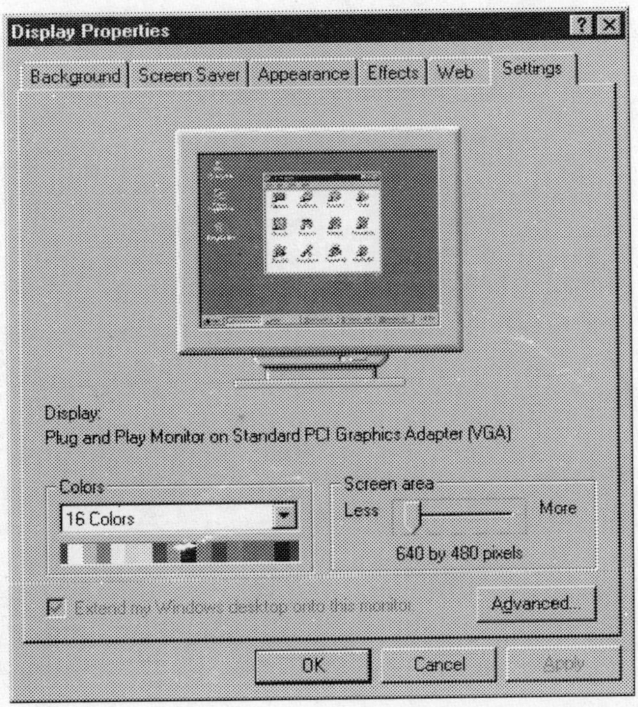

FIGURE 24.5 Windows 9x Display Properties Settings Window.

Figure 24.5 shows the Display Properties Settings window for the second time in this book—and for good reason. The current as well as past A+ Operating System exams focus on your ability to resolve display-related issues with this graphic. For example, If you are running a 640 ×4 80-pixel display, as shown in Figure 24.5, and you are unable to view entire Web pages through your Internet browser, or you want to fit more icons on your Desktop, simply use the mouse to move the "Screen area" bar to 800 × 600 pixels or more. If your video card supports a higher resolution, you will be able to fit more into the viewable screen area with this method. If you select the Advanced > Performance button, you will have the option of changing the Graphics Hardware acceleration settings.

NOTE *The exam may try to confuse you here. Another way to navigate to the Graphics Hardware acceleration settings is Control Panel > System > Performance > Graphics.*

Changing these settings can be useful if you are having trouble with how fast your system is handling graphics. If you select Advanced > Adapter, the system's video Adapter/Driver information will look like that shown in Figure 24.6. If you

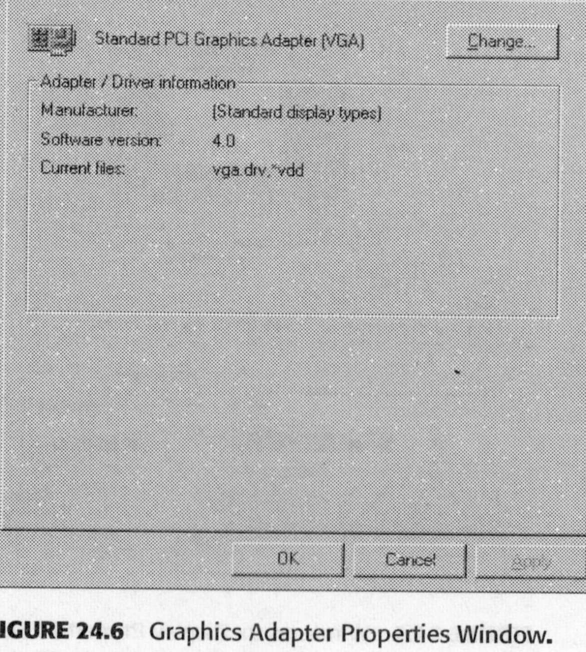

FIGURE 24.6 Graphics Adapter Properties Window.

select the Change radio button on this screen, the Update Device Driver Wizard window will appear and lead you through the process of updating the video adapter driver. Remember, there are usually several ways to achieve a single goal in a Windows operating system. You can update your video adapter driver, as well as many other device drivers, through Device Manager.

Virtual Memory Settings

In Chapter 23, we discussed virtual memory and swap files. You should recall that Windows 9x has the ability to use a portion of free hard disk space as a temporary storage area or memory buffer area for programs that need more memory than is available in RAM. This temporary hard disk memory area is called virtual memory or swap file. The actual name for this memory in Windows 9x is called WIN386.SWP.

To view or change your virtual memory settings in Windows 9x, select Start > Settings > Control Panel > System > Performance > Virtual Memory. You will be presented with a window similar to that shown in Figure 24.7. As stated in the Virtual Memory window, you should be very cautious when changing your system's virtual memory settings. If you are not sure of what these settings should be, you should obviously let Windows manage your settings for you. If Windows is managing your virtual memory settings for you, it allocates around 12MB above the amount of physical RAM installed in your system. For example, if you have

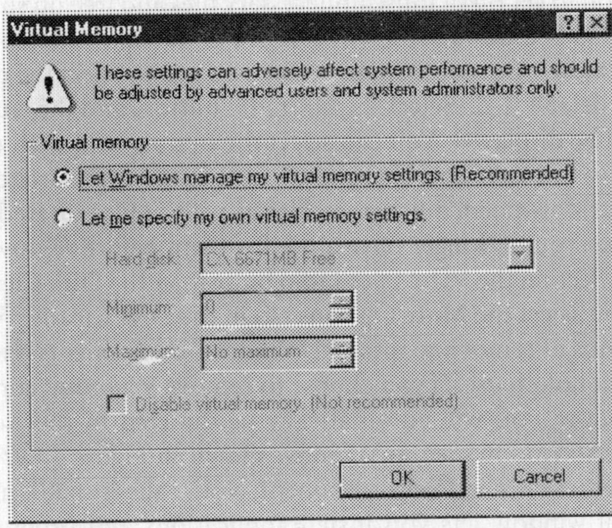

FIGURE 24.7 Windows 9x Virtual Memory Settings.

64MB of RAM installed in your system, Windows will create and manage a swap file of around 76MB of hard drive space.

The Recycle Bin

The Windows 9x Recycle Bin is a Desktop icon that represents a directory in which files are stored on a temporary basis. When you delete a file from a computer system's hard drive, it is moved to the Recycle Bin. To restore a file that has been deleted to its original location on the hard drive, right-click on the file in the Recycle Bin and select Restore, or select File from the menu bar and then select Restore. If you want to remove a file from the Recycle Bin to free up hard drive space, select File from the menu bar, and select Empty Recycle Bin. You can also delete entries in the Recycle Bin by selecting File from the menu bar and selecting Delete. When you delete a file from the Recycle Bin, its associated entry in the hard drive's FAT is removed. It is still possible to recover the deleted file with many available third-party utility programs.

Disk Cleanup Utilities and More

Your hard drive can get bogged down after a while with unnecessary files. Applications and programs can leave temporary files scattered on your hard drive, temporary Internet files and cookies are left behind when you surf the Internet, and all those downloaded 'shareware' programs that you haven't used in ages can take up precious hard drive space.

Windows 98 has an excellent tool known as Disk Cleanup. This built-in utility allows you to get rid of those unnecessary files and free up space. To access the Disk Cleanup in Windows 98, click Start > Programs > Accessories > System Tools > Disk Cleanup. A window appears that asks you to select the drive you want to clean up. The default is C:. Select the OK radio button, and the window shown in Figure 24.8 will be displayed. You can select the options you wish to have removed from your drive by inserting a check mark next to the appropriate selections. Always review your downloaded program files as well as files located in the Recycle Bin to verify that you no longer have a use for them before removing them. You can do this by selecting the View Files radio button on the Disk Cleanup window.

If you select the More Options tab in the Disk Cleanup window, you will have the options of removing optional Windows components and other programs that you do not often use. If you choose to remove Windows components from within this window, you will automatically be directed to the Add/Remove Programs Properties/Windows Setup Window shown in Figure 24.9. This window lets you add or remove a Windows component. Notice the Install/Uninstall tab. The Install/Uninstall window lets you install applications and programs from a floppy or CD-ROM, or uninstall registered software that you do not use. The Add/Remove

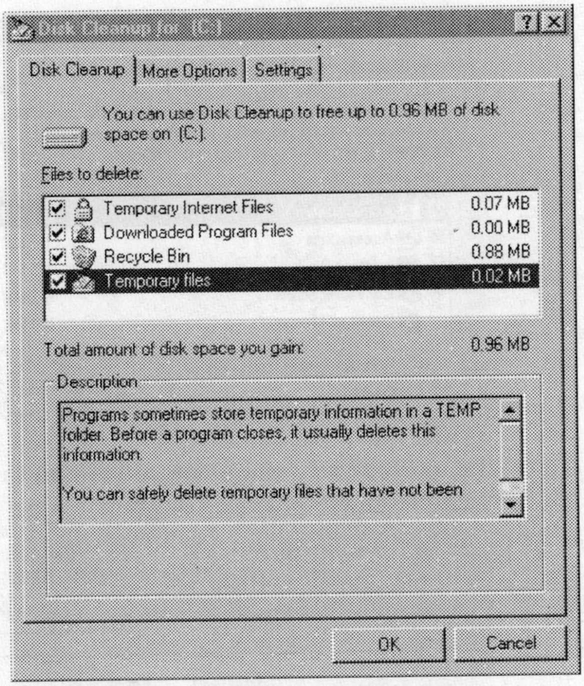

FIGURE 24.8 The Disk Cleanup Window.

Programs Properties window can also be accessed by clicking Start > Settings > Control Panel > Add/Remove Programs.

You should also take note of the Startup Disk tab in Figure 24.9. With the Startup Disk window, you can create a Windows 9x bootable troubleshooting floppy disk that you can use later for diagnostic purposes.

Windows 9x allows you to schedule routine maintenance jobs easily through the use of the Maintenance Wizard. This utility is a handy tool that can be used to automatically run utilities such as Defrag, ScanDisk, or Disk Cleanup at times that are convenient for the computer user. In Windows 9x, the Maintenance Wizard utility can be run by selecting Start > Programs > Accessories > System Tools > Maintenance Wizard.

Backup Utility

Windows operating systems come with a Backup utility program that is used to backup information to a tape storage device for future restoration. It is of utmost importance that you backup your critical information in the event of an operating system failure or accidental deletion of files.

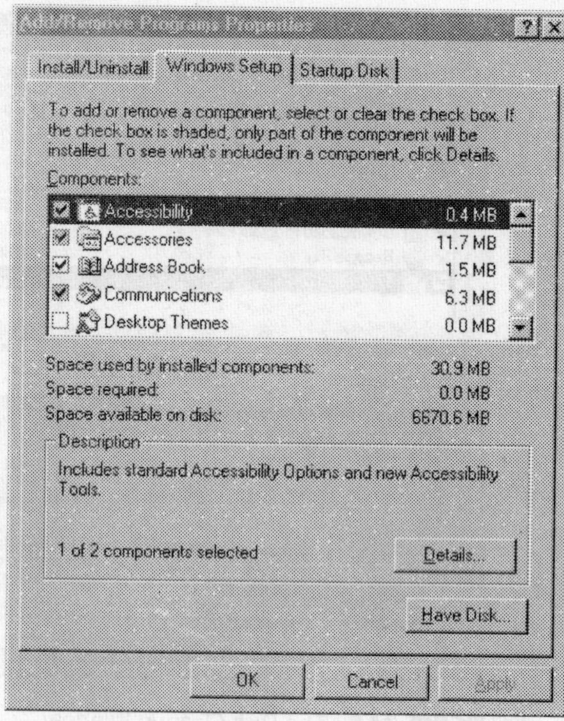

FIGURE 24.9 Add/Remove Programs Properties Window.

A good backup program consists of a backup schedule that can be created using the Backup utility or a third-party backup utility program. In Windows 9x, the Backup utility can be accessed by selecting Start > Programs > Accessories > System Tools > Backup. If the Backup utility is not installed, you can install it through the Add/Remove programs applet located in the Control Panel.

There are several backup types and strategies that you can implement. The backup type and strategy that you use depends on the amount of storage capacity you have, the time it takes to back up files, and the time it takes to restore files. The following types of backups can be used to build your own personalized backup strategy.

- *Copy* backs up only selected files. The Copy backup turns the Backup archive bit off or resets it.
- *Full backup* backs up everything on your hard drive. If you have to restore an entire system, it is the best backup to have. During this backup, the backup archive bit is turned off. This simply means that every file will be backed up again whether or not its contents have changed. The disadvantages of this type

of backup are that it takes longer to run and it is often redundant because most system files do not change.

- *Incremental backup* backs up all the files that have changed or been created since the last backup job and have their archive bits set to on. This backup type uses less tape storage space and spreads the storage of files across several tapes. With an incremental backup, files are backed up much faster than with a differential backup, but they take much longer to restore. To do a proper incremental restore, you will need the last full backup tape and multiple incremental tapes.
- *Differential backup* backs up all files that have been created or have changed since the last backup and does not reset the archive bit. The archive bit is left on. Differential backup takes much longer to do, but is much faster to restore. To do a proper restore, you will need the last full backup tape and the last differential backup tape.

A Zip drive is a popular information storage device. The average Zip drive can hold about 100MB of data, which can be very useful for the daily storage and backup of important files. Users of Windows can use a third-party utility, such as WinZip™, to store files in compressed form and then back them up. Windows stores compressed files in .ZIP format.

PRINTERS

The current A+ Operating Systems Technologies exam is likely to make sure that you are familiar with file and printer sharing, as well as methods used to create and rename printer shares and change printer properties.

In Windows 9x, if you want to add a printer, rename a printer, share a printer, connect to or disconnect an already shared network printer, or change a currently installed printer's properties, you can select Start > Settings > Printers, or My Computer > Printers, or Control Panel > Printers. Once you have navigated to the printer's applet, you can right-click an already installed printer and rename it, change its shared name, cancel current print jobs, or select Properties to change advanced features and settings for a printer. If you want to add a local or networked printer, simply select the Add Printer icon, select Next, and choose Local Printer or Network Printer. If you select Local Printer, you will be required to choose a printer manufacturer and printer, or choose the Have Disk option and insert your local printer's driver disk or CD-ROM. If you select Network Printer, you will need to specify the UNC name for the location of the shared Network Printer or browse to the printer on the network with the Browse radio button. Remember for the exam that the proper UNC syntax to browse to a shared network printer is "\\Computername\Printername".

A shared printer can utilize spooling techniques. When spooling is implemented, print jobs are stored on a networked computer system's hard drive. The print jobs are sent to a printer when it is available to print. If you want to print directly to a printer without print jobs being spooled, you can change a printer's spool settings to "Print directly to the printer." This can be accomplished by right-clicking a currently installed printer, selecting Properties > Advanced, and choosing the "Print directly to the printer" option.

So that others can access your locally installed printers and files, you must enable File and Print Sharing on your local system in the Network applet in the Control Panel. The same is true if others in a Windows 9x workgroup or network wish to share their printers and files. Besides printers and files, you can also share CD-ROM devices and modems in Windows 9x.

WINDOWS 9X NETWORKING

Windows 9x clients can be part of a workgroup or a domain. A *workgroup* is typically implemented when a network consists of 10 or fewer computers. A workgroup, otherwise known as a peer-to-peer network, utilizes share-level security (password-protected shares) and does not require the use of high-end server computers. Three components that must be present and properly configured for a computer to operate successfully in a peer-to-peer network are a NIC, a protocol, and the ability to share resources. A *domain* is implemented when the number of computers exceeds 10. A domain utilizes high-end server computers that hand out or serve resources to users who are authenticated through the use of user-level security.

Computers must have a common language or protocol in order to communicate with one another over a network. Windows 9x provides built-in support for several commonly used protocols. These protocols and their descriptions follow:

TCP/IP: This is the most widely used protocol on the planet. Every computer using the Internet has a unique TCP/IP numeric address. This protocol can be used in a Windows 9x network to share information. If you are currently connected to a network, you can view your own TCP/IP address information in Windows 9x by selecting Start > Run, entering "WINIPCFG" on the Open line, and clicking OK. Your computer's IP configuration will appear, including the NICs MAC address, IP address, Subnet Mask, and Default Gateway.

NOTE

To display your IP address information in Windows NT, enter "IPCONFIG" in place of "WINIPCFG".

IPX/SPX: This is a Novell protocol that allows Windows clients to communicate with resources on a Novell network. IPX/SPX and its Windows counterpart, NWLink, can be used to share information in a Windows 9x network.

NetBIOS: Don't be fooled on the exam—NetBIOS is not used to share printers and files on a network. It is actually an API program that allows computers within a LAN to communicate.

NetBEUI: This is a small, fast, efficient transport protocol that is well suited for small networks. NetBEUI can be utilized to share information in a Windows 9x network.

Connecting a Windows 9x system to a network is a fairly basic task. The first thing to do is navigate to the Network applet located in Control Panel or right-click the Network Neighborhood icon on the Desktop and select Properties. A network configuration window will appear, similar to that shown in Figure 24.10.

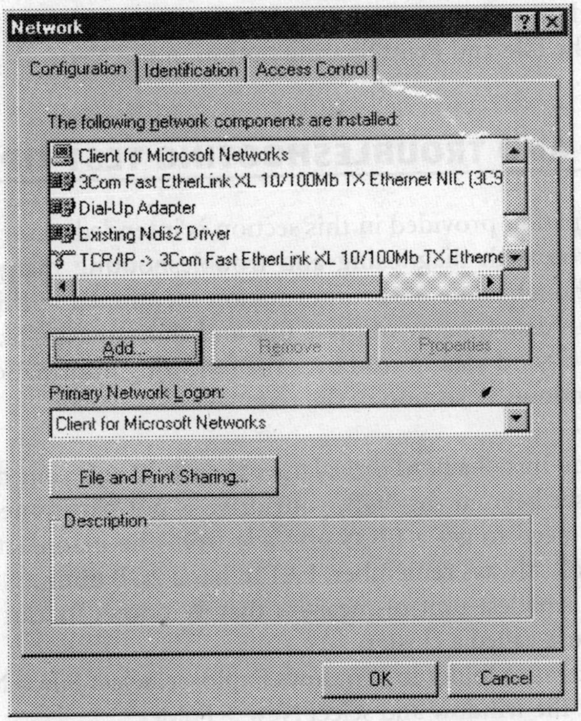

FIGURE 24.10 Network Configuration Window for Windows 9x.

The second step is to install Client for Microsoft Networks. You do this by clicking on the Add radio button and selecting Client from the type of network components you want to install. Click the Add button again, and select Microsoft and Client for Microsoft Networks from the list of manufacturers and network clients. Once the client for Microsoft Networks is installed, highlight it in the network components configuration window, and click Properties. The Client for Microsoft Networks Properties General tab appears, from which you can choose to log on to a Windows NT domain.

Next, you must install any special protocols necessary to communicate and share information with other computers on the network. Remember, if you want to communicate with Novell systems, install IPX/SPX. TCP/IP and NetBEUI are installed by default if you chose to install networking during the Windows Install and Setup routine. These two protocols can be used to communicate with other Windows systems on a network. If you did not install networking when you installed the OS, select the Add button on the Network Configuration window. Highlight Protocol and click the Add button. Select a manufacturer and protocol, and then click OK.

Finally, if you want to share your resources with others, you will need to install the file and print sharing service, and make sure you give access to your resources by selecting the File and Print Sharing button in the Network configuration window.

DIAGNOSING AND TROUBLESHOOTING TEST TIPS

The information provided in this section is intended to serve as a quick reference to assist you with diagnosing and troubleshooting many Windows 9x-related issues. Although some of the information mentioned in this section has not been discussed in detail, many of these tips and shortcuts are likely to show up on the exam. It is a good idea to read over the following information in final preparation for the Windows 9x section of the test:

- ✓ If you install a hard drive larger than 2GB and your operating system doesn't see beyond the 2GB, your drive is not partitioned as FAT32. You may also need to get a BIOS upgrade from the manufacturer of your motherboard. Always remember, FAT16 has a 2GB limit.
- ✓ The smallest unit of measure that Windows 9x can work with on a hard drive is called a cluster.
- ✓ To create a folder in Windows Explorer, select File > New > Folder or right-click the window and select New > Folder.

- ✓ To create a shortcut on your Windows desktop, right-click the desktop and select New > Shortcut.
- ✓ In Windows 9x, the file MSDOS.SYS should be at least 1K.
- ✓ Installation files in Windows 95 are called cabinet or .CAB files. The proper name syntax used for Windows 95 .cab files is Win95_xx.cab (xx = a numeric value, such as 13).
- ✓ In order for a mapped network drive to retain its mapping on reboot, you must check the "Reconnect at Logon" box when establishing the mapping.
- ✓ The End key is used to access the interactive startup menu during the Windows 98 boot sequence.
- ✓ The Alt+Tab key sequence allows you to toggle between applications that are currently running on your system.
- ✓ The Shift+F8 keystroke sequence can be used to refresh your desktop in Windows.
- ✓ Menus within Windows programs, such as Word or Windows Explorer, designate hot keys with an underscore (for example, Files, Edit, and View).
- ✓ You can get a system configuration printout from a Windows 9x command prompt by entering "MSDN" and pressing the Print Screen key.
- ✓ If you want to access a printer by its UNC name, the proper syntax is \\computername\printername.
- ✓ If you have installed a new modem and your previous dial-up networking configuration does not work, go to the dial-up networking properties of your original entry and configure them for the new modem.
- ✓ The DOSSTART.BAT file is automatically executed when you restart your system in MS-DOS mode.
- ✓ The correct starting order for Windows 9x is IO.SYS, MS-DOS.SYS, CONFIG.SYS, COMMAND.COM, AUTOEXEC.BAT.
- ✓ SCANREG can be used to restore a Registry from DOS. If you want to replace the Registry with an older Registry, use SCANREG/RESTORE. If you want to fix the current loaded Registry, use SCANREG/FIX.
- ✓ If you have recently installed Client for Microsoft networks, IPX/SPX, and File and Print Sharing and are still unable to browse your network, verify that "File and print sharing" is checked. Without this setting enabled, you will not be able to see other workstations in Windows 9x.
- ✓ In order to make a network dial-up connection to the Internet in Windows, you need two important network components. TCP/IP and a Dial-up Adapter.
- ✓ If you want to configure a dial-up connection to the Internet, you must have the network protocol TCP/IP bound to a dial-up adapter.

- ✓ If you are using a laptop computer with a NIC and the NetBEUI protocol, "File and print sharing" must be enabled on the NIC if you want to share information.
- ✓ If you are having difficulty moving a window between two monitors connected to the same computer system, you may already have the window maximized.
- ✓ To remove unneeded items from the Windows 98 Start menu, right-click the item in the Start menu and choose Delete or right-click on the taskbar, select Properties, navigate to the Customize Start Menu Options, and use the Remove button to eliminate unwanted Start menu items. It should be noted that items in the Start folder are loaded in alphabetical order.
- ✓ Client, Adapter, Protocol, and Service are network components that can be added through the Windows 9x Network applet.
- ✓ If you are having trouble detecting USB devices, you are most likely running the original version of Windows 95, which doesn't support USB without an update. Alternatively, you may not have USB support enabled in your BIOS settings. Again, Windows 95 does not support USB without additional software.
- ✓ If your system hangs at the Windows 9x splash screen on boot-up, hold down the Shift key on startup to stop possible corrupt startup folder programs from loading.
- ✓ If items on your desktop look different from usual or are unidentifiable, the first step for resolving this problem is to refresh the desktop by right-clicking the desktop and selecting Refresh.
- ✓ If you are having trouble installing or updating Windows system files, you should try disabling any Antivirus features in your systems BIOS as well as your antivirus real time protection. Then attempt to reinstall the software.
- ✓ If you need to restore an OS file that has been deleted from your system, you can use the EXTRACT command to restore a file from the Windows 9x Installation CD.
- ✓ Windows 98 comes with a powerful FAT32 drive conversion utility program called Drive Converter, which has the ability to convert an already formatted FAT16 partition into a FAT32 or NTFS partition.
- ✓ If you double click a shortcut on your Windows desktop and nothing happens, it is likely that the application program that is tied to the shortcut has been moved, removed, or is corrupted.
- ✓ If you have two printers installed on your Windows 9x system and you delete your default printer, the remaining printer will automatically become your default printer.

- ✓ If you have just completed a Windows 9x operating system installation and you are having difficulties adjusting your screen resolution, the first things you should do are update your Windows and video drivers.
- ✓ Windows 9x is not compatible with NTFS.
- ✓ The root directory under Windows 9x supports a maximum of 512 entries.
- ✓ Common protocols that are used to share printers in Windows 9x are TCP/IP, IPX/SPX and NetBEUI.
- ✓ The Windows 9x Registry is a hierarchical database made up of special Key entries.
- ✓ If you wish not to have your print jobs spooled in Windows 9x, you can choose to print directly to the printer in the spool settings dialogue box.
- ✓ The undocumented Microsoft utility MKCOMPAT.EXE can be used to assist older Windows 3.1 applications to run in a Windows 9x environment.
- ✓ The statements PROMPT PG and LH C:\Windows\COMMAND\MSCDEX are commonly found in the autoexec.bat file.
- ✓ The navigation path to capture a printer port in Windows 9x is: My Computer > Control Panel > Printer applet > File > Properties > Details.
- ✓ A ".CPL" file is a (Control Panel Extension) file. If you ever receive an invalid page default (kernel32) error when opening Control Panel, you will need to determine which .CPL file is damaged or corrupt and replace it.
- ✓ To create a Startup Disk in Windows 9x navigate to Control Panel > Add/remove programs and select Create Disk from the Startup Disk tab.
- ✓ The first thing you should do if you receive the "out of memory error" while using Windows 9x is to check the system resources in the system control panel for any applications or processes that are using up valuable system resources.
- ✓ If a memory manager cannot provide an application with requested memory, a memory page fault occurs.
- ✓ To increase graphics acceleration speed in Windows 9x, navigate to Control Panel, System, Performance, Graphics.
- ✓ Windows 98SE is the only version of Windows 9x that offers ICS (Internet Connection Sharing) capabilities.
- ✓ Windows 9x is fully capable of being upgraded to Windows 2000 Professional.
- ✓ The correct booting order for a system is POST, BIOS, BOOT SECTOR, GUI.
- ✓ The Windows 9x System Monitor can be used to monitor virtual memory and networked client and server info.
- ✓ If Windows 9x finds a damaged or corrupt Registry upon booting, it will attempt to automatically repair the damaged Registry.

- ✓ If you select "N" for large disk support while running FDISK, a fat16 partition will be created.
- ✓ If the "Starting Windows 98" logo screen is missing at startup, it is likely that the file logo.sys is missing or corrupt.
- ✓ You should never share more than 300 folders in Windows 9x. If you do, the folders may not appear to be shared when displayed in Explorer.

CHAPTER SUMMARY

This chapter introduced many of the Windows 9x concepts, utilities, shortcuts, and file systems that you will be required to know for the A+ exam.

It is impossible to identify every detail that the current exam will cover; therefore, it is very important that you practice with the tools mentioned in this chapter in order to back up your knowledge with hands-on experience and give you the best chance of passing the exam. There are many details of Windows 9x that are beyond the scope of this book. Use all the resources you can get your hands on to pass this exam. It is suggested that you scan the Microsoft White Pages at *http://www.Microsoft.com*; they refer to all the Windows operating systems mentioned in this book. The following review questions are a great preparation tool. If you do not understand the concepts behind one of the review questions, use your operating system's Help utility or the Internet to give you more details.

REVIEW QUESTIONS

1. You are interested in using the Windows 98 Drive Converter to convert your FAT16 partition to FAT32. What can you gain from this conversion? (Choose Three)

- □ A. Your applications will load quicker.
- □ B. You will utilize fewer resources.
- □ C. You will gain file level security.
- □ D. You will lose valuable storage space based on smaller 4K clusters.
- □ E. Your storage space overall will become more efficient.

Correct Answers = A, B, and E

Answers A, B, and E are all benefits that can be achieved when you convert to FAT32. File level security is a feature of NTFS (Net Technology File System), which is available only with Windows NT and Windows 2000. Choice D is incorrect because smaller 4K clusters will allow you to gain more storage space.

2. You plan on using only the OEM Windows 95 CD-ROM to install Windows on a blank hard drive. Why won't this work?

- o A. The Windows 95 OEM Installation CD-ROM is not bootable.
- o B. You do not have enough hard drive space.
- o C. You are using a nonregistered OEM version.
- o D. You must partition the drive as NTFS5 first.

Correct Answer = A

The Windows 95 OEM installation CD is not bootable. If you plan on using this CD-ROM with a hard drive that is not bootable (in this case blank), then you will need a bootable floppy disk with supporting CD-ROM device drivers installed to successfully install this Windows version.

3. What doesn't Windows 95A support?

- o A. COMMAND.COM
- o B. Defragmenter
- o C. FAT32
- o D. FAT16

Correct Answer = C

Windows 95 release A does not support FAT32. It does utilize COMMAND.COM, comes with a Defragmenter utility, and provides support for FAT16.

4. Which is considered the easiest upgrade path?

- o A. Windows NT to Windows 98
- o B. Windows 95 to Windows 98
- o C. Windows NT to Windows 2000 Professional
- o D. Windows 2000 Professional to Windows 3x

Correct Answer = B

Windows NT cannot be upgraded to Windows 98. Choice D is out of the question. Although the transition from Windows NT to Windows 2000 Professional is fairly straightforward, upgrading from Windows 95 to Windows 98 is considered the easiest upgrade path.

5. **Which are considered the safest ways for common users to edit or make changes to the Registry in Windows 95? (Choose Two)**
   - □ A. REGEDT32
   - □ B. REGEDIT
   - □ C. Device Manager
   - □ D. Control Panel
   - □ E. REGEDT34

   Correct Answers = C and D

   Using the Windows 9x Device Manager and Control Panel options to change settings and devices is considered the safest ways for common users to make edits to the Registry. Common users should not have the ability to make direct edits to the Registry using REGEDT32 or REGEDIT.

6. **The Windows 9x Registry is considered to be what?**
   - o A. A big spreadsheet
   - o B. A hierarchal database made up of keys
   - o C. A multi-tiered tree text file
   - o D. A national database

   Correct Answer = B

   The Windows 9x Registry, as well as the Registries implemented in Windows NT and Windows 2000, are hierarchal databases made up of special Registry keys that hold most of the operating system's software, hardware, and application settings.

7. **You are currently running Windows 95A on a 2GB hard drive. You install a new 10GB drive and configure it as a slave drive. You can see only 2.0GB of the new drive when running FDISK. What is the problem?**
   - o A. Windows 95A has a 2GB limit.
   - o B. Windows 95A is good for only a one-hard-drive system.
   - o C. Windows 98 was previously installed.
   - o D. Hard drive manufacturers have been doing cost cuts and are keeping the other 8GB.

   Correct Answer = A

   Windows 95A provides support for only up to 2GB partitions on a hard drive. If you wish to utilize partitions greater than 2GB, you should install Windows 95B or Windows 98.

8. You want to empty all of the files in your Recycle Bin but you are not quite sure what will happen to them. What happens to files located in the Recycle Bin when it is emptied?

- o A. They are converted from FAT to NTFS.
- o B. They are bound to the IPX/SPX protocol.
- o C. Only the entries in the FAT are removed.
- o D. The hard drive sector is wiped out and marked bad.

Correct Answer = C

When you empty the Recycle Bin, only the entries in the file allocation table are removed. This gives you the ability to recover these files using third-party recovery tools.

9. You are interested in renaming a printer in Windows 9x. What paths could you take? (Choose Two)

- □ A. Start > Settings > Printers
- □ B. Start > Run > Printers > Rename
- □ C. My Computer > Printers
- □ D. Start > Control Panel > Label Printer

Correct Answers = A and C

Answers A and C are valid paths to renaming a printer in Windows 9x. Choices B and C are invalid options.

10. You have installed a new program on your Windows system that is configured to start up automatically when your system starts. When you reboot, the system hangs at the Windows logo screen. What should you do in order to get into Windows?

- o A. Turn the system off and back on. Hold the Shift key down after seeing the Windows logo screen.
- o B. Reinstall Windows.
- o C. Use Alt+Print Screen and present the error to a senior technician.
- o D. After you see the logo screen, count to three and press the Esc key.
- o E. Boot to an antivirus disk and run a full virus scan with updated virus definition files.
- o F. All of the above.

Correct Answer = A

The Shift key is often used at boot-up to bypass applications that start automatically. Reinstalling Windows will help you get into Windows; however, it is not the logical choice here. Choices C, D, and E are invalid selections that will not accomplish the goal of getting into Windows.

REFERENCES

http://www.microsoft.com/whdc/hcl/search.mspx. This site is the home of the Microsoft Windows Hardware Compatibility List. This list can be used to see if your hardware is compatible with a specific Microsoft operating system.

http://windowsupdate.microsoft.com/. You should keep your Windows operating system up to date with the most recent Microsoft updates and security patches. This can be accomplished from this Microsoft Windows Update site.

http://www.Microsoft.com. It is suggested that you visit the Microsoft.com Web site and sharpen up on as many operating systems white pages as possible before taking the A+ Operating Systems Technologies exam.

25 Windows NT

In This Chapter

- Overview of Windows NT
- NT Server vs. NT Workstation
- Installation and Upgrading
- The Windows NT Start-Up Process
- The Windows NT Registry
- Windows NT Networking and Administration
- Resource Sharing and Drive Mapping
- Utilities and Settings
- Printers
- Diagnosing and Troubleshooting Test Tips
- Chapter Summary
- Review Questions
- References

OVERVIEW OF WINDOWS NT

In 1993, Microsoft introduced Windows NT to the world in order to meet the great demand for a true network operating system business solution. The original implementation of NT came in the form of Windows NT Server 3.1. After several modifications, Windows NT Server 3.51 was released. In 1996, Windows NT Server 4.0 and NT Workstation 4.0 were released.

Windows NT was originally designed with the following concepts and features in mind:

Compatibility: It was imperative that Windows NT be able to support and communicate with other file systems, such as FAT, OS/2 HPFS (High Performance File System), Mac OS, CDFS (Compact Disc File System), Unix, Novell

Netware, and other NTFS (NT File System) operating systems. To be compatible with such file systems, NT was designed to provide support for networking protocols such as TCP/IP, IPX/SPX, NWLink, AppleTalk, DLC, and NetBEUI.

Reliability and stability: Windows NT was designed to protect the major components of the operating system from other programs and applications that might fail. It was also designed to protect each program and application from all others by allowing each to run in its own Virtual Machine (VM). Windows NT is also considered the first truly fault-tolerant operating system. It was designed to provide built-in support for redundant storage through the use of Redundant Array of Independent Disks (RAID).

Security: Unlike a peer-to-peer network that uses password-protected shares, Windows NT was designed to centralize the control of user access to network resources through the use of special domain controller computers that authenticate users. These controller computers are known as *primary* and *backup domain controllers.*

Performance: Windows NT was designed to provide support for the use of multiple processors and true multitasking abilities. It can support true 32-bit preemptive multitasking while maintaining backward support for 16-bit cooperative programs.

Internet Explorer and Web services support: Windows NT has built-in support for Internet Explorer and a personal Web server.

The current A+ Operating Systems Technologies exam will most likely focus on your ability to troubleshoot Windows NT boot operations, emergency repair operations, and file system compatibility issues. To give you the best possible chance of passing the exam, it is highly recommended that you support the knowledge you will gain in this chapter with hands-on experience. In other words, follow along with the examples provided in this chapter on a real computer system running Windows NT Server or Workstation 4.0.

NT SERVER VS. NT WORKSTATION

The current A+ exam is likely to refer to Windows NT Server 4.0 and Windows NT Workstation 4.0 simply as Windows NT or Windows NT 4.0. Many of the procedures for carrying out specific tasks are similar in both operating systems.

For example, a Windows NT question relating to the creation of an Emergency Repair Disk (ERD) may come in the following form:

Q. You want to create an Emergency Repair Disk in Windows NT 4.0. What command would you use to do this?

o A. FDISK/ERD

o B. ERD/MAKE

o C. RDISK.EXE

o D. ERD/RDISK

Correct Answer = C

Notice that the question does not focus specifically on Windows NT Server or Windows NT Workstation; an ERD can be created using either operating system. Although you should know the difference between a server computer and a client workstation, focus your studies on the capabilities of the operating system technology as a whole.

Windows NT Server

Windows NT was designed for client/server-based network environments. In a client/server environment, the client computer or workstation requests information from the server computer. For our purposes, the client computer can be Windows 9x, Windows NT Workstation, Windows Me, Windows 2000 Professional, or Windows XP. The server computer can be Windows NT Server or Windows 2000 Server. This section focuses on Windows NT Server.

A Windows NT Server computer is used to provide access to network resources and provide print/file sharing, database, e-mail, and fax services. Windows NT Server can also act as a gateway to mainframe computing systems or act as an Internet gateway server for client computers.

Before a user can log on to a Windows NT domain, the user must be assigned a user ID, which allows him or her to be authenticated on the Windows NT domain. The user ID is assigned specific rights to resources such as directories, files, and printers. This method of assignment provides centralized control of network access and serves as a way to control and secure network file and printer sharing. A *domain* is defined as a group of networked computer systems that share a common Security Accounts Manager (SAM) database that is used as a reference to grant users network access. When a new user is added to a Windows NT domain through the User Manager for Domains administrative tool, the user ID is stored in the Primary Domain Controller's (PDC's) SAM database. This database is replicated to all Backup Domain Controllers (BDCs) that exist in the same domain as the PDC. The purpose of a BDC is to improve network performance by load balancing the network authentication process and provide backup to the PDC in case of failure. In other words, users or clients can be granted access to the network through a BDC or a PDC. The BDC stores an identical copy of the SAM database in case the PDC suffers a crash. There can only be one Windows NT PDC server in a single Windows NT domain. There can be several BDC servers in a single Windows NT domain. The amount of BDCs needed in a domain is directly tied to the amount of users requiring authentication. Microsoft recommends having one BDC for every 2,000 user accounts.

A well-trained network administrator or technician is usually assigned the duties of managing a Windows NT Server domain. The typical duties of a Windows NT network administrator include the following:

- **Managing network access and user permissions:** This includes adding and removing user accounts from the SAM database, managing groups of users, and assigning permissions for users or groups of users to access network resources.
- **Installing and upgrading software:** The administrator is usually responsible for installing and fine-tuning operating system software, such as Windows NT Server or Windows NT Workstation. This may also require software service pack installations, patches, and upgrades. Depending on the business needs of a company, the administrator may also be required to support and integrate many forms of third-party software.
- **Backups and virus protection:** It is the responsibility of the network administrator to provide backup and fault-tolerant systems in the event of an emergency or system failure. In some cases, federal law and business contracts require proof that regular backups and backup procedures are in place in order for business to be conducted or contracts to be maintained. The recent onslaught of damaging computer viruses has created the need for enterprise-wide antivirus business solutions and skilled administrators that can maintain them properly. If you do not have a good backup plan and virus protection implemented, your entire business is at serious risk.
- **Network monitoring and utilization:** It is important that a network be properly monitored for maximum utilization and possible problem areas that may decrease overall network performance. Several tools included with Window NT are used for network monitoring; these will be discussed later in this chapter.

Windows NT Workstation

The majority of clients or computer users never actually see server computers or domain controllers. They access resources on server computers from desktop workstations or laptops that are running client operating systems, such as Windows

9x, Windows Me, Windows NT Workstation, Windows 2000 Professional, or Windows XP.

Windows NT Workstation was developed to be the client-side workhorse of the Windows NT domain. It is designed to handle multitasking operations and support processor-intensive applications and programs. A Windows NT Workstation computer can act as a standalone operating system in a peer-to-peer network or be joined to a Windows NT domain. Many of the administrative functions available in Windows NT Server are also available in Windows NT Workstation. Workstations are thought to have less functionality and are only useful at the local operating system level.

INSTALLATION AND UPGRADING

Many factors must be considered as you prepare for a successful installation or upgrade of Windows NT. The installation processes for Windows NT Workstation and Windows NT Server are quite similar. Shortly, you will be guided through a full installation of Windows NT Server. Before the installation process is explained, there are several factors you need to consider; these important factors are explained next.

Before You Start

Microsoft provides strict minimum hardware requirements for the installation of Windows NT Workstation and Windows NT Server. You should verify that your system meets or exceeds the minimum recommendations before installation. The minimum hardware requirements for a typical Windows NT Workstation installation are a 486 processor, 12MB of RAM, a VGA display adapter, 110MB of available hard drive space, a CD-ROM device, and 3.5-inch floppy drive. The recommended requirements for a Windows NT Workstation installation are a Pentium processor, 16MB of RAM, SVGA support, 300MB of available hard drive space, a CD-ROM device, a 3.5-inch drive, and an NIC.

As mentioned in Chapter 24, you should always consult the manufacturer's specifications before installing any software. Minimum and recommended hardware requirements for Windows NT Server as well as other Microsoft operating systems can be found at the Microsoft Web site (*http://www.microsoft.com*). It is also important to verify that your installed hardware is supported by the operating system you are installing. If you are installing a Windows operating system, you should check your installed hardware against the hardware compatibility list at *http://www.microsoft.com/whdc/hcl/default.mspx*.

Before installing Windows NT on a hard drive, you must also consider which type of file system the operating system will use. Windows NT works with FAT16 and NTFS. It is not compatible with FAT32 partitions unless you utilize special third-party programs. If you are planning a clean install of Windows NT on a hard drive, you should use NTFS in order to take full advantage of its many benefits. The benefits of NTFS include its overall ability to recover from system failure; support for RAID mirroring, which enables data to be written to two hard drives simultaneously, resulting in a complete hard disk backup; smaller cluster size than FAT16, which enables NTFS to support larger partitioned drive volumes and make better overall use of disk space; and the ability to provide file-level security and auditing.

If you are installing Windows NT on the same hard drive as Windows 9x or DOS, you will want to use FAT16. FAT16 gives you the ability to see files across operating systems and partitions located on the same hard drive. You can always convert a FAT16 partition to NTFS later from a command prompt by entering the following command:

```
CONVERT C:/FS:NTFS
```

The Windows NT command prompt can be accessed by selecting Start >Run and entering "CMD" at the Open line. CMD.EXE is the actual command prompt in Windows NT, Windows 2000, and Windows XP. You can also navigate to the Windows NT command prompt by selecting Start > Programs > Command Prompt.

If you want to create a dual boot scenario, which will allow you to boot into either the Windows 9x or Windows NT operating systems (assuming they are installed on the same hard drive), you must have a bootable FAT system partition.

NOTE

If you have Windows NT installed on the same hard drive as Windows 9x, and you cannot view files between the operating system's partitions, you most likely have Windows 9x installed on a FAT32 partition.

Another important fact about NTFS and FAT32 partitions is that if you copy files from an NTFS partition or 'volume' to a FAT32 partition or 'volume,' the files will retain their file attributes and long file names. They will also retain any information stored in the file. However, they will lose their compression status, file permissions assigned from within Windows NT, and any encryption status.

This may seem like an awful lot to consider before installation, but it is important to consider all these items in order to achieve your operating system goals.

The Installation Process

The Windows NT Server installation process can be started in one of two ways.

To initiate an *over-the-network installation*, do the following:

1. Share a networked CD-ROM device and place the Windows NT Server CD-ROM in the shared device. Alternatively, copy the I386 directory and its contents to a local or shared network drive.
2. If you are using Windows or DOS, use the WINNT.EXE command from the client computer to execute the start-up process. If you are upgrading from an older Windows NT version, use the WINNT32.EXE command from the client computer. You will be presented with the Windows NT Setup screen. From this point on, follow the instructions in the next section.

To initiate the installation process *using the three Windows NT installation floppy disks and the Windows NT Server CD-ROM*, do the following:

1. Assuming that your system is configured to boot first to a floppy drive, insert the installation floppy disk labeled "Setup Boot Disk" into the floppy drive, place the Windows NT Server installation CD-ROM into the CD-ROM device, and restart the system.
2. The Windows NT Setup screen appears. The installation will continue until you are prompted for the second installation floppy disk. While the information on the second disk is processed, you will see the Windows NT kernel loading the version and associated build number. The "Welcome to Setup" screen appears, which gives you the options to Continue, Repair, or Exit the installation process. In this case, you want to choose the Continue option and proceed with installation. Next, the license agreement appears. Page down to the end and press the F8 key to acknowledge your acceptance.
3. You will be asked to insert the third installation floppy disk. The installation process continues searching your system for installed hardware devices. At this point, the installation process has gathered enough information to determine if an older Windows NT operating system has been installed on the hard drive. If the process finds evidence of an earlier version, you will be prompted with the following options:

   - To upgrade, press Enter.
   - To cancel upgrade and install a fresh copy, press "N".

   Since we are doing a clean install, the second option is appropriate. The installation process continues, displaying the system type, video card, keyboard, and mouse information. The installation process continues until a list appears of the available partitions the program has found on your hard drive. If you have multiple partitions, you must select one on which to install Windows NT. Be careful not to install NT onto a partition that currently contains a file system with information you want to keep. If you have one partition, select it and press Enter.

4. Next, you are given several options, including a choice of file system to format the partition with.
   - Format the partition using the FAT file system.
   - Format the partition using the NTFS file system.

   As explained above, format with FAT if you wish to maintain compatibility or dual boot with a DOS or Windows 9x partition. Use NTFS if you are interested in performance, program protection, file-level security, and support for file names of up to 254 characters in length. Choose the file system you want to format with and press Enter.
5. After the partition has been formatted, you are asked for the location in which to install the Windows NT files. The default location provided for you is \WINNT. Accept the default by pressing Enter. You will then be prompted for permission to scan the hard drive for corruption. Press Enter to continue. The Setup program will continue to copy files to the hard drive, and you will eventually be asked to press Enter again to restart the system. As the system starts back up, you will notice the "Last Known Good Menu" pass by. This feature will be available every time you restart the operating system in the future. It is used to assist you with restoring the last known good system configuration stored on your drive in case you make operating system configuration mistakes.
6. You are asked for the type of installation you would like, including Typical, Portable, Compact, or Custom. It is best at this point to choose the Typical installation and click Next. You will then be asked to supply a name and company name. Enter the appropriate information and continue. Next, you are asked to provide a CD key, which is provided with the installation CD-ROM kit. Enter it and continue. Then you must enter the type of licensing you would like to use. The two licensing options are per seat and per server.
   - **Per seat means per device:** If you have a 300 per-seat license, 300 users can sign on to and legally use any of the Windows NT servers in your business.
   - **Per server:** If you purchase 50 per-server licenses, or CALS, as Microsoft calls them, any 50 devices can connect to the specific server simultaneously.

   If you need more help determining which license type to use, go to the following Microsoft Web site: *http://www.microsoft.com/resources/sam/licensing/cal_guide/default.asp.*

Enter the appropriate license type, select the number of licenses you have purchased, and continue. Next, you will be asked to specify a computer name of 15 characters or less for your server and to choose whether it will be a PDC, BDC, or standalone server. If this is the first server on your network, you should choose the PDC option. If it is the second domain controller installed, choose the BDC option. If the server is going to be used for exchange (e-mail), SQL (database), fax, or as a file and print server, you should choose the standalone server option. After you have chosen the type of server that will be created, the installation process will ask you to configure a password of 14 characters or less for the administrator account. Confirm the password by entering it a second time, and click Next.

7. You are now prompted to create an ERD. If you choose the "Yes" option, Setup will ask you to insert a blank floppy disk into the floppy drive, and the ERD is created. You can select the "No" option and create an ERD later by entering RDISK/S at the Start > Run > Open line in the Windows NT GUI. The ERD disk contains valuable system configuration information that can be used to restore your system if it fails. The /S switch used with the RDISK command is used to back up the SAM database.
8. After you have created an ERD, Setup offers you the opportunity to install additional components, such as accessories, communications options, games, multimedia, and Windows messaging. Select the components you wish to add and click Next.
9. Windows NT Setup then informs you that you are entering the Windows NT Networking portion of Setup. You are asked to choose how to connect the server from the following choices:

   - Do not connect this computer to a network at this time.
   - This computer will participate on a network:
     - Wired to the network
     - Remote access to the network

   To connect to a network and allow the installation process to continue, select "This computer will participate on a network:" and choose "Wired to the network." Setup then asks if you would like the Internet Information Server (IIS) installed. Do not select this option unless you want the server to provide Web services.
10. Next, you are prompted to allow Setup to automatically detect your Network Interface Card (NIC).
11. Assuming that Setup has found the NIC, and it has been configured properly, you are then asked which network protocols you would like to install. By default, Windows NT Setup chooses TCP/IP, NetBEUI, and IPX/SPX for you. Accept the defaults, unless you require additional protocols. Setup

then asks if you require special services. Accept the default unless you have special needs, and continue. Next, you will be asked if the system will be part of a workgroup or a domain. If this is the first server in a new domain, you will not be presented with this option. If you are joining this server to an existing domain, you can add it with a domain administrator's user ID and password.

12. Finally, you will need to set your system's time zone and adjust video display options. After this, the system will restart at least once, and you boot directly into the Windows NT GUI.

Installation Notes

Windows NT can use a unique database file and an answer file to automate the setup of multiple Windows NT installations. If you use these two files to automate your installation, you will be required to include within these two files most of the responses to the installation questions described above.

There are several important switches that you can use in combination with the Windows NT Setup commands. Some of these important switches and useful installation notes are described here:

- Windows NT can be installed on the same hard drive as Windows 9x, but Windows 9x cannot be upgraded to Windows NT. Windows NT uses a different Registry and operating system structure. If you are installing Windows NT on the same hard drive as Windows 9x, you must specify a different location for Setup to install the necessary files to; otherwise, Setup will overwrite your previous Windows 9x installation.
- If you want to create the three Windows NT installation floppy disks after Setup has completed, you can use the command WINNT32.EXE with the switch /OX from a Windows NT command prompt. You can install Windows NT without being prompted for the three installation floppy diskettes by entering the command WINNT/B2 from a command prompt. This assumes that you have the Windows NT CD-ROM inserted in a CD device.
- The /I:inf_file switch is used with the WINNT command to identify the name of the Setup information file to be used for an automated installation. The default file name is DOSNET.INF. The /udf switch is used during an unattended installation to specify unique settings for specific computers in the uniqueness database file.

THE WINDOWS NT START-UP PROCESS

In order to support and troubleshoot the Windows NT operating system, it is very important to understand the Windows NT boot sequence and what really happens behind the scenes before the Windows NT GUI appears.

The following steps detail the Windows NT start-up process:

1. When you push the power button on your system unit or select "Restart the computer?" from the Shut Down Windows menu, the system BIOS executes the POST (Power-On Self-Test).
2. The BIOS then looks to load the MBR (Master Boot Record), which is located on the hard disk. The MBR, which is actually a small program, is used to locate the active partition on the hard drive, which holds the operating system's boot sector.
3. The MBR runs the operating system program boot instructions, which are located in the boot sector.
4. The file Ntldr (NT Loader) that is stored in the root directory of the system partition (C:\) is executed. Ntldr is the first Windows NT operating system file loaded during the start-up process. It is the main file used to see that the OS boot process is carried out properly. It can be compared to the IO.SYS file that is utilized with Windows 9x.
5. Ntldr changes the operating system processor mode from Real Mode to 32-bit mode. This allows a 32-bit file system to be loaded. Keep in mind that Windows NT is a 32-bit operating system. In order for Ntldr to read both FAT and NTFS, the processor mode must be altered to run in 32-bit mode.
6. Ntldr reads the BOOT.INI file, which displays a choice of operating system boot-up options to the screen. By default, the choices are:
   - Windows NT Workstation Version 4.00 (or Windows NT Server if installed)
   - Windows NT Workstation Version 4.00 [VGA mode]

   These options display for a default of 25 seconds. If you do not choose an option, the system will boot to the option that is selected in the System Startup section of System Properties in the Windows NT Control Panel (Figure 25.1). As shown in Figure 25.1, you can change the amount of time that the System Startup menu list is displayed. You can also change the location of where the MEMORY.DMP file stored if a "STOP" error occurs during system startup. Please note that the MEMORY.DMP file is stored in the system root by default.

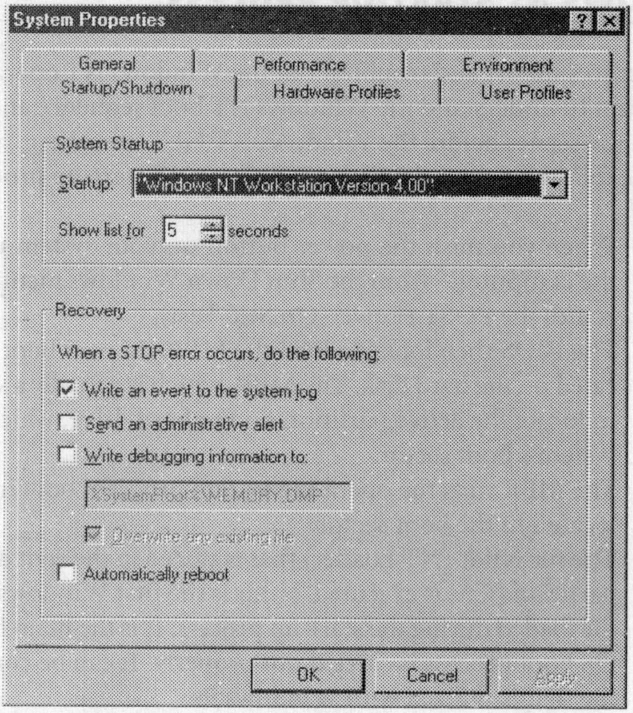

FIGURE 25.1 The Startup/Shutdown tab of the System's Properties window.

7. If the option to boot into "Windows NT Workstation (or Server) Version 4.00" was chosen in the previous step, Ntldr will call on the program Ntdetect.com to gather information on hardware that is connected to the OS. This information will later be loaded into the Windows NT Registry. If another option was chosen in step 6, such as an option to boot into DOS or Windows 9x (assuming that a dual boot scenario was created), Ntldr will call on the file Bootsect.dos to handle the responsibility of loading alternative operating systems.
8. In this step, Ntldr reads the system archive that is located in the Windows NT Registry for all hardware devices and associated drivers. Ntldr also loads the files NTOSKRNL.EXE and HAL.DLL. Ntoskrnl is known as the Windows NT kernel. It resides in main memory at all times after it is loaded. It is the core or central module of the Windows NT operating system, and is responsible for memory management and all tasks associated with the OS. The Windows NT Hardware Abstraction Layer (HAL) is a device-level layer of code that allows programs for the operating system to be utilized without

the overhead of APIs. The HAL is a required operating system component that provides a seamless connection from the Windows NT kernel to hardware devices.

9. Ntldr hands complete control of the operating system over to Ntoskrln. This completes the start-up process.

Resolving Nt Boot Issues

Many things can cause Windows NT Server or Windows Workstation to boot up improperly, including incorrectly configured IRQ and I/O settings, problems with NTLDR, and important system files being deleted or overwritten. Following are some of the most common boot issues and the proper methods of troubleshooting or resolving them.

- If you can't boot into your Windows NT operating system, you should always first attempt to use the "Last Known Good Configuration" option on start-up. You can initiate this option by pressing the space bar when you see the "Last Known Good Configuration" option displayed at start-up. As stated earlier, when you choose this option on start-up, the system attempts to restore the last good operating system configuration load. This option is not useful if you have already booted into a configuration that is corrupt.
- If you receive the error message "Boot could not find NTLDR. Please insert another disk." on start-up, it is advisable to run the ERD process. The ERD process restores important system files. In order for Windows NT to boot properly, the files NTLDR, BOOT.INI, and NT DETECT.COM must be located in the root directory of the system partition.

NOTE

NTLDR, BOOT.INI, and NT DETECT.COM are the same three files that must be on a Windows NT boot disk in order for it to be bootable.

- If you receive an error message stating that Windows NT could not start because the file NTOSKRNL.EXE could not be found, it will be necessary to install a backup copy of this file from the ERD.

THE WINDOWS NT REGISTRY

The Windows NT Registry is very similar to the Registry used with Windows 9x. The main difference is that the Windows NT Registry is a 32-bit program. The Windows 9x Registry is a 16-bit program. Windows NT stores Registry information in a file

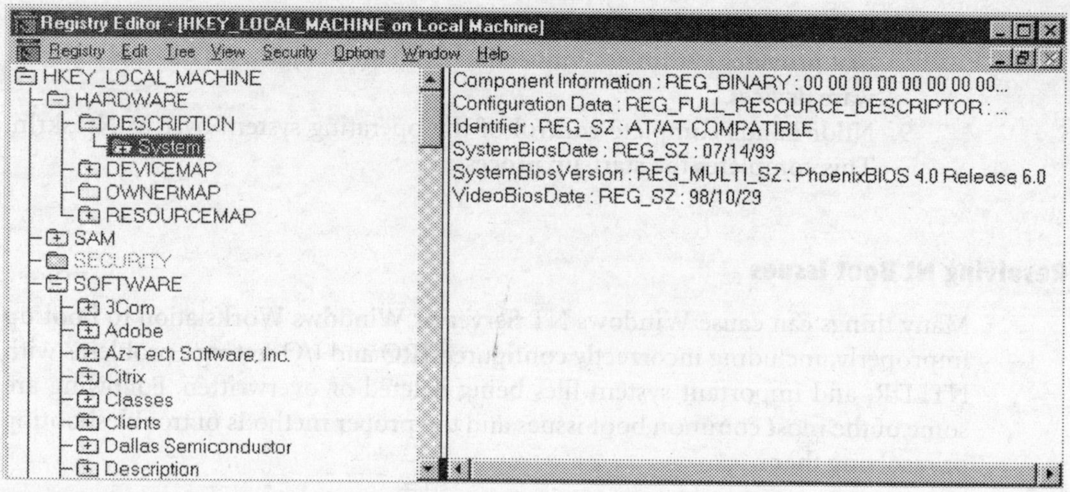

FIGURE 25.2 Windows NT Registry Editor displaying subkeys and values.

called REG.DAT. To maintain the ability to modify and communicate with older 16-bit programs, Windows NT supports the 16-bit registration database program editor REGEDIT.EXE that is used with Windows 9x. REGEDT32.EXE is the Windows NT Registry editor that displays the Registry Keys in the right pane of the display and the Registry values in the left pane (Figure 25.2).

You can use either REGEDIT.EXE or REGEDT32.EXE to make changes to the Registry in Windows NT. Make sure that you update your ERD disk using RDISK /S from a Windows NT command prompt before making any changes to the Registry.

If you would like more information about the differences between REGEDIT.EXE and REGEDT32.EXE, visit the Microsoft Product Support Web site at *http://support.microsoft.com/support/kb/articles/Q141/3/77.ASP*.

WINDOWS NT NETWORKING AND ADMINISTRATION

As mentioned earlier in this chapter, a Windows NT Workstation can participate in a workgroup or a domain environment. In a workgroup, each computer system houses its own SAM database. In a domain environment, the SAM database is located in a more central location, such as a PDC or BDC. This allows administrators to control user access to the network and provide for the sharing of network resources from a centralized location. A workgroup model mirrors a peer-to-peer network in which security and the sharing of resources is controlled at every machine. Imagine organizing a workgroup of 200 users—you would have to control user access to the workgroup and password-protected shares at every single system!

User Account Creation and Management

Windows NT comes with an administrator account that is used to manage and maintain the operating system. You were asked to create a password for this account during the Windows NT installation process. Keep in mind that a Windows NT administrator account can be renamed, but it cannot be deleted. Once you are logged on as the administrator, you can create user accounts (or user IDs), which grant users access to a Windows NT network.

User accounts are created in User Manager on Windows NT Workstation. User Manager can be accessed by selecting Start > Programs > Administrative Tools [Common] > User Manager. Selecting User Manager brings up the window shown in Figure 25.3. If you are using Windows NT Server, you will administer user accounts with User Manager for domains. User Manager for Windows NT Workstation is a scaled-down version of the more complex User Manager for Domains.

Following are guidelines for creating Windows NT User IDs and passwords:

- User IDs can be up to 20 characters long and are not case sensitive.
- User IDs can be made up of numbers, letters, and allowable characters.
- Passwords can be up to 14 characters long and are case sensitive.
- Passwords can be made up of numbers, letters, and allowable characters. The following characters can be used to make up a password: ` ~ ! @ # $ % ^ & * () _ + - = { } | [ ] \ : " ; ' @ : ? , . /
- As shown in Figure 25.3, User Manager has several built-in groups. These groups are designed for ease of administration. A Windows NT built-in group

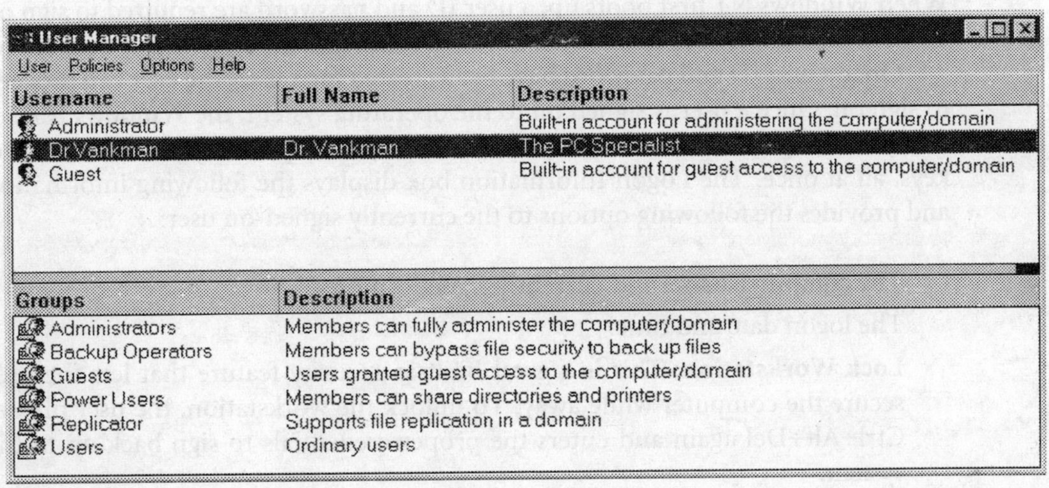

FIGURE 25.3 The Windows NT User Manager.

has pre-assigned user rights. Windows NT user rights allow users or groups of users to carry out specific tasks, including the right to backup the system, shut down the system, or change the system time. After a user ID has been created in User Manager, it can be placed in a group. When the user ID is placed in a group, the ID inherits all the rights associated with that group. For example, if the user ID BSAWYER were created and added to the Administrator Group, the user BSAWYER would inherit all the user rights associated with the Administrator Group.

Every Windows NT Workstation or Server has a set of built-in local groups. If a user has been placed into a local group, it is possible for the user to access resources and be granted rights on the local system. To ease domain-level administration efforts, Windows NT Server also makes use of global groups. Many users can be placed in a global group, and the global group can then be added to a local group located on a workstation or server. The end result is that it is possible for all users in the global group to access resources assigned to the local group on a particular workstation or server.

In addition to creating user IDs and assigning user rights, User Manager also has the ability to audit the success and failure of events that occur on the system. An administrator can audit access to files and objects, users who have logged on or logged off the system, and security policy changes, just to name a few. The results of the events that have been audited are displayed in the Windows NT Event Viewer. Event Viewer is described under "Utilities and Settings," later in this chapter.

Logon

When Windows NT first boots up, a user ID and password are required to sign on to the local computer system or the network (domain) the system is connected to.

Once a user ID and password have been created for a user, the user can proceed to sign on. Once a user is signed on to the operating system, the Windows NT Security and Logon Information box can be displayed by pressing the Ctrl+Alt+Del keys, all at once. The Logon Information box displays the following information and provides the following options to the currently signed-on user:

The computer name and currently signed-on user.

The logon date and time.

Lock Workstation: This is a great built-in security feature that lets the user secure the computer while away. To unlock the workstation, the user presses Ctrl+Alt+Del again and enters the proper credentials to sign back on to the system.

Logoff: The option to end the current Windows NT session is available. Simply select the Logoff radio button. The message "This will end your Windows NT session" appears. Select the OK button, and you will be logged off the system.

Shut Down: If you select the Shut Down option, you are presented with the option to shut down the system or shut down and restart. These options are the same as the options offered by selecting Start > Shut Down from the Windows NT Desktop display. The only exception is that you are also offered the ability to close all programs and log on as a different user if you use Start > Shut Down.

Change Password: If you have been granted the right to change your own password by a network administrator or network security person, you can select the Change Password radio button to change your sign-on password (user rights are discussed shortly).

Task Manager: Similar to Windows 9x, Windows NT comes with a built-in Task Manager. (Task Manager is discussed in more detail later.) You can enter the Task Manager by selecting the Task Manager radio button.

Cancel: The last option is the Cancel radio button. If Cancel is selected, you are directed back to the Windows NT Desktop.

It is important to note that the same Windows Security and Information display can be accessed in Windows 2000 Professional and Windows NT Server by following the same procedures. The information and options available are identical.

LSA, SID, and ACL

Security access to resources and the entire security sign-on process that takes place when a user logs on to Windows NT is very complicated and beyond the scope of this book. However, a basic explanation of the process is in order.

When a user logs on to Windows NT Workstation, the Local Security Authority (LSA) generates what is called a Security Access Token (SAT). This SAT is assigned a SID (Security ID for the user). The unique user SID contains access rights and privileges that have been assigned to the user's ID that was created in User Manager or User Manager for Domains (explained in the next section). Windows NT maintains an *Access Control List* (ACL) for all objects on the Windows NT domain. An object can be a file, a folder, or a printer share, just to name a few. In order for a user to be granted access to an object on the domain, the user's SAT must be accepted by the ACL. It is improbable that the A+ Operating System Technologies exam will address detailed questions on this subject.

User Profiles and System Policies

A Windows NT local user profile is created when a user first logs on to a Windows NT system. The local user profile is a configuration of the environmental settings and preferences that have been established by the user. In simple terms, a user profile is a combination of Desktop configuration settings the user sees every time he or she logs on. An administrator may implement a roaming user profile for an individual if he or she wishes to use the particular configuration settings assigned to the user at any other computer.

With a roaming user profile, the user's profile information is stored on a server computer and is presented to the user wherever he or she logs on to the network.

Windows NT has a useful tool for controlling user environments, called the System Policy Editor. With the System Policy Editor tool, an administrator can configure system policies for computers, users, or groups of users. For example, let's say you wanted all users who signed on to the network as the user ID GUEST to be restricted from changing the screen saver and wallpaper, and editing the Registry. You can use the built-in settings within System Policy Editor to create a policy for the user ID GUEST and apply the restrictions above. You would then need to copy the file NTCONFIG.POL (which is the policy you have saved in System Policy Editor) to the NETLOGON share on the authentication server. When the user GUEST logs on to the network, the policy takes effect.

Profiles and system policies are basically tools used by administrators to control a Windows NT network.

Dial-Up Networking

Dial-up networking allows you to connect to remote networks using a modem or ISDN connection from within Windows NT. If you did not choose the Remote Access to the Network option during the Windows NT installation process, dial-up networking is not installed on your system. If this is the case, you can add dial-up networking by accessing the Network applet located in the Control Panel, select the Services tab, and click the Add radio button. A list of network services opens. Choose Remote Access Service, and click OK. Remote Access Service must be installed to utilize dial-up networking. You will be asked for the location of the I386 folder, which contains Windows NT installation .CAB files. Insert the Windows NT installation CD-ROM if you have not copied the I386 directory to the C:\ drive (which, by the way, is common practice among NT administrators; this avoids the need to use the installation CD-ROM to install services and drivers). Select Continue, and the Remote Access Service will attempt to find a modem connected to your system. Simply follow the instructions for the modem identification and associated COM port, and reboot the system when prompted. This process also installs a network dial-up adapter, which can be seen in the Network applet of the Control Panel once you have rebooted.

After you have rebooted your system, navigate to My Computer > Dial-Up Networking. You will be required to set up a phone book entry and configure the proper protocols and authentication methods used to communicate with the Dial-up Server. From here, it's as simple as clicking the phone book entry you have created to access a server remotely.

If you are using dial-up networking in Windows 9x or Windows NT, and cannot connect to a dial-up server—or an ISP, for that matter—you should first try to establish a new connection within dial-up networking. For Windows 9x, select the New Modem option from the Dial-Up Networking Connection Properties. For Windows NT, attempt to create and configure a new phone book entry from within the Dial-Up Networking applet in My Computer.

NOTE

In order to establish a dial-up connection with the Internet, you must have TCP/IP and a network dial-up adapter.

RESOURCE SHARING AND DRIVE MAPPING

The procedures for sharing folders, printers, and other resources in Windows 9x, Windows NT, and Windows 2000 are all relatively similar.

To share a folder within the Windows NT operating system, navigate to Windows NT Explorer by clicking Start > Programs > Windows NT Explorer, or right-click the Start button and select Explore. Once in Explorer, right-click on a folder to be shared with other users, then select the Sharing tab. If the folder has been previously shared, the Shared As button will be selected, and a Share Name will appear, as shown in Figure 25.4. You will also notice that in Windows Explorer, a previously shared folder is displayed with a hand holding it so as to share its contents. If a folder is not shared, the Not Shared button will be selected. Simply select the Shared As button and enter a Share Name. Select Apply, then OK, and the folder will be shared.

Notice the Permissions button shown in Figure 25.4. If you click Permissions from within the OS, you will see the users who have access to the newly created share. By default, the Everyone Group in Windows NT has access and full control of newly created folder shares and printer shares. You can choose the Add or Remove options in the Access Through Share Permissions box to grant or disallow specific users to access your share. You can also change the type of access a particular user or group of users has to your share. The types of access rights that can be assigned to folder-level shares in Windows NT are No Access, Read, Change, and Full Control.

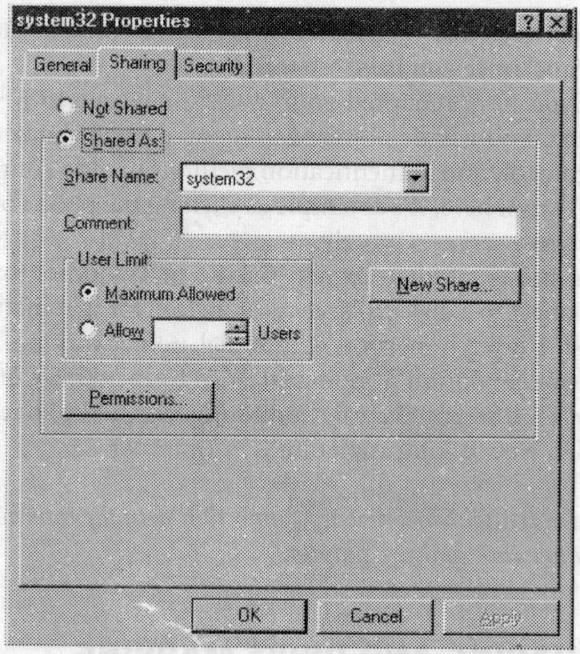

FIGURE 25.4 Sharing a folder in Windows NT.

So far, we have discussed folder sharing and permissions. If you look at Figure 25.4 once again, you will notice the Security tab. The presence of this Security tab indicates that the system has been configured with NTFS. We can use the Security tab to apply file-level permissions, implement auditing, or take ownership of selected items (Figure 25.5). These features are available only with Windows NT and Windows 2000. File-level permissions and auditing are not available in Windows 9x.

Establishing drive mappings in an operating system allows you to connect to other computers, printers, and network resources. Having static drive mappings comes in very handy for displaying, moving, and copying information from one location to another.

To map a network drive in Windows NT, follow these instructions:

1. Right-click on the Network Neighborhood icon on the Desktop.
2. Select Map Network Drive. The Map Network Drive dialog box will appear.
3. From the Drive list, select the drive letter you wish to map.
4. Enter a path for your mapping. You need to enter the UNC name for the location of the server and share you wish to map to—for example, \\Servername\Sharename.

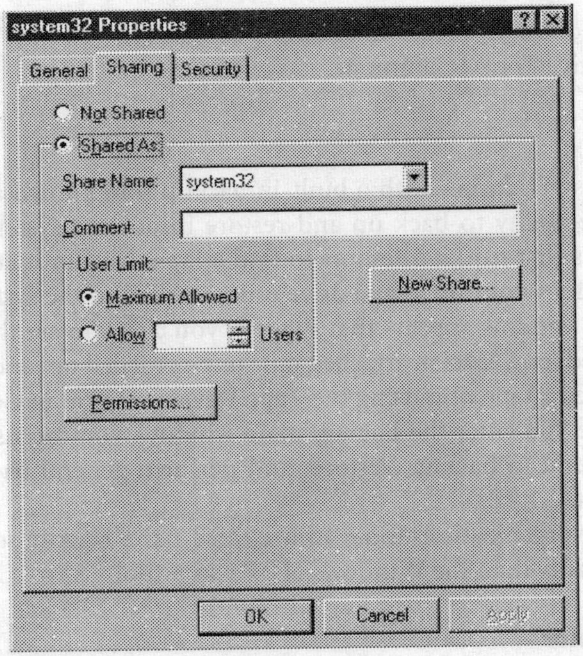

FIGURE 25.5 Windows NT Security tab.

5. Select Reconnect at login to retain your mappings when you reboot the system.
6. Click OK.

Another way to access the Map Network Drive dialog box is to navigate to Windows NT Explorer and select Tools from the menu bar. You will have the option to Map Network Drive or Disconnect Network Drive.

After you have mapped to a resource on the network, your drive mappings can be located in Windows NT Explorer or My Computer.

UTILITIES AND SETTINGS

Windows NT offers utilities and tools for such tasks as formatting hard drives and assigning drive letters to volumes; monitoring and logging the performance of workstation or server computers; viewing system, security, and application event logs; and backing up critical information. Some of the more commonly used tools and their functions are described next. All the following tools are located in the Administrative

Tools [Common] area, which can be accessed by selecting Start > Programs > Administrative Tools [Common].

Backup

Windows NT comes with a built-in backup tool known as Backup. Backup provides the ability to back up and restore important system files and data. When Backup is first run, it attempts to find a tape drive unit attached to the system. If Backup does not find a tape drive unit attached to the system, a Tape Drive Error Detected window appears that suggests you check to see that the proper cables are connected, power to an attached tape unit is turned on, and that you have properly configured a tape unit using the Tape Devices option in Control Panel.

Once you enter the Backup main window, you can use the Operations drop-down menu to backup, restore, and perform general backup tape maintenance functions.

Most organizations today utilize third-party backup software that offers more functionality than the Windows NT Backup tool.

Disk Administrator

The Windows NT Disk Administrator is a very useful administrative tool that lets you format drive space, assign and change drive labels, and implement fault-tolerant systems by establishing disk mirror sets and disk stripe sets.

Disk Administrator is located in the Administrative Tools [Common] area. Once you open the Disk Administrator, the window shown in Figure 25.6 appears.

From the Partition drop-down menu, you can delete, create, or extend partitions and create volume sets or stripe sets. From the Tools drop-down menu, you can format a displayed drive or volume, assign a drive letter to a disk or volume, or display the properties of a drive.

Explaining every function of the Windows NT Disk Administrator is beyond the scope of this book; however, it is important for you to understand the terms mentioned here for the A+ Operating Systems Technologies test.

Fault Tolerance and Raid

Fault tolerance is the ability of a computer system to recover from a hardware or software failure or crash. There are several types of fault-tolerant hard disk configurations and specifications known as RAID levels.

Several levels of RAID are available today that provide fault-tolerant systems. It is important that you have a basic understanding of the following three levels of RAID.

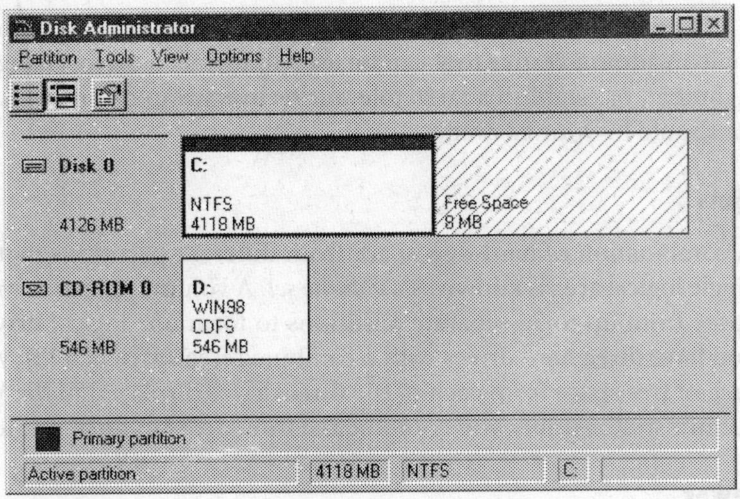

FIGURE 25.6 Windows NT Disk Administrator.

RAID level 0, or disk striping without parity: With this level of RAID, data is spread or written over multiple hard disks. This technique provides better performance of read-and-write operations than other levels of RAID, but it is not considered fault tolerant.

RAID level 1, disk mirroring, or disk duplexing: To use RAID level 1 and establish what is called a disk mirror with the Windows NT Disk Administrator, you need two installed hard drives. After you have established a mirror within Windows NT Disk Administrator, all data written to your first hard drive is also written to the second hard drive. This provides true fault tolerance. If one of your hard drives fails, the other drive can be used to recover data. With disk mirroring, only one hard drive controller card is used to support both hard drives. *Disk duplexing* is the same as disk mirroring, with one exception: a second hard drive controller card is used; therefore disk duplexing is more fault tolerant than disk mirroring.

RAID level 5, otherwise known as disk striping with parity: RAID level 5 is one of the most widely used fault-tolerant implementations. This RAID level requires a minimum of three hard drives installed in a single system and can support up to 32 hard drives. With RAID level 5, all information and parity data are spread across the disks. If one disk crashes, the information needed to implement a complete recovery by the system can be gathered from the other two disks.

If you encounter a question on the OS exam that asks which Windows NT built-in administrative tool can be used to format a drive, change a drive letter assignment, or establish a fault-tolerant recovery implementation, *Disk Administrator* should be your answer.

Volume Sets

A combination of hard disk space from different partitions that is used to form a single logical area is known as a *volume set*. A volume set can combine the free drive space from up to 32 separate partitions to form one logical drive. For example, if you have three hard drives with a combined free space of 4GB, you can select each area of free space from each of the three drives displayed in the Windows NT Disk Administrator utility and combine the three areas to form one logical drive.

Event Viewer

The Windows NT Event Viewer, also located in the Administrative Tools [Common] area, is used to monitor and evaluate significant events that occur within the operating system. Event Viewer maintains three separate event logs, each of which has its own unique purpose for monitoring and troubleshooting important events.

The three main event logs that can be viewed with Event Viewer are the System Log, the Security Log, and the Application Log.

System Log: This maintains information pertaining to important system events, such as services that have been stopped or started within the operating system. Some of these services may include the Event Log service, the computer browser service, DHCP service, or any other service run by the system. The System Log also maintains useful start-up information that can be used to troubleshoot components that are attached to the system.

Security Log: As mentioned earlier in the User Manager sections, enabled events in the Audit Policy are displayed in the Security Log. The Security Log can keep a record of successful and unsuccessful logon attempts to the domain or network. It can also track file and object access, as well as system restarts and shutdowns.

Application Log: The application log keeps track of important information about system-related applications. These applications may include Microsoft Office, antivirus software, and Windows Update.

Over time, the event logs that are maintained within the Event Viewer can use up important hard drive space and cause your system to run slowly or crash. A good practice is to change the default settings from "Overwrite events older than 7 days" to "Overwrite events as needed."

Performance Monitor

Windows NT includes an important add-on utility that can be used to track and monitor the performance of system components and the overall performance of a workstation or server computer. This tool is called the Windows NT Performance Monitor. Some of the most useful information that can be gathered and logged by performance monitor includes processor utilization, memory utilization, memory page faults per second, percentage of free disk space, and real-time server counters to keep track of important server utilization.

Windows Nt Diagnostics

Yet another very useful tool included with Windows NT is the Windows NT Diagnostics utility. This utility can be used to view and troubleshoot system resources, such as IRQs, I/O ports, DMA channels, memory, and devices. All system services as well as environmental variables can also be viewed through Windows NT Diagnostics.

The Windows NT Diagnostics utility can be accessed through the Administrative Tools [Common] area or by selecting Start > Run and entering "WINMSD" on the Open line. The Windows NT Diagnostics utility is not meant to be used for updating or changing system or environmental settings; it is simply a representation of settings and information stored in the Registry, and used for diagnostics and troubleshooting.

TCP/IP Utilities

Several important utilities are part of the TCP/IP package and are installed with Windows NT Workstation and Windows NT Server by default. These utilities are used to troubleshoot and test network connectivity issues. Following are descriptions of the most commonly used TCP/IP utilities and their functions. Note that all these utilities work in a similar manner in Windows 2000.

PING

Short for Packet Internet Groper, PING is a utility used to test the connection between two computers. The following syntax is used to PING a computer by IP address or by name:

```
PING 209.15.176.206
PING CHARLESRIVER.COM
```

The PING utility works by sending a TCP/IP packet to a destination IP address and waiting for a reply. If the destination host receives the packet of information, four echo replies are received at the computer that initiated the PING command.

PING is most commonly used to test connections to the Internet and ISPs. If you want to test a particular connection to a host IP address over a period of time (persistent), you can use the PING -t command. For example, to run a persistent PING to test your connection to the Charles River Media Web site, enter the following at a command prompt:

```
PING -t 209.15.176.206
```

To stop your connection test, simply press the Ctrl+C key combination.

IPCONFIG

You should recall from Chapter 24 that the WINIPCFG command is used at a Windows 9x command prompt to display TCP/IP information, such as a system's IP address, subnet mask, and default gateway. Windows NT and Windows 2000 utilize the TCP/IP utility IPCONFIG to display the same information. You can display a system's IP address and additional information by navigating to a Windows NT or Windows 2000 command prompt and entering "IPCONFIG."

The following results are from entering the IPCONFIG command at a Windows 2000 command prompt:

```
Windows 2000 IP Configuration
Ethernet adapter Local Area Connection 3:
      Connection-specific DNS Suffix . : srst1.fl.home.com
      IP Address . . . . . . . . . . . : 192.168.1.101
      Subnet Mask . . . . . . . . . . . : 255.255.255.0
      Default Gateway . . . . . . . . . : 192.168.1.1
```

TRACERT

The TCP/IP TRACERT utility is used to troubleshoot connections between routes that a packet will take before reaching its destination address. In other words, TRACERT measures the time it takes for a packet of information to move between routers in hops until it reaches its destination. You can view the results of TRACERT and the time it takes for the packet to move between routers to see where the slow response is located. To run a TRACERT to the Charles River Media Web site, enter the following command at a command prompt:

```
TRACERT CHARLESRIVER.COM
```

The results from a system running a TRACERT to the Charles River Media Web site are displayed next. The TRACERT results end when you see "Trace complete."

```
Tracing route to CHARLESRIVER.COM [209.15.176.206]
over a maximum of 30 hops:
1 10 ms 10 ms 10 ms 10.101.0.1
2 20 ms 10 ms 20 ms atm5-0-953.tampflerl-rtr2.tampabay.rr.com
[65.32.11.146]
3 10 ms 10 ms 10 ms srp8-0.tampflerl-rtr4.tampabay.rr.com [65.32.8.228]
4 10 ms 10 ms 10 ms pop2-tby-P0-1.atdn.net [66.185.136.185]
5 10 ms 10 ms 20 ms bb1-tby-P0-3.atdn.net [66.185.138.208]
6 30 ms 30 ms 30 ms bb2-atm-P7-0.atdn.net [66.185.152.245]
7 30 ms 30 ms 30 ms pop2-atm-P5-0.atdn.net [66.185.138.43]
8 30 ms 30 ms 30 ms level3.atdn.net [66.185.138.34]
9 30 ms 30 ms 50 ms so-4-1-0.bbr2.Atlanta1.level3.net [209.247.9.169]
10 40 ms 50 ms 50 ms so-0-0-0.bbr1.Washington1.level3.net [64.159.1.2]
11 40 ms 51 ms 50 ms so-6-0-0.edge1.Washington1.Level3.net
[209.244.11.10]
12 40 ms 70 ms 60 ms qwest-level3-oc48.Washington1.Level3.net
[209.244.219.182]
13 40 ms 41 ms 50 ms dca-core-03.inet.qwest.net [205.171.209.113]
14 40 ms 50 ms 41 ms dca-core-02.inet.qwest.net [205.171.9.49]
15 60 ms 70 ms 60 ms atl-core-02.inet.qwest.net [205.171.8.153]
16 60 ms 60 ms 60 ms atl-core-01.inet.qwest.net [205.171.21.149]
17 51 ms 60 ms 80 ms atx-edge-01.inet.qwest.net [205.171.221.18]
18 70 ms 61 ms 60 ms genesis2net.net-gw.qwest.net [63.237.0.30]
19 50 ms 60 ms 60 ms 64.224.0.72
20 50 ms 61 ms 60 ms charlesriver.com [209.15.176.206]
Trace complete.
```

The output, or 'results' of using PING, IPCONFIG, or TRACERT can be directed to a text file for future reference, documentation, and further troubleshooting purposes. To direct the results of any of these utilities to a text file, simply add the greater than sign (>) followed by any name you choose to the end of the command. For example, to direct the results of a persistent PING to CHARLESRIVER.COM to a text file named publisher, enter the following command at a command prompt:

```
PING -t CHARLESRIVER.COM >publisher
```

To view the results in the text file named publisher, navigate to C:\ and edit the file named publisher. You can also view these results by opening the text file "publisher" using Notepad in Windows.

NSLOOKUP

NSLOOKUP is used to query a DNS for a host name to IP address resolution. In simple terms, when the NSLOOKUP command is given, a request is issued to resolve a fully qualified domain name, such as CompTIA.com, to an IP address.

From a command prompt, enter "NSLOOKUP CompTIA.COM". The results of this command would be:

```
Name: Comptia.com
Address: 216.219.103.72
```

Telnet

Telnet is a TCP/IP terminal emulation program/protocol that allows a user to access another system by entering the command "telnet" at a command prompt followed by a valid host name. For example, if you wanted to access a program or directory on a computer named joeshmo.edu, you would enter the following command at a command prompt:

```
telnet joeshmo.edu
```

You would then be welcomed and challenged for a user name and password. If you enter the proper credentials, you will be able to access information as a normal user of the system named joshmo.edu.

For an excellent and detailed description of how the Telnet protocol really works, visit the following www2.rad.com Web site: *http://www2.rad.com/networks/1997/telnet/proj.htm#INTRODUCTION*.

PRINTERS

The current A+ Operating System Technologies exam will most likely make sure that you can resolve basic Windows NT or Windows 2000 printing problems. Troubleshooting printing-related issues from within either of these two operating systems is basically the same.

There are several questions that you should ask yourself and/or your customer who is having difficulty printing.

Is the printer you are sending a document to set as the default printer in the Printers applet of My Computer or Control Panel? If the desired printer is not set as the default printer, you can rectify this situation by right-clicking the installed printer icon located in the Printers applet and selecting "Set as Default

Printer." Print the document again. Another way to direct a print job to a specific printer is to select the File menu option from within the document you wish to print. Next, select the Print option, and from the Printer Name drop-down menu option, select the installed printer to which you would like to direct the print job.

Is there enough memory installed on the Print Server or user's workstation to handle the print job or jobs that have been submitted to print? It is very common to experience "out of memory" errors when attempting to print to a locally installed or networked printer. More often than not, there is simply not enough physical memory installed on the system to handle the transition of the print job from the system to the printer. This can be resolved by installing more memory in the system itself.

Is the printer spooler service stalled on the shared network printer? The printer spooler service is a service that manages print jobs sent to a Windows NT or Windows 2000 shared network printer. If a print job or multiple print jobs are stalled on a network print server running the spooler service, the simple solution is to stop and start the printer spooler service. In Windows NT, the Services applet is located in the Control Panel. In Windows 2000, the Services applet is located within the Control Panel/Administrative Tools applet.

Do you or the customer have rights to print to the shared printer? As discussed earlier in this chapter under "Resource Sharing and Drive Mapping," file, folder, and printer shares can all be assigned access rights within Windows NT and Windows 2000. If you or a customer cannot access a certain printer share on a network, you may not have been granted the proper rights.

DIAGNOSING AND TROUBLESHOOTING TEST TIPS

The following information is designed to assist you with last-minute study preparation for the current CompTIA A+ Operating Systems Technologies exam. Not all of these tips are described within this chapter. However, they are very relevant to the exam, and you should review these important Windows NT diagnosing and troubleshooting test tips before taking the test.

✓ Windows NT is a multitasking, multithreaded operating system that can run applications in their own NTVDMs or virtual memory spaces. NTVDMs (NT Virtual DOS Machines) are part of a built-in Windows NT subsystem that allow 16-bit applications to act as if they are running in their own memory-protected DOS environment. If you are running an application or program that interferes with another application or program, you should attempt to run the offending program in its own protected memory space.

- ✓ It is not possible to upgrade to Windows NT 4.0 from Windows 9x. You can install Windows NT on the same hard drive but not in the same directory as Windows 9x. However, you can upgrade to Windows 4.0 from Windows NT 3.1 or Windows NT 3.51 operating systems.
- ✓ Dr. Watson is a Windows NT diagnostic tool that takes a picture, or 'snapshot,' of a system during an error state or fault. The Windows NT Workstation Dr. Watson log files are stored in C:\WINNT.
- ✓ Programs and files with the extensions .EXE, .COM, and .BAT can be run from the Windows NT command prompt.
- ✓ Windows NT supports port replication through the use of hardware profiles. If you want to ensure that the port replicator works on your laptop while at the office but is ignored while out of the office, you will need to enable Hardware Profiles in the System applet of Control Panel.
- ✓ Windows NT supports FAT16 and NTFS partitions. It does not include support for FAT32.
- ✓ Windows NT does not have a native Disk Defragmenter utility.
- ✓ Windows NT does not have the Device Manager utility that was implemented with Windows 9x.
- ✓ If you ever receive the message "Boot could not find NTLDR. Please insert another disk" while booting into Windows NT, you will need to run the emergency repair process.
- ✓ The best way to remove a virus from Windows NT, or any other Windows operating system for that matter, is to boot to a virus-free floppy disk and run antivirus software with up-to-date virus definition files.
- ✓ You need the files NTLDR, NTDETECT.COM, and BOOT.INI on a boot disk for Windows NT, Windows 2000, and Windows XP.
- ✓ If you are using an Internet browser in Windows NT or any other Windows operating system to access a secure Internet site, Your URL line will most likely begin with HTTPS://.
- ✓ If you receive an error message stating that a service failed to start upon booting Windows NT, you can check to see what particular service didn't start in the System Event Log in Event Viewer.
- ✓ The file NTBOOTDD.SYS is used by the operating systems Windows NT, Windows 2000, and Windows XP to support SCSI hard drives. It must be present at Windows boot-up for SCSI to be supported.
- ✓ The BOOT.INI is a required file used by Windows NT, 2000, and XP at start-up.
- ✓ If a user can't log on to the network in a Windows NT or 2000 domain environment, the first thing you should check is the user's network credentials, such as their user ID and password.
- ✓ If there is no sound coming from your speakers, you should first check the Volume Control applet and verify that no devices are muted.

- ✓ There are three easy ways to set the system time: Control Panel > Date/Time; Open the clock in the system tray; and from a command prompt, type in the word Time.
- ✓ In Windows NT 4.0, the command line utility RDISK.EXE can be used to create an ERD (Emergency Repair Disk).
- ✓ You can use the PING command to verify the presence of a remote system.
- ✓ Windows NT does not provide native support for USB, FireWire (IEEE 1394), or plug and play.
- ✓ PING, TRACERT, and NSLOOKUP are TCP/IP utilities that can be used to determine the IP address of known Internet domain names.
- ✓ To change a computer name or join a workgroup or domain in Windows NT, right-click on Network Neighborhood, then Select Properties, and under the Identification tab select Change.
- ✓ After installing a new hard drive, you can prepare the drive for use by accessing the Windows NT utility Disk Administrator and format the drive.

CHAPTER SUMMARY

By reading this chapter, you should have gained enough understanding to install, upgrade, and troubleshoot the Windows NT operating system. At this point, you should also have a basic understanding of the following:

- How to create an ERD from within Windows NT.
- How the Windows NT domain model is structured.
- How the Windows NT authentication process works.
- How security and access rights are implemented and supported in Windows NT.
- How to access and use some of the many important utilities associated with Windows NT, including User Manager, Task Manager, and Event Viewer, to name a few.
- Sharing network resources and establishing drive mapping.
- Diagnosing basic printing problems from within Windows NT and Windows 2000.

Although it is beyond the scope of this book to cover every detail of this complex operating system, you should now have enough knowledge to answer the following review questions, which are designed to fine-tune your skills in preparation for the real CompTIA exam. As always, if you do not understand a topic, or if you require more information, the Microsoft Web site is an invaluable resource.

REVIEW QUESTIONS

1. **You have installed Windows NT Workstation on a computer that is already running Windows 9x. You cannot see Windows 9x files from within Windows NT Workstation. What is most likely the problem?**

   o A. The Windows NT Workstation partition is FAT32.
   o B. The Windows NT Workstation partition is FAT16.
   o C. You need to select View and Show All Files in Explorer.
   o D. The Windows 9x partition is FAT32.

   Correct Answer = D

   NTFS and FAT32 are incompatible file systems. You cannot see across these two partitions when they are installed on the same hard drive. This question states that you cannot see the Windows 9x files from within Windows NT Workstation. The obvious choice would be that the Windows 9x partition is FAT32.

2. **You have just installed Windows NT. You attempt to boot into the operating system and receive the message "Boot could not find NTLDR. Please insert another disk." What should you do?**

   o A. Make a copy of NTLDR from another NT computer and use it in yours.
   o B. Run the Emergency Repair process.
   o C. Restart and use the Last Known Good Configuration.
   o D. Insert a blank floppy and type "RDISK /S."

   Correct Answer = B

   If you receive the error message "Boot could not find NTLDR. Please insert another disk." on boot-up, it is advised that you run the Emergency Repair process. The ERD process will restore your important system files.

3. **Which important files must be located in the root directory of the system partition for Windows NT to boot properly? (Choose Three)**

   □ A. COMMAND.COM
   □ B. NTLDR
   □ C. MSDOS.SYS
   □ D. BOOT.INI
   □ E. NTDETECT.COM
   □ F. IO.SYS

   Correct Answers = B, D, and E

In order for NT to boot properly, the files NTLDR, BOOT.INI, and NT DETECT.COM must be located in the root directory of the system partition.

4. What should you always try first if you can't boot into your Windows NT operating system?

o A. Reformat the boot partition with FAT16.

o B. Press F8 on boot-up to enter Safe Mode.

o C. Reinstall from three setup floppies and installation CD-ROM.

o D. Use the Last Known Good Configuration.

Correct Answer = D

If you can't boot into your NT operating system, you should always first attempt to use the "Last Known Good Configuration" option on boot-up. You can initiate this option by pressing the space bar when you see the "Last Know Good Configuration" option displayed on the screen at boot-up.

5. You are currently running Windows NT and would like to convert your FAT16 partition to NTFS in order to provide for a more secure OS. What command would you enter at a DOS prompt to do this?

o A. FDISK /MBR

o B. CONVERT C:/FS:NTFS

o C. CONVERT C:/FS:NTFS

o D. FORMAT C:/ FAT16:NTFS

Correct Answer = C

You can always convert a FAT16 partition to NTFS from a command prompt by entering the command CONVERT C:/FS:NTFS. FDISK /MBR will format your master boot record. Choices B and D are invalid.

6. What command can you use to bring up the command prompt in Windows NT?

o A. CMD.EXE

o B. COMMAND.COM

o C. Ctrl+Alt+Del

o D. SYSPOL.EXE

Correct Answer = A

The Windows NT command prompt can be accessed by selecting Start > Run and entering CMD at the Open line. CMD.EXE is the actual command prompt in Windows NT and Windows 2000.

7. You wish to transfer files from within a Windows NT Workstation volume that is formatted with NTFS, to a Windows 9x volume that is formatted with FAT32. Which of the following will happen to your files? (Choose Three)

- □ A. They will retain any information stored in the file.
- □ B. They will retain their Long File Names.
- □ C. They will retain their File Attributes.
- □ D. They will retain their compression status.
- □ E. They will retain their encryption status.
- □ F. They will retain file-level permissions.

Correct Answers = A, B, and D

If you transfer files from an NTFS volume to a FAT32 volume, you will retain information saved within the file, the files LFN (Long File Name), and the file attributes. However, the files will not remain compressed, will not remain encrypted, and will lose file-level permissions.

8. This service must be installed in order to utilize Dialup Networking with Windows NT. What is the service?

- o A. Dialup Networking service
- o B. Dialup Networking Monitor service
- o C. Remote Access service
- o D. Windows Installer service

Correct Answer = C

The Remote Access service must be installed to utilize Dialup Networking with Windows NT. All other choices are incorrect.

9. You have a 20GB hard drive with Windows NT installed. You are interested in formatting the free space available on the drive, labeling the newly formatted space with a drive letter, and exploring opportunities for a fault-tolerant implementation. Which Windows NT tool would you use?

- o A. Drive Converter
- o B. Backup
- o C. Disk Administrator
- o D. Partition Administrator

Correct Answer = C

The Windows NT Disk Administrator is a very useful administrative tool that offers the abilities to format drive space, assign and change drive labels, and implement fault-tolerance systems by establishing Disk Mirror sets and Disk Stripe sets.

10. You believe that your customer is unable to print documents because the wrong printer is set as the Default Printer in the Printer applet of Control Panel. What suggestions do you have to assist with the customer's printing issue? (Choose Two)

□ A. Ask the customer to print to a different networked printer.

□ B. Navigate to the proper printer and "Set as Default Printer."

□ C. Tell the customer a reboot should take care of the problem.

□ D. Reinstall the printer drivers.

□ E. Have the customer use the Print option from the document File menu and choose a specific printer.

Correct Answers = B and E

If the wrong printer is set as the default printer, you will not be able to print documents. The simple solution is to set the desired printer as the default printer. Answers B and E are the proper procedures for setting a default printer or directing a print job to a specific printer.

11. Which file must be present at Windows NT boot-up for SCSI devices to be supported?

o A. CMD.EXE

o B. NTBOOTDD.SYS

o C. NTVDM.VXD

o D. NTCONFIG.POL

o E. None of the above

Correct Answer = B

The file NTBOOTDD.SYS is used by the Windows NT, 2000, and XP operating systems to support SCSI hard drives. It must be present at Windows boot-up for SCSI to be supported.

CMD.EXE is the 32-bit command interpreter for Windows NT, Windows 2000, and Windows XP. NTVDM.VXD is an invalid selection that is in place to fool you. NTCONFIG.POL is the name of the Windows NT policy that is created by using the System Policy Editor.

12. Where does Dr. Watson store his log files in Windows NT?

o A. C:\Windows

o B. C:\

o C. C:\WINNT

o D. On a highly fault tolerant RAID 5 Array

o E. None of the above

Correct Answer = C

Dr. Watson is a Windows NT diagnostic tool that takes a picture or "snapshot" of a system during an error state or fault. The Windows NT workstation Dr. Watson log files are stored in C:\WINNT. All other choices are invalid.

REFERENCES

http://www.microsoft.com. This site contains the minimum and recommended hardware requirements for Windows NT Server as well as other Microsoft operating systems can be found at this Microsoft Web site.

http://www.microsoft.com/whdc/hcl/default.mspx. This Microsoft Web page offers access to the Hardware Compatibility List that can help you verify if your hardware is supported by Windows NT.

http://www.microsoft.com/resources/sam/licensing/cal_guide/default.asp. This Microsoft Web site describes CAL (Client Access Licensing) in great detail.

http://support.microsoft.com/support/kb/articles/Q141/3/77.ASP. This Microsoft site compares the differences between REGEDIT.EXE and REGEDT32.EXE.

http://www2.rad.com/networks/1997/telnet/proj.htm#INTRODUCTION. This www2.rad.com Web site has an excellent description of how the Telnet protocol really works.

26 Windows 2000

In This Chapter

- Overview of Windows 2000
- Windows 2000 Installation Process
- Windows 2000 Upgrade Procedures
- Windows 2000 Start-Up Process
- Windows 2000 Tools and Utilities
- Profiles
- Printers
- Windows 2000 Networking and the Internet
- Diagnosing and Troubleshooting Test Tips
- Chapter Summary
- Review Questions
- References

OVERVIEW OF WINDOWS 2000

In case you haven't heard, Windows 2000 was built on Windows NT technology.

If you have used Windows 2000 Professional or Windows 2000 Server to any extent, you may have noticed that the Windows 2000 family of operating systems was built with a combination of the best Microsoft operating system technologies available, including Windows 9x and Windows NT.

As you may recall, Windows 9x is suitable for client workstation use and supports only FAT16 and FAT32 partitions. Unlike Windows NT, it does not support file-level security. Windows 9x offers built-in Disk Defragmenter and Device Manager utilities, which are very useful tools for maintaining hard drives and troubleshooting hardware devices and drivers, respectively.

Windows NT was developed for a domain structure environment and offers better security and administration capabilities than Windows 9x, but it only provides support for FAT16 and NTFS partitions. Windows NT does not have a native Disk Defragmenter utility and does not offer the Device Manager that was available in Windows 9x.

Windows 2000 combines the functionality of Windows 9x and Windows NT by including the following features:

- Support for FAT16, FAT32, NTFS, and CDFS file systems (Windows 2000 does not support HPFS)
- A built-in Disk Defragmenter utility
- A built-in Device Manager utility
- Safe Mode support similar to Windows 9x
- File-level and folder-level security
- Full administrative support for a client/server environment

In addition to the combined features included from the previous operating systems, Windows 2000 offers many new technologies and improvements. We will discuss many important Windows 2000 advances in this chapter. Here are some of the most notable:

Improved security: Windows 2000 offers file- and folder-level encryption with Encrypting File System (EFS). EFS makes use of public and private encryption keys. In order to decrypt a file or folder, you must be the one who originally encrypted it or be a recovery agent.

Better support for hardware: Windows 2000 offers better overall support for plug and play, USB, and infrared.

Better support for laptops: Windows 2000 assists with the overall performance of laptop computers by providing Advanced Configuration and Power Interface (ACPI) and smart battery.

Active Directory: Windows 2000 Server provides Active Directory, which gives administrators a single point to manage network objects and resources.

Better disk management capabilities: Windows 2000 makes use of disk quotas, which allow administrators to restrict the amount of hard drive space a particular user can use. Disk quotas can be applied to volumes or users.

Better support for the Internet: Windows 2000 supports Dynamic HTML (DHTML) as well as Extensible Markup Language (XML), which helps Web developers create better solutions for businesses.

Windows 2000 file system protection: Windows 2000 has a built-in backup feature called Windows File Protection that keeps a backup of important system files. If you write over important system files with programs or applications, Windows File Protection prompts you that it needs to restore the important system files you just replaced.

WINDOWS 2000 INSTALLATION PROCESS

Before installing Windows 2000 or any other Windows operating system, you must verify that your computer meets the minimum hardware requirements. The minimum hardware requirements for Windows 2000 Professional are as follows:

- 133MHz Pentium processor
- 2GB hard drive with 650MB of free drive space
- 64MB of RAM
- VGA monitor
- Keyboard
- Mouse
- 12x CD-ROM (not required for over-the-network installation)

The second pre-installation step is to verify that your hardware is in compliance with the Hardware Compatibility List (HCL) located at *http://www.microsoft.com/whdc/hcl/search.mspx.*

NOTE

The Windows 2000 Professional installation CD-ROM contains a copy of the HCL, but this HCL is outdated. Your best bet is to visit the Web site to review the most recent hardware compatibility updates.

Next, you need to choose one of three Windows 2000 Professional installation methods. The three installation methods and their general descriptions are as follows.

CD-ROM Installation

Installing Windows 2000 Professional by CD-ROM is by far the easiest method. If your system BIOS supports the ability to boot to CD-ROM, all you have to do is place the installation CD-ROM in your CD drive and reboot. The installation process will begin by copying the installation files to your hard drive. Your system is then rebooted, and the GUI phase of the installation process begins.

Four Setup Disks

The Windows 2000 Professional CD-ROM can create four installation floppy disks to be used for installation if your system cannot boot from a CD-ROM.

If you are currently running DOS or Windows 3x, open the Bootdisk folder located on the Windows 2000 Professional Installation CD-ROM and run the makeboot.exe program. If you are currently running Windows 9x, Windows NT, or Windows 2000, run the makebt32.exe program, which is also located in the Bootdisk folder on the installation CD-ROM. After you have created all four floppy diskettes, place the first diskette in the floppy drive and restart the system.

Network Installation

To implement an over-the-network installation of Windows 2000 Professional, you need to copy the entire contents of the Windows 2000 Professional CD-ROM to a shared network folder. It is advisable to have this shared location on a server computer. In Windows 2000 lingo, this server is called a *distribution server*.

To begin an over-the-network installation from a Windows 9x client or Windows NT Workstation, connect to the shared folder and execute the winnt32.exe program. To perform an over-the-network installation from a blank hard drive, boot the system from a bootable network floppy disk and execute the winnt.exe program from the distribution server.

No matter which installation method you choose, the Windows 2000 installation process will progress through the following modes and steps:

Text mode setup:

- A partition for Windows 2000 is created.
- A file system is chosen.
- The partition on which the file system will be installed may need to be formatted.
- The installation files are copied to the hard drive.
- Setup Wizard (GUI mode of setup) commences.
- Choose your regional settings.
- Enter the name and organization.
- Enter the product key.
- Enter a 15-character computer name.
- Select and enter a local administrator account password.
- Enter the date and time.
- Network configuration commences.
- Setup attempts to autodetect installed NICs and proceeds to install Windows networking protocols and services, including TCP/IP, file and print sharing, and Client for Microsoft Networks.
- You are prompted to join the computer to a workgroup or a domain.

Final phase of installation:

- Startup menu shortcuts are created.
- Installation configurations are saved to the hard drive.
- Temporary installation files are removed.
- The system restarts.

Automated Installation

Although you will not be tested on the finer details of carrying out an automated installation of Windows 2000, it is important that you have a basic understanding of the tools used to carry out this type of installation. Passing the A+ exam is an important step toward a career in the computer industry. Understanding and implementing the newest operating system tools is just as important.

Like Windows NT, Windows 2000 offers the ability to carry out automated, unattended installations. In order to configure and carry out these types of Windows 2000 Professional installations, you need to understand the following three important installation tools—Setup Manager, SYSPREP, and RIS—and you must do some planning.

Setup Manager

The Windows 2000 installation CD-ROM comes with a utility called Setup Manager. Setup Manager can be used to create an unattended installation file called UNATTEND.TXT. UNATTEND.TXT is a file that Setup Manager uses to store and automate answers to installation questions that would normally have to be answered by a person sitting at a computer.

To install Setup Manager and implement the UNATTEND.TXT file, you must first extract Setup Manager from the Windows 2000 installation CD-ROM. To do this, navigate to the Support\Tools folder located on the CD-ROM and double-click the file DEPLOY.CAB. Next, you extract the file's SETUPMGR.EXE and SETUPMGR.DLL to a common folder located on the hard drive. To do this, right-click each file (separately) and select the extract option. After this process is complete, executing the SETUPMGR.EXE file on the hard drive starts a wizard program that allows you to create the UNATTEND.TXT file and asks you which options you would like UNATTEND.TXT to perform. You can also use UNATTEND.TXT to create an automated installation of SYSPREP or RIS.

Here are some of the installation questions that can be answered by using UNATTEND.TXT.

- Confirmation to the End-User License Agreement (EULA)
- Name and organization

- Computer name
- Password for the local administrator account
- Display settings, such as monitor refresh rate and number of colors
- Network settings, such as protocols, services, and IP address settings
- Whether to join a workgroup or a domain
- Time zone settings

If you recall the installation process mentioned earlier in the chapter, the bulleted items above should look familiar to you.

System Preparation Tool (SYSPREP)

The System Preparation Tool (SYSPREP) is a Windows 2000 utility that allows you to prepare for the creation of a Windows 2000 disk image by making sure that the Security Identifiers (SIDs) are unique for all target systems that will have an image copied to them.

With the use of third-party disk imaging software, such as Symantec Ghost, an exact duplicate or mirror image of a system can be made and distributed to multiple systems on a network. SYSPREP prepares a system for this image. Besides generating a unique computer SID, SYSPREP contains a mini-setup wizard that is used to specify settings such as computer name, regional settings, network settings, time zone, and workgroup or domain membership.

SYSPREP is a very useful tool for configuring many computers with the same operating system, configuration settings, and software. The process for installing SYSPREP as well as RIS was described under "Setup Manager," earlier in this chapter.

Remote Installation Service (RIS)

RIS is a Windows 2000 Server utility service that is used to deploy Windows 2000 Professional to connected client computers over a network. You can use RIS to deploy the images you have created with third-party software to connected systems, or to repair bad or corrupted installations you have already deployed.

WINDOWS 2000 UPGRADE PROCEDURES

Windows 2000 offers several upgrade paths. The following operating systems can be upgraded to Windows 2000:

- Windows 95 (All Versions)
- Windows 98 (All Versions)

- Windows NT 3.51
- Windows NT 4.0

Before upgrading to a new operating system, your first consideration should always be to make a complete backup of the current operating system and data. This is crucial if you wish to have a path back to your current operating system and information. Next, you should scan your current operating system with updated antivirus software so that any viruses are not transferred during the upgrade process. Finally, you should uncompress any compressed drives.

Upgrading from a previously installed operating system to Windows 2000 is a fairly simple task. The most important thing to keep in mind for a successful upgrade is that the Windows 2000 setup program must be run from within the operating system you want to upgrade in order for your settings and information to be transferred to Windows 2000. To upgrade from Windows 9x or Windows NT using the Windows 2000 installation CD-ROM, do the following:

1. Boot your system into Windows 9x or Windows NT.
2. Insert the Windows 2000 installation CD-ROM.
3. If your system autodetects the installation CD-ROM, your current operating system is detected, and you are asked if you want to upgrade to Windows 2000. Select "Yes" if you want to upgrade, and continue with the upgrade process. If the installation CD-ROM is not autodetected, select Start > Run, and type in the CD-ROM drive letter, followed by "\I386\WINNT32.EXE", and click OK.

To upgrade from Windows 9x or Windows NT to Windows 2000 over a network, do the following:

1. From within the operating system you want to upgrade, connect to a network share that contains the Windows 2000 installation or setup files.
2. Navigate to and run \I386\WINNT32.EXE from the shared network location.
3. Answer "Yes" to perform the upgrade, and follow the installation instructions provided.

NOTE

If you have trouble running a previously installed application after you have upgraded to a new operating system, you are advised to reinstall the application on the upgraded operating system.

If you would like more information on upgrading to Windows 2000 from Windows 9x or Windows NT visit: *http://www.microsoft.com/windows2000/professional/howtobuy/upgrading/path/win9x.asp.*

What About Windows Me (Millennium Edition)?

There is no recommended upgrade path provided by Microsoft to upgrade from Windows Me to Windows 2000. This is because Windows 2000 was actually released before Windows Me. That's right, Windows 2000 is not a supported upgrade from Windows Me.

If you attempt to upgrade to Windows 2000 Professional from within the Windows Me operating system, you will most likely encounter a message stating that the version of Windows you are attempting to install is newer, and will ask you if you want to upgrade. If you select OK to the upgrade, you will most likely encounter the following error message:

```
Cannot load C:\windows\upgdlls\w95upg.dll\WIN9XUPG\W95UPG.DLL.
```

This is because Windows 2000 is looking for the upgrade path from Windows 9x! Windows Millennium will be described in much more detail in Chapter 27.

For more information regarding this unsupported Microsoft upgrade, visit the following Microsoft site: *http://support.microsoft.com/default.aspx?scid=kb;en-us;272627.*

WINDOWS 2000 START-UP PROCESS

The current A+ exam will most likely focus on your ability to utilize the Windows 2000 tools that are available during the start-up process or boot sequence to complete or troubleshoot a system that will not completely boot into the operating system. Pay special attention to such tools as the Last Known Good Configuration option in the Advanced Options menu (described immediately after the start-up process). It is more likely that the exam will target your ability to utilize these tools than expect you to have memorized the finer details of the Windows 2000 start-up process.

The steps in the Windows 2000 start-up process are as follows:

1. The POST (Power-On Self-Test) is run.
2. The start-up process begins, and plug-and-play devices are recognized.
3. The MBR (Master Boot Record) is located and processed.
4. NTLDR.COM (bootstrap loader) is loaded. The hardware detection phase begins.
5. The BOOT.INI is loaded, and the operating systems are detected. If multiple operating systems are located in the BOOT.INI, BOOTSECT.DOS is processed, allowing a system to boot with Windows 9x, Windows Me, or

DOS. Remember for the exam that multiple boot options are specified in the BOOT.INI file at system start-up.

6. NTDETECT.COM runs. Hardware and hardware profiles are detected.
7. The Windows 2000 kernel (NTOSKRNL.EXE) is loaded.
8. HAL.DLL is loaded, which creates the hardware abstraction layer.
9. The system reads the Registry and loads all necessary device drivers.
10. The logon process begins with the execution of WINLOGON.EXE.

Advanced Options Menu

You should recall from Chapter 24 that Windows 9x offers a start-up menu that provides several boot configuration options to be used for troubleshooting purposes. Windows 2000 offers a similar feature called the Advanced Options menu. When the Windows 2000 boot sequence is in its final phase, the Starting Windows screen appears. At this point, the option to press the F8 key and enter the Advanced Options menu is presented. If you press the F8 key, you will be offered the following options:

- Safe Mode
- Safe Mode with Networking
- Safe Mode with Command Prompt
- Enable Boot Logging
- Enable VGA Mode
- Last Known Good Configuration
- Directory Services Restore Mode (Windows 2000 domain controllers only)
- Debugging Mode
- Boot Normally

You should already be familiar with the functions of several of these options from our previous discussions of the Windows 9x start-up menu. The most important point that can be made here is that you should not completely advance into the Windows 2000 operating system if you have experienced trouble at start-up. Instead, press the F8 key and choose the Last Known Good Configuration option. This loads the last known good Registry settings and allows you to boot into the operating system successfully if you have not already logged on to the system with a bad configuration.

Recovery Console

The Windows 2000 installation CD-ROM comes with a utility called the Windows 2000 Recovery Console. The Recovery Console can be used to assist with the recovery of a computer system that is having problems starting or will not boot into an operating system at all.

The Windows 2000 Recovery Console can be installed so that it is available at system start-up by navigating to the i386 folder located on the installation CD-ROM and entering the command WINNT32/CMDCONS. This makes the Recovery Console option available when Windows 2000 boots up. The Recovery Console can also be used to copy system files to a hard drive and configure services that will be available when the system boots into the operating system.

Dual Booting

With Windows 2000, you can set up your computer for several different dual-booting scenarios. Windows 2000 can be dual booted with DOS, Windows 3x, Windows 9x, Windows Me, and Windows NT. However, some very strict rules apply to dual booting with Windows 2000, depending on the booting scenario you want to create.

Here are some general rules to consider before installing multiple operating systems in a dual-boot scenario with Windows 2000:

- Each operating system you install must be installed and configured on a separate volume. Microsoft does not support multiple operating systems installed on the same volume with Windows 2000. This is mainly to ensure that each operating system can maintain separate configuration settings and file structures. Each operating system is considered separate. All programs and drivers installed on one particular operating system are considered separate from any other installed operating systems.
- The volume that the system is booted from must be formatted with the proper file system to support the dual-boot configuration. For example, if you are going to dual boot between Windows 2000 or Windows NT and Windows 9x, the volume that the system boots to must be formatted as FAT.
- Windows 2000 should be installed after DOS, Windows 95, or Windows Me. If you install Windows 2000 first and then attempt to install DOS, Windows 95, or Windows Me, you will write over important system and boot files.

The following section describes the proper order of operating system installations necessary to achieve specific dual booting goals:

- To dual boot between DOS, Windows 95 or Windows 98, or Windows Me and Windows 2000, install DOS first, followed by Windows 95 or Windows 98, or Windows Me followed by the Windows 2000 installation.
- To dual boot between Windows NT 4.0 and Windows 2000, install Windows NT 4.0 first, followed by Windows 2000. If you are using an NTFS partition

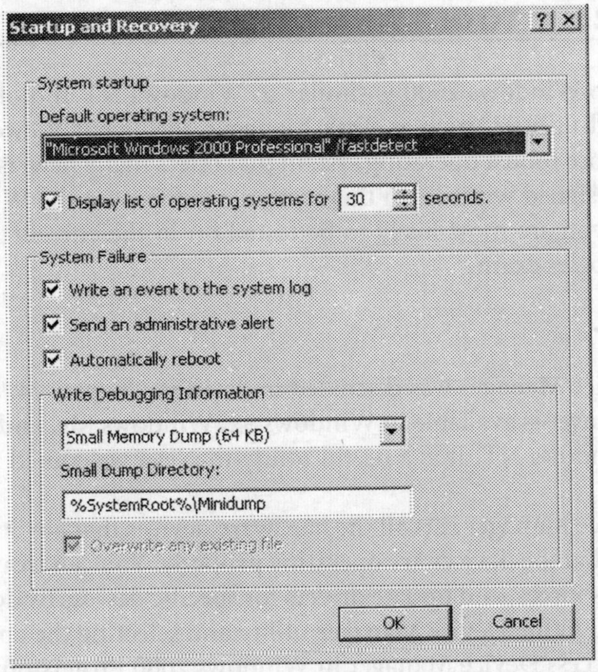

FIGURE 26.1 Choosing a default OS in the Startup and Recovery window.

with Windows NT 4.0, make sure that you have installed a minimum of NT Service Pack 4 so that your Windows NT 4.0 NTFS partition can access files on the Windows 2000 NTFS 5 partition.

After you have installed multiple operating systems on your hard drive, you can navigate to the Startup and Recovery Window and choose a default operating system. The default operating system displayed in Figure 26.1 is Windows 2000 Professional. The default operating system is the one that will be booted into when your system boots up. You can change the default operating system by selecting the drop-down menu under "Default operating system:" and selecting the installed operating system to be used as the default. You can also change the time limit for which the list of operating systems is displayed at system start-up. To access the system Startup and Recovery window, navigate to Control Panel > System > Advanced > Startup and Recovery.

WINDOWS 2000 TOOLS AND UTILITIES

Although Windows 2000 is similar to Windows NT and offers many of the same tools and utilities, such as Task Manager and Event Viewer, Windows 2000 is a much more robust operating system that offers many new useful utilities, tools, and newly designed wizards. In this section, we focus on the Windows 2000 tools and utilities you are most likely to be tested on in the current A+ Operating Systems Technologies exam.

Device Manager

The Device Manager was discussed in detail in Chapter 24. As you may recall, Device Manager is available in Windows 9x, Windows Me, and Windows XP, but not with Windows NT. It is a useful utility that is a welcomed feature with Windows 2000.

Device Manager lists all the hardware devices that are attached to a system and ensures that the devices are operating properly. You can troubleshoot devices, view device resources, and update drivers for specific devices by double-clicking on a device listed in the Device Manager utility and selecting the appropriate option.

To access Device Manager in Windows 2000 Professional, navigate to Control Panel > System > Hardware > Device Manager, or Control Panel > Administrative Tools > Computer Management > Device Manager.

DRIVER SIGNING

Windows 2000 offers Driver Signing options that allow you to prevent or block users from installing software and device drivers that are not digitally signed or approved by Microsoft. This is a very useful feature that can save administrators and technicians from having to reconfigure systems that have been corrupted by unsigned or unapproved software or driver installations. To navigate to and block the installation of unassigned drivers, select Start > Settings > Control Panel > System > Hardware > Driver Signing. The Driver Signing Options window appears (Figure 26.2). By default, the option to warn users when an unsigned driver or file is installed is selected. Choose the option to block the installation of unsigned files, and select OK.

Administrative Tools and Computer Management

There are many ways to access administrative programs and carry out administrative tasks in Windows 2000. You can use individual utilities and programs, create your own administrative console with Microsoft Management Console and snap-in programs, or use preconfigured tools, such as Computer Management, to carry

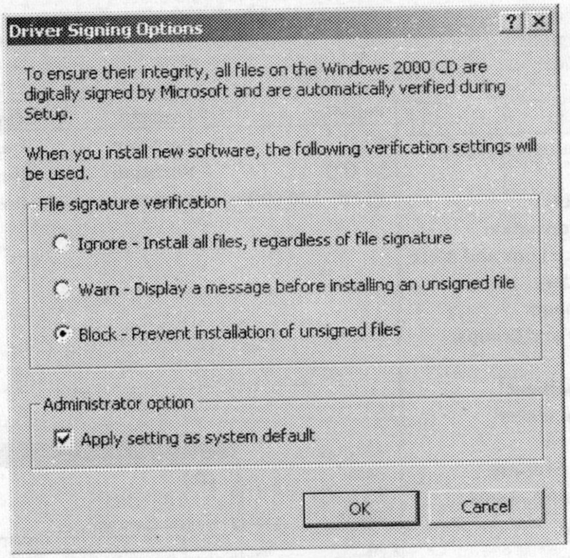

FIGURE 26.2 The Driver Signing Options window.

out many administrative duties from one central location. The Microsoft Management Console will be discussed in more detail later in the chapter.

On the Windows 2000 Control Panel is the Administrative Tools folder. This folder contains many useful tools that were present with Windows NT 4.0, such as Performance Monitor, Event Viewer, Services, and Local Security Policy. This folder also contains an icon for a very useful administrative tool known as Computer Management. Computer Management is a prepackaged group of administrative programs, otherwise known as *snap-ins*, which can be administered from one central location. As shown in Figure 26.3, Computer Management provides quick access to system resources and tools such as Device Manager, Event Viewer, System Information, and Local Users and Groups. You can also manage disks and logical drives, and run Disk Defragmenter from the Storage section of the Computer Management tree. You can quickly access the Computer Management window by right-clicking on the My Computer Desktop icon and selecting Manage.

Local Users and Groups

The Local Users and Groups snap-in (see Figure 26.3) is the Windows 2000 Professional replacement for the User Manager, which was available with Windows NT 4.0 Workstation. Using this tool, you can add and remove users, make new local groups, add users to groups, assign user profiles (profiles are discussed later in this chapter), set passwords, and disable or unlock user accounts.

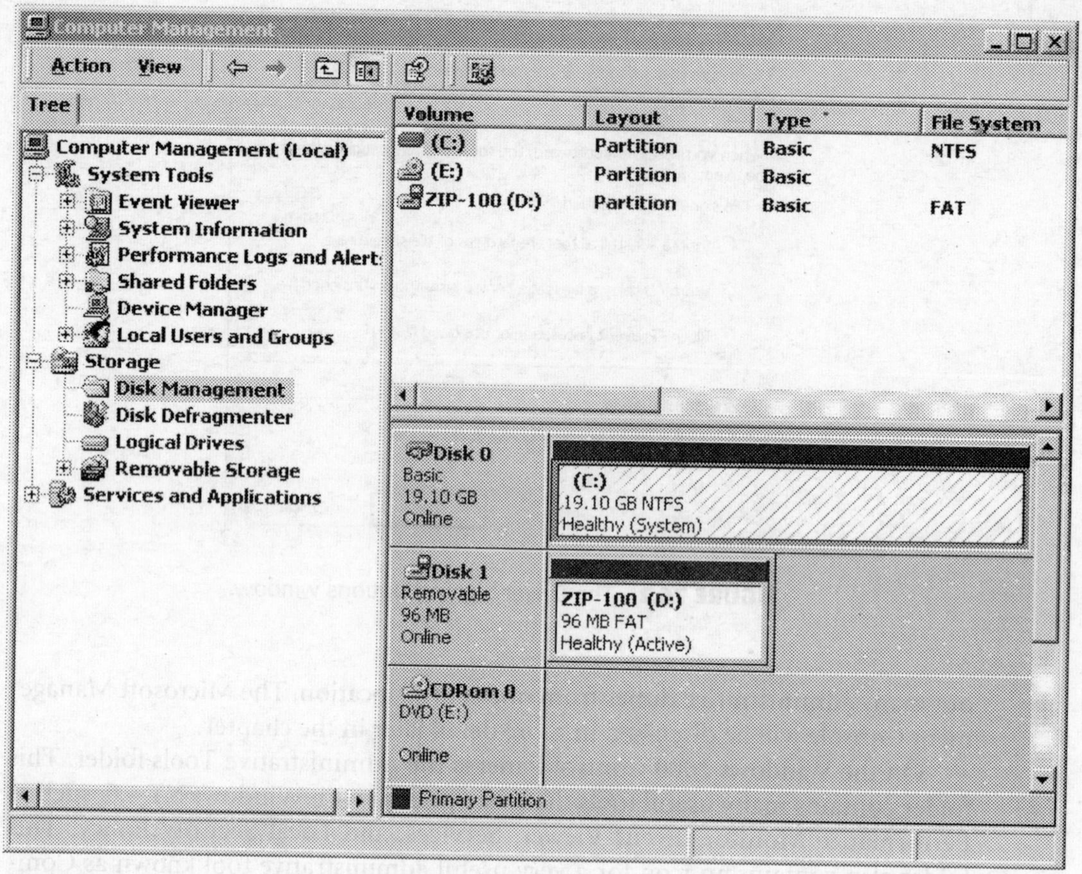

FIGURE 26.3 The Computer Management window.

Windows 2000 Professional comes with built-in accounts for Administrator and Guest. The built-in groups available with Windows 2000 Professional are Administrator, Power Users, Backup Operators, Replicator, Users, and Guests. Each of these groups has built-in, pre-assigned permissions that allow user accounts assigned to a particular group to have special rights. The most powerful group is the Administrator group. Administrators have the privileges to carry out all tasks. Power Users have some administrative privileges and can install legacy applications. Backup Operators can backup and restore files and folders. The Replicator group is used for replicating directories. The Users group has very basic privileges. All users of the system are automatically added to the Users group.

The Guest group is similar to the Users group and has very limited rights to the system.

Backup Utility

The Backup utility has been revamped and included with Windows 2000. The newly designed Backup utility provides useful backup and restore wizards that can be used to design a backup or restoration job for files on a local machine or over the network.

As displayed in Figure 26.4, the Backup utility also offers the ability to create an ERD (Emergency Repair Disk).

NOTE

Windows 2000 does not offer the ability to create an ERD using the Windows NT 4.0 utility RDISK.EXE.

You can use the Windows 2000 Backup utility to backup information from one file system type and restore the information to another file system type. For example, you can backup files located on an NTFS partition and restore the files to a

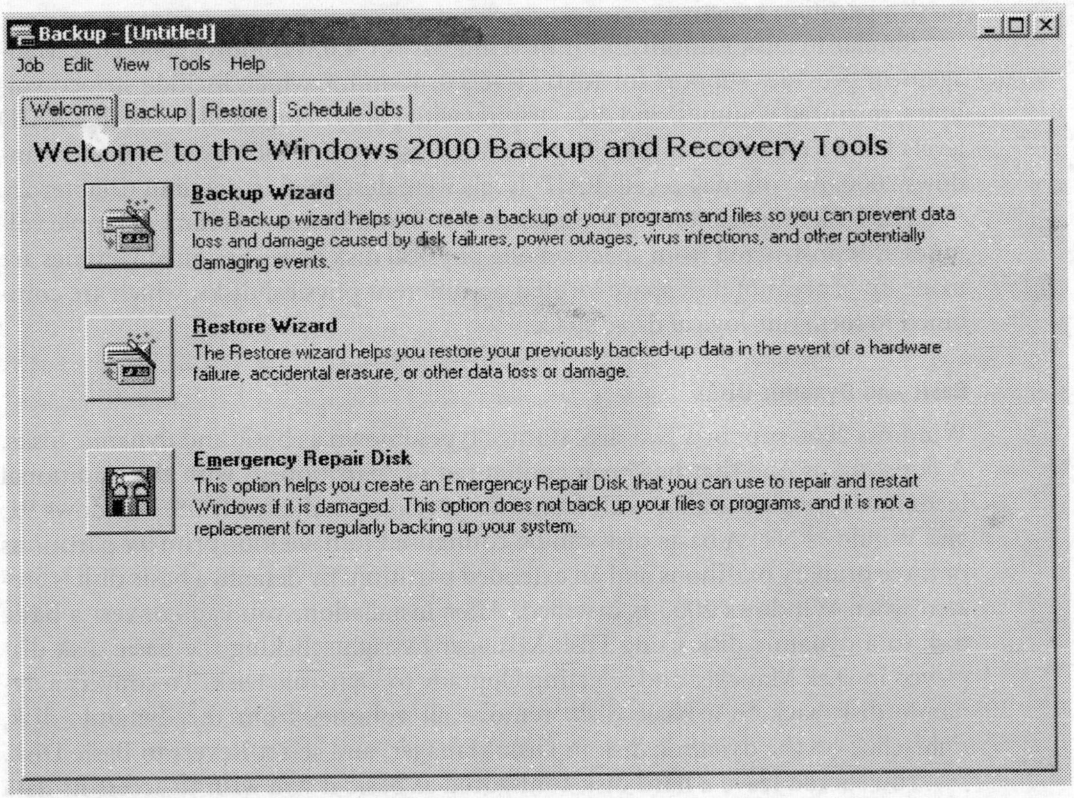

FIGURE 26.4 The Windows 2000 Backup utility.

FAT32 partition, but you must keep in mind that NTFS and FAT32 are not compatible file systems. If you restore to FAT32 from NTFS, you will retain long file names and file attributes, but you will lose file properties such as compression, encryption, and permission values.

Disk Management and Volume Types

As discussed in Chapter 25, Windows NT 4.0 uses the Disk Administrator tool to manage hard disks and logical drives. Windows 2000 has a similar tool called Disk Management, which offers the ability to manage hard disks, logical drives, and dynamic disks (discussed in the next section).

To access the Windows 2000 Disk Management tool, open Control Panel > Administrative Tools > Computer Management > Storage > Disk Management. The Disk Management tool gathers information about local physical drives and displays information similar to that shown in Figure 26.3.

With the Disk Management tool, you can change the drive letter and path for a disk or logical drive, format a drive, delete a logical drive, delete a partition, or mark a partition as active.

Similar to Disk Administrator in Windows NT 4.0, Windows 2000 Disk Management provides support for RAID levels 0, 1, and 5, which include striped volumes, mirrored volumes, and disk striping with parity. You should note that RAID levels 1 and 5 are only available in the Server versions of Windows NT 4.0 and Windows 2000. As you may recall, RAID levels were described in detail in Chapter 25.

The Disk Manager tool also supports simple and spanned volumes. Simple volumes are constructed from space on one physical disk drive. Spanned volumes are made up of areas of disk space located on different physical disks, which are combined to form one logical drive space.

Basic and Dynamic Disks

Windows 2000 supports two disk storage types known as basic and dynamic disks. A *basic disk* is one that has been configured or 'partitioned' with the traditional techniques we are familiar with from our previous studies of DOS, Windows 9x, and Windows NT. A basic disk can be configured to have four primary partitions or three primary partitions and an extended partition. By default, a basic disk is created when Windows 2000 is installed. After installation, you can convert a basic disk to a dynamic disk using Disk Manager by right-clicking the basic disk displayed in Disk Manager and selecting Upgrade to Dynamic Disk. To convert a dynamic disk back to a basic disk, remove all volumes from the dynamic disk, right-click on the dynamic disk in Disk Manager, and select Revert to Basic Disk.

You should leave a hard disk configured as basic if you wish to access its data from DOS or Windows 9x.

Dynamic disks are areas of space on a single disk, or areas combined from multiple disks, created and organized using volume techniques to organize areas instead of traditional partitioning techniques. Disks that have been configured with DOS or Windows 9x cannot access dynamic disks. Dynamic disks can be created and managed using Disk Manager. You can create five types of dynamic disks: simple, mirrored, spanned, striped, and RAID level 5 volumes.

Disk Quotas

Disk quotas can be implemented in Windows 2000 to track and control the amount of disk space used by a particular user or disk volume. To enable quota management, right-click on the disk from Windows Explorer or My Computer, select Properties, choose the Quota tab, and choose the appropriate options to suit your administrative needs. Disk quotas can be used only for volumes configured with NTFS.

With disk quotas, an administrator can do the following:

- Limit the amount of disk space used by a user and create an event log message if this limit has been met.
- Create an event log message if a user or volume has met a warning level set for the amount of disk space specified.

Compression and Encryption

If your Windows 2000 system is configured with the NTFS file system, you can take advantage of compression and encryption. *Compression* allows the size of files and folders to be reduced so they do not use as much disk space as they would if they were uncompressed. To compress or uncompress a file or folder in Windows 2000, simply right-click on a file or folder from within Windows Explorer and select Properties. From the General tab, click the Advanced button. The Advanced Attributes window appears (Figure 26.5). From this window you can compress a file or a folder in the Compress or Encrypt attributes section.

NOTE *If files are compressed, they will be displayed in a different color in Windows Explorer. The default color for compressed files and folders is blue.*

Files and folders created on NTFS partitions can be encrypted. *Encryption* is a feature of EFS that allows you to secure volumes, files, and folders. You can set the encryption attribute for a file or folder to secure its contents from the Compress or Encrypt attributes section (see Figure 26.5). To decrypt a file or folder, you must be the creator of the file or folder, or be an Encrypted Data Recovery Agent (EDRA). EDRAs are discussed in the following section.

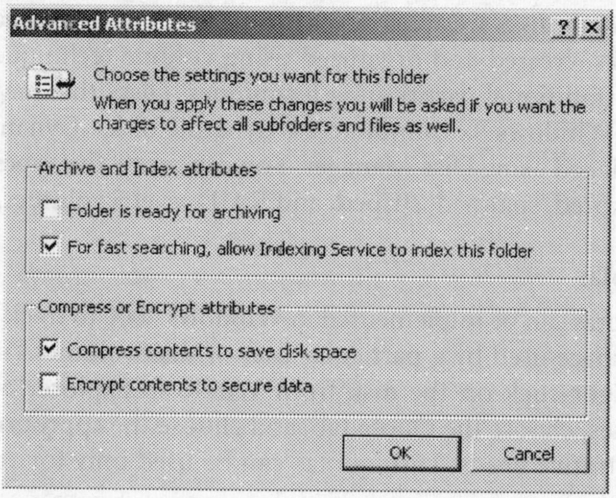

FIGURE 26.5 Setting compression and encryption attributes.

Local Security Policy

As mentioned at the beginning of this section, the Local Security Policy icon can be accessed from the Administrative Tools folder located in the Windows 2000 Control Panel. Policies are used in Windows 2000 to enforce certain rules and restrictions on user accounts in order to protect the integrity of the operating system and to provide administrators with the ability to audit important events.

If you open the Local Security Policy icon, you will see that you can make policy and settings changes for the following policies:

Account Policies: You can use the Account Policies section to create and apply a Password Policy and an Account Lockout Policy. This allows you to apply policies that force the implementation of such items as minimum or maximum password age, password length, and account lockout after so many failed password attempts.

Local Policies: These policies include an Audit Policy, User Rights Assignment, and Security Options. This is where you enable the auditing of events, such as File and Object Access and System events in Windows 2000. You can also make changes to the rights that users and groups have on the local machine from this area.

Public Key Policies: This policy is part of the Windows 2000 EFS that allows the recovery of lost data by designated Recovery Agents. In this area, administrators can create and add EDRAs, which can be used to unlock or decrypt encrypted files and folders that have been encrypted by other users.

Microsoft Management Console

Windows 2000 offers a new feature called Microsoft Management Console (MMC). The MMC is used to provide a personalized central location for administration through the installation of snap-ins. Snap-ins are applications that represent the various utilities and tools available in Windows 2000, such as the Disk Defragmenter, Device Manager, Computer Policies, Event Viewer, Services, and Certificates, just to name a few. To navigate to and personalize your own Management Console, select Start > Run and enter "MMC" in the Open line. Click OK. A somewhat empty-looking Management Console appears. To add or remove snap-in programs, select Console from the menu options bar. Next, select Add/Remove Snap-in, and from the Stand Alone tab, select Add. A list of available stand-alone snap-in programs is presented. Simply choose the programs you wish to design your own console.

Registry Editors

Like Windows NT 4.0, the Windows 2000 Registry holds system configuration and environmental settings that can be directly edited with utilities such as REGEDIT.EXE and REGEDT32.EXE. To edit the Windows 2000 Registry directly using either of these utilities, select Start > Run and enter either "REGEDIT" or "REGEDT32" on the Open line, and select OK. The REGEDIT utility is an easy tool to use if you need to locate a specific Registry Key. The REGEDT32 utility is more useful for editing specific Registry Keys.

NOTE: *Normal users should never have the ability to directly edit the Registry.*

System Configuration Utility

The System Configuration utility, known as MSCONFIG.EXE in Windows 9x, is also available in Windows 2000. It provides a graphical display of important system information, such as hardware resources, components, software, and Internet Explorer settings and information. One of the most useful features of the System Configuration utility is the System Summary. The System Summary gives detailed information about the system, including the installed operating system, system name, BIOS version, time zone, total physical memory, physical memory available, and many other important system values.

The System Configuration utility also gives you the ability to quickly launch programs, such as Disk Cleanup, Dr. Watson, Hardware Wizard, and the Windows Backup utility.

To access the System Configuration Utility in Windows 2000, select Start > Programs > Accessories > System Tools > System Information, or select Start > Run, enter "WINMSD" at the Open line, and press Enter. The System Summary appears by default. If you wish to launch any of the other tools, such as Disk Cleanup, from the menu bar, select Tools > Windows > Disk Cleanup or any of the other programs listed.

Power Management and Options

In the Windows 2000 Control Panel, you will notice an icon for Power Options. From within Power Options you can configure power schemes that are designed to help reduce the amount of power consumed by devices attached to your system. The built-in power schemes available from the drop-down menu in the Power Options Properties/Power Schemes window are these:

- Home/Office Desk
- Portable Laptop
- Presentation
- Always On
- Minimal Power Management
- Max Battery

You can change the default power settings for each of the power schemes displayed by selecting the appropriate power scheme and changing the settings listed in the "Settings for" section, below the Power Schemes section. The three built-in options that can be changed are Turn off monitor, Turn off hard disks, and System standby.

Active Directory

Windows 2000 Server offers a directory service known as Active Directory. Active Directory provides a hierarchical view of network objects and provides a central location from which all resources on a network can be managed. With Active Directory, administrators can easily view and make changes to user IDs, permissions, rights, computer systems, printers, and any other objects listed in Active Directory. It is not likely that you will encounter many questions about Active Directory on the A+ exam, for it is a Windows 2000 server component that is so robust it could, in fact, have its very own exam.

PROFILES

Windows NT and Windows 2000 utilize user profiles to customize and provide Desktop environments for computers and users. Specific settings for the network, printers, modems, and display options, as well as many other settings can be configured to provide special Desktop atmospheres for users. Three types of user profiles can be implemented in Windows 2000: local profiles, roaming profiles, and mandatory profiles.

Local profiles: When a user first logs on to a Windows 2000 system, a local user profile is automatically created for that specific user. This profile is stored on the local machine on the system partition in the ROOT\Documents and Settings folder. For example, if Windows 2000 were installed on the C drive, and a user named JoeShmo logged on to the system, a local profile for JoeShmo would be created. The profile and its settings would be stored in C:\Documents and Settings\JoeShmo. A local user profile is created for any other user who logs on to the same system. Their profile will also be stored in the C:\Documents and Settings folder.

Roaming profiles: Roaming user profiles are created and stored on network servers in order to provide identical environments for users wherever they log on to the network. For example, an administrator could create a profile for a user named SteveBleile. The administrator would then copy the profile for SteveBleile to a profile server. The profile would then be automatically copied to any system that the user SteveBleile logs on to. Any settings or changes that have been made by the user SteveBleile will be copied back to the profile server and presented the next time the user logs on to the network.

Mandatory profiles: A mandatory profile is similar to a roaming user profile. The main difference is that changes to settings made by the user are not copied back to the profile server when the user logs off the system. Administrators provide a controlled environment for users by implementing mandatory user profiles. A user gets the same Desktop (which was created by the administrator) wherever he or she logs on to the network.

Hardware Profiles

When you install Windows 2000, a hardware profile named Profile 1 is automatically created. This profile is used to tell your operating system what hardware devices (and their settings) are to be used when your system is started.

Hardware Profiles are commonly implemented with the use of laptop or portable computer systems. Laptops are often used with docking stations, which are typically configured with devices such as printers, modems, NICs, or CD-ROMs. A *docked hardware profile* can be created on a laptop system to automatically recognize all devices attached to a docking station when the laptop is inserted into the docking station. Docking stations are typically used at home or at the office. A more suitable hardware profile, called *undocked*, can be created for a laptop when the laptop is not being used with a docking station. This hardware profile loads only the devices, drivers, and settings needed when you are not connected to the docking station. Hardware profiles can be managed by selecting Control Panel > System > Hardware > Hardware Profiles.

PRINTERS

Installing and managing printers in Windows 2000 is not difficult if you have already carried out similar tasks using Windows 9x, Windows Me, or Windows NT.

Windows 2000 utilizes an Add Printer Wizard to assist with the installation of local or network printers. To add a new printer using the Add Printer Wizard, select Start > Settings > Printers, or open Control Panel > Printers. Next, double-click Add Printer. The Add Printer Wizard will start. After clicking Next, you will be asked if the printer is connected locally or on the network.

If the printer you wish to install is connected directly to your system, select Local Printer and click the radio button to automatically detect and install a plug-and-play printer. If the printer and associated printer driver are detected, continue with the instructions to finish the installation. If the printer and associated printer driver are not detected, a message like the one in Figure 26.6 appears, and you will be asked to click Next to configure your printer manually. You will need to configure a printer port and provide the printer drivers from the printer manufacturer so that the operating system can recognize your printer.

If the printer you wish to connect to is located on a network, select Network Printer from the Local or Network Printer window and click Next. Then you will need to locate the network printer by entering the proper UNC name for the system to which the network printer is connected and the share name of the printer. Alternatively, you can click Next to browse for the printer on the network. The proper UNC for locating a printer share on a network is \\Servername\Printername.

If the printer you wish to connect to is located on the Internet or your intranet, select the "Connect to a printer on the Internet or your Intranet" radio button and enter the appropriate URL address to connect to the printer.

If you want to change the printer properties for installed printers in Windows 2000, simply right-click on a printer and select Properties. You will be able to change printer port settings, sharing options, security, and color management settings, just to name a few options.

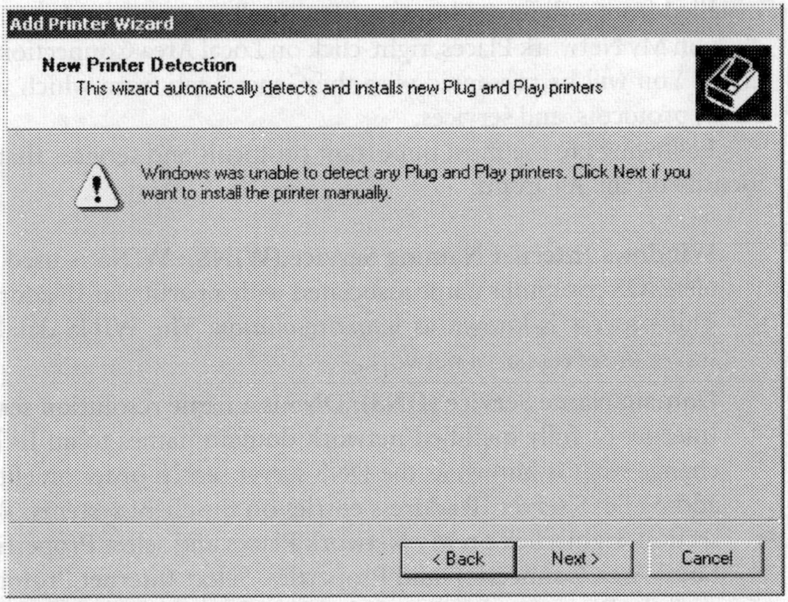

FIGURE 26.6 The Add Printer Wizard suggesting a Manual Mode printer installation.

WINDOWS 2000 NETWORKING AND THE INTERNET

The current A+ Operating Systems Technologies exam will most likely focus on your ability to configure network settings and protocols from within the Windows 2000 Professional operating system. The configurations of Windows 2000 Server and Advanced Server operating systems for network support are beyond the scope of this book. However, the exam will expect you to have a general understanding of network services such as WINS (Windows Internet Naming Service), DNS (Domain Name Service), DHCP (Dynamic Host Configuration Protocol), and FTP (File Transfer Protocol). In this section, we focus on Windows 2000 Professional network connectivity and define some of the important protocols and services used in networks, including the largest network of all—the Internet.

Important Network and Internet Protocols and Services

In the previous operating system chapters, we have discussed protocols in some detail. In Chapter 25, you learned how to install protocols and services from within the Network applet of Control Panel. In Windows 2000 Professional, protocols and services are installed in much the same way, with the exception that they are installed from a different location. To install protocols and services, simply right-click on My Network Places, right-click on Local Area Connection, and select Properties. You will be presented with the General tab from which you can configure NICs, protocols, and services.

Following are the most important protocols and services that you may have to identify on the A+ exam:

Windows Internet Naming Service (WINS): WINS is used to determine the NetBIOS computer name associated with a particular IP address on a network. This process is known as *name resolution*. The WINS database resides on a server or servers on a network.

Domain Name Service (DNS): DNS is a name resolution service that resolves Internet or fully qualified network domain names to an IP address. You can change what is known as the DNS server search order on client computers by adding DNS server IP address entries on the client systems. To navigate to this section, right-click on My Network Places and select Properties, right-click on Local Area Connection and Properties. Select Internet Protocol (TCP/IP) and click the Properties button, click the Advanced button, select the DNS tab, and select Add under the DNS Server addresses in the order of use section. Enter the IP addresses of the DNS servers you wish to use to resolve domain names. It's that simple! This tells the client computer in which order DNS servers should be used to resolve domain names. On another DNS note, domain names have extensions that identify an associated affiliation. .EDU is used for schools and colleges, .COM is for commercial use, .ORG is reserved for nonprofit groups, .GOV is reserved for the United States government, and .NET is used for networking systems or as a replacement for .COM.

Dynamic Host Configuration Protocol (DHCP): DHCP is a protocol used to assign IP addresses automatically on a TCP/IP network. The DHCP server hands out IP addresses to client computers configured to use DHCP. The alternative to DHCP is configuring your system to use a static IP address. To use a static IP address, you will need an IP address, a default gateway, and a subnet mask. If you are using DHCP and need to renew your current dynamically assigned IP address, you should enter the following at a Windows 2000 command prompt:

```
IPCONFIG /RENEW.
```

Internet Connection Sharing (ICS): ICS is a feature of dial-up networking that allows all the computers in a home or small business to share one connection to the Internet. In Windows 2000 Professional, ICS can be configured by selecting Start > Settings > Network and Dial-up Connections, right-clicking on an icon configured for an Internet connection, selecting Properties, selecting the Sharing tab, and clicking Enable Internet Connection Sharing for This Connection. You will then be presented with settings that you can customize for your connection.

NOTE *It is very important for you to remember that ICS is available in Windows 98 SE, Windows 2000, Windows Me, and Windows XP. ICS allows two or more connected computers to share one Internet connection, whether it be a dial-up, DSL, cable, ISDN, satellite, or T1 connection.*

Automatic Private IP Addressing (APIPA): APIPA is a service used with Windows 98 and Windows 2000 Professional that allows client computers to configure themselves automatically with the IP address and subnet mask for network connectivity if a DHCP server fails or is not found. If a DHCP server fails, APIPA uses an IP address in the range of 169.254.0.0 through 169.254.255.254.

Hypertext Transfer Protocol (HTTP): HTTP is an Internet protocol used to define consistent connections.

Hypertext Transfer Protocol Secure (HTTPS): HTTPS is a secure protocol used to transmit information over the Internet. To access a secure Internet site, such as ChristopherCrayton.com, you would need a URL entry of HTTPS://ChristopherCrayton.com. HTTPS is concerned with the secure transmission of individual messages between client and host by using TPC port 443 as opposed to the port 80 that is normally used to transmit HTTP data. It is important to note that HTTPS and SSL (described shortly) compliment each other for secure Internet connectivity. Once again, please note that you will know you are using HTTPS when you make a request through your Internet browser and the URL begins with HTTPS://.

SSL (Secure Sockets Layer): SSL is a protocol that uses public and private keys to secure data transmitted over the Internet. With SSL, a secured connection is established between a client and a server. SSL is a commonly used security protocol that provides transport security through Internet browsers provided by Netscape and Microsoft. SSL is a session-based X.509 digital certificate supporting protocol that uses a public and private key exchange to encrypt the passing of data between client and server systems. The SSL protocol supports RSA, DES, IDEA, 3DES, and MD5. SSL can be used by services such as HTTP, FTP, SMTP, IMAP, POP, and Telnet. SSL uses a combination of the SSL Record protocol and the SSL Handshake protocol to provide security. The Handshake protocol provides authentication services, while the Record protocol provides for a secure connection. Many Internet Web sites utilize SSL as a secure means of obtaining confidential customer information, such as bank account numbers and other personal information. It provides confidential Web sessions and authentication services for Web servers.

Simple Mail Transport Protocol (SMTP): SMTP is a protocol used for transferring e-mail between client computers and e-mail severs. For a client to send e-mail messages using SMTP successfully, a client computer should be configured with an IMAP (Internet Message Access Protocol) or POP (Post Office Protocol) server address. POP and IMAP accounts use SMTP to allow a person using a dial-up or Internet connection to gain access to mail on a mail server computer. In most cases, SMTP is used for sending mail only. This is based on its inability to handle message queuing properly at the mail-receiving end. In order to receive stored messages properly from a mail server, most client-side systems are set up for POP or IMAP.

NOTE: *You send mail with SMTP. You download or receive mail with POP or IMAP.*

SMTP: This is most often used with TCP port 25. SMTP Relay is when an intermediary mail server (relay server) is used to accept any incoming mail and forward it to another mail server or final destination. This final destination is typically the e-mail server where the user's e-mail account is stored. There can be many relay servers involved with the relaying of e-mail. The problem here is that mail servers that implement SMTP Relay usually accept most mail received and deliver or relay outgoing mail without verifying or authenticating the sender or receiver. Spammers, spoofers, and unauthorized users can take advantage of this vulnerability by faking a sender's address, and using just about any receiving address they wish. This can cause great a proliferation of junk mail or 'spam,' and it usually does. A common problem among companies that use improperly configured e-mail and SMTP Relay servers is that they are unknowingly being used as hosts to spam other servers and hosts. This can result in a company's mail server being black holed—meaning they are banned or 'blocked' from using e-mail services provided by ISPs. This can then result in major downtime and loss of productivity. SMTP Relay anyone?

NNTP (Network News Transfer Protocol): NNTP is a protocol included with Internet browsers such as Internet Explorer and Netscape, which allows clients and server systems to post and retrieve Usenet newsgroup messages. A program called a newsreader is often used on the client side for this purpose.

File Transfer Protocol (FTP): FTP is a protocol used to transfer data between computers on a TCP/IP network. Special file servers known as FTP servers are used to handle FTP functions. Users are typically authenticated anonymously on FTP file servers, which means that users can read and update information stored on the FTP server without being authenticated or authorized to access the server. The FTP server does care who the user is.

Here are some good practices when configuring and using FTP:

- ✓ Configure your FTP server to run FTP services only; do not run unnecessary services that can be exploited.
- ✓ Do not store valuable data that cannot be recovered on your FTP server.
- ✓ Use a secure file transfer package, such as SSL, and encrypt all important data.
- ✓ Disallow unnecessary access to your FTP server; do not use a 'blind' or anonymous FTP.
- ✓ Audit and log events on your FTP server.

TFTP (Trivial File Transfer Protocol): TFTP is a scaled down, simplistic version of FTP. Instead of using the TCP (Transmission Control Protocol) that FTP uses, TFTP use the UDP (User Datagram Protocol). Unlike FTP, TFTP does not use authentication and doesn't provide any security features whatsoever. It is commonly used by servers as a mechanism to reboot diskless systems and X-terminals.

S/FTP (Secure/FTP): There are many third-party programs available today that assist in making your FTP server more secure. Many of these programs are Java based and allow for an SSL encrypted connection to your FTP server. For very secure FTP, X.509 certificates and the use of asymmetric public key cryptography is often used to encrypt public keys. For larger file transmissions, symmetric keys are used to encrypt and decrypt data sessions. There are many algorithms that are used in securing FTP. A few of these include: DES, 3DES, and Blowfish. In conclusion, S/FTP is meant to provide strong authentication and encryption services, and support for FTP.

Workgroup or Domain?

If you have installed Windows 2000 Professional and are not currently attached to a workgroup or domain, you can join your system to a workgroup or domain, or change your system's name by right-clicking on the My Computer icon, selecting the Network Identification tab, and choosing the Properties button. You will then have the options of changing your computer name or becoming a member of a workgroup or a domain. In order to join your system to a workgroup or domain, you must have administrative privileges.

Internet Connectivity

Configuring your system to connect to the Internet is not difficult. You need a Local Area Connection, TCP/IP, an Internet browser (such as Internet Explorer or Netscape Navigator), a modem, and an ISP.

You can use the Internet Connection Wizard to connect your system to the Internet. To do this, right-click on the Internet Explorer icon located on the Desktop, select Properties, select the Connections tab, and click the Setup button. You will be offered several options for configuring and finally making your connection. Follow the instructions presented by the wizard.

Viruses

Computer viruses are becoming more and more of a threat to the integrity of computer systems and computer data. If a virus has wiped out your important personal information or destroyed your business' data, then you are probably already aware of how critical it is to have a good antivirus package, updated antivirus DAT files, and a good backup plan.

Viruses are easily spread via the Internet, through e-mail attachments, infected floppy disks, and network shares. The most common types of viruses are the following:

Trojan: A virus that comes disguised as a useful file or program, the file or program is used to deliver the Trojan virus to the system.

Macro: Often spread through e-mail, a macro virus is one that infects programs, files, and templates associated with applications such as Microsoft Word or Excel. Macro viruses usually insert undesired objects or words into documents. They are usually programmed to be triggered by a specific action or event.

Boot sector: These viruses infect the MBR on hard disks. They can easily make the hard disk unbootable. Thus, it is always good practice to have a bootable floppy virus-scanning disk available to assist with recovery from this type of virus.

Polymorphic: This is a very popular type of virus that mutates so that it is virtually undetectable by antivirus software.

File infectors: These types of viruses typically attach to executable programs, such as files with a .COM or .EXE extensions.

Worm: A worm virus resides in computer memory and duplicates itself until it finally consumes enough system resources to render the system inoperative.

Stealth: A stealth virus can infect partition tables, boot sectors, and executable programs, and hides from antivirus detection software.

The recommended way to clean a virus from an infected computer is to boot the system to a virus-scanned boot disk that includes an updated DAT (virus definition) file, and which cleans the virus from the infected system by running the antivirus cleaning software program from the boot disk.

The current A+ operating system technologies exam is likely to test your knowledge regarding the types of media and software that can actually be infected by viruses. For the exam, please note that floppies cannot be infected when they are write-protected, CD-ROMs cannot be infected, hard drive boot sectors can be infected, system and network files can be infected.

DIAGNOSING AND TROUBLESHOOTING TEST TIPS

Windows 2000 introduced many changes to the operating system world. It is much more robust than its predecessors. For that reason, you will face a vast array of questions regarding Windows 2000 technology when you take the current A+ Operating Systems Technologies exam. This chapter is designed to prepare you with as many diagnosing and troubleshooting test tips as possible to prepare you for the test. Please use the following items, as well as the review questions and A+ Operating Systems Technologies Cumulative Practice Exam, to sharpen your skills in final preparation for the Windows 2000 portion of the exam:

- ✓ Windows 2000 components can be added to the operating system from the Windows 2000 Installation CD-ROM by using the Add/Remove Programs applet in the Control Panel.
- ✓ If you are trying to connect to an ISP through a dial-up connection and receive the error message "Server cannot negotiate an appropriate protocol," this is most likely the result of an improperly configured or corrupt TCP/IP configuration.
- ✓ By default, files with the extensions .INI, .INF, and .DLL not are displayed in Windows 2000 Explorer. If you want hidden files and folders to be displayed, choose Tools > Folder Options > View, and select "Show Hidden Files and Folders" in the Advanced Settings box of the View section.
- ✓ To assign or 'map' a drive letter to a network folder in Windows 2000, simply right-click My Network Places or My Computer and select Map Network Drive.
- ✓ Windows 2000 provides network protocols for communication with other networked systems. Remember for the exam that Windows 2000 supports TCP/IP, NWLINK, NetBEUI, and AppleTalk. TCP/IP is used for most networks, including the Internet. NWLINK is used for communication with Novell Networks. NetBEUI is a fast, efficient Microsoft network protocol. AppleTalk is used for communicating with Apple Macintosh systems.
- ✓ If you have the ability to send e-mail and attachments over the Internet, but cannot receive e-mail and attachments from others, you should verify that your SMTP settings and mail server settings are accurate.

- ✓ If you want to connect to a specific news group on the Internet via an ISP, you will need to acquire the IP address associated with the Network News Transfer Protocol (NNTP) server for that ISP.
- ✓ In Windows 2000, a hidden Start Menu can be displayed by pressing Ctrl+Esc.
- ✓ You can create a shortcut for a program from within Windows Explorer by right-clicking the program and selecting Create Shortcut. To create a shortcut that will be placed on the Windows Desktop, right-click the program from within Windows Explorer, select Send to, and select Desktop (create shortcut).
- ✓ You can use the Alt+Tab keyboard sequence to switch between applications running in Windows 2000.
- ✓ In Windows 2000, your network interface card type can be displayed in Device Manager. Device Manager can be accessed through the System applet in the Windows 2000 Control Panel.
- ✓ To set a default printer in Windows 2000, navigate to Start > Settings > Printers, right-click on the printer, and check "Set as Default Printer".
- ✓ You can prevent Windows 2000 users from installing unsigned device drivers by navigating to System Properties > Hardware > Driver Signing. You may then select from the Ignore, Warn, or Block options.
- ✓ Virtual memory uses swap file space on a hard drive for storage.
- ✓ If you are running out of memory while running multiple programs in Windows 2000, you can increase the size of your paging file by navigating to System Properties > Advanced > Performance Options > Change...
- ✓ If you delete files that are stored on removable media such as a floppy disk, CD-RW, or removable hard drive, the files will be immediately deleted. They will not go into the Recycle Bin.
- ✓ If you restore data to a FAT32 partition that was originally backed up from an NTFS partition, you will only retain file attributes and the long file names. You will lose any file-level permissions, compressions, or encryption. These are only supported under NTFS.
- ✓ The Windows 2000 operating system provides support for FAT16, FAT32, NTFS, and CDFS file systems.
- ✓ You can use the Disk Cleanup Wizard or navigate to Internet Explorer > Tools > Internet Options to clean up temporary Internet files.
- ✓ In Windows 2000, user profiles are stored in C:\Documents and Settings.
- ✓ Hypertext Transport Protocol Secure (HTTPS) is a very popular, secure protocol used to transmit messages over the Internet.

- ✓ FTP sessions by default are not encrypted. User names and passwords are transmitted in clear text. FTP user IDs and passwords can be easily grabbed with a network packet sniffer.
- ✓ Adding a DNS server's IP address to a local system's DNS server search order will tell the local system where the DNS server is located.
- ✓ If you have an application that ran just fine and under Windows 95 but won't run after upgrading to Windows 2000, you should reinstall the application.

CHAPTER SUMMARY

On completion of this chapter, you should have gained the information and skills necessary to carry out the following tasks and understand the following concepts:

- Install Windows 2000 Professional.
- Upgrade to Windows 2000 Professional from Windows 9x or Windows NT 4.0.
- Prepare for dual-boot scenarios with Windows 2000, Windows 9x, Windows Me, and Windows NT 4.0.
- Understand the steps and progression of the Windows 2000 start-up process.
- Implement Windows 2000 tools and utilities to carry out specific tasks and maintain operating system integrity.
- Understand the different user profiles that can be implemented with Windows 2000.
- Configure general file and folder options.
- Install and configure printers in Windows 2000.
- Diagnose and troubleshoot basic operating system problems.
- Have a general understanding of networking protocols and Internet connectivity.

It is very important that you have a solid understanding of the operating systems information provided to you thus far. In the two remaining chapters of this book, we will explore Windows Millennium (Me) and Windows XP, which are included in CompTIA's new 2003 Operating Systems Technologies Objectives. Stay alert, you will need to apply the information you have learned so far to these remaining chapters. But first, more questions...

REVIEW QUESTIONS

1. Windows 2000 provides support for which of the following file systems? (Choose Three)

- □ A. FAT32
- □ B. OS/2
- □ C. CDFS
- □ D. CFDS
- □ E. NTFS
- □ F. HPFS

Correct Answers = A, C, and E

Windows 2000 provides support for FAT32, CDFS, and NTFS. The OS/2 operating system uses HPFS (High Performance File System), which Windows 2000 does not support.

2. Which operating systems can you upgrade to Windows 2000 Professional? (Choose Three)

- □ A. Windows 95
- □ B. Windows 98
- □ C. OS/2
- □ D. Windows 3x
- □ E. Windows NT 4.0

Correct Answers = A, B, and E

From the choices listed, only Windows 95, Windows 98, and Windows NT can be upgraded to Windows 2000 Professional.

3. You just wrote over important Windows 2000 system files after installing a third-party application. Windows 2000 prompts you with the message "Files that are required for Windows to run properly have been replaced by unrecognized versions. To maintain system stability Windows must restore the original versions of these files." Where did this message come from?

- o A. System Protector 2000
- o B. Windows 2000 File Protection
- o C. Windows 2000 File Authentication
- o D. Windows 2000 File and Object Auditor

Correct Answer = B

Windows 2000 has a built-in backup feature called Windows File Protection that keeps a backup of important system files. If you write over important system files with programs or applications, Windows File Protection will prompt you that it needs to restore the important system files you just replaced.

4. What should you always consider first before upgrading to a new operating system?

o A. Verify that you have the most current service pack.

o B. Back up the system partition.

o C. Back up your current operating system and data.

o D. Back up only critical information.

Correct Answer = C

Before upgrading to a new operating system, your first consideration should always be to make a complete backup of your current operating system and data. This is crucial if you wish to have a path back to your current OS and information.

5. If you want to upgrade Windows 9x or Windows NT to Windows 2000 Professional, what must you do?

o A. Insert the Windows 2000 installation CD-ROM and reboot.

o B. Insert the first Windows 2000 installation floppy diskette and reboot.

o C. Run the Windows 2000 setup program from within Windows 9x or Windows NT.

o D. Connect to a network share that has the Windows 2000 setup program and reboot.

Correct Answer = C

In order to perform an upgrade to Windows 2000 Professional, you must run the setup program from within an existing operating system. Choices A and B are valid options for a full Windows 2000 installation. D will not perform an upgrade or a full installation.

6. You want to install the Windows 2000 Recovery Console so that it is available at system startup. Assuming that your CD-ROM has a drive letter of D, what command would you use?

o A. D:\i386\INSTALL/CMDCONS

o B. D:\i386\WINNT32 /CMDCONS

o C. D:\i386\WINN/EXECMDCONS

o D. D:\i386\WINDOWS/EXECMDCONS

Correct Answer = B

The Windows 2000 Recovery Console is a useful tool that can be used to troubleshoot a system that will not boot, copy system files to a hard drive, and configure services. To install the recovery console so that it is available at system startup, insert the Windows 2000 installation CD-ROM and enter the command "WINNT32 /CMDCONS" from the i386 folder. You can then select the Recovery Console option when your system restarts.

7. Windows 2000 provides support for dynamic volumes. Which of the following dynamic volume types does Windows 2000 support? (Choose Four)

□ A. Duplicated volumes

□ B. Multi-homed volumes

□ C. Spanned volumes

□ D. Raid Level 5 volumes

□ E. Mirrored volumes

□ F. Striped volumes

Correct Answers = C, D, E, and F

Windows 2000 provides support for five different types of dynamic volumes. The five dynamic volumes supported are spanned, Raid-5, mirrored, striped, and simple.

8. Which are valid paths to creating a network drive mapping in Windows 2000? (Choose Two)

□ A. Open My Computer, right-click on System, and select Map Network Drive.

□ B. Open My Computer, right-click on C:, and select Map Network Drive.

□ C. Right-click on My Computer and select Map Network Drive.

□ D. Navigate from Explorer > Tools > Folder Options > Map Network Drive.

□ E. Right-click on My Network Places and select Map Network Drive.

Correct Answers = C and E

Only choices C and E will enable you to establish a drive mapping.

9. Where in Windows 2000 can you verify that a recently installed device is functioning properly?

○ A. Control Panel > Add/Remove Hardware

○ B. The Windows 2000 HCL

○ C. Hardware Profiles

○ D. Device Manager

Correct Answer = D

Similar to Windows 9x, Windows 2000 provides the Device Manager utility. The Device Manager will place a yellow field containing a black exclamation point on devices that are having a problem or a red "X" on devices that are disabled. To troubleshoot a device, double-click on the device and use the Troubleshooter utility.

10. Where in Windows 2000 are settings for local user profiles located?

- o A. C:\Documents and Settings
- o B. C:\Winnt\System32\Repl\Import
- o C. C:\Windows\Profiles\Settings
- o D. C:\Documents and Settings\Profiles

Correct Answer = A

Local user profiles are stored in the C:\Documents and Settings folder by default in Windows 2000.

11. Several Windows 2000 and Windows 98 computers on your network are configured with DHCP and TCP/IP. What will happen to these computers if they are unable to acquire IP addresses from a DHCP server?

- o A. The computers will not be able to communicate on the network.
- o B. Automatic Private IP Addressing will assign IP addresses to the computers from the 169.254.0.0 range.
- o C. The computers will acquire valid IP addresses from a local WINS server.
- o D. The computers will acquire valid IP addresses from a remote DNS server.

Correct Answer = B

A built-in feature of the Windows 98 and Windows 2000 DHCP client is Automatic Private IP Addressing (APIPA). This feature will automatically assign an IP address from the Class B IP range 169.254.0.0.

12. Which of the following operating systems cannot be upgraded to Windows 2000 Professional?

- o A. Windows 95
- o B. Windows 98
- o C. Windows Me
- o D. Windows NT Workstation
- o E. All of the above

Correct Answer = C

Windows 2000 is not a supported upgrade from Windows Me.

13. What must you do to begin the upgrade procedure from Windows 9x or Windows NT to Windows 2000?

o A. Insert the Windows 2000 installation CD-ROM and reboot.

o B. Insert the Windows 2000 installation floppy disk and reboot.

o C. Boot your system into Windows 9x or NT. Insert the Windows 2000 CD-ROM and select Yes to upgrade.

o D. Insert the Windows 2000 installation recovery CD-ROM and reboot.

o E. All of the above will begin the upgrade procedure to Windows 2000.

Correct Answer = C

To upgrade from Windows 9x or Windows NT to Windows 2000, boot your system into Windows 9x or Windows NT. Next, insert the Windows 2000 installation CD-ROM. Select Yes when asked if you want to upgrade. Inserting the Windows 2000 CD-ROM and rebooting would perform a fresh Windows 2000 installation, making choice A incorrect. Choices B, D, and E are invalid.

14. Which of the following is a protocol that uses public and private keys to secure data transmitted over the Internet?

o A. MMC

o B. POP

o C. IMAP

o D. SSL

o E. All of the above

Correct Answer = D

SSL (Secure Sockets Layer) is a session-based X.509 digital certificate-supporting protocol that uses a public and private key exchange to encrypt the passing of data between client and server systems. MMC (Microsoft Management Console) is used to provide a personalized central location for administration through the installation of snap-ins. POP (Post Office Protocol) and IMAP (Internet Message Access Protocol) accounts use SMTP to allow a person using a dial-up or Internet connection to gain access to mail on a mail server computer.

15. What is used to resolve a domain name to an IP address?

o A. Forward DNS

o B. DNS

o C. WINS

o D. SMTP

o E. None of the above

Correct Answer = B

DNS (Domain Name Server or Service) is used to resolve fully qualified domain names to a node or IP address. Choice A is invalid. WINS (Windows Internet Naming Service) is used to determine the NetBIOS computer name associated with a particular IP address on a network. SMTP (Simple Mail Transport Protocol) is a protocol used for transferring e-mail between client computers and e-mail servers.

16. Which of the following can be easily infected by a virus? (Choose Three)

- □ A. Network files
- □ B. CD-ROM
- □ C. Write-protected floppy disk
- □ D. Boot sectors
- □ E. System files
- □ F. Ink-jet cartridge
- □ G. All of the above

Correct Answers = A, D, and E

Write-protected floppies cannot be infected, CD-ROMs cannot be infected, hard drive boot sectors can be infected, and system/network files can be infected. Ink-jet cartridges and other consumable printer items cannot be infected by computer viruses.

17. What type of server would you connect to through your ISP for newsgroup information?

- o A. NNTP
- o B. DNS
- o C. HTTPS
- o D. Polymorphic
- o E. None of the above

Correct Answer = A

NNTP (Network News Transfer Protocol) is a protocol included with Internet browsers such as Internet Explorer and Netscape that allows clients and server systems to post and retrieve Usenet newsgroup messages. DNS (Domain Name Server or Service) is used to resolve fully qualified domain names to a node or IP address. HTTPS (Hypertext Transfer Protocol Secure) is a secure protocol used to transmit information over the Internet. A polymorphic virus is a very popular type of virus that mutates so that it is virtually undetectable by antivirus software.

18. You can send e-mail messages with any problems. Unfortunately, you cannot receive e-mail. What settings should you check?

- o A. SMTP
- o B. POP or IMAP
- o C. C:\WINNT\SYSTEM32\REPL\IMPORT
- o D. Local user account password
- o E. None of the above

Correct Answer = B

You send mail with SMTP. You download or receive mail with POP or IMAP. In this situation, you need to check your incoming mail settings for POP or IMAP. All other choices are invalid.

REFERENCES

http://www.microsoft.com/whdc/hcl/search.mspx. The Microsoft Hardware Compatibility Web site.

http://www.microsoft.com/windows2000/professional/howtobuy/upgrading/path/win9x.asp. This Microsoft Web site offers directions on upgrading from Windows 9x to Windows 2000. From this page, other OS upgrading instructions can be located as well.

http://support.microsoft.com/default.aspx?scid=kb;en-us;272627. This Microsoft Web site describes why there is no supported upgrade path from Window Me to Windows 2000.

27 Windows Me

In This Chapter

- Overview of Windows Me
- Windows Me Installation Process
- Windows Me Upgrade Process
- Windows Me Start-Up Process
- Windows Me Tools and Utilities
- Profiles
- Printers
- Windows Me Networking and the Internet
- Diagnosing and Troubleshooting Test Tips
- Chapter Summary
- Review Questions
- References

OVERVIEW OF WINDOWS ME

Windows Millennium (Me) was originally introduced in the summer of 1999, and was released to the general public in September of 2000 as a follow up to the very successful Windows 98 Second Edition.

Windows Me is based on the Windows 9x kernel, with an updated front end that makes it look more like Windows 2000. While Windows Me may look a little different than Windows 98 SE, it is basically the same.

Windows Me was not a major release, and was mostly viewed as an incremental update to the Windows 9x family. Upon installing Windows, the first thing you will notice is that there is no sign that AUTOEXEC.BAT or CONFIG.SYS files attempt to load; this was done to reduce start-up time. Another big difference that you may notice is the absence of DOS; though rest assured, it's still there. Microsoft decided to remove access to (Real Mode) DOS "to prevent customers [from] having trouble with the DOS features and to make the computer boot up and shutdown more quickly." True, you can no longer reboot into DOS (from the Start menu) or use F8 in the boot sequence to go directly to a DOS prompt, but it is still easy enough to make a boot disk to accomplish this task. There is only one version of Windows Me (with two different installation types: Full and Upgrade). New features included in Windows Me are:

Auto-Update: This is a feature added to Me which basically tries to determine when your modem isn't being used to download content from the Internet and uses that time to find (and notify you) if any updates are available for your system.

System Restore: Available in Windows for the first time, System Restore will make a 'save point,' collecting all of your current system and Registry settings (including drivers for your hardware), which you can choose to return to, should a newly installed feature be causing you grief.

MS Driver Signing: This notifies you when a driver you are attempting to install is Microsoft certified by WHQL (Windows Hardware Quality Labs).

Home Networking Wizard: This was also added for ease of setting up home networking features, such as PC-to-PC connectivity and Internet sharing. The Home Network Wizard takes much of the grief out of setting up a home-based network and installs the appropriate drivers for your networked components.

System File Protection: Also included with Windows Me, this feature works to ensure that new programs being installed cannot overwrite critical system files with their own, possibly incompatible files.

Expanded Multimedia Content: A newer version of Windows Media Player (version 7.0) was included with Windows Me. It includes better support for MP3 and DVD playback. Also included for the first time in this version of Windows is Windows Movie Maker, a great tool for editing digital video.

Scanner and Camera Wizard: This wizard was included to streamline the process of adding such devices without having to use the interface software included with the device.

Enhanced USB and FireWire Support: The growing demand for expansion devices and their ever-changing connectivity types brought better support for USB devices, and finally brought FireWire (or IE 13394) support to Windows 9x. FireWire is a high-performance serial bus that can connect upwards of 60 devices in a daisy chain configuration. FireWire supports connection speeds of up to 400Mbps.

Most of the enhancements that Windows Me offers over Windows 98 SE revolve around digital media content. It came with an updated Windows Media player (version 7.0), and DVD playback software, as well as Windows Movie Maker. Included with Windows Me, is the Scanner and Camera Wizard, which makes adding such devices much easier, and generally a walk-through procedure (as opposed to having to use the interface software included with the device). Other enhancements included updates to USB and FireWire support for better functionality.

WINDOWS ME INSTALLATION PROCESS

Manufacturers of operating systems provide minimum and recommended hardware specifications that should be considered before installing or upgrading an OS. The minimum system requirement for Windows Me can be found on Microsoft's Windows Me site at: *http://support.microsoft.com/default.aspx?scid=253695.*

The basic system requirements are:

- Pentium 150MHz processor or better
- 32MB of RAM
- Minimum 320MB of hard drive space (formatted as FAT32)
- CD/DVD-ROM drive

NOTE *These are the very basic system requirements. Different hardware is required for some of Windows Me features (e.g., Movie Maker requires more memory).*

Before You Start

As always, you should check the manufacturer's recommended hardware requirements for operating system installation. Next, make sure that you have the correct version of the Windows Me installation CD-ROM that fits your needs. There are two version of Windows Me available, the full version and the upgrade version. The upgrade version requires a previous version of Windows 95, 98, or 98 Second Edition installed on your hard drive for installation. (At the very least, you must have the CD-ROM with one of those operating systems on it to verify that you are doing an upgrade.) Both the upgrade and the full version can be installed on a hard drive on a separate partition from a nonupgradeable OS (such as Windows NT); but only the full version can be used to install on a completely blank hard drive, should you not own a copy of Windows 95, 98, or 98 Second Edition (more on that later). Remember, OEM disks were designed for specific systems and do not work as a full installation on all systems (which can subsequently cause problems with trying to use nonbootable OEM CD-ROMs in the installation process).

WINDOWS ME UPGRADE PROCESS

The full installation and upgrade processes aren't all that dissimilar from other Windows 9x installations (e.g., Windows 98).

If you are performing an upgrade from an older version of Windows, simply place the Windows Me upgrade CD-ROM into the CD-ROM drive while in the current version of Windows. You will be presented with the Windows Me installation prompt: "This CD-ROM contains a newer version of Windows than the one you are presently using. Would you like to upgrade your computer to this new version of Windows Millennium now?"

NOTE

If you are using a version of Windows 3x or have Auto Insert Notification turned off, you will not be prompted with this query box. You can browse to the setup.exe using the file manager; or if you are using Windows 9x, you can go to Start > Run > then type (if D: is the correct drive letter for the CD-ROM that the upgrade CD-ROM is in) D:\win9x\setup.

After you choose to upgrade, your system will check to ensure that no programs are running (and if they are, prompt you to close them). After that, a routine check will run to determine if your disk has any errors and corrects them as necessary. You'll be greeted by the Windows Millennium Setup Wizard screen followed by the license agreement and finally the Product key entry screen. (Make sure to enter it excluding any dashes.) From here, Windows Me will determine what hardware you currently have installed and will initialize the system's Registry file. A check will determine if you have enough disk space for the upgrade, and you will be prompted to save your system files. This is important, as should you choose not to save your system files, you will be unable to revert to your current operating system should Windows Me not completely fit your needs. It is recommended that you always choose to backup system files at this point, as you can always remove them later. (Should you run out of disk space, removing the files will free up 50–100MB.)

Should the installation determine that backing up your files would leave too little space, you will be alerted and prompted with the option of skipping the backup in order to free up disk space.

You will now be prompted to create an Emergency Startup Disk that can be used should the hard drive be damaged or system files are lost or corrupted. Since these things happen to the best of us, it is highly recommended that you have Windows create this disk, and have it handy at all times. Also, should this installation fail, this disk is necessary to uninstall Windows Me. Click on Finish, and you'll go on to the meat of the installation, the file copy process. A status bar lets you know just how much progress has been made in copying files from the CD-ROM to your hard drive. After the copying is complete, your PC will need to reboot. Remove the floppy disk from the drive (you did make the Emergency Startup Disk, right?) and reboot. Once rebooted, your system will begin installing drivers for various devices and reboot as necessary. This process is completely automated; you should be ready to go in about 30 minutes.

If you want a little more control over what exactly Windows Me installs and where, you can choose to do the install from the command prompt. Using a boot disk (refer to the Windows 9x installation section to review components necessary for boot disk), boot up your PC to the command prompt. Type "D:" (or whichever drive letter represents the CD-ROM where your Windows Me disk is being installed from), then type "Setup" to start the Setup program.

NOTE *If you have previously copied the Windows Me installation files to your hard drive, you enter the address of the folder to where you copied the files.*

Once the Startup program has started, an instance of ScanDisk checks out the hard drive for errors; and after a few moments, you will be greeted by the familiar GUI mode (with mouse support). You will be taken from the license agreement through the Product key entry, just as in the upgrade. Next, you will be prompted to enter the installation directory where you want Windows Me to be installed (the default is C:\Windows). Following this, provided that you are installing on a formatted hard drive, you will be prompted to save existing system files. Moving through familiar paces, you will be prompted for creation of a boot disk, which is highly recommended. If you are installing to a previously unused Windows folder (or if you changed the default installation directory) you will be prompted to pick the type of installation: Typical, Portable, Component, or Custom.

You will then be prompted for your Name/Company Name, select the components you wish to install, followed by the various network options (IDs, workgroups, etc.). Much like the 9x family, it is highly recommended that you wait until your computer is finished with the OS installation to configure network options (a choice made that much easier with the ease of Home Network Wizard). After choosing country, time, and date, you should be all but finished.

The installation process really doesn't differ too much between an upgrade and a full install. The same basic differences existed in Windows 9x (e.g., making sure the hard drive is formatted for the particular operating system you are trying to install, creation of a boot disk, etc.); so while the command prompt portion of the installation section focuses on a full installation, rest assured it is the same for the upgrade installation.

Dual Booting

It is possible for Windows 9x (as well as Windows Me) to be set up in a dual-boot situation with another operating system from the Windows NT/2000 family on the same hard drive. There will be a few complications that you can expect, due to the fact that Windows 9x wants to be the only operating system, and will often overwrite system files. If Windows NT or 2000, for example, is installed on a FAT16-partitioned drive, you will receive an error when installing Windows Me that Windows NT system files are present. If Windows NT is installed on an NTFS partition, Windows Me will report that it is damaged and will not let you continue the installation (as interactive reparation is not allowed during Setup). Should you have a Windows NT or 2000 installation on a FAT16-partitioned drive and choose to install Windows Me anyway, the Windows NT or 2000 boot files will be overwritten with the Windows Me files. Windows NT and Windows 2000 do come with repair tools to correct the problem, though, so there's a solution to the problem. Before you get started, you should realize that you will need to make or have a copy of the boot disk for Windows Me (or Windows 95 or 98, should you be trying to dual-boot with those).

NOTE *Do not attempt to use a boot disk for another operating system; that is, if you are trying to set up Windows Me in a dual-boot situation, do not try and use a Windows 98 boot disk. Boot disks are fairly regimented in terms of revision control and their own particular internal files and utilities.*

To install Windows Me (or any of the Windows 9x family, for that matter):

1. Ensure that your Windows NT installation is up to date. Make sure that you have all the latest service packs and any hot fixes that are pertinent to your system. Windows 2000 comes ready out of the box to be able to see Windows 9x (Windows 95, 98, or Me), but you should be updated to at least Service Pack 1 for other reasons.
2. Create a Repair Disk for either Windows NT or Windows 2000. This disk contains copies of key Registry entries, along with a description of the partition geometry of the disk.
   - To build a Repair Disk(s) in Windows NT, use the RDISK.EXE command line and follow the prompts.
   - To build a Repair Disk(s) in Windows 2000, run the Backup utility and click the Emergency Repair Disk option on the Welcome tab.
3. Create a FAT32 partition for the Windows Me installation. It does not have to be the boot partition, but it does have to be a DOS-accessible partition for the installation to succeed.

NOTE *Windows NT can recognize FAT16 partitions, but not FAT32 partitions. If no such partition exists, use a third-party tool like Partition Magic to create one.*

4. Using Windows NT or 2000, insert your Windows Me CD-ROM and copy the SETUP folder to your FAT32 partition. You should use the same folder name to copy installation files, but should SETUP already exist, try using NEW SETUP or something similar.
5. It is time to restart your computer and boot from your Windows Me boot disk. At the command prompt, type: SYS C: to transfer the boot files. This should return the command line SYSTEM TRANSFERRED.
6. Switch to the folder where you installed the Setup files (remember the syntax: drive name:\folder name), and type Setup.exe to start the Setup process.
7. You will receive the aforementioned warning about Windows NT system files being present (or possibly files from another operating system, depending on what else you have installed). In any event, ignore these messages for now. Otherwise, the installation process shouldn't be all that different from a normal Windows Me installation. The only difference is that the location of the Windows installation cannot be on the same partition as your Windows NT installation (which can cause inconsistencies in your Programs folder).
8. Once the installation finishes, you need to ensure that your system boots to Windows Me normally. If it does not boot normally, unrepaired disk problems may have occurred during installation.
9. We are now ready to repair the NT boot files, which will allow you to use the NT boot loader so you can choose between Windows NT, Windows 2000, or Windows Me. Boot the computer using your Windows NT or 2000 setup disks or CD-ROM (if you can boot from a CD-ROM), and choose "R" for Repair. Choose to Repair only the Windows NT boot sector, nothing else.

NOTE

If your Windows NT or 2000 installation is not found, you can use the Repair Disk made in step 2 to correct the problem.

10. Once the Repair operation is finished, boot the computer, and you should see the Windows NT or 2000 boot menu option menu with Windows Me at the bottom.

NOTE

Should you not receive the boot option, you will have to edit your BOOT.INI (should be a read-only file in the root directory of your boot drive). You'll need to modify the permissions so that you can edit the file. Add the line: C:\Windows Me, and reboot. (Actually, you can add whatever you like in the description after C:\, as long as it is different from the other menu choices.

Using DOS

As stated earlier, no real-mode DOS comes included with Windows Me. You can boot to a command prompt, though, and you may find it easy to troubleshoot and add/delete certain files from here. To boot into DOS, you will need a start-up disk. Here is how you can create a start-up disk:

- Go to Start > Settings > Control Panel.
- Double-click Add/Remove Programs.
- Click the Start-Up Disk tab, then choose to Create Disk (you will need a formatted floppy disk).

Restart your PC with the disk in the floppy drive. Make sure that your BIOS is set to boot from the floppy drive first, or you will just be taken back into Windows Me. If all goes well, you will be taken to the Microsoft Windows Millennium Startup Menu. From here, you can press Shift+F5 to go to the command prompt.

WINDOWS ME START-UP PROCESS

Windows Me is a member of the Windows 9x family and as such uses the exact same start-up process, with the notable exclusion of AUTOEXEC.BAT and CONFIG.SYS. Windows Me finally did away with legacy support for these files. In previous iterations of Windows 9x, Windows was actually using its own 32-bit versions instead of these files; they were only used for backward compatibility. Please refer to Chapter 24 on Windows 9x for a full description of the start-up process.

WINDOWS ME TOOLS AND UTILITIES

The tools utilized in Windows Me remain largely unchanged from the tools offered in the earlier versions of Windows 9x. Windows Me does add some notable exceptions, though, such as PCHealth tools (including the very helpful System Restore utility). Let's take a look at some of the new tools as well as some of the best tools to help you troubleshoot errors.

Display Settings

Display settings are accessed the same way across all of the Windows 9x family of operating systems by either right-clicking on the Desktop and choosing Properties or by going through Start > Settings > Control Panel, and clicking the display icon. From either of these avenues, you are taken to the Display Properties applet (see

Figure 27.1). Click on the Settings tab to change Desktop resolution (which may be featured on the exam) and color depth. If you click the Advanced button, and then the Monitor tab, you can adjust your monitor's refresh rate, which by default is typically set to 60Hz. Did you note the checkbox toggle on/of for "Hide modes that this monitor cannot display" option on the Monitor tab? It should stay checked (toggled on), because running your monitor at unsupported refresh rates can seriously affect the life span of a monitor. When changing the Desktop resolution, Windows Me will automatically set the refresh rate for the lowest possible setting (equal to or greater than 60Hz) that the monitor can handle at that particular resolution (i.e., it may be possible to run your monitor at 75Hz at 1024 × 768, but Windows Me will typically default to 65Hz at this resolution). Make sure that you are running the highest possible refresh rate for your monitor in order to avoid headaches, strained eyes, and other physical ailments that can be caused by prolonged use of a monitor with a low refresh rate.

DXDIAG

DXDIAG is another useful command line that is run from the Run prompt in the Start menu to utilize the DirectX Diagnostic tool. The DirectX Diagnostic tool is

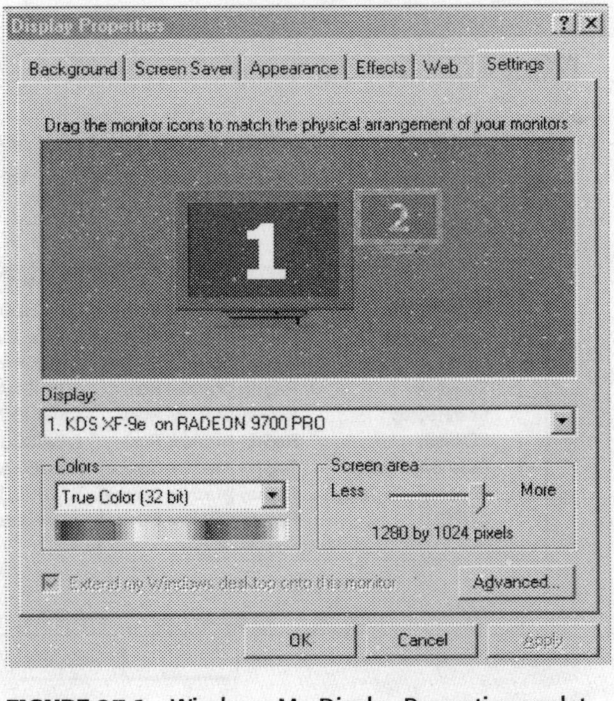

FIGURE 27.1 Windows Me Display Properties applet.

another display applet relating specifically to DirectX, a 3D API that is directly supported by Microsoft. Most computers have some form of 3D processing unit in the video card, either on-board or as AGP/PCI, and Windows Me comes with a version of DirectX automatically installed. Direct Draw and DirectX capabilities can be tested from the DirectX Diagnostics applet, and general information can be found by clicking the General tab.

MSCONFIG

Windows Me, being a member of the Windows 9x family, shares many of the qualities found in Windows 95 and Windows 98 SE. Unfortunately, it contains many of the same issues that plague its older siblings, as well. Boot times have been improved from those found in Windows 95 and 98, but booting can still be slowed by having too many services running at start-up. To check exactly what you have starting within the boot-up process, go to Start > Run, and type in "MSCONFIG" (not case sensitive) on the Open line. This will bring up the System Configuration Utility (see Figure 27.2), which contains several system tabs, including System.ini, Win.ini, and Startup. The one we're interested in is Startup. From here, you can choose what applications will start with Windows, with checkboxes to the left indicating if you wish them to be toggled on or off. For optimal performance, only leave

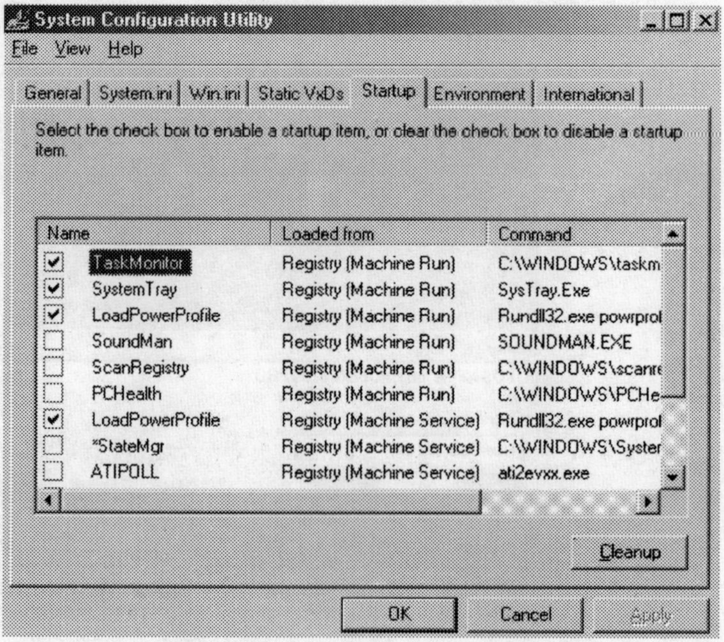

FIGURE 27.2 Windows Me System Configuration Utility.

enabled what is absolutely necessary at start-up. Most programs, Microsoft Office included, have a tendency to leave start-up files as a part of the boot sequence, which (when compounded with several other start-up enabled programs) can seriously slow down the amount of time it takes to boot into Windows.

Device Manager

While not specific to Windows Me, the Device Manager is one of the most useful tools you have at your disposal when trying to troubleshoot hardware difficulties. By right-clicking My Computer, which will bring up the System Properties applet, and choosing the Device Manager tab, you have access to your entire list of hardware. From here, you can uninstall, re-install, and update drivers for all of your hardware. When in doubt, in dealing with malfunctioning devices, turn to the Device Manager first.

PCHealth Tools

Windows Me has a variety of PCHealth features that are used to monitor and correct problems with your system. All of the resources used by the 9x family are carried over and can be found in the same locations. Some of the more useful tools that can be utilized are:

Viewing System Information: This can be accessed through Start > Programs > Accessories > System Tools > System Information. From here, you will be given a folder tree on the left, with +/– boxes that let you expand/contract any particular category. When in the System Information applet, pay special attention to the Tools menu, which gives you access to:

System Restore: We will discuss this in the next section.
Fault Log: Fault Log provides a comprehensive error log for troubleshooting issues.
Network Diagnostics: This is a helpful little utility that diagnoses problems with network connectivity.
DirectX Diagnostics: Discussed earlier in this section, The DirectX Diagnostics utility contains tools for testing 3D system drawing capabilities, as well as DirectX sound functions.
Update Wizard Uninstall: This utility aids in uninstalling downloaded updates using the Windows update feature.
Signature Verification Tool: This tool is useful in troubleshooting when you need to ensure that certain critical system files have not been modified since installation
Registry Checker: The Registry Checker scans your Registry for errors that could be causing issues.

Automatic Skip Driver Agent: This is a wonderful tool if you are trying to diagnose problems with Windows' start-up. This utility identifies problems with drivers loaded at start-up that keep Windows Me from starting correctly, and it allows you to skip them.

Dr. Watson: Dr. Watson™ is a program error debugger tool used in Windows 9x, NT, and 2000 to detect and log critical error information pertaining to system halts. Dr. Watson also attempts to point you in the right direction by offering possible tips for problem and error resolution.

System Configuration Utility: This gives you the ability to change start-up services and programs that load at start up.

ScanDisk: Discussed in Chapter 23, ScanDisk is a Microsoft disk analysis and repair utility that is used to recover and repair lost or bad clusters on a disk. Windows 9x and Windows Me utilize a GUI version of ScanDisk that can be accessed and run by selecting Start > Programs > Accessories > System Tools > ScanDisk.

WMI Control: WMI (Windows Management Implementation) Control lets you take control of remote PCs on a network for security and maintenance.

Resource Meter: The Resource Meter is a great tool for monitoring your GDI (Graphical Device Interface), system resources, and user resources. This tool can be found by navigating Start > Programs > Accessories > System Tools > Resource Meter.

System Monitor: A more complex version of the Resource Meter, the System Monitor can be used to graph Kernel usage (by default), File System, Memory Manager, and Microsoft Network Client. To change the graph target, choose Edit > Add Item, then choose another statistic to graph.

NOTE

You can also remove items from the graph using the Edit menu.

Windows Update: This utility automatically keeps your operating system up to date with current patches, fixes, security updates, service releases, and other information offered by Microsoft (see Chapter 24 on Windows 9x for an in-depth discussion).

Auto Update: This feature runs from the system tray. Auto Update uses downtime (time when you are using the Internet) and downloads what it deems to be appropriate updates, then prompts you to install them. To disable this feature, go to the Control Panel and double-click the Automatic Updates icon. From here you can choose to:

1. Automatically download updates and notify me when they are ready to be installed. (On by default).

2. Notify me before downloading any updates and notify me again when they are ready to be installed.
3. Turn off automatic updating. I will update my computer manually.

System Restore: System restoration is accomplished in Windows Me using the new System Restore tool. It can be found by navigating Start > Programs > Accessories > System Tools > System Restore. System Restore essentially takes a snapshot of your current system setup (e.g., current drivers, installed programs, etc.) which it can revert to previous settings at any point. System Restore compresses these files and saves them as .cab files in C:\Restore\Archive. It's a good tool to use prior to a major driver update for your hardware, before installing new software (or major updates to current software), or any other action that might cause your system to function incorrectly as a result of an upgrade. Using the System Restore tool before doing any such action allows you to capture a working image of your current setup, so that if something does go wrong in the process of upgrading, you can always revert back to a working setup.

NOTE *Windows automatically captures an image of your machine once a day and holds it for a period of about two weeks. You can always choose from one of Windows' Restore Points, or choose to revert to one you've specifically made.*

From the System Restore applet's initial screen you are asked if you want to restore your computer to an earlier setup or create a new Restore Point. To create a Restore Point:

1. Go to Start > Programs > Accessories > System Tools > System Restore.
2. Choose "Create Restore Point."
3. Click Next.
4. You are then prompted to enter a description of your Restore Point. You can enter anything you like (up to 64 characters). When you've entered your desired description, click Next to continue.
5. Windows will create the Restore Point and indicate that it is complete. A time/date display is listed with your personalized description (as entered in the previous step).

To revert to an earlier Restore Point:

1. Go to Start > Programs > Accessories > System Tools > System Restore.
2. Choose "Restore My Computer to an Earlier Time."
3. Click Next.
4. The next screen has a calendar on the left and an option box on the right. Choose from the dates displayed in bold to open the available Restore

Points made on those given days/dates. The Restore Points available appear in the option box to the right. Choose the appropriate Restore Point, and click Next to continue (see Figure 27.3). You will be prompted with a cautionary message that reads, "Before restoring your computer, save and close all open files, and close all open programs. Do not alter, open, or delete any files or programs until the restoration is complete." Click Next to continue.

5. The following screen will display the progress of the System Restore and restart the system.
6. The System Restore screen will appear when the system restarts. Click Close to continue.

NOTE

The system restoration tool is completely reversible. If for any reason you are displeased with the image you chose, you can always go back to where you were before you restored.

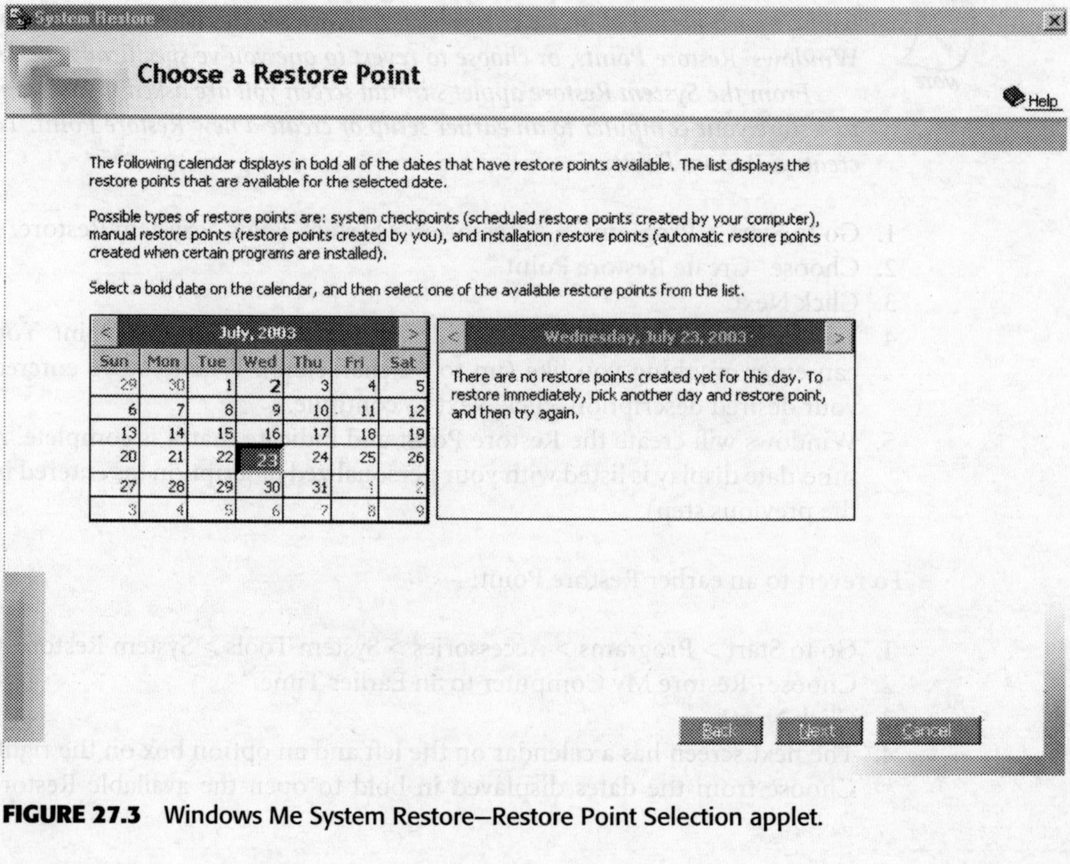

FIGURE 27.3 Windows Me System Restore—Restore Point Selection applet.

It is also possible to start the System Restore tool from a command prompt. You would want to consider this when you cannot start Windows Me normally or in Safe Mode. To do this you must:

1. Boot your PC using a Windows Me start-up disk.
2. From the Startup menu, choose Minimum Boot
3. You will be given a command prompt, type "edit c:\windows\system.ini" (provided that this is your Windows directory), and press Enter.
4. Edit the "shell =" line so that it reads, "shell =program.exe."
5. Press ALT+F, then "S" (to save changes made to the system.ini).
6. Press ALT+F again, then "X."
7. Remove the Windows Me start-up disk and restart the computer.
8. The Program Task Manager should start. If it doesn't, repeat the previous steps, making sure you follow the instructions exactly.
9. From the File menu, click Run, type "MSCONFiG" (is not case sensitive) in the command line, and press Enter.
10. Click Launch System Restore, to begin restoring you computer to a previous, functional Restore Point.

NOTE

Once you configure your computer to start Program Manager (progman.exe), you can also start the System Restore tool with the command line C:\windows\system\restore\rstrui.exe.

PROFILES

Profiles in Windows Me can be broken down into two categories, Hardware and User.

Hardware Profiles are useful when you are using a machine under different circumstances, where it's beneficial to load different devices at different times. A perfect example would be a laptop, because you are not always connected to a network. It takes several seconds for your network connection to time out when you start a laptop that is not connected to the network. By disallowing Windows to start up with network connectivity, boot times can be greatly increased. You can create several different hardware profiles, disabling certain devices on your system. When you set up these profiles, Windows will prompt you at start-up which profile you would like to use at that time. To set up a hardware profile:

1. Go to Start > Settings > Control Panel > System to open the System Properties applet. Click the Hardware Profiles tab (see Figure 27.4).

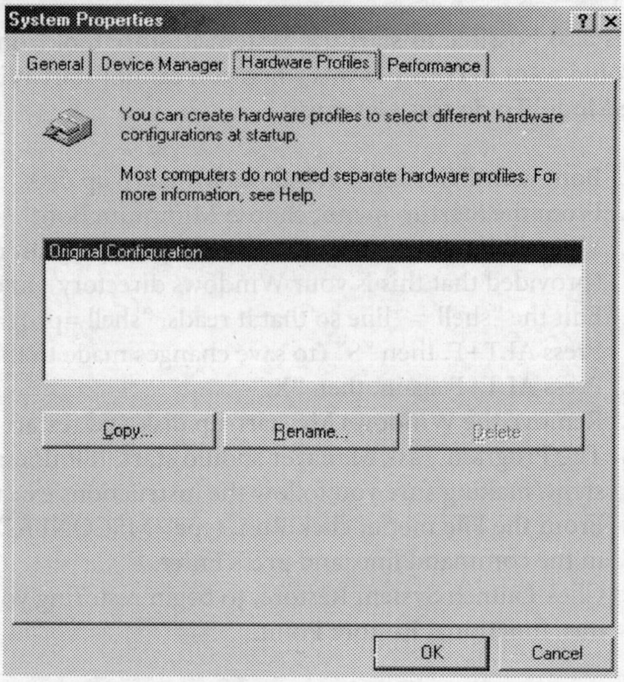

FIGURE 27.4 Windows Me System Properties applet-Hardware Profiles tab.

2. Select the profile that you wish to use as the basis for the new profile you will be setting up. Click Copy to open the Copy Profile dialog applet, and create a duplicate.
3. Enter a name for the copied profile and click OK. (The new profile file appears in the Hardware Profiles list.)
4. Restart the PC, and when prompted, select your new profile.
5. Choose the individual hardware drivers for your new profile by going to Start > Settings > Control Panel > System, and select the Device Manager.
6. Click the + sign next to a device to expand the selection to all devices under it.
7. Double-click the device you want to edit (which will bring up a Properties box). Choose to Disable or leave that particular device enabled in this hardware profile.
8. Click OK.
9. Close the Device Manager tab to exit.

User Profiles are created if you wish to allow different user accounts to customize their own Desktop settings and passwords. By default, Windows Me is installed as a single-profile system, where all users get the same settings every time they log on, regardless of the username and password they use. To set up User Profiles:

- Go to Start > Settings > Control Panel > Passwords. You will now be at the Password Properties dialog box.
- Select the User Profiles tab, which prompts you with two options:

1. **All users of this computer use the same preferences and desktop settings.** On by default, this is the option you'd use if you did not want to have customized User Profiles.
2. **Users can customize their preferences and desktop settings. Windows switches to your personal settings when you log on.** This is the option you want to set up customized Desktop settings for multiple users (see Figure 27.5). When you select this option, you will be given two other options: **Include Desktop Icons and Network Neighborhood contents in User Settings:** Allows Desktop icons and Network Neighborhood contents to be

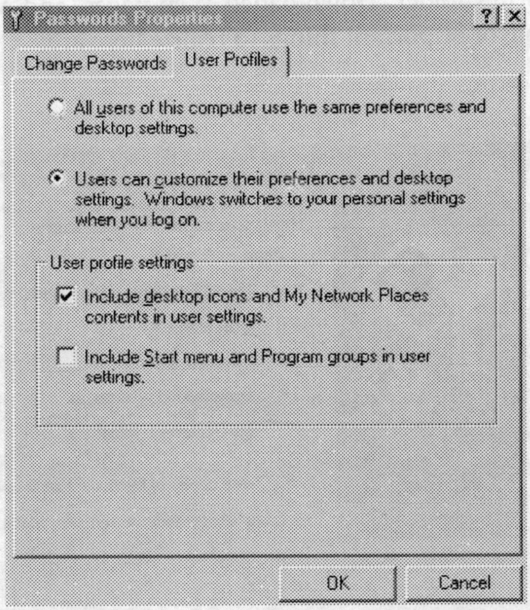

FIGURE 27.5 Windows Me Password Properties User Profiles tab.

customized for the individual user (can include Desktop colors, fonts, and passwords).

Include Start Menu and Program Groups in User Settings: Allows the contents of the Start menu and the options in the Program menu to be customized by the user.

3. After you have made your choices for permissions regarding Desktop icons, Network Neighborhood, the Start menu, and Program groups, you are ready to set up User Profiles through the Users icon in the Control Panel at Start > Settings > Control Panel > Users.
4. This screen will show you all existing users and the ability to add a new user, delete an existing user, or make a copy of an existing User Profile. To create a new user, click the New User button to the right.
5. You will be taken through the Add User Wizard, which will walk you through the process of adding a new user. First, you will be prompted to enter a new user name and password. Next, you will be prompted with the Personal Items Settings dialog, where you can choose to select the items you want to personalize for that account, which is also the same menu you'd get if you had clicked Change Setting (see Figure 27.6) on the previous screen, and how you want them to be created. The options for personalization include: Desktop folder and Documents menu, Start Menu, Favorites folder, Downloaded Web pages, and My Documents folder. A couple of important things to realize here are:

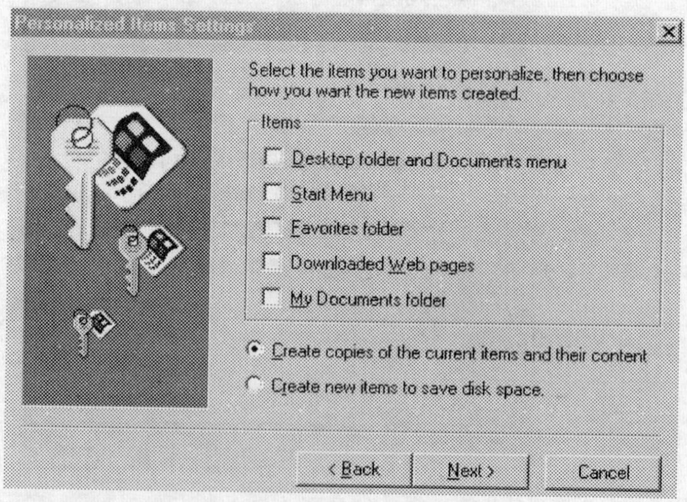

FIGURE 27.6 Windows Me Users Personalized Items Settings selection.

Should you choose to personalize these items, you must realize that the changes made to these items are only for this User Profile. If you enabled Start Menu for example, and the user changed the icons around or removed shortcuts, it would only be reflected there when the user logged on to their User Profile (not others).

When choosing to create copies of current items and their contents, or when creating new items to save disk space, you need to realize that should you choose to create new items to save disk space, users will not have access to what you already have installed. If you had Favorites created to save disk space, they would not see any favorites currently in other profiles; they would be starting from scratch.

6. Close the Wizard, and you're done. You can log off or log on to that new account at any time.

It should be mentioned that this is the most daunting method of setting up a new User Profile. In fact you can just follow steps 1–3 above, then choose to restart. When you log on, choose to log-in with a different user name (any name you choose) and password (again, any of your choosing), and you will be prompted with a Windows message that reads "*You have not logged on at this computer before. Would you like this computer to retain your individual settings for use when you log on here in the future?*" If you choose "yes," you have created a new User Profile (which can be edited in the Users menu from the Control Panel). Editing, deleting, and copying User Profiles can all be handled through the Control Panel > Users menu, as well.

NOTE *Creating User Profiles with different editable properties requires a lot of hard drive space for storage. If you are going to be creating separate profiles, each with their own settings (as in step 2 of User Profiles, above), make sure you have at least 500MB of free hard drive space.*

PRINTERS

Printer maintenance in Windows Me isn't all that dissimilar from the other Windows 9x OSs. The Printer applet can be found in Start > Settings > Printer or My Computer > Control Panel > Printer, and it functions the same as in Windows 98. From here, you can choose to either rename or delete an existing Printer, or access the Add Printer Wizard. To change the name of an existing printer, simply right-click and choose the Rename option. When you select the Add Printer Wizard, you are prompted with two choices: add a Local printer or add a Network printer.

Adding a Local Printer

This option allows you to add a printer that is local (attached directly) to your computer. To add a local printer:

- Choose the Local printer option and click Next.
- You will be prompted to choose the manufacturer/model number for your printer. Choose from the manufacturer names on the left, followed by the model number on the right. The Have Disk box can be used if you have the printer software provided by the manufacturer. Click on the Have Disk option to be taken to a browser screen where you can select a device to scan for appropriate drivers, or you can use the Browse option to scan through your files (media) for the exact location of the driver file. (Remember syntax when typing in the location line instead of browsing.)

NOTE *You should always check to see that the drivers you are installing are the most up-to-date versions. Check with your printer manufacturer's Web site for support information and updates to your software before installation.*

- Click Next to continue.
- Choose your printer port on the next screen. Click Next to continue.
- Enter the name that you want Windows to refer to the selected printer as. Click Next to continue.
- Windows will now prompt you to print a test page. It is your option to print a test page or not, but it's always good to know as soon as possible if you are having any difficulty installing a printer, so it is recommended that you do.
- You will be returned to the Printers applet. You will notice that a printer icon with the name you assigned appears. You can now choose to rename this printer, add a new printer, or just close the Printer applet to continue.

Adding a Network Printer

Adding a network printer is as easy as adding a local printer:

- Choose the Network printer option and click Next.
- Enter the correct network path or click Browse if you are not sure of the correct path to the desired printer. There is an option on the lower portion of this screen that asks if you will be using any MS-DOS programs to print. Choose which option best suits your needs.
- Click Next to continue.
- Type the name you wish to associate with this printer, also choose if you wish this to be the default printer for this computer.

- Click Next to continue.
- You are now prompted to run a test page. Do so if you deem necessary.

Sharing a Printer

You can share a printer using the Home Networking Wizard, even if you've used it previously. You can also set this up manually by going to Start > Control Panel > Network.

- Choose File and Printer Sharing.
- Verify that the checkbox is filled in for Printer Sharing.
- Click OK (rebooting the machine may be necessary at this point).
- Go to Start > Settings > Printer, or My Computer > Control Panel > Printer.
- Right-click the desired printer's icon, and choose Sharing.
- Choose the name you wish to be associated with the printer on the network (you can choose to enable a password for the printer by filling out a password in the appropriate field).
- Click OK.

WINDOWS ME NETWORKING AND THE INTERNET

Windows Me offers the Home Networking Wizard to set up local connections and the Internet Connection Wizard to help you establish a connection to the Internet. In previous versions of the Windows 9x family, you had to manually configure your network card and install necessary protocols and clients through the Network applet in the Control Panel. This can all still be done the same way, but the Home Networking and Internet Connection Wizards will accomplish all of this for you, including setting up and installing necessary protocols for features like Internet Sharing. All of the protocols handled by Windows 9x are supported in Windows Me (e.g., NetBEUI, TCP/IP, etc.) and are handled the same. For information on these protocols please refer to Chapter 24 on Windows 9x.

First, we will take a look at the steps necessary to create an Internet connection in Windows Me.

Create an Internet Connection

Creating an Internet connection can be started in several ways. You can:

- Go to Start > Programs > Accessories > Communication > Internet Connection Wizard.

- Go to Start > Settings > Control Panel > Internet Options, then open the Internet Properties applet and choose the Connections tab and then the Setup button.
- If you do not currently have an Internet connection setup, you can simply start an instance of Internet Explorer to start the Internet Connection Wizard.
- From Internet Explorer, go to Tools > Internet Options, and then select the Connections tab, followed by the Connect button. You will start the Internet Connection Wizard, which will guide you through the process of starting a new Internet connection. From this applet, the first three options will be:
    - **I want to sign up for a new Internet account. (My telephone line is connected to my modem.)** This option dials you into Microsoft's Referral Service using your modem, then gives you a list of recommended ISPs to set up a new account. You are led through several screens of data entry—everything from credit card information to address/zip code for local dial-up numbers. At the end, you will have an established Internet account.
    - **I want to transfer my existing Internet account to this computer. (My telephone line is connected to my computer.)** This option is for those who already have an existing service or who are signing up with a service not listed on Microsoft's Referral Service page. To do this, you will need all of the information provided by the ISP for that particular account (e.g., dial-up phone numbers, user names, passwords, POP and SMTP information for your mail account, etc.).
    - **I want to set up my Internet connection manually, or I want to connect through a Local Area Network (LAN).** Both this and the previous option are identical in nature in terms of the steps you will have to complete. Should you choose one of these last two options, the process will continue on as follows:

1. You will be prompted to choose if you connect through a phone line and a modem; click Next.
2. The next screen will ask you to enter the telephone number for your ISP. (Make sure you uncheck the box for "Dial using the area code and country code" if it is not necessary in your area.)

NOTE

Most ISPs do not require you to enter static or specific DNS or IP addresses. However, should your ISP require it, you can click on the Advanced tab to enter these numbers.

3. Click Next to continue.
4. Enter your username and password in the appropriate fields, and click Next.

5. Enter a name that you wish to associate with this particular connection. This should be something that you can easily identify; it does not necessarily have to be the name of the ISP.
6. Click Next to continue.
7. You are now prompted to set up an e-mail account. Click Yes and Next to continue.
8. Should Windows find an existing e-mail account, you are prompted to either edit that account or set up a new one. Choose "Create New Internet Account" and click Next to continue.
9. Enter your display name in the appropriate field (the name that will be attached to all outgoing e-mail that you send). Click Next to continue.
10. Enter the e-mail address for sending/receiving e-mail messages. Click Next to continue.
11. This screen will have you fill out your incoming mail server type (usually POP3), as well as enter your POP3 (IMAP or HTTP) server name and your SMTP server name. Click Next to continue.
12. You will be prompted for your user name and password. Enter these then click Next to finish to process.

Essentially, what you have done by using the ICW (Internet Connection Wizard) is avoid having to set your TCP/IP and dial-up networking settings manually (and installed Dial-Up Networking, had it not been installed previously). Should you need to edit the settings or set up a new dial-up connection, you can do so from the Dial-Up Networking folder located at Start > Settings > Dial-Up Networking (which is possible if your ISP requires you to change settings due to connection failure).

Dial-Up Networking

Dial-up networking is handled exactly in the same way as it is for the rest of the Windows 9x family. Again, it can be found at Start > Settings > Dial-Up Networking. From there, you will have access to any previous connections or the ability to create a new one. If you are modifying an existing connection, right-click on it from the Dial-Up Networking folder, and click Properties. Dial-up networking handles standard modem connections, ISDN connections, and null-modem connections between serial ports. From the General tab, you can choose from the following:

General tab: You choose the phone number to dial, whether to use an area code and country code when dialing, or choose a different modem for the connection from the drop-down menu. (Click the Configure button to open the Properties for the selected modem, and edit them if necessary.)

Networking tab: TCP/IP, NetBEUI, and IPX/SPX Compatible protocols can be easily selected/deselected, and you can choose to specify an IP or DNS address (see Figure 27.7).

Security tab: Modify your username and password. Check mark the box if you want your Internet connection to connect automatically and log on to network options.

Dialing tab: Select/Deselect the default Internet connection, retry settings (in case of a failed connection), and idle disconnect settings.

NOTE *You can actually change the default Internet connection much more easily by going to Internet Explorer > Tools > Connections, and choosing which connection should be the default from there.*

Creating a Peer-To-Peer Network

Creating a peer-to-peer Network in Windows Me is just as easy as setting up an Internet connection. To start, go to Start > Programs > Accessories > Communications > Home Networking Wizard. At the introductory screen, click Next.

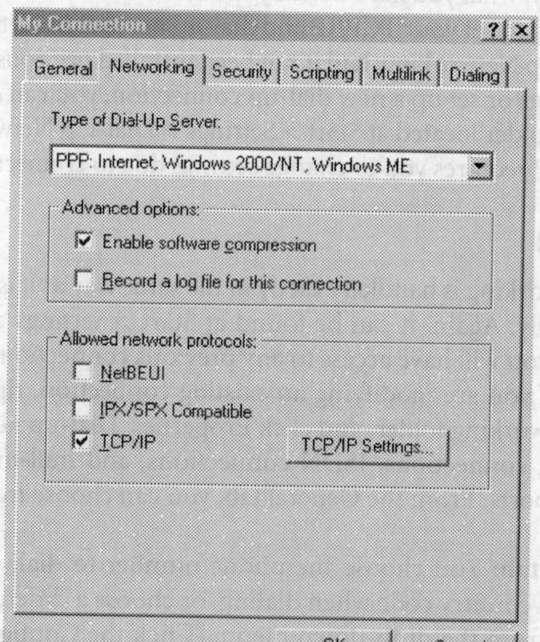

FIGURE 27.7 Windows Me dial-up networking connection properties Networking tab.

- Choose if your computer is currently connected to the Internet, and in what manner. Click Next to continue.
- Depending how you answered in the previous step, you'll be asked if you wish to share your connection with the Internet. If you do, then choose the Network Adapter to share (that is the NIC you have installed to connect your home network). Click Next to continue.
- Enter a name that you wish to be associated with this computer on your network. You will also be choosing the workgroup name. (You can leave it at the default or change it as you feel necessary, but do realize that all computers must use the same workgroup name.) Click Next to continue.
- Next will be the TCP/IP screen, and you will be prompted to choose whether to share certain folders and printers associated with this PC. Choose which items you would like to share and click Next to continue.
- You will be prompted to create a setup disk. Should you have any other Windows 9x machines on your network, choose YES. If the other computers are running Windows Me, or Windows 2000 or NT, you will not require the disk.
- When you reach the Completing the Home Networking Wizard Screen, choose Finish, and the necessary files will be copied.
- If you are prompted to restart your machine, do so. When you restart, you will be prompted for a username and password (just make them up if you don't have them already), and your computer is now networked.

NOTE *Use the disk created in this process to set up networking on Windows 95 and 98 machines. (Run it from the My Computer menu in that operating system.)*

NOTE *You can still manually install network drivers if you do not wish to relinquish control to the Home Network Wizard, or if you find it necessary to use other protocols. Manual installation of network drivers starts with:*

- Go to Start > Settings > Control Panel, then double-click Network.
- Review the list of components on the Configuration tab (see Figure 27.8). Should Client for Microsoft Networks not appear there:
  1. Click Add, followed by Client, and click Add again. A list of provided Microsoft Clients appears.
  2. Choose Client for Microsoft Networks, and click OK.

NOTE *You may be prompted to insert the Windows Me CD-ROM. Do so if necessary.*

- From here, choose your desired protocol (ATM, ATM LAN Emulation, IPX/SPX compatible, NetBEUI, PPP over ATM, or TCP/IP). Click the protocol to install, and click OK to continue.

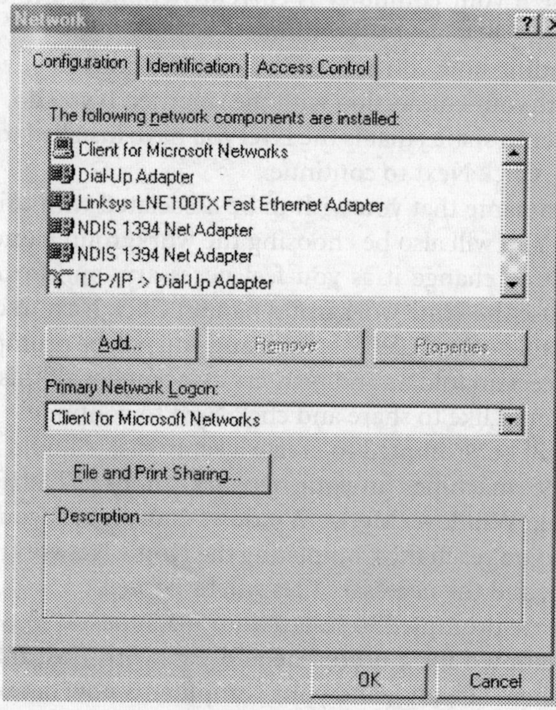

FIGURE 27.8 Windows Me Network Configuration tab.

- Open the network logon drop-down list and choose the client for the network (e.g., Client for Microsoft Networks).
- Click File and Print sharing to choose your file and print sharing permissions (make sure both boxes are checked to share both of them).
- Click OK to finish. The system may require you to reboot; do so if necessary.

Connecting to a Windows NT or 2000 Server

You can still connect to a Windows 2000 or NT server using the Home Networking Wizard. However, you must take the following into consideration:

- If the Windows NT Server is a domain server, you need to create a user account on the NT server for every Windows Me user who will need to access resources on the NT server.
- If you are using Windows NT Workstation, make sure you have the same workgroup name entered as you do for each Windows Me station that will be in that workgroup.

- If you are using Windows NT Server, you must set the Windows Me PC to log on to the Windows NT domain and enter the correct domain in the domain entry field at each station. To do this:
    1. Go to the Control Panel > Network Properties, and choose Client for Microsoft Windows Networks.
    2. Click the domain checkbox, and enter the name of your Windows NT domain.

Creating a Firewire Subnet

Users who have created an Ethernet or modem network and use a mobile device or laptop may want to consider setting up a subnet (or secondary network) using IEEE 1394 (FireWire) or wireless connection so that they can move about freely with the mobile device while having access to all resources. If you are using an external DSL or cable modem, you will require two Ethernet cards on your primary ICS (Internet Connection Sharing) machine where the Internet is shared from. Otherwise, you will need only one to connect to the rest of your network. Make sure that you have ICS set up on your primary ICS server before you begin. To create this subnet:

- Go to Start > Settings > Control Panel > Internet Options.
- Click on the Connections tab.
- On the LAN (Local Area Network) tab, click Sharing.
- Choose the device that connects you to the secondary network from the list.

NOTE *If sharing is not an option, you have not enabled ICS on your system. Follow the steps in the Home Networking Wizard to set up this feature.*

- Click OK, and you will be prompted to restart your computer.

Cookies

A cookie is a message that is sent or 'transmitted' to a Web server from a Web browser. It is important to note that a cookie can also be referred to as a state object or persistent cookie. The cookie is used to provide the Web server with unique information that is used to identify where the request to the server is coming from. In other words, the cookie provides information about you. When you access pages on the Internet and enter your personal information into Web forms, that information along with other prepared information is combined into a file called a cookie. Most often, server-side scripts known as CGI (Common Gateway Interface) scripts are used to control what happens with the cookie. The next time you happen upon the same Web site, your Internet browser will automatically forward the locally stored cookie to that Web site's server. If set up to do so, the server will provide you with a prepacked, customized page that targets you for specific advertisements. In other words, you will get 'spammed.'

Many Web servers use trusted cookies as their only form of authentication. This widespread misuse of cookies has spawned a major security threat to both Web servers and users alike. If an attacker, or 'cookie hijacker,' is able to infiltrate a user's session while the user is logged on to a server service, the attacker can steal the user's cookie and use it to access such things as account information. A common practice that attackers use to grab cookies during an active session is to execute a fake JavaScript routine on an unprotected server.

Although many servers are open to this cookie authentication exploitation, most servers that provide important financial information and extremely sensitive data have more secure authentication mechanisms and devices in place.

There are several good ways to protect your system from the threats to security provided so nicely by the use of cookies. You can set up your Internet browser to alert you when a cookie is present, you can direct your browser to only download cookies from trusted sites, or you can disable cookies altogether. Depending on your operating system and Internet browser, this procedure will vary.

Javascript

JavaScript is a programming script language that is supported by Internet browsers provided by Netscape and Microsoft. JavaScript is commonly used by Web developers to interact with Web pages, which are typically created using HTML or XML source codes. In simple terms, JavaScript allows developers to spruce up Web pages by adding features such as self-updating software packages, pop-up windows, link-to pages, and 3D interactive worlds to new or existing Internet Web pages. JavaScript is considered to be a portable, object-oriented, robust and secure scripting language.

The productive tools that we manufacture to design and create a better, more intuitive Internet experience all seem to come with a heavy price tag concerning security. Java, JavaScript, and Java applets (little programs sent with Web pages that do not require user interaction) are no exception. They all provide transportation mechanisms that can allow attackers to insert code to infiltrate and destroy your system. JavaScript, applets, and Java are programs that actually run on your system.

Hijackers and attackers often create scripts and applets, which are oftentimes able to circumvent network security parameters. They can be used to manipulate files on users' computers.

Signed Applets

As mentioned earlier, applets are small programs that contain scripts that are sent with Web pages to users. Applets, such as Java applets, allow calculations, animations, and other functions to take place on a user's system without a need for communication to take place with the applet-providing server.

Applets can contain malicious code that can easily destroy a system if allowed to run. A popular technique known as sandboxing is often used to quarantine applets that appear suspicious or malicious.

Signed applets are applets that contain a digital signature. They are a means of proving that an applet has come from a trusted location, author, or site. Signed applets receive permission to access local system resources. Plain applets only have access to the directories from which they originally run. Some books state that signed applets cannot be altered. This is simply not true. Anyone can create or forge a signed applet. This makes them very dangerous and provides a huge security vulnerability to local as well as networked systems.

NOTE

It is important to note that most applets on the Web are unsigned applets. These applets can be assigned various security levels, which include untrusted, high, medium, and low levels of security. Please refer to Table 27.1 for the various levels of unsigned applet security.

ActiveX

ActiveX is a set of object-oriented programs, technologies, and tools that are Microsoft's answer to Java technology, which, by the way, was created by Sun Microsystems. ActiveX is basically a combination, or 'outgrowth' of the Microsoft technologies known as OLE (Object Linking and Embedding) and COM (Component Object Model). When this technology is used in a networked environment that provides directory support and other services, the COM technology becomes DCOM (Distributed Component Object Model).

The goal of this technology is to create a self-sufficient program, known as a component or ActiveX control, which can be run anywhere your ActiveX network exists.

ActiveX's controls, or 'components,' can be compared to Java applets, and can be reused by applications and other systems throughout your network.

ActiveX provides a power tool for developers and programmers. Unfortunately, ActiveX carries with it security risks, as JavaScript and applets do. But, the ActiveX security model is quite different from the security controls in place for Java and Java applets. As you may recall, Java applets are restricted based on a set of

TABLE 27.1 Applet Security Levels

Applet Security Level	Action Taken
Untrusted	Untrusted applets do not have permission to run on a system at all. They only have the ability to start.
High	Applets with this security rating run under what are considered safe restrains and are only permitted certain functions. They are not permitted to carry out unsafe actions. They cannot access most browser settings. They cannot read, write, delete, or change files. They can only listen to network ports located above port 1024. They cannot access a system's printer queue or clipboard.
Medium	These applets can run under safe restraints. By default, if one of these applets attempts to read, write, change, or perform any of the other "High" restraints, you will prompted (warned) by your Internet browser. Next, you may grant the requested permission to the applet if you choose.
Low	This level carries the greatest security risk. Applets with Low security run under minimum restraint. Your browser will not warn you the actions listed above unless the applet attempts to start local applications.

actions that are considered safe. The ActiveX security model does not limit an application package to a set of individual restrictive controls. Instead, its controls are based on digital signatures. These digital signatures are registered and certified with a trusted digital authority, such as VeriSign. When a person registers a software package or application with a trusted CA (Certificate Authority), they are agreeing that the package or 'ActiveX Control' is free of malicious code. From that point on, the risks involved with downloading the controls are totally the responsibility of the user.

In simple terms, the main weaknesses or problems associated with ActiveX controls are:

- Once the user has accepted the certificate, responsibility for the control's actions are placed completely on the user. If an uneducated user on your network happens to accept a certificate from an unknown or unofficial CA Authority, you may not have many systems left operable by the end of the day.

- Users can change browser settings to allow unsigned ActiveX controls to be downloaded with a warning.
- There is no good logging or audit trail available to track down what an ActiveX control has done to your system.

If you need help troubleshooting problems associated with active content such as JavaScript and ActiveX using Internet Explorer, Microsoft provides an excellent white paper on the subject. You will also be shown how to disable dangerous active content altogether in this white paper: *http://support.microsoft.com/default.aspx?scid=KB;EN-US;Q154036*.

To access the ActiveX settings for Internet Explorer, navigate to Internet Explorer > Tools > Internet Options > Security Settings. Choose the network resource where you wish to edit ActiveX settings (e.g., Internet, Local Intranet, Trusted Sites, Restricted Sites), and Reset custom settings (see Figure 27.9). From here, you will be able to Disable/Enable/Prompt settings to:

- Download signed ActiveX controls
- Download unsigned ActiveX controls

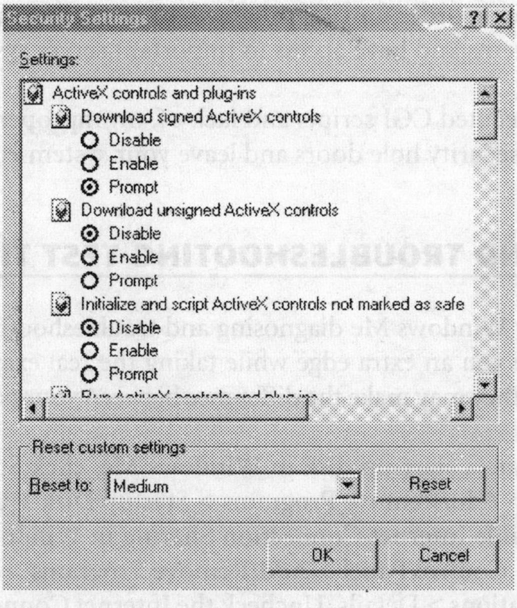

FIGURE 27.9 Windows Me Internet Explorer Security Settings window.

- Initialize and script ActiveX controls not marked as safe
- Run ActiveX controls as plug-ins (this also has an option for Administrator approved)
- Script ActiveX controls marked safe for scripting

CGI

The Common Gateway Interface is a language-independent interface or standard that Internet Web servers use to pass a user's request to an application program and forward a response back to the Web server, which in turn provides the results to the user. In English, when a user fills out an HTML form on a Web page, a CGI program is typically used to process the form's data behind the scenes and get the information back to the server. This allows Web servers to dynamically serve and interact with the users. The actual method of passing data between a server and an application is called the CGI.

CGI programs run on Web servers and are considered to be server-side applications. JavaScript, applets, and ActiveX controls are run on individual systems and are considered client-side programs. A disadvantage with using CGI programs is that they start a new service on a Web server every time a CGI program runs. This can result in a major decrease in the performance of a Web server.

The use of CGI programs allows the vulnerabilities associated with HTTP to be exploited. Also, in order for CGI programs to work, they are written to run on most operating systems and have access to important server system files, as well as connected hosts.

Poorly executed CGI scripts and lack of, or improper, file system permissions can open the security hole doors and leave your system vulnerable to attack.

DIAGNOSING AND TROUBLESHOOTING TEST TIPS

The following Windows Me diagnosing and troubleshooting test tips have been included to give you an extra edge while taking the real exam. Pay close attention to these tips, for they may make the difference between your passing or failing the exam.

- ✓ To create a start-up disk in Windows Me, click Start > Settings > Control Panel > Add/Remove Programs > Startup Disk > Create Disk > OK.
- ✓ To disable Internet Connection Sharing in Windows Me, click Start > Settings > Control Panel > Add/Remove Programs > Windows Setup > Communications > Details. Uncheck the Internet Connection Sharing checkbox, and click OK.

- ✓ To place encryption on a compressed folder in Windows Me, right-click on the Compressed folder and select "Encrypt." Type a password in the Password box and verify the password by entering it again in the Confirm Password box.
- ✓ System Monitor can be used in Windows Me to monitor dial-up networking connections and measure download and upload speeds.
- ✓ To maximize ISP/Internet and dial-up networking connection speeds, you should disable any unused or unnecessary protocols. To do so, navigate to Dial-Up Networking and right-click on your connection icon. Next, select Properties > Networking tab, and uncheck NetBEUI and IPX/SPX compatible. These protocols are not normally used for ISP connections.
- ✓ In Windows Me, you can print out your system configuration summary by clicking Start > Programs > Accessories > System Tools > System Information. On the File menu, click Print.
- ✓ To associate a file with a program in Explorer, right-click on the file, select "Open With," and choose the program you wish to open the file with. You can change the start order of items in the Windows Me Start menu by dragging them to a different location.
- ✓ To increase your capacity for temporary Internet page storage, simply navigate to Internet Explorer > Tools > Internet Options > General tab > Settings. You can then increase your storage space for temporary Internet pages by moving the slider to the right.
- ✓ To undo a previous system restoration or restoration point prior to your last system restoration in Windows Me, Click Start > Programs > Accessories > System Tools > System Restore. For undoing your last system restoration, select "Undo my last restoration," and select Next. For rolling back to a restoration point prior to your last system restoration, click "Start the System Restore Wizard," and navigate through the Wizard instructions.
- ✓ A default install of Windows Me does not have Direct Memory Access (DMA) enabled for CD-ROM devices and hard drives. Enabling DMA for these devices will improve the overall CPU access time to these devices. To enable DMA support in Windows Me, select Start > Settings > Control Panel > System. Next, select the Device Manager tab and then double-click on your desired hard drive or CD-ROM device. Select the Settings tab and place a check mark in the DMA box. A message, "Unsupported hardware alert", will be displayed. Select OK, and reboot your system.
- ✓ To turn off 32-bit PC card support in Windows Me, select Start > Settings > Control Panel > System. Next, select the Device Manager tab, and verify that "View devices by type" is selected. Select the plus sign (+) next to PCMCIA

Socket and select your PC card controller. Next, under device usage place a check mark in the "Disable in this hardware profile" box, and select OK.

- ✓ To disable the Smart Start menu in Windows Me, select Start > Settings > Taskbar. Next, select Start Menu and remove the check mark from the "Use Personalized menus" checkbox.
- ✓ To reset your Internet Explorer settings to their default installation settings, select Internet Options on the Internet Explorer Tools menu. Next, select the Programs tab and click the Reset Web Settings button.
- ✓ To add or modify a device driver in Windows Me, navigate to the System Properties icon in the Control Panel, select the Device Manager tab, select the plus sign (+) next to hardware type, and double-click on the hardware. Select the Driver tab and click Update Driver. You will then need to follow the specific instructions displayed on the screen.
- ✓ In most cases, Windows Me will detect and repair a bad or corrupt Registry. If you need to do a manual restore of the Windows Me Registry, you should first boot to a start-up disk. Then, from a command prompt, type "cd\ windows\command" and press Enter. Next, at the command prompt, type "scanreg /restore". You will then need to select the Registry to be restored, and press Enter. You will be told whether or not you have restored a good, working Registry. You will then need to reboot your system.
- ✓ Disk Defragmenter is still located in the same location: Start > Programs > Accessories > System Tools > Disk Defragmenter. Don't forget to use it if your programs are slow to load, and you haven't done it in a while.
- ✓ Shortcuts are handled exactly the same way they were in previous versions of the Windows 9x family. Don't forget that special symbols (e.g., \ / @ > | : " ? *) are not allowed.
- ✓ Programs being installed often like to create unnecessary shortcuts in your Start menu. Removing them is as easy as right-clicking the desired shortcut and selecting Delete. (This will not uninstall the program, only remove the shortcut to its destination file.)
- ✓ Should you lose mouse support, you can begin troubleshooting by bringing up the Start menu using CTRL+ESC.
- ✓ The Start menu Favorites contain the exact same Favorites found in Internet Explorer. Should you wish to disable them in the Start menu, go to Control Panel > Settings > Task Bar & Start Menu > Advanced, and disable them there.

DCC (Direct Cable Connection) is still supported by Windows Me, however the fact that the absolute fastest port supported is the parallel port (or the even slower serial port), they are not a very attractive solution. However if you are using a laptop and just want to quickly connect to zip a file, or if your need an external drive that is not available to you, it will do the trick. To set up a DCC connection, go to Start > Programs > Accessories > Communications to make sure DCC is installed. (If it is not installed, install it from the Add/Remove Programs section of the Control Panel; you will need the Windows Me CD-ROM). To start the DCC applet, go to Start > Programs > Accessories > Communications > Direct Cable Connection. The DCC setup process will guide you through the rest of the setup.

CHAPTER SUMMARY

Upon completing this chapter, you should have obtained a good basic understanding of the Microsoft Me operating system and the specific areas of the operating system that are most likely to appear on the CompTIA A+ Operating Systems Technologies exam. It is important to remember that Windows Me has been added to the A+ Operating Systems Technologies exam as CompTIA 2003 Objective. For that reason, it is a sure bet that CompTIA will ask several Windows Me-related questions on the exam. At this point, you should be familiar with the following processes and tools:

- The Windows Me installation and upgrade processes and procedures.
- The Windows Me start-up process.
- Basic navigation skills from within Windows Me, including using and locating windows, applets, and associated shortcuts.
- Be able to establish an Internet connection and have knowledge of the associated Internet tools and settings from within Windows Me.
- Familiarity with Windows Me tools such as DXDIAG, System Restore, PCHealth tools, and MSCONFIG.
- You should know the diagnosing and troubleshooting test tips by heart and be able to answer all of the review questions correctly.

As a final note regarding your Microsoft Me exam preparation, you should think of Windows Me as an extension of Windows 9x. In other words, Windows Me is very similar to Windows 98, with the exception of a few new features and support for such technologies as USB and FireWire.

Windows Me was intended to be the next supercharged version of Windows 98, with all new bells and whistles. But, as recent history has shown, the real supercharged operating system of choice award belongs to Windows XP, and Windows Me stands as more of an incremental update from Windows 9x. We will cover Window XP next in Chapter 28.

REVIEW QUESTIONS

1. When you access a Web page on the Internet, what can be placed in your system that is used as a sort of tracking device to uniquely identify you?

o A. Acceptor
o B. Cookie
o C. A Multi-Purpose Internet Extension
o D. UNC

Correct Answer = B

A cookie is a unique identifier that Web servers place in your system to identify you. Choices A and C are invalid. A UNC name is used to access a particular share on a particular workstation or server on a network.

2. Which of the following are potentially harmful to the welfare of a system?

o A. Cookies
o B. Signed applets
o C. Java Scripts
o D. All of the above

Correct Answer = D

Many Web servers use trusted cookies as their only form of authentication. This is a major security risk. Hijackers and attackers often create scripts and applets, which at times are able to circumvent network security parameters. They can be used to manipulate files on users' computers.

3. Concerning applet security levels, please select the choice that best represents the most restrictive to the least restrictive applet security level.

o A. Low, Untrusted, Medium, High
o B. Untrusted, High, Medium, Low
o C. High, Medium, Low, Untrusted
o D. None of the above

Correct Answer = B

Applets can be assigned various security levels, which include untrusted, high, medium, and low levels of security. Please refer to Table 27.1 for the various levels of unsigned applet security and their levels of restriction. All other choices are invalid.

4. **Which of the following would you consider using in the event of a failed software installation for new hardware?**

   o A. System Restore

   o B. Disk Defragmenter

   o C. ScanDisk

   o D. None of the above

   Correct Answers = A

   Disk Defragmenter would be used if you were experiencing unusually long load times for programs (hard drive thrashing), while ScanDisk should be used if you think you may have errors on your hard drive.

5. **If you were interested in setting up user profiles that you wanted to be completely independent of each other (where all the Favorites, Start Menu, etc., were different), where would you go first to specify that you wanted such accounts created?**

   o A. Start > Settings > Control Panel > System

   o B. Start > Settings > Control Panel > Passwords

   o C. Command line DXDIAG

   o D. None of the above

   Correct Answer = B

   The first option takes you to the system applet, which is where you'd go to set up a Hardware Profile, not a User Profile. DXDIAG actually brings up the DirectX diagnostic tool.

6. **You can access a real DOS prompt using Windows Me (not a Window applet). What is required to do so?**

   o A. A Windows Me startup disk

   o B. A version of Windows XP installed opposite your Windows Me installation

   o C. To install DOS from Add/Remove Programs list

   o D. None of the above

   Correct Answer = A

   A version of XP installed on your machine won't help you access a DOS prompt. Unfortunately, DOS cannot be added or removed from within Windows Me.

7. Which of the following does not come enabled with an installation of Windows Me? (Choose Two)

- □ A. System Restore
- □ B. DMA support for hard drives
- □ C. Remote Assistance
- □ D. Device Manager

Correct Answers = B and C

Both System Restore and Device Manager are set up and enabled after a Windows Me installation.

8. When you're using Windows Me to connect to an NT domain server, which of the following is true?

- o A. Windows Me cannot connect to an NT domain server.
- o B. You will be unable to use System Restore while connected to the NT domain server.
- o C. A loss of performance will be felt when you access NT network resources.
- o D. User accounts must be created on the NT server for every Windows Me user who will need to access resources on the NT server.

Correct Answer = D

It is possible to connect to an NT domain server as long as the user accounts are created for every Windows Me user. System Restore still works fine, and no performance loss is present when you access networked resources.

9. Which two files are noticeably absent from the Windows Me startup process?

- o A. AUTOEXEC.BAT
- o B. CONFIG.SYS
- o C. All of the above
- o D. None of the above

Correct Answer = C

In fact, these two missing-in-action files are the only noticeable difference between Windows Me start-up and other Windows 9x applications.

10. When setting up a subnet on a machine that is a client (or station that receives) Internet Connection Sharing from another machine (server), how many network cards will you need?

- o A. One
- o B. Two.
- o C. You cannot set up a subnet from a machine that is not the server for Internet Connection Sharing.
- o D. None of the above.

Correct Answer = C

You must set up the subnet on the machine that is the server for Internet Connection Sharing when setting up a subnet.

REFERENCES

http://support.microsoft.com/default.aspx?scid=KB;EN-US;Q154036. This Microsoft Web site describes how to disable Active Content in Internet Explorer.

http://support.microsoft.com/default.aspx?scid=253695. This Microsoft Web site gives the minimum system requirements for Windows Me.

http://support.microsoft.com/search/preview.aspx?scid=kb;en-us;Q279736. This Microsoft Web site explains the process of starting System Restore from a command prompt in Windows Me.

28 Windows XP

In This Chapter

- Overview of Windows XP
- Windows XP Installation Process
- Windows XP Upgrade Procedures
- Windows XP Start-Up Process
- Windows XP Tools and Utilities
- Profiles
- Printers
- Windows XP Networking and the Internet
- Diagnosing and Troubleshooting Test Tips
- Chapter Summary
- Review Questions
- References

OVERVIEW OF WINDOWS XP

On October 25, 2001, Microsoft finally accomplished what had been sought after for approximately six years; with the release of Windows XP, the consumer-oriented Windows 9x and business-oriented Windows NT families had been successfully merged into one Windows platform based on Windows 2000.

Windows XP comes in two flavors: Home and Professional. Windows XP Home Edition is the replacement for Windows 98, Windows 98 Second Edition, and Windows Millennium Edition. Windows XP Professional serves as an upgrade for the same versions Windows Home Edition supports, as well as including Windows NT 4.0 Workstation and Windows 2000 Professional. The Professional edition offers extra networking capabilities and hardware/software options not found in the Home Edition. It is important to note that neither version of Windows XP will support an upgrade from Windows 95 or versions of Windows NT prior to 4.0.

Windows XP Home Edition includes some key new features, while expanding on some of the existing Windows Me and 2000 features:

System Restore: System Restore allows the OS to be turned back to a saved point in time, restoring lost or changed data and Registry entries.

Remote Assistance: Windows XP Home provides software to grant an authorized technician or friend (using Windows XP Professional) to assist you with troubleshooting or demonstrate procedures.

Network Setup Wizard: This wizard provides a step-by-step, end-user interface for installing or setting up networked printers, sharing files, adding network connections, and performing Internet Connection Sharing (ICS).

Codename Luna and Common Tasks: The new looks of the Start menu and Explorer allow the most frequently used programs and commands to be accessed quickly and consistently.

Windows File Protection: As mentioned in Chapter 26, WFP protects critical operating system files from being changed or deleted improperly.

Expanded Multimedia Support: Windows Media Player 8, enhanced DVD playback, built-in CD writer, and audio CD ripping support, all provide users with rich multimedia experiences.

Internet Explorer 6 (IE6): IE6 contains enhanced security and encryption, per-site third-party cookie blocking, and integrated multimedia capabilities using Windows Media Player 8.

Internet Connection Firewall (ICF): ICF is the first integrated firewall included in a consumer version of Windows, guarding the computer from intrusion from the Internet.

Fast User Switching: User switching allows multiple local user accounts to be active and running software simultaneously on a single computer.

Roll Back Driver: In the event that a hardware driver causes a software or hardware problem, you now have the option of returning to the previous driver, or like previous versions of Windows, completely uninstalling the existing one.

Windows XP Professional also includes the following supplemental features for business or workstation use:

Encrypted File System (EFS): Windows XP Professional offers key-encryption transparently for sensitive data and for multiple users, simultaneously.

Remote Desktop: Windows XP Professional can create a virtual machine of a remote computer on your local machine via a network or the Internet, allowing you to see and control it.

Hibernation and Fast Resume: Hibernation is a battery-saving mode similar to Standby, freezing the running processes and reducing energy usage until you are ready to quickly resume them again. However, with Hibernation, processes and system memory are dumped to the hard drive, and the computer is shut down. When you start the system again, Windows XP then loads the image from the hard drive.

IEEE 802.1x: This offers secure wireless networking through authentication and key management.

Enhanced Driver Signing and Verification: This version of driver signing is based on Windows 2000; however, it provides tougher stress-testing and more rigorous standards for device driver certification, such as WHQL (Windows Hardware Quality Labs).

IP Security (IPSec): IPSec provides enhanced data protection and security, which is especially vital to Virtual Private Networks (VPNs).

Kerberos Support: Kerberos is an Internet industry-standard high-strength authentication for Windows 2000, Windows XP, and enterprise-level resources.

Windows XP also supports up to 4GB of RAM and two Symmetric Multiprocessors (SMP).

WINDOWS XP INSTALLATION PROCESS

To use Windows XP Professional or Windows XP Home, your system needs to meet or exceed the following requirements:

- 233MHz Pentium-compatible processor
- Approximately 1.5GB of free drive space (however, it depends on the features and software you choose to install)
- 64MB of RAM (bare minimum; some features may be unavailable or limited)
- Super VGA monitor (800x600)
- Keyboard
- Mouse
- CD-ROM

As with all Windows NT-based operating systems, it is always wise to ensure that your hardware is in compliance with the Hardware Compatibility List (HCL). You may search for your specific hardware by visiting the latest HCL, available at *http://microsoft.com/whdc/hcl/search.mspx*.

Consider upgrading your BIOS. Windows XP, like Windows 2000, attempts to use ACPI compliance to its fullest. Windows XP more strictly follows ACPI standards, so it is a good idea to look to your motherboard manufacturer's Web site for an upgrade. An old BIOS with buggy ACPI support is likely to cause Windows XP to behave erratically (e.g., you choose Standby and your system reboots instead).

CD-ROM Installation

If your BIOS supports CD-ROM booting, then you may insert the CD-ROM and reboot your system. After a delay while setup inspects your hardware, the typical blue text-mode installation screen is shown. If you have any RAID devices or third-party SCSI adapters, you must press F6 when you see a message at the bottom of the screen requesting this in black-on-gray text. After this, you may press F2 to begin Automated System Recovery (ASR), which will allow you to recover an existing, nonbooting Windows XP system. ASR is not included in Windows XP Home. Otherwise, you are presented with options for installing or repairing an existing Windows XP system using Recovery Console. After you choose to install and accept the licensing agreement, setup will display the current partition(s) of your hard disk drive(s). You are able to create or delete partitions as necessary. Select either an existing partition or unpartitioned space, and the options for formatting to either an NTFS or FAT file system will appear. If you selected an existing partition, you may have extra options; you can choose not to format it or convert a FAT file system to NTFS. After this step has been completed and Windows copies files to the partition you selected, your system will restart into GUI mode to continue setup.

SIX Setup Disks

Unfortunately, Microsoft has taken away the last crutch from rapidly dying legacy systems. You are no longer able to create any setup floppy disks from the CD-ROM. However, due to the demand for the disks, Microsoft has released two utility downloads on the Internet. They are both a self-extracting compressed file that will generate six floppy disks, rather than four, for either Windows XP Home or Windows XP Professional. The Windows XP Professional disk creation utility will not allow Windows XP Home to boot, and vice-versa. Microsoft has now made it clear that floppy disk support will be entirely absent from the future Windows product lines.

The Windows XP Home disk creation utility can be downloaded from: *http://www.microsoft.com/downloads/details.aspx?FamilyID=E8FE6868-6E4F-471C-B455-BD5AFEE126D8*.

The Windows XP Professional disk utility can be obtained at: *http://www.-microsoft.com/downloads/details.aspx?FamilyID=55820edb-5039-4955-bcb7-4fed408ea73f.*

NOTE

You cannot perform an upgrade to Windows XP from start-up disks.

WINDOWS XP UPGRADE PROCEDURES

Although it is recommended to perform a clean install of any operating system, if you have an existing upgradeable version of Windows, such as Windows 98, 98, SE, or Windows Me, then you may choose to insert the CD-ROM for Windows XP Home at your Windows Desktop. If you have Windows 2000 or Windows NT 4.0, then you must upgrade to Windows XP Professional. Windows 98, Windows 98 SE, and Windows Me may also be upgraded to Windows XP Professional.

Once you insert either CD-ROM, autorun will launch a menu allowing you to choose from several options. It is advisable to start with Check System Compatibility. This executes the Windows XP Upgrade Advisor. It will scan your current hardware and software for known conflicts or bugs that have cropped up during Microsoft's initial testing of the operating system. The first step of the Advisor (if a network connection is detected) is to prompt you for permission to download the updated setup files, which is a great way to expand the list of incompatible software and hardware the Advisor searches for. The final report from the Upgrade Advisor may seem daunting or disappointing at first, but it is really not as critical as it sounds. Most of your hardware will obviously require drivers built for Windows XP (or Windows 2000 drivers that are compatible with Windows XP), and your incompatible software will most likely be superseded by software that either ships with Windows XP already, or the software manufacturer may have created a newer version that supports Windows XP directly. If you decide to install a Windows 2000 driver that is compatible with Windows XP, you must understand that there is a potential to cause system instability. Some drivers may work, but they are not guaranteed as a signed driver would be. The Advisor saves its report in the C:\WINDOWS directory by default.

NOTE

It is important to note that while the networking protocol NetBEUI is technically not supported and will show up in the Advisor's report, NetBEUI for Windows XP is actually available as an extra from the CD-ROM.

If you are interested in upgrading to Windows XP from another version of Windows, consult Table 28.1 to find the proper upgrade path.

TABLE 28.1 Microsoft Windows XP Upgrade Chart

Previous Windows Version	Windows XP Home	Windows XP Professional
Evaluation (any versions)	No	No
Server (any versions)	No	No
Windows 3x	No	No
Windows 95	No	No
Windows 98/98 SE	Yes	Yes
Windows Me	Yes	Yes
Windows NT Workstation 4.0	No	Yes
Windows NT Workstation prior to 4.0	No	No
Windows 2000 Professional	No	Yes
Windows XP Home	N/A	Yes
Windows XP Professional	No	N/A

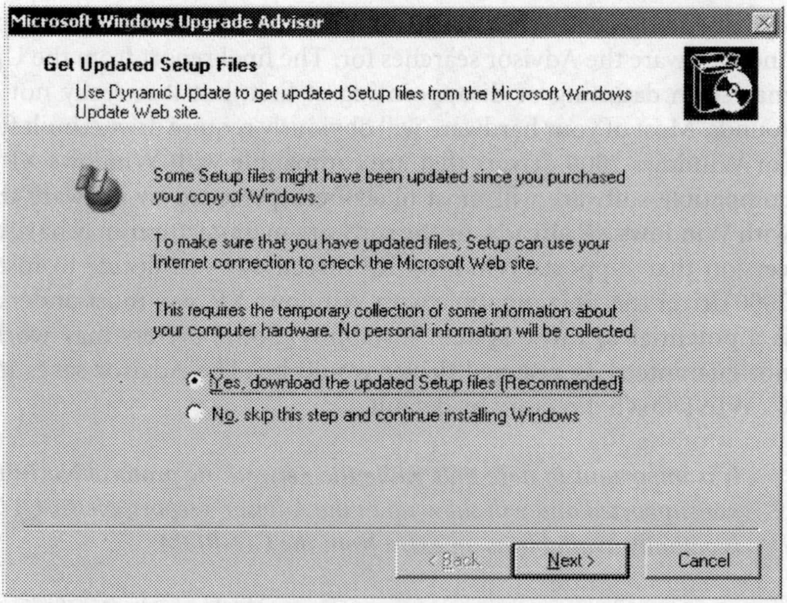

FIGURE 28.1 The Windows XP Upgrade Advisor: updating the setup files.

As you can see, the options for upgrading to Windows XP Home are somewhat limited. However, Microsoft currently offers a special price plan for consumer power users seeking an upgrade from Windows XP Home to Windows XP Professional.

Automated and Network Installations

There are several ways to deploy Windows XP over a network or to multiple computers:

- Unattended, answer file-based installation
- Unattended, cloned image installation (Sysprep)
- Remote Installation Services (RIS)
- Systems Management Server (SMS)

If you plan to install Windows XP on multiple computers with differing hardware and software configurations, then an unattended answer file installation will probably be most beneficial. You or your users will not have to answer the typical questions during setup, saving time and money. It is possible, however, to create a cloned image of an existing installation that will be deployed to all computers, which is useful if all of the client computers will have the same hardware and software configurations. Windows XP can be automatically installed using a variety of methods. The first we will discuss is the unattended answer file method.

An answer file automates the setup procedure. it provides the answers to the typical prompts you would receive during a manual installation of Windows XP. The i386 folder on your Windows XP installation media comes with a sample answer file named Unattend.txt. The actual name of the file does not matter, as long as it is plain text format and spelled correctly when used in conjunction with the setup command (e.g., winnt.exe or winnt32.exe). For instance, winnt.exe /u:mysetup.txt or winnt32.exe /unattend:computer.txt are both valid commands to start an unattended installation. This allows you to possibly create multiple answer files, one for each section of your organization.

An answer file is made up of sections, keys, and values. A section is a word enclosed in square brackets, such as [GuiUnattended]. A key is a string of text following a section that has no spaces. The key is simply an option for the installation. A typical key could be "TimeZone." It is followed by an equals sign (=), then the answer, which is known as a value. So a line just under the [GuiUnattended] section could read TimeZone=5, specifying Eastern Standard Time for the unattended installation. If the value after the key and the equal sign is longer than one word, you must enclose it in quotation marks, for example, OrgName="This is my organization." Some sections may not contain key/value combinations, but rather just a list of files, such as in the [OEMBootFiles] section. Comments start with a semicolon (;) and these lines are ignored by the setup program. They are for your personal information or explanation purposes only.

To get started, simply insert the Windows XP installation CD-ROM in a computer that is already running Windows XP and choose Perform Additional Tasks. Then choose Browse this CD. You should now see the contents of the media. Open the Support folder, and then the Tools folder. Now make a new folder on your Desktop or in a place that you can access easily. In the Tools folder you are browsing, find and double-click the file DEPLOY.CAB. Choose Edit, Select All. Click Edit again, choose Copy, and then navigate to the new folder you created. Finally, choose Edit, then Paste, and you will now have the Setup Manager and everything you need to create an answer file with ease.

NOTE

Microsoft has released a newer version of the Setup Manager and deployment utilities on their Web site. It is considered part of Windows XP Service Pack 1. You can find the newer DEPLOY.CAB here: http://www.microsoft.com/downloads/details.aspx?familyid=7a83123d-507b-4095-9d9d-0a195f7b5f69.

Ref.chm and deploy.chm in your folder contain instructions and help on the answer file process. When you launch setupmgr.exe, a wizard will begin which will walk you through the creation or modification of an answer file. This wizard will help you create an answer file for an unattended installation, a Sysprep installation, or an RIS installation. Sysprep is a utility that prepares an existing Windows XP installation for cloning. If your computer systems are identical in hardware and software, you can create an 'image' or 'clone' of an existing Windows XP installation and install it on multiple systems using Sysprep. Remote Installation Services allows you to deploy the operating system over a network to multiple clients from one or more remote locations.

The Setup Manager can help you create an answer file for Windows XP Home, Windows XP Professional, Windows 2002 Server, Windows 2002 Advanced Server, and Windows 2002 Data Center Edition. The next step in the Setup Manager requests the amount of interaction to be used during an answer file installation. There are currently five types:

Provide defaults: This option will fill in any info you have supplied in your answer file, but allows interaction to change any and all information if necessary. This is not an unattended method.

Fully automated: There are no prompts for information and there are no chances to review or change any information.

Hide pages: This is similar to fully automated, except that it will prompt for information not supplied in the answer file. Any pages and information supplied by an answer file are not shown at all.

Read only: Pages and information provided by an answer file can be reviewed, but they cannot be changed.

GUI attended: The text mode portion of the installation is automated, but the graphical portion of the installation is not.

After choosing an interaction type, you are given a choice as to the medium of installation. You may choose a CD-ROM based installation or a distribution folder installation. A distribution folder has advantages over a CD-ROM installation in that you are able to add files, such as drivers, that are not normally part of the installation. You are also able to store the distribution folder locally on the computer or on a network share.

Once you have chosen a medium, Setup Manager prompts for all of the information that will be provided by the answer file. These are typical questions asked during an attended installation; however, the answers will be saved and used for all of your unattended installations. After the initial questions about time zone, display settings, and product key, the network settings are next.

The network settings portion of the answer file wizard first prompts you for computer names. You have the option of making Setup Manager create computer names based on the organization name. If you do not choose auto-generated names, and you enter more than one computer name, Setup Manager creates a Uniqueness Database (UDF) file. A UDF is simply an answer file that modifies the main answer file by overriding values according to the parameters with which you began the installation. For example, if you launch Windows XP Setup with the switch "/udf:1,myfile.udf", then Setup will look inside the file myfile.udf for ID #1 and use that particular ID's answers, overriding your answer file's defaults. You can create an ID for each instance that you need to override answers in your answer file, and then use them on a case-by-case basis.

The next important step is to include the local Administrator account's password. If you choose a fully automated install, obviously it will not be able to prompt the user for one. You will have to specify a password here. It is recommended that you choose the option to encrypt the password in the answer file so that the password will not be in plain text inside the answer file. There is a limit of 127 characters to a password. You can also choose to have the Administrator account log on automatically each time the computer is started.

Next, you may add or remove networking components, such as Client for Microsoft Networks, File and Printer Sharing, and networking protocols. The final page of the network settings section is the Workgroup or Domain page. If you choose to include this computer in a domain, you may also have Setup create the account on the domain server if one has not already been created for it.

The final phase of the Setup Manager questions allow you to choose telephony settings, regional settings, languages, browser and shell settings, the folder in which Windows will be installed, network printers, 'run once', and additional commands. Run once is a list of commands that will only be executed during the first logon of a newly installed Windows XP system. 'Additional commands' allow you to specify commands that will be run after the end of an unattended setup. You may only specify commands that do not require you to log on.

After you have completed all of the questions, Setup Manager will prompt you to create a .txt file in the directory you extracted Setup Manager to. You may change the location and file name. Again, if multiple computer names were specified, Setup Manager also creates a UDF file. Depending on the type of answer file created, Setup Manager may also create a sample batch file (.bat) script. The batch file will automatically launch setup with the proper parameters to use your new answer file.

Remote Installation Services

Remote Installation Services allows Windows XP deployment from a network server, such as Windows 2000 (or 2002) Server, Advanced Server, or Datacenter, using a setup wizard. This guide will assume you have access to Windows 2000 Server; however Windows 2002 Server will have mostly similar prompts and dialogs. Before you enable RIS on a Windows Server machine, it is wise to install the RIS update Microsoft has provided on their Web site if you have not already installed Service Pack 1 (SP1): *http://www.microsoft.com/downloads/details.aspx?FamilyID=4C7A0E4A-A0DC-46B3-9FDE-8149E223A494*.

You must install RIS on either a member server or a domain controller. It does not matter which. The Windows Server must have DNS, DHCP, and Active Directory, as RIS relies heavily on these services to function. The client computers must have either a PXE boot ROM enabled network adapter or a network adapter supported by the boot floppy that can be created by a remote boot floppy generator (RBFG.exe). The Windows XP images must be stored on a shared volume other than the volume that Windows Server is installed on, and has to be formatted with NTFS 5.

To enable RIS, you must log on to the Windows Server with Administrator privileges and navigate to the Control Panel > Add/Remove Programs. Choose Add/Remove Windows components, and be sure that you have access to either an i386 folder or the Windows 2000 Server CD-ROM. At the Add/Remove Windows components screen, you will check mark Remote Installation Services. This will automatically install RIS on the server. If the i386 files cannot be located, you will be prompted for them. Unfortunately, the server must be restarted after RIS is finished installing.

To begin RIS configuration, you may either navigate back to Add/Remove Windows components, or run RIS Setup from a command prompt, such via the Run command found under the Start menu. When you begin, you are prompted for the destination of the RIS files and Windows installation images. Again, this location cannot be a system drive (i.e., the C: drive), it must be formatted with NTFS 5, and it must have enough hard drive space to hold multiple installation images. RIS installations are quite in-depth, and are more thoroughly explained on Microsoft's TechNet Web site, here: *http://www.microsoft.com/technet/treeview/default.asp?url=/TechNet/prodtechnol/winxppro/reskit/prbc_cai_facb.asp.*

It is not likely that the test will be in-depth about RIS.

WINDOWS XP START-UP PROCESS

Aside from the standard power-on self-test performed during the initial start-up of a PC, Windows XP has a much more complicated boot process than its sister operating system family, Windows 9x. Ntldr, located in the root of the C: drive, performs several tasks critical to start-up:

1. The x86-based processors always start out in Real Mode. Real Mode disables certain processor features to enable backward compatibility with software designed for 8-bit and 16-bit processors. Ntldr switches the processor to 32-bit Protected Mode, enabling access to large amounts of RAM and all extended processor functions.
2. Ntldr also contains code to enable read and write access to file systems such as NTFS or FAT16/FAT32. Once this is parsed and loaded, Ntldr reads the BOOT.INI, also located in the root of the C: drive, to determine the location of the operating system.

3a. For dual-booting systems, your old master boot record sector was saved to a file in the root of the C: drive during initial installation of Windows XP, and that file is called BOOTSECT.DOS. When BOOT.INI detects multiple operating systems, you are prompted with a menu that will enable you to choose your operating system. If you choose an operating system other than Windows XP, 2000, or NT, then Ntldr executes BOOTSECT.DOS as if it were read from the actual master boot record sector, loading that operating system. The hidden file C:\BOOTSECT.DOS contains the boot sector to your old operating system, which was backed up during Windows XP installation. The file system boot sector is the first sector of a logical volume or partition, and is not to be confused with a master boot record, which begins with the first physical sector on a hard drive itself.

3b. If your system is single-booting or you chose Windows XP, 2000, or NT through a multiboot menu, then Ntdetect.com loads and performs basic device detection. Ntdetect.com detects hardware profile information, as well as Advanced Power Management Interface (ACPI) tables. Once that has completed, Ntldr passes BOOT.INI, Registry information, and hardware detection information obtained from Ntdetect.com on to Ntoskrnl.exe.

4. For non-ACPI systems, your hardware's firmware and your BIOS provide the resources such as Interrupt Requests (IRQs) to Windows XP. For ACPI-compliant systems, Windows XP is able to assign and manage all necessary resources. After Ntldr launches Ntoskrnl.exe, the Hardware Abstraction Layer (HAL) is loaded into memory, providing secured access to hardware and their associated resources. A hardware abstraction layer catches all requests to hardware made by software and ensures security by preventing unauthorized direct access to hardware. All hardware interaction must be done via kernel-level system calls and Application Programming Interfaces (API). Depending on your type of computer, Windows XP setup installs a custom HAL. To see which HAL your system will have, consult Table 28.2.

5. The kernel and HAL initiate a group of software components known as the Windows Executive. The Executive processes Registry configuration data, and starts services and hardware drivers. The Registry information parsed by the Executive contains the common control sets, such as the Last Known Good control set. The CurrentControlSet entry in the Registry is a clone of the control set created upon every boot of Windows XP. Ntldr

TABLE 28.2 The Different HAL Files

Computer's Description in Device Manager:	HAL File Copied:
ACPI Multiprocessor PC	Halmacpi.dll
ACPI Uniprocessor PC	Halaacpi.dll
Advanced Configuration and Power Interface (ACPI) PC	Halacpi.dll
MPS Multiprocessor PC	Halmps.dll
MPS Uniprocessor PC	Halapic.dll
Standard PC	Hal.dll
Compaq SystemPro Multiprocessor or 100% Compatible	Halsp.dll

searches the Services subkey of the Registry to find drivers and services with a Start key value of 0, such as hard disk controllers. Ntoskrnl.exe searches for and starts drivers with a Start key value of 1, such as network protocols. After all of the drivers and services have been loaded in memory, started, or both, the kernel starts Session Manager (known as Smss.exe).

6. Smss.exe performs the following functions, in this order:
   a. Creates system environment variables.
   b. Starts Win2k.sys, the kernel-mode portion of Windows, which switches Windows XP from text to graphics mode.
   c. Starts the user-mode portion, Csrss.exe.
   d. Starts the Logon Manager (Winlogon.exe).
   e. Creates virtual memory swap files.
   f. Replaces pending files that were in use during the last boot (such as when you are requested to restart Windows after installing a driver).
7. After Winlogon.exe executes, it launches several subsystems that provide security and functionality for services. The first thing that Winlogon launches is Services.exe, also known as the Service Control Manager (SCM). Next, the Local Security Authority (LSA, or Lsass.exe) is executed. Finally, Winlogon waits for and parses the CTRL+ALT+DEL key combination at the logon prompt. The Local Security Authority is responsible for validating local credentials, such as the user name and password, using the appropriate security protocol (e.g., Kerberos V5).
8. The control sets mentioned in step 5, above, are updated during the next phase of Winlogon.exe. Group Policy settings take effect after logging on, and then the user's local start-up items, login scripts, and services are executed.

Plug-and-Play detection runs asynchronously with the logon phases, and Windows XP extracts necessary drivers for new hardware from Driver.cab. If the drivers are not found, Windows XP prompts you to provide them. The logon and plug-and-play processes are the final steps in the start-up process.

WINDOWS XP TOOLS AND UTILITIES

Windows XP has taken Windows 2000's Microsoft Management Console (MMC) a step further. Some of the Windows 2000 utilities have been redesigned to be only available through the MMC as a 'snap-in.' The Services control panel applet, Disk Management, and Device Manager have now been integrated into the MMC. Even when launched as a separate entity, they still load MMC first. The MMC is a fully customizable utility for organizing commonly used administrative functions. Computer

Management, as discussed in Chapter 26, is a preconfigured MMC with the most common utilities already 'snapped-in.' With only two clicks of the mouse, you are able to access the Device Manager, Services, Disk Management, or many other common administrative tools. Simply right-click My Computer, choose Manage, and Computer Management appears. It is always important that you know the Microsoft way to access utilities, as it is more likely to appear on the test than the aforementioned shortcut method. You would simply navigate to Start (or Settings, for 'Classic Start Menu' users) > Control Panel > Administrative Tools > Computer Management.

In this chapter, we will discuss the new, as well as improved, Windows system utilities.

Device Manager

Device Manager has always been an invaluable tool for troubleshooting Windows systems. Windows XP includes a similar version of Windows 2000's Device Manager; and just like in Windows 2000, it is only available as a Microsoft Management Console snap-in. It features a new utility called Roll Back Driver. If you install an upgraded or alternate driver over an existing one, Windows XP will backup the old driver in case there is a problem. At any time, you may access a device's driver Properties pane and choose to revert to the older driver (see Figure 28.2). Obviously, this is a worthwhile addition to existing troubleshooting methods. To access Device Manager, navigate to Control Panel > System > Hardware tab > Device Manager button, or use Computer Management under Accessories > Administrative Tools, or Control Panel > Administrative Tools.

Driver Signing

As with Windows 2000, Windows XP offers advanced Driver Signing options that will prevent unapproved device drivers from being loaded by unauthorized users. The Microsoft Driver Signing (also known as Windows Logo Testing) standards are much more rigorous and stress testing than ever before. This is to ensure compatibility and stability regardless of computer configuration. You may choose to ignore, warn, or completely disable unsigned driver installations. The default setting is 'warn,' which displays a dialog requesting action when an unsigned driver installation is attempted. You may then choose the system default through this Properties pane. To access the Driver Signing Properties page, visit System Properties either through the Control Panel or by right-clicking on My Computer and choosing Properties. Once you are in System Properties, you should choose the Hardware tab, and then you will see the Driver Signing button.

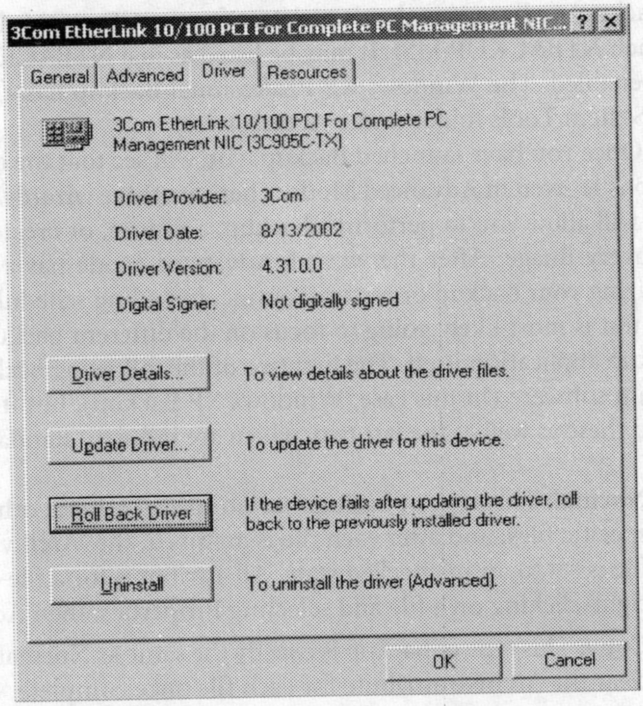

FIGURE 28.2 The enhanced Driver tab featuring the new Roll Back Driver.

Microsoft Management Console

As discussed in Chapter 26, the Microsoft Management Console is a handy way to centralize your administrative tasks. Windows XP has modified several existing standalone applications to be only accessible as a snap-in. Event Viewer, Disk Defragmenter, Disk Management, Device Manager, Local Users and Groups, Performance Logs and Counters, and Services are only available in Windows XP through the MMC. You can open a blank MMC window by choosing Start > Run, typing "MMC" in the Open box, and then pressing OK. You may add the aforementioned tools or several other advanced administrative programs by selecting File > Add/Remove Snap-in.

Backup

Windows XP Home Edition does not include Backup by default. You can install it by delving deep into the installation CD-ROM. Navigate to X:\Valueadd\msft\

ntbackup\ (where X is the drive letter for the CD-ROM drive you are using) and launch NTBACKUP.MSI. It may be listed as just NTBACKUP if file extensions are not enabled. The Windows XP Professional Backup has a Start Menu shortcut in the System Tools folder under Accessories.

Once you have launched Backup, you will see that the opening interface is very simplistic, even in Advanced Mode. There are three wizards on the main dialog page that will allow you to perform a backup, a restore, or create an Automated System Recovery image. After the wizard, Advanced Mode has a lot of options for customizing your backup or restore routine, including scheduling automatic backups. The test is most likely going to focus on the different backup types rather than the Backup application itself. The first two of the following backup types are specific to certain software (in this case, Windows XP Backup), but it is important to understand these as well as the last two, which are industry standard types:

Normal: This type of backup has no special criteria other than the selection of specific files; and after each file is archived, the 'Archive' attribute bit for each file is set to an unchecked state. All attributes for a file or folder are viewed by right-clicking on a file and selecting Properties, then Advanced (if necessary).

Copy: This type of backup is exactly the same as Normal, except that it does not clear the Archive attribute for each file once complete.

Incremental: Incremental is an industry-standard term for files that have been created or modified since the last backup. When you create a file or modify an existing one that has been backed up previously (which clears its Archive attribute), Windows automatically turns on the Archive bit for that file, telling the backup software that it needs to be backed up again. After each file is backed up using Incremental, the Archive bit is cleared again.

Differential: Differential is also an industry-standard term, and it performs the same as Incremental, except that the Archive bit is not cleared, much like Copy.

NOTE

It is very important to remember from Chapter 26 that NTFS and FAT are not compatible file systems. NTFS contains extended features, such as compression, encryption, and security permissions. All of these extended attributes will be lost during the copy from NTFS to FAT. Long file names and regular attributes such as Read-Only and Archive will be retained, however.

System Restore

System Restore, first introduced in Windows Me, is a valuable tool for 'turning back the clock.' Think of System Restore as an expanded 'Last Known Good configuration.' Windows Me and Windows XP keep track of certain 'milestones'; for example, if you install a new driver or use Windows Update to upgrade system software, Windows will create a 'Restore Point' that allows you to revert back to a previous date's Registry configuration (including replaced files) in case of a problem. You may also create a Restore Point at any time you wish. It is found in the Start menu under Accessories > System Tools. You are presented with a calendar that contains system Restore Points for each milestone.

You can disable or re-enable System Restore by visiting System Properties, either in Control Panel > System, or by right-clicking on My Computer and selecting Properties. You will see a System Restore tab that allows you to disable it completely or adjust the amount of hard drive space (for each drive letter) that will be used to backup files during each milestone. The more hard drive space you allocate, the more fault tolerance your system will have. If there is not enough allocated hard drive space, certain files may be excluded from backup; System Restore becomes much less effective in this situation.

Windows Imaging Architecture

Windows Imaging Architecture (WIA) is a new standard set forth by Microsoft for imaging devices (e.g., scanners or digital cameras) to communicate directly with the operating system. It was first introduced in Windows Me, and it offers internal support for many popular cameras and scanners. It provides a much more simplified interface for scanning or downloading digital images than TWAIN. According to the TWAIN group, TWAIN is not actually an acronym, but rather a take-off on the Kipling quote, "never the twain shall meet." It implies that the hardware and the imaging software will never directly communicate, but a device driver acting as a middleman will relay information and messages. TWAIN is the standard driver type for the majority of imaging devices prior to Windows Millennium. WIA is Microsoft's replacement for TWAIN.

Event Viewer

As with all Windows NT-based operating systems, Event Viewer is a vital tool for troubleshooting software, hardware drivers, and services failure. You can find the Event Viewer in Administrative Tools in the Control Panel.

All events are logged to disk and time-stamped for organization. There are three main categories of events: Application, Security, and System. Under Application, you will find errors and warnings having to do with setup programs (such as with InstallShield or the installer service for Microsoft, MSI) and regular applications (e.g., crashes, missing data, etc.). If you double-click on an entry, data useful for troubleshooting will appear, usually followed by a Web site address to Microsoft.com that will either attempt to explain the event in more detail or lead you to a fix or solution for a particular known issue. If you are looking for a particular log in any of the three sections, you should use Filter, which is found in the View pull-down menu.

In the Security section of the Event Viewer, you will find successful and unsuccessful logins, as well as items chosen by the administrator to be 'audited.' By default, security logging is turned off. You can use Group Policy to enable security logging. To do this, navigate to Administrative Tools in the Control Panel and choose Local Security Settings (see Figure 28.3). The main two items of importance to the Security log are listed under Local Policies, and they are called Audit Policy and Security Options. For example, if you enable Failure auditing for the Audit logon events in the Audit Policy subcategory, Security logs will be created in the Event Viewer when a logon error occurs.

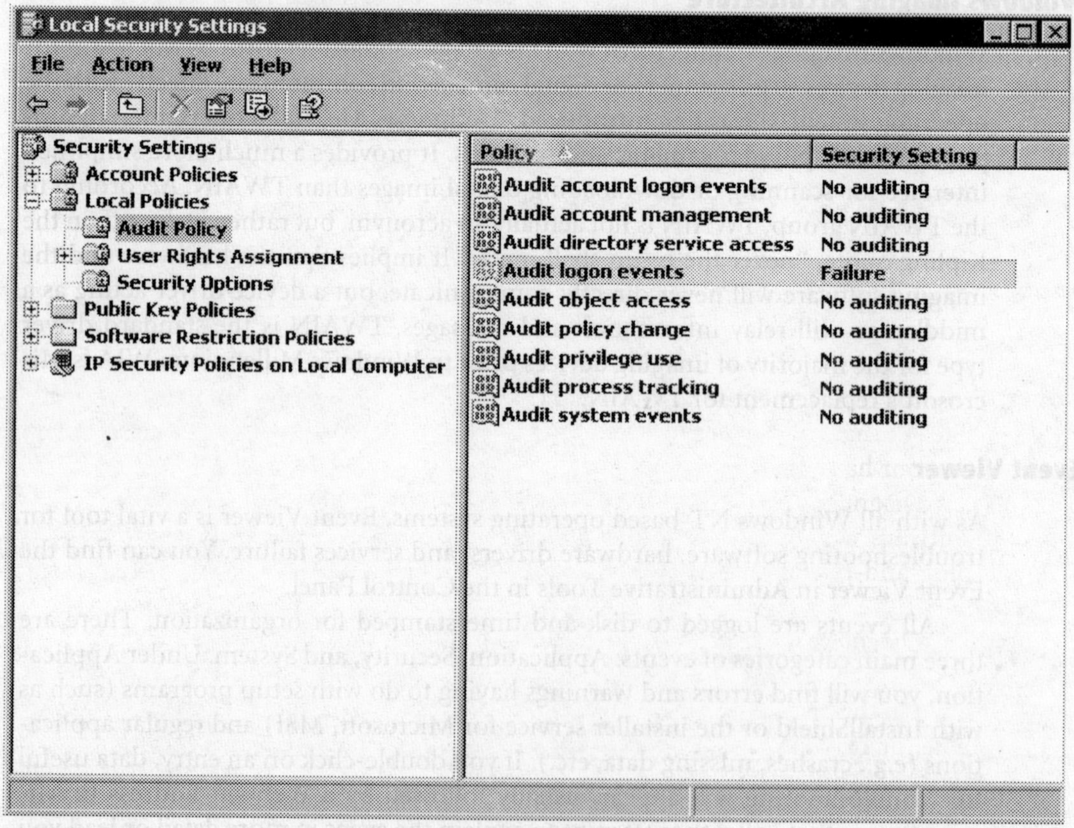

FIGURE 28.3 Enabling Auditing with Local Security Policies.

Last, but not least, under the System section there will be events pertaining to information or errors from device drivers, services problems, and other Windows XP system components.

For computers configured as a domain controller, there will be two additional logs: Directory Service and File Replication. They will probably not be important for the test. Domain Name System (DNS) computers will also record a DNS server log.

MSCONFIG (Microsoft Configuration Utility)

Since Windows 98, MSCONFIG has been an advantage to all technicians due to its compact interface and optimized layout. The first thing you will notice about it is that you are able to quickly select the type of start-up from the very first tab (General). This has always been helpful, because it is the first step to narrowing the spectrum of possibilities for a given issue. If there is a software problem in the system, the first step is usually to disable third-party or background software to ensure that it is not user software that is causing the particular problem. You can do so by choosing Selective Startup on the General tab and then fully unchecking the Load Startup Items box. This is a three state checkbox. If you have used MSCONFIG before, and you previously visited the Startup tab and disabled specific items, then your Load Startup Items checkbox will be checked but grayed out. It is not disabled; however, it means that there are specific items that are loading and specific ones that are not. If you were to completely uncheck this field, MSCONFIG would forget which particular items you had chosen to load, and it would completely unload all items. If you see a grayed checkbox, you should visit the Startup tab and write down the items that are not checked. That way, if you have to clear the Load Startup Items checkbox, you will be able to restore your old configuration when you have solved your problem. More will be discussed about MSCONFIG in the troubleshooting section of this chapter. The General tab also has a button called Expand File . . . that will extract files from Windows XP installation media or any location on your hard drive.

Diagnostic Startup causes Windows XP to interactively load device drivers and software when you restart the system. All Microsoft Services (e.g., networking, plug-and-play, Event Logging, etc.) are temporarily disabled in this mode.

NOTE *Diagnostic start-up permanently deletes ALL System Restore points.*

On the SYSTEM.INI and WIN.INI tabs, you are able to specifically disable, enable, or rearrange lines from those particular files. SYSTEM.INI commonly contains 386-Enhanced virtual device and legacy device driver entries, such as text mode fonts, keyboard and display drivers, and password lists (PWL files). WIN.INI contains Windows and software settings that have not yet migrated to the Windows

Registry. These files are mainly used for backward compatibility with 16-bit and old Windows programs.

The BOOT.INI tab contains options for starting the operating system, such as the paths to each Windows operating system you may have. You are also able to enable special options such as a safe VGA video driver (/BASEVIDEO) or specify the type of Safe Mode launch (/SAFEBOOT). You may change the amount of time Windows XP gives you to make an operating system selection by modifying the Timeout value.

The Services tab contains individual check marks for all services, including third party. Unchecking a service is the same as selecting Disabled for a service's properties in the Services section of Computer Management. There is a handy checkbox available for hiding all Microsoft services. This way, you can easily see third-party services. During troubleshooting, it is often wise to disable third-party services that are not required for your computer to function.

The last tab, Startup, contains the items from the Registry that are going to launch whenever Windows XP boots. You may specifically disable or enable start-up items here. If there is a start-up item that has been removed during an upgrade from a previous version of Windows, you will be able to use the button marked Restore Startup Programs . . . to bring them back. Windows XP Setup commonly disables start-up items that it knows have been replaced with newer software, such as an entry for Windows 9x power management or video driver utility software (not to be confused with the actual driver).

Remote Desktop

Windows XP includes an interesting tool called Remote Desktop for troubleshooting a remote computer. Other common uses for it are accessing your data or controlling a machine from a remote location, such as an office computer while you are out of the office. The computer you are going to control is known as the *host computer*. The computer you will connect from is called the *client*. Your client computer can have Windows 9x or Windows NT 4.0 and higher installed, provided that it has the Remote Desktop Connection client software installed. The host computer you will be controlling must have Windows XP Professional installed. Obviously, an Internet or network connection is required.

In order for a remote computer to connect for Remote Desktop session, the Administrator or a user from the Administrator group must have enabled it. Right-click on My Computer, select Properties, and choose the Remote tab. You must check the checkbox with the text "Allow users to connect remotely to this computer" under the Remote Desktop section. After that, it is advisable to select the remote users that will be connecting to the machine, unless you are the Administrator or part of the Administrator group.

Both Windows XP Home and Windows XP Professional install the Remote Desktop client software by default. If you are running a previous version of Windows, such as Windows 98, then you will have to insert the Windows XP Home or Windows XP Professional CD-ROM into the drive and select Perform Additional Tasks from the autorun menu. Then you will choose Set up Remote Desktop Connection. Follow the on-screen directions, and the client will be installed.

Once you have enabled Remote Desktop on the host and installed client software on a Windows-based client machine, you are ready to set up a virtual private network connection or remote access service connection to the host machine. Navigate to Start > Programs (or All Programs) > Accessories > Communications > Remote Desktop Connection. At the prompt screen, you will enter either the Universal Naming Convention (UNC) name (e.g., \\CRAYTON; the \\ is optional) or an IP address. You may either choose to connect or refine your parameters by choosing "Options >". Options will show you many new settings, including display settings, audio settings, and user name, password, and domain settings. Choose Connect and the Log On to Windows dialog pane should appear to request your user name, password, and optional 'domain' (if you have not specified them already in the advanced Options area). You now have control over the host computer. The remote host computer will be locked so that no passersby can see what you are doing to it. Local users will still be able to log on if they have a proper user name and password.

Remote Assistance

Remote Assistance is similar to Remote Desktop, but with a few exceptions. It is an interactive connection in which the host computer will display what the client computer is controlling. Remote Assistance also requires that there be someone at the host computer to send an invitation for a connection. To use Remote Assistance, both computers must either be running Windows XP Home or Windows XP Professional. Remote Assistance can happen in one of three ways:

1. If both machines have Windows Messenger installed, you can navigate to the Tools menu of Windows Messenger and choose Ask for Remote Assistance. All online contacts will be displayed with their e-mail addresses. If your friend accepts the invitation, you will be prompted for confirmation. Although the remote computer will have temporary control over your machine, you will still be able to end the session by clicking on the Stop Control button or by pressing the escape (ESC) key. The person you chose to control your machine will receive a password confirmation dialog to initiate the Remote Assistance session. After that, they can either watch your display or chat with you, or they can click on Take Control to begin controlling your computer.

2. Remote Assistance can also begin via e-mail. Click Start > Help and Support. When the Help and Support Center opens, you will choose "Invite a friend to connect to your computer with Remote Assistance" under the Ask for assistance heading. Click Invite someone to help you, and then enter the e-mail address of the person you are inviting. Choose Continue, and enter your name and a brief summary of the issue. For security reasons, you are able to set an expiration date for this session, which will disallow Remote Assistance connections after that date. You must also specify a password, which you will have to give to the person in a separate communication. Choose Send Invitation. Your friend will receive an e-mail with an attachment. They must open the attachment, enter the password in the dialog box, and choose Yes.
3. If you use Web-based e-mail or prefer not to send the request over the Internet, you may save the request to a file. During the e-mail type of Remote Assistance (step 2, above) you may opt to Save Invitation as a file instead of Send Invitation. This way, you could transport the request via another means than e-mail, if you have to. You can also use Web-based e-mail and attach it as a file, avoiding the necessity for Outlook Express (or similar e-mail clients).

Recovery Console

Recovery Console is a tool used to repair a damaged system, such as a boot problem. Windows 2000 and Windows XP both have the Recovery Console on their installation CD-ROMs. To use the Recovery Console for Windows XP, simply insert the installation CD-ROM and boot it as you normally would to install Windows XP. Press "R" at the blue screen to repair a Windows XP installation using Recovery Console. You will be prompted to select which installation to repair. Although there is usually just one, this gives you the option to access other Windows 2000 or Windows XP installations. You will then be prompted for the Administrator password. After logging on, you will be at a screen similar to an MS-DOS prompt, but it is actually a CMD.EXE-style prompt. If you type HELP at the prompt, you will be presented with a list of all possible commands. If you type a command followed by a slash and a question mark (e.g., ATTRIB /?) you will be presented with the syntax and options specific to that command.

Although you are logged on as an Administrator, it is more secure an environment than an MS-DOS or command prompt. You are able to:

1. View the root directory of all disk drives
2. View the Windows directory and all subdirectories
3. Access removable media, such as floppy disks and CD-ROM drives

4. Copy files from a floppy or CD-ROM to the accessible directories
5. Extract files from cabinet (.CAB) files
6. Write a new boot sector or write a new master boot record using FIXBOOT and FIXMBR, respectively
7. Manage disk partitions using DISKPART
8. List, enable, or disable services using LISTSVC, ENABLE, and DISABLE, respectively

You are not able to do the following:

1. View any directory or access files in any place other than the root of any drive and the Windows directory
2. Copy files to a floppy or CD-ROM from the accessible directories

There are eight different attributes possible for files and folders when in the console. Here is a quick run-down of those attributes:

1. "D" is for directory. Files will show a dash (-).
2. "A" is for a file or directory that has its 'archive' bit turned on (see the previous section on Backup).
3. "R" is for files and directories that are set to 'read-only.'
4. An "H" means the file or directory is hidden.
5. An "S" on a file or directory means it has its 'System' attribute on.
6. "E" is for encrypted files or directories.
7. "C" stands for compressed files or directories.
8. "P" means 'reparse point.' Reparse points are special NTFS file stubs that contain user-controlled data. The format of this data is understood only by the program, which stores the data as well as a file system filter that you install to interpret the data and process the file. The test is not likely to ask any questions about reparse points.

PROFILES

In order to more efficiently organize Windows, Microsoft has created user profiles. Windows XP profiles are stored in a centralized location on the system drive. Profiles specify shortcuts, settings, retain 'most recently used' information, as well as storing My Documents and other common folders. By default, local user profiles are stored in C:\Documents and Settings\. Each folder under that folder is a user's name, such as Administrator. In addition to your documents and settings, Internet Explorer history, cache, cookies, and Favorites are also stored here. There is a folder under your user name called Desktop that stores all of the shortcuts that will appear on your Desktop.

The 'All Users' profile provides system-wide settings and shortcuts that all users will receive. It can only be modified by the system Administrator. In contrast, the Default User profile only specifies default settings given to each newly created user. When a user is created, the contents of the Default User profile are copied to the new user's profile folder to provide a template. Only the Administrator may edit the Default User profile.

The hidden folders Application Data and Local Settings under your user name folder is commonly where all Microsoft Internet programs store their information. Outlook and Outlook Express, Internet Explorer, and MSN/Windows Messenger all store data here, except for cookies and Favorites, which are found directly under your user name folder. Application Data stores credentials and certificates, while Local Settings stores a copy of the credentials, an icon cache, a 'temp' folder, your history, and Internet Explorer's Temporary Internet Files. Desktop.ini, which you will find nearly everywhere, is a file that specifies the current look and settings of the given folder in Explorer, whether icons are shown as simply icons, Details, Thumbnails, or whether to show hidden files or system folders, and so forth. If a special icon is chosen for a folder, or if there is wallpaper applied, then it is stored in Desktop.ini as well.

When you log on to a domain controller with your user name, a roaming profile is copied from your network profile's home directory to the local hard drive, and it is combined with the All Users' profile. When you are done working, any changes made to your profile are saved back to the network profile's home directory so that you may access your changes from any workstation. You can see or modify a list of profiles by right-clicking on My Computer, choosing Properties, navigating to the Advanced tab, and under the User Profiles section, click the Settings button. You will be able to change a roaming profile to a local profile (provided that there is a roaming profile for you), or copy and delete profiles from this screen. It will also list how large the profile is in megabytes, which is helpful if you are in a network environment with space limitations.

A 'mandatory' user profile is a roaming profile that is not updated when the user logs off. The system Administrator sets up a profile of specific settings and shortcuts that is delivered to a user or group of users. Only members of the Administrator group may change the mandatory profile, as it is designed to provide consistent or job-specific functionality to your profile.

PRINTERS

Microsoft has yet again expanded the ease of use and installation of peripherals in Windows XP. For those already familiar with Windows 2000 printer procedures, there will be little differences other than slight wording changes or merged dialogs and buttons.

There are two main types of printer installations: hot-pluggable and standard. Hot-pluggable refers to newer technologies, such as infrared, IEEE 1394 (FireWire), and Universal Serial Bus (USB). Standard usually refers to serial, parallel, or Centronics connectors. Hot-pluggable printers are the easiest to install.

To ensure accurate detection of hot-pluggable devices, connect them directly to your computer's main ports, rather than through an external USB or FireWire 'hub,' which is designed to expand the amount of ports available. If your printer came with a CD-ROM that supports Windows XP, it is a good idea to attempt to install the driver prior to connecting and powering on the printer for the first time. An even better idea is to download the latest Windows XP driver from the printer manufacturer's Web site and install it.

Once your printer is connected and powered on, Windows should automatically detect the brand and model of printer, and begin searching for drivers. If Windows does not have a driver in its database, and you have not already installed one, Windows will prompt you for it. You may insert the CD-ROM at the first Found New Hardware screen and Windows will automatically begin searching the entire CD-ROM for it. If the hardware wizard is cancelled mid-way through, or if there is an error, your printer will no longer be detected as a brand new device from then on. It will be listed in Device Manager with a black exclamation point on a yellow field. You should right-click on it and choose Uninstall. This usually allows Windows to start over when you detach and reconnect the printer. There are some instances where this will not work; and in those cases, you should refer to the printer's documentation and the manufacturer's technical support channels.

Parallel printers are not usually plug and play (though on very rare occasions, it has been possible). Once you connect one and power it up, you have to manually install the driver for it yourself and hope that Windows can communicate with it. If your printer is very old, then you may have to use the Add Printer Wizard. Navigate to the Start menu > Printers and Faxes. Then choose Add Printer. A wizard will appear that will walk you step-by-step through the installation of your printer. You may choose to install a local printer (connected directly to your machine) or a network printer (set up as a network share). You have the option to disable plug-and-play detection for your printer, and it is a good idea to do so if your printer is not new. After you choose "Local printer," you will have to select a port that the printer is connected to. If your printer is on a special port (such as infrared), then you will be able to select it here (although most of the time, infrared printers are detected as plug and play). Standard parallel printers on standard PCs will most likely communicate on LPT1 (short for Line PrinTer 1, a now archaic term). There are ways to print to Communications (COM) ports (such as fax drivers and serial connection printers) or even straight to a file. There are many other instances where there can be a special port to print to, such as an Adobe Acrobat Portable Document Format (PDF) Writer; or if a USB printer driver has been installed but not added to the Printers folder, then you may see a special USB port here.

If your serial, parallel, or Centronics printer is fairly recent, then it probably came with a CD-ROM or diskettes that you can install from, which will add the printer to the Printers folder (and the Add Printer Wizard list), as well as installing informative printer monitor software and other miscellaneous tools. Again, it is always recommended to download the latest drivers from a manufacturer's Web site instead of using the included driver disks.

WINDOWS XP NETWORKING AND THE INTERNET

Windows XP includes expanded networking technologies not found in any other previous version of Windows. We will discuss the new and upgraded features of Windows XP networking in this section.

The first thing to know is how to view your IP configuration. There are two main ways. If you are familiar with or prefer the command prompt, you can launch CMD (Start > Run > CMD.EXE) and type "ipconfig". This will give you an overview of your network adapter(s) and their IP configurations. Instructions about the advanced options for ipconfig are available if you type "ipconfig /? | more". If you prefer to see your statistics inside Windows, then you may double-click on an active connection's lights in the notification area (near the clock). You may also visit Network Connections in the Control Panel and double-click on an active connection icon. If you double-click on a disabled connection, then Windows will attempt to enable it.

Network Setup Wizard and New Connection Wizard

As with most common tasks in Windows XP, Microsoft has created wizards to guide users through the setup of a small home or office network, or manage Internet connections. The first wizard we will discuss guides you through setting up Internet Connection Sharing (ICS) using the included Internet Connection Firewall, and sharing files, folders, and printers. The Network Setup Wizard (Figure 28.4) is located in Network Connections, which can be found in the Control Panel. The Wizard is quite self-explanatory, and there are included diagrams that will try to describe your current or desired network setup so that you can easily configure it.

The New Connection Wizard, which is also available in Network Connections, gives you more flexibility and also allows you to perform Internet connectivity tasks not available in the Network Setup Wizard, such as selecting PPP over Ethernet (PPPoE). PPPoE is a technology used to encapsulate Point-to-Point Protocol

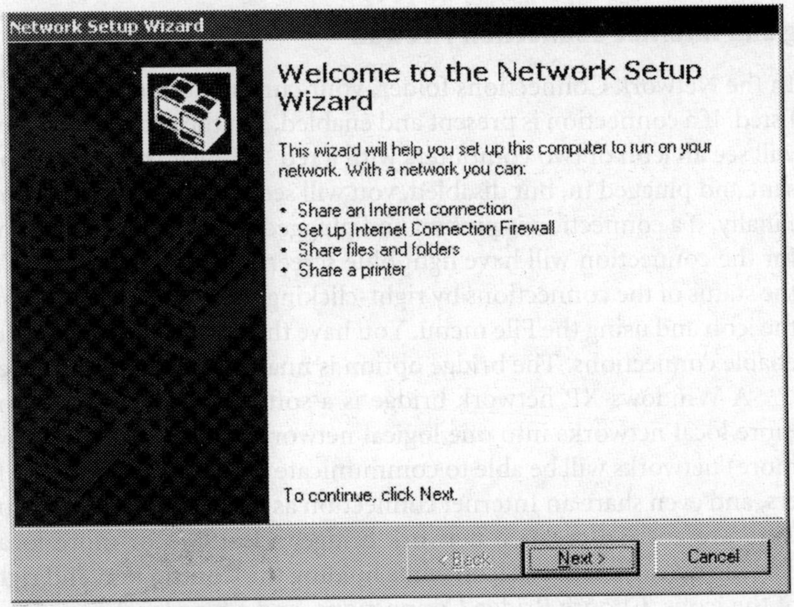

FIGURE 28.4 The Network Setup Wizard.

(PPP) frames in an Ethernet packet. This is the networking frame type most commonly used with Asymmetric Digital Subscriber Line (ADSL) connections. In the previous versions of Windows, third-party software had to be deployed in order for Windows to support the PPPoE frame type, allowing your system to connect using ADSL. Windows XP now includes a built-in implementation of PPPoE that is more stable, compatible, and easier to use than most third-party PPPoE software. The New Connection Wizard is the best method for connecting a new computer to the Internet, as it has the most options available. If you choose the manual setup of an Internet connection in the New Connection Wizard, you can select from three types of connections. You may connect via a dial-up modem, using a broadband connection that requires a user name and password (most commonly used in ADSL or PPPoE), or just a simple broadband connection that is always on (such as a high-speed cable modem). The New Connection Wizard also allows you to easily set up a Virtual Private Network (VPN) or business-oriented dial-up connection. Finally, if you choose to set up an advanced connection to another computer, you have direct connection options such as serial, parallel, and infrared, or you may configure your computer to be a host for incoming direct cable connections.

Bridging and Internet Connection Firewall

In the Network Connections folder, your current connections and their status are listed. If a connection is present and enabled, but the actual cable is unplugged, you will see an icon of two computers with a red "X" over them. If a connection is present and plugged in, but disabled, you will see an icon with gray computer screens. Finally, if a connection is present and plugged in, and is working properly, the icon for the connection will have light blue screens on the computers. You can change the status of the connections by right-clicking on their respective icons, or selecting the icon and using the File menu. You have the options to repair, bridge, disable, or enable connections. The bridge option is unavailable via the File menu.

A Windows XP network bridge is a software solution for combining two or more local networks into one logical network. Computers on each of the two (or more) networks will be able to communicate with each other, share files and printers, and even share an Internet connection as though a hardware router or gateway were present. To create a network bridge, select two or more local networks by clicking on each network icon while holding the Control key, and right-click on one of the icons. Choose Bridge Connections, and a new local area connection icon is created. When a local network is added to a bridge, it loses its normal properties, such as IP address, client software, protocols, and so forth. The bridged connection will keep track of all IP settings, clients, protocols, and the list of local area connections that are included in the bridge in its Properties.

Windows XP includes a new feature that no other version of Windows has included before. There is a built-in Internet Connection Firewall (ICF) that can protect your network from unwanted incoming connections and traffic (see Figure 28.5). It cannot protect you from unwanted outgoing connections, such as those coming from spyware, malware, Trojan horse virus programs, and other hacker tools, and it is not designed for use on computers that are not directly connected to the Internet. Only users of the Administrator group can enable or disable ICF. You must also understand that if Internet Connection Firewall is enabled on a local area network connection with other computers, it will prohibit file and printer sharing.

To enable ICF, navigate to Network Connections, right-click on an Internet connection, and choose Properties. On the Advanced tab of the connection's properties there will be a checkbox to enable ICF; and once enabled, the Settings button below it allows you to configure ICF further. On the first tab of Advanced Settings, called Services, you can enable access from the Internet to certain services on your firewalled machine. This basically prevents these services from being firewalled (blocked). The next tab, Security Logging, allows you to choose whether to log dropped packets, successful connections, or change the location and size of the log file. The log file is called PFIREWALL.LOG, and it is stored in C:\WINNT or C:\WINDOWS (depending on your installation) by default. The last tab, ICMP,

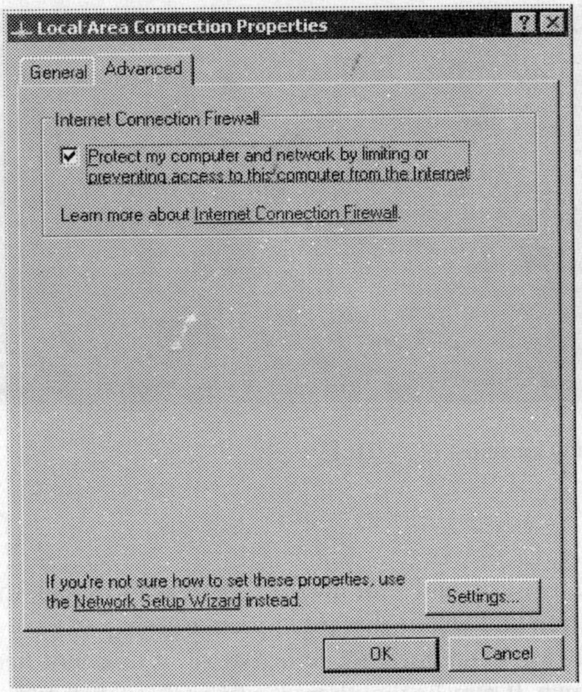

FIGURE 28.5 Enabling Internet Connection Firewall.

contains options for enabling or disabling incoming Internet Control Message Protocol (ICMP) packets. ICMP is a special error message, status, and diagnostics protocol; and in contrast to TCP, it is connectionless. The common ICMP messages listed here, such as echo, are used to relay error and diagnostics information. ICMP echo, also known as PING (for use with the PING program), is used to determine whether a remote computer is responding, and to check the latency and integrity between your computer and the destination. Any ICMP echo data sent to a remote computer will be returned unmodified as soon as possible. The PING program will also report how long it took to relay the information and will even glean how many route hops a given packet had to take. The Time-To-Live (TTL) value reported by the PING program refers to how long the packet will route around the Internet before it is discarded (see Figure 28.6). If there were no TTL, packets would float aimlessly on the Internet for eternity. An example of a practical use for the PING TTL is as follows: if your PING packet's TTL value is 255, and a PING response comes back with a TTL of 240, then you will know it took 15 hops through routers and other computers on the Internet before your packet reached its destination. Most TTL values are based on powers of two, with the exception of 255. Common TTLs

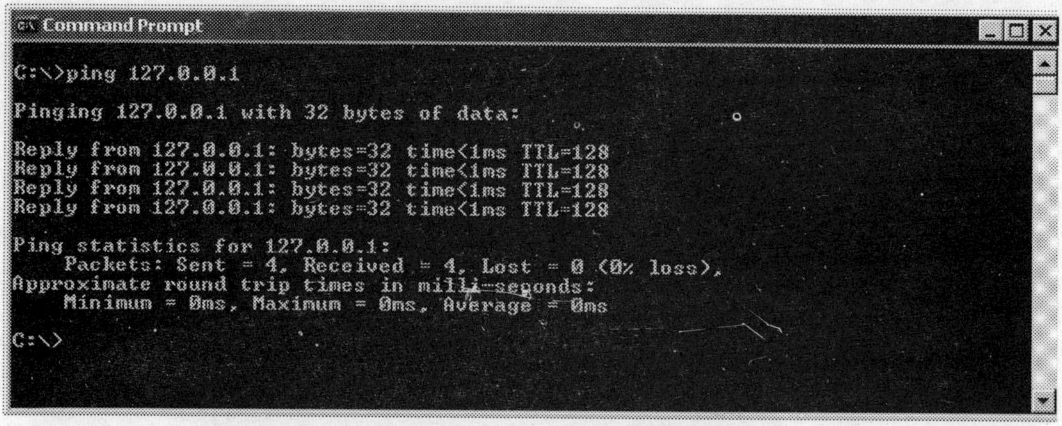

FIGURE 28.6 Pinging localhost (127.0.0.1)

include 32, 64, 128, and 255. If a TTL value is too small, the packet will not reach its destination and will be discarded prematurely.

If an ICMP echo does not return at all, it does not necessarily mean the machine is down. It may be that there is a firewall, such as ICF, on the destination machine that is blocking ICMP echo (PING) requests. This tab is where you would specify whether you wish to block such messages. Other ICMP messages you can block deliver routing, status, and troubleshooting data, such as "destination unreachable," and "parameter problem." The practical uses for the other ICMP types listed here are beyond the scope of the test. At the most, you will only need to understand ICMP echo and the use of the PING program.

File and Printer Sharing

Like previous versions of Windows, Windows XP includes a peer-to-peer file and printer sharing client. It uses a packet protocol called Server Message Block (SMB). NetBIOS relies heavily on SMB packets to access network shares, networked printers, and send network messages. You can install File and Printer Sharing as a 'client' via the Properties of any connection icon in the Network Connections folder.

Windows XP Home contains only simple file sharing, but Windows XP Professional has two levels of detail for file and printer sharing. When you first enable File and Printer Sharing in Windows XP Professional, it is in simple mode. In simple mode, you do not specify which users and permissions will go to which files, folders, and printers. All users have access to all shares. Windows XP prefers that you use the Network Setup Wizard to safely share files and printers. To share files locally, you simply drag files or folders into the Documents folder for the All Users profile (located in C:\Documents and Settings\). If you wish to share files or printers remotely, Microsoft recommends you use the Network Setup Wizard.

For more power and flexibility in sharing files, folders, and printers, you can enable Advanced File Sharing (in Windows XP Professional only). To do this, open any folder (or My Computer), choose the Tools menu, then Folder Options. Under the View tab there is a list of checkboxes for folder options. The very last item is usually "Use simple file sharing (Recommended)". If you uncheck this checkbox, you will have enabled Advanced mode. In Advanced mode, you must right-click on a folder or printer, choose Sharing and Security . . . , and you will be able to change all the typical settings for shared folders, such as the name of the share, the users, groups, and permissions for each object you are sharing, and even shared files caching (for offline use). The test is not likely to go into shared files caching. This type of sharing uses an Access Control List (ACL), just like all of the other secured objects in a Windows NT family operating system.

DIAGNOSING AND TROUBLESHOOTING TEST TIPS

Windows XP is quite a complicated operating system. Merging the best of all Windows worlds into a single platform creates a mammoth burden of information you will have to study and remember for the new A+ Operating Systems Technologies exam. The following refresher tips, as well as the review questions and practice exams on the CD-ROM, are designed to give you an edge in the exam room.

- ✓ Windows XP merges the Windows 9x and Windows NT families into a set of two operating systems, mostly based on Windows 2000: Windows XP Home Edition and Windows XP Professional.
- ✓ Windows XP Home can upgrade the following Windows operating systems: Windows 98, 98 SE, and Windows Millennium Edition.
- ✓ Windows XP Professional can upgrade the same ones as Windows XP Home, as well as: Windows NT 4.0 Workstation, Windows 2000 Professional, and Windows XP Home.
- ✓ You cannot upgrade any evaluation version or server version of Windows to Windows XP.
- ✓ Automated System Recovery requires Microsoft Backup, and ASR is only present in Windows XP Professional. Microsoft Backup for Windows XP Home is installable separately from the installation CD-ROM. Still, ASR is not available for Windows XP Home, even if you install Backup for Windows XP Home from the CD-ROM.
- ✓ You cannot create installation floppy disks from a Windows XP installation CD-ROM; you must download them from Microsoft.

- ✓ Windows XP Upgrade Advisor saves its reports to the WINDOWS directory by default.
- ✓ The protocol NetBEUI is no longer supported. It can be installed separately via the CD-ROM, however, but it is still officially unsupported by Microsoft.
- ✓ ACPI is an industry standard for controlling power management features, such as Standby and Hibernate, as well as assigning resources such as IRQs, DMAs, and I/O addresses to plug-and-play operating systems.
- ✓ WDM refers to a driver model supported in Windows Me and Windows XP. VxD files (virtual device drivers) are not supported in any Windows NT platform, including Windows XP. WHQL is the name of the Microsoft lab that performs driver testing and driver signing.
- ✓ WIA, developed by Microsoft, is a replacement technology for TWAIN, a driver model for scanners, cameras, and other imaging input devices.
- ✓ MSCONFIG's Diagnostic Startup permanently deletes all System Restore points.
- ✓ Point-to-Point Protocol over Ethernet (PPPoE), used for most ADSL or DSL installations, is supported internally by Windows XP.
- ✓ Microsoft recommends using the Network Setup Wizard to share files, folders, and printers, but you can enable Advanced file sharing by opening a folder window, choosing the Tools menu > Folder Options > View tab, and removing the check from "Use simple file sharing."
- ✓ Internet Connection Firewall will block file and printer sharing if used on a local network connection. ICF logs are stored in C:\WINDOWS (or C:\WINNT) as PFIREWALL.LOG, by default.

CHAPTER SUMMARY

Although Windows XP is a groundbreaking version of Windows that combines the best features of every version of the entire Windows family, it is by no means an easy task to apply and understand all of the possible technologies available. With the help of this chapter, you should now be well-versed in the intricate utilities and networking technologies present in Windows XP. Windows XP has been added to the A+ Operating Systems Technologies exam as a CompTIA 2003 Objective, and you should expect to see several questions regarding this operating system. You should now have a good understanding of the following ideals:

- The Windows XP installation and upgrade processes; specifically, which versions can be upgraded and which cannot.
- The Windows XP start-up process, including HAL and its functions.
- The basics of Remote Installation Service, unattended, and answer file based installations.

- Windows XP administration utilities, such as MMC, Backup, System Restore, Event Viewer, Device Manager, Remote Desktop, Remote Assistance, Recovery Console, and MSCONFIG.
- Profiles: local, roaming, and mandatory.
- Printer installation and troubleshooting.
- How to use Network Setup Wizard to configure networking components.
- How to use New Connection Wizard to connect to the Internet, especially with broadband adapters.
- How to install Internet Connection Firewall and understand what it can and cannot do.

The best way to assert your skills is to ensure that you understand not only which answer is the correct answer, but why a particular answer is correct and others are not. The following review questions will give you an opportunity to test your comprehension of this chapter, as well as help prepare you for the exam.

REVIEW QUESTIONS

1. While installed on a local area connection, an Internet Connection Firewall will do which of the following? (Choose Two)

□ A. Block unwanted outgoing traffic

□ B. Block unwanted incoming traffic

□ C. Block file and printer sharing traffic

□ D. Block unwanted cookies

Correct Answers = B and C

Internet Connection Firewall cannot block outgoing traffic. Cookies are documents created by Web pages that wish to store information about your visit to a particular site, and therefore are not blocked by ICF. File and printer sharing traffic is blocked only if you install ICF on a local area connection (instead of an Internet connection).

2. PPPoE is a technology used for which of the following connection types?

o A. Broadband

o B. Cable

o C. Dial-up

o D. ADSL

Correct Answer = D

Broadband is a general term that refers to carrying several data channels across a common wire. Cable TV, cable Internet, and DSL are all broadband technologies. The specific connection type that uses PPPoE is typically ADSL. PPPoE allows users to experience the same traditional login that they were used to on dial-up, as well as keeping Internet service provider costs down. PPPoE is very easy to implement on both the ISP and the end-user side.

3. To create a new user account you must navigate to:

o A. Control Panel > User Accounts

o B. User Manager > User Accounts

o C. Control Panel > Users

o D. Settings > Users

Correct Answer = A

Users are located in "User Accounts" and they are in the Control Panel. All other answers are invalid.

4. The acronym for the central administration utility is:

o A. MCA

o B. MCC

o C. MMC

o D. MAC

Correct Answer = C

MMC stands for Microsoft Management Console.

5. Time to Live references which of the following?

o A. The amount of route hops before a packet is discarded

o B. The time available to activate a Windows evaluation product

o C. The amount of latency between source and destination

o D. The contrast of Time to Die

Correct Answer = A

Without Time to Live, packets could float around the Internet for eternity. You can see a Time-to-Live value when you PING a remote computer. Latency is a value in milliseconds, also reported by the PING program. All other answers are invalid.

6. **The BOOT.INI tab of MSCONFIG shows you which of the following?**
   - o A. The boot paths of each Windows operating system installed
   - o B. Boot options for troubleshooting, such as /SAFEBOOT, /SOS, and /BASEVIDEO
   - o C. All of the above
   - o D. None of the above

   Correct Answer = C

   The BOOT.INI tab of MSCONFIG can show you the menu delay time-out, the default operating system, the settings for each operating system, and a button to diagnose and repair invalid BOOT.INI boot paths as well.

7. **Which folder commonly stores local profiles (e.g., Application Data)?**
   - o A. C:\My Documents\
   - o B. C:\Profiles and Settings\
   - o C. C:\Documents and Settings\
   - o D. C:\Documents and Profiles\

   Correct Answer = C

   Documents and Settings is the name of the folder that houses each user's My Documents, Application Data, Temporary Internet Files, cookies, and more. The rest are invalid responses. My Documents has been moved to Documents and Settings under your user name.

8. **Which version of Windows cannot be upgraded to Windows XP Professional?**
   - o A. 0Windows 98
   - o B. Windows NT 4.0
   - o C. Windows 2000 Professional
   - o D. Windows 3.1

   Correct Answer = D

   The only version of Windows listed here that cannot be upgraded to Windows XP Professional is Windows 3.1.

9. **Which file allows you to extract Setup Manager for creating answer files?**
   - o A. EMPLOY.CAB
   - o B. SETUPMGR.CAB
   - o C. ANSWER.CAB
   - o D. DEPLOY.CAB

   Correct Answer = D

An updated DEPLOY.CAB is available on Microsoft's Web site, but the original file on the installation CD-ROM (Support:Tools) also allows you to install Setup Manager. The other answers are fictitious.

10. BOOTSECT.DOS is:

- o A. A backed up copy of your old operating system's master boot record
- o B. A backed up copy of your old operating system's file system boot sector
- o C. A backed up copy of your old AUTOEXEC.BAT
- o D. A backed up copy of MS-DOS 6.22

Correct Answer = B

Not to be confused with the master boot record, a file system boot sector is an operating system partition's program that loads the operating system into RAM. A master boot record is your hard drive's overall table of contents, including partitions, and a program that actually loads the desired operating system partition's boot sector in order to launch the operating system. The master boot record is the first physical sector on a drive, and a file system boot sector is the first sector in any given logical volume or partition.

REFERENCES

http://microsoft.com/whdc/hcl/search.mspx. The latest Hardware Compatibility List from Microsoft.

http://microsoft.com/downloads/details.aspx?FamilyID=E8FE6868-6E4F-471C-B455-BD5AFEE126D8. The Windows XP Home floppy disk creation utility.

http://microsoft.com/downloads/details.aspx?FamilyID=55820edb-5039-4955-bcb7-4fed408ea73f. The Windows XP Professional floppy disk creation utility.

http://microsoft.com/downloads/details.aspx?familyid=7a83123d-507b-4095-9d9d-0a195f7b5f69. Updated Setup Manager to create answer files.

http://microsoft.com/downloads/details.aspx?FamilyID=4C7A0E4A-A0DC-46B3-9FDE-8149E223A494. Remote Installation Service (RIS) patch for Windows 2000 Professional/Server/Advanced Server.

http://microsoft.com/technet/treeview/default.asp?url=/TechNet/prodtechnol/winxppro/reskit/prbc_cai_facb.asp. Microsoft's in-depth article on installing using RIS.

ppendix About the CD-ROM

VIDEOS

Title	Filename
Opening Different Types of Cases and Accessing Internal Parts	Opening_the_Case.mpg
Installing Memory	Installing_Memory.mpg
Removal and Replacement of Expansion Cards	Removal_and_Replacement_of_Expansion_Cards.mpg
Installing CPUs	Installing_CPUs.mpg
Motherboard Installation	Motherboard_Installation.mpg
Vacuuming	Vacuuming.mpg

Video System Requirements

- Sound card
- Windows 95 or later
- A media player such as Windows Media Player (Start > Programs or All Programs > Accessories > Entertainment > Windows Media Player), available free from *microsoft.com/windowsmedia* if you don't already have it), or QuickTime (*apple.com/quicktime/products/qt*)
- Pentium 1 or equivalent and higher
- 16MB RAM

DOCUMENTS AND DOCUMENT SYSTEM REQUIREMENTS

These two documents are available in two file formats: .doc, which can be opened by Microsoft Word, Microsoft Wordpad (Start > Programs (or All Programs) > Accessories > Wordpad), and many other word processing programs; and in PDF format, which can be opened by Adobe Acrobat and Acrobat Reader. (The reader is available free from *adobe.com.*)

Beep Codes

Beep Codes.doc, Beep Codes.pdf, Beep Codes.htm

Industry Contacts

Industry Contacts.doc, Industry Contacts.pdf, Industry Contacts.htm

README

The README document is in .rtf, text, and .pdf formats. The text version (readme.txt) will open automatically in Microsoft Notepad. Any text editor or word processing program can open it. It can even be viewed by using the *Type* or *More* commands (see Appendix C, "Command-Line Tutorial," for instructions). The RTF file (readme.rtf) can be viewed in any word processing program, including Wordpad. The .pdf file can be opened in Adobe Acrobat and Adobe Reader. All of these documents are viewable on any PC with any of the aforementioned programs.

IMAGES AND IMAGE SYSTEM REQUIREMENTS

All of the images that appear elsewhere in Section 1 of this book are on the accompanying CD-ROM, in color. Any PC running Windows 95 and later with the default Windows component *Imaging* (Start > Programs or All Programs > Accessories > Imaging), or any other image-viewing program, and a minimum of 16MB of RAM can open the image files.

NOTE

The CD-ROM should autostart and open to an HTML index with hyperlinks to all the files. If not, open My Computer, double-click the optical drive, and double-click on the index.html file icon. You can also double-click individual files to open them.

A+ PRACTICE EXAMS

The CD-ROM included with this book contains A+ practice exams that will prepare you well for the CompTIA A+ Hardware Service Technician and Operating Systems Technologies examinations.

The practice exams included with the CD-ROM were created by the author specifically and exclusively for this book. Each practice exam is an interactive, timed test that features a review to identify incorrect answers and areas of weakness.

There are four practice exams. The first two exams contain practice questions for the A+ Core Hardware Service Technician test (Section 2A, Chapters 2 through 9). The second two exams contain practice questions for Operating Systems Technologies test (Section 2B, Chapters 10 through 15). Each exam has 80 questions. It is recommended that you take these tests until you score 100% every time. This will ensure your best chance to score well on the real CompTIA A+ examinations.

A+ Exam System Requirements

- CD-ROM drive
- Pentium 1 or equivalent and higher
- 16MB RAM
- SVGA or better video adapter
- Windows 95 or later
- Mouse or compatible pointing device
- Internet Explorer 5.0 or greater with JavaScript enabled. To download IE 6.0, go to *microsoft.com/windows/ie/*
- *downloads/ie6/default.asp.*

Installation

No installation is required. Simply insert the CD; it should autostart. Click on the hyperlink to start the exam. If the CD does not autostart, navigate to your CD-ROM drive letter, and double-click "A+ Practice Exam" to start the program. You can copy the program to your hard drive by copying the program file and "Include" folder to a local drive.

General Operation

Each exam contains 80 questions and must be completed within 90 minutes. You must correctly answer 64 of the 80 questions in each exam in order to pass. You will receive a score at the end of the exam or at any point you elect to end the exam.

At the end of each exam, a review option is available to check your answers. Exam scores are displayed on the startup page for the last practice of each exam.

Keyboard Shortcuts

There are two keyboard shortcuts available once a practice exam has been started.

To navigate to the next question after starting a practice exam, use Alt+N for Next.

To go back to the previous question, use Alt+B for Back.

SECURITY+ EXAM SAMPLE MATERIAL

Sample chapter, *Security+ Exam Guide* (TestTaker's Guide Series by Christopher A. Crayton). This sample chapter is included for those interested in pursuing the CompTIA Security+ Exam SY0-01. The filename is SecurityPlusC.pdf. This document can be opened in Adobe Acrobat and Adobe Acrobat Reader only.

Glossary

95 Microsoft Windows 95.

98 Microsoft Windows 98. Includes both the original and second editions unless otherwise noted.

98SE Microsoft Windows 98 Second Edition.

2000 Microsoft Windows 2000 Professional.

%systemroot% The Windows\System folder in 9x, and the Winnt\System32 folder or Windows\System32 folder in 2000 and XP. The actual folder used can vary. The percent marks indicate that the term is a variable.

AC (Alternating Current) Current that changes from a positive voltage to a negative voltage during one cycle. An example is household electricity in the United States, which is 110V at 60Hz.

ACPI (Advanced Configuration and Power Interface) A power management specification that makes better use of power by letting the operating system control the power provided to peripheral devices.

ADC or A/D (Analog-to-Digital Converter) A component on a sound card that converts analog sound to a digital bit stream.

ADSL (Asymmetric Digital Subscriber Line) A newer transmission technology in the global broadband access market. ADSL supports data rates from 1.5–9 Mbps when receiving data (known as the downstream rate) and from 16–640 Kbps when sending data (known as the upstream rate). Not only is ADSL winning devout followers with its impressive speed, but also quite impressively, such increased data flow occurs over existing copper telephone lines (POTS). With more than half the worlds broadband subscribers now using one variation of the technology or another, the long-term potential for this market is basically every phone line in the world.

AGP (Accelerated Graphics Port) A 32/64-bit expansion interface available on newer PCs that supports fast, three-dimensional graphics and provides the video controller card with a dedicated path to the CPU. The most common internal standard (as of this writing) for computer video. Uses SVGA connectors for monitors.

algorithm A mathematical formula designed to solve a problem by accounting for expected occurrences.

AMR (Audio Modem Riser) A new architectural design for motherboards developed by Intel. This new design places the analog I/O audio functions along with a codec chip on a small board, or 'riser.' This separation of the analog functions from the motherboard means higher audio quality and more flexibility for manufacturers' further design advancements, thus allowing them a way to side step the lengthy certification process of new motherboard designs.

ANSI (American National Standards Institute) A nonprofit organization whose primary purpose is to develop standards for the information technology industry.

API (Application Program Interface) A set of uniform routines or rules that allow programmers and developers to write applications that can be used to interact with various operating system platforms. APIs define system calls for service, and are the building blocks and tools used by programmers in building software applications.

APM (Advanced Power Management) User-level program found in all modern laptop computers and most modern desktop systems. Its features, which can be disabled, include system standby and hibernate. For the best results, Microsoft recommends that you disable advanced power management in the BIOS, since BIOS may have settings that Windows cannot override.

applet A small program within Windows that is used to configure certain aspects of hardware and software. The items in Control Panel are called applets—literally, "small applications."

application A computer program.

ARP (Address Resolution Protocol) A TCP/IP protocol used to determine the hardware MAC address for a network interface card.

ASCII (American Standard Code for Information Interchange) Specifies a 7-bit pattern that assigns numeric values to letters, numbers, punctuation marks, and certain other characters by standardizing the values used. ASCII enables communication between computers and peripherals by using numbers in place of characters.

ASR (Automated System Recovery) Backup tool in Windows XP that creates an image of your boot partition for restoration in case of failure or replacement of the boot hard drive.

AT (Advanced Technology) A discontinued form factor of case, motherboard, and power supply. IBM's name for its 80286 PC that was introduced in 1984. The AT form factor refers to the layout of the components on a motherboard.

ATA (Advanced Technology Attachment) The American National Standards Institute standard for IDE drives.

ATAPI (Advanced Technology Attachment Packet Interface) Interface standards that allow devices such as CD-ROM drives, Iomega Zip drives, and tape backup drives to utilize IDE/ATA controllers. The standard for IDE optical drives.

ATX (Advanced Technology Extensions) A more recent motherboard form factor that has replaced the AT form factor. ATX and its variations are the most commonly used form factors of case, motherboard, and power supply as of this writing. Variations include MicroATX and others

base video The minimum video Windows displays, usually 640x480 resolution with 16 colors. A PC can provide base video without any of the video drivers being loaded into memory, such as early in the boot process.

beta Early version of a program that is not ready to be sold. Users often can obtain a free beta version of a program to test its performance and report bugs to the developer.

BIOS (Basic Input/Output System) The BIOS is software built in to a ROM BIOS or flash BIOS chip that is used to control hardware devices such as hard drives, keyboards, monitors, and other low-level devices before a computer system boots into an operating system. It is a program that works as soon as the computer is powered on to test hardware, locate the operating system (OS) startup files on the hard drive in order to start the OS, and support the transfer of data among hardware devices.

bitmap A format of an image file that stores a map of each pixel along with the color information for each. Because of all this stored information, the files are rather large. In Windows, bitmap files have the extension .bmp. There are color, and black and white bitmaps.

blue screen of death The nickname of a Windows 2000 or XP stop error. When Windows detects a serious problem with the system, it shuts down the computer and dumps the contents of the memory to a file. It also displays a blue screen with the error data.

BNC (Bayonet Nut Connector, Bayonet Neil-Concelman, or British Naval Connector) A connector used to connect a computer to a coaxial cable in a 10Base2 Ethernet network.

bps (Bits Per Second) A standard measurement of the speed at which data is transmitted; for example, a 56K modem has the ability to transmit at a rate of 56,000 bps.

broadband High-speed Internet connection such as DSL or cable Internet, or faster business connections.

buffer underrun error An error that happens when burning an optical disc that causes the media to become useful as a beverage coaster. This error was prevalent with old CD burners.

bug A design flaw in a program.

burn-in test A series of individual tests used to make sure a new computer is running properly. A computer that passes the burn-in test is ready to sell to the customer.

cache (pronounced "cash"): 1. High-speed memory that is used on various types of hardware components. It is designed to enhance the performance of these devices by storing data in such a way as to make sure that it is transmitted smoothly to and/or from the device. Generally, the more cache a device has, the better it performs. Disk drives and CPUs are examples of devices with caches. Synonym: *buffer*. 2. An area in memory or on a disk drive that holds frequently accessed data.

CAD/CAM (Computer-Aided Design/Computer-Aided Manufacturing) Software designed with dual functionality—not only as a designing system, but also for controlling manufacturing processes.

case The cabinet that holds all parts of the computer. Most cases come with power supplies.

CAT (Computerized Adaptive Testing) An efficient testing process in which a test taker's selections of subsequent questions are based on the correctness or incorrectness of the previously answered questions. Therefore, the test is adapted to the test taker's ability, eliminating the possibility of too many items that are either too easy or too hard for them.

Cat5/Cat5e A standard for Ethernet network cables. Cables that don't meet the standard might not work well in networks, but should be adequate for voice telephone connections.

CCD (Charge-Coupled Device) A light-sensitive circuit in a device, such as a digital camera or optical scanner, which stores and displays the color representation of a pixel in electronic format. CCD arrays are made up of CCDs whose semiconductors connect.

CD (Compact Disk) A round metallic disk that stores information such as text, video, and audio in digital format.

CD-R (Compact Disk-Recordable) A type of compact disk that can be written or recorded to once, but read many times.

CD-RW (Compact Disk Read/Write) A type of compact disk that can be written to several times.

CEE power cord A three-conductor power cord used to connect computers, monitors, and many other devices to AC power. These are probably the most standard part of a computer, as almost every non-laptop computer power supply, CRT monitor, and many other devices use these.

CGA (Color Graphics Adapter) The first color graphics adapter for IBM PCs. CGA can only produce a resolution of 640 × 480 and two colors. CGA has been replaced by VGA for the most part.

check box A small square box within a dialog box that enables an event when there is a checkmark inside. Add a checkmark by *selecting* the check box. Remove the checkmark by *clearing* it. You can normally have any combination of selected and cleared check boxes in a dialog box.

chipset The set of integrated circuits used on a particular device.

CMOS (Complementary Metal-Oxide Semiconductor) Nonvolatile RAM that is used to hold hard drive, DRAM, and other necessary start-up information to boot a computer system. Modern CMOS is typically stored in flash RAM.

CNR (Communication and Networking Riser) A new riser card developed by Intel to meet open industry specifications. Besides its original purpose to reduce the cost of implementing LAN, modem, and audio subsystems, it also has the ability to keep electrical noise interference to a minimum.

coaster A failed optical disc burn resulting in a useless disc.

color depth Number of different shades of color that can be reproduced by a monitor or imaging device. In computers discussed in this book, color depth ranges from 16 to 4,294,967,295 colors.

COM port See *serial port.*

command-line interface See *text-based interface.*

composite video An analog video signal that is carried through one cable. The same signal that is used by all standard VCRs and by many computer video capture and video output devices.

compressed file A file that has been altered so that it takes up no unnecessary space. For example, a *bitmap* image file is one in which every picture element in the entire picture contains color or grayscale information. Because there are hundreds of thousands or millions of picture elements in various types of bitmap files, the files take up a lot of disk space. However, if you have a bitmap file containing an image that is mostly solid yellow with only a small drawing in one corner, the compression technique might use an *algorithm* that sets a range of all the picture elements that should be yellow and assigns yellow to all of them, rather than assigning yellow to each individual element. Such techniques make for a much smaller file. Some compressed files are self-extracting; that is, they open themselves when double-clicked. Others need some type of "unzip" program to open them. Still others are compressed and decompressed by Windows.

configure Make changes to device, software, or firmware settings.

cookie 1. A small file placed on a computer when the user visits and/or enters data into a Web page. The cookie is used to customize the Web page for the next time the user visits the page, sometimes by identifying the user, sometimes by remembering the information the user entered into a Web form. 2. The magnetic disk inside a floppy disk case.

CPU (Central Processing Unit) The CPU is the brain or central element of a computing system. The chip that performs all the calculations necessary for the computer to do its job. Intel's *Pentium* and *Celeron*, and AMD's *Athlon* and *Duron* are names of popular lines of CPUs. Synonym: *processor.*

CPU family Set of processors of a similar design made by one company. *Pentium 4* and *Athlon* are examples of CPU families.

CRT (Cathode Ray Tube) A vacuum tube located inside a monitor that houses beams of electrons used to illuminate phosphors and produce graphic images.

CSMA/CD (Carrier Sense Multiple Access with Collision Detection) A contention-based protocol used to detect collisions of packets in Ethernet networks. If a collision occurs, the information is retransmitted.

current folder When using a command interpreter such as the MS-DOS prompt or the Windows 2000, XP command prompt, the *current folder* is the one that most commands will affect unless another folder is specified in the command's syntax.

cursor The small image on the screen of a document that indicates the location where keyboard or other input will go. To illustrate the difference between a cursor and a pointer, note that the cursor in a document doesn't move along with the pointer until the pointing device is clicked, and that moving the cursor with any of the keyboard keys doesn't move the pointer. See also *pointer.*

DAC (Digital-to-Analog Converter) A device used to convert digital information to analog signals. A DAC is typically used by a modem to prepare information for analog phone line transmission.

DC (Direct Current) DC is the unidirectional movement or flow of electrons. DC is necessary for most electronic computer components.

Desktop The Windows screen that opens when the computer is booted. Contains the Start menu, the Task Bar, the System Tray, and all the icons.

desktop computer Originally meant to mean a computer in a horizontal case, it has come to mean any personal computer that is not portable.

developer Company or individual who makes software.

DHCP (Dynamic Host Configuration Protocol) A protocol used to dynamically assign IP addresses to computer systems in a TCP/IP network. DCHP eases administrative overhead by reducing the need to assign individual static IP addresses.

DHTML (Dynamic Hypertext Markup Language) A new form of HTML programming code that allows developers to create more-interactive or responsive Web pages for users.

dialog box A rectangular window containing configuration controls.

DIMM (Dual Inline Memory Module) A 64-bit data path memory module. In Pentium computers, one DIMM can be installed in a memory bank.

DIN AT The wide 5-pin plug/socket used to connect a keyboard to an AT motherboard.

DIP switch A tiny switch used for configuring some hardware devices, especially older devices.

directory See *folder*.

display See *monitor*.

DMA (Direct Memory Access) A technique used by computer devices to access and move data in and out of memory without interrupting the CPU. It is used by certain hardware devices such as hard drives, floppy drives, and sound cards to interact directly with system memory rather than burden the processor. Enable or disable DMA in a device's system property page.

DNS (Domain Name System) An Internet service that translates fully qualified domain names to computer IP addresses.

dongle A small cable with a telephone or Ethernet jack on one end, the other end of which plugs into a PC Card network adapter or modem. Dongles are usually fragile, especially at the plug that plugs into the PC Card. Many newer PC Cards have built-in jacks, making dongles unnecessary. See *PC Card*.

DOS (Disk Operating System) A 16-bit operating system developed by Microsoft that does not support true multitasking capabilities.

dpi (Dots Per Inch) A measurement of image resolution. The number of dots per horizontal inch is used to calculate the dpi that a device, such as a printer, is able to produce.

DRAM (Dynamic Random Access Memory) A popular type of memory used to store information in a computer system. DRAM chips must be electronically refreshed continuously to hold their data.

drive cage An assembly in a computer that holds disk drives.

driver, device A piece of software that allows the OS and programs to communicate with a hardware device. Hardware devices can't work without some type of driver, even if Windows' Device Manager indicates that no driver is necessary.

driver, generic A device driver that is designed to work with most or all devices in a general category of hardware devices, such as a video adapter or modem. Generic drivers usually don't allow all of a device's features to work. An example of a generic driver is the video driver that provides minimum video resolution and color depth when a computer first starts to boot.

DSL (Digital Subscriber Line) A popular high-speed technology that uses phone lines for Internet connectivity. The two most widely used forms of DSL are ADSL (Asymmetric Digital Subscriber Line) and SDSL (Symmetric Digital Subscriber Line).

dual-boot A computer with two separate OSs that are selectable at the time of boot.

DVD (Digital Versatile Disk or Digital Video Disk) A type of CD technology developed for full-length motion pictures that can hold 4.7GB to 17GB of information.

DVI Digital Video Interface. The standard interface for digital video on PCs. Digital monitors and video adapters have DVI connectors.

DVO The digital video header connector on a motherboard for connection of a digital video adapter.

ECC (Error Correction Code or Error Checking and Correction) A technique used to test data for errors as it passes out of memory. If errors are found, ECC attempts to make the necessary corrections.

ECP (Extended Capabilities Port) An IEEE 1284 bidirectional parallel port standard that offers faster transfer rates than traditional parallel port standards. ECP is most often used for communication between computer systems and printers or scanners.

EDO (Extended Data Output) A type of DRAM that has the ability to read more information before needing to be refreshed. EDO is much faster than its predecessor, FPM DRAM.

EEPROM (Electrical Erasable Programmable Read-Only Memory) A type of PROM chip whose can be changed or erased with an electronic charge. EEPROM chips were very popular before the introduction of flash ROM chips.

EFS (Encrypting File System) A feature first fully implemented with Windows 2000 that enables any file or folder to be stored in an encrypted format by making the encryption an attribute of that file or folder. Only an individual user or an authorized recovery agent can decrypt the file or folder. This feature is extremely useful for storing highly sensitive data.

EGA (Enhanced Graphics Adapter) IBM introduced EGA in 1984. The EGA standard for video adapters offers a resolution of up to 640 × 350 and supports up to 16 colors. EGA has been replaced by VGA and is for the most part obsolete.

EIDE (Enhanced IDE) An enhancement to the IDE hard drive standard that offers access to hard drives larger than 528MB through the use of LBA support. The EIDE standard also offers support for DMA, for up to four attached devices (including tape drives and CD devices), and for faster hard drive access time.

El Torito specification A standard for CD-ROM drives that allows the computer to boot from a CD-ROM.

EMI (Electromagnetic Interference) An electronic phenomenon that occurs when the signal from two or more electronic devices interferes with each other. EMI can occur when one data cable is placed too close to a second cable. If the electrical signals cross, the integrity of the information passing along the data cable may be affected.

EMS (Expanded Memory Specification) A memory management tool used to gain access to memory above the 640K-memory limitation in an MS-DOS-based environment. Advances in the ways that Windows manages access to memory has for the most part eliminated the need for EMS.

environment variable In Windows and DOS, the setting of the path that enables the system to locate certain Windows program files and commands when entered into the command prompt or Run dialog. Although the term *environment variable* technically means anything that can be changed in a computer, the aforementioned definition represents the most important and common use of the term. See *path.*

EPP (Enhanced Parallel Port) An IEEE parallel port interface standard. Also known as IEEE 1284, EPP supports bidirectional or half-duplex data transmission methods.

EPROM (Erasable Programmable Read-Only Memory) A ROM chip whose contents can be erased by shining an ultraviolet light through a hole in the top of the chip.

ESD (Electrostatic Discharge) The movement or transfer of electrons from one location to another. Static electricity can be transferred from the human body to an electronic component, causing damage to the components. ESD can be avoided by wearing an ESD-protective wrist strap when working with components.

Ethernet The most common network system, usually making use of unshielded twisted-pair cables with RJ-45 connectors.

expansion slots Slot connectors on the motherboard for attaching various components. Motherboards typically have several expansion slots.

extension, filename Character(s) after the final period in a filename. The extension tells the OS what type of file it is, and Windows associates certain programs with each known file extension so that the file can be opened with minimum delay. For example, in the file chapter1.txt, "txt" is the extension, and it indicates a text file that would normally be opened by a text editor such as Notepad. Most file extensions are hidden by default in Windows; change this setting by going to Control Panel > Folder Options > View tab and clearing the "Hide file extensions for known file types" check box.

FAT (File Allocation Table) A table consisting of clusters that are logical units of information located on a hard drive and used by the operating system to identify the location of stored entries or files.

FIFO (First-In, First-Out) A data storage method in which the oldest information is read or used first.

file system System of storing data on a disk. File systems discussed in this book are FAT16, FAT32, NTFS, and various optical drive file systems. Not all versions of Windows can access all file systems.

firewall A hardware- or software-based mechanism for blocking unwanted access to a computer over a network or the Internet.

FireWire A high-throughput hardware interface standard that allows many devices to be connected to a single port with only the FireWire controller using any Device Manager resources. Synonym: *IEEE 1394*.

firmware Flash memory that is used to manage the basic operation of hardware devices. The most well-known example of firmware is a computer's BIOS. Other devices, such as optical drives, have firmware. Firmware can be updated via a process called *flashing*.

flash memory Expensive memory that holds its data indefinitely after the power has been disconnected, but the data can be changed in a process called *flashing*. Flash memory chips are used for devices such as digital cameras, data storage devices on computers, and BIOSs.

flat panel monitor A physically thin monitor, such as a laptop monitor, that uses light-emitting semiconductors rather than a glass picture tube. Contrast with *CRT monitor*.

flat screen monitor A CRT monitor in which the viewable portion of the glass picture tube is flat, not curved. Not to be confused with a *flat panel monitor*.

floppy disk drives Devices that store data on removable magnetic disks. Virtually all floppy drives sold since the mid-1990s have been of the 3.5-inch variety. These floppy disks are enclosed in a thin, hard, plastic shell. Because of this, they are sometimes confused with hard drives. Because of their limited capacity, their susceptibility to data loss, and other reasons, floppy disks have become much less useful in recent years. However, floppy disks can be indispensable for certain repairs. Synonyms: *floppies, diskette drives, FDDs*.

folder A virtual container used by Windows to organize files. Formerly called *directories*.

form factor A standard of shapes, sizes, and mounting designs of hardware devices such as cases, power supplies, motherboards, hard drives, and others.

FPM (Fast Page Mode) A DRAM memory type that makes use of memory paging, which increases overall memory performance. Most DRAM memory types are FPM.

FPU (Floating-Point Unit) A math coprocessor that is built into the CPU. An FPU is designed to handle higher-end mathematical equations that assist with today's complex formulas and graphical calculations.

Front Side Bus (FSB) The channel that connects the processor with main memory. The faster the FSB, the better the performance. As of this writing, this number will range between 33 and 800 MHz.

FRU (Field-Replaceable Unit) An interchangeable or replaceable computer part or component that can be installed at a customer's site or remote business location by a computer technician.

FTP (File Transport Protocol) A transfer protocol primarily used on the Internet to transfer files from one location to another.

GB (Gigabyte) A measurement of computer system data storage space. One gigabyte is equal to 1024MB, or approximately 1 million kilobytes.

GPS (Global Positioning System) A worldwide satellite navigational system that was designed originally for the U.S. military under the name NAVSTAR (Navigation System with Timing and Ranging).

Even though its utility has crossed over into the civilian sector, it is still operated by the U.S. Department of Defense. Twenty-four GPS satellites continuously transmit digital radio signals of data, such as the satellite's location and the exact time, to their corresponding earth-bound receivers. By knowing how far away a satellite is from its receiver and its location on an imaginary sphere, GPS can be used to calculate longitude, latitude, and even altitude.

graphics adapter See *video card.*

graphics card See *video card.*

GUI (Graphical User Interface, pronounced *"gooey"*) The Windows interface that makes use of graphical elements for controls, using such objects as buttons to click and the procedure of clicking and dragging. Contrast to *text-based interface.*

HAL (Hardware Abstraction Layer) Allows an operating system to interact with hardware devices at a more general or abstract level.

hang When a program or OS process gets stuck at a certain point and doesn't continue.

hard drive A device that stores data on permanently enclosed magnetic disks. The vast majority of computers have at least one hard drive. Data stored on a hard drive remains after the power is disconnected. The OS (such as Windows), along with programs and data, are almost always stored on a hard drive. Synonyms: *hard disk drive,* HDD.

HCL (Hardware Compatibility List) A document that contains a list of all hardware compatible with a specific OS.

heat sink A small metal radiator used to allow heat to dissipate from heat-producing electrical devices, especially processors. Fans are often mounted on heat sinks to facilitate dissipation of heat.

hex number See *hexadecimal number.*

hexadecimal number A base-16 number. With decimal numbers, after 9 comes 0, and the 1 is carried over into the next column. Hex numbers include the following digits: 0123456789ABCDEF. After F comes 0, and the 1 is carried over into the next column. For example, F *hex* equals 15 in decimal, and 10 *hex* equals 16 in decimal. The purpose of hex numbers is to shorten what would otherwise be very long decimal numbers when referring to random access memory addresses and input/output addresses on a computer.

hibernate Saving the desktop as it is with all open programs and applets the way they are to the hard drive, and then shutting off the power. When power is resumed, the desktop should appear exactly as it was when it was hibernated. Synonym: *suspend.*

HMA (High Memory Area) The memory location consisting of the first 64K of the extended memory area. The HMA is controlled by the software driver HIMEM.SYS.

hot-pluggable Capable of being connected or disconnected from the computer or peripheral without risk of damage. Synonym: *Hot-swappable.*

HTML (Hypertext Markup Language) A programming language that is used to create pages or hypertext documents on the World Wide Web. HTML is a scripting language that uses tags to define the way Web pages are displayed. E-mail messages using anything more than plain text use HTML.

HTTP (Hypertext Transport Protocol) A fast Internet application protocol used for transferring data.

HVD (High-Voltage Differential) A now obsolete form of 'differential' signaling that is commonly used for long runs in noisy areas. LVD (Low-Voltage Differential) is the new technology replacing HVD.

IDC (Insulation Displacement Connector) A type of connector that displaces the insulation on a cable, allowing an electrical contact between the terminal and conductor. Insulation displacement occurs as the cable is pressed into a terminal slot smaller than the conductor diameter. Insulation displacement technology has become a highly effective alternative to stripping and soldering wire in thousands of applications, with its greatest benefit being placement spread.

IDE (Intelligent or Integrated Drive Electronics) A specification for hard disk and CD-ROM drive interfaces whose drive controllers are integrated onto the drive itself. IDE provides support for up to two drives per system, whereas EIDE supports up to four drives per system. Today, the more common reference used for this technology is ATA.

IEEE (Institute of Electrical and Electronics Engineers) The world's leading international standards organization whose primary purposes are the development of information technology standards and the welfare of its members.

IEEE 1284 A standard for parallel cables. IEEE 1284-certified cables are more likely than noncertified cables to work reliably.

IEEE 1394 See *FireWire.*

initialize To start a hardware device.

I/O (Input/Output) A term used to describe devices and programs that transfer information into and out of a computer system. Input devices can include keyboards, mice, and touch screens. Output devices can include printers, monitors, and plotters.

I/O address A location of a hardware device communication channel in a motherboard. Expressed in a hex number. I/O address ranges must be different for each hardware device installed in a computer.

IP (Internet Protocol) A TCP/IP protocol used primarily to allow computers to be connected in a local area network or to the Internet.

IPX/SPX (Internetwork Packet Exchange/Sequence Packet Exchange) A Novell networking protocol used primarily with Novell Netware.

IRQL or IRQ (Interrupt ReQuest Line or Interrupt Request) A channel from a hardware device to the processor used to get the processor to respond to the device's request for attention. There are a limited number of IRQs on a computer, and two devices cannot use the same IRQ at the same time. If two devices attempt to use the same IRQ to communicate with the CPU, an IRQ conflict will most likely occur.

ISA (Industry Standard Architecture) An industry standard that describes the expansion bus architecture for the IBM AT and XT PCs. ISA expansion slots can still be found in some systems today, although they are steadily being replaced by PCI and AGP technology.

ISDN (Integrated Services Digital Network) A digital communications standard that allows data and voice to be used on the same phone line connection. ISDN provides support for up to 128Kbps transfer rates and is intended to replace traditional analog technology.

ISP (Internet Service Provider) A company whose primary business is to provide access to the Internet for other companies and individuals.

jumper A small connector used to connect two pins together on a circuit board for the purpose of configuration.

KB (Kilobyte) 1,024 bytes.

Kbps (Kilobits Per Second) A measurement of data transfer rate. One kilobit per second is equivalent to 1,000 bits per second.

key 1. A notch or other physical feature that prevents a devices from being inserted into a slot the wrong way 2. The top level portions of the Windows registry.

knowledge base A collection of all technical information about a manufacturer's or developer's products. Almost always searchable on the Web.

LAN (Local Area Network) A network of computers that are typically connected in a central location, such as a building. In a LAN, computers are connected by wires or other media and share common resources, such as printers, files, and modems.

laptop A small portable computer. Although laptops are generally considered larger than *notebooks,* the two terms are often used interchangeably, including in this book.

LBA (Logical Block Addressing) An enhanced BIOS translation method used for IDE and SCSI disk drives that allows accessibility beyond the 504MB limit imposed by traditional IDE. LBA is a way of addressing hard drives by assigning numbers to each sector on the drive. These numbers run sequentially, with zero representing the first sector. Originally used with SCSI drives, IDE drives began to support LBA with the advent of larger (over 504MB) IDE drives. Basically, it is a translation of the cylinder, head, and sector specifications of a drive into addresses that can be used by a 'translating' BIOS.

LCD (Liquid Crystal Display) A technology for flat screen displays that uses polarized sheets and liquid crystals to produce images. LCD technology was originally used for laptop computers and watches, but is becoming very popular for desktop computers.

LED (Light-Emitting Diode) A highly efficient, long-lasting light that illuminates when electrical current passes through it. Most LEDs are usually a monochromatic red. Benefits of LEDs include ability to display images, low power requirements, long life, and high efficiency. However, they require more power than LCDs.

legacy Of or pertaining to any hardware using standards older than the computer on which they are to run. Also refers to versions of software that have been replaced by a newer version and data files created on such software.

load Automatically copy files from disk into memory. When Windows or a program starts, it's actually loading into memory.

lockup Situation in which the computer stops responding. The screen image and pointer freeze, keyboard lights get stuck, and hard drive activity stops.

LSA (Local Security Authority) The LSA is a key component of the logon process in both Windows NT and Windows 2000. For example, in Windows 2000, the LSA validates users for both local and remote logons.

LVD (Low-Voltage Differential) An Ultra2 subset of the SCSI-3 standard, LVD increases the maximum burst transfer rates to 80Mbytes/sec, which is a requirement for multiple drive applications. Such increases in bandwidth means optimal performance for server environments where rapid response is required. LVD uses less power (3.3V DC) than high-voltage differentials (5.0V DC).

malware Programs that can cause various problems on a computer or can steal your personal data.

MAN (Metropolitan Area Network) A network that is smaller than a WAN, but larger than a LAN. It is usually confined to a city block or a college campus.

map a network drive Assigning a drive letter to a folder or drive partition on a remote computer on the network.

MAPI (Messaging Application Programming Interface) A Microsoft application programming interface that provides the ability to send e-mail and attachments from within programs such as Word, Excel, PowerPoint, and Access.

MAU (Multistation Access Unit) A special hub used in a Token Ring network that is used to connect computers for a star topology network while maintaining Token Ring capabilities. It is also known as MSAU.

MB (Megabyte) 1,024 kilobytes or 1,048,576 bytes.

MBR (Master Boot Record) The MBR is the first sector on a hard drive. A small program on the MBR contains information about the partitions, indicating which one is bootable, in case there are more than one.

MCA (Micro Channel Architecture) A proprietary 32-bit expansion bus developed by IBM for its PS/2 computers.

MDA (Monochrome Display Adapter) A standard for monochrome adapters introduced by IBM. Monochrome is only capable of displaying text.

Me Microsoft Windows Millennium Edition. Microsoft uses the lower-case "e," so we do too.

media Disks, flash memory, or other materials used for data storage.

memory Chip assemblies that store data for very quick recall. The main memory in a computer requires constant power to be able to hold data. Every task performed by a computer requires the program and data to be loaded into memory. Information that is held in memory can be quickly accessed by the computer's CPU without the need to read the data preceding the required information. Synonym: *random access memory (RAM).*

MFD (Multifunction Device) Any device that is capable of multiple functions. For example, with printers, you can have a laser (or ink-jet) printer capable of all the following: print, copy, scan, and fax.

MicroATX A small, commonly used (as of this writing) form factor of case, motherboard, and power supply. Based on *ATX*.

MicroDIMM (Micro Dual Inline Memory Module) Commonly used in subnotebook computers, each 144-pin MicroDIMM provides a 64-bit data path, so they are installed singly in 64-bit systems.

MIDI (Musical Instrument Digital Interface) A standard or protocol used for the interface between a musical instrument or device and a computer system. It is used in digital synthesizers for playing and manipulating sound.

MMC (Microsoft Management Console) Management application that draws upon a graphical user interface and a programming framework to allow the creation and saving of consoles. This is particularly important, since consoles are used to manage Windows-based software and hardware.

MMX (Multimedia Extensions) A multimedia technology developed by Intel to improve the performance of its Pentium microprocessor. MMX technology included 57 new processor instructions and is said to improve multimedia application performance up to 60%.

Modem (Modulator-Demodulator) A communication device used to convert signals so they can be transmitted over conventional telephone lines. A modem converts incoming analog signals to digital format and outgoing digital signals to analog format. It allows the computer to access a telephone line for the purpose of faxing, Internet access, data transfer between computers, or other telecommunications-related uses. Internal modems plug into expansion slots, while an external modem connects to a port on the computer.

monitor A device resembling a television that displays the computer's video images. Synonyms: *screen, display.*

motherboard The large printed-circuit board to which all other parts are connected. Synonyms: *system board, main board, desktop board.*

MPEG (Motion Picture Experts Group) A standards group that works with the ISO to establish rules and standards for audio and video compression. MPEG technology is used to make high-quality compressed files.

MSCDEX (Microsoft CD-ROM Extensions) A software driver used in Windows 3x and DOS to allow the operating systems to communicate with CD-ROM devices. The actual file that contains the driver is called MSCDEX.EXE. More-efficient 32-bit CD-ROM drivers, such as CDFS, have replaced MSCDEX.EXE.

MSDS (Material Safety Data Sheet) Designed to provide employers, employees, and EMS personnel with the proper procedures for various substances and chemicals, the data sheet is broken down into 10 sections: General Information; Ingredients; Physical Data; Fire and Explosion Data; Health Hazard Data; Reactivity Data; Spill, Leak, and Special Disposal Features; Special Protection Information; Special Precautions; and Transportation Data. Access to MSDSs include workplace laboratories, universities, the product's distributor, and online.

multimedia The combination of sound and various forms of graphics including video and animation. Although the prefix "multi" indicates more than one, many people incorrectly use the term to refer to sound only.

multiple-boot A computer with three or more OSs that can be selected when booting.

multitester A device used to test various properties of electrical currents and circuits such as voltage, continuity, and resistance. Most commonly used in computer repair for testing power supplies.

NetBEUI (NetBIOS Extended User Interface) An extended or enhanced version of the NetBIOS protocol.

NetBIOS (Network Basic Input Output System) An application programming interface (API) protocol that expands the utility of the DOS BIOS by adding special functions for Local-Area Networks (LANs). The message format (SMB) provides the foundation for NetBIOS.

network A collection of two or more computers and other devices that can communicate with each other so that the users and computers can share information and hardware devices such as printers.

network card A device that connects the computer to the network. Network cards come in the form of a separate card or are built in to the motherboard. It is an electronic circuit board that attaches a computer to a network. It connects to a wire that typically leads to a networked hub, router, or bridge. Synonyms: *network adapter, network interface card, NIC.*

newsgroup A group of subscribers who can post and reply to messages over the Internet using a newsreader program such as Outlook Express. Microsoft and other companies make use of newsgroups for professional and peer technical support. See *Usenet.*

NIC (Network Interface Card) See *network card.*

NLX (InteLex Form Factor) A computer motherboard form factor designed to provide more room for components than the LPX form factor.

NNTP (Network News Transfer Protocol) A protocol used to manage messages that are posted to Usenet newsgroups.

notebook A small portable computer. Although notebooks are supposed to be smaller than laptops, the two terms are often used interchangeably, including in this book.

NTFS (NT File System) A Windows NT hard drive file system that offers file- and object-level security features, file compression, encryption, and long file name support. A new version of the NTFS file system, called NTFS5, is offered with the Windows 2000 operating system.

OEM (Original Equipment Manufacturer) Refers to any product that is designed for manufacturers and retail computer builders to supply with their equipment. For example, Microsoft requires end users of OEM versions of Windows to get technical support from the manufacturer or computer builder rather than from Microsoft.

OLE (Object Linking and Embedding) A specification created by Microsoft that allows objects created in one program or application to be embedded or linked to other applications. With OLE, if a change is made to an application, the change is also made to the second application.

optical drives Includes *CD-ROM, CD-RW, DVD-ROM,* and various writable DVD drives. Optical drives are devices that read, or read *and* write data from or onto discs using laser beams.

option button One of at least two small round circles within a dialog box that can be *selected* (a dot placed inside) or *cleared* (the dot removed). With option buttons, normally only one in a group can be selected at a time. Originally referred to as "radio buttons," which came from old car radios with mechanical station preset buttons, in which only one button could be pushed in at a time.

OSI (Open Systems Interconnect) The OSI reference model is a networking model developed to provide network designers and developers with a model that describes how network communication takes place.

page file The file used by Windows for virtual memory. Synonym: *swap file.*

paging When Windows moves data between memory and the page file for the use of virtual memory.

parallel An interface used for external devices such as printers and scanners. Parallel devices communicate with the system by sending as many as eight electrical pulses simultaneously.

patch Software designed to fix problems in other software.

path 1. The hierarchy of drives, folders, and subfolders that indicates the location of a file, folder, printer, or other element. In a network, the path can include the computer, usually in the form of the computer name preceded by two backslashes. The indication of the location of commands in a command prompt or Run dialog. Usually called *the path*. When you change an *environment variable* related to the path to commands or Windows program files, you change the path to those commands or files.

PC Card A credit card-sized hardware device that plugs into a slot in a laptop or the occasional desktop with a PC Card slot. The most common PC Card devices are modems and network adapters. The term *PC Card* replaced the term *PCMCIA* because nobody wanted to pronounce a six-syllable term. There are three main types of PCMCIA cards. Type I is used mainly for RAM, Type II is used for modems, and Type III is used for hard disks.

PCI (Peripheral Component Interconnect) A 32- to 64-bit expansion bus created by Intel and used in most modern computers. Today, most NICs, sound cards, and modems are connected to a motherboard through a PCI expansion bus.

PCI Special Interest Group (SIG) Originally formed as the Peripheral Component Interconnect Special Interest Group, PCI SIG is the industry organization chartered with the development and management of the PCI bus specification, the industry standard for a high-performance I/O interconnect to transfer data between a CPU and its peripherals. Founded in 1992, PCI SIG stands at the forefront of its field and can tout an active membership base of 850 industry-leading companies. To reach PCI SIG, visit them online at *http://www.pcisig.com*, or by phone at (800) 433-5177, or by fax at (503) 693-8344.

PCMCIA (Personal Computer Memory Card Industry Association) See *PC Card*.

PDA (Personal Data Assistant) A small handheld mobile computing device that provides functions similar to a desktop or laptop computer. Most PDAs today use a pen or stylus in place of a keyboard to input data.

PDF (Portable Document Format) A file format developed by Adobe Systems. PDF captures all the formatted elements of a printed document from a multitude of desktop publishing applications and converts them into an electronic image. Therefore, it is easier and to view, print, and send the formatted documents to others. To view the files, you need the free Acrobat Reader. PDF files are most beneficial when needing to maintain the online graphic appearance, quality, and clarity of documents, such as for brochures, maps, and magazines.

PIF (Program Information File) A file that is used to provide settings for 16-bit DOS applications. A PIF file has a .PIF extension and stores information such as window size and memory that should be allocated to an application or program.

pins Conductive metal pieces that are part of electrical connectors.

pixel The smallest picture element in a video display or an image file.

PnP (Plug and Play) A technology introduced in Windows 95 that has the ability to autodetect devices that are attached to a computer system. In order for a system to be fully PnP compliant, there must be a PnP operating system, a PnP BIOS, and PnP devices.

pointer The image on a computer screen that indicates the location of the pointing device control.

pointing device A device that is used to move the on-screen pointer and choose or select screen elements. A mouse is the most common pointing device.

port Connector on the outside of a computer to which peripheral devices can be connected. Examples are parallel, serial, PS/2, VGA, USB, and FireWire. Not to be confused with the networking term.

POST (Power-On Self-Test) A program that tests computer components at system start-up, such as RAM, disk drives, and peripherals. If the POST finds a problem during its diagnostic testing, it usually reports a numeric error to the screen or sounds a series of beep error codes.

POST card A card that can be plugged into an expansion slot and contains a small display to a show a problem code. A POST card is ideal for diagnosing computers that won't boot. It can be a great timesaver.

POTS (Plain Old Telephone Service) Also known as the Public Switched Telephone Network (PSTN), most homes have this telephone service. This standard service is in comparison to high-speed, digital services such as ISDN. Speed and bandwidth are the criteria that differentiate between POTS and non-POTS services. Generally, the standard speed for POTS is limited to about 52Kbps.

power supply A box-shaped device that converts wall-outlet AC power to low-voltage DC used to power the devices in the computer.

processor See *CPU.*

PROM (Programmable Read-Only Memory) A ROM chip that can be written to once.

properties, property page A dialog box that presents information about a device, folder, or file, usually allowing one or more configuration options.

protocol, network A piece of software containing rules for a particular networking purpose. Every network connection requires all parties to be using the same protocol in order to communicate.

PS/2 Interface for keyboards and pointing devices on most ATX-based motherboards.

RAID (Redundant Array of Independent (or Inexpensive) Disks) A way of storing the same data in different places on a category of disk drives that employ two or more drives. This allows for a combination of increased fault tolerance and improved performance. RAID disk drives are more frequently used on servers rather than personal computers. There are a number of different RAID levels, with the three most common being RAID 0, RAID 3, and RAID 5.

RAM See *memory.*

RAMDAC (Random Access Memory Digital-to-Analog Converter) A chip on a video card that converts binary digital data into analog information, which can then be output to a computer monitor.

RDRAM (Rambus Dynamic Random Access Memory) A type of fast DRAM memory originally developed by Rambus, Inc. for today's Pentium computers.

read Detect data from storage media. Technically, transfer data from a file into memory.

readme file File that comes with software or hardware that contains useful information to the user.

rewritable An optical disc that can be written to, erased, and written to again. Includes CD-RWs and recordable DVDs.

RGB (Red, Green, and Blue) The three primary colors of light that are used in PC monitors. A color monitor has three electron guns. Each of the electron guns represents one of the three primary colors of light to produce a final color image to computer screen.

RJ-11 A modular one-line telephone connector with two wires: red and green. An RJ11 connector has the same plastic shell as an RJ-14 connector.

RJ-14 A modular two-line telephone connector with four wires: red and green for line 1, and black and yellow for line 2. An RJ-14 connector has the same plastic shell as an RJ11 connector.

RJ-45 A modular telephone or network connector with eight wires. In order to be used with Ethernet networks, RJ-45 connectors must adhere to the Cat5 or Cat5e standard.

ROM (Read-Only Memory) A computer chip whose information cannot be deleted or erased, but which can be read by the system many times. ROM is nonvolatile memory that holds the system BIOS.

root folder The highest-level folder in a disk partition. If you open My Computer, and then any drive, you are looking at the root folder. For example, C:\ is the root directory of the C drive. Any files or folders you see with C:\ open are said to be in the root folder. Often called *root directory.*

SAM (Security Accounts Manager) A built-in Windows NT and 2000 component that is used to manage the security of user accounts.

SAT (Security Access Token) A security token that allows users access to resources in a Windows environment. A token carries access rights that are associated with a user's account.

SCSI (Small Computer System Interface) A standard that applies to fast electronic hardware interfaces in computer systems. SCSI technology can be used to allow up to 15 devices to be daisy-chained together. SCSI is most commonly used to connect hard drives, CD-ROM devices, scanners, and printers to computer systems.

SDRAM (Synchronous Dynamic Random Access Memory) A type of DRAM that synchronizes itself with the internal clock speed of the computer's processor.

SE (Single Ended) One of two kinds of parallel SCSI technology, the second kind being differential ended. Single-ended SCSI was the original technology used and has shorter distances than its counterpart. They are incompatible, although converters can bridge single ended to differential. It can also be used to refer to the physical signal circuitry used on the SCSI bus.

SEC (Single Edge Connector) Intel's chip package design that uses a circuit board with a single edge connector. A processor and memory cache are integrated onto the circuit board and inserted into the computer system's motherboard.

SEP (Single Edge Processor) A processor chip package design similar to SEC.

Serial ATA (S-ATA) A completely new standard based on serial signaling technology that will eventually make PCs even smaller and more efficient. Serial ATA only requires seven wires per device (as compared to 40 wires for IDE ribbon cables), and its cables are capable of lengths of one meter (as compared to 40 centimeters for IDE). S-ATA will eventually render the old IDE ribbon cables obsolete, resulting in an industry-wide move over to new hard drives, controllers, and connectors.

serial port A port through which electrical pulses are sent one at a time. Used for external modems and other devices. Original IBM PCs had four serial ports, with each assigned a logical address called a *COM port.*

server A computer that provides services to other computers on a network, called *clients* or *workstations.* Servers tend to be high-powered machines.

service A small program or part of a program whose purpose is supporting larger programs or OS components. In 2000 and XP, access Services in Administrative Tools from Control Panel, Start menu, or Manage.

setup The installation of software, including Windows. Synonym: *installation* (only of software).

setup program The BIOS configuration program.

SGRAM (Synchronous Graphic Random Access Memory) A single-ported type of video RAM that is synchronized with the CPU's clock to achieve high speeds.

shell The system that gives the user control of the OS. In the case of Windows, the shell is the *GUI.*

SID (Security Identifier) A unique security number that is associated with users, groups, and accounts in a Windows NT and 2000 Network. Access to processes that run in Windows NT and 2000 require this unique SID and a token.

SIMM (Single Inline Memory Module) A type of circuit board on which DRAM chips are mounted. The circuit board is inserted into the motherboard. A SIMM module has a 32-bit wide data bus.

slot A horizontal multi-pin electrical connector that accepts a card-type connector. Expansion cards such as PCI, AGP, and ISA are slots. In addition, some processors, including many Pentium IIIs, plug into slots.

S.M.A.R.T. (Self Monitoring Analysis and Report Technology) An example of a computer's start-up program or BIOS and the computer's hard disk proactively working together. If enabled during computer setup, it has the ability to automatically monitor a disk drive's health and report potential problems. The BIOS receives analytical information from the hard drive and determines whether to send the user a warning message about possible future failure of the hard drive.

SMB (Server Message Block) A protocol used by DOS and Windows for sharing files, directories, serial ports, printers, and other devices. SMB works in a client server, request-response format. Such servers make file systems and other resources available to clients over a network. SMB can be used over TCP/IP, NetBEUI, and IPX/SPX.

socket A flat electrical connector with holes. A device such as a socket processor has pins that plug into the holes.

SODIMM (Small-Outline Dual Inline Memory Module) Commonly used in laptop computers because of their thinner profiles than DIMMs.

sound card A device whose primary function is to allow a computer to play and record sound. A sound card can either be a separate card that plugs into an expansion slot, or a component built into the motherboard. Sometimes called a *multimedia device.*

SQL (Structured Query Language) A programming language used to gather or query information from various computer databases. IBM developed SQL in 1974.

SRAM (Synchronous Random Access Memory) A fast type of memory that does not have to be refreshed over and over to maintain its contents. SRAM is faster than DRAM and is used mostly for cache memory in computer systems. SRAM is also referred to as static RAM.

standby Saving the desktop as it is with all open programs and applets the way they are to memory, and then operating on low power. In most cases, you can resume from standby by moving or clicking the pointing device, or by pressing any keyboard key.

stop error See *blue screen of death.*

STP (Shielded Twisted Pair) A type of copper cabling used in networks in which pairs of wires are twisted around one another to extend the length that a signal can travel on the cable and reduce the interference of signals traveling on the cable.

surge suppressor A device designed to absorb increases in voltage that can damage computers, peripherals, or other devices. Most very inexpensive models provide little or no protection.

suspend See *hibernate.*

SVGA (Super Video Graphics Array) A video display standard that applies to any resolution or color depth higher than the VGA standard of 640x480 and 16 colors. Based on its predecessor, VGA, which uses the same connectors.

swap file See *page file.*

syntax The proper way to type commands with their parameters and switches.

tab A graphical depiction of the tab on a paper file folder. Click a tab to select a different page in a dialog box or property sheet. Sometimes used to represent the entire page that a tab is on.

TB (Terabyte) 1,024 gigabytes, approximately 1 million megabytes, or 1,099,551,627,776 bytes.

TCP/IP (Transmission Control Protocol/Internet Protocol) The primary set of protocols used by the Internet and most networks. TCP/IP allows different networks and computers to communicate with one another.

text-based interface Interface that involves typing commands rather than using graphical elements. Contrast with *GUI.* Synonym: *command-line interface.*

throughput Measurement of the speed of data transfer.

toggle Turn a software or hardware element on or off. For example, pressing the <Caps Lock> key on the keyboard toggles uppercase letters on or off.

touchpad A flat pointing device that works by sliding a fingertip across its surface. Software can provide additional features such as tapping to click. Synonym: *trackpad.*

trackball A pointing device that has a partially enclosed ball that the user rolls to move the pointer.

trackpad See *touchpad.*

TSR (Terminate-and-Stay-Resident Program) A program that remains resident in computer memory and can be run repeatedly without having to be reloaded into memory. Most TSR programs are loaded into memory by the DOS file AUTOEXEC.BAT. DOSKEY is a TSR program.

UART (Universal Asynchronous Receiver/Transmitter) A chip that converts data from serial information to parallel information, and vice versa. UARTs are used for equipment or devices that are attached to serial ports.

UMA (Upper Memory Area) The first 640K to 1024K of memory addresses reserved for device drivers and system use.

UMB (Upper Memory Block) A reserved memory block in the UMA used to load device drivers and TSR programs.

UPS (Uninterruptible Power Supply) Provides a continuous supply of power to a computer system when a primary power source fails. A UPS can also protect a system from power sags. It is indispensable when making changes to a computer's BIOS, because a power failure during a BIOS update will render a computer useless unless a replacement BIOS chip is obtained and installed, which isn't always possible. UPSs almost always include surge suppression. Synonym: *battery backup.*

URL (Uniform Resource Locator) A URL is an address that points to a resource or another URL located on the World Wide Web. An example of a URL is *http://www.charlesriver.com.*

USB (Universal Serial Bus) An interface standard that supports up to 127 devices using one system resource (IRQ). With USB, PnP peripheral devices can be attached to a computer system while the power is on and the operating system is up and running. Only the USB controller uses IRQs or other Device Manager resources; the connected devices don't.

Usenet A system of communication on the Internet in which subscribers to newsgroups can post and reply to messages that all subscribers can see.

UTP (Unshielded Twisted Pair) A common type of twisted-pair cable used in most networks. There are five categories of UTP that support different data transmission speeds. Unlike STP, UTP does not have a protective shielding.

VGA (Video Graphics Array) See *SVGA.*

video card A device whose primary function is to generate a video signal ("picture") to be shown on the monitor. A video card can either be a separate card that plugs into a slot on the motherboard, or a device built into the motherboard. Synonyms: *video adapter, graphics adapter, display adapter.*

virtual memory System used by Windows that uses hard disk space as additional memory in a process called *paging.* The file where Windows stores virtual memory data is called the *page file* or the *swap file.*

VL-Bus (VESA local bus) A 32-bit expansion bus that has been replaced by PCI expansion bus technology.

voltmeter A device that tests only the voltage of a circuit.

VPN (Virtual Private Network) A way to provide secure network access to the individual users and remote offices of an organization without the excessive expenses associated with owning or leasing the lines. This is done via the Internet by using a shared public infrastructure and tunneling. Additional security features can be utilized to enhance privacy.

VRAM (Video Random Access Memory) A special type of dual-ported memory that is used in video adapters to produce graphic images on a computer monitor.

VRM (Voltage Regulator Module) A small, replaceable module that is installed on the motherboard to sense the microprocessor's voltage requirements and regulate the voltage fed to the microprocessor. Nearly all motherboards have either a built-in voltage regulator or VRM. Therefore, if the computer's microprocessor is changed, a VRM may need to be added to the existing voltage regulator to keep consistent with the voltage requirements of the new microprocessor.

VxD (Virtual Device Driver) A 32-bit device driver used in Windows. Virtual device drivers have a .VXD extension.

WAN (Wide Area Network) A WAN is typically made up of two or more LANs linked together to form a larger network. WANs are usually spread over large areas. The Internet is a WAN.

WHQL (Windows Hardware Quality Labs) WHQL tested refers to driver qualifications with regards to the Windows Hardware Assurance team.

WINS (Windows Internet Naming Service) A Windows Networking service that provides a computer NetBIOS name to IP address resolution.

WLAN (Wireless Local-Area Network) A type of local-area network that allows a user to connect/communicate between nodes by using high-frequency radio waves (wireless connection). Wireless LAN adapter cards have been created for use with laptop computers.

WRAM (Window Random Access Memory) A very fast type of dual-ported video memory that has the ability to read and write larger sections of memory than VRAM.

write Record data to a storage medium.

writable Refers to a disc that can have data recorded on it.

WWW (World Wide Web) A system of servers on the Internet that provide support for pages and documents created with HTML and other scripting languages. You can access the WWW by using such tools and Web browsers as Internet Explorer, FTP, Telnet, HTTP, and Netscape Navigator.

XGA (Extended Graphics Array) A video display standard developed by IBM that has the ability to support a resolution of 1024 × 768. XGA can also support up to 65,536 colors.

XMS (Extended Memory Specification) The first 64K of memory located above 1MB.

XP Microsoft Windows XP Home and Professional editions.

XP Home Microsoft Windows XP Home Edition.

XP Pro Microsoft Windows XP Professional Edition.

ZIF (Zero Insertion Force CPU socket) Allows a CPU to be inserted into a socket without applying much pressure. Uses a locking lever to hold the processor in place.

Zip file A file compressed with the algorithm developed by the inventor of the Zip file. The file's extension is *.zip*. See *compressed file*.

Index

D

W

X

Y

Z

ISBN	TITLE	AUTHOR	PRICE	PAGES
8170087503	**Cisco IP Routing Protocols: Troubleshooting Techniques**	V. Anand, K. Chakrabarty	Rs. 295.00	409
	DATABASES			
8170087147	**DBMS-Complete Practical Approach**	Sharad Maheshwari, Ruchin Jain	Rs. 230.00	530
8170082404	**Learn to Program Visual Basic-Examples**	John Smiley	Rs. 295.00	500
8170082412	**Learn to Program Visual Basic-Databases**	John Smiley	Rs. 325.00	670
8170082420	**Learn to Program Visual Basic-Objects**	John Smiley	Rs. 325.00	700
817008475X	**IT Resources-Access 2002 VBA Programming Access**	Michele Amelot	Rs. 195.00	424
8170084512	**The Power of Oracle 9i**	Rajiv Parida, Vinod Sharma	Rs. 475.00	1100
	DOEACC 'O' LEVEL			
8170088089	**DOEACC 'O' Level Model Test Papers**	Ramesh Bangia	Rs. 175.00	296
8170085640	**Programming and Problem Solving Through "C" Language**	Harsha Priya, R. Ranjeet	Rs. 95.00	306
8170084474	**IT Tools and Applications**	Ramesh Bangia	Rs. 145.00	392
8170085594	**Business Systems**	Ramesh Bangia	Rs. 175.00	452
8170085454	**Internet & Web Design**	Ramesh Bangia	Rs. 120.00	321
	ELECTRONIC COMMERCE			
8170085497	**Electronic Commerce**	Pete Loshin, John Vacca	Rs. 295.00	472
817008119X	**E-Commerce**	Mamta Bhusry	Rs. 95.00	215
8170083524	**Marketing in The Cyber Age**	Kurt Rohner	Rs. 295.00	250
	HARDWARE/EMBEDDED SYSTEMS			
8170087473	**Essentials Electronics for PC Technicians**	John W. Farber	Rs. 295.00	546
8170086264	**Grid Computing: A Practical Guide to Technology and Applications**	Ahmar Abbas	Rs. 295.00	408
8170088186	**CD Cracking Uncovered Protection Against Unsanctioned CD Copy**	Kris Kaspersky	Rs. 295.00	422
8170083435	**Practical Linux Programming: Device Drivers, Embedded Systems**	Ashfaq A. Khan	Rs. 295.00	420

ISBN	TITLE	AUTHOR	PRICE	PAGES
8170083575	**TCP/IP Application Layer Protocols for Embedded Systems**	M. Tim Jones	Rs. 295.00	350

INTERNET

ISBN	TITLE	AUTHOR	PRICE	PAGES
8170083206	**The Internet Hand Book for Writers, Students & Teachers**	Mary McGuire, Linda Stillborne	Rs. 195.00	288
8170084776	**Way in-Internet Getting Started**	Elizabeth Bramire	Rs. 95.00	165

KEEPING AHEAD SERIES

ISBN	TITLE	AUTHOR	PRICE	PAGES
8170084652	**Keeping Ahead Exchange 2002 Server**	Philippe Levesque	Rs. 145.00	285
8170084660	**Keeping Ahead Windows 2000 Professional**	Jose Dardoigne	Rs. 175.00	388
8170084679	**Keeping Ahead Windows 2000 Server**	Philippe Mathon	Rs. 175.00	360
8170084687	**Keeping Ahead Linux Administration Kernel Version 2.0 to 2.2**	Bruno Guerin	Rs. 125.00	240
8170084695	**Keeping Ahead Using Linux Kernel Version 2.0 to 2.2**	Bruno Guerin	Rs. 125.00	258
8170084709	**Keeping Ahead Java 2**	Benjamin Aumaille	Rs. 145.00	284
8170084717	**Keeping Ahead SQL Server 7**	Joelle Mosset	Rs. 145.00	329
8170084725	**Keeping Ahead Java Script and VB Script**	Benjamin Aumaille	Rs. 145.00	313
8170084733	**Keeping Ahead C++ Programming Language**	Bruno Dubois	Rs. 125.00	234
8170084741	**Keeping Ahead TCP/IP in the NT Environment**	Bruno Ferec	Rs. 125.00	230

MCSE

ISBN	TITLE	AUTHOR	PRICE	PAGES
817008489X	**MCSE-Administering SQL Server 7.0**	Jerome Gabillaud	Rs. 295.00	580
8170084903	**MCSE-Networking Essentials**	Jose Dordoigne	Rs. 245.00	453
8170084911	**MCSE-Windows 2000 Professional**	Jose Dordoigne	Rs. 325.00	665
817008492X	**MCSE-Windows 2000 Server**	Philippe Mathon	Rs. 345.00	712

MULTIMEDIA AND ANIMATION

ISBN	TITLE	AUTHOR	PRICE	PAGES
8170088208	**3 DS Max 6 Animation with Character Studio 4 and Plug-Ins**	Boris Kulagin, Dmitry Morozov	Rs. 175.00	216
8170088216	**Adobe Audition: Soundtracks for Digital Video**	Roman Petelin, Yury Petelin	Rs. 195.00	278

ISBN	TITLE	AUTHOR	PRICE	PAGES
8170086205	**Building A Digital Human**	Karl Brilliant	Rs. 295.00	380
8170086213	**Making Digital Videos**	Ben Long	Rs. 295.00	284
8170087171	**Illustrating with Macromedia Flash TM MX 2004**	Robert Firbaugh	Rs. 245.00	366
8170082439	**Multimedia Basics-Technology (Vol. I)**	Andreas Holzinger	Rs. 195.00	285
8170082447	**Multimedia Basics-Learning (Vol. II)**	Andreas Holzinger	Rs. 195.00	300
8170082455	**Multimedia Basics-Design (Vol. III)**	Andreas Holzinger	Rs. 195.00	280
8170083532	**Maya Feature Creature Creations**	Todd Palamar	Rs. 295.00	450
8170083540	**Sound Forge Power**	Scott R. Garrigus	Rs. 195.00	250
8170086116	**Multimedia and Web Technology**	Ramesh Bangia	Rs. 295.00	706

NETWORKING

ISBN	TITLE	AUTHOR	PRICE	PAGES
817008721X	**Networking Essentials**	Jose Dordoigne	Rs. 195.00	453
8170087023	**Computer Networks**	Ajit Kumar Singh	Rs. 95.00	181
817008203X	**Telecom & Networking Glossary**	Robert Mastin	Rs. 300.00	250
8170082048	**Data Networking Made Easy**	Karen Patten	Rs. 360.00	350
8170082056	**Digital Convergence**	Andy Covell	Rs. 300.00	250

OFFICE AUTOMATION

ISBN	TITLE	AUTHOR	PRICE	PAGES
8170088003	**Desk Top Publishing**	Dinesh Maidasani	Rs. 125.00	210
8170087805	**Learning Computer Programming, MS Office and Internet & Web Tech.**	Dinesh Maidasani	Rs. 95.00	318
8170087686	**MS Word 2000 Thumb-Rules and Details**	Snigdha Banerjee	Rs. 175.00	390

ON YOUR SIDE SERIES

ISBN	TITLE	AUTHOR	PRICE	PAGES
8170084830	**On your side-Powerpoint 2002**	Andrew Blackburn	Rs. 145.00	282
8170084849	**On your side-Excel 2002**	Adrienne Tommy	Rs. 125.00	275
8170084857	**On your side-Word 2002**	Adrienne Tommy	Rs. 125.00	289
8170084865	**On your side-Access 2002**	Adrienne Tommy	Rs. 125.00	303
8170084873	**On your side-Frontpage 2002**	Andrew Blackburn	Rs. 95.00	220
8170084881	**On your side-Windows XP**	Adrienne Tommy	Rs. 125.00	310

OPERATING SYSTEMS

ISBN	TITLE	AUTHOR	PRICE	PAGES
8170087236	**Linux-A Practical Approach**	B. Mohamed Ibrahim	Rs. 95.00	187
8170083427	**The MS-Windows XP Professional Handbook**	Louis Columbus	Rs. 295.00	330
8170084784	**Way in-Windows XP Home Edition**	Andrew Blackburn	Rs. 95.00	183

Please write for a free color Firewall Media Catalog for details on the above books.

ISBN	TITLE	AUTHOR	PRICE	PAGES
8170086221	**Cyber Rookies—Operating System Fundamentals**	D. Irtegov	Rs. 295.00	498

PROGRAMMING

ISBN	TITLE	AUTHOR	PRICE	PAGES
8170087791	**The Art of Programming Through Flowcharts & Algorithms**	Anil Bikas Chaudhuri	Rs. 95.00	160
8170086248	**Preventative Programming Techniques**	Brian Hawkins	Rs. 295.00	322
8170083443	**Learning Computer Programming : It's not about Languages**	Mary Farrell	Rs. 295.00	375
8170086256	**Object-Oriented Programming From Problem Solving to Java**	Jose M. Garrido	Rs. 295.00	360
8170088038	**Assembly Language Programming for Intel Processors Family**	Vasile Lungu	Rs. 295.00	577
8170088178	**The Assembly Programming Master Book**	Vlad Pirogov	Rs. 395.00	726

PROGRAMMING - C#, C, C++

ISBN	TITLE	AUTHOR	PRICE	PAGES
8170083702	**The Power of C#**	Rajiv Parida	Rs. 295.00	592
8170085632	**Mastering Graphics Programming in 'C'**	Sudhir Dawra	Rs. 145.00	286
8170087074	**Mastering C Programs**	J.B. Dixit	Rs. 195.00	434
8170081262	**Programming in C**	J.B. Dixit	Rs. 245.00	505
8170087619	**Unix and C Programming**	Ashok Arora, Shefali Bansal	Rs. 295.00	606
8170086140	**Data Structure for 'C' Programming, 2nd Edition**	Ajay Kumar	Rs. 145.00	290
8170081270	**Programming in C++**	J.B. Dixit	Rs. 260.00	601
8170088194	**Hackish C++ Pranks & Tricks**	Michael Flenov	Rs. 245.00	326
8170082889	**Basics of C++ Programming**	Nishant Kundalia	Rs. 95.00	168
8170083648	**Mastering C++ Programs**	J.B. Dixit	Rs. 295.00	614
817008623X	**Cyber Rookies—C++ Programming Fundamentals**	Chuck Easttom	Rs. 295.00	417

SECURITY

ISBN	TITLE	AUTHOR	PRICE	PAGES
8170083419	**Computer Forensics : Computer Crime Scene Investigation**	John Vacca	Rs. 445.00	600
8170083494	**Firewall Architecture for the Enterprise**	Norbert Pohlmann, Tim Crothers	Rs. 295.00	480
8170086272	**Net Spies**	Andrew Gauntlett	Rs. 195.00	210

Please write for a free color Firewall Media Catalog for details on the above books.

ISBN	TITLE	AUTHOR	PRICE	PAGES
	SOFTWARE ENGINEERING AND TECHNOLOGY			
817008718X	**Human Aspects of Software Engineering**	James E. Tomayko, Orit Hazzar	Rs. 195.00	338
8170087899	**Management Information Systems**	Avdhesh Gupta, Anurag Malik	Rs. 175.00	362
8170087953	**Human Computer Interaction**	Rajendra Ranjan Kumar	Rs. 95.00	210
8170088097	**System Analysis and Design**	Preeti Gupta	Rs. 125.00	192
817008802X	**Autocad 2005 for Engineers**	Ionel Simion	Rs. 175.00	271
8170088054	**Digital Signal Processing Fundamentals**	Ashfaq A. Khan	Rs. 295.00	391
817008363X	**Practical Project Management**	Ivan Bayross	Rs. 195.00	342
	STRAIGHT TO THE POINT SERIES			
8170084601	**STTP : Word 2002**	Corinne Hervo	Rs. 45.00	154
817008461X	**STTP : Excel 2002**	Corinne Hervo	Rs. 45.00	153
8170084628	**STTP : Dreamweaver 4**	Corinne Hervo	Rs. 45.00	135
8170084636	**STTP : Flash 5**	Corinne Hervo	Rs. 45.00	126
8170084644	**STTP : Photoshop 6**	Corinne Hervo	Rs. 45.00	152
8170084482	**STTP : MS Office 2000**	Ramesh Bangia	Rs. 95.00	300
8170086108	**STTP : MS Office 2003**	Ramesh Bangia	Rs. 145.00	288
8170087651	**STTP : MS Word 2003**	Ramesh Bangia	Rs. 60.00	150
8170088011	**STTP : Photoshop CS**	Firewall Media	Rs. 60.00	150
8170088143	**STTP : MS Excel 2003**	Firewall Media	Rs. 60.00	150
8170088151	**STTP : Coreldraw 12**	Firewall Media	Rs. 60.00	150
	STUDIO FACTORY			
8170084792	**Studio Factory-Photoshop 6**	Christophe Aubry	Rs. 175.00	364
8170084806	**Studio Factory-Flash 5**	Sami Ben Yahiya	Rs. 145.00	314
8170084814	**Studio Factory-Dreamweaver Ultradev 4**	Philippe Chatellier	Rs. 95.00	240
8170084822	**Studio Factory-Dreamweaver 4**	Christophe Aubry	Rs. 175.00	373
8170087627	**Studio Factory-Flash MX**	Arnaud Blanche	Rs. 145.00	337
8170087643	**Studio Factory-Dreamweaver MX**	Christophe Aubry	Rs. 195.00	407
817008766X	**Studio Factory-Photoshop 7**	Cyril Guerin	Rs. 175.00	390
	WEB TECHNOLOGY			
8170087163	**Web Design with Macromedia Studio MX 2004**	Eric Hunley	Rs. 295.00	558

Please write for a free color Firewall Media Catalog for details on the above books.

ISBN	TITLE	AUTHOR	PRICE	PAGES
8170083400	**Professional Web Design (Techniques and Templates)**	Clint Eccher	Rs. 295.00	425
8170088046	**HTML, XHTML, CSS and XML**	Teodoru Gugoiu	Rs. 195.00	355
8170083583	**FrontPage 2000 for Visual Learners**	Chris Charuhas	Rs. 95.00	200
8170083591	**HTML & Java Script for Visual Learners**	Chris Charuhas	Rs. 95.00	200
8170083605	**The Visual Learner's Guide to Managing Web Projects**	Chris Charuhas	Rs. 95.00	130
8170083613	**Dreamweaver 4 for Visual Learners**	Chris Charuhas	Rs. 95.00	200
8170084768	**IT Resource-Implementing XML: Managing and Formatting Data**	Johhny Brochard	Rs. 125.00	279
8170085470	**Design Your Web World**	Sunil Jalota	Rs. 45.00	103

ORDER FORM

LAXMI PUBLICATIONS (P) LTD.

7/19, Ansari Road, Daryaganj, New Delhi-110002
Phones : 23262368, 23262370 ; *Faxes* : 011-2325 25 72, 2326 22 79
Email : colaxmi@hotmail.com
Website : www.laxmipublications.com

Please send me the following books by V.P.P. I have sent Rs. .... by M.O./Draft on Date ....

☐ ____________________

☐ ____________________

☐ ____________________

☐ ____________________

☐ ____________________

☐ ____________________

☐ ____________________

(Please use separate sheet if you need more books)

Fill in this coupon in BLOCK letters only.

Name ____________________

Address ____________________

____

P.O. ____________________ Distt. ____________________

State ____________________ Pin Code ☐☐☐☐☐☐

Phone ____________________ Email ____________________

Please do not refuse to accept the V.P.P. Honour it and write to us if there is any complaint. We shall set right your complaint, if any.

Our books are available at all leading bookshops.

Please mention Name of Books, clearly.

It is necessary to send Rs. 50.00 per book as an advance. Without advance order will not be sent.

Terms and Conditions for the supply of Books by V.P. Parcels to Students

1. Mention your name, address and nearest post office, with Pin Code No., in capital block letters for quick compliance of your order.
2. You can also send complete payment in advance by Money Order.
3. V.P. Parcels are detained by the Postal Authorities for only 5 days. Hence the same should be honoured on receiving intimation to avoid legal action against the defaulter.
4. Half Postage free.
5. All disputes will be settled in Delhi Courts only.
6. V.P. Parcels are not accepted for stations served by A.P.O. 56 and A.P.O. 99. While ordering for our Books from these stations, please ascertain and send the amount in full, in advance, on receipt of which, the books will be sent by registered post.
7. (*i*) V.P.P. Orders should be accompanied with advance of Rs. 50.00 per book. Without advance, ordered book(s) will not be sent.

   (*ii*) While sending advance by money order, please write your requirements on the last part of money order (space for communication). On its reverse side write your complete name and address.

   (*iii*) **Please note that the upper part of the money order form here you have written your address, remains with post office. So it is necessary to write your address again on last part of the M.O. form.**
8. Order placed will not be cancelled.
9. For books which are not supplied to you due to their being out of stock, please write again after 30 days with 25% advance.
10. Requests for our Books from students who did not honour their previous order will not be considered unless they send us full advance payment plus the postage charges for the returned parcel.
11. Prices are subject to change without notice.

Please write your letters to :

LAXMI PUBLICATIONS (P) LTD.

7/19, Ansari Road, Daryaganj, New Delhi-110002

Phones : 23262368, 23262370 ; *Faxes* : 011-2325 25 72, 2326 22 79

Email : colaxmi@hotmail.com

Website : www.laxmipublications.com